WITHDRAWN

Although much has been written about the American West, especially the frontier, this is the first book-length assessment of historical writing about the region. *Historians and the American West* surveys the entire field: what has been done, how well it has been done, and what needs to be done. Such an appraisal of the rich historiography of the region is long overdue, for the West has inspired some of the finest historical writings the United States has produced, a tradition rooted in the works of Bancroft, Turner, Bolton, and Webb.

Eighteen historians of the West (defined here as the region west of the 98th meridian, excluding Alaska and Hawaii) have contributed chapters on a broad variety of topics. More than bibliographical essays, these are wide-ranging discussions of the key books, articles, interpretations, and themes that characterize each subject.

Readers interested in the West will find in this book a handy and valuable guide to the state of the art in the historiography of the region. Taken together, the essays reveal a literature which, although still influenced by the grand tradition of Bancroft, Turner, Bolton, and Webb, has adopted newer approaches and techniques that draw it ever deeper into the mainstream of United States historiography.

Michael P. Malone is Dean of Graduate Studies and a professor of history at Montana State University. His publications include *Montana: A History of Two Centuries* (with Richard B. Roeder, 1976) and *The Battle for Butte: Mining and Politics on the Northern Frontier, 1864–1906* (1981).

Historians and the American West

Edited by
Michael P. Malone
Foreword by
Rodman W. Paul

University of Nebraska Press: Lincoln & London

The paper in this book meets the guidelines for
permanence and durability of the Committee on
Production Guidelines for Book Longevity of
the Council on Library Resources.

Library of Congress Cataloging in Publication Data

Main entry under title:

Historians and the American West.

Includes index.
1. West (U.S.) – Historiography – Addresses, essays,
lectures. I. Malone, Michael P.
F591.H68 1983 978 82-17550
ISBN 0-8032-3071-0

Contents

83-5171

Foreword

Recent trends have provided two quite different justifications for the preparation of a book of this kind. First has been the immense increase in the volume of writing about the West. As historical journals have multiplied and universities and historical societies have insisted upon having their own presses, manuscripts have found it easy to reach a printer; and while the current economic recession will doubtless reduce temporarily the number of releases by commercial publishers, the slack will be taken up by other, smaller outlets that operate on subsidies or low overheads.

Thus the overworked reader will welcome this as an annotated guide that will help show what is of first importance and what is secondary among the innumerable offerings of our greatly expanded output. But this book has a second purpose also. As the editor, Michael P. Malone, states in his excellent introduction, the "aim here is to decide what has been done, how well it has been done, and what needs to be done." That is, a team of historians have been asked to drop their own scholarly work long enough to make a critical examination of past and present while ruminating about the future; they have been asked to appraise the state of the art.

This second objective may ultimately prove to be even more important than the first, for since World War II western historians have been moving gradually into new topics, new ways of looking at old themes, new methodologies, and new bodies of evidence. This is a good time to pause and take stock. The present volume should stimulate a good deal of overdue soul searching. Are we as open to innovation as we should be? Or, conversely, are we being swept by current fads into approaches that ultimately will prove unrewarding? In the current zeal for numbers and social theory, are we forgetting the importance of style, clarity, and grace?

Editor Malone worries that "historians of the West have been noticeably slow in taking up the newer methodologies that became popular during the 1970s." In 1980 the American Historical Association published a notable volume entitled *The Past Before Us: Contemporary Historical Writing in the United States,* edited by Michael Kammen. Anyone who compares the chapters in that survey with the essays in the present book will sense that we in western history have as yet ventured only cautiously and partially into the ferment of new thinking that has characterized the profession nationally.

Doubtless we will find ourselves giving far more consideration to the new approaches if and when we finally begin serious work on the most neglected era of western history, the twentieth century. In our efforts to explain the complex happenings of recent decades, the ideas and methods of the social science-minded historians will prove essential. It is understandable that most of us have felt more comfortable when dealing with periods before 1900, because in those days the West was a relatively distinct entity whose historical experience was manageable, whereas in our own century western history blends into national history to such a degree as to lose its identity. But if specialists in the history of the West do not take on the job, then national historians will, and developments in the West will be reduced to local illustrations of national trends. Studies in urban history are already showing this tendency.

The impression that as yet we have accepted only a limited involvement in the new ways may be exaggerated by the age grouping, and hence the unconscious outlook, of the eighteen scholars who have contributed to this useful volume. The oldest was born in 1915, the youngest in 1942; eleven were born between the beginning of the Depression and the beginning of World War II. With one exception, they took their doctoral degrees in the 1960s or earlier. That means that they were trained too soon to catch the full force of the new ideas and new methodologies that were then fighting for recognition. It would be interesting to solicit the views of scholars who are now in their thirties or even late twenties—the oncoming generation, so to speak.

In an important respect the selection of contributors reflects a decided change in the education of historians. Whereas before the war a very few great universities dominated graduate training, in this volume doctoral degrees from fourteen different universities are represented among the eighteen essayists, and most of the universities are west of the Mississippi.

A few characteristics of the book deserve special comment. One is the continuing towering presence of Frederick Jackson Turner, Herbert Eugene Bolton, and Walter Prescott Webb. Including Malone's introductory analysis of the three, thirteen of the eighteen essayists bring on stage one or the other of these challenging figures. Some do so casually, some to praise, some to criticize. Criticism of Turner is especially prevalent. Thus, Bradford Lucking-ham shows that Turner was well aware of the potentialities of western urban history but failed to pursue the subject. Sandra Myres protests the heavily masculine character of Turner's West. Kenneth N. Owens suggests the lack of attention to "territorial administration and frontier politics . . . during the generation of Turner and the generation of Webb." Clark C. Spence feels that in part the long neglect of mining history stems from "the Turnerian empha-sis" on other subjects.

By contrast, Donald C. Cutter and Gordon B. Dodds are warmly admiring in their comments on Bolton, while Gilbert C. Fite is carefully factual in his brief remarks on Webb. Richard W. Etulain, the only author save Malone to discuss all three figures, points to the lack of interest in cultural history shown by all three.

It would seem, then, that while none of these modern western historians view Turner, Bolton, and Webb with the scorn shown by some critics of a generation ago, most find serious lacks now that western history has pro-duced a whole congeries of subfields that seem to demand attention. Perhaps it is worth pointing out that the most effective use of the thinking of any of the three is Frederick C. Luebke's brilliant demonstration of the appropriate-ness for ethnic studies of the methodology of Turner the sectionalist, as dis-tinct from Turner the frontiersman.

Rather surprising is the absence of comments on studies in social mobility, which are for the western historian one of the most illuminating uses of the new quantitative methods. Geographically scattered impressions in studies such as those already published by Merle Curti, Peter R. Decker, Howard Chudacoff, and Ralph E. Mann have given us tantalizing insights that suggest how great are the potentialities here.

Finally, the editor speaks briefly of the "West that wasn't" and of its most prominent offspring, the cowboy Western. In the course of essays on more substantial subjects, Gilbert C. Fite refers in passing to interpretations of the cowboy, and Richard W. Etulain calls attention to the importance of "myth and symbol" interpretations. But as the late Ray A. Billington's *Land of Savagery, Land of Promise* has demonstrated for Europe, the mythical West, the fake West, has influenced millions who have never read an honest history. Had a historian undertaken an essay for this volume on the uses of the West in fiction, film, and television, it might easily have grown into a book itself.

Instead, these historians have stuck to the facts, achieving the big accomplishment of giving western history a highly informative and decidedly interesting guidebook and self-appraisal. This volume represents hard work by busy people who have taken time to help all of us. Professional and amateur historians alike will find that this is the place to start from when they set out on a new journey of historical exploration.

RODMAN W. PAUL

Acknowledgments

All works of history are joint endeavors in some sense or other, but this one is especially so. To the eighteen historians who have collaborated with me in producing this volume, I am grateful indeed, not only for their prompt and persevering workmanship and assistance, but also for all that I have learned in working with them. Thanks are due, as well, to the late Ray Allen Billington for his encouragement and advice in the initial, planning stages; to Martha Edsall for her secretarial help in the many phases of mailing, typing, and copying; and especially to Kathleen Campbell for her exceptional assistance. I owe a special debt to Emeritus Professor Rodman Paul of the California Institute of Technology, both for his willingness to write the foreword for the volume and even more so for his great help to me in reading and criticizing the essays. This book has been a team effort; however, it must be said that the choice of contributors and the responsibility of editing their work have been entirely my own.

In a lighter vein, the reader should know that the nineteen of us who contributed to this volume struggled long and strenuously to come up with an original yet descriptive title. The best suggestion, which I simply lacked the courage to use, came from Clark Spence, to whom I am nonetheless grateful for the idea: "WRITERS OF THE PURPLE SAGE."

M. P. M.

Chapter One

Michael P. Malone

Introduction

Like all regions of all nations, the western United States has produced a history which is in part an aspect of the larger national mosaic and is in part a singular entity. Regional history is a composite of local, national, even global factors that have merged, diverged, and recombined over time to form a distinctive, yet also a familiar pattern. The great challenge facing all regional historians is to analyze the particular while visualizing the universal, to render that which is unique while casting it in the proper and broader perspective. This is a difficult and demanding task, and it requires a true blending of artistic and scientific endeavors. Many western regionalists have failed at it, but, as the following pages will reveal, many have succeeded as well.

More than such compact and geographically distinct regions as New England, the Deep South, or the Upper Midwest, the West is a sprawling amalgamation of diverse subregions. It may, indeed, be no region at all. After all, how much does the forested and humid coastal region of the Pacific Northwest, which Richard Maxwell Brown aptly calls "the Great Rain Coast of North America," have in common with the distant and arid deserts of the Far Southwest? What does urban and balmy southern California have in common with the cold, windy, and underpopulated northern Great Plains? We may or may not accept Walter Prescott Webb's famous argument that the West is geographically bound into an identifiable region by the factor of the desert: the fact that, with relatively few exceptions, the vast lands west of the 98th meridian are either semiarid or are real deserts in nature.[1] There is considerable truth in this, even though it can easily be exaggerated to yield a barren sort of environmental determinism.

It is best to follow Webb in taking the broad view. In several respects, both geographic and historical, the West should indeed be defined to embrace the entire region lying west of the 98th meridian, the line of diminishing rainfall which runs from the eastern Dakotas on the north through central Texas on the south. This large area has, in addition to certain shared geographic and climatological factors, a common history as well. After all, the nineteenth-century frontier did not engulf the region in a simple wavelike sweep from east to west. It reached at first across the Rocky Mountains, and the arid lands flanking them, to the verdant valleys of the Pacific Coast, then moved eastward to the Rockies, and finally ended with the taking of the drylands of the western Plains and the arid Southwest early in this century.

Thus John Gunther was quite correct when he argued in 1947 that the "West's heart line" runs, not down the Pacific Coast, but rather up the eastern shadow of the continental divide from El Paso and Santa Fe, through the "Front" region of Colorado, northward through Laramie and Great Falls. This mountain-plains region is much more self-consciously western than are the cosmopolitan cities of the coast. So the West is loosely united not only by the environmental factors of aridity and vast resources, but also by a common frontier past, with which it is preoccupied, and by a common "colonial" history of economic exploitation, with which it is also preoccupied on a more subliminal level. As Gunther concluded: "the West still carries the stigmata of a frontier civilization—it is the newest part of the nation, the most sparsely settled, the most individualistic, the friendliest. This is all shirt-sleeve country, he-man country, where the beds are usually double and where you drink beer straight from the bottle."[2]

This common history and historiography of the West—its evolution, current state, and future prospect—is the subject of this volume. In seventeen historiographic essays, each by a historian of the West who is accomplished in his or her field, the reader will find assessments of the "state of the art" of historical writing and interpretation on a wide range of subjects. Our aim here is to describe what has been done, how well it has been done, and what needs to be done as we see it. The volume is not meant to be an annotated bibliography, but rather a gathering of critical appraisals of the historical literature on subjects as diverse as western mining, western transportation, western women, Indians and minorities, and western politics and economic development. Out of the assembled essays, we hope, will emerge a better understanding of what several generations of western historians have accomplished and failed to accomplish, and of the legacy and tasks they have left to this and to future generations.

The legacy of western historical writing reveals a range of styles from the highly personal and romantic to the most studious and scientific. Our first historical glimpses of the little-known West were those recorded by contemporary observers. They include some of the most fascinating and valuable eyewitness accounts ever produced in North America, among them the narratives of the sixteenth-century travels of Cabeza de Vaca, Coronado, and other Spanish explorers of the Southwest; the fascinating journals of the great Lewis and Clark expedition of 1804–06; Richard Henry Dana's widely read account of his seaward journey to California, *Two Years Before the Mast*; Josiah Gregg's description of the Santa Fe trade, *Commerce of the Prairies*; the immensely popular reports of the self-promoting explorer John Charles Frémont; and Francis Parkman's *The Oregon Trail*, the classic rendering of his struggle against failing health to learn of the Plains and their peoples. From these and from many other firsthand accounts, Americans and Europeans came to envision the West as a land of epic proportions, exotic peoples, exciting adventure, and great promise.[3]

The West as wild frontier, as the romanticized domain of the heroic and unrestrained individual: this image, once implanted, waxed with time as nineteenth-century pioneer movements swept across the vast trans-Mississippi expanses. Popular literature abounded with larger-than-life frontiersmen-heroes, from mountain men to cowboys, whose exploits were a mélange of fact, fiction, fantasy, and sheer nonsense. As we all know, the fantasized Wild West evolved into the most conspicuous strain of our national folklore, first through the media of the dime novel and the bizarre Buffalo Bill touring shows, and then through the adventure novels of Zane Grey, Louis L'Amour, and their brethren and the formula epics of Hollywood and television.[4] It became difficult, nearly impossible, for the rest of the world to understand the West as a real place, inhabited by real people. And that problem endures to the present, even as the once-colonized West, with its boundless space and its wealth of energy resources, threatens to upstage its older sister regions to the east. Westerners are still asked, on occasion, if Wyoming has network television or if there is federal mail delivery in New Mexico.

Surrounded by this aura of legend and folklore, the new communities of the West began to produce histories of themselves during the late nineteenth and early twentieth centuries. Most of these early histories shared the same romantic traits which so colored the fiction of the era. Witness the heroic, adventurous *Winning of the West*, written by one-time Dakota stockman Theodore Roosevelt during 1889–96, or the Colorado-California writer Helen Hunt Jackson's *A Century of Dishonor* (1881), a highly sentimentalized account of the Indian's fate. In truth, most of the early histories were local works done by local amateurs, and they usually typified the local-history genre of the age, as aptly described by Kathleen Neils Conzen: "It [the local history] recounted a tale of progress and communal harmony in a conventional formula whose elements included surprisingly elegiac accounts of the Indians whom the community had dispossessed; heroic tales of the sufferings and achievements of the early settlers; chronological narrative of political and governmental milestones; recitation of the community's contributions to such national events as wars and economic crises; brief chronicles of the main economic, social, and cultural institutions of the town; and often a 'mug book' celebrating the lives of leading citizens."[5]

Of course, this is not to say that no serious history was written during these Indian summer days of the ebbing frontier. One must, for instance, always take account of that weighty shelf of volumes produced by Hubert Howe Bancroft and his associates. A wealthy San Francisco businessman and book collector, Bancroft assembled a team of coworkers in the 1870s and began a mass-production effort to gather the source materials and write the histories of Mexico and the western United States. His 39-volume *Works* sold widely and offered readers highly detailed and reliable histories of the western states; his fine collections formed the nucleus of the prized Bancroft Library at the University of California at Berkeley. While less than gripping as historical narratives, the Bancroft histories are still useful as rich and trustworthy sources of fact and as studies that are more than just antiquarian tomes.[6]

Given this, the point remains that truly scholarly history of the West is a product of the past ninety years that has been fostered mainly in university, college, research library, and historical society professional settings. Three people merit special attention as the "founding fathers" of a truly serious frontier-western historiography: Herbert Eugene Bolton, Frederick Jackson Turner, and Walter Prescott Webb. Of the three, Herbert Bolton (1870–1953) had the least impact upon the historiography of the West as a broader region but the greatest impact upon that of any specific subregion—namely, the Southwest. First at the University of Texas, then briefly at Stanford, and finally during most of his productive years at the University of California at Berkeley, the enthusiastic and indefatigable Bolton gathered source materials like a tireless frontier entrepreneur, turned out book after book, and trained more than one hundred Ph.D.s who carried on his work. His reputation rests upon his thesis that the Americas share a common, transnational history, and even more upon his many studies of what he called the "Borderlands," where the Spanish, the Anglo-American, and the French frontiers mingled. As Donald Cutter's essay reveals, this remarkable scholar left his imprint so indelibly upon the Southwest that historians still refer to it as the "Bolton-lands."[7]

The two people who, more than any others, really shaped the historio-graphic tradition of the West were Turner and Webb. Frederick Jackson Turner (1861-1932) of the University of Wisconsin first stated his far-reach-ing thesis concerning "The Significance of the Frontier in American History" at the annual meeting of the American Historical Association at Chicago in 1893. He restated and refined it many times thereafter, and no interpretation of American history has ever had a more lasting or decisive impact. Simply stated, the "Turner thesis" argued that readily available land and the wester-ing frontier worked over the course of three centuries to form a uniquely American character and civilization. Conceding that the "germs" of European society were first rooted to the Atlantic Coast of the future United States, Turner argued that the leavening conditions of one semiwilderness frontier after another caused the Americans to shed some traits and to adapt others as they moved westward, until they had evolved an essentially new civilization. To Turner, the distinctively American traits which the frontier experience imparted to the young nation were most notably individualism, democracy, nationalism, and mobility. While not discounting the hereditary factors of European tradition, Turner emphasized the decisive impact of a new environ-ment upon those traditions.

Turner's thesis met a truly remarkable reception, for it told a maturing and expansive young nation what it wanted to hear: that it was not a mere appendage of a decadent Europe, but rather was a unique and great civiliza-tion in its own right. Disciples like Avery Craven, Orin G. Libby, Frederick Merk, and Frederick L. Paxson, many of whom had studied with Turner at Wisconsin or later at Harvard, carried the message to all parts of the nation. And during the four decades which ended in the Great Depression, the Turner thesis enjoyed a widespread, consensual acceptance among American histor-ians, even among the wider reading public. During the economically depressed 1930s and the internationally minded 1940s, however, many historians came to reject the thesis as being too simplistic, too imprecise, too preoccupied with a rural and agrarian past that ignored the urban-industrial present, or too chauvinistic in its celebration of American uniqueness. Yet the Turner tradition enjoyed a resurgence after World War II, and it lives on, especially among historians of the West who have modified it, refined it, and placed it in a credible context of a multiplicity of historical factors that shaped American civilization. Among these neo-Turnerians, the most formidable was Turner's biographer Ray Allen Billington (1903-81), a highly influential historian of the frontier who in many writings made a more complex and subdued interpretation of the frontier hypothesis plausible to modern generations.[8]

While Turner's name will always seem synonymous with the frontier, that of Walter Prescott Webb (1888–1963) will always be associated with the Great Plains. Unlike the midwesterner Turner, the Texan Walter Webb was a westerner who wrote about the West itself. And unlike Turner, whom he resembled in his environmental interpretation, Webb wrote less like a social scientist than a poet, or at least a liberated artist. An unknown historian at the University of Texas, Webb created a sensation in 1931 with his monumental *The Great Plains,* a sweeping and highly original book that depicted the Plains as not just a place but an overarching environmental presence that broke or bent men and institutions when they failed to conform to its realities. *The Great Plains* taught American historians to think of the arid West in terms that were close to environmental determinism, an approach which well fit the "dust bowl" years of the 1930s. In this sense, it reinforced the environmental interpretation of Turner.

In later writings, like his provocative *Harper's* essay of 1957, "The American West, Perpetual Mirage," Webb elaborated upon his earlier thesis, always graphic in his message that man is futile in his efforts to transform the western desert into a garden. He completed his other major book in 1952, *The Great Frontier,* another work of impressive creativity, which viewed the expansion of Europe after Columbus as a "400 Year Boom" during which the expanding global frontiers fed their wealth into a burgeoning European "metropolis." This book never achieved the renown of *The Great Plains,* in part because Webb did not flesh it out as well, but its thesis, which in a sense is Turnerian in a worldwide setting, is worthy of lasting study.[9]

Both Turner and Webb were exceptional teachers who left behind armies of devoted students and disciples to carry on their work. The quintessence of their enduring legacy to western historiography is twofold: an environmental interpretation which sometimes approaches real determinism and, especially in Turner's case, a preoccupation with the frontier. This preoccupation, which is a hallmark of western historical writing, stems from more than merely Turner's influence. It arises even more directly from the folklore of the frontier, which modern mass media have institutionalized. The frontier era is our heroic age, and that in part has colored our historical writing about it. Much of what we call "western history" is really popularized, antiquarian, frequently half-fictionalized lore: did Daniel Boone slip out unnoticed to

Idaho? Which Indian killed Custer? Who shot first at the O.K. Corral?

Despite our romantic fascination with the western frontier, some of the best serious works in all of American historical literature are studies of the frontier or of frontiersmen. For example: Bernard De Voto's beautifully written *Across the Wide Missouri* (1947) and *The Year of Decision: 1846* (1942), both of which celebrate the tough individuality of the frontiersman; Dale Morgan's *Jedediah Smith and the Opening of the West* (1953), which convincingly does the same; the authoritative histories of the mining frontier by Rodman Paul, *Mining Frontiers of the Far West: 1848-1880* (1963), and William Greever, *The Bonanza West* (1963); Gilbert Fite's *The Farmers' Frontier: 1865-1900* (1966); Edgar Stewart's close analysis of the West's most famous battle, *Custer's Luck* (1955); Robert Utley's demythologizing *Frontier Regulars: The United States Army and the Indian, 1866-1890* (1973); and Robert Athearn's exemplary economic history, *Union Pacific Country* (1971).[10] The list might be extended at length. In fact, the frontier has attracted the attention of some of this country's most distinguished historians.

Yet, no doubt inevitably, time took its toll against both the Turner thesis itself and the frontier preoccupation of western historiography. Since the early 1930s, and even before, Turner had had his critics: economic determinists like Louis Hacker, who disliked Turner's noneconomic interpretation; internationalists like Carlton Hayes, who scored Turner's thesis for encouraging a national introspection when we should have been assuming our international obligations; more thoughtful critics like George Wilson Pierson and Benjamin F. Wright, Jr., who accused Turner of sloppiness in terminology and argument and of understating the influence of cultural heritage.[11] But until well after World War II, historians of the frontier and of the West usually defended or at least did not challenge the thesis.

By the 1950s, though, doubts slowly began to surface as highly respected figures in the field began to raise objections. Two examples stand out. In 1950, Henry Nash Smith's superb and highly influential *Virgin Land: The American West as Symbol and Myth* burst upon the scene. This book, one of those few which truly changed the way we think, dealt with the West as viewed in the American and European imagination and treated brilliantly and insightfully such subjects as the dime novel hero, popular expansionism, the myths of the West as desert and garden, and the legends of agrarianism. In his final chapter, Smith placed the Turner thesis in this context of legend and mythmaking, arguing that Turner had accepted such myths as fact and written them into history. Earl Pomeroy, one of the most distinguished of western historians, dealt with Turner more directly and more philosophically. In several writings he argued against the narrow limitations of the Turnerian approach and urged western historians to broaden their conceptualization and methodology. Like the cultural historian Louis B. Wright, Pomeroy stressed the social and cultural continuities and imitativeness of the frontier; like growing numbers of other new leaders in the field, he stressed the role of cities in shaping the West.[12]

The writings of historians like Smith and Pomeroy were actually less significant for the doubts they raised about the Turner Thesis than for their catalytic roles in raising new questions, setting forth new insights, and inviting emulation. A number of fine books have come forth in the interdisciplinary, literary-cultural style of analysis of Smith's *Virgin Land* during the past three decades: Leo Marx's *The Machine in the Garden* (1964), Roderick Nash's *Wilderness and the American Mind* (1967), Richard Slotkin's *Regeneration Through Violence: The Mythology of the American Frontier, 1600–1860* (1973), William H. Goetzmann's *Exploration and Empire* (1966), Kevin Starr's *Americans and the California Dream* (1973), and Ray Allen Billington's *Land of Savagery, Land of Promise: The European Image of the American Frontier* (1981) being among the best.[13] Similarly, Pomeroy has trained a number of leading western historians, who carry on his style of carefully researched and closely reasoned historical analysis.

Beyond dispute, the past quarter-century has witnessed a true transformation in the writing of western history, a vast expansion and enrichment of the field. At the root of this productivity is not really a repudiation of Turner. In fact, many western historians continue to embrace his interpretation in one form or another, and even more maintain a fondness for Webb's less controversial environmental thesis. More to the point is the simple and indisputable fact that the broad and far-reaching trends which have transformed all of American historiography have also had their impact upon the study of this particular region. The leavening of American historiography, like most national trends, has rippled westward in its impact.

One finds examples of such innovation and enrichment in all directions. In his acclaimed study of *The Cattle Towns* (1968), Robert R. Dykstra takes a close look at five major Kansas cattle towns during the period 1867–85 and asks the right questions about violence and order. His findings dispel many legendary assumptions. In his refreshingly questioning and insightful *The Great Columbia Plain* (1968) and *Imperial Texas* (1969), historical geographer

D. W. Meinig offers more traditional historians a lesson in how to comprehend regional development. Leonard J. Arrington does the same in a different
manner in *Great Basin Kingdom: An Economic History of the Latter-day
Saints, 1830–1900* (1958). Mark Wyman's *Hard-Rock Epic: Western Miners
and the Industrial Revolution, 1860–1910* (1979), a superb and multifaceted
study of industrial miners, takes western labor history to a new high.[14]

Howard Lamar's highly regarded territorial histories, *Dakota Territory,
1861–1889: A Study of Frontier Politics* (1956) and *The Far Southwest,
1846–1912: A Territorial History* (1966), serve as models for others; and
Kenneth Owens's studies of frontier politics bring to the subject a degree of
sophistication seldom seen in such writings on the West. Among state and
regional histories, which in a sense are a genre apart, we now have volumes of
real distinction that are important to the history of the entire nation. T. A.
Larson's widely respected *History of Wyoming* (1965, 1978), Walton Bean's
California: An Interpretive History (1968, 1978), and Dorothy Johansen and
Charles Gates's *Empire of the Columbia: A History of the Pacific Northwest*
(1957, 1967) are good examples.[15]

As the essays in this volume by Sandra Myres, Bradford Luckinghan, and
Frederick Luebke reveal, the increasing interest of American historians in
women, the family, and social history, as well as in urban and ethnic history,
is finding more and more reflection in the West. Julie Roy Jeffrey's *Frontier
Women: The Trans-Mississippi West, 1840–1880* (1979) and Sandra Myres's
Westering Women and the Frontier Experience (1982) are in the vanguard
of histories opening the neglected yet promising field of women's history
in the West. And the late John D. Unruh's masterful *The Plains Across:
The Overland Emigrants and the Trans-Mississippi West, 1840–1860* (1979)
and John Mack Faragher's controversial feminist interpretation in *Women and
Men on the Overland Trail* (1979) are among the best known of recent works
which take a new look at social relationships in frontier settings. Books such
as Gunther Barth's *Instant Cities: Urbanization and the Rise of San Francisco
and Denver* (1975) and John W. Reps's *Cities of the American West: A History of Frontier Urban Planning* (1979) are indicative of the fast rising
interest in western cities.[16]

Yet much remains to be done, even to be begun. The entire vast field of
the twentieth-century West, in all its many facets, is still largely neglected and
untreated. Only Gerald Nash's outline history, *The American West in the
Twentieth Century* (1973, 1977), has so far attempted even an overview.
Even the basic political and economic topics of the post-1900 era, as the
essays below by William Lang and F. Alan Coombs so clearly demonstrate,

are mostly yet untouched. Of all the newly emerging fields in the history of the West, none is more promising or exciting than the comparison of America's frontier experience with those of Rome, Russia, China, Australia, or other expanding states. Jerome O. Steffen's broadly conceptual *Comparative Frontiers: A Proposal for Studying the American West* (1980) offers some provocative thoughts on directions to be followed, and so does the recent research of W. Turrentine Jackson.[17]

Historians of the West have been noticeably slow in taking up the newer methodologies that became popular during the 1970s. Take, for instance, the trend toward computerized quantification and the "new political" and "new economic" histories which apply it. Few western specialists have embraced quantified research, but those who do can find admirable models in Frederick Luebke's highly regarded study of politics, *Immigrants and Politics: The Germans of Nebraska, 1880-1900* (1969), or Richard Peterson's successful use of collective biography to describe *The Bonanza Kings: The Social Origins and Business Behavior of Western Mining Entrepreneurs, 1870-1900* (1977). With interesting results, psychohistory has recently been applied to a likely patient—George Armstrong Custer. And the application of oral history is expanding rapidly in this as in all fields of American history, one of the best examples being Joseph H. Cash and Herbert T. Hoover, *To Be an Indian: An Oral History* (1971).[18]

The American West is a field of historical study that has a proud tradition and commands a remarkable public interest, as can be seen at the lively conventions of the Western History Association or by noting the circulation of journals like the *Western Historical Quarterly,* the *Pacific Historical Review,* or *Montana: The Magazine of Western History.* The field has changed drastically in the two decades that have elapsed since the death of Walter Webb in 1963. Yet it is also an underdeveloped area, an exciting field to be working in at this time.

So it seems appropriate to the group of western historians represented in this volume that we pause at this time and survey the traditions of our field of study, the work of recent decades, and the work which in our opinions needs to be done. In the following pages the reader will find a variety of historiographic assessments—some encyclopedic, others more selective and critical. It is our intent and our hope that the essays will serve several purposes: to set forth at length the "state of the art" in the writing of western history, to provide informed assessments of the quality of what has been done, and, by pointing out the gaps, shortcomings, and opportunities, to help facilitate the improvement and enlargement of the field. This is the first such historiographical volume to attempt an appraisal of the entire West as a region. We hope that bountiful harvests of the future will justify and assure many successors to it.

Notes

1. Richard Maxwell Brown, "The Great Rain Coast of North America," paper presented to Pettyjohn Symposium on Northwest Regional History, Washington State University, Pullman, 30 October 1980; Walter P. Webb, "The American West, Perpetual Mirage," *Harper's*, May 1957, pp. 25-31.

2. John Gunther, *Inside U.S.A.* (New York and London: Harper and Brothers, 1947), pp. 145-47; see also Bernard De Voto, "The West: A Plundered Province," *Harper's*, August 1934, pp. 355-64; Gene M. Gressley, "Colonialism: A Western Complaint," *Pacific Northwest Quarterly* 54 (January 1963): 1-8.

3. On the Spanish explorers, see chap. 2 below; Bernard De Voto (ed.), *The Journals of Lewis and Clark* (Boston: Houghton Mifflin, 1953); Richard Henry Dana, *Two Years Before the Mast*, several eds. (New York: Modern Library, 1945); Josiah Gregg, *Commerce of the Prairies*, ed. Max Moorhead (Norman: University of Oklahoma Press, 1954); Donald Jackson and Mary Lee Spence (eds.), *The Expeditions of John Charles Frémont*, 2 vols. (Urbana: University of Illinois Press, 1970-); Francis Parkman, *The Oregon Trail* (Madison: University of Wisconsin Press, 1969).

4. Henry Nash Smith best placed the western hero in context in *Virgin Land: The American West as Symbol and Myth* (Cambridge: Harvard University Press, 1950; paperbound ed., 1970); see also Kent L. Steckmesser, *The Western Hero in History and Legend* (Norman: University of Oklahoma Press, 1965), and William W. Savage, Jr., *The Cowboy Hero: His Image in American History and Culture* (Norman: University of Oklahoma Press, 1979).

5. Kathleen Neils Conzen, "Community Studies, Urban History, and American Local History," in Michael Kammen (ed.), *The Past Before Us: Contemporary Historical Writing in the United States* (Ithaca, N.Y.: Cornell University Press, 1980), p. 271; Theodore Roosevelt, *The Winning of the West*, 6 vols. (New York: G. P. Putnam's Sons, 1900); Helen Hunt Jackson, *A Century of Dishonor* (Boston: Roberts Brothers, 1885).

6. *The Works of Hubert Howe Bancroft*, 39 vols. (San Francisco: History Co., 1882-90).

7. On Bolton's writings and impact, see chap. 2 below.

8. Turner's seminal essays are available in many editions. Among the most useful are George R. Taylor (ed.), *The Turner Thesis*, 3d ed. (Lexington, Mass.: D. C. Heath, 1972), and R. A. Billington (ed.), *The Frontier Thesis* (New York: Holt, Rinehart and Winston, 1966), both of which include Turner's writings and also selections from his critics and supporters. The authoritative biography is Billington, *Frederick Jackson Turner: Historian, Scholar, Teacher* (New York: Oxford University Press, 1973); the best statement of the neo-Turnerian position is Billington, *America's Frontier Heritage* (New York: Holt, Rinehart and Winston, 1966; paperbound ed., Albuquerque: University of New Mexico Press, 1974). Among many other studies, see Wilbur R. Jacobs, *The Historical World of Frederick Jackson Turner* (New Haven: Yale University Press, 1968), and Jacobs *et al.*, *Turner, Bolton, Webb* (Seattle: University of Washington Press, 1965; paperbound ed., 1979).

9. Walter P. Webb, *The Great Plains* (Waltham, Mass.: Ginn, 1931; paperbound ed., Lincoln: University of Nebraska Press, 1981); Webb, *The Great Frontier* (Boston: Houghton Mifflin, 1952; paperbound ed., Austin: University of Texas Press, 1964); Webb, "The American West: Perpetual Mirage"; Necah S. Furman, *Walter Prescott Webb: His Life and Impact* (Albuquerque: University of New Mexico Press, 1976); Gregory M. Tobin, *The Making of a History: Walter Prescott Webb and "The Great Plains"* (Austin: University of Texas Press, 1976).

10. Bernard De Voto, *The Year of Decision: 1846* (Boston: Houghton Mifflin, 1942; De Voto, *Across the Wide Missouri* (Boston: Houghton Mifflin, 1947); Dale L. Morgan, *Jedediah Smith and the Opening of the West* (New York: Bobbs-Merrill, 1953; paperbound ed., Lincoln: University of Nebraska Press, 1964); Rodman W. Paul, *Mining Frontiers of the Far West: 1848–1880* (New York: Holt, Rinehart and Winston, 1963; paperbound ed., Albuquerque: University of New Mexico Press, 1980); William S. Greever, *The Bonanza West: The Story of the Western Mining Rushes, 1848–1900* (Norman: University of Oklahoma Press, 1963); Gilbert C. Fite, *The Farmers' Frontier: 1865–1900* (New York: Holt, Rinehart and Winston, 1966; paperbound ed., Albuquerque: University of New Mexico Press, 1977); Edgar I. Stewart, *Custer's Luck* (Norman: University of Oklahoma Press, 1955); Robert M. Utley, *Frontier Regulars: The United States Army and the Indian, 1866–1890* (New York: Macmillan, 1973; paperbound ed., Bloomington: Indiana University Press, 1977); Robert G. Athearn, *Union Pacific Country* (New York: Rand McNally, 1971; paperbound ed., Lincoln: University of Nebraska Press, 1976).

11. These and other critiques are handily gathered in Taylor (ed.), *The Turner Thesis.*

12. Smith, *Virgin Land*; Earl Pomeroy, "The Changing West," in John Higham (ed.), *The Reconstruction of American History* (New York: Harper and Row, 1962), pp. 64-81; especially Pomeroy, "Toward a Reorientation of Western History: Continuity and Environment," *Mississippi Valley Historical Review* 41 (March 1955): 579-600; Pomeroy, *The Pacific Slope: A History of California, Oregon, Washington, Idaho, Utah, and Nevada* (New York: Knopf, 1965; paperbound ed., Seattle: University of Washington Press, 1975); see also Louis B. Wright, *Culture on the Moving Frontier* (Bloomington: Indiana University Press, 1955; paperbound ed., New York: Harper and Brothers, 1961).

13. Leo Marx, *The Machine in the Garden: Technology and the Pastoral Ideal in America* (New York: Oxford University Press, 1964; paperbound ed., 1967); Roderick Nash, *Wilderness and the American Mind* (New Haven: Yale University Press, 1967; paperbound ed., 1973); Richard Slotkin, *Regeneration Through Violence: The Mythology of the American Frontier, 1600-1860* (Middletown, Conn.: Wesleyan University Press, 1973); William H. Goetzmann, *Exploration and Empire: The Explorer and the Scientist in the Winning of the American West* (New York: Knopf, 1966; paperbound ed., New York: W. W. Norton, 1978); Kevin Starr, *Americans and the California Dream: 1850-1915* (New York: Oxford University Press, 1973; paperbound ed., Santa Barbara and Salt Lake City: Peregrine Smith, 1981); Ray A. Billington, *Land of Savagery, Land of Promise: The European Image of the American Frontier* (New York: W. W. Norton, 1981).

14. Robert R. Dykstra, *The Cattle Towns* (New York: Knopf, 1968; paperbound ed., New York: Atheneum, 1970); D. W. Meinig, *The Great Columbia Plain: A Historical Geography, 1805-1910* (Seattle: University of Washington Press, 1968); Meinig, *Imperial Texas: An Interpretive Essay in Cultural Geography,* paperbound ed. (Austin: University of Texas Press, 1969); Leonard J. Arrington, *Great Basin Kingdom: An Economic History of the Latter-day Saints, 1830-1900* (Cambridge: Harvard University Press, 1958; paperbound ed., Lincoln: University of Nebraska Press, 1966); Mark Wyman, *Hard-Rock Epic: Western Miners and the Industrial Revolution, 1860-1910* (Berkeley and Los Angeles: University of California Press, 1979).

15. Howard R. Lamar, *Dakota Territory, 1861-1889: A Study of Frontier Politics* (New Haven: Yale University Press, 1956); Lamar, *The Far Southwest, 1846-1912: A Territorial History* (New Haven: Yale University Press, 1966; paperbound ed., New York: W. W. Norton, 1970); Kenneth N. Owens,

"Patterns and Structure in Western Territorial Politics," *Western Historical Quarterly* 1 (October 1970): 373-92; T. A. Larson, *History of Wyoming* (Lincoln: University of Nebraska Press, 1968, 1978); Walton Bean, *California: An Interpretive History*, 3d ed. (New York: McGraw-Hill, 1978); Dorothy O. Johansen and Charles M. Gates, *Empire of the Columbia: A History of the Pacific Northwest* (New York: Harper and Row, 1957, 1967).

16. Julie Roy Jeffrey, *Frontier Women: The Trans-Mississippi West, 1840-1880* (New York: Hill and Wang, 1979); Sandra L. Myres, *Westering Women and the Frontier Experience* (Albuquerque: University of New Mexico Press, 1982); John D. Unruh, *The Plains Across: The Overland Emigrants and the Trans-Mississippi West, 1840-60* (Urbana: University of Illinois Press, 1979); John Mack Faragher, *Women and Men on the Overland Trail* (New Haven: Yale University Press, 1979); Gunther Barth, *Instant Cities: Urbanization and the Rise of San Francisco and Denver* (New York: Oxford University Press, 1975); John W. Reps, *Cities of the American West: A History of Frontier Urban Planning* (Princeton: Princeton University Press, 1979).

17. Gerald D. Nash, *The American West in the Twentieth Century: A Short History of an Urban Oasis* (Englewood Cliffs, N.J.: Prentice-Hall, 1973; paperbound ed., Albuquerque: University of New Mexico Press, 1977); Jerome O. Steffen, *Comparative Frontiers: A Proposal for Studying the American West* (Norman: University of Oklahoma Press, 1980); David H. Miller and J. O. Steffen, *The Frontier: Comparative Studies* (Norman: University of Oklahoma Press, 1977); W. Turrentine Jackson, "A Brief Message for the Young and/or Ambitious: Comparative Frontiers as a Field for Investigation," *Western Historical Quarterly* 9 (January 1978): 5-18; Howard Lamar and Leonard Thompson (eds.), *The Frontier in History: North America and South Africa Compared* (New Haven: Yale University Press, 1981).

18. Frederick C. Luebke, *Immigrants and Politics: The Germans of Nebraska, 1880-1900* (Lincoln: University of Nebraska Press, 1969); Richard H. Peterson, *The Bonanza Kings: The Social Origins and Business Behavior of Western Mining Entrepreneurs, 1870-1900* (Lincoln: University of Nebraska Press, 1977); Charles K. Hofling, *Custer and the Little Big Horn: A Psychobiographical Inquiry* (Detroit: Wayne State University Press, 1981); Joseph H. Cash and Herbert T. Hoover, *To Be an Indian: An Oral History* (New York: Holt, Rinehart and Winston, 1971).

Chapter Two

Herbert T. Hoover

**American Indians
from Prehistoric Times
to the Civil War**

Few if any noteworthy groups in the society of the United States have received as little attention from historians as have American Indians.[1] Before the 1930s, their historic plight was described mainly by amateurs and professional writers in disciplines other than history, and the few reliable publications to appear treated them mainly as obstacles to the progress of Anglo-American civilization or as antiquarian curiosities. During the past half-century or so, small groups of professional historians and ethnologists finally have assumed responsibility for the Indians' presence in history and have begun to recognize them as a cultural force deserving treatment in a separate field of interest. Unfortunately, these groups have not been large enough to keep pace with other bodies of professionals who have been engaged in the improvement of American historiography—those who have worked on labor history, for example, or on modern techniques such as cliometrics, oral research, and psychohistory. Indeed, so few bona fide scholars have been attracted to Native Americans that unwary readers still are supplied almost as much semifictional literature as soundly written history. So few have been engaged in the work that the consuming public has yet to receive even elementary guidance by qualified authors on the complexities of the field as a whole or of its several subdivisions.[2]

American Indian history contains three distinct components: the histories of the internal affairs of all the tribes from the Atlantic seaboard to the Pacific slope since prehistoric times; the history of policies devised by non-Indian political leaders and reformers, and enforced by colonial and later by federal officials, from the founding of Hispanic settlements in the Southeast during the sixteenth century to the present; and the history of contact between Indian and non-Indian groups across the country from the arrival of the first

European colonials in the United States to the early 1980s.[3] The three parts are closely intertwined, for they all deal with the experiences of American Indian people. Yet they are so different from each other that the research and writing of each calls for special preparation and unique perspective. And the assessment of past publications about each of the three components must be presented in a separate context.

As background for writings about the several subdivisions of Indian history from the sixteenth century to the Civil War, there have appeared several types of literature in ancillary but important areas of interest. Scores of studies on the origins of the tribes have appeared, in varying lengths and qualities. Fortunately, two general works were published in the 1960s to draw most of them together. Historian Lee Huddleston wrote one, which traces the historiography of the subject from 1492 to 1729. Anthropologist Robert Wauchope published the other, which synthesizes and describes theoretical categories ranging from illogical ramblings of "crank pseudoscientists" to plausible writings by exponents of the Bering Land Bridge hypothesis. Using archaeological evidence as a principal basis for his text, Jesse D. Jennings supplied valuable descriptions of prehistoric societies, whatever their origins; he discussed relationships between their cultures and the land and resources available to them before non-Indians arrived. Two students of demography have reproduced summaries of early population counts: fifty-four careless guesses prepared between 1677 and 1789. These were followed by numerous provincial compilations, plus statistical estimates included in Henry R. Schoolcraft's multivolume survey for the period 1790–1860.[4]

Additional background information is found in the dozen general surveys of American Indian history that have appeared since 1900. Unfortunately, each of these surveys attempts generalizations and draws conclusions that cannot yet be substantiated. Spadework of sufficient depth to support this type of survey doubtless will not be completed much before the beginning of the twenty-first century. Together, these works nevertheless provide valuable background information and serve as guides for scholars and general readers alike. Among the most useful is Angie Debo's *A History of the Indians of the United States*, which dwells excessively upon the history of the Five Civilized Tribes. Another of similar quality is Wilcomb E. Washburn's *The Indian in America*, which in places supplies almost as much conjecture as objective analysis in the effort to explain how American Indians surrendered their independence during three centuries of contact with whites. The best to appear so far is Arrell M. Gibson's *The American Indian: Preehistory to the Present,* which offers in textbook organization fairly accurate outlines of the histories of policy and intercultural contact but is deficient for its author's propensity to confuse fact with fiction in the survey of ethnohistory.[5]

Within the scope of premature publications such as these, reliable literature about the internal affairs of the tribes is in very short supply. This is not the result of faulty scholarship. On the contrary, in ethnography the percentage of total works with lasting value has been inordinately high, partly because a number of superior scholars have been attracted to it, and partly because raw materials for this subfield have been gathered over so long a time. Centuries ago, participants in Hispanic colonial experiments in the Southeast, in French-Spanish imperial competition along the Gulf Coast, in the conquest expeditions across the arid Southwest, and in Euro-American colonial enterprises on the Atlantic seaboard all took time to record data on Native American societies.

After colonial vanguardsmen grew secure on the seaboard, their successors moved over the eastern mountain chain across the Appalachian plateau and Great Lakes plains and created records of still greater value. The principal group of missionaries kept careful records, which have been published in seventy-three volumes as *The Jesuit Relations and Allied Documents.* Franciscan Louis Hennepin, who "fell captive" to some Sioux in the spring of 1680 and then "was rescued" by Daniel Greysolon Duluth a short time later, wrote reminiscences on the society of his hosts, about whom he understood very little but for whom he preserved information of remarkable veracity. Forty years later, a trader in the same region composed an essay that corroborated and enlarged upon subjects covered by Hennepin.[6] These and other early modern chronicles supplied a firm base of information about the political, economic, social, and philosophical nature of major Indian groups that dwelled east of the Mississippi as they existed during initial contacts with whites.

Imperial wars then raged between non-Indian colonial forces, precipitating fights between pioneers and Indians on several fronts. Until they were over, few writings appeared on the nature of Indian life. Cadwallader Colden prepared *The History of the Five Nations Depending on the Province of New York,* a treatise on the roles of Indians in imperial competition that contained some anthropological data. James Adair wrote his study of the Five Civilized Tribes and the Catawba federation, which will be described in the text below. Aside from these, few studies of importance appeared until the outset of the nineteenth century.[7]

As whites turned their attention to the development of the trans-Mississippi West, however, and made frequent contacts with the aboriginal owners of the resources contained therein, a spate of published documents and secondary sources appeared. Many included ethnographic material of enormous value. Those produced at federal expense have become classics. The first was Jedediah Morse's *A Report to the Secretary of War.* . . . The second was Henry R. Schoolcraft's *Information Respecting the History, Condition and Prospects of the Indian Tribes of the United States.*[8] The latter was by far the better of the two because Schoolcraft was the more perceptive observer, because he took more time for the preparation of his work, and most of all because he published almost verbatim the reports turned in by non-Indians who had lived with the tribes over long periods of time. The literate trader Philander Prescott, for instance, who had Indian wives and held the job of head U.S. farmer for the eastern Sioux, was a prime informant.

In the years between the appearances of these official works, others of substantial importance were also created. Philander Prescott marked down his impressions in detail before he met a violent death during the Minnesota Sioux War of 1862, and these have been printed in several places. Edwin Thomas Denig, another trade operative who lived like Prescott, left valuable records about five tribes situated farther west, and they have been published in book form. William W. Warren, who grew up among Indians surrounding the headwaters of the Mississippi and then dealt with their plight while a member of the Minnesota territorial legislature, surveyed the ethnohistory as well as the contact history of an important federation in his *History of the Ojibwa Nation.* Rudolph Friedrich Kurz wrote an excellent journal from impressions he gathered among fur traders, which contained ethnographic as well as commercial information.[9]

During the third quarter of the nineteenth century, there was again a paucity of work because of wars—wars across the trans-Mississippi West between Indians and whites that disrupted most ethnographic efforts until the late 1870s. But scholarship was then revived, and it flourished with encouragement and some funding from the new Bureau of American Ethnology. Albert S. Gatschet worked on the federation that had controlled the Mississippi Delta. John R. Swanton accomplished pioneering research among numerous tribes on the Gulf Coast. Alice Fletcher, James Owen Dorsey, and Stephen Return Riggs wrote landmark studies on the tribes of the central and northern Great Plains region.[10]

The efforts of scholars such as these continued into the twentieth century. Meanwhile, writers of Indian extraction, who had been educated under the U.S. government's "civilization plan," started to produce ethnographic reminiscences about their respective tribes. Among the most successful and prolific was Charles Alexander Eastman. Working with his non-Indian wife and former education inspector for the western Sioux, Elaine Goodale, he published many works of value. One was *The Soul of the Indian,* about religious philosophies and practices. Another was *Wigwam Evenings: Sioux Folk Tales Retold.* Representing the same federation of tribes, Ella C. Deloria produced *Dakota Texts* a short time later. Luther Standing Bear generated reminiscences for his *My People the Sioux* after that.[11]

By the end of the 1930s, the academic professions in the United States had matured sufficiently to produce anthropologists capable of drawing this great body of raw material on American Indian tribal cultures together into readable syntheses. First in the succession of academics to accomplish this was Clark Wissler, who wrote *Indians in the United States: Four Centuries of their History and Culture,* an enduring work that identified all major groups, described their ancient cultures, and interpreted changes that had occurred through four hundred years of contact with non-Indians. A few years later John Swanton produced the first in a succession of three exemplary works to come out on the southeastern tribes. *The Indians of the Southeastern United States* introduced modern readers to the old cultural values and practices of that region in some detail. Historian Robert F. Berkhofer then supplied historical context and interpretive remarks for the reprinting of James Adair's *The History of American Indians* as he had known them in 1775. This was especially valuable to historiography, for it supplied cultural information about the Five Civilized Tribes and the Catawba federation from an eighteenth-century "noble savage" point of view. Finally, Charles Hudson drew together and expanded the substance of previous accounts with his recent survey, *The Southeastern Indians,* in which he dealt sequentially with prehistory, social institutions, and contact history, giving the greatest attention to early modern belief systems, social organization, subsistence, ceremonies, art, music, and recreation.[12]

Though not yet graced by scholarship of equal quality, the tribes of several trans-Mississippi provinces have received excellent ethnographic treatment, too, in the 1960s and 1970s. Drawing upon Hispanic colonial records as well as archaeological and anthropological surveys, William W. Newcomb, Jr., described the early cultures of several small federations in *The Indians of Texas: From Prehistoric to Modern Times.* Using similar sources, Edward Holland Spicer supplied information about early modern culture (as well as change through interracial contact) among southwestern groups in his *Cycles of Conquest.* More recently W. R. Wood and Margot Liberty edited essays by leading authorities in their new *Anthropology on the Great Plains.*[13]

Along with these important regional studies have come a few general accounts, to update and enlarge the work of Wissler. Oliver LaFarge gave the subject visual appeal in *A Pictorial History of American Indians.* Harold E. Driver combined ethnography with contact history in his *Indians of North America.* Spicer tried with limited success to deal with cultural experiences in the tribes by writing *A Short History of the Indians of the United States.*[14]

A remarkable quantity of information about the internal affairs of the tribes and federations has been assembled since colonial Hispanic chroniclers wrote their reports on the societies they encountered in the Southeast. To date, no work has appeared to tie it all together with mature insights, generalizations, and conclusions, but this is likely to happen within the next quarter-century.

Still greater amounts of information have been preserved, by even more writers, on the second subdivision of Indian history identified above—the history of policies devised and implemented by non-Indians to govern the lives of original Americans. All but a few of the significant works have been published in the past half-century.

None deserving recognition has ever been written on the colonial era. At that time, no policies devised by the Spanish and French had lasting impacts, of course, beyond their influence on imperial designs and the shaping of intercultural contacts. And no significant policies were ever employed by British leaders. Individual colonies were left mainly to their own devices until the 1740s. By the time parliament and the cumbersome ministries worked out a general plan thereafter, it was too late to accomplish much but to influence intercultural alignments in the trans-Appalachian country and to hasten the coming of the American Revolution.

More than a score of studies have appeared, however, to explain federal Indian policies that were shaped and applied between the founding of the United States and the Civil War. Together, four of these supply an overview sufficient to guide the work of scholars and to satisfy the curiosities of most general readers. Although now dated in many ways, Laurence F. Schmeckebier's *The Office of Indian Affairs: Its History, Activities, and Organization* remains useful as a source of information on the genesis of the U.S. Indian Office and the Indian Field Service and their early dealings with various Indian groups. George Dewey Harmon's *Sixty Years of Indian Affairs, Political, Economic, and Diplomatic, 1789-1850* supplies added material on administrative networks and discusses the application of federal policies in the communities of specific tribes and federations. William T. Hagan's *American Indians* provides appropriate interpretations on the evolution of early federal influence in tribal life. S. Lyman Tyler's semiofficial publication, *A History of Indian Policy*, reviews the emergence of federal policies and their early application, even though it deals mainly with affairs in the twentieth century.[15]

Other historians have written about Indian-government relations during shorter time periods. Walter H. Mohr supplied background in his *Federal Indian Relations, 1774–1788.* In two publications, Francis Paul Prucha dealt with trade policy, the evolution of the Jacksonian "civilization plan," and the application of the plan down to mid-century. Bernard W. Sheehan and Father Prucha dwelled upon the benevolent intentions of Jeffersonians and Jacksonians who devised the civilization plan, challenging the "Devil theorists," who have identified greed, land lust, and cultural imperialism as the major influences in shaping early American Indian policies. Ronald Satz wrote a valuable description of government relations with Indians during the Jackson era. Robert A. Trennert and Edmund J. Danziger described the establishment of the civilization plan on reservations in the late 1840s and the 1850s.[16]

A dozen short studies or more have appeared that trace the application of early federal policies in specific regions before the Civil War: in the South, the Old Northwest, Sioux country, Arkansas and Missouri, Texas, the Mexican Cession Lands, and the Pacific Northwest. Though a jumble of monographs of irregular quality, this body of literature supplies a penetrating look into the impacts of federal administration, as well as a review of the treaty-making process and a summary of problems surrounding the establishment of reservations. Two books by former federal officials—Indian Commissioner Francis E. Leupp and administrator for the Bureau of Indian Affairs D'Arcy McNickle—have appraised the early policies in retrospect.[17]

Additional studies have come out on more specific aspects of early relationships between the tribes and the federal government. In *A History of the United States Indian Factory System, 1795–1822,* Ora Peake wrote one of several pieces to appear on national policy before the Jackson era. Even more literature has been published about the removal of trans-Appalachian tribes across the Mississippi. Reginald Horsman supplied background in a brochure, *The Origin of Indian Removal, 1815–1824.* Grant Foreman wrote separate surveys on the relocation of the Five Civilized Tribes from the Southeast and of Algonquian peoples from the Great Lakes plains in his *Indian Removal* and *The Last Trek of the Indians.* Mary Young examined the involvement of land companies and an early nineteenth-century allotment system offered to

Indians as an alternative to the trail of tears in her *Redskins, Ruffleshirts, and Rednecks.* Michael Paul Rogin published a provocative though unconvincing study of Jackson's support for removal as a Freudian manifestation in his *Fathers and Children: Andrew Jackson and the Subjugation of the American Indian.*[18]

Works about groups who implemented federal policies have supplied yet another view. R. Pierce Beaver's *Church, State and the American Indians* tells how public officials long employed missionaries to accomplish the "civilization" as well as the Christianization of Indians. William M. Neil's "The Territorial Governor as Indian Superintendent in the Trans-Mississippi West" describes problems that confronted ranking field administrators as they endeavored to mollify tensions that grew out of conflict between the expectations of policymakers and the practicalities of local circumstances. John L. Loss's "William Clark, Indian Agent" and Jerome O. Steffen's *William Clark: Jeffersonian Man on the Frontier* deal with the most effective superintendent to coordinate policies in the field during the first half of the nineteenth century. Willoughby Maynard Babcock drew attention to problems at the grass roots in related articles about the first and foremost agent ever to serve at Fort Snelling: "Major Lawrence Taliaferro, Indian Agent" and "Talliaferro Map of the St. Peters Agency."[19]

Considerable work has been accomplished on higher-ranking officials. Father Prucha has supplied a brief evaluation of one central figure in *Lewis Cass and American Indian Policy.* Herman J. Viola has prepared a reprint of the autobiography of the first Indian commissioner in *Memoirs, Official and Personal* of Thomas L. McKenney. Archivist Robert Kvasnicka and Viola have gathered brief but useful essays on many others in their encyclopedic *The Commissioners of Indian Affairs, 1824-1977.*[20]

Roles and problems of U.S. Army leaders in the management of Indian affairs have also been summarized and explained successfully. Prucha related half of the story in *The Sword of the Republic: The United States Army on the Frontier, 1783-1846.* Robert Utley told the rest in *Frontiersmen in Blue: The United States Army and the Indians, 1848-1865.* And Richard White has called attention to how western tribes became worthy opponents to hinterland garrisons, through the development of military prowess in protracted wars with their Indian neighbors, in "The Winning of the West: The Expansion of the Western Sioux in the Eighteenth and Nineteenth Centuries."[21]

Other aspects of policy history in pre–Civil War times still are conspicuous for the paucity of scholarship they have attracted. There has been little work on the early evolution of educational systems, for example, as Estelle Fuches and Robert J. Havighurst have implied by the historical survey contained in their analysis of the 1960s, *To Live On This Earth: American Indian Education.* There is need for extensive exploration of the histories of laws and treaties, as is evidenced in uninterpreted material printed on these subjects.[22]

Many topics in policy history have yet to attract scholars, but considering that the study of policies has been pursued as a special subdivision of Indian history by bona fide scholars for less than half a century, progress in the study of pre-Civil War times has been remarkable. A similar observation is appropriate to the assessment of the third subdivision—Indian-white contact history—although this requires some qualification. Thus far, scholarship on relationships between Indian and non-Indian groups has not compared favorably with that accomplished in the subdivisions of ethnography and policy history, in large degree for a lack of objectivity. The quality of publications about contact history has long been limited by the emotions surrounding the issue of whites' culpability for the cultural deterioration and threats of genocide experienced by the tribes. Often using Helen Hunt Jackson's intemperate polemic as a standard by which to judge the injustices, historians and ethnologists alike have made a game of weighing evidence for and against the Devil theory.

Bernard Sheehan has assembled various opinions about the subject for pre-Civil War times in his article "Indian-White Relations in Early America: A Review Essay." An illustration of the dichotomy of opinion that has evolved may be found in literature on colonial years. Alden Vaughn has argued with his description of war between the races that Indians of seventeenth-century New England suffered more due to differences between cultures than from cruelty on the parts of Puritan aggressors. David Beer has insisted, on the other hand, that a careful examination of colonial literature leads to another conclusion. After a brief run of "noble redman" publications, colonials betrayed their growing rancor in print by using such terms as "savage," by including reports of the torture of white captives, and by interpreting warfare as an expression of blood lust on the parts of the original American participants.[23]

More than a dozen other writers have prepared publications that have dealt with the various dimensions as well as the morality of early contact history. Among the first to speculate on the nature and possible consequences of the confrontation were Thomas McKenney and John Nicolay (Abraham Lincoln's personal secretary), who recommended in the years 1846 and 1863 the establishment of a separate state or territory for Indians out of fear that they might be exterminated by avaricious whites. Commissioner Francis

Leupp implied, more than half a century later, that insensitive non-Indians had long engendered cultural deterioration in the tribes. Then, as contact history began to attract serious scholars during the 1930s, Jennings C. Wise wrote on Indian-white relations before the Civil War as an inevitable clash of political systems and religious philosophies, in which Indians were the losers. Donald McNicol dwelled upon impressions that the two cultural forces had developed about each other by the middle of the ninteenth century.[24]

More recently, Harold Fey and D'Arcy McNickle surveyed highlights of contact history and blamed public policy for negative effects; Edward Spicer supplied a detailed analysis of the consequences of contact in the Southwest in his *Cycles of Conquest*; and Robert Munkres expressed the belief that prior to 1840 the interface had caused little change in trans-Mississippi tribes, for up to that time only itinerant traders showed up on a regular basis. But subsequently tribal traditions began to fade as many groups of white pioneers filed across the Mississippi, demanding the concentration of Indians on reserves to make way for the exploitation of natural resources. Then McNickle appraised changing conditions in tribal life due to intercultural relations from early to modern times. And William Hagan enlarged on McNickle's theme with a review of the history of tribalism as the target of aggressive attacks. Hagan concluded that Indians have proven the strengths of their ancient cultures by sustaining their affinities for tribal life in the face of long and concerted effort by whites to render their cultural values and institutions extinct.[25]

While these and other authors have written contact history with Indian cultural attrition and survival as a central focus, others have altered the scope by describing whole experiences of particular tribes and federations in their dealings with non-Indians. Mislabeled "tribal history" more often than not, these studies represent the kind of penetrating research that must be accomplished nationwide before the subfield can approach maturity. Among the earliest twentieth-century scholars to participate in the study of federations was Doane Robinson, who published *A History of the Dakota or Sioux Indians* three-quarters of a century ago. Grant Foreman then wrote *The Five Civilized Tribes,* as academicians developed their interest in the 1930s. A little later Randolph Downes described the tribes of Algonquian country in his *Council Fires on the Upper Ohio.* And Roy W. Meyer attempted a contact history of the four *Isanti* groups of Sioux in the 1960s, under the erroneous title *History of the Santee Sioux.*[26]

Others have narrowed their research to deal with contact history in one tribe at a time. Grace Woodward has prepared a readable account of the pre–Civil War years in *The Cherokees.* Arthur DeRosier offered a sequel to Grant Foreman's collective works on the Five Civilized Tribes in *The Removal of the Choctaw Indians.* William Unrau wrote *The Kansa Indians* and R. David Edmunds *The Potawatomis* about contact experiences down to the Civil War.[27] Tribal and federation studies such as these have begun to supply vital information on the intricacies of Indian-white relations down to 1860. Their shortcomings result not from deficient scholarship, for the most part, or from any particular errors in judgment about events that transpired at major points of contact, but rather from the failure of the authors to interpret their findings adequately, and their resulting reluctance to shed light upon the effects of early American contact on both races down to the present.

Similar defects appear in the examination of contact by special white groups before the 1860s. Many fine studies deal with relationships between fur traders and Indians from the Great Lakes to the Rocky Mountains, for example. Harold A. Innis's *The Fur Trade in Canada* traces the activities of merchants who worked the Great Lakes region for New France as far west as the semiarid prairies. Marjorie Gordon Jackson's "The Beginning of British Trade at Michilimackinac" tells how British-Canadian operatives took over from the French and, in a deliberate effort to substitute monopoly for free trade, organized the North West Company. W. L. Morton's "The North West Company: Pedlars Extraordinary" assesses the nature of that trade while tracing the history of the Nor'westers from 1774 to 1821. Wayne Stevens's "The Fur Trade in Minnesota During the British Regime" contains a brief but learned treatise on the commerce that flowed between the St. Lawrence and Prairie du Chien. Grace Lee Nute's "Forts in the Minnesota Fur Trading Area, 1660-1880" surveys the history of trading posts down to the time when they were replaced by agency stores. Richard Oglesby's *Manuel Lisa and the Opening of the Missouri Fur Trade* explains, better than any other work, the beginnings of northern Great Plains commerce under St. Louis merchants. John E. Sunder's *Joshua Pilcher: Fur Trader and Indian Agent,* on Lisa's successor, carries the story to the early 1840s; his *The Fur Trade on the Upper Missouri, 1840-1865* traces northern Plains trade through the heyday and waning years of the company founded by Pierre Choteau, Jr., to the time of the founder's death and the company's collapse in 1865, after which agency stores soon replaced trading posts and itinerant operatives. In superficial but important efforts to interpret the interface, Lewis O. Saum's *The Fur Trader and the Indian* supplies evidence about traders' impressions of Indians with whom they dealt west of the Mississippi; Preston Holder's "The

Fur Trade as Seen from the Indian Point of View" provides a glimpse from the other side.[28]

Recently two scholars initiated studies of family life among traders and began to shed light not only upon economic affairs and social attitudes but also on the plight of the mixed-blood progeny in camps of Hudson's Bay Company and North West Company workers. Although written about the Canadian frontier, these studies have obvious application where the two companies operated in the north central United States. With "Women and the Fur Trade," Sylvia Van Kirk described services rendered by the Indian and mixed-blood common law wives of traders in commercial liaison and cultural instruction as well as in personal companionship among the men who worked on the hinterland. In *Strangers in Blood: Fur Trade Company Families in Indian Country,* Jennifer Brown examined family life that evolved from the merger of two societies with different traditions; in "Ultimate Respectability: Fur-Trade Children in the 'Civilized World,'" she described how traders sent their progeny away for education and "civilization" to assure them secure niches either in non-Indian society or in fur trade areas.[29]

On contact between white soldiers and Indians at the grass roots, there are several reliable studies. Father Prucha's *Broadax and Bayonet: The Role of the United States Army in the Development of the Northwest, 1815-1860* deals with the upper Mississippi River region, for example. Robert Athearn's *Forts of the Upper Missouri* describes army operations from the James River to the northern Rockies.[30] These and other studies of contact by fur traders and white soldiers provide reliable information about the intruders, but unfortunately they supply a limited amount of information about the effects of the protracted relationships of the two groups with each other, and they fail to assess long-range impacts of that contact upon both Indians and whites.

Publications about the activities and influences of missionaries have had similar strengths and weaknesses. For the early years, R. Pierce Beaver's "Methods of American Missions to the Indians in the Seventeenth and Eighteenth Centuries: Calvinist Models for Protestant Foreign Missions" advances the notion that conversion efforts in colonial times had few lasting results and tells how colonial ecclesiastics developed methods and procedures used by missionaries in the nineteenth century. Robert F. Berkhofer's *Salvation and the Savage* attempts with success encumbered by narrow perspective to explain why missionaries' achievements in "civilization" and Christianization fell short of expectations through early modern times. Sister M. Acquinas Norton's "Missionary Activity in the Northwest under the French Regime, 1640-1740" provides a sketch, with little interpretation, for the years from

Hennepin's expedition to the mid-eighteenth century. Stephen Return Riggs's *Mary and I* is an eyewitness account of the problems and achievements of nineteenth-century missionaries who came west under the auspices of the American Board of Commissioners for Foreign Missions.[31]

So far there has been a dearth of effort to explain specific causes for trouble throughout the history of contact. Reginald Horsman's "American Indian Policy in the Old Northwest" and other writings deal with the influence of land lust. Francis R. Packard's "Epidemic Sickness and Mortality in the English Colonies in North America from Its Earliest Discovery to the Year 1800" enumerates the worst of the plagues imported by whites. Hiram Chittenden's "The Smallpox Scourge of 1837," in his general study of the fur trade, is one of a number of articles about specific epidemics. J. Francis Nolan's "The Liquor Problem and the Jesuit Missions in New France" and a chapter in William Johnson's *The Federal Government and the Liquor Traffic* are among the few articles to deal with whiskey and drugs in an historical context.[32]

One other type of inquiry stands out in Indian-white contact historiography; there have been many biographical studies of principal Indian leaders. Perhaps Francis Parkman's classic on the Algonquian organizer Pontiac was the first of high quality to appear. R. David Edmunds's important anthology, *American Indian Leaders,* is the most recent. It contains life stories of several pre-Civil War Indian leaders that cut across subject areas in all of the three subdivisions of American Indian history.[33]

As was indicated earlier, research and writing on each of the major components of this field of history require special preparation and unique perspective, and each should be presented in its own context. The historiography of each should be assessed by itself, according to its own requirements and its own themes.

To date, policy history has been written best. This results partly from the existence of such large volumes of primary source materials and the ready access to them provided by the National Archives and other repositories. The advanced condition of historiography in this subdivision stems, too, from the better preparation of scholars. Because this subject area calls for the very training supplied by most graduate programs in history and because it requires little interdisciplinary knowledge or experience, almost anyone with training in a respectable graduate program in history might qualify to write about it proficiently.

Ethnography suffers from an obvious defect, despite the availability of substantial quantities of materials and the participation of capable ethnologists. Quality has been eroded by the refusal of all but a few scholars in this subdivision to make more than token gestures toward the acquisition of interdisciplinary understanding. Trained mainly in anthropology, most have been stubborn in their refusal to study the methods and lessons offered by historians, and the value of their writings has suffered accordingly. With few exceptions, they have written culture studies on particular time periods and have either ignored the impacts of change through intercultural contact and time, or have given these dimensions of the study no more than token recognition in preliminary chapters and epilogues. Out of this disposition has flowed isolated study after isolated study comprising little information about relationships between Indian ethnography and Anglo-American mainstream culture throughout the recorded history of American life.

Indian-white contact historiography is hampered by a similar malady. Just as most anthropologists have refused to incorporate the lessons of professional history into their studies, so have Indian-white contact historians spurned the need for training and field experience in the ethnologies of the "other cultures." In the main, this subdivision of Indian history has been dominated by non-Indian scholars—many of considerable ability—who have presumed to understand the causes, the progress, and the effects of intercultural attrition over long periods of time without the slightest experience with the habits and philosophies of the Indians engaged in the prolonged contact. Non-Indian scholars have, for example, presumed to judge the impacts of mission activities with little or no knowledge about the religions the white ecclesiastics were attempting to supplant. Lacking this information, which is available only through extensive field work, they have failed to understand either the philosophical attrition that took place at the time or the cross-cultural religions that have evolved from periods of initial contact to the present. Native Americans with academic competence who have attempted to write contact history have been guilty of the same fault. They have endeavored to perceive history at the grass roots without fully understanding whence the invaders came, what they represented, and how they were postured in the interface. This defect inherent in Indian-white contact study can be remedied only by interdisciplinary training in both history and ethnology, through active participation by writers of both cultures in the systematic study of the "other culture," and ideally by cross-cultural collaboration and joint authorship.

Added to shortcomings in the scholars themselves, there are deficiencies in Indian historiography caused by the infancy and the complexity of the field. A plethora of topics exists in the several subdivisions that must be explored by serious scholars. There are no studies of the "colony" movement in federal Indian policy, for example, which in Sioux country alone goes back to Eatonville on Lake Calhoun (1829). There are no sound publications of historical scope on agency farmers, on field matrons, or on field nurses, who were far more important to the application of policies and intercultural contact than any groups of higher ranking officials. There is no meritorious study of the history and the roles of mixed-bloods. There is no scholarly work about the important efforts of nuns and other female ecclesiastics who served so effectively throughout contact history in Indian education and health care delivery. There is no sound analysis of the history of conflict and cooperation between medicine men and white physicians. There are no good studies of "regular" and "irregular" labor in reservation societies. There are no good reviews of the processes of land allotment, land lease, and surplus land sales, or of treaties, or law, or education; and so the list goes on.

Because of the newness of the field, regional emphasis remains out of balance. By far the greatest concentration has been on Indian history for the southern and eastern parts of the United States. There is need to accelerate efforts to study the histories of the northern and far western tribes and federations.

Finally, American Indian historiography suffers for a paucity of systematic direction. Before 1970, the only extensive bibliography in print was George Peter Murdock's *Ethnographic Bibliography of North America.* Fortunately, a number of others have appeared over the past decade, and several efforts are still in progress. The *Index to Literature on the American Indian* came out annually during the early 1970s. Dwight Smith then produced *Indians of the United States and Canada: A Bibliography* of recent periodical publications with annotations. William Hodge published *A Bibliography of Contemporary North American Indians* in 1976. In 1977 Father Prucha compiled *A Bibliographical Guide to the History of Indian-White Relations in the United States* for the University of Chicago Press. It contained the best list of guides to primary sources on American Indian history in print, followed by an extensive compilation of books and articles subdivided into subject categories. And Father Prucha has brought it up to date with a supplement published by the University of Nebraska Press in 1982. Along with these came lists of official reports and publications on literature, economic development, urban affairs, and other special interests. In the middle of the 1970s, Francis Jennings became general editor of the Newberry Library series, published by

Indiana University Press, which on completion in 1983 will include thirty volumes dealing with special subjects and particular regions as well as certain tribes and federations. These have been designed for the general reader as well as for the scholar. Each volume identifies approximately one hundred of the best books and articles on its subject, supplies a short list of recommended readings for the buff, then treats each entry in a substantial historiographical essay for the academician.

More recently, this writer and Jack Marken introduced a series of larger volumes with the publication of *Bibliography of the Sioux,* which presents more than thirty-three hundred citations on the subject, part of which are annotated. It establishes a model for an ongoing series, which Marken will edit and which to date has contracted some twenty other volumes for various subjects, regions, and tribes across the United States.[34]

The appearance of bibliographies that deal as a matter of course with early American Indian history as well as with recent affairs signals the emergence of the whole field of interest from infancy into adolescence. Because Indian history for the years preceding the Civil War is remote, relatively undramatic, and to some degree beyond the reach of oral and anthropological field work, it has received far less attention from scholars than has the history of the last one hundred years or so. The signs are promising, nevertheless. The whole field is emerging from the clutches of amateurs and scholars in other disciplines and is at last coming into the grasp of professional historians and ethnographers. By the outset of the next century, it should have matured to keep pace with more traditional fields of study in the history of the United states.

Notes

1. Substance for this chapter comes mainly from files of a project funded by the National Endowment for the Humanities, entitled "History of the Sioux Federation."

2. Articles on American Indian historiography have been published from time to time. Perhaps the most provocative have been two that appeared under one cover in 1971: Wilcomb E. Washburn's "The Writing of American Indian History: A Status Report," and Robert F. Berkhofer's "The Political Context of a New Indian History," *Pacific Historical Review* 40 (August 1971): 261–81, 357–82. Both seem simplistic in retrospect, for their themes went little beyond recognition of the need for historians and anthropologists

to borrow from each other. Historian Berkhofer blamed anthropologists for the lack of cooperation, while ethnologist Washburn pointed an accusing finger at historians. Other articles have had equally narrow scope. Berkhofer derided academicians for treating Indians only as obstacles to the Anglo-American frontier and called for "Indian-centered" history in "Native Americans and United States History," *The Re-interpretation of History and Culture* (Washington, D.C.: National Council for the Social Studies, 1973): 37–52. More recently, Francis Jennings criticized scholars for the same error and prescribed greater interdisciplinary cooperation as a remedy, in "A Growing Partnership: Historians, Anthropologists, and American Indian History," *History Teacher* 12 (November 1980): 87–104. Steven C. Schulte complained about the paucity of interest in pre–Civil War times in "American Indian Historiography and the Myth of the Origins of the Plains Wars," *Nebraska History* 61, no. 4 (Winter 1980): 437–44. Each of these publications raised a significant issue, but none explained the dimensions or defined the central needs of the field.

3. Assumptions advanced below about these subdivisions pertain only to federally recognized tribes. Comments about intratribal affairs and Indian-white contact apply also to the past experiences of nonfederal tribes, of course, given allowances for limitations on sources available pertaining to their histories for their lack of official dealings with the United States.

4. Lee Eldridge Huddleston, *Origins of the American Indians: European Concepts, 1492–1729* (Austin: University of Texas Press, 1967); Robert Wauchope, *Lost Tribes and Sunken Continents: Myth and Method in the Study of American Indians* (Chicago: University of Chicago Press, 1962); Jesse D. Jennings, *Prehistory of North America* (New York: McGraw-Hill, 1968, 1974); Evarts Boutell Greene and Virginia D. Harrington, *American Population Before the Federal Census of 1790* (New York: Columbia University Press, 1932); Henry R. Schoolcraft, *Information Respecting the History, Condition and Prospects of the Indian Tribes of the United States,* 6 vols. (Philadelphia: Lippincott, Grambo and Company, 1851–57).

5. Angie Debo, *A History of the Indians of the United States* (Norman: University of Oklahoma Press, 1970); Wilcomb E. Washburn, *The Indian in America* (New York: Harper and Row, 1975); Arrell Morgan Gibson, *The American Indian: Prehistory to the Present* (Lexington, Mass.: D. C. Heath, 1980).

6. Reuben Gold Thwaites (ed.), *The Jesuit Relations and Allied Documents,* 73 vols. (Cleveland: Burrows Brothers Company, 1896–1901); Thwaites (ed.), *A New Discovery of the Vast Country in America* . . . , 2 vols. (Chicago:

A. C. McClurg Company, 1903); Edwin D. Neill (ed.), "The 'Sioux or Nadouesis,'" *Minnesota Archaeologist* 39, no. 4 (December 1980): 199–206 (reprint from the obscure *Macalester College Contributions*, 10 [1890–92]). The writer draws many examples from the historiography of the region between the Great Lakes plains and the Rocky Mountains for several reasons. One is that here have lived the Sioux, one of four or five major tribal federations in the United States, about whom more than four thousand books and articles have been published over the years. Another is that the writer has channeled most of his scholarly interest into Sioux-white contact history and hence is most familiar with the historiography of sources on this federation and the region it has occupied. Still another is that writers of general works have in the past drawn excessively upon the histories of southern and eastern tribes and federations at the expense of the histories of major groups elsewhere in the country. It seems time for scholars to begin to structure American Indian literature to include the people of all major cultures and regions.

7. Cadwallader Colden, *The History of the Five Nations Depending on the Province of New York* (Ithaca, N.Y.: Cornell University Press, 1964); James Adair, *The History of the American Indians*, ed. Robert F. Berkhofer (San Francisco: Johnson Reprint Corporation, 1968).

8. Jedediah Morse, *A Report to the Secretary of War . . .* (New York: Augustus M. Kelley, 1970); Henry R. Schoolcraft, *Information Respecting the History. . . .*

9. See *Collections of the Minnesota Historical Society* 6 (1894): 475–91; Donald Dean Parker (ed.), *The Recollections of Philander Prescott, Frontiersman of the Old Northwest, 1819–1862* (Lincoln: University of Nebraska Press, 1966); John Ewers (ed.), *Five Indian Tribes of the Upper Missouri: Sioux, Arikaras, Assiniboines, Crees, Crows* (Norman: University of Oklahoma Press, 1961); William W. Warren, *History of the Ojibwa Nation* (Minneapolis: Ross and Haines, 1970); John N. B. Hewitt (ed.), *Journal of Rudolph Friedrich Kurz* (Washington, D.C.: Government Printing Office, 1937).

10. Albert S. Gatschet, *The Shetimasha Indians of St Mary's Parish Southern Louisiana* (n.p., 1883); John R. Swanton, *Indian Tribes of the Lower Mississippi Valley and Adjacent Coast of the Gulf of Mexico* (St. Clair Shores, Mich.: Scholarly Press, 1976); for examples of Great Plains studies, see Alice Fletcher, *Indian Ceremonies* (Salem, Mass.: Salem Press, 1884); James Owen Dorsey, "Siouan Sociology: A Posthumous Paper," *Annual Reports of the Bureau of American Ethnology* 2 (1897): 205–44; and Stephen Return Riggs, *Dakota Grammar, Texts, and Ethnography* (Washington, D.C.: Government

Printing Office, 1893, 1977; reprinted for distribution without introduction or revision in 1977 by Blue Cloud Abbey, Marvin, S.Dak.).

11. Charles Alexander Eastman, *The Soul of the Indian* (New York: Houghton Mifflin, 1911); Charles Alexander and Elaine Goodale Eastman, *Wigwam Evenings: Sioux Folk Tales Retold* (Eau Claire, Wis.: E. M. Hale. 1937); Ella C. Deloria, *Dakota Texts,* ed. Agnes Picotte and Paul N. Pavich (Vermillion, S.Dak.: Dakota Press, 1978); Luther Standing Bear, *My People the Sioux* (Boston: Houghton Mifflin, 1928; paperbound ed. Lincoln: University of Nebraska Press, 1975).

12. Clark Wissler, *Indians in the United States: Four Centuries of their History and Culture* (New York: Doubleday, Doran, and Company, 1940); John R. Swanton, *The Indians of the Southeastern United States,* Bureau of American Ethnology Bulletin no. 137 (Washington, D.C.: Government Printing Office, 1946); Adair, *The History of the American Indians*; Charles Hudson, *The Southeastern Indians* (Knoxville: University of Tennessee Press, 1976).

13. William W. Newcomb, Jr., *The Indians of Texas: From Prehistoric to Modern Times* (Austin: University of Texas Press, 1961); Edward Holland Spicer, *Cycles of Conquest* (Tucson: University of Arizona Press, 1962); W. Raymond Wood and Margot Liberty, *Anthropology on the Great Plains* (Lincoln: University of Nebraska Press, 1980).

14. Oliver LaFarge, *A Pictorial History of American Indians,* ed. Alvin M. Josephy, Jr. (New York: Crown Publishers, 1974); Harold E. Driver, *Indians of North America* (Chicago: University of Chicago Press, 1969); Edward Holland Spicer, *A Short History of the Indians of the United States* (New York: Van Nostrand-Reinhold Company, 1969).

15. Laurence Schmeckebier, *The Office of Indian Affairs: Its History, Activities, and Organization* (Baltimore: Johns Hopkins University Press, 1927); George Dewey Harmon, *Sixty Years of Indian Affairs, Political, Economic, and Diplomatic, 1789-1850* (Chapel Hill: University of North Carolina Press, 1941); William T. Hagan, *American Indians* (Chicago: University of Chicago Press, 1961); S. Lyman Tyler, *A History of Indian Policy* (Washington, D.C.: Bureau of Indian Affairs, 1973).

16. Walter H. Mohr, *Federal Indian Relations, 1774-1788* (Philadelphia: University of Pennsylvania Press, 1933); Francis Paul Prucha, *American Indian Policy in the Formative Years: The Indian Trade and Intercourse Acts, 1790-1834* (Cambridge: Harvard University Press, 1962; paperbound ed. Lincoln: University of Nebraska Press, 1970), and "American Indian Policy in the 1840s: Visions of Reform," *The Frontier Challenge: Responses to the*

Trans-Mississippi West, ed. John G. Clark (Lawrence: University Press of Kansas, 1971): 81-111; Bernard W. Sheehan, *Seeds of Extinction: Jeffersonian Philanthrophy and the American Indian* (Chapel Hill: University of North Carolina Press, 1973); Prucha, "Andrew Jackson's Indian Policy: A Reassessment," *Journal of American History* 56 (December 1969): 527-39; Ronald Satz, *American Indian Policy in the Jacksonian Era* (Lincoln: University of Nebraska Press, 1975; paperbound ed. 1976); Robert A. Trennert, Jr., *Alternative to Extinction: Federal Indian Policy and the Beginnings of the Reservation System, 1846-51* (Philadelphia: Temple University Press, 1975); Edmund J. Danziger, Jr., *Indians and Bureaucrats: Administering the Reservation Policy during the Civil War* (Urbana: University of Illinois Press, 1974).

17. Kenneth Coleman, "Federal Indian Relations in the South, 1781-1789," *Chronicles of Oklahoma* 35 (Winter 1957-58): 435-58; Reginald Horsman, "American Indian Policy in the Old Northwest, 1783-1812," *William and Mary Quarterly* 18 (January 1961): 35-53; Lucy Elizabeth Textor, *Official Relations Between the United States and the Sioux Indians* (Palo Alto, Calif.: Stanford University Press, 1896); Howard W. Paulson, "Federal Indian Policy and the Dakota Indians, 1800-1840," *South Dakota History* 3 (Summer 1973): 285-309; James C. Malin, "Indian Policy and Westward Expansion," *Bulletin of the University of Kansas Humanistic Studies* (Lawrence: University of Kansas, 1921): 1-108; George Dewey Harmon, "The United States Indian Policy in Texas, 1845-1860," *Mississippi Valley Historical Review* 17, no. 3 (December 1930): 377-403; Lena Clara Koch, "The Federal Indian Policy in Texas, 1845-1860," *Southwestern Historical Quarterly* 28 (January 1925): 223-34; (April 1925): 259-86; 29 (July 1925): 19-35; (October 1925): 98-127; Edward Everett Dale, *The Indians of the Southwest: A Century of Development Under the United States* (Norman: University of Oklahoma Press, 1949); Alban Hoopes, *Indian Affairs and Their Administration, with Special Reference to the Far West, 1849-1860* (Philadelphia: University of Pennsylvania Press, 1932); F.C. Coan, "The First Stage of the Federal Indian Policy in the Pacific Northwest, 1849-1852," *Oregon Historical Society Quarterly* 22, no. 1 (March 1921): 46-89, and "The Adoption of the Reservation Policy in the Pacific Northwest, 1853-1855," *Oregon Historical Society Quarterly* 23, no. 1 (March 1922): 1-38; William H. Ellison, "The Federal Indian Policy in California, 1846-1860," *Mississippi Valley Historical Review* 9, no. 1 (June 1922): 37-67; Francis E. Leupp, *The Indian and His Problem* (New York: C. Scribner's Sons, 1910); D'Arcy McNickle, *They Came Here First: The Epic of the American Indian* (Philadelphia: J. B. Lippincott Co., 1949).

18. Ora Peake, *A History of the United States Indian Factory System, 1795-1822* (Denver: Sage Books, 1954); Reginald Horsman, *The Origin of Indian Removal, 1815-1824* (East Lansing: Michigan State University Press, 1970); Grant Foreman, *Indian Removal* (Norman: University of Oklahoma Press, 1972), and *The Last Trek of the Indians* (New York: Russell and Russell, 1972); Mary E. Young, *Redskins, Ruffleshirts, and Rednecks* (Norman: University of Oklahoma Press, 1961); Michael Paul Rogin, *Fathers and Children: Andrew Jackson and the Subjugation of the American Indian* (New York: Knopf, 1975).

19. Robert Pierce Beaver, *Church, State and the American Indians* (St. Louis, Mo.: Concordia Publishing House, 1966); William M. Neil, "The Territorial Governor as Indian Superintendent in the Trans-Mississippi West," *Mississippi Valley Historical Review* 43, no. 2 (September 1956): 213-37; John L. Loss, "William Clark: Indian Agent," *Kansas Quarterly* 3, no. 4 (Fall 1971): 29-38; Jerome O. Steffen, *William Clark: Jeffersonian Man on the Frontier* (Norman: University of Oklahoma Press, 1977; paperbound ed., 1977); Willoughby M. Babcock, Jr., "Major Lawrence Taliaferro, Indian Agent," *Mississippi Valley Historical Review* 11, no. 3 (December 1924): 358-75, and "Talliaferro Map of the St. Peters Indian Agency," *Minnesota Archaeologist* 11, no. 4 (October 1945): 115-47.

20. Francis Paul Prucha, *Lewis Cass and American Indian Policy* (Detroit: Wayne State University Press, 1967); Thomas L. McKenney, *Memoirs, Official and Personal,* 2 vols. (New York: Paine and Burgess, 1846; paperbound ed. of vol. 1 Lincoln: University of Nebraska Press, 1973); Robert Kvasnicka and Herman J. Viola (eds.), *The Commissioners of Indian Affairs, 1824-1977* (Lincoln: University of Nebraska Press, 1979).

21. Francis Paul Prucha, *The Sword of the Republic: The United States Army on the Frontier, 1783-1846* (New York: Macmillan, 1969; paperbound ed., Bloomington: Indiana University Press, 1977); Robert M. Utley, *Frontiersmen in Blue: The United States Army and the Indian, 1848-1865* (New York: Macmillan, 1967; paperbound ed., Lincoln: University of Nebraska Press, 1981); Richard White, "The Winning of the West: The Expansion of the Western Sioux in the Eighteenth and Nineteenth Centuries," *Journal of American History* 65, no. 2 (September 1978): 319-43.

22. Estelle Fuchs and Robert J. Havighurst, *To Live on This Earth: American Indian Education* (Garden City, N.Y.: Doubleday, 1972); Felix S. Cohen, *Handbook of Federal Indian Law* (New York: HMS Press, 1972); Charles J. Kappler, *Indian Affairs: Laws and Treaties,* 7 vols. (Washington, D.C.: Government Printing Office, 1904-41).

23. Bernard Sheehan, "Indian-White Relations in Early America: A Review Essay," *William and Mary Quarterly* 26 (April 1969): 267–86; Alden Vaughan, *New England Frontier: Puritans and Indians, 1620–1675* (Boston: Little, Brown, 1965); David F. Beer, "Anti-Indian Sentiment in Early Colonial Literature," *Indian Historian* 2, no. 1 (Spring 1969): 29–33, 48.

24. Thomas L. McKenney, *On the Origin, History, Character and the Wrongs and Rights of the Indians with a Plan for the Preservation and Happiness of the Remnants of the Persecuted Race,* vol. 2 of his *Memoirs*; John Nicolay, *Lincoln's Secretary Goes West,* ed. Theodore C. Blegen (LaCrosse, Wis.: Sumac Press, 1965); Francis Leupp, *Red Man's Land: A Study of the American Indian* (New York: Fleming H. Revell Company, 1914); Jennings C. Wise, *The Red Man in the New World Drama: A Politico-Legal Study with a Pageantry of American History* (New York: Macmillan, 1971); Donald M. McNicol, *The Amerindians: From Acuera to Sitting Bull, from Donnacona to Big Bear* (New York: Frederick A. Stokes Company, 1937).

25. Harold E. Fey and D'Arcy McNickle, *Indians and Other Americans: Two Ways of Life Meet* (New York: Harper and Bros., 1959); Edward Holland Spicer, *Cycles of Conquest*; Robert L. Munkres, "Indian-White Contact Before 1870: Cultural Factors in Conflict," *Journal of the West* 10, no. 3 (July 1971): 439–73; D'Arcy McNickle, *Native American Tribalism: Indian Survivals and Renewals* (New York: Oxford University Press, 1973); William T. Hagan, "Tribalism Rejuvenated: The Native American Since the End of Termination," *Western Historical Quarterly* 12, no. 1 (January 1981): 7–16.

26. Doane Robinson, *A History of the Dakota or Sioux Indians* (1904; reprinted Minneapolis: Ross and Haines, 1974); Grant Foreman, *The Five Civilized Tribes* (Norman: University of Oklahoma Press, 1934); Randolph Downes, *Council Fires on the Upper Ohio* (Pittsburgh: University of Pittsburgh Press, 1940); Roy W. Meyer, *History of the Santee Sioux* (Lincoln: University of Nebraska Press, 1967; paperbound ed. 1980).

27. Grace Woodward, *The Cherokees* (Norman: University of Oklahoma Press, 1963); Arthur H. DeRosier, Jr., *The Removal of the Choctaw Indians* (Knoxville: University of Tennessee Press, 1970); William E. Unrau, *The Kansa Indians* (Norman: University of Oklahoma Press, 1971); R. David Edmunds, *The Potawatomis* (Norman: University of Oklahoma Press, 1978).

28. Harold A. Innis, *The Fur Trade in Canada* (New Haven: Yale University Press, 1930); Marjorie Gordon Jackson, "The Beginning of British Trade at Michilimackinac," *Minnesota History* 11 (September 1930): 231–70; W. L. Morton, "The North West Company: Pedlars Extraordinary," *Minnesota History* 40 (Winter 1966): 157–65; Wayne E. Stevens, "The Fur Trade in

Minnesota during the British Regime," *Minnesota History Bulletin* 5 (February 1923): 3-13; Grace Lee Nute, "Forts in the Minnesota Fur-Trading Area, 1660-1880," *Minnesota History* 11 (December 1930): 353-85; Richard Edward Oglesby, *Manuel Lisa and the Opening of the Missouri Fur Trade* (Norman: University of Oklahoma Press, 1963); John Edward Sunder, *Joshua Pilcher* (Norman: University of Oklahoma Press, 1968), and *The Fur Trade on the Upper Missouri* (Norman: University of Oklahoma Press, 1965); Lewis O. Saum, *The Fur Trader and the Indian* (Seattle: University of Washington Press, 1965; paperbound ed. 1966); Preston Holder, "The Fur Trade as Seen from the Indian Point of View," *Frontier Re-examined,* ed. John Francis McDermott (Urbana: University of Illinois Press, 1967), pp. 129-39.

29. Sylvia Van Kirk, "Women and the Fur Trade," *The Beaver* 303, no. 3 (Winter 1972): 4-21; Jennifer Brown, *Strangers in Blood: Fur Trade Company Families in Indian Country* (Vancouver: University of British Columbia Press, 1980); Brown, "Ultimate Respectability: Fur Trade Children in the 'Civilized World,'" *The Beaver* 308, no. 3 (Winter 1977): 4-10; 308, no. 4 (Spring 1978): 48-55.

30. Francis Paul Prucha, *Broadax and Bayonet: The Role of the United States Army in the Development of the Northwest, 1815-1860* (Madison: State Historical Society of Wisconsin, 1953); Robert Athearn, *Forts of the Upper Missouri* (Englewood Cliffs, N.J.: Prentice-Hall, 1967; paperbound ed. Lincoln: University of Nebraska Press, 1972).

31. Robert Pierce Beaver, "Methods of American Missions . . . ," *Journal of Presbyterian History* 47, no. 2 (June 1969): 124-48; Robert F. Berkhofer, Jr., *Salvation and the Savage* (New York: Atheneum Press, 1972); Sister M. Acquinas Norton, "Missionary Activity. . . ," *Acta et Dicta* 6, no. 2 (October 1934): 141-60; Stephen Return Riggs, *Mary and I* (Boston: Congregational Sunday-School and Publishing Society, 1887).

32. Horsman, "American Indian Policy in the Old Northwest, 1783-1812," Francis R. Packard, "Epidemic Sickness and Mortality . . . ," *History of Medicine in the United States* (New York: Hafner Publishing Co., 1963), pp. 59-159; Hiram M. Chittenden, "The Smallpox Scourge of 1837," *The American Fur Trade of the Far West,* 2 vols. (Stanford, Calif.: Academic Reprints, 1954), 2:619-27; J. Francis Nolan, "The Liquor Problem and the Jesuit Missions in New France," *Acta et Dicta* 3, no. 1 (July 1911): 91-141; William Johnson, "The Aborigines," *The Federal Government and the Liquor Traffic* (Westerville, Ohio: American Issue Publishing Co., 1911), pp. 160-209.

33. Francis Parkman, *The Conspiracy of Pontiac and the Indian War after the Conquest of Canada,* 2 vols. (1851; reprinted New York: AMS Press,

1969); R. David Edmunds (ed.), *American Indian Leaders* (Lincoln: University of Nebraska Press, 1980).

34. George Peter Murdock, *Ethnographic Bibliography of North America* (New Haven: Human Relations Area Files, 1941, 1960, 1975); *Index to Literature on the American Indian* (San Francisco: Indian Historian Press, 1970-); Dwight L. Smith, *Indians of the United States and Canada: A Bibliography* (Santa Barbara, Calif.: ABC-Clio Press, 1974); William Hodge, *A Bibliography of Contemporary North American Indians* (New York: Interland Publishing Company, 1976); Francis Paul Prucha, *A Bibliographical Guide to the History of Indian-White Relations in the United States* (Chicago: University of Chicago Press, 1977); Prucha, *Indian-White Relations in the United States: A Bibliography of Works Published 1975-1980* (Lincoln: University of Nebraska Press, 1982); Francis Jennings (ed.), The Newberry Library Center for the History of the American Indian Bibliographical Series (Bloomington: Indiana University Press, 1976-83); Jack W. Marken and Herbert T. Hoover, *Bibliography of the Sioux* (Metuchen, N.J.: Scarecrow Press, 1980).

Chapter Three

Donald C. Cutter

The Western Spanish Borderlands

Fields of historical research and writing frequently owe their existence to a single dominant figure who not only made an impact during his lifetime, but who by the forces he unleashed also transmitted his influence to later generations. Herbert Eugene Bolton stands so clearly as the monolith in any consideration of Borderlands research that it is occasionally hard to see the other columns that support a superstructure that has been growing since 1920.

So great was Bolton's importance to the development of Hispanic Southwest historiography that the question might be asked whether the area was the Borderlands or the Boltonlands. His early imprint on the study of the region where the northward extension of Hispanic civilization and the westward movement of the Anglo-American frontier converged is so great that the field is shaped largely by the area and intensity of that great teacher's interest. From the *Debatable Land* of Georgia on the east to the *Outpost of Empire* by the Golden Gate on the west, and from the days of Vásquez de Coronado, the *Knight of Pueblo and Plains,* to the Age of Carlos III, Bolton spun a magic tale of explorers, of Jesuit and Franciscan priests, of more than one *Pageant in the Wilderness,* and of long treks by humble but heroic pioneers.[1] His copious research and writing has been emulated by others, and there can be little doubt that many themes for research and publication were predetermined by Bolton's preferences as reflected in his own investigations. Exploration, colonization, international rivalry, dramatic events, and, above all, biography of heroic figures motivated much of Bolton's work and that of his disciples. Events that might otherwise have been neglected or forgotten were recalled and magnified, but the overall effect was to give dimension to a significant portion of national history. Yet it was a national history that included multicultural input, and thereby it was a reflection of Bolton's second side.

Bolton's historiographical dominance is multifaceted. He wrote prolifically, was a teacher of large classes, had seminars at which students were two and three deep around a large circular custom-built desk at which Knights and Ladies of the Roundtable received training and inspiration, was departmental chairman, directed the Bancroft Library, and prepared a still-useful guide for archival research. For a normal scholar this would have been more than enough, but Bolton was also an innovative thinker about the nature of American history. His new approach found fulfillment in his course on the history of the Americas (of which the Borderlands were but a small, illustrative point). His expression of that hemispheric view of American history is summarized in "The Epic of Greater America," his 1932 presidential address to the American Historical Association annual meeting at Toronto, in which he emphasized the similarities of New World history rather than the differences.[2] A considerable number of Bolton's disciples followed him into this "big picture"—the hemispheric view—rather than along the desert trails of Southwestern explorers. In a sense Bolton was a split personality—the Borderlands regionalist and the hemispheric generalist.

Important as Bolton was to the study of the Borderlands area, which he helped to shape, some of his ideas served unintentionally to limit the field in both time and geographical coverage. In all of Bolton's writing, he seldom concerned himself with any aspect of the Borderlands that did not lie north of the international boundary between modern Mexico and the United States. Only in his interest in *The Padre on Horseback*, Jesuit Father Eusebio Francisco Kino, did Bolton dip below the border for his subject matter, and even then it was to treat a heroic individual whose acknowledged contribution to Arizona history is of first magnitude.[3] Nor did Bolton deal with the decline of imperial Spain in the late colonial period.

Though later Borderlands scholars tend to make a rather rigid division between the Eastern Borderlands and the Western Borderlands, with Louisiana, Mississippi, Alabama, Georgia, and Florida forming the first subdivision and Texas, New Mexico, Arizona, and California making up the western portion, Bolton freely worked both sides of the Mississippi River. The major division of the field between east and west is not merely a geographic, ethnographic, or even ecological division, though there is something of each in such differentiation. Whether appropriately or inappropriately, the determining factor is the administrative operation of those areas during the Spanish period, with what is today the southeastern United States having its immediate headquarters in the captaincy generalship of Cuba. As a result, administration and planning for that eastern sector, as well as the repositories for documentation generated in or concerning that area, bear only scant relationship to the portion that today forms the northern Mexican states and the southwestern United States. The Eastern Borderlands were appendages of the Caribbean holdings of Spain. They abut that sea and are embued with subtropical characteristics and Caribbean orientations such as slavery, plantation activity, concern for coastal defense, and great attention to international rivalry.

The Western Borderlands, except for the Texas Coast, are oriented toward Sonora-type life, with attention to such primary activities as mining, ranching, missionary work, and Indian control on a wide front. Arguments for treating all of the Spanish Borderlands as a single unit have been advanced from various sources, principally because they reflect a common Hispanic cultural contribution to United States history. Despite such an attractive argument, the documentation is so separate, the colonial administration was so distinct, and the environments are so dissimilar that individuals are discouraged from entering both fields. Jack D. L. Holmes and William S. Coker—who are leading scholars of Eastern Borderlands study—and their associates find more common ground between the areas than do most Western Borderlands exponents.[4] The contributions of Holmes and Coker have been significant, and certainly Bolton found no difficulty in any larger concept of Borderlands study embracing the South Atlantic Coast and the Gulf of Mexico littoral.

Even when divided, the Borderlands area to the west—which has had the greater amount of research attention and which as a result has become a focal point for academic study as well as for research and publication—is not a totally homogeneous area. Scholars of Western Borderlands study have enjoyed the luxury of disagreement concerning the parameters of legitimate concern. Some would limit the Borderlands to areas that are today part of the United States and that have had a sustained Hispanic input in such measurable terms as population origins, placename geography, land titles, and Spanish language use. Some include Oklahoma in the Spanish Southwest and exclude California and the Pacific Coast. Others, the writer of this essay included, expand the Spanish Borderlands to all of those areas where Spanish colonial efforts and institutions had impact. Certainly the short-lived Spanish settlement at Santa Cruz de Nootka on the west coast of Vancouver Island (1789-95) is a result of Spanish Borderlands expansion, as are Spanish explorations to Valdez and Cordova in Alaska, to Rosario Channel, the San Juan Islands, and into the Strait of Juan de Fuca.

To divorce from the Borderlands the late eighteenth-century Spanish Northwest Coast activities would be administratively and historically untenable. The Spanish Naval Department of San Blas on the coast of Nayarit and the great Pacific galleon port of San Diego de Acapulco can also be considered as parts of the Spanish Borderlands, and from those maritime portals the Borderlands can extend as far as Hawaii, Guam, and the Philippine Islands.[5]

The web of Borderlands research is a loose fabric, and equally elastic is the spidery veil of which it is made. Like the classic cartoon character Mr. Anyface, the Borderlands take on different shapes depending on time and circumstances, and there is no compelling reason why it should be otherwise. Such flexibility may be strange, but it is convenient from an archival viewpoint. It also fits the Borderlands into a wider range of historical activity than the parochial orientation frequently found in regional history. It would not be erroneous to extend Borderlands historiography to all areas touched by the indelible colors of colonial Spain as it was administered out of the viceregal capital at Mexico City.

Lest the idea be gained that writings on the Spanish Southwest began with Bolton's rise to prominence, in all fairness to some notable precursors it is well to commence any overview of such historiography with the contributions of some early historical writers who recognized the value and uniqueness of the field of southwestern study. First to mind comes that great collector and publisher of North American materials Hubert Howe Bancroft. Using assembly-line techniques and squads of writers, between 1882 and 1900 he published his monumental, thirty-nine-volume *Works of Hubert Howe Bancroft*. The emphasis of his work was on California, though he ranged from Central America to Alaska and eastward to Texas. His great collections later became the nucleus of what is today the Bancroft Library of the University of California.

There exists a very close relationship between the acquisition of Bancroft's materials, the recruitment of Bolton to the University of California, and the creation there of the leading school of Borderlands history. As for Bancroft, he was not a professional historian. His work suffered from great inconsistency, and it lacked the perceptive analysis that characterizes later Borderlands study. Nevertheless, most Borderlands history begins with Bancroft and the voracious collecting mania that motivated him. The Spanish Borderlands are particularly emphasized in the following Bancroft volumes: *History of California*, volumes 1 and 2; *The North Mexican States and Texas*; *New Mexico and Arizona*; and the early chapters of both *Oregon* and *The*

Northwest Coast.[6] Each massive tome is accompanied by a long but difficult bibliography, and by so many footnotes as to make one believe the text to be a mere vehicle to support the notes. Some of Bancroft's compilers and writers must share credit for being in the vanguard of Borderlands historiography, for they were probably more conversant with the history of the area than was the mastermind who collected and organized the material for subsequent writing. Such a procedure as Bancroft utilized made for some duplication, occasional contradiction within his several works, and an otherwise unaccountable variety of emphasis. He is also noteworthy in his use of oral history—not by today's tape recording, but in dictated pioneer reminiscences in both Spanish and English.

In summary, Bancroft was the first case of anything like organized study of the Borderlands, and his bibliography has been fundamental to subsequent efforts of both past and present Borderlands research. Additions to the original Bancroft collections have been made in all areas. The Bancroft Library at the University of California, Berkeley, has kept pace with the expansion of the field, adding many manuscript and microfilm collections from foreign and domestic archives, and it has become the Mecca of Borderlands scholars. The University of California history department has not kept pace with its special library and has largely abdicated the role of leadership that it earlier had during the halcyon days of Bolton, Herbert I. Priestley, Charles E. Chapman, and subsequently Lawrence Kinnaird and George P. Hammond.

Outside of the Bancroft influence, but highly motivated to contribute to posterity an understanding of the Hispanic role in the Southwest and its literature, were other nonprofessionals. Both Adolph F. A. Bandelier, a Swiss-born, midwestern-raised banker, and Charles Fletcher Lummis, a journalist, began their fruitful writings about Indian and Hispanic New Mexico at a time when few were interested in the area and when the availability of documentation and the opportunity for field work were unparalleled. The two men became close personal and professional friends. Bandelier is sometimes called the Father of Southwestern Anthropology and Archaeology, although admittedly infrequently by anthropologists, and his contributions have been given partial recognition in the National Monument named in his honor. Later in life he was joined by his second wife, Fanny Bandelier, who translated the story of Alvar Núñez Cabeza de Vaca.[7]

As a popularizer of the Southwest and its Hispanic and Indian heritage, the one-time invalid Lummis divided his writing between history, fiction, and ethnography. After contributing from time to time to the magazines of his day, Lummis wrote his first book in 1891, *A New Mexico David,* followed almost immediately by *Pueblo Indian Folk Tales* (later released as *The Man Who Married the Moon*). He was an unabashed publicist at a time when such persons were in short supply and almost no demand. His book *Some Strange Corners of Our Country* (later retitled *Mesa, Cañon and Pueblo*) was a valuable handbook, and his *Land of Poco Tiempo* won the plaudits of his contemporaries. His *Spanish Pioneers* was a corrective to the prevalent misconception of rapacity of the Iberian conquest. Lummis did not confine his Borderlands contributions to his own writings alone. Following a trip to Peru and establishment of his home in Los Angeles, he edited the *Land of Sunshine,* a popular history magazine later rechristened *Out West,* and became the founder of the Southwest Museum in Highland Park, Los Angeles.[8] As a crusader, editor, museum founder, writer, and publicist, Lummis ranks high among those who brought interest and status to the Spanish contribution to regional development, and in so doing he generated effective support. The Southwest Museum today stands as a monument to his zealous activity and as a treasure house of material reflecting the manifold interests of the irrepressible journalist who gave early vitality to regional study.

Though the phrase "Spanish Borderlands" has been used frequently here and elsewhere to describe the area under consideration, the catchall title was not actually invented until 1921. It is not surprising that Bolton was involved, though there is reason to believe that he was not the originator of the expression. Rather, it seems that the phrase came out of the editorial office of the Yale Chronicles of America series, to which Bolton was at that time under contract to produce a small volume. This work, *The Spanish Borderlands: A Chronicle of Old Florida and the Southwest,* is Bolton at his best—vivid, stimulating, and abreast of the large body of detailed factual material of which this volume is a sweeping synthesis. Certainly it did not treat comprehensively the vast field of Borderlands history, but it did introduce the concept of area study by the man who was to become the Master of the Borderlands. Master that he was of the story of Spanish influence in the southern tier of states, Bolton never again attempted a synthesis of that vast area's history. The closest he had ever come was a joint effort with one of his students, Thomas Maitland Marshall, entitled *The Colonization of North America, 1492-1783,* and that predated his *Spanish Borderlands.*[9] The Bolton and Marshall work was used primarily as a supplementary reading book for Bolton's popular History of the Americas course and as an alternate text in the University of California course, History of North America. In it there was considerable attention to the Borderlands, but in the broad sense in which the struggle for control of the continent takes precedence over local affairs or institutional developments.

It fell to one of Bolton's most apt students to do what Bolton felt was not his role, the writing of an overview of the Borderlands. The task was undertaken by Father John Francis Bannon, S.J., then professor of history at St. Louis University. The book was part of the Holt, Rinehart and Winston series Histories of the American Frontier under the general editorial supervision of Ray Allen Billington and its title was simple: *The Spanish Borderlands Frontier, 1513-1821.*[10] Space considerations necessary for fitting the study into the prearranged format of the commercial series limited the author to 238 pages of text. Without notable changes, publication of the Histories of the American Frontier series was transferred from Holt, Rinehart and Winston to the University of New Mexico Press. One of the books of that series which has enjoyed the greatest sales, the Bannon book will remain in print for the forseeable future. It is not only the best comprehensive survey of the Borderlands, it also includes copious footnotes and a useful bibliography of published and unpublished works.

Bannon also edited many of Bolton's significant brief writings in a single volume entitled *Bolton and the Spanish Borderlands.* The biographical portion of that book was superceded and amplified by Bannon in his complete, appreciative biography, *Herbert Eugene Bolton: The Historian and the Man.* Very few other works have focused on the Borderlands in survey style. Odie B. Faulk's *Land of Many Frontiers,* W. Eugene Hollon's *The Southwest: Old and New,* Lynn I. Perrigo's *The American Southwest: Its Peoples and Cultures,* and, in a more literary vein, David Lavender's *The Southwest* give the Spanish period moderate coverage by way of background.[11] In general, however, the Spanish era in the Southwest has not effectively penetrated either western history textbooks or national textbooks, despite a rather large body of appropriate literature.

The appearance of books of readings on the Spanish Borderlands is a sign of approaching maturity. Two have appeared in English. The earlier volume of the two is now out of print, even though it was used as supplemental reading in several university courses on the Borderlands. This pioneer effort, *The Spanish Borderlands—A First Reader,* was edited by Oakah L. Jones, Jr. All the articles had previously appeared in the quarterly *Journal of the West,* the historical periodical providing maximum Borderlands coverage during that period. More recently, a new anthology has supplanted the Jones book. Edited by David J. Weber, *New Spain's Far Northern Frontier: Essays on Spain in the American West, 1540-1821* has the advantage of including essays from a wide variety of sources. It also has useful introductory material by the editor and a succinct but pertinent bibliography of the general Borderlands field. The breadth and focus of Weber's book make it unusually appropriate for use as a textbook or as collateral reading for courses in Southwest history. It was preceded in time but not in availability by his abbreviated Spanish-language version, *El México perdido.*[12]

The number of Borderlands publications emanating from Mexico and Spain is not great, particularly studies focusing on the western area in the colonial period. The Mississippi Valley and Florida are areas of special attention of the History Department of the Universidad de Zaragoza, and both in the *Anuario* of that institution and in separate volumes there has been writing of merit based on sources in the several archives of Spain. Spanish scholars of the Zaragoza school are Fernando Solano Costa, José Antonio Armillas Vicente, and Juan José Andreu Ocariz. The outlet for their studies is often the annual *Estudios del departamento de historia moderna.*

The outstanding single contributor to Spanish study of the Borderlands is Luis Navarro García of the Universidad de Sevilla, an institution which is almost literally in the shadow of the Archivo General de Indias, largest single repository of original Borderlands documentation. His oft-cited *Don José de Gálvez y la Comandancia General de las Provincias Internas del norte de Nueva España* is massive, well documented, and includes a large collection of maps of the Spanish Borderlands. The same author has also produced *Las Provincias Internas en el siglo XIX* (1965), *Sonora y Sinaloa en el siglo XVII* (1966), and *La Conquista de Nuevo México* (1978). Mario Hernández Sánchez-Barba of the Universidad Complutense de Madrid is another notable Spanish contributor, especially in his *La Ultima expansión española en América* and *Juan Bautista de Anza: un hombre de frontera.* A brief bibliography of works in several languages is contained in Francisco Morales Padrón, *Historia del descubrimiento y conquista de América.* Also in Spain, the documentary series *Chimalistac* has many volumes dealing with the Borderlands. Published by José Porrúa, these limited editions of significant research materials, with notes frequently added, provide source documents for regional study. An example is volume 13, *Documentos para servir a la historia del Nuevo México, 1538-1778.*[13]

The existence of publications abroad and in Spanish introduces a consideration of one element of Borderlands investigation not generally found in other western historical research. This is the problem of cultural, linguistic, palaeographic, and archival considerations that derive in great measure from non-English sources, which results in two factors not common to most other research fields. The first is the need to make available in good English translation extensive material for serious study. Borderlands historical investigation has been enhanced by a large number of translations of important documents or collections of documents, the origin of which is Spanish. Again, Bolton was a leader in this regard with his translations of *Spanish Explorations in the Southwest; Arrendondo's Historical Proof of Spain's Title to Georgia; Historical Memoirs of New California;* and *Anza's California Expeditions.* [14]

In this translating effort Bolton was preceded by others who made worthwhile efforts, was aided in his own work by various able research assistants, and was emulated by both his own students and by many others who, all told, have brought forth an increasing library of translated and edited volumes of basic and interesting documents. These publications permit persons not versed in the arts of transcribing, deciphering, and translating Spanish historical documents to have access to a much wider variety of material than would otherwise be possible. Some of these important translated documents have appeared in extended cooperative documentary studies or series as described below, while others have reached publication as individual contributions. In rare cases of especially important translated documents, more than one version has been published, generally, though not always, with a considerable time gap between editions. An example is the journal of the Domínguez-Escalante exploring expedition of 1776, which was early translated by Bolton in his *Pageant in the Wilderness* (1951); later, thanks to the influence of bicentennialism, two more editions appeared in 1976. One was edited by Ted Warner with a translation by Angelico Chavez; the other was basically a reprinting of the Bolton translation, edited by Walter Briggs as *Without Noise of Arms.* [15]

A second uncommon element in Borderlands research is the need to aid the uninitiated and even rather advanced researchers in learning those skills required to reach maximum efficiency in such specialized effort as is involved in archival research in non-English materials. Acquisition of research competence for Hispanic archives has long been part of Borderlands academic training. An early small volume that helped many southwestern students in their efforts to attain such skill was J. Villasana Haggard, *Handbook for Translators of Spanish Historical Documents.* Utilized for many years and therefore helpful in standardizing translation efforts, as well as imparting palaeographic and other skills, the small book has for a long time not been available. To fill the gap, Thomas C. Barnes, Thomas H. Naylor, and Charles W. Polzer have teamed up to produce *Northern New Spain: A Research Guide.* This handbook for researchers provides a guide to collections, a breakdown of archival sources both at home and abroad, information on palaeography, weights, measures, coinage, racial terminology, Indian names, and a good bibliographical section on guides to archival collections. The greatest drawback is regionalism. Haggard is oriented strongly toward Spanish documentation concerning the Texas area, whereas *Northern New Spain* is heavy on Jesuit documentation and on mining activity appropriate to the Sonora-Arizona area but somewhat alien to most other Borderlands study. However, in the absence of other available tools for the special research competence needed in the study of the Spanish Southwest, *Northern New Spain* will be useful to nearly everyone.[16]

Academically oriented support groups such as the Fulbright program, the Social Science Research Council, and the Treaty of Friendship and Cooperation between Spain and the United States have given financial encouragement to research which in turn has resulted in significant publication as well as in guides to archival holdings concerning the Spanish Southwest. Particularly important in the matter of archival guides to aid in Borderlands research were those inventories of the contents of foreign archives which bore on the history of the United States. While Bolton was yet at the University of Texas in the first phase of his career, J. Franklin Jameson asked him to do a guide to the Mexican archives for the Department of Historical Research of the Carnegie Institution. Bolton's efforts south of the border resulted in his still-useful *Guide to Materials for the History of the United States in the Principal Archives of Mexico*. A companion volume in spirit but not in sponsorship or format, and one long used by Borderlanders, was compiled by one of Bolton's first doctoral candidates, Charles E. Chapman. This catalog of more than six thousand items of manuscript material in Sevilla was published in 1919 as *Catalogue of Materials in the Archivo General de Indias for the History of the Pacific Coast and the American Southwest*.[17] Oriented strongly to California, the book lists the Spanish archival holdings that are the core of the Bancroft Library Foreign Microfilm Collection of AGI materials.

A recent useful summary, certainly not in the detail of the Bolton or Chapman catalogs but of far-reaching importance, is Henry Putney Beers, *Spanish and Mexican Records of the American Southwest: A Bibliographical Guide to Archive and Manuscript Sources*.[18] Broken down into individual states, the book provides an easement to archival repositories at all levels from the upper echelons of government to the modest holdings of administrative subunits. Both the focus and the comprehensiveness of Beers's work make it indispensable.

In any survey of Borderlands publications, several important series stand out. One of Bolton's most capable students, George P. Hammond, shepherded several publication programs. He was the impetus for the Quivira Society Publications, which between 1929 and 1958 added much to the bibliography of the Borderlands. As the series name suggests, almost all titles concerned the Western Borderlands, with the place of publication of individual volumes determined by the academic appointment held by Hammond at the time of issue. The list embraced eleven appropriate titles as follows (with title listed first, followed by editor, place of publication, and the date thereof): *Diego Pérez de Luxán, Expedition into New Mexico made by Antonio de Espejo, 1582-83*, George P. Hammond, Los Angeles, 1929; *Sigismundo Taraval, The Indian Uprising in Lower California*, Marguerite E. Wilbur, Los Angeles, 1931; *Carlos de Sigüenza y Góngora, The Mercurio Volante . . .*, Irving A. Leonard, Los Angeles, 1932; *Gaspar Pérez de Villagrá, History of New Mexico*, Gilberto Espinosa, Los Angeles, 1933; *Francisco Céliz, Diary of the Alarcón Expedition into Texas, 1718-1719*, Fritz L. Hoffman, Los Angeles, 1935; *Juan Agustín Morfi, History of Texas, 1673-1779* (2 vols.), Carlos E. Castañeda, Albuquerque, 1935; Henry Raup Wagner, *The Spanish Southwest: An Annotated Bibliography* (2 vols.), Albuquerque, 1937; *Juan de Montoya, New Mexico in 1602*, Hammond and Agapito Rey, Albuquerque, 1938; *Three New Mexico Chronicles* [Pino, 1812; Barreiro, 1832; Escudero, 1849], H. Bailey Carroll and J. Villasana Haggard, Albuquerque, 1942; *Instructions for Governing the Interior Provinces of New Spain by Bernardo de Gálvez*, Donald Worcester, Berkeley, 1951; and *Nicolás de Lafora, The Frontiers of New Spain*, Lawrence Kinnaird, Berkeley, 1958.

Hammond's direction of the Coronado Cuarto Centennial Publications series of the University of New Mexico Press resulted in a similar set of volumes concerning the Spanish Southwest. These embraced: Herbert E. Bolton, *Coronado and the Turquoise Trail*, 1949; Hammond and Agapito Rey, *Narratives of the Coronado Expedition, 1540-1542*, 1940; Hammond and Rey, *The Rediscovery of New Mexico, 1580-1594*, 1966; Frederick W. Hodge, Hammond, and Rey, *The Benevides Memorial of 1634*, 1945; Hammond and Rey, *Don Juan de Oñate, Colonizer of New Mexico, 1595-1628* (2 vols.), 1953; Charles W. Hackett and Charmion Sibley, *Revolt of the Pueblo Indians of New Mexico and Otermín's Reconquest, 1680-1682* (2 vols.), 1942; José M. Espinosa, *The First Expedition of Vargas into New Mexico*, 1940; Alfred B. Thomas, *The Plains Indians and New Mexico, 1751-1778*, 1940; and Theodore E. Treutlein, *Pfefferkorn's Description of Sonora, 1756-1767*, 1949. Almost all of the contributors except for Hodge, Sibley, and Rey were Bolton men. The series is deficient in that there is no seventh volume. This omission of "New Mexico in the Latter 17th Century" is permanent and results from the recent death of France V. Scholes of the University of New Mexico, who though not trained in the Bolton school was considered by Bolton to be an adopted knight of the roundtable. A midwesterner trained at Harvard, Scholes was a Borderlands contributor who in turn trained a number of top scholars in the history of New Spain, since his interest in the northern Borderlands was subordinate to his dedication to Cortés and the conquest of Mexico.

Among its many publications in western history, the Arthur Clark Company of Glendale (earlier of Cleveland) has one series dedicated specifically to Borderlands history. This series, *Spain in the West,* has up to the present date (1982) twelve volumes that have appeared between its inception in 1914 and the latest publication in 1977. Significant titles and authors have been: Herbert E. Bolton (ed.), *Kino's Historical Memoir of Pimería Alta* (2 vols.), 1919; Marguerite Eyer Wilbur (ed. and trans.), *Juan María de Salvatierra of the Company of Jesus by M. Venegas,* 1929; Herbert I. Priestley, *Franciscan Explorations in California,* 1946; Peter Gerhard, *Pirates on the West Coast of New Spain, 1575-1742,* 1960; Maurice G. Holmes, *From New Spain by Sea to the Californias, 1519-1668,* 1963; Michael E. Thurman, *The Naval Department of San Blas: New Spain's Bastion for Alta California and Nootka, 1767 to 1798,* 1967; and Janet R. Fireman, *The Spanish Royal Corps of Engineers in the Western Borderlands, 1764 to 1815,* 1977.

The prominent University of Oklahoma Press at Norman has two series listings in which important Borderlands studies have appeared. The Civilization of the American Indians series includes two books by Alfred B. Thomas: *Forgotten Frontiers: A Study of the Indian Policy of Juan Bautista de Anza, Governor of New Mexico, 1777-1787* (1932), and *After Coronado: Spanish Exploration Northwest of New Mexico, 1696-1727* (1935). In Oklahoma's American Exploration and Travels series, Thomas also edited *Teodoro de Croix and the Northern Frontier of New Spain, 1776-1783* (1941); Abraham P. Nasatir and Noel Loomis presented *Pedro Vial and the Roads to Santa Fe* (1967); and the present writer prepared *The California Coast: A Bilingual Edition of Documents from the Sutro Collection* (1969).

Notable contributors of single volumes from the same press, though not included in any series format, are Jack D. Forbes, *Apache, Navaho and Spaniard* (1960); Oakah L. Jones, Jr., *Pueblo Warriors and Spanish Conquest* (1966) and *Los Paisanos: Spanish Settlers on the Northern Frontier of New Spain* (1979); and Max L. Moorhead, *The Presidio: Bastion of the Spanish Borderlands* (1975). Except for Noel Loomis, all of the Oklahoma Press listings are by Boltonians of the first, second, or third generation. A recent non-Boltonian listing is Arthur L. Campa, *Hispanic Culture in the Southwest* (1979).

Dealer-publishers with Borderlands interest have produced important works, generally in limited editions and geared in large measure for the collector's market. Glen Dawson of Los Angeles has published a fifty-title series of small books on Early California Travels and more recently has been involved in a Baja California Travels series of an even greater number of titles, the majority of which are Borderlands contributions. Warren Howell, of John Howell, Books, in San Francisco, has published some of the most elegant examples of the art of fine printing. Aided by collector-author-editor John Galvin, Howell has published a series of luxury editions on various phases of regional history.[19]

The California Historical Society, with books by W. Michael Mathes and Edwin A. Beilharz, and the Arizona Historical Society (formerly known as the Arizona Pioneers' Historical Society), with titles by Fathers Peter M. Dunne and Ernest J. Burrus, have long been involved in publishing in the Borderlands field. In Washington, D.C., the Academy of American Franciscan History has produced such significant studies as Francis F. Guest, *Fermín Francisco de Lasuén* and the several works of Maynard Geiger on Father Junípero Serra. A major effort has long been under way at the academy to publish the collected writings of all of the father presidents of the California Franciscan missions. To date, the most notable are the writings of Serra in four volumes and the writings of Lasuén in two volumes, edited by Antonine Tibesar and Finbar Kenneally, respectively.[20]

In writing of the northern extension of the Borderlands, the early pioneer was Henry Raup Wagner, bibliophile and collector, who published *Spanish Voyages to the Northwest Coast of America in the Sixteenth Century*; *Cartography of the Northwest Coast of America*; and *Spanish Explorations in the Strait of Juan de Fuca*. More recently, other significant works have appeared. Warren Cook's *Flood Tide of Empire*, Iris Wilson Engstrand's two books, *Noticias de Nootka: An Account of Nootka Sound to 1792 by José Mariano Moziño* and *Spanish Scientists in the New World: The Eighteenth Century Expeditions*; and Derek Pethick's *The Nootka Connection: Europe and the Northwest Coast, 1790–1795*, all deal with facets of northward advance and retrenchment in the final years of the Spanish colonial empire.[21]

Other noteworthy contributors to regional colonial study have been John Kessell with *Mission of Sorrows, Jesuit Guevavi and the Pimas, 1691–1767*; *Friars, Soldiers and Reformers*; *Kiva, Cross and Crown*; and *The Missions of New Mexico since 1776*; Robert Weddle with *The San Saba Mission: Spanish*

Pivot in Texas; San Juan Bautista: Gateway to Spanish Texas; and Wilderness Manhunt: The Spanish Search for La Salle; Felix D. Almaraz, Jr., with Tragic Cavalier: Governor Manuel Salcedo of Texas, 1808-1813; and anthropologist Edward H. Spicer with Cycles of Conquest: The Impact of Spain, Mexico and the United States on the Indians of the Southwest.[22] Any reasonably complete listing of worthwhile reading on Borderlands topics would extend this section beyond its allotted space, but many of the books previously listed will through their notes and bibliographies lead the reader to an awareness of the great range and variety of works already published in the field.

A vast majority of these bibliographical items have been written by persons influenced by Bolton directly or indirectly. It is no wonder then that such a great teacher was honored by his students in the inevitable Festschrift, but in the case of Bolton, with a duplication of the honor, we have a rare case. The first series of essays done in his honor by his disciples was the two-volume New Spain and the Anglo American West, while the second, a huge volume, was entitled Greater America: Essays in Honor of Herbert Eugene Bolton. In both works the Borderlands were well represented, though in neither was that the only area of concern. Bolton's bibliography, lists of his graduate students, and even of their writings appeared in the Greater America volume. A final list of Bolton's academic progeny and a definitive list of his writings are also contained in the Bannon biography of Bolton.[23]

Bolton's research and the avalanche of writing on Borderlands topics he stimulated have never been the subject of great criticism, but his "Greater America" concept has suffered such a fate. Some have seriously questioned the thesis of a unity of the Americas. Evidence pro and con was marshalled by Lewis Hanke in Do the Americas Have a Common History? A Critique of the Bolton Theory.[24] No similar effort has been made concerning Bolton's less theoretical and more practical contribution to Borderlands history, certainly not among practitioners of that specialized field of study. They can only marvel at the vitality and productivity of his work in regional history. Largely through his pioneer efforts, combined with the subsequent activities of his students, and of his students' students, and on into the fourth and even fifth academic generations, the status of Borderlands research seems secure. That much of the present research bears only faint resemblance to Bolton's own emphasis would never have bothered the founding father. On the contrary, he would probably point the way to even other fields, yet insufficiently tilled and susceptible to production of abundant harvests of new understanding. Though some may claim that Borderlands study has made a far-off corner of Spain's colonial empire, and one of the least important corners at that, into the most studied part of Latin America, there is still much to be done. The field offers seemingly inexhaustible possibilities. Furthermore, Borderlands study aims in great measure to enrich the comprehension of American national heritage rather than to illumine Spanish colonial history, though it may do both. The Spanish Southwest—the Borderlands or the Boltonlands—is an area where cultural pluralism is commonplace and where Cortés, Cabrillo, Coronado, Oñate, Vizcaíno, Kino, and Serra replace Pilgrims and Puritans, Quakers and Cavaliers as figures of primary importance in an aspect of national history that in its beginnings predates Jamestown and Plymouth Rock.

Notes

1. Herbert E. Bolton with Mary Ross, *The Debatable Land: A Sketch of the Anglo-Spanish Contest for the Georgia Country* (Berkeley: University of California Press, 1925); Bolton, *Outpost of Empire: The Story of the Founding of San Francisco* (New York: Knopf, 1931); Bolton, *Coronado: Knight of Pueblo and Plains* (New York: Whittlesey House, 1949); Bolton, *Pageant in the Wilderness: The Story of the Escalante Expedition to the Interior Basin* (Salt Lake City: Utah State Historical Society, 1951).

2. Bolton, "The Epic of Greater America," *American Historical Review* 38 (April 1933): 448-74.

3. Bolton, *The Padre on Horseback* (San Francisco: Sonora Press, 1932).

4. See for example: Jack D. L. Holmes, *Gayoso: The Life of a Spanish Governor in the Mississippi Valley, 1789-1799* (Baton Rouge: Louisiana State University Press, 1965) and *Honor and Fidelity: The Louisiana Infantry Regiment and the Louisiana Militia Companies, 1766-1821* (Fort Worth: Arrow Printing, 1965); William S. Coker (ed.), *The Military Presence on the Gulf Coast* (Pensacola: Gulf Coast History and Humanities Conference, 1978).

5. For Spain in the Pacific Northwest, see Warren L. Cook, *Flood Tide of Empire: Spain and the Pacific Northwest, 1540-1795* (New Haven: Yale University Press, 1973).

6. Hubert Howe Bancroft, *The Works of Hubert Howe Bancroft*, 39 vols. (San Francisco: A. L. Bancroft and Co., 1882-1900).

7. Adolph F. A. Bandelier, *The Gilded Man (El Dorado) and Other Pictures of Spanish Occupancy of America* (New York: D. Appleton and Co., 1893) and *The Delight Makers* (New York: Dodd, Mead and Co., 1890).

8. Charles F. Lummis, *A New Mexico David and Other Stories and Sketches of the Southwest* (New York: C. Scribner's Sons, 1891); Lummis, *The Man Who Married the Moon and Other Pueblo Indian Folk-stories* (New York: The Century Company, 1894); Lummis, *Mesa, Cañon and Pueblo: Our Wonderland of the Southwest, Its Marvels of Nature, Its Strange Peoples, Its Centuried Romance* (New York and London: The Century Company, 1925); Lummis, *The Land of Poco Tiempo* (New York: C. Scribner's Sons, 1925); Lummis, *The Spanish Pioneers* (Chicago: A. C. McClurg and Co., 1893).

9. Bolton, *The Spanish Borderlands: A Chronicle of Old Florida and the Southwest* (New Haven: Yale University Press, 1921); Bolton and Thomas Maitland Marshall, *The Colonization of North America, 1492-1783* (New York: Macmillan, 1920).

10. John Francis Bannon, *The Spanish Borderlands Frontier, 1513-1821* (New York: Holt, Rinehart and Winston, 1970).

11. Bannon (ed.), *Bolton and the Spanish Borderlands* (Norman: University of Oklahoma Press, 1964); Bannon, *Herbert Eugene Bolton: The Historian and the Man* (Tucson: University of Arizona Press, 1978); Odie B. Faulk, *Land of Many Frontiers: A History of the American Southwest* (New York: Oxford University Press, 1968); W. Eugene Hollon, *The Southwest: Old and New* (New York: Knopf, 1961; paperbound ed., Lincoln: University of Nebraska Press, 1968); Lynn I. Perrigo, *The American Southwest: Its Peoples and Cultures* (New York: Holt, Rinehart and Winston, 1971); David Lavender, *The Southwest* (New York: Harper and Row, 1980).

12. Oakah L. Jones, Jr. (ed.), *The Spanish Borderlands—A First Reader* (Los Angeles: Journal of the West Publishing Co., 1974); David J. Weber, *New Spain's Far Northern Frontier: Essays on Spain in the American West, 1540-1821* (Albuquerque: University of New Mexico Press, 1979); Weber, *El México perdido: Ensayos escogidos sobre el antiguo norte de México* (Mexico: SEP/SETENTAS, 1976).

13. Luis Navarro García, *Don José de Gálvez y la Comandancia General de las Provincias Internas del norte de Nueva España* (Sevilla: Escuela de Estudios Hispano-Americanos, 1964); Navarro, *Las Provincias Internas en el siglo XIX* (Sevilla: Escuela de Estudios Hispano-Americanos, 1965); Navarro, *Sonora y Sinaloa en el siglo XVII* (Sevilla: Escuela de Estudios Hispano-Americanos, 1966); Navarro, *La Conquista de Nuevo México* (Madrid: Ediciones Cultura Hispánica, 1978); Mario Hernández Sánchez-Barba, *La Ultima expansión española en América* (Madrid: Instituto de Estudios Políticos, 1957); Hernández, *Juan Bautista de Anza: un hombre de frontera* (Madrid: Editorial Gráfica Espejo, 1962); Francisco Morales Padrón, *Historia*

del descubrimiento y conquista de América (Madrid: Editorial Nacional, 1963); *Documentos para servir a la historia del Nuevo México, 1538-1778* (Madrid: Ediciones José Porrúa Turanzas, 1962).

14. Bolton, *Spanish Explorations in the Southwest* (New York: Scribner's, 1916); Bolton, *Arredondo's Historical Proof of Spain's Title to Georgia* (Berkeley: University of California Press, 1925); Bolton, *Historical Memoirs of New California,* 4 vols. (Berkeley: University of California Press, 1926); Bolton, *Anza's California Expeditions,* 5 vols. (Berkeley: University of California Press, 1930).

15. Ted J. Warner (ed.), *The Domínguez-Escalante Journal: Their Expedition through Colorado, Utah, Arizona and New Mexico in 1776,* trans. Fray Angelico Chavez (Provo: Brigham Young University Press, 1976); Walter Briggs (ed.), *Without Noise of Arms: The Domínguez-Escalante Search for a Route from Santa Fe to Monterey* (Flagstaff, Ariz.: Northland Press, 1976).

16. J. Villasana Haggard, *Handbook for Translators of Spanish Historical Documents* (Austin: University of Texas Press, 1941); Thomas C. Barnes, Thomas H. Naylor, and Charles W. Polzer, *Northern New Spain: A Research Guide* (Tucson: University of Arizona Press, 1981).

17. Bolton, *Guide to Materials for the History of the United States in the Principal Archives of Mexico* (Washington, D.C.: Carnegie Institution of Washington, 1913); Charles E. Chapman, *Catalogue of Materials in the Archivo General de Indias for the History of the Pacific Coast and the Spanish Southwest* (Berkeley: University of California Press, 1919).

18. Henry Putney Beers, *Spanish and Mexican Records of the American Southwest: A Bibliographical Guide to Archive and Manuscript Sources* (Tucson: University of Arizona Press, 1979).

19. Fr. Francisco Garcés, *A Record of Travels in Arizona and California, 1775-1776,* ed. John Galvin (San Francisco: John Howell, Books, 1967); Galvin (ed.), *The First Spanish Entry into San Francisco Bay* (San Francisco: John Howell, Books, 1971).

20. W. Michael Mathes, *Vizcaíno and Spanish Expansion in the Pacific Ocean, 1580-1630* (San Francisco: California Historical Society, 1968); Edwin A. Beilharz, *Felipe de Neve: First Governor of California* (San Francisco: California Historical Society, 1971); Peter Masten Dunne, *Jacobo Sedelmayr, Missionary, Frontiersman, Explorer* (Tucson: Arizona Pioneers' Historical Society, 1955); Dunne, *Juan Antonio Balthasar, Padre Visitador to the Sonora Frontier, 1744-45* (Tucson: Arizona Pioneers' Historical Society, 1957); Ernest J. Burrus, *Kino's Plan for the Development of Pimería Alta, Arizona and Upper California: A Report to the Mexican Viceroy* (Tucson:

56 *The Western Spanish Borderlands*

Arizona Pioneers' Historical Society, 1961); Francis F. Guest, *Fermín Francisco de Lasuén* (Washington, D.C.: Academy of American Franciscan History, 1973); Antonine Tibesar (ed.), *Writings of Junípero Serra,* 4 vols. (Washington, D.C. Academy of American Franciscan History, 1955); Finbar Kenneally (trans. and ed.), *Writings of Fermín Francisco de Lasuén,* 2 vols. (Washington, D.C.: Academy of American Franciscan History, 1965).

21. Henry Raup Wagner, *Spanish Voyages to the Northwest Coast of America in the Sixteenth Century* (San Francisco: California Historical Society, 1929); Wagner, *Cartography of the Northwest Coast,* 2 vols. (Berkeley: University of California Press, 1937); Wagner, *Spanish Explorations in the Strait of Juan de Fuca* (Santa Ana: Fine Arts Press, 1933); Iris Wilson Engstrand (ed. and trans.), *Noticias de Nutka: An Account of Nootka Sound in 1792 by José Mariano Moziño* (Seattle: University of Washington Press, 1970); Engstrand, *Spanish Scientists in the New World: The Eighteenth-Century Expeditions* (Seattle: University of Washington Press, 1981); Derek Pethick, *The Nootka Connection: Europe and the Northwest Coast, 1790–1795* (Vancouver: Douglas and McIntyre, 1980).

22. John Kessell, *Mission of Sorrows: Jesuit Guevavi and the Pimas, 1691-1767* (Tucson: University of Arizona Press, 1970); Kessell, *Friars, Soldiers and Reformers: Hispanic Arizona and the Sonora Mission Frontier, 1767-1856* (Tucson: University of Arizona Press, 1976); Kessell, *Kiva, Cross and Crown* (Washington, D.C.: Government Printing Office, 1979); Kessell, *The Missions of New Mexico Since 1776* (Albuquerque: University of New Mexico Press, 1980); Robert Weddle, *The San Saba Mission: Spanish Pivot in Texas* (Austin: University of Texas Press, 1964); Weddle, *San Juan Bautista: Gateway to Spanish Texas* (Austin: University of Texas Press, 1968); Weddle, *Wilderness Manhunt: The Spanish Search for La Salle* (Austin: University of Texas Press, 1973); Felix D. Almaraz, Jr., *Tragic Cavalier: Governor Manuel Salcedo of Texas, 1808-1813* (Austin: University of Texas Press, 1971); Edward H. Spicer, *Cycles of Conquest: The Impact of Spain, Mexico and the United States on the Indians of the Southwest* (paperbound; Tucson: University of Arizona Press, 1962).

23. *New Spain and the Anglo American West,* 2 vols. (Los Angeles: privately printed, 1932); *Greater America: Essays in Honor of Herbert Eugene Bolton* (Berkeley: University of California Press, 1945); Bannon, *Herbert Eugene Bolton,* pp. 275-90.

24. Lewis Hanke (ed.), *Do the Americas Have a Common History? A Critique of the Bolton Theory* (New York: Knopf, 1964).

Chapter Four

Gordon B. Dodds

The Fur Trade
and Exploration

Historians of the fur trade and of exploration in the trans-Mississippi West resemble in many respects the traders and explorers themselves. Some undertook large projects sustained by sweeping visions; others were more modest in their objectives. Some left a literary record that was clear and ample; others, one that was opaque and sparse. The contributions of some were enduring; of others, fleeting. Some were influential; others, forgotten. Some depended heavily on the work of predecessors; others opened new areas. This essay examines many of the important works in the historiography of the fur trade and of exploration but does not attempt to include every title.

Despite the widespread interest in the subject of the western fur trade and hundreds of publications about it, there are only a few volumes that attempt to survey its history. First among these in both time and stature is Hiram Martin Chittenden's *The American Fur Trade of the Far West* (1902).[1] This massive work, originally published in three volumes, is divided into five sections. Part One, on the organization and financing of the fur trade, is followed by a section that is the heart of the work. In this part, which comprises almost one-half of the book, Chittenden presents a detailed history of the major American companies operating in the trans-Mississippi West to the year 1843. Parts Three and Four discuss, respectively, "Contemporary Events Connected with the Fur Trade" and "Notable Incidents and Characters in the History of the Fur Trade." Part Five of the book describes the natural environment of the trans-Mississippi West. It is followed by eight appendices that contain source selections and miscellaneous materials.

Chittenden based the *History of the American Fur Trade* principally upon the extensive papers of the Chouteau family of St. Louis, which were in private hands when he wrote. He supplemented these records with a wide range of newspaper sources and other materials that encompassed the major sources then known. His style is clear and his judgments fair. Chittenden's philosophy of history partook both of the older, romantic histories, in the mode of Parkman, Irving, and Theodore Roosevelt, and of the newer scientific approach of Beard and Turner. That is, he stressed the role of great men in shaping history and used much space depicting the dramatic incidents of the trade. On the other hand, he was assiduous in gathering sources, attempted to weigh them objectively, and understood the role of wealth and influence in shaping governmental policies.

Chittenden's work was flawed by inadequate citation of authorities, a curious organizational structure, errors of omission, and a few factual mistakes. He was also unaware of important bodies of material that have subsequently come to light. But despite these deficiencies, *History of the American Fur Trade* presented an objective, detailed, and comprehensive account of the fur trade of the trans-Mississippi West that remains the standard.

Inexplicably, no one has attempted to rewrite Chittenden. There are some works, however, that approach certain broad aspects of his theme. The closest approximation is Paul Chrisler Phillips's *The Fur Trade*.[2] In this ample work the author attempted to interpret the entire fur trade of North America from its colonial origins through the middle 1830s. His emphasis was on the international aspects of the fur trade, how as an imperial phenomenon it affected the politics of nations. The book was a courageous attempt to reach an ambitious goal, but one that was not fully realized. In a work of fifty chapters, Phillips devoted only eight to the trans-Mississippi West. He used only secondary works or published original sources, and even most of these were in print before 1940. The style of the work was infelicitous and the biographical dimension was muted. Phillips's major achievement was his attempt to place the fur trade, more fully than had Chittenden, in its international context.

The broad approaches of Chittenden and Phillips necessarily sacrificed many of the details of the working lives of mountain men. This lacuna was partially overcome in Bernard De Voto's *Across the Wide Missouri*.[3] De Voto's spirited book, illustrated with paintings of Alfred Jacob Miller that are the only real record of how the mountain man looked, focuses upon the career (1832–38) of William Drummond Stewart in the Rockies. For the limited period it discusses and for the evidence it provides about the appearance and equipment of the mountain men, the book is excellent.

Four years after Phillips published his masterpiece, LeRoy R. Hafen presented the first volume of his *Mountain Men and the Fur Trade of the Far*

West. The first volume contains Hafen's "Brief History of the Fur Trade of the Far West." It is an excellent summary—probably the best short account— for the years 1825–40; but the reader must be mindful that it is not a history of the business element of the trade, but rather is concerned with "fur gathering and with the men engaged in it; with routes they blazed, the resources discovered, the frontiers advanced. Those men take on importance as we recognize their contributions to geographical exploration, control of Indians, and ultimate acquisition of the land."[4]

Historians have been reluctant to synthesize and interpret the narrower topic of St. Louis–based American fur traders, although several excellent studies on the individuals and companies operating from the great fur capital have appeared. This brief review cannot treat all of the solid studies but will examine several meritorious ones. In 1918 (revised slightly in 1941) Harrison Clifford Dale edited several important source works in his *Ashley-Smith Explorations and the Discovery of a Central Route to the Pacific, 1822–1829.*[5] The editor made available a selection of sources unavailable to Chittenden, the most important of which were Ashley's record of his journey to the Green River in 1824–25 and Smith's letter describing his second expedition through California to Fort Vancouver in 1828.

Oddly, for almost three decades, little substantial effort was made to follow up Dale's pioneering work until *Across the Wide Missouri* appeared. Dale's real successor, and the first distinguished work on the American fur trade since Chittenden, was Dale Morgan's *Jedediah Smith and the Opening of the West* (1953). Although Morgan's book was not marked by the discovery or identification of important new sources, except for the diaries of Archibald R. McLeod and William H. Ashley (which Chittenden and all earlier scholars had confused with that of William Sublette), it was a major contribution in synthesis and interpretation. Morgan went beyond the career of Jedediah Smith to encompass the whole history of the trans-Mississippi trade. He stressed the trader's contribution to geographic knowledge, writing of Smith: "He entered the West when it was still largely an unknown land; when he left the mountains, the whole country had been printed on the living map of the trappers' minds. . . ."[6] In the use of these new sources, in his focus upon the international dimensions of the trade, and in his greater accuracy, Morgan surpassed Chittenden. Indeed, he produced a volume that remains the closest approximation ever written to a comprehensive one-volume account of the U.S. trade.

John Sunder in his *Bill Sublette: Mountain Man* (1959) also dealt with the fur trade in its larger context—this time the relationship of the fur trade to local business interests in St. Louis and to the ancient dream of the Edenic West. Sunder stressed Sublette's role as geographer, competitor with John Jacob Astor, and the first to take wagons as far as the Popo Agie River. The sources are the expected ones but the portrait is fresh and striking. Two years after Sunder's book appeared, the western novelist Don Berry wrote *A Majority of Scoundrels: An Informal History of the Rocky Mountain Fur Company*.[7] Ignored by professional historians, the book is worthy of consideration as a skillfully written summary of the years 1822–34. Berry used the major secondary sources, and some of the original ones, to present a book that makes up in verve for its lack of originality. The book, its author declared, is "informal" because its language is "insufficiently academic" to qualify as traditional history.

In 1964 Dale Morgan published one of the best edited volumes in the historiography of the American West. In his *West of William H. Ashley*, Morgan arranged, annotated, and provided links for material that illuminates the trans-Mississippi fur trade from 1822 to 1838.[8] Focusing on the international context of this trade, Morgan divided his work into two parts, "The Bloody Missouri" and "Beyond the Continental Divide." He supplied an introduction to the entire volume entitled "Fur Trade and Exploration before the Ashley Era," a brilliant summary of the topic. Using journals, letters, newspaper reports, and his own scholarly interpretations, Morgan furnished a scholarly narrative that the reader may follow with ease and interest. Although the narrative focuses on Ashley, it encompasses the work of his American rivals as well as his British competitors.

A few years later Morgan and Eleanor T. Harris provided a companion volume of comparable editorial excellence, the overland journal of William Marshall Anderson, who accompanied William Sublette to the Rockies in 1834.[9] Anderson's journal contains a valuable description of landmarks of the trail; the only eyewitness account of the founding of Fort Laramie; the first day-by-day record of a fur trade rendezvous; the only chronicle of the merger of Fitzpatrick, Sublette, and Bridger with Fontenelle, Drips, and Co.; and (with one exception) the only daily record of a descent of the Missouri River in a pirogue in the 1830s. The editors followed Anderson's journal with forty-five biographical sketches of mountain men, some of which are superior in quality to those in Hafen's *Mountain Men*.

Out of a rather slender array of documents, Richard Oglesby has traced the career of Manuel Lisa. Lack of sources prevented him from drawing a full portrait, but he has brought together better than has anyone else the Missouri River trade from 1807 to 1820. He also showed Lisa's attempts to penetrate the city of Santa Fe and to contend with the British in the northern Rockies. Like William Sublette, who followed him, Lisa exemplified not only his livelihood as a trader but his aspirations as an American expansionist. Lisa, as did his St. Louis competitors and successors, provided clear evidence to the British and the Spanish that, in Frederick Merk's phrase, "fur trade and empire" go hand in hand. More specifically, Oglesby showed that Lisa preceded Ashley and Henry by about fifteen years in using white trappers rather than Indians. Rounding out the collection of biographies of the St. Louis traders are solid studies of Joshua Pilcher, a man of many mysteries, and William H. Ashley, who, like William Sublette, used his wealth as a trader to finance other business ventures.[10]

The financial arrangements of St. Louis fur traders were affected for several decades by the business pursuits of the American Fur Company. The historiography of this great concern begins with the oldest work in fur-trade history, Washington Irving's *Astoria.*[11] Alternately hailed by champions such as Chittenden and assailed by critics such as H. H. Bancroft, *Astoria* has emerged over the years as a generally sound and vivid account of the Pacific Fur Company's short-lived venture at the mouth of the Columbia. Chittenden and Kenneth W. Porter, in his biography of Astor, also dealt competently with this offshoot of the American Fur Company, with Porter providing the most detailed financial account of it. The parent American Fur Company is portrayed in several of Chittenden's chapters as a heroic enterprise guided by a financial genius. Yet Chittenden also recognized the rapacious wastefulness and the political machinations of the traders. All in all, however, he saw the trade as a grand venture marred only by the destruction of Indian culture.

Kenneth Porter in 1931 published a book on Astor that attempted a new direction in American biography. As author of the first volume in a projected series sponsored by the school of business at Harvard, he had the task of emphasizing Astor's economic activities rather than his personal life. Overall, the book is an outstanding account that has never been superseded. Its treatment of the work of the American Fur Company and its various departments, and of the Pacific Fur Company, is thorough and judicious in the use of sources and in careful presentation. Porter regarded Astor sympathetically, but not uncritically. The only major deficiency of the book is in its rather brief account of the relationship of Astor's company to his British and American competitors. Thirty-three years after Porter's book appeared, David Lavender published *The Fist in the Wilderness.*[12] The work of a gifted amateur who had published many volumes on various aspects of western history, this book is a partial rewriting of Chittenden (whom Lavender criticized in an unspecified way as "careless and prejudiced") and Porter. Although he employed for the most part the usual sources and contributed little new in interpretation, Lavender told the familiar story in more vivid ways than had earlier writers. His most original contributions were to use the life of Ramsey Crooks, Astor's longtime associate, as a vehicle for his narrative and to stress more than had previous scholars the importance of the American Fur Company as a factor in Indian relations. In this last respect his manuscript was enriched by his use of Records of the Office of Indian Affairs in the National Archives.

Scholars have not neglected the foreign corporations operating in the trans-Mississippi West. From the great mass of writings on the North West Company and the Hudson's Bay Company, only a few works stand out. These tend to focus upon the imperial implications of the fur trade, the theme that Phillips grappled with only with partial success. One splendid volume is Frederick Merk's edition of George Simpson's journal of his journey to the Pacific Northwest in 1824–25. The first edition, published in 1931, contains a brief introduction surveying the history of the two great British firms in the Oregon country until the time of Simpson's journey. It is clear, scholarly, and succinct. The notes to the journal and the appendices containing selected Hudson's Bay Company documents throw much light upon the subject. In 1968 Merk prepared a revised edition that contained a new introduction entitled "The Strategy of Monopoly." This essay, consistent with the author's long-standing interest in the diplomacy of the Oregon question, shows brilliantly the competition between the British and American fur companies—the similarities and differences reflected in their rivalry—and its significance for the demise of the Hudson's Bay Company south of the 49th parallel.[13] It is a study of economics, public opinion, and international conflict.

John S. Galbraith's *The Hudson's Bay Company as an Imperial Factor, 1821–1869* deals with some of the same themes.[14] One of the four sections is entitled "The Oregon Question and Its Aftermath." Galbraith skillfully examined the Oregon dispute between 1821 and 1838; the foundation of the Puget's Sound Agricultural Company; the making of the treaty of 1846 and its two relicts, the possessory rights question and the nationality of the San Juan Islands; and company control of Vancouver Island. He traced the forces and events that caused the British government eventually to sacrifice the interests of the company to the larger national interest of Anglo-American harmony.

The introductions and annotations to the Pacific Northwest publications of the Hudson's Bay Company Records Society—for example, the journals of Peter Skene Ogden and John Work—are most useful. In these volumes the editors brought order out of the disparate geographical and trading activities of the men in the field. Gloria Griffen Cline published a solid life of Ogden, and Richard Glover edited and introduced David Thompson's records of his explorations in North America. William Sampson provided the best brief biography of John McLoughlin in his introduction to *John McLoughlin's Business Correspondence, 1847–48*. Several chapters in E. E. Rich's ponderously written *History of the Hudson's Bay Company* present an accurate overview.[15]

The fur trade in the Southwest, on the other hand, has been neglected by historians. Chittenden paid it almost no attention and Phillips slighted it. The only respectable survey is that of Robert G. Cleland, *This Reckless Breed of Men*, in which the author stressed the American trade in the region as an imperial factor leading to U.S. sovereignty. David Lavender's *Bent's Fort* documents the largest mercantile firm in the Southwest. Max Moorhead made available an annotated edition of Josiah Gregg's classic *Commerce of the Prairies*. Howard Lamar illuminated the influence of the trader in this region in his monograph on the trader. A detailed monographic study of a very difficult subject is David Weber's *The Taos Trappers*. Weber carried his account of the trappers operating out of this most important fur-trading center between St. Louis and Fort Vancouver from the Spanish period to the end of the Mexican War. He wove together often fragmentary records of a series of small companies to form a coherent narrative of a neglected topic.[16]

In addition to the general histories of the fur trade, the accounts of specific companies, and the biographies, there are scholarly treatments of several specialized aspects of the business. One of the most ambitious of these is LeRoy Hafen's *Mountain Men and the Fur Trade of the Far West*. Distributed through ten volumes are Hafen's brief history of the trade (referred to above), 292 biographical sketches of the trappers and traders written by eighty-five contributors, a statistical view of the mountain men, and an extensive bibliography. The geographical focus of the work "is the area of the Central Rockies and operations from the fur emporium at St. Louis."[17] The intellectual framework is the daily life of the fur traders, their geographical discoveries, and their relationships with the Indians. Hafen, in the main, developed his ambitious plan successfully. The selections include all of the important and many of the minor figures of the trade. He selected competent authors for his biographies. Most of the essays are clearly written. Yet many of the authors relied on secondary sources alone and some were given more or less space for their subjects than is warranted in comparison with other persons included in this work.

An approach almost diametrically contrasting to Hafen's is that of David J. Wishart in *The Fur Trade of the American West, 1807–1840.* Rather than emphasizing the actions of individual men, or even individual companies, Wishart attempted "a new synthesis which adopts an interdisciplinary approach and focuses on the interrelationships between the biological, physical, and cultural environments of the fur trade."[18] In this work of historical geography, modeled upon the seminal approaches of Donald W. Meinig, Wishart argued that for two decades the fur traders worked out an adjustment to the natural environment of the Plains and Rockies and to national and international markets that "crystallized into a steady state" by the mid-1820s. By that time (and surviving for the next two decades) there were two production systems. The Rocky Mountain trading system was based upon the beaver, the white trapper, the rendezvous, and the Platte River overland supply route. The Upper Missouri system was based upon the bison, the Indian, the trading post, and the Missouri River supply route. In the middle of the 1830s these systems became disrupted and the fur trade took new shape. Wishart concluded that the fur trade was destructive to the American environment, unimportant to the American economy but important to that of the West (especially St. Louis), useful in exploring the West and forming the vanguard of its settlement, and influential for the geography of the missionary and military frontiers. These conclusions, although dressed up in modish jargon (e.g., "biosphere people," "Euro-Americans") have long been familiar to historians.

The aspirations of the mountain men, and how scholars have perceived them, is a source of controversy. William H. Goetzmann saw them as expectant capitalists who took advantage of the social and economic fluidity of the frontier to rise in wealth and status. Mountain men were, Goetzmann contended, neither romantic heroes nor escapists from the constraints of civilization, as they had been perceived by earlier writers. Goetzmann's conclusions, in turn, were attacked by Harvey Lewis Carter and Marcia Carter Spence, who found them less accurate than the two older views.[19]

Indians were of course essential to many of the fur traders, who frequently regarded them as suppliers, guides, or potential enemies. Most books on western Indians treat the fur trade in one degree or another, but no one has attempted a comprehensive history of this relationship that encompasses the Indians, the traders, and the natural environment in the manner of Calvin Martin's brilliant monograph for the area east of the Mississippi River,

Keepers of the Game: Indian-Animal Relationships and the Fur Trade.
What have been done are several superficial works and a few outstanding
studies or sections of works with other primary foci. Lewis Saum's *The Fur
Trader and the Indian* is an excellent study in intellectual history. The theme
of the book is the manner in which the British, French, and American fur
traders applied their preconceptions of the Indians in their actual intercourse
with them. Saum investigated the three myths of the noble savage, the bestial
red man, and the degenerate trapper who becomes a "white Indian." He
found that the trappers' perception of the Indian varied among men of the
same and different nationalities and eras, but that as a group they admired
two aspects of the Indians: their absence and their furs. In breadth of
material, sophistication of interpretation, and lucidity of style this work is a
model.[20]

Another solid treatment of the Indian and the fur trade is contained in
Alvin Josephy's *The Nez Perce Indians and the Opening of the Northwest*.
Unlike many popular writers, Josephy pointed out the benefits to the Indians
of the initial Caucasian contacts. The traders gave the Indians guns and other
material objects that added to their wealth and power. The Indians, he wrote,
"had as much of the trade as they wanted, and could acquire what they
needed from the American trappers without being made to feel subservient."
That the fur trade was not always of such benefit to the Indians, however, is
clear in John Ewers's fine study "The Influence of the Fur Trade on Indians
of the Northern Plains." Another excellent study of the Indians and the fur
traders in the context of historical geography is contained in D. W. Meining's
Great Columbia Plain. The mutual impact for another region of the West is
well told in Oscar Lewis's *The Effects of White Contact Upon Blackfoot Culture*. A trailbreaking work on an important subject is Jennifer L. Brown's
Strangers in Blood: Fur Trade Company Families in Indian Country, which
concentrates on the Canadian Northwest. Another pioneering work is Mary
C. Wright's fine essay "Economic Development and Native American Women
in the Early Nineteenth Century."[21]

Most standard histories of the fur trade stop with the last rendezvous. The
trade's continuance for another two decades is the substance of John E.
Sunder's *Fur Trade on the Upper Missouri, 1840–1865*. This trade, primarily
in bison robes, was the domain of the American Fur Company. Sunder
showed the company in its economic role, its relationship to the Indians, and
even its assistance to natural scientists. He demonstrated fully the relationship
of the trade, its development and decline, to the other forces in American
life such as the advance of the farmer's frontier, declining robe markets,

transportation changes, and the Civil War. In lesser compass, Rhoda R. Gilman examined the final years of the trade on the Upper Mississippi River.[22]

Finally, there is one fine novel of the fur trade that is of real assistance to the historian. A. B. Guthrie's *The Big Sky* is the story of Boone Caudill, the mountain man whose quest for untrammeled freedom in the fur trade ends in tragedy.[23] The mountain man's attitudes toward nature and the Indian, his equipment, and his jargon are depicted splendidly in this story of a Kentucky youth whose personal rise and fall parallels those of the classic Rocky Mountain trade.

The historiography of exploration overlaps that of the fur trade, and many of the works previously mentioned treat the fur trader as explorer. For example, A. P. Nasatir investigated the tangled interrelationships of the early Spanish and English trader-explorers on the waters of the Upper Missouri and Mississippi rivers. Beginning with a series of articles published fifty years ago and culminating in his monumental *Before Lewis and Clark: Documents Illustrating the History of the Missouri, 1785-1804,* Nasatir dealt with the history of exploration and trading in this region from 1763 to 1804. His assiduous pursuit of documents, especially in Spanish archives, his meticulous translations, and his precise editorial paraphernalia make this last work definitive. On the other hand, scholars have slighted the French explorers of the trans-Mississippi West, especially the exploits of the Vérendryes, although De Voto dealt with them briefly in *The Course of Empire,* and so does a new volume by G. H. Smith.[24]

The epic story of the missionary and military explorers in the Far Southwest and the Spanish Borderlands appears in many volumes. The most impressive of these are Herbert Eugene Bolton's biographical studies. In his volumes on Anza, Coronado, and Kino, Bolton carefully traced the ventures of the Spanish into the unknown country of the southern Plains, the Rockies, and Arizona and California. Bolton emphasized the sweep and drama of the subject, but in no superficial way: for he grounded his works carefully not only in the documents but on his personal exploration of the region. For the latter period of American interest in the opening of the Southwest there is a good deal of descriptive material contained in the twelve-volume Southwest Historical Series edited by Ralph A. Bieber, especially in Bieber and Averam B. Bender's *Exploring Southwestern Trails, 1846-1854.*[25]

W. Eugene Hollon in 1949 did a substantial biography of Zebulon Pike, but one that lacked a personal dimension because of the absence of personal papers. Further information on Pike's career is contained in Donald Jackson's edition of *The Journals of Zebulon Montgomery Pike with Letters and*

Related Documents. This scholarly work attempts to establish that "Pike's expedition to the West ranks second in significance to that of Lewis and Clark (a statement he would have contested strongly), but neither Pike nor his men rank second to anyone in courage or endurance." Jackson's book is important as the first edition of Pike's documents that contains the confiscated records returned by Mexico in 1910, in addition to other previously unpublished materials. Richard G. Wood gave biographical treatment to Pike's successor as a military explorer, and further proponent of the myth of the Great American Desert, Stephen H. Long.[26]

For the northern portion of the nation, no subject has received more attention than the explorations of Lewis and Clark. So far as sources are concerned, no one has yet redone Reuben Gold Thwaites's edition of the original journals of the Lewis and Clark expedition, but additional material has come to light since that time. Much of it was collected and edited by Donald Jackson in his *Letters of the Lewis and Clark Expedition, with Related Documents, 1783–1854.* The most important contribution of this notable work, which also has a second edition containing new material, lies in showing exactly how closely Jefferson worked with the expedition from its origin until the publication of its reports. In *The Field Notes of Captain William Clark,* Ernest Staples Osgood skillfully annotated Clark's rough notes of the expedition's preparations at Camp Dubois and the journey to the Mandan villages and the winter encampment there. What will be the definitive edition of Lewis and Clark documents is now being prepared in ten volumes under the editorship of Gary E. Moulton and will be published by the University of Nebraska Press. It will contain an atlas, all the journals and field notes from the members of the Corps of Discovery, and a natural history of the expedition. John Bakeless produced the best short history of the expedition in his *Lewis and Clark: Partners in Discovery,* although Bernard De Voto's introduction to his condensation of the journals is illuminating for evaluating the objectives, success, and international context of the expedition.[27]

Two newer monographs are exemplary. Paul Cutright's *Lewis and Clark: Pioneering Naturalists* deals with the achievements of the explorers not only as scientists but as anthropologists and physicians. Cutright argued convincingly that, despite their lack of scientific training, Lewis (especially) and Clark were careful observers whose reports, sketches, and specimens were of high quality. John Logan Allen's study, *Passage Through the Garden: Lewis and Clark and the Image of the American Northwest,* is a model in intellectual history. Allen defined the early nineteenth-century geographical image of the Pacific Northwest, discovered how Lewis and Clark reshaped it during their expedition, and speculated on how their revised image affected future conceptions of the region. In this book of "conceptual" as distinct from "real" geography, Allen showed how older visions of the Pacific Northwest, such as a Garden of Eden easily approachable through a single range of mountains, were punctured by the great expedition. These symbols were succeeded, however, by "new editions of the ancient myths," especially that of a rich commerce with Asia.[28] In the process of his research Allen made a discovery of enormous significance, being the first to identify and discuss Nicholas King's map of 1803, ordered by Albert Gallatin, which compiled all available knowledge about the American West.

The most important of Lewis and Clark's successors in the central and northern portions of the continent was John C. Frémont. Allan Nevins did his biography twice, but the best recent scholarship is contained in Donald Jackson and Mary Lee Spence's edition of *The Expeditions of John Charles Frémont*. The editors point out that Frémont was fortunate in the timeliness of his explorations, and their edition is scholarly testimony to exactly how the explorer appealed to the American public. This attraction is demonstrated both in the first volume, which deals with his travels from 1834 to 1844, and in the second, which appraises his role in the conquest of California and his subsequent court-martial.[29] One notable feature of this edition is a series of excellent maps.

Frémont's colleagues appear in fresh light in William Goetzmann's original and stimulating study of *Army Exploration in the American West, 1803-1863*. This book, which concentrates upon the history of the Corps of Topographical Engineers (1838-63), makes the military explorer as significant a western type as the trapper, farmer, miner, and cowboy. But the contribution of this notable book goes beyond narrative and description. Goetzmann's greatest insight was to place the corps within the context of romanticism as expression of nationalism, of science as the pursuit of cosmic knowledge, as "urge toward diversity," and as ally (through reports, drawings, and paintings) of art and literature. "The total picture of the Corps operating on the West is," wrote Goetzmann, "more than anything else, a picture of the cultural mind in action."[30] His integration of western exploration with national culture was masterful.

Two other monographs deal in part with the role of exploration and surveying in the West. Oscar Winther's *Old Oregon Country* devotes a limited amount of space to the wagon roads of the region. A rather different work, with its primary focus upon exploration, is W. Turrentine Jackson's *Wagon Roads West*, a study of "the role of the federal government in the location, survey, and improvement of routes for wagons in the trans-Mississippi West before the railroad era."[31] Jackson traced the impact (especially in the years 1846-69) of the Corps of Topographical Engineers, the Office of Exploration and Surveys of the War Department, and the Pacific Wagon Road Office of the Department of the Interior in improving the routes both of those settlers going west and of those who had arrived. The government built roads to connect western military forts, to speed the mails, and to facilitate the transportation of freight. The routes it developed in many cases became the highways of the late nineteenth and twentieth centuries. Throughout his monograph, Jackson emphasized that the actual construction of roads was relatively limited, that the major contribution was in the selection of routes.

Discoverers and explorers, of course, communicated their findings by way of maps as well as literary reports. The first of the great historical cartographers was Henry R. Wagner, who prepared a collection of maps of the Pacific Northwest tied together by essays discussing their development. Wagner's pioneering work was carried on in much greater compass in Carl I. Wheat's five-volume *Mapping the Trans-Mississippi West*. This work, like Wagner's, is a narrative and bibliocartography. It is a monumental and definitive work which, in its range and thoroughness, provides the historian with an indispensable resource.[32]

As in the case of the fur trade, there are but few works of synthesis on western exploration. Two skillful works dealing with John Wesley Powell have appeared, each taking a sophisticated and broad approach to his work in its many ramifications. Wallace Stegner emphasizes the western dimension of Powell's career in his *Beyond the Hundredth Meridian: John Wesley Powell and the Second Opening of the West*. William Culp Darrah deals not only with this subject but also with other phases of Powell's life in his *Powell of the Colorado*.[33]

Richard Bartlett attempted a survey of the surveys in 1962. His book contains a treatment of the great exploring expeditions headed by Clarence King, F. V. Hayden, John Wesley Powell, and George Wheeler. Based on original sources, the book gives the main outlines of the life and demise of the expeditions. It brings to light neglected individuals like Hayden and Wheeler. A somewhat comparable work is Gloria Griffen Cline's *Exploring the Great Basin*, which makes able use of the work of many scholars. Its strength lies in the comprehensive sweep of its treatment from the era of the Indians to the arrival of the Mormons, in its clarity of style, and in its lucid organization.[34]

The interpretive power and literary brilliance, lacking in earlier analyses of exploration, are among the many admirable features of William H. Goetz-mann's *Exploration and Empire*. This rarity of historical scholarship, a truly original book (and one of the best works ever written about the American West), reaches a height that hitherto only Chittenden and Morgan have scaled. Goetzmann argued that the American West, as the nation itself, was the result of an attempt of easterners to replicate their culture in a new country. The western experience, he wrote, "offered a theater in which American patterns of culture could be endlessly mirrored." But the West had to be discovered before it could be used and explored after it had been discovered. And it was the use of the concept of "exploration" that was most original about Goetz-mann's work. He pointed out that an area once "discovered" may successive-ly be "explored" by men seeking different uses for it. These people, in computer terminology, are "programmed" in advance to look for certain uses, a concept that ties exploration into the old American belief in "mis-sion."

Goetzmann argued that nineteenth-century American western exploration passed through three "mission" eras. The first, the period of imperial rivalry among the powers, lasted from Lewis and Clark to the mid-1840s. The second, from 1845 to 1860, saw the explorer fostering Manifest Destiny as settlement and investment replaced international conflict. From 1860 to 1900 occurred the era of the great surveys, a time of "more intensive scien-tific reconnaissances and inventories," but also one that germinated the idea of conserving as well as exploiting natural resources. In developing his thesis, the author used not only literary sources but also evidence from maps, draw-ings, paintings, and photographs.[35] After Goetzmann, no one will again look at Lewis and Clark, and Frémont, and Stevens, and Powell, and Hayden, and the others in the old ways. He has raised a high standard in examining explor-ation from the vantage point of weighing culture and environment in the frontier process, in using sources in an imaginative and exhaustive way, and in integrating the American West with world history.

The historiography of the fur trade and of exploration reflects that of the West and the nation. There is no orthodox school of interpretation; indeed, there is no school at all. Scholars have selected and examined their subjects from diverse vantage points. In this process a few notable books have ap-peared and many competent ones. Each generation has answered its questions to its satisfaction. For the future, taking our cue from Goetzmann, we may be assured that there will be many new explorations if few discoveries. Per-haps nothing else should be required.

Notes

1. Hiram Martin Chittenden, *The American Fur Trade of the Far West: A History of the Pioneering Trading Posts and Early Fur Companies of the Missouri Valley and the Rocky Mountains and of the Overland Commerce with Santa Fe*, 3 vols. (New York: F. P. Harper, 1902). Stallo Vinton annotated Chittenden (St. Paul: Press of the Pioneers, 1935), an edition later reprinted (Fairfield, N.J.: A. M. Kelley, 1976).

2. Paul Chrisler Phillips, *The Fur Trade*, 2 vols. (Norman: University of Oklahoma Press, 1961).

3. Bernard De Voto, *Across the Wide Missouri* (Boston: Houghton Mifflin, 1947; paperbound ed. n.d.).

4. LeRoy R. Hafen, *The Mountain Men and the Fur Trade of the Far West: Biographical Sketches of the Participants by Scholars of the Subject with Introductions by the Editor*, 10 vols. (Glendale, Calif.: Arthur H. Clark, 1965-72), quote on p. 1:15. Together, the various entries in this work comprise the best bibliography of primary sources.

5. Harrison Clifford Dale, *The Ashley-Smith Explorations and the Discovery of a Central Route to the Pacific, 1822-1829* (Cleveland: Arthur H. Clark, 1819; rev. ed., Glendale, Calif.: Arthur H. Clark, 1941).

6. Dale L. Morgan, *Jedediah Smith and the Opening of the West* (Indianapolis: Bobbs-Merrill, 1953; paperbound ed. Lincoln: University of Nebraska Press, 1964), quote on p. 9.

7. John E. Sunder, *Bill Sublette: Mountain Man* (Norman: University of Oklahoma Press, 1959); Don Berry, *A Majority of Scoundrels: An Informal History of the Rocky Mountain Fur Company* (New York: Harper and Bros., 1961).

8. Dale L. Morgan, ed., *The West of William H. Ashley* (Denver: The Old West Publishing Company, 1964).

9. Dale L. Morgan and Eleanor Towles Harris (eds.), *The Rocky Mountain Journals of William Marshall Anderson: The West in 1834* (San Marino, Calif.: Huntington Library, 1967).

10. Richard E. Oglesby, *Manuel Lisa and the Opening of the Missouri Fur Trade* (Norman: University of Oklahoma Press, 1963); John E. Sunder, *Joshua Pilcher: Fur Trader and Indian Agent* (Norman: University of Oklahoma Press, 1968); Richard M. Clokey, *William H. Ashley: Enterprise and Politics in the Trans-Mississippi West* (Norman: University of Oklahoma Press, 1980).

11. The best edition is *Astoria; or., Anecdotes of an Enterprise Beyond the Rocky Mountains,* ed. Edgeley W. Todd (Norman: University of Oklahoma Press, 1964).

12. Kenneth W. Porter, *John Jacob Astor: Business Man,* 2 vols. (Cambridge: Harvard University Press, 1931; reprinted, New York: Russell and Russell, 1966); David Lavender, *The Fist in the Wilderness* (Garden City, N.Y.: Doubleday, 1964; paperbound ed., Albuquerque: University of New Mexico Press, 1979).

13. Frederick Merk, *Fur Trade and Empire* (Cambridge: Harvard University Press, 1931; rev. ed., 1968); Merk, *The Oregon Question: Essays in Anglo-American Diplomacy and Politics* (Cambridge: Harvard University Press, 1967).

14. John S. Galbraith, *The Hudson's Bay Company as an Imperial Factor, 1821-1869* (Berkeley and Los Angeles: University of California Press, 1957; paperbound ed., New York: Octagon Books, 1977).

15. K. G. Davies (ed.), *Peter Skene Ogden's Snake Country Journal, 1826-27* (London: Hudson's Bay Record Society, 1961); William R. Sampson (ed.), *John McLoughlin's Business Correspondence, 1847-48* (Seattle: University of Washington Press, 1973); E. E. Rich, *The History of the Hudson's Bay Company, 1670-1870,* 2 vols. (London: Hudson's Bay Record Society, 1958-59); Gloria Griffen Cline, *Peter Skene Ogden and the Hudson's Bay Company* (Norman: University of Oklahoma Press, 1974; paperbound ed., n.d.); Richard Glover (ed.), *David Thompson's Narrative, 1784-1812* (Toronto: Champlain Society, 1962).

16. Robert G. Cleland, *This Reckless Breed of Men: The Trappers and Fur Traders of the Southwest* (New York: Knopf, 1950; paperbound ed., Albuquerque: University of New Mexico Press, 1976); David S. Lavender, *Bent's Fort* (Garden City, N.Y.: Doubleday, 1954; paperbound ed., Lincoln: University of Nebraska Press, 1972); Howard R. Lamar, *The Trader on the American Frontier: Myth's Victim* (College Station: Texas A&M University Press, 1977); David J. Weber, *The Taos Trappers: The Fur Trade in the Far Southwest, 1540-1846* (Norman: University of Oklahoma Press, 1971); Max L. Moorhead (ed.), *The Commerce of the Prairies by Josiah Gregg* (Norman: University of Oklahoma Press, 1954).

17. Hafen, *Mountain Men,* 1:14.

18. David J. Wishart, *The Fur Trade of the American West, 1807-1840: A Geographical Synthesis* (Lincoln: University of Nebraska Press, 1979), quote on p. 9.

19. William H. Goetzmann, "The Mountain Man as Jacksonian Man,"

American Quarterly 15 (1963): 402-15; Harvey Lewis Carter and Marcia Carpenter Spence, "Stereotypes of the Mountain Man," *Western Historical Quarterly* 6 (1975): 17-32; "Mountain Man Stereotypes," *ibid.*, 295-302. The last essay continues the discussion of the subject by the three authors.

20. Calvin Martin, *Keepers of the Game: Indian-Animal Relationships and the Fur Trade* (Berkeley and Los Angeles: University of California Press, 1978) (for dissenting views see Shepard Krech [ed.], *Indians, Animals, and the Fur Trade: A Critique of Keepers of the Game* [Athens: University of Georgia Press, 1981]); Lewis O. Saum, *The Fur Trader and the Indian* (Seattle: University of Washington Press, 1965; paperbound ed., 1966).

21. Alvin M. Josephy, Jr., *The Nez Perce Indians and the Opening of the Northwest* (New Haven: Yale University Press, 1965, quote on p. 78; abridged paperbound ed., Lincoln: University of Nebraska Press, 1979); John C. Ewers, "The Influence of the Fur Trade on Indians of the Northern Plains," in Malvina Bolus (ed.), *People and Pelts: Selected Papers of the Second North American Fur Trade Conference* (Winnipeg, Manitoba: Peguis Publisher, 1972), pp. 1-26; D. W. Meinig, *The Great Columbia Plain: A Historical Geography, 1805-1910* (Seattle: University of Washington Press, 1968), pp. 34-95; Oscar Lewis, *The Effects of White Contact Upon Blackfoot Culture with Special Reference to the Role of the Fur Trader* (New York: J. J. Augustin, 1942); Jennifer L. Brown, *Strangers in Blood: Fur Trade Company Families in Indian Country* (Vancouver: University of British Columbia Press, 1980); Mary C. Wright, "Economic Development and Native American Women in the Early Nineteenth Century," *American Quarterly* 33 (Winter 1981): 525-36.

22. John E. Sunder, *The Fur Trade on the Upper Missouri, 1840-1865* (Norman: University of Oklahoma Press, 1965); Rhoda R. Gilman, "Last Days of the Upper Mississippi Fur Trade," in Bolus (ed.), *People and Pelts*, pp. 103-35.

23. A. B. Guthrie, *The Big Sky* (Boston: Houghton Mifflin, 1947; paperbound ed., Bantam, 1972).

24. A. P. Nasatir, "Anglo-Spanish Rivalry on the Upper Missouri," *Mississippi Valley Historical Review* 16 (1929, 1930): 359-82; 507-28; Nasatir, "The Anglo-Spanish Frontier on the Upper Mississippi, 1780-1796," *Iowa Journal of History and Politics* 29 (1931): 155-232; Nasatir, *Before Lewis and Clark: Documents Illustrating the History of the Missouri, 1785-1804* (St. Louis: St. Louis Historical Documents Foundation, 1952); see also Bernard De Voto, *The Course of Empire* (Boston: Houghton Mifflin, 1952; paperbound ed., 1962), pp. 195-216; G. Hubert Smith, *The Explorations of*

the La Vérendryes in the Northern Plains, 1738–1743, ed. W. Raymond Wood (Lincoln: University of Nebraska Press, 1980).

25. Herbert Eugene Bolton, *Anza's California Expeditions*, 5 vols. (Berkeley: University of California Press, 1930–31); Bolton, *Rim of Christendom: A Biography of Eusebio Francisco Kino, Pacific Coast Pioneer* (New York: Macmillan, 1936); Bolton, *Coronado: Knight of Pueblos and Plains* (New York and Albuquerque: Whittlesey House and the University of New Mexico Press, 1949); see also Ralph A. Bieber and Averam P. Bender, *Exploring Southwestern Trails, 1846–1854* (Glendale, Calif.: Arthur H. Clark, 1938; reprinted, Philadelphia: Porcupine Press, 1974).

26. W. Eugene Hollon, *The Lost Pathfinder: Zebulon Montgomery Pike* (Norman: University of Oklahoma Press, 1949; paperbound ed., Westport, Conn.: Greenwood Press, 1981); Donald Jackson (ed.), *The Journals of Zebulon Montgomery Pike with Letters and Related Documents*, 2 vols. (Norman: University of Oklahoma Press, 1966); quote on p. 1:x; Richard G. Wood, *Stephen Harriman Long, 1784–1864: Army Engineer, Explorer, Inventor* (Glendale, Calif.: Arthur H. Clark, 1966).

27. Reuben Gold Thwaites (ed.), *Original Journals of the Lewis and Clark Expedition, 1804–1806*, 8 vols. (New York: Dodd, Mead and Co., 1904–05; reprinted, New York: Arno Press, 1969); Donald D. Jackson (ed.), *Letters of the Lewis and Clark Expedition, with Related Documents, 1783–1854* (Urbana: University of Illinois Press, 1962; 2d rev. ed., 1978); Ernest S. Osgood (ed.), *The Field Notes of Captain William Clark* (New Haven: Yale University Press, 1964); John E. Bakeless, *Lewis and Clark: Partners in Discovery* (New York: W. Morrow, 1947); Bernard De Voto (ed.), *The Journals of Lewis and Clark* (Boston: Houghton Mifflin, 1953; paperbound ed., n. d.).

28. Paul R. Cutright, *Lewis and Clark: Pioneering Naturalists* (Urbana: University of Illinois Press, 1969); John L. Allen, *Passage Through the Garden: Lewis and Clark and the Image of the American Northwest* (Urbana: University of Illinois Press, 1975), quote on p. 398.

29. Allan Nevins, *Frémont, the West's Greatest Adventurer*, 2 vols. (New York: Harper, 1928); Nevins, *Frémont, Pathmarker of the West* (New York: D. Appleton-Century Co., 1939; 2d rev. ed., 1955); Donald Jackson and Mary Lee Spence (eds.), *The Expeditions of John Charles Frémont*, 2 vols. (Urbana: University of Illinois Press, 1970–73).

30. William H. Goetzmann, *Army Explorations in the American West, 1803–1863* (New Haven: Yale University Press, 1959; paperbound ed., Lincoln: University of Nebraska Press, 1979), quotes on pp. 18, 431.

31. Oscar Osburn Winther, *The Old Oregon Country: A History of Fron-*

tier Trade, Transportation, and Travel (Stanford, Calif.: Stanford University Press, 1950; paperbound ed., Lincoln: University of Nebraska Press, 1969); W. Turrentine Jackson, *Wagon Roads West: A Study of Federal Road Surveys and Construction in the Trans-Mississippi West, 1846–1869* (Berkeley and Los Angeles: University of California Press, 1952; paperbound ed., Lincoln: University of Nebraska Press, 1979), quote on p. vii.

32. Henry R. Wagner, *The Cartography of the Northwest Coast of America to the Year 1800*, 2 vols. (Berkeley: University of California Press, 1937; reprinted, Amsterdam: N. Israel, 1968); Carl I. Wheat, *Mapping the Trans-Mississippi West, 1540–1861*, 5 vols. (San Francisco: Institute of Historical Cartography, 1957–63).

33. Wallace Stegner, *Beyond the Hundredth Meridian: John Wesley Powell and the Opening of the West* (Boston: Houghton Mifflin, 1954; paperbound ed., Lincoln: University of Nebraska Press, 1982); William Culp Darrah, *Powell of the Colorado* (Princeton: Princeton University Press, 1951).

34. Richard A. Bartlett, *Great Surveys of the American West* (Norman: University of Oklahoma Press, 1962; paperbound ed., 1980); Gloria Griffen Cline, *Exploring the Great Basin* (Norman: University of Oklahoma Press, 1963; paperbound ed., n.d.).

35. William H. Goetzmann, *Exploration and Empire: The Explorer and the Scientist in the Winning of the American West* (New York: Knopf, 1966; paperbound ed., New York: W. W. Norton, 1978), quotes on pp. xi, xiii. This book is the best reference for primary sources on the subject.

Chapter Five

Dennis E. Berge

Manifest Destiny
and the Historians

Ray Allen Billington's *The Far Western Frontier, 1830-1860* appeared in 1956 as a volume in the New American Nation Series; the editors, Henry Steele Commager and Richard Morris, introduced the volume with a commentary on the westward expansion of the United States. "No other nation," they noted, "had ever expanded so rapidly, or expanded so far without putting an intolerable strain upon the existing political and economic fabric," adding that "what is most impressive about the American expansion is the ease, the simplicity, and the seeming inevitability of the whole process."[1]

The forces that shaped this American expansionism have generally been placed within the context of what the journalist John O'Sullivan referred to in 1845 as the "manifest destiny" of the United States, a destiny, he said, which was "to overspread the continent allotted by Providence for the free development of our yearly multiplying millions."[2] O'Sullivan's catchwords provided a framework within which expansionist issues came to be viewed by his own generation and several that followed, and they have also served as a focus for the attention of scholars—historians, in particular—who have attempted to explain what American expansionism has been all about.

Taken at face value the term "manifest destiny" carries with it a sense of the inexorable that is akin to the assertion of Commager and Morris that there was a "seeming inevitability" to the process of American expansionism. And while it is evident that the forces that produced this expansionism were powerful enough to shape history, both their identity and their inevitability have been subject to debate among historians. At frequent issue has been whether American territorial growth was motivated by a genuine expansionist impulse, or whether the message of manifest destiny was merely rhetoric to rationalize such motives as land hunger or a desire for western ports and the

Orient trade. The aim of southern expansionists to extend the area of slavery by acquiring Mexican territory has also been advanced, as has the argument that the attitudes of Americans in general toward the seizure of Mexican lands was influenced strongly by racist or ethnocentric convictions. It is this territorial conflict between Mexico and the United States that has attracted the greatest attention from historians, and because of the focus on this subject, it has furnished the dominant element in the historiography of American expansionism.

The first historical studies to reflect the influence of manifest destiny were thus the early histories of the Mexican War. A number of such studies appeared in the first year or so after the war. They lacked the sense of objectivity, historical perspective, and breadth of research that later scholars would bring to the subject, but they also reveal the kinds of perceptions different segments of the manifest destiny generation had gained as a consequence of their own experience. Not surprisingly, the writers disagreed over the legitimacy of the American role in the war, as well as over the causes of the conflict. They wound up in two fairly distinct camps—one that condemned the war on moral grounds, and one that defended it in terms of Mexican provocation or celebrated the conflict as a demonstration of American military prowess. With some exceptions, both groups tended to underplay the role of a simple desire for territory as a major cause of the war.

One of the first Mexican War histories was that of John Frost, a Philadelphia high school teacher and popular historian who showed little interest in what caused the war and only remarked casually that it somehow came about because of the annexation of Texas. Frost was more interested in the emergence of the United States as a military power. He glamorized the role of the American army during the course of the war, and although he admitted that the Treaty of Guadalupe Hidalgo gave to the United States "an immense tract of fine territory," Frost argued that the real importance of the war was in demonstrating to the Western world that the United States was now a military power to be reckoned with. "Europe has long contemplated us as a mere commercial and business-loving nation," he concluded, but "the war in Mexico has dissolved this vain dream, and taught astonished Europe a lesson, whose precepts will be remembered in every one of her belligerent assemblies for ages . . . the Mexican War is an episode in history, having but few parallels."[3]

Nathan Covington Brooks echoed Frost's martial views in his *Complete History of the Mexican War,* but Brooks attributed the conflict to a sense of outrage in the United States over provocative actions by Mexico. He, like Frost, demonstrated a sense of appreciation over the territory gained as a result of the war but said that its greatest importance was that "it has given our country a prominent rank among the nations of the earth." John S. Jenkins offered a similar interpretation in his *History of the War between the United States and Mexico.* Although he conjectured that the annexation of Texas may have been "the original moving cause of the war," he did not attempt to analyze the motives of Americans in making the annexation and only argued that the United States' claim to the right to do so seemed reasonable. He did argue, however, that "Mexico herself invited hostilities by a refusal to negotiate"; like Brooks, Jenkins demonstrated considerable contempt for the actions of the Mexican government and people during the events that led to the war.[4]

A more critical approach to the Mexican War was offered by Edward Mansfield, a West Point graduate who dealt with the war largely in military terms. But to Mansfield the conflict *was* basically a struggle over territory, and he traced its origins in those terms. The problem began, he explained, because Texas was essentially unoccupied at a time when American expansionism was coming into full swing. When Mexican immigration policies encouraged the influx of American adventurers and settlers it consequently set the stage for what came to be almost a battle for the continent. "It was natural for them [the Texans] to pursue these new objects," he said, "and it was equally natural that they should desire to remain politically and socially connected with the land of their birth and the home of their associations." Mexico responded as well as she could to the challenges that followed, but in a spirited and agonizing conflict the Anglo-Saxon of the north, who was essentially "a conqueror over nature," prevailed, and the eagle supplanted the vulture in dominion over the lands that now comprise the southwestern quadrant of the United States.[5] Mansfield made no secret of the aggressiveness of the United States nor the legitimacy of Mexico's defense of her territory, and if there is any work among the early histories of the Mexican War which gives recognition to territorial encroachment it is his.

A different depiction of the demand for territory emerged from other early critics of the Mexican War. Abiel Abbot Livermore, whose study was published by the American Peace Society, condemned American expansionism as being simply "an incessant grasping after more territory," also arguing that "the passion for land . . . is a leading characteristic of the American people." Livermore regarded expansionist demands to be largely the product of the South and West, however, and he noted the difference between the peaceful and compromise settlement of the Oregon question with Great Britain and the more aggressive actions taken toward the territory belonging to Mexico. Was that explained simply because Great Britain was strong and Mexico weak, he asked, "or, in the further fact that Oregon was a free territory and was not wanted, and that Texas was a slave state and was wanted, and wanted, too, up to the extreme limit to which she had ever swelled her revolutionary pretensions?" His own conclusion was that "had it not been for the institution of slavery Texas would never have been conquered and annexed; and . . . had it not been for the annexation of Texas, and the desire for more Mexican soil, not a drop of human blood would have been shed." A similar judgment was made by the son of diplomat John Jay, William Jay, who also published an extremely critical account of the war. Jay focused upon slavery sentiment even more strongly than did Livermore and insisted that the desire to create more slave states in order to strengthen and protect that institution was the sole reason for expansion into Mexican territory.[6]

In sum, then, early histories of expansionism focused largely upon its relationship to the Mexican War, and most of these attributed the origins of that war to other causes than a drive for territory—to Mexican provocations, on the one hand, or to the desire to buttress the institution of slavery, on the other hand. Edward Mansfield's study was an exception to the pattern, and Mansfield came close to identifying a drive for territory as a natural attribute of man, while other opponents of expansionism argued that the acquisition of western territories was essentially a means to an end: the extension of slavery.

Following the burst of Mexican War scholarship there was a considerable hiatus in expansionist-oriented histories, as Civil War and Reconstruction issues and the emergence of a modern American society attracted the greater attention of historians. Then Hubert Howe Bancroft published his remarkable collection of studies of western North America, dealing separately or in varying combination with the histories of Texas, the Rocky Mountain and trans-Rocky Mountain states, the northern states of Mexico, and the nation of Mexico itself. U.S. expansion into the Far West became a frequent subject of the Bancroft *Works,* as he alternately praised and condemned Anglo-Americans for their aggressiveness, their genius for self-government, their harsh treatment of "lesser" peoples, and their habits of industry and inventiveness that turned a wilderness into an empire. He identified some of those in the vanguard of the westward movement as "adventurers, pure and simple; reckless, daring, and unprincipled men," some as "political adventurers, whose reward was to be . . . glory and wealth, under a reformed political system," and some as "enthusiastic Americans, who believed in the manifest destiny of their nation to possess this land." Bancroft's assessment of the actual process of possession was frequently less flattering. He was also critical of the role of the United States in the Mexican War and, much like earlier critics, rooted the causes of the war in the desire of southerners to strengthen the institution of slavery.[7]

Despite these observations Bancroft also advanced a larger and more compelling reason for American expansionism that overrode a causation as specific as the desire to expand slavery. He expressed this idea largely in Malthusian terms. The filling of the American West, he argued, was but the culmination of a worldwide movement of people from east to west that had begun in earliest times, and probably in Asia. As the population of mankind grew and as settled areas in the east became crowded, the movement of people began, with the most energetic or mobile cultures spearing westward, following the sun into new and untenanted lands and there beginning anew. With the seizure of the American West, however, he believed that the historical process had come to an end. "True," he said, "our western lands for the present will hold many more people, . . . but all the same the end will come—the end of the world, it may be, as it is noticeable that in the more advanced stages of national age and culture, increase is first arrested, and then population retrogrades."[8]

At the turn of the century a different type of historical work began to enter into the library of American history—the monograph, or book-length study, devoted to a specific aspect of the nation's past. The American Nation series included a number of such volumes, including George Garrison's *Westward Extension, 1841-1850*, the first significant attempt to assess American expansionism of the 1840s as a subject in itself. It is an oddity that Garrison was able to devote more than three hundred pages to this theme without once mentioning the term "manifest destiny," and it is also true that he structured his study largely within the confines of political and diplomatic history. Yet Garrison defined the issues of expansionism into both Oregon and the Southwest with care, and he approached his subject with an air of objectivity. To Garrison, as to Bancroft, the root cause of American expansion was the push of population from Europe against the American seaboard, and the result was an "expansion impulse" that was abetted by the extraordinary adventurousness and aggressiveness of the Anglo-American people.[9]

Garrison argued that sectional disagreements between North and South, caused by their contrasting economic systems, began to make inroads into the sense of unity with which Americans viewed expansion. But when the push to Oregon and the Mexican Southwest took place, majority opinion in the two sections supported both moves. Antislavery groups voiced opposition to the prospect of extending the area of slavery by annexing Texas, but this was not enough to control "the instinct of expansion" even in the North, and Texas was annexed. When this act resulted in war with Mexico, the war, too, received majority support and thus "was essentially a popular movement." It was not until the Wilmot Proviso highlighted differences in ideals and interests between North and South and began to intensify northern opposition to the further extension of slavery that the "expansionist proclivities" of Americans started to come under rein. This growing antislavery sentiment in the North was ultimately responsible for bringing the war to a close, with territorial gains short of what most expansionists now wanted. In this sense, Garrison argued, the issue of slavery did more to curtail than to cause "the expansion impulse."[10]

Other studies of American expansion, particularly as it related to Texas, followed Garrison's work. In 1911 Justin Smith published a tightly argued account of the Texan experience from its original colonization through annexation in which he rejected both slavery extension and territorial ambition as motives for developments there. He argued instead that they were the logical outcome of Mexican colonization policies and political mismanagement, aggravated by cultural differences between Anglo-American colonists and Mexican overlords. Annexation was eventually accepted by the United States as a matter of right, but only after some hesitation; Smith concluded that "gradually the American people, though not extremely thoughtful, well-informed or high-minded on the subject, reached the sound conclusion that it was for the national advantage to bring about annexation without further delay," and Texas was annexed.[11]

Wilfred Binkley also produced a study of expansionism in Texas, focusing upon the Texans themselves, and he began his examination of Texan behavior with the establishment of the Texas Republic in 1836. What he discovered was a series of assertive policies on the part of Texans in which they first pushed their boundary claims against Mexico to the Rio Grande River and then embarked upon a series of plans—some only formulated, some actually attempted—to extend Texan sovereignty over New Mexico, northern Mexico, and even as far as California. These efforts were motivated by desires such as that of obtaining a militarily defensive boundary or by the perception that control of California ports would be an asset in gaining acceptance of annexation by the United States. But Binkley was also impressed by the aggressiveness of the Anglo-American Texans and by the "expansionist propensity" that guided their actions. In the end, this propensity paid off in the favorable boundary agreement she was able to establish following annexation in the Compromise of 1850, as well as in retention of her own public lands and a cash settlement with which to pay her public debt.[12]

In 1919 Justin Smith returned to print with his second major study bearing upon the subject of expansionism, this one a two-volume history of the Mexican War. It was the most vigorous defense of the U.S. role in that war yet—or perhaps ever—published, and it was in addition a monumental work. Based upon exhaustive archival research in the United States, Mexico, and elsewhere, and upon practically every previously published source, Smith's account was masterfully synthesized and persuasively written. It was also highly ethnocentric. Smith attributed the causes of the war solely to Mexican misconduct, provocation, insult, and martial spirit, while the U.S. response, initially one of forbearance and patience, turned warlike only when injuries became too much to bear. It was only then that the United States rose in arms to chastise her irresponsible neighbor to the south. Smith denied, however, that the question of expansionist goals had anything to do with the U.S. decision to go to war. War came, he said, because Mexico wanted it. The United States annexed Texas as a matter of right, the right of two independent republics to amalgamate if they chose. As for the territorial cessions made at the end of the war, they occurred only because Mexico had no other means with which to pay for past injuries. "Besides," he concluded, "while ours could perhaps be called a war *of* conquest, it was not a war *for* conquest—the really vital point. We found it necessary to require territory, for otherwise our claims and indemnity could not be paid. The conflict was forced upon us."[13]

In view of the extremity of Smith's position and of his considerable influence upon later students of expansionism and the Mexican War, we might take note at this point of his rejection of the entire notion of territorial gain as a cause of the Mexican War. A somewhat different assessment, however, can be made of the work of Bernard De Voto, who published a stirring account of American expansion in 1943 with his *The Year of Decision: 1846*. De Voto viewed frontier expansion as a folk movement with heroic overtones and neither denied nor apologized for the aggressive behavior of the United States toward England and Mexico in the rush to occupy the American West. As far as the colonization of Texas was concerned, for example, he argued that "it penetrated not a populous, developed, and organized civilization but an empty waste. Few Mexicans lived there in '46, practically none when the colony was made. The occupation of Texas neither usurped nor absorbed a community, a culture, or an economy. Instead, it created all three." De Voto found something inexplicable yet irresistible about the lure of the West for Americans, and for mankind in general. Like Hubert Howe Bancroft some sixty years before, he detected a universal appeal in the westward movement that cut across time and culture. "When the body dies," he noted reverently, "[as] the Book of the Dead relates, the soul is borne along the pathway of the setting sun. Toward that Western horizon all heroes of all peoples known to history have always traveled." Whether the passageway be the Gates of Hercules, the Western Ocean, or, presumably, the Oregon Trail, the objects of this movement were the same: open country, freedom, and the unknown. Like Bancroft, De Voto also realized that even this process must eventually come to an end, simply because the West must eventually be used up, but while Bancroft had become depressed over the prospect De Voto became mystical. "Westward lies the goal of effort," he concluded. "And, if either Freud or the Navajo speak true, westward we shall find the hole in the earth through which the soul may plunge to peace."[14]

One of the trends among twentieth-century students of American expansionism thus far had been a greater tendency to try to establish the role of public opinion, but there still had been no attempt to define or measure systematically the actual components of manifest destiny. This situation was corrected in 1935 when Albert K. Weinberg published his *Manifest Destiny: A Study of Nationalist Expansionism in American History,* a seminal work based on wide-ranging research that endures as the most important study in this field. Weinberg found, for one thing, that the spirit of manifest destiny which crystalized so noticeably in the 1840s was in actuality a pervasive factor throughout American history, that some of its elements could be detected among Americans as early as the revolutionary generation, and others traced through American behavior and attitudes up to Weinberg's own generation.

Included among the objects of American expansionist interest were thus not only Oregon and the Southwest, but at various times Canada, Latin America, and the Philippines. There was consequently a thread of continuity that ran from America's early expansionism to the age of imperialism and beyond. Weinberg's intent was to enter into what he called "the wonderland of nationalism" in an effort to identify and analyze the different justifications Americans advanced as they pursued their different expansionist aims. He found that these justifications fell into thematic patterns, and that while some of the themes were more lasting than others, they combined to form an expansionist fabric. Americans justified expansion on the basis of natural right, or of geographical predestination. They argued that Americans would make more effective use of the soil than did Indians or Mexicans, or that they would regenerate those same societies and bring them up to their own level of civilization, or that they would do the same for the people of the Philippines. These and a dozen similar arguments were advanced along a broad front and over a long course of time as explanations for American interest in other lands.

But the question remained: Did these arguments constitute a series of conditioning factors through which Americans persuaded each other to do something they would not otherwise do, or were they simply rationalizations for something they were going to do anyway? Weinberg struggled constantly with this question, and as he moved from one manifest destiny argument to another he found continued reason to doubt that the arguments advanced were the actual basis of American expansionism. "Why did extension of freedom mean to the American of the middle 'forties less the liberation of other peoples than the aggrandizement of his own freedom—and territory," he asked. "Undoubtedly one explanation was the American's healthy-minded egoism, a matter of instinct rather than of logic. Another was the fact that the American philosophy of individualism blessed egoism in its affirmation of a natural right to the pursuit of happiness."[15]

Elsewhere Weinberg noted that "the inconsistency between the doctrine of beneficent territorial utilization and its largely unbeneficent practice is probably significant of another inconsistency between ideology and motive. . . . The discrepancy is between the nationalist's pretension to interest in the use of territory and his fundamental interest in its possession. It is because of the possessive instinct and not the plough that the soil is destined for the race using the cannon rather than the bow and arrow." Weinberg complained repeatedly that the complexities of manifest destiny had dropped him into the world of Lewis Carroll, and that "nature is 'so full of a number of things' that anyone impartially observant does not know what to follow." In the end, however, Weinberg had to come down someplace, as he did when he said of the imperialist spirit that "apparently the fundamental cause was neither international fellowship nor objective need, but the appeal to instinct and impulse in the glorious prospect of world empire."[16]

In structure, if not always in point of view, Weinberg's book has influenced the work of other scholars. John Douglas Pitts Fuller, for example, soon published a study entitled *The Movement for the Acquisition of All Mexico, 1846-1848,* in which he utilized Weinberg's concepts. Fuller's work was useful in demonstrating that such a growth in sentiment did take place between 1846 and 1848, and that the greatest opposition to this movement emerged from antislavery New England and the slaveholding states of the southeast, the latter because they feared the acquisition of extensive territories not suited for slavery. He also concluded that "in the minds of many expansionists, professed motives probably had little force in themselves, but were merely used to glorify those acquisitive tendencies which are rooted in human nature," and that as far as the doctrines of manifest destiny were concerned "the conclusion seems to be that the desire created the ideal and the created soon became as great as the creator."[17]

Another historian who accepted much of Weinberg's structure, but this time not his point of view, was Frederick Merk. Merk devoted the greater part of his professional career to the study of American expansionism. He published his findings, which were related mainly to the settlement and acquisition of Oregon, in a series of articles and monographs over a period of some thirty-five years. These were not highly interpretive works, but in 1963 Merk turned to interpretive synthesis in his *Manifest Destiny and Mission in American History.* Like Weinberg, Merk delineated the components of the spirit of manifest destiny, although in a more caustic tone; like Fuller, he traced the rise and fall of the all-Mexico movement. To Merk, however, the message of manifest destiny was not simply a reflection of American expansionist sentiment. It was a cause, indeed the leading cause, of American expansionism. There were genuine expansionists, to be sure. These were the ones who used the press, which Merk believed to be highly effective in molding public opinion in the mid-nineteenth century, and other "agencies of mass propaganda" to popularize expansionist views.[18] They were successful, at least until the demise of the all-Mexico movement, which signaled the beginning of the end of the spirit of continentalism in the United States.

Continentalism was followed in the latter years of the century by the emergence of a spirit of imperialism, particularly in business circles, and Merk again attributed the growth of this sentiment to the use of propaganda. In this instance, however, a counter-propaganda campaign was effective in limiting the scope of the expansionist crusade. The doctrines of imperialism were, in addition, less palatable to Americans than the doctrines of continentalism, for they necessarily involved either the subjugation or amalgamation of other races and cultures. Hawaii was annexed, but America was literally jolted into its war with Spain; when that war was over, the acceptance of Spanish insular territories was both limited and tentative. With this, the American spirit of expansionism passed from the scene.[19]

Merk concluded his study with the assertion that "continentalism and imperialist doctrines were never true expressions of the national spirit" of the United States. "A better-supported thesis," he said, "is that Manifest Destiny and imperialism were traps into which the nation was led in 1846 and in 1899, and from which it extricated itself as well as it could afterward."[20]

One further response to Weinberg's work was that of Norman Graebner, who presented his findings in a study called *Empire on the Pacific.* Graebner accepted in part the thesis that manifest destiny helped propel Americans westward, but he argued that a stronger lure bringing Americans across the continent was found in the ports and harbors of the Pacific and that it was "the pursuit of commercial empire" that determined the course of the American advance. He conceded the importance of the role played by frontiersmen in the annexation of Texas; but insofar as expansion to the Pacific Coast was concerned, he believed that it was a much more calculated and deliberate process than Texas had presented and that it was formulated by politicians acting in response to travelers' reports and commerical interests. It was thus the location of Puget Sound and the San Diego harbor that determined the northern and southern boundary demands of the United States along the Pacific.

In many ways, however, the Graebner study appears to be a corrective to Weinberg's thesis more than a revision. "Historians have tended to exaggerate the natural urge of the American people to expand in the forties," he argued, adding that neither public opinion nor the pressure of pioneers determined the eventual limits of the United States. "Indeed," he concluded, "manifest destiny is an inadequate description of American expansionism in the forties. The mere urge to expand or even the acceptance of a destiny to occupy new areas on the continent does not create specific geographic objectives. . . . It was not by accident that the United States spread as a broad belt across the continent in the forties. It was rather through clearly conceived policies relentlessly pursued that the United States achieved its empire on the Pacific."[21] In a later essay entitled "The Mexican War: A Study in Causation," Graebner demonstrated how these "clearly conceived policies" led the United States into war with Mexico—a war, he argued, that the United States entered at her own option and solely for territory, but which Mexico fought because she had no choice.[22] This view was reinforced only in part by Gene Brack in his *Mexico Views Manifest Destiny, 1821-1846,* a study of Mexican perceptions of American expansionism. Brack found that Mexicans of that era were keenly aware of the dangers to them from this expansionism, and from American feelings of racial superiority over Mexicans. He defined manifest destiny as an "ethnocentric notion" held by many Americans that had a powerful influence in causing the confrontation with Mexico, but Brack also argued that the Mexican War was not caused by actions of the United States alone. "Mexico after all did not present a model of enlightened humanitarianism toward her own Indians," he stated, "and in their attitudes toward the United States Mexicans appeared in their own way ethnocentric."[23]

The work of Weinberg, Merk, Fuller, Graebner, and Brack represents an attempt to isolate the spirit of manifest destiny from related concerns and to analyze it as a subject in itself. One consequence of such studies has been to highlight the importance of manifest destiny upon the many facets of American expansionism. Recent studies of related subjects generally include at least passing—and sometimes puzzled—reference to the importance of manifest destiny, while others have gone after the subject with some seriousness. Recent Mexican War histories have frequently been included in the latter group.

Perhaps the most successful of the newer Mexican War studies is Otis Singletary's *The Mexican War,* a well-written and skillfully synthesized effort drawn largely from previously published works. Singletary attributed the war to a variety of causes that included the nagging claims question between the United States and Mexico, Mexican political instability, a perception in the United States that Mexico had performed brutally in her relations with Texas, and the pressures of American expansionism. Singletary defined manifest destiny as "bumptious expansionism" and a "disease" that had emerged as early as the Jefferson administration, and which lingered on even after the war with Mexico was over. He denied, however, that either expansionism or the annexation of Texas by themselves caused the war. Annexation, he concluded, "was one, but by no means the sole cause of the war. The bad feelings that had slowly but surely grown out of the encroachments of one power and the brutalities of the other set the stage for war; political instability increased its probability; the failure of diplomacy made it inevitable."[24] A somewhat sharper assessment was made by Charles L. Dufour in *The Mexican War: A Compact History, 1846–1848.* Dufour agreed with Singletary on the mixed causation of the war, but he focused more heavily upon manifest destiny as a motivating factor behind the actions of the United States. He disapproved of the spirit of manifest destiny, and he accepted Merk's argument that the respectable aura surrounding it was largely a creation of propaganda. "Manifest Destiny," Dufour concluded, "was, nevertheless, a land-grabbing scheme, pure and simple, no matter how eloquently or altruistically it appeared in public under the auspices of editors, politicians, business and professional leaders, and ministers of the Gospel."[25]

A far different view of manifest destiny was presented by Seymour V. Connor and Odie B. Faulk in their *North America Divided: The Mexican War, 1846-1848*. The authors of this work defined the concept "in its original sense" as "one of spreading democratic government to the people of the western hemisphere"; while they conceded that expansionism played a role in provoking the war between Mexico and the United States, they probed the Mexican political scene to demonstrate that Mexican centralists, particularly those associated with Santa Anna, had done more to cause the war through their brutal policies toward Texas and their bellicose attitudes toward the United States.[26] K. Jack Bauer, in his more recent study *The Mexican War, 1846-1848,* agreed that Mexican leaders must bear a large share of responsibility for the war. "Many, if not most," he charged, "used the popular resentment over the fancied *gringo* aggression which they themselves largely created as a stepping-stone to power. Once in power those politicians found themselves captives of that propaganda." Yet Bauer also blamed the war in part on inept political leadership in the United States and, in particular, indicted James K. Polk for his policy of "gradual escalation" that simply invited Mexico to follow suit. Here he likened Polk's efforts to the ill-fated U.S. policies in Vietnam. Bauer found it difficult to envision any set of circumstances, however, that would have reduced expansionist pressure upon Mexican lands, "since they stood in the way of the inexorable movement westward of the American frontier and the American settlers." He attributed this movement largely to the spirit of manifest destiny and, echoing Frederick Merk, described this spirit as a self-induced messiah complex "which warped the American view of her role into a divine mission to evangelize the rest of the world with her own true way."[27]

A parallel can be drawn between Bauer's findings and those of David Pletcher, whose *The Diplomacy of Annexation: Texas, Oregon, and the Mexican War* ranks as the most scholarly and perceptive diplomatic study bearing on the expansionism of the 1840s. Like Bauer, Pletcher emphasized the role of propaganda in stimulating an "artificial fury" over manifest destiny doctrines, and in promoting a belief among Americans that they possessed a "divine favoritism" when it came to possession of western lands. He balanced this propaganda against the "natural expansionist pride" of the American people and viewed Polk as a true representative of the resultant expansionist spirit. Like Bauer, too, Pletcher condemned Polk's policy of gradual escalation in his actions toward Mexico. Pletcher argued that if Polk had relied upon skillful professional diplomacy rather than using "bluff and a show of force" in foreign relations, American expansion to the Pacific could have been achieved without war and would have resulted in less divisiveness within American society.[28]

The conflict with Mexico aside, it was the Far West—California and the Pacific Northwest—that provided the target for much of the manifest destiny message; here was terminus, the place that would provide the logical culmination of the westward march of the American people. Historians of the settlement of the area have dealt with this theme in various ways. John Walton Caughey, in his durable and popular history of California, presented manifest destiny as one of several factors that excited the interest of the U.S. government in California, the others being the wealth of that province, the inadequacy of Mexican control, fear of French and English designs on the area, and the strategic value of San Francisco Bay. Also of interest to Caughey was the influence of manifest destiny upon the flurry of filibustering southward from California that followed, for, he said, "many Americans and particularly many Californians of the fifties were reluctant to believe that this much expansion was all that had been ordained" by manifest destiny.[29] A similar connection was made by Andrew Rolle in his *California: A History,* when he argued that filibustering in Mexico and South American was taken on by "rootless adventurers" who were still pushing manifest destiny toward what they considered to be the nation's "natural frontiers." He also noted that "during the 1850s it was frequently as unpopular for a Westerner to be opposed to filibustering as it was for a Southerner to be against slavery." Rolle regarded manifest destiny as a mixture of individualism, religious conviction, and incurable nationalism, and also as a peculiarly western trait. He indicated that American fear of foreign acquisition of California was partly responsible for the assertive actions taken by the U.S. government in pursuit of its own interests there, but the important factor, said Rolle, was the increasing swarm of American settlers into Mexican California, and he stated that "the rate of American migration to California in the 1840s seemed almost to forecast its future control by *Yanquis.*"[30] Robert Glass Cleland agreed with this contention in his *From Wilderness to Empire: A History of California.* Cleland emphasized the role of "an extraordinary advertising campaign" in exciting the interest of Americans in settling and acquiring California. The western settler, he said, had become "almost fanatical in his belief in manifest destiny and the expansion of the United States to the Pacific." This archetypal settler found a responsive agent in James K. Polk, a westerner rather than a southerner, said

Cleland, and a true believer in manifest destiny—"as deep-rooted in his convictions as the rigid Calvinist theology to which he subscribed." And so it was that Polk, in addition to his confrontation with Mexico over the Texan affair, "quickly initiated a program within California itself that promised to bring about ultimate annexation."[31]

Acquisition of the Pacific Northwest involved at least two ingredients that differed from those which led to the penetration of the American Southwest. One of these was the role of Protestant missionaries as advance agents of migration, and the other was the nearly direct confrontation with Great Britain that took place over the Oregon country. Oscar Winther, the historian perhaps most closely connected with the history of the Pacific Northwest, tried to balance these factors out in his *The Great Northwest: A History,* which was published in 1947. He credited the missionaries with transforming the region south of the 49th parallel from a fur trade empire to an agricultural frontier, and he said that publicists such as Hall Jackson Kelley and Washington Irving had created such an attractive image of the Oregon country that it "brought the name 'Oregon' to the lips of nearly every American man, woman, and child." The result was "Oregon fever," a regional variation of manifest destiny that lured increasing numbers of American settlers to Oregon in the years following the migration of 1841, and which ultimately buried British claims to anything south of the 49th parallel through sheer weight of numbers.[32] Winther repeated this theme in *The Old Oregon Country,* published in 1950, while a somewhat different assessment was made by Dorothy O. Johansen in her *Empire of the Columbia.* Johansen argued that the common western fear of British domination of the Pacific Northwest had a great deal to do with settler immigration to the Oregon country, and she also drew from the findings of Norman Graebner to demonstrate that the lure of Pacific harbors helped determine the course of expansionism in that area.[33]

David Lavender, however, ranged more widely through the motives of Oregon migrants than either Winther or Johansen in his *Land of Giants: The Drive to the Pacific Northwest, 1750-1950,* published in 1956. Addressing the sizable overland migration of 1843, Lavender noted that it was composed mostly of farmers and family men who were prosperous enough to buy the costly outfits needed to transport them to Oregon, and that they stood small chance of financial gain by exchanging their substantial farms back east for what they would find in the Pacific Northwest. Had it been cheap virgin land they were after, said Lavender, they would have been better off to buy in Iowa or Wisconsin for $1.25 an acre. Yet they passed up that opportunity in order to travel two thousand miles to the "unknown x" of Oregon. Why? Partly, he said, it was simply for a promise, and a fulfillment—"a westering bent so strong among the bulk of the movers that it amounted almost to an instinct." Partly, too, it was a determination to keep the British from winding up with Oregon, and partly, at least on the part of some migrants, the desire to escape the presence of Negro labor. There were also speculative urges involved, and the realization among some that the harbors of the Oregon country opened to the markets of Asia; above all, there was the spirit of romance. And this, to Lavender, added up to the feeling of manifest destiny—much maligned, perhaps, but a movement in which "the strands of idealism and opportunism were inextricably intertwined." "Northward," Lavender said, "in a Canadian jumping-off point called Red River, there were no such convictions. The lack is not without its import in our history."[34]

But did the spirit of manifest destiny die away with the acquisition of California and the Pacific Northwest? Frederick Merk, as we have seen, saw a connection between the continentalism of the 1840s and the imperialism of the 1890s. Julius Pratt, whose *Expansionists of 1898* is a landmark study of that imperialism, also saw the connection. The manifest destiny of the 1840s, he believed, was largely a matter of emotion, an expression of half-blind faith in the superior virility of the American race and the superior beneficence of American political institutions. Between then and the 1890s, he explained, this emotional concept had been given a philosophical foundation through the work of theorists in the fields of economics, social Darwinism, Anglo-Saxon supremacy, and Protestant evangelism. And to all this Alfred Thayer Mahan added a new dimension by linking overseas possessions and naval strategy.[35]

Walter Millis, in his *Martial Spirit: A Study of Our War with Spain,* noted the use of manifest destiny doctrines by the Republican party in its pursuit of an "energetic foreign policy" that included control of the Hawaiian Islands and the "independence" of Cuba, but of greater import to Millis was the fact that the decade of the 1890s saw the final filling in of the American frontier. With this, he said, came something more than a release of energy: a realization on the part of the newly industrialized society that it had passed through a muddled period of national development in which it had been preoccupied with self. Millis argued that there was a sudden new awareness, and a new interest, in adventurous interaction with the outside world. "The frontier had dissolved suddenly into the past," said Millis, "and we looked up to find nothing before our eyes save salt water and the nations of the earth that lay beyond it."[36]

While Millis found that the imperialist behavior of Americans in the 1890s represented a break with the past, others have found a stream of continuity between the two. David Healy, for example, in his *U.S. Expansionism: The Imperialist Urge in the 1890s,* emphasized this factor. Healy noted that the latter part of the nineteenth century was in fact an age of international imperialism, and that the United States took lessons on this score from Great Britain and other colonial powers of the day. However, the United States was also following in her own traditions as she began to spread overseas. Citing the post–Civil War interest of Americans in places such as Cuba, Puerto Rico, Greenland, Iceland, and Alaska, Healy claimed that "the idea of expansionism never really died in the United States; neither was it ever found entirely separated from the concepts of progress and mission." Yet Healy saw nothing unusual about American expansionist behavior and compared it to that of regional or global powers such as Germany, Italy, China, Japan, Indonesia, Russia, Great Britain, France, and others. He placed it within the context of the normal behavior of nation states and concluded by noting that "to possess great potential power without eventually seeking to apply it toward desired ends would be a queer condition indeed."[37]

That the spirit of manifest destiny was a uniquely American phenomenon seems clear enough, but its causes as well as its influences have not been issues upon which all historians have agreed. Nineteenth-century American historians tended to focus upon the more general theme of "expansionism" when addressing subjects related to the war with Mexico or the American occupation of the trans-Mississippi West. Issues such as the extension of slavery, the fear of British or other European intrusion, or a simple desire to demonstrate that the United States was now a world power also frequently came into play. It was not until the appearance of George Garrison's *Westward Extension* in 1906 that the subject of expansionism began to receive more serious attention.

The most significant contributions to the study of manifest destiny have undoubtedly been made by Albert Weinberg and Frederick Merk, with an important addition by Norman Graebner. The basic disagreement between Weinberg and Merk came over the question of whether or not the spirit of manifest destiny represented a fundamental human drive for territorial acquisition, which is what Weinberg came to believe, or whether, as Merk argued, it was simply a process through which Americans persuaded themselves that the acquisition of territory at the expense of other people was a good thing. Beyond this lies the question of the influence of the spirit of manifest destiny upon the age of filibustering that came in the two decades following the Mexican War, and upon American imperialism during the 1890s. What is evident, however, is that the spirit of manifest destiny, elusive as it may have been, and both maligned and praised, has been measured as an important ingredient in American history.

Notes

1. Ray Allen Billington, *The Far Western Frontier, 1830-1860* (New York: Harper and Row, 1956; paperbound ed., 1962), p. xiii.

2. Quoted in Albert K. Weinberg, *Manifest Destiny: A Study of Nationalist Expansionism in American History* (Baltimore: Johns Hopkins Press, 1935; paperbound ed., Chicago: Quadrangle, 1963), p. 112. O'Sullivan seems to have used the term "manifest destiny" for the first time in the July issue of the *Democratic Review* in 1845, but he used similar phraseology as early as 1839, when he stated that "the nation of many nations is destined to manifest to mankind the excellence of divine principles; to establish on earth the noblest temple ever dedicated to the worship of the Most High." For this see Norman A. Graebner (ed.), *Manifest Destiny* (Indianapolis: Bobbs-Merrill, 1968), p. 17.

3. John Frost, *The Mexican War and Its Warriors; Comprising a Complete History of All the Operations of the American Armies in Mexico: With Biographical Sketches and Anecdotes of the Most Distinguished Officers in the Regular Army and Volunteer Force* (New Haven: H. Mansfield, 1850), pp. 9, 331-32 (quote).

4. Nathan Covington Brooks, *A Complete History of the Mexican War: Its Causes, Conduct, and Consequences* (Philadelphia: Grigg, Elliot and Co., 1849), pp. 538-39; John S. Jenkins, *History of the War between the United States and Mexico from the Commencement of Hostilities to the Ratification of the Treaty of Peace* (Auburn: Derby, Miller and Company, 1849), p. 499.

5. Edward D. Mansfield, *The Mexican War: A History of its Origin, and a Detailed Account of the Victories Which Terminated in the Surrender of the Capital; with the Official Despatches of the Generals . . .* (New York: A. S. Barnes and Burr, 1848), pp. 14, 322-23.

6. Abiel Abbot Livermore, *The War with Mexico Reviewed* (Boston: American Peace Society, 1850), pp. 12, 53, 180-81; William Jay, *A Review of the Causes and Consequences of the Mexican War* (Boston: Benjamin B. Mussey and Co., 1849), p. 269.

7. See, for instance, Hubert Howe Bancroft, *The Works of Hubert Howe*

Bancroft, 39 vols. (San Francisco: A. L. Bancroft and Company, 1882-90), vol. 22: *History of California*, pp. 84-88; vol. 13: *History of Mexico*, pp. 308, 325.

8. *Ibid.*, vol. 38: *Essays and Miscellany*, pp. 39-44.

9. George Pierce Garrison, *Westward Extension, 1841-1850*, vol. 17 of *The American Nation: A History* (New York: Harper and Bros., 1906), pp. 3-4, 332.

10. *Ibid.*, pp. 96-97, 201, 251, 266-68, 332.

11. Justin H. Smith, *The Annexation of Texas*, corrected ed. (1911, New York: Barnes and Noble, 1941), pp. 28-33, 469.

12. William Campbell Binkley, *The Expansionist Movement in Texas, 1836-1850*, University of California Publications in History, vol. 13 (Berkeley: University of California Press, 1925), pp. 11, 214-22.

13. Justin H. Smith, *The War with Mexico*, 2 vols. (New York: Macmillan, 1919), 2:322-23.

14. Bernard De Voto, *The Year of Decision: 1846* (Boston: Little, Brown, 1943; paperbound ed., n.d.), pp. 12, 49.

15. Weinberg, *Manifest Destiny*, pp. 125-26.

16. *Ibid.*, pp. 99, 457.

17. John Douglas Pitts Fuller, *The Movement for the Acquisition of All Mexico, 1846-1848*, The Johns Hopkins University Studies in Historical and Political Science, series 54, no. 1 (Baltimore: Johns Hopkins Press, 1936), p. 160.

18. For a collection of Merk's Oregon essays see his *The Oregon Question: Essays in Anglo-American Diplomacy and Politics* (Cambridge: Belknap Press of Harvard University Press, 1967); Merk, *Manifest Destiny and Mission in American History: A Reinterpretation* (New York: Knopf, 1963; paperbound ed., n.d.), p. 55. (Merk's assessment of manifest destiny is found on pp. 24-60.) For additional work by Merk utilizing this theme, see his *The Monroe Doctrine and American Expansion, 1843-1849* (New York: Knopf, 1966) and his *Slavery and the Annexation of Texas* (New York: Knopf, 1972).

19. Merk, *Manifest Destiny and Mission*, pp. 235-48, 256-57.

20. *Ibid.*, p. 266.

21. Norman A. Graebner, *Empire on the Pacific: A Study in American Continental Expansion* (New York: Ronald Press Company, 1955), pp. 3, 226-28. A good discussion of primary sources is also contained in Graebner's bibliographical essay on pp. 258-65. Also, for a further critique along the line suggested above, see Shomer S. Swelling, *Expansion and Imperialism* (Chicago: Loyola University Press, 1970).

22. Graebner, "The Mexican War: A Study in Causation," *Pacific Historical*

Review 49 (August 1980): 115.

23. Gene Brack, *Mexico Views Manifest Destiny, 1821-1846: An Essay on the Origins of the Mexican War* (Albuquerque: University of New Mexico Press, 1975), pp. 181-82.

24. Otis A. Singletary, *The Mexican War* (Chicago: University of Chicago Press, 1960; paperbound ed., n.d.), pp. 14, 20.

25. Charles L. Dufour, *The Mexican War: A Compact History, 1846-1848* (New York: Hawthorn Books, 1968), p. 290.

26. Seymour V. Connor and Odie B. Faulk, *North America Divided: The Mexican War, 1846-1848* (New York: Oxford University Press, 1971), pp. 7, 31-32.

27. K. Jack Bauer, *The Mexican War, 1846-1848* (New York: Macmillan, 1974), pp. 392-93, 1-3.

28. David M. Pletcher, *The Diplomacy of Annexation: Texas, Oregon, and the Mexican War* (Columbia: University of Missouri Press, 1973), pp. 334, 609-11.

29. John Walton Caughey, *California* (New York: Prentice-Hall, 1953), pp. 219, 300-301.

30. Andrew F. Rolle, *California: A History* (New York: Thomas Y. Crowell, 1963; text ed., Arlington Heights, Ill.: Harlan Davidson, 1978), pp. 250-51, 186.

31. Robert Glass Cleland, *From Wilderness to Empire: A History of California* (New York: Knopf, 1960), pp. 86-87, 104-5.

32. Oscar Osburn Winther, *The Great Northwest: A History* (New York: Knopf, 1947, 1950), pp. 120-21, 124.

33. Oscar Osburn Winther, *The Old Oregon Country: A History of Frontier Trade, Transportation, and Travel* (Stanford: Stanford University Press, 1950; paperbound ed. Lincoln: University of Nebraska Press, 1969), pp. 98-100; Dorothy O. Johansen and Charles M. Gates, *Empire of the Columbia: A History of the Pacific Northwest* (New York: Harper and Row, 1957, 1967), pp. 197-99.

34. David Lavender, *Land of Giants: The Drive to the Pacific Northwest, 1750-1950* (Garden City, N.Y.: Doubleday, 1956; paperbound ed., Lincoln: University of Nebraska Press, 1979), pp. 224-26.

35. Julius W. Pratt, *Expansionists of 1898: The Acquisition of Hawaii and the Spanish Islands* (Baltimore: Johns Hopkins Press, 1936), pp. 3-25.

36. Walter Millis, *The Martial Spirit: A Study of Our War with Spain* (Boston: Houghton Mifflin, 1931), pp. 55-56, 5.

37. David Healy, *U.S. Expansionism: The Imperialist Urge in the 1890s* (Madison: University of Wisconsin Press, 1970), pp. 37, 255.

Chapter Six

Clark C. Spence

Western Mining

In one sense, at least until comparatively recently, the historian's approach to the mineral West has been like that of early Nevada miners toward the materials with which they worked. For years prospectors had toiled away along the Truckee and the Carson, gaining a modest amount of gold but sweating and cursing the "damned blue stuff" that clogged their rockers. Finally in 1859, when assays were run in California, this "damned blue stuff" proved far more valuable than the gold they were getting and the rush was on—for silver. But previously, Nevada miners had washed only the dirt in which gold glittered; they ignored the unfamiliar, more complex silver deposits, unaware of their real value. In like fashion, the historian has long tended to be preoccupied with the drama and the excitement of the mining rushes, until the mid-twentieth century ignoring in large measure the "damned blue stuff"—the more prosaic but, in the long run, more important mineral industry.

Even in the 1980s the public continues to be thrilled by the colorful rowdiness of the precious metal stampedes, by ghost-town guide books and romantic accounts of Lost Breyfogle or Lost Dutchman or countless other misplaced deposits of fabulous wealth.[1] The average reader is much more interested in the bad man from Bodie, the light ladies who followed the heavy money, or the gambling and swilling of rotgut whiskey in some root-hog-or-die mining camp than in a three-dollar-a-day mucker toiling in the bowels of the earth, the capitalization of a joint-stock company, or the evolution of a new smelting process. Despite this popularity of the gaudy and the sensational, however, since World War II serious scholarly study of the western mineral industry has proceeded at a steady but measured pace, the product of a small but gradually expanding fraternity of writers.

In part, the past neglect of the history of mining stems from the impact of the Turnerian emphasis on things political, on individualism, democracy, environmental influence, and on the pre-Appomattox era. In part it is the outgrowth of the belief that the glamor rush periods will pay larger dividends with smaller investments, that publishers and the reading public prefer descriptions of spectacles over accounts of the tunneling process or the growth of an industry. In part, too, the historian's relatively primitive equipment has not been well suited by itself to a field that may require some technical knowledge of geology, mining and milling, even metallurgy, not to mention economics, accounting, or law. Only since World War II have professional historians begun to acquire the necessary tools, including some of those of the modern social sciences.

There are many gaps in the historiography of mining. There is no general history of American mining—no overarching assessment of the total picture in the way Geoffrey Blainey's splendid *The Rush That Never Ended* deals with Australia. Nor is there any full-fledged history of mining in the American West, no tying of the nineteenth and twentieth centuries into an integrated whole. One of the first general efforts, that of Walter Crane in 1908, purported to be an economic history of mining in the United States but actually devoted most of its space to western regions. Crane drew with scissors and paste from contemporary mining periodicals and his material remained raw and undigested, lacking in analysis.[2]

What bibliographers label as the standard history of American mineral development was written nearly half a century ago by engineer-editor Thomas A. Rickard, a Cornishman and a kind of stormy petrel of mining literature. Except for brief sections on Lake Superior copper and lead in the Mississippi Valley, Rickard's *History of American Mining,* too, is purely western in scope. Emphasizing technology, it is an uneven collection of articles, wanting in integration and interpretation and with vast gaps, including most of the twentieth century.[3] Clearly, a general history of American mining is much needed.

Although popular writers mined the surface deposits and on occasion turned out anecdotal books about the mineral West, it was not until 1963 that broad scholarly histories appeared. In one volume of that year, *The Bonanza West,* William Greever attempted the most comprehensive survey to date. In a narrative approach, he tied together the political, social, and economic aspects of the nineteenth-century rushes from California to the Yukon, omitting without explanation only those of the Southwest.[4]

A second book of 1963, *Mining Frontiers of the Far West* by Rodman W. Paul, was the first synthesis of western mining to emphasize the "whys" and to focus on scientific and technological advances in charting the transition from individual to corporate enterprise down to 1880. Paul establishes logical patterns, with California gold playing a key role in the extension of placer and quartz techniques; with the Comstock pioneering large-scale, corporate, deep-level operations that hastened exploitation as well as speculation; and with Colorado and its rich silver-lead ores ultimately combining with European reduction methods to replace the Comstock in preeminence and lay the foundation for a western mineral economy more integrated into the national structure. Less important than Paul's and Greever's books, but superb in its own way, is the more recent coffee-table quarto of T. A. Watkins, *Gold and Silver in the West,* which brings together some magnificent illustrations and an exceptionally good text on gold and silver mining.[5]

These are all limited to the nineteenth century. Specialized and corporate studies do range well into recent times, but there are no comprehensive studies of the post-1900 era, no work comparable to Marvin Bernstein's on the Mexican mining industry, for example. Russell Elliott's book *Nevada's Twentieth-Century Mining Boom* gives an excellent portrayal of gold and copper developments in one state, but only to 1920. One of the few American studies to span both centuries is Duane A. Smith's black-and-white photographic history of Colorado mining, which includes not only an intriguing selection of pictures but also a sensible, perceptive narrative for the 1848 to 1970 period.[6]

All this is not to say that the pre–World War II era lacked sound studies of mineral development. The numerous (and voluminous) county, state, and regional histories of the late nineteenth century include much on western mining but submerge it in a sea of other information. The good monographs that were written tended to be about fragments of the mineral West, some of them still of considerable value. Eliot Lord's *Comstock Mining and Miners,* for example, although done for the U.S. Geological Survey nearly a hundred years ago, remains a readable, balanced history based on sources some of which are no longer available. Also in the 1880s, Dan De Quille (William Wright), whose brawny *Big Bonanza* would take its place alongside Mark Twain's *Roughing It* as a Comstock classic, would produce also a less anecdotal but excellent and enduring historical description of the lode.[7]

It was in 1885 that Scribner's published *Mining Camps: A Study in American Frontier Government,* the work of a young Californian, Charles Howard Shinn, who was an advocate of the "germ" theory taught at Johns Hopkins

University. The extraordinary attempts at self-government by California miners, Shinn argued, could be traced back to remote Teutonic ancestors, an idea that would take root but would be twisted and attributed not to the remote Germanic background but to the frontier environment by Frederick Jackson Turner and his disciples. Before the century came to a close, Shinn would also produce a much less original volume on the Comstock lode, in which he drew heavily upon and watered down Lord.[8]

In 1914 William J. Trimble's pioneering *Mining Advance into the Inland Empire* appeared. Original in research and conception, Trimble's study compared the sociopolitical, institutional, and technological developments of the mineral frontiers of British Columbia and of the northwestern United States during the 1850s and 1860s. In what is still a provocative analysis, Trimble put new emphasis on the role of the California "Yon-siders," who joined eastern adventurers to push these frontiers.[9]

Trimble stands as a model of excellence, a beacon for scholars, and some of the best mining history of our time has been done on a regional basis, often at the state or even district level. Though neither range beyond 1873, John Caughey's *Gold Is the Cornerstone* and Rodman Paul's *California Gold* are still, after a third of a century, the definitive studies of the budding mineral industry of California. More recent writers have emphasized that during the initial stampede "the glory was in the going"; hence, the routes have been well described. Literally hundreds of published gold rush diaries indicate, if nothing else, that the Forty-niners were literate men with aspirations and that those who came in their wake had only to follow trails plainly marked with pencil stubs.[10]

Phyllis F. Dorset's detailed description of Colorado gold and silver rushes to 1910 is solid but lacks some of the technical grasp of Caughey and Paul and is not set as well into the national setting. Building upon Lord, Shinn, and the more popular George Lyman, Grant Smith in 1943 published the indispensible and still standard history of the Comstock lode. Watson Parker has written a perceptive account of the 1874–79 Black Hills gold excitement; Merle Wells has provided brief but reliable analyses of early mining in Idaho; and Alaska and the Yukon, despite their remoteness, are blessed with at least five solid studies.[11]

From the beginning the mining West was an urban frontier, with population centers playing important roles, a fact of which modern historians have not been unaware. In his broad investigation *Rocky Mountain Mining Camps,* Duane A. Smith points the way for more detailed study of the component parts of the urban story—law enforcement, fire protection, sanitation, recreation facilities, municipal government, church organizations, business enterprise, and all the many aspects of town living that Lewis Atherton has depicted for a more midwestern area. Amid many accounts of mining camps, often of the hell-for-breakfast variety, several stand out. W. Turrentine Jackson's *Treasure Hill* is a model social, political, and economic case study of White Pine, Nevada, and at the same time a splendid example of how local history can be given much broader meaning. Other excellent monographs include Duane A. Smith's description of the birth, maturation, and gradual demise of a small Colorado silver community, Caribou; the Griswolds' lively portrayal of early Leadville; Marshall Sprague's sprightly volume on Cripple Creek; Larry Barsness's on Alder Gulch and Virginia City, Montana; Watson Parker's fine study of Deadwood; and Paul Fatout's low-keyed account of little-known Meadow Lake, California. There is much on mining in James B. Allen's straightforward survey of company towns in the West and surprisingly little in Gunther Barth's analysis of "instant cities," Denver and San Francisco. Several other writers have had more success in relating mining areas and rail links with them to the growth of Spokane.[12]

Still others have studied specific facets of town life. Using quantitative methodology, Ralph Mann has discussed both the social and the political structure in the California mine centers of Grass Valley and Nevada City. Others have taken a close look at elements as diverse as architecture or the mining camp theater, while Elliott West has broken with tradition by seriously studying the saloon, not only in terms of social and economic roles but also to assess the background and characteristics of its proprietors. In the same debunking vein, sociologist Marion Goldman perceptively evaluated the grim real world of prostitution on the Comstock.[13] No doubt historians will soon "discover" others of the mining town's "little people with dirty faces"— teachers, ministers, restaurateurs, liverymen, barbers, and all the rest.

Michael P. Malone has completed a study of Butte mining and politics, a fitting subject, given the role of that copper city in Montana's political life. Anaconda's domination of the state—the wearing of the "old copper collar"— is the usual example cited of the direct impact of a mining corporation upon government, but surely other studies might be done on the influence of major copper firms in Arizona, the Bunker Hill and Sullivan in Idaho, the Guggenheim interests in Alaska, or the combined efforts of mine owners' associations in any of half a dozen western states. And even with several studies of free silver politics, the actual political role of the mineral interests in the 1890s has not always been clear.[14]

Pertinent, too, would be some consideration of attitudes of the mining community toward the role of state or federal governments. What of the legislative battles, conducted in most western capitals, on the question of taxation of mineral resources? What of the relations of the industry with federal agencies like the U.S. Geological Survey or the Bureau of Mines? What of mine inspection and safety legislation, at both the state and national level? No western study exists that is comparable to William Graebner's history of coal mining safety legislation of the Progressive Era. Historians have left largely untouched the question of western mining during two world wars, ignoring manpower problems, price controls, production of strategic metals, and discontinuance of gold operations as unessential in 1942. Or what of the industry during the New Deal or the special federal concerns with uranium after 1945? Apart from Robert Kelley on the California debris controversy, little attention has yet been paid to the environmental impact of wresting ores from the earth, although Duane Smith is at work on the subject—one which has assumed even more relevancy with the advent of large-scale strip mining in Wyoming and Montana.[15]

Mining is, of course, an economic endeavor, and its investment and corporate side provides challenging opportunities for the historian. At any given time, companies which incorporated to exploit western ore pockets (or perhaps eastern pants pockets) numbered in the thousands. An 1865 guidebook listed 2,080 mining and milling concerns registered in San Francisco; in a single twelve-month period of the Cripple Creek excitement of the 1890s, 632 new mining firms were recorded in Colorado. Yet few companies in any period enjoyed an active, productive life over any appreciable length of time. Of the approximately four thousand mining companies described in the 1956 edition of *The Mines Register* as operative in the Western Hemisphere, only twenty-two of those in the trans-Mississippi West had been in existence prior to 1900, only five before 1890.

Fortunately for scholars, the records, accounts, and correspondence of countless of these defunct companies are readily available in repositories around the country, although the major producing companies have not often opened their archives for historical use. The western mineral industry in general has been slow to learn what oil and railroad companies learned some time ago—namely, that historical damnation often varies inversely with access to corporate files. Histories of mining corporations are not plentiful; good ones are even harder to find. Some studies of specific mines tell us much about the companies that operated them; examples are the Horn Silver mine and the Bingham Copper mine, both in Utah. There are occasional studies of small business enterprises or of individual British concerns, and there is a detailed treatment of the precursors of the Colorado Fuel and Iron Company, with another volume on the way. There is an excellent history of the rich Hercules in the Coeur d'Alenes, and another of the Chisos Mining Company, a quicksilver producer in the Big Bend country of Texas with much light cast on Howard Perry, its dominant but hardly admirable central figure.[16]

Corporate historians sometimes leave much to be desired. Robert Glass Cleland's history of Phelps Dodge and Robert Ramsey's story of the fifty years of the Newmont Mining Corporation are lightly documented and uncritical. Isaac Marcosson's histories of Anaconda and of American Smelting and Refining Company may be flattering to the corporations involved but not to any scholarly pretensions of the author. The great Homestake Mining Company, in operation since 1877, is without a real written history, except for a few official pamphlets and one monograph on its labor policies. Anaconda, Homestake, ASARCO, Bunker Hill and Sullivan, and other major enterprises cry out for scholarly business histories; anyone undertaking such a project has before him the paragon of David Lavender's graceful and objective treatment of Cyprus Mines Corporation, an American-run enterprise in the far-off Mediterranean.[17]

Only gradually are we learning more about capital formation, investment, and speculation in western mines. K. Ross Toole has touched briefly and thoughtfully upon the migration of capital to Butte and of the relation of Anaconda to world copper economics, the latter in itself a topic worthy of a major study. Clark C. Spence and W. Turrentine Jackson have both written of the flow of British capital, an important element in placing western mining in its international context; Joseph E. King has described the financing of Colorado mining to 1902, challenging the idea that eastern investors did little more than exploit the resources of the Rockies. Apart from these volumes and a few case studies of individuals, the historical information on promotion, corporate organization, or mine share dealings mounts slowly, although a recent broad study of mining stock exchanges helps put such matters into perspective.[18]

Still lacking is any history of representative promoters in the manner of David Pletcher's *Rails, Mines, and Progress* for the Mexico of Porfirio Díaz, but the literature of the West includes a growing number of revealing studies of individual promoters. These range from Thomas Lamoreaux, the typical and somewhat marginal operator described by Lewis Atherton, to John Fahey's more successful Charles Sweeney, who pyramided companies, one upon another, to control one of the major Coeur d'Alene producers, and on to the flamboyant "Colonel" William Cornell Greene, who built and lost an industrial empire at Cananea in northern Sonora amidst fiscal, legal, and political manipulation that spread from Washington, D.C., to the Mexican border and beyond.[19]

Other promoters merit investigation. Newsworthy ones like William J. Sutherland, George D. Roberts, and Asbury Harpending led exciting lives; that of Anglo-American promoter Whitaker Wright was colorful enough to have been dramatized by a major radio network in the 1960s. And it would be revealing to know more about lesser figures like the Reverend Calvin A. Poage, a Californian who provided the motivating force behind the formation of several Arizona mining ventures in the 1870s, the capital coming from other clergymen and their flocks. "A Saintly Syndicate," commented the editor of the San Francisco *Chronicle* (November 19, 1877): "Presbyterian Preachers in a Prodigious Pool. . . . They stir UP the Arizona Wild cat with the Gospel Rake, and He Scampereth Like Sampson's Foxes."

Historians are paying more attention to other players besides promoters on the mineral scene, although none has yet studied in depth and in a scholarly way the ubiquitous prospector and his role over a century or so. For the mining nabobs, however, Richard Peterson has done in his *Bonanza Kings* what Atherton did for the cattlemen—a prosopographical analysis of fifty owner-entrepreneurs of the late nineteenth century—in which he demonstrates their kinship with eastern counterparts, albeit with more economic and social mobility. In a separate article Allan Weinstein debunks the idea that large bonanza mine owners supported remonetization of silver in the seventies.[20] Good beginnings as they are, such studies tell us little about the last eighty years.

Colorful mining figures collect biographers as pay dirt did prospectors, and there are excellent biographies of William Ralston, Horace A. W. Tabor, Winfield Scott Stratton, John Mackay, and William Boyce Thompson. The biography of Adolph Sutro is reasonably objective; that of Augustus Heinze, the Montana manipulator, less so. Completion of Russell Elliot's work on William M. Stewart will provide the first full biography of an important mining man said to have towered over his Nevada contemporaries "like the Colossus of Rhodes," and, it was added, "with as much brass in his composition."[21]

Important families like the Guggenheims have hardly received their due; certainly the Lewisohns and the Douglases have not. George Hearst, as powerful a mine magnate as ever bought a seat in the U.S. Senate, has to date warranted only a beautifully printed but fawning *Life,* penned by the editor of one of his son's newspapers. Hearst teamed with two other Californians, Lloyd Tevis and James Ben Ali Haggin, to control more than a hundred western mines, among them the wealthy Homestake, Anaconda, and Ontario. Lacking are definitive biographies either of them or of other such influential men as John Percival Jones, Marcus Daly, William Andrews Clark, John Greenway, or Samuel Newhouse, to name a few.[22]

No persons in western mining are more interesting than the technical experts who directed the emerging industry. Clark C. Spence has focused in detail on the host of mining engineers who guided the transition from a "by guess and by God" approach to a scientifically oriented business. Not all of this society of specialists were as famous as Herbert Hoover, but many did operate on a global scale and carried technology in their baggage as they traipsed from one end of the world to another. And many of them justify full biographies: John Hays Hammond, millionaire associate of Cecil Rhodes who knew every U.S. president from Grant to Hoover, except one; Daniel Jackling, pioneer in the low-grade copper techniques that revolutionized the industry; Thomas A. Rickard, engineer-editor of three of the most important mining periodicals of the world at one time or another and author of more than two dozen books; or Rossiter W. Raymond, described as "Consulting mining engineer; practicing lawyer, sailor, soldier, writer, orator, editor, theologian, teacher, novelist, chess player."[23]

Much remains to be written about the developing technology of mining and smelting, especially after the brief labor-intensive placer era had passed. Subsequent hydraulic, deep-level, dredge, or low-grade copper approaches would require heavy capital and corporate endeavor. With promoters and engineers as midwives, the change occurred at first by trial and error, later on a more systematic and scientific basis. Historians have yet to study all of this analytically and in depth. They have not, however, ignored early mining methods, including stamp milling, Nevada silver processing, or Philipp Deidesheimer's square-set timbering. Rodman Paul is convincing in placing Colorado in the forefront of nineteenth-century mine advances.[24]

In volumes that sometimes overlap, Otis E. Young, Jr., traces the European antecedents of western mining and milling techniques and is effective in pulling together the specific processes and equipment in use before 1900. By implication, Young points the way to dozens of areas that historians of technology might fruitfully investigate in detail. For example, what of the development of mine surveying, or of techniques and machinery for pumping, draining, ventilating, hoisting, boring, and tunneling? What of the evolution of underground transport systems by endless rope, mule, and locomotive? Or what of advances in power drills or the application of electricity for lighting, signaling, and energy? What of the ubiquitous assayer and the changing nature of his profession over a century and a half? Robert L. Kelley deals with hydraulic mining in California, but his emphasis is on the debris controversy, rather than on the industry or its technology. Some of the company histories, especially Arrington and Hanson's work on Bingham Copper, give an excellent idea of the low-grade copper techniques, but missing is any overall view of their application for the West in general—or for the world. Nor has much been written on the history of gold dredging, a mass-production approach that brought rapid change after the 1890s. Two recent volumes, both by engineers or geologists, have provided insight into dredging in parts of Alaska and the Klondike. And a pilot article by Clark C. Spence anticipates a full-scale monograph on the subject, with western America as but one locale in the expansion of dredge technology to various parts of the globe.[25]

Also of importance to the historian are the innovations in dressing ores and in separating minerals, processes such as basic amalgamation through chlorination, cyanidation, flotation, leaching, or smelting with complex converters and furnaces of many kinds. Time brought vast improvements: ore tonnage handled increased a hundredfold, electric power replaced steam, automatic weighers and samplers combined to increase the percentage of metal recovered. Between 1895 and 1945, for example, Homestake gold recovery went from 75 to 95 percent; Bunker Hill and Sullivan silver rose from 72 to 92 percent. Yet despite its significance, minerals separation and processing has remained a terra incognita to historians until very recently, when James E. Fell's study of the Colorado smelting industry stressed the impact of European processes and eastern capital in the 1859–1910 era.[26] This is a beginning, but comprehensive investigation is needed to pull together the story for Montana, Utah, Arizona, and Colorado, especially with due attention to the running battles over pollution that were so evident at Butte, Anaconda, and the Deer Lodge Valley of Montana.

Another potentially rich field of study, closely allied to the technological, is that of the ancillary industries connected with mining. The manufacture and sale of mining and milling equipment constituted a highly important industry in itself. San Francisco early became the center of machinery production for far-western mining and would subsequently manufacture for the world over. Among its important firms was the Union Iron Works, founded in 1849, which built mining equipment of all kinds, eventually including dredges, not to mention the battleship *Oregon*. A reorganized Union Iron and another major plant, the Risdon Iron Works, would merge in 1911 and eventually become part of Bethlehem Steel, which maintained its mine machinery division well into the mid-twentieth century.

Two other California businesses, the Joshua Hendy Iron Works and Harron, Rickard and McCone, both spanned much of the period from 1875 to 1950. Elsewhere, such companies as Hendrie and Bothoff and Stearns-Rogers (both of Denver), Allis Chalmers of Milwaukee (formerly Fraser and Chalmers), and the Marion Steam Shovel Company of Ohio have been producing mining equipment for over a century. Another, Bucyrus-Erie Company of Milwaukee, is the subject of a good business history, which does justice to its role in the mineral West. A recent study of a much more modest mine and mill machinery producer in Central City, Colorado, throws light on the small-scale entrepreneur, of which there were undoubtedly many.[27] But the important large firms, apart from Bucyrus-Erie, have been neglected. Many of them, with intimate western connections, taken individually or collectively as a mine machine industry, merit serious consideration from business and economic historians.

In the West the old saying "It takes a mine to run a mine" was true in many cases figuratively and in some instances literally. In addition to capital, mines and mills required a variety of supplies for everyday operation. Mercury, for example, was universally used in the simple gold separation processes and has long been regarded as the handmaiden of the gold mining industry. Its production centered in California, where the New Almaden mine held a virtual monopoly from 1845 to 1858, when it closed temporarily because of a legal struggle over ownership. Its closing pushed quicksilver prices upward and provided incentive for the opening of competing mines, the most powerful of which subsequently combined with the New Almaden to regulate output and prices and to control the bulk of the American market against Spain, the only real competitor, until 1873, when the monopoly disintegrated. The history of the New Almaden is covered in a few articles and a slim volume devoted to the snarled legal questions of title in the 1840-63 era.[28] Nor is there any historical study of the larger California quicksilver industry nor of the national and international setting within which it functioned

The supplying of chemicals, blasting powder, timber, even candles and other commodities has also been neglected by scholars. Entire West Coast industries, especially explosives, developed to meet mining needs. One Nevada company in 1877 used nearly two million pounds of ice, costing $22,000, to cool the lower levels of its mine. The annual statement of another firm in the same area five years later shows $14,000 paid out for sulphate of copper, $11,000 for ordinary salt (both used in milling), $11,000 for candles, more than $67,000 for mine timbers, and $74,249 for quicksilver. It has been estimated that over a thirty-year period, the Comstock lode swallowed up eight hundred million feet of lumber—enough to build fifty thousand ranch-type houses, each with two baths and a double garage. Timber was so important that expensive V-flumes were built, some a dozen miles long, to move logs rapidly to the mines. Much of this timber, and that for fuel or charcoal, came illegally from the public domain. When Land Commissioner William A. J. Sparks cracked down in the mid-1880s, no wonder screams of corporate anguish filled the air and western senators rode to the rescue, not without some success, as K. Ross Toole has indicated in one of the few analyses of a fragment of this story, a story that needs telling in its entirety.[29]

Another relatively unexplored auxiliary industry has been litigation. No industry in any country was ever subject to as much or as complicated legal activity as mining in western America. In five years the twelve leading mines of the Comstock were embroiled in a total of 245 lawsuits, absorbing directly about $10 million—roughly one-fifth of the lode's entire output for that period. Expert witness fees alone ran more than $100,000 in one case settled in the Helena district court in 1893. But apart from Shinn's early study and a scattered handful of articles concerned with local miners' laws, with the impact of Nevada on federal mine legislation, and with questions of mineral taxation, few historical studies have centered on mining law or mining lawyers. Admittedly these are intricate and highly technical fields, but materials abound, both manuscripts and documented treatises by legal experts. Historians cannot wait for attorneys to write legal history any more than they can expect farmers to produce agricultural history.[30]

One area that has received considerable attention in recent years is mine labor, in part perhaps because of the violence and drama of the early union movement, and in part because of a growing interest in workers' history, i.e., the everyday life and labor of the average person. Studies of the Industrial Workers of the World and its leadership stress the turbulence and radicalism of the "Wobblies" and their antecedents in the western mines. Vernon Jensen's broad history of the nonferrous industries gives fair and thorough coverage to the struggle for unionization. But like Robert Wayne Smith on the Coeur d'Alene troubles of 1892 and George Suggs on the destruction of the Western Federation in Colorado, Jensen emphasizes the "labor war" aspect of the contest and the hostile actions of state and corporate officers.[31]

The standard works on the bloody upheavals in the Colorado coal fields in 1913-14 ("the most ferocious conflict in the history of American labor and industry," former senator George McGovern calls it) are in the same vein, and a recent cryptic study of Montana, 1917-21, clearly demonstrates how the response of Anaconda combined with war hysteria and antiradicalism to stifle the labor movement in that state. Others have viewed the Bisbee deportation of 1917, though reprehensible and inconsistent with basic democratic tenets, predictable given citizens' norms and attitudes of that time.[32]

On the other hand, a number of labor studies since World War II have been more optimistic and have broken with the tradition that violence was a western phenomenon. For example, Joseph H. Cash stresses the Homestake's paternalism toward its employees, a policy that kept out unions but maintained high productivity and profits with general labor peace from 1877 to 1942. Others have pointed to the role of federal mediation in bringing an amicable settlement of the 1917 Western Federation strike at Clifton-Morenci. In an important volume of 1974, *The Hardrock Miners,* Richard E. Lingenfelter sees militant unions as a necessary response to industrial mining prior to 1893. He argues that previous writers placed too much emphasis on labor violence, which imitated eastern patterns, and that they ignored the fact that most labor-management relations were peaceful and conducted with understanding.[33]

In 1979 both Mark Wyman and Ronald C. Brown described miners' adjustments to the changes of the industrial revolution, especially the new technologies. Wyman especially looks at unionization, self-help movements, political action, and a brief labor flirtation with radical syndicalism. Brown, too, sees the western miner as a part of the changing national economy and analyzes his reaction to industrialization, capitalism, urbanization, and the frontier environment to give a revealing composite portrait of a wage miner or mill hand and his life and work.[34]

As in the case of technology and capital flow, mine labor had its international dimensions, along with an ethnic mix. Historians have described the early Mexicans and South Americans who brought traditional methods and equipment to early California, but they have done little with the extensive Spanish-speaking population that provided a vast mining labor pool for the late nineteenth and twentieth centuries. A well-documented article reveals the employment of Native Americans to a surprising extent in the early California mines, and Rudolph Lapp has written an objective study, rich in detail and perspective, of blacks in the California rush. But not much has been made available on these groups for the later period.[35] Seldom significant as wage miners but always in evidence as independent placer miners and as targets for racist agitation, the Chinese have received attention at the local level and in more general histories; yet still missing is a specific study of the Chinese and western mining. The Cornish, the ever-present "Cousin Jacks," have been described in three books, the best by John Rowe, who devotes two-thirds of his space to the West. Less and more scattered consideration has been given to other groups—Irish, Italians, Greeks, and East Europeans—so far as their role in mining over a sustained period is concerned.[36] One can envision, for example, a fascinating and illuminating monograph on the ethnic and national mélange that made up the labor force of the city of Butte for half a century or more.

It is clear that historians have traditionally favored the "glamor" metals, silver and gold. No one has attempted a serious history of western copper mining or smelting, despite the tremendous importance of these industries. Although the history of lead and zinc production farther east has been studied, little has been done with these minerals in the West. The same has been true of coal, iron, aluminum, and molybedenum, not to mention semi-precious stones like turquoise, or precious gems, except for the infamous diamond swindle of 1872.[37] Generally ignored are the "Cinderella minerals," including building stone, gypsum, clay, salt, potash, phosphate, cement rock, and sand and gravel. Uranium has still not found its historian. But it has its occasional articles and one competent volume on the Colorado Plateau, which argues that most of the finds of the post–World War II period were actually rediscoveries—old claims or new claims in old areas going back to the earlier radium and vanadium eras.[38]

It is encouraging that historians of the mining West have moved away from the romance and narrowness of the early frontier years to put more emphasis on the industry, the complexities of economic and technological change, and the reaction of workers and communities to diverse parts of the transition process. Surprisingly little of the "new" social history has so far been applied to western mining, although some excellent social history has been a part of the steadily growing bibliography on the subject. Recent trends have viewed western mining as an integral part of national development or as a component of the larger international scene, with personnel, capital, and technology drawn from many quarters. This suggests a need for both continuity and comparative studies. Jerome Steffen has recently called for a closer look at pre-California mining frontiers to determine their impact on those of the Far West. Such historians as W. Turrentine Jackson have been interested in the comparative frontiers of the American West and of Australia; and Jay Monaghan has tied the 1849–53 gold rushes of the two continents together in a book that is more narrative than analytically comparative. Back in 1940, Englishman William Parker Morrell published an admirable book on world gold rushes, among them the important ones of the trans-Mississippi West.[39]

With the many new monographs on mining everywhere since that time, surely the way is open for other imaginative comparisons across national lines: comparative studies of mining camps, specific mines, corporate organizations and management, advancing technology, or environmental impact, for example. At whatever level, historians will find the mineral West challenging and fascinating. Deceptively complex, it blends the rawness and newness of a rich and rugged terrain with sophisticated mechanization, capital formation, and labor policies of an increasingly industrial America. It is at once isolated, yet urban and cosmopolitan; typical, yet somehow distinctive from the mainstream of national development.

Notes

1. A few of the ghost town books have real merit. One example exceptional for its superb historical photographs is Stanley W. Paher, *Nevada Ghost Towns and Mining Camps* (Berkeley: Howell-North, 1970). For three excellent volumes, illustrated by artists' sketches, see Muriel Sibell Wolle, *Stampede to Timberline: The Ghost Towns and Mining Camps of Colorado* (Boulder: the author, 1949); *The Bonanza Trail: Ghost Towns and Mining Camps of the West* (Bloomington: Indiana University Press, 1953);*Montana Pay Dirt: A Guide to the Mining Camps of the Treasure State* (Denver: Sage Books, 1963). Of the more than eleven hundred authors who have written on lost mines and buried treasures of the West, probably the most respectable is Harry Sinclair Drago, *Lost Bonanzas: Tales of the Legendary Lost Mines of the American West* (New York: Dodd, Mead and Co., 1966); Thomas Probert, *Lost Mines and Buried Treasures of the West: Bibliography and Place Names— From Kansas to California, Oregon, Washington, and Mexico* (Berkeley: University of California Press, 1977).

2. Geoffrey Blainey, *The Rush That Never Ended*, 2d ed. (Carlton, Victoria: Melbourne University Press, 1969); Walter R. Crane, *Silver and Gold: Comprising an Economic History of Mining in the United States, the Geographical and Geological Occurrence of the Precious Metals, with Their Mineralogical Associations, History and Description of Methods of Mining and Extraction of Values, and a Detailed Discussion of the Production of Gold and Silver in the World and in the United States* (New York: John Wiley and Sons, 1908). There is no general published bibliography of the history of western mining that is up-to-date and all-embracing, combining

both primary and secondary sources. An extensive winnowing of primary materials is possible from the bibliographies of a number of books. See especially: William S. Greever, *The Bonanza West: The Story of the Mining Rushes, 1848–1900* (Norman: University of Oklahoma Press, 1963); Rodman W. Paul, *Mining Frontiers of the Far West, 1848–1880* (New York: Holt, Rinehart and Winston, 1963; paperbound ed., Albuquerque: University of New Mexico Press, 1974); Clark C. Spence, *Mining Engineers and the American West: The Lace-Boot Brigade, 1849–1933* (New Haven: Yale University Press, 1970); Richard H. Peterson, *The Bonanza Kings: The Social Origins and Business Behavior of Western Mining Entrepreneurs, 1870–1900* (Lincoln: University of Nebraska Press, 1977); Otis E. Young, Jr., with the technical assistance of Robert Lenon, *Western Mining: An Informal Account of Precious-Metals Prospecting, Placering, Lode Mining, and Milling on the American Frontier from Spanish Times to 1893* (Norman: University of Oklahoma Press, 1970); Ronald C. Brown, *Hard-Rock Miners: The Intermountain West, 1860–1920* (College Station: Texas A & M University Press, 1979).

3. Thomas A. Rickard, *A History of American Mining* (New York: McGraw-Hill, 1932).

4. Examples, none of them enduring, might include Glenn Chesney Quiett, *Pay Dirt: A Panorama of American Gold Rushes* (New York: D. Appleton-Century, 1936); Carl B. Glasscock, *The Big Bonanza: The Story of the Comstock Lode* (Indianapolis: Bobbs-Merrill, 1931); George F. Willison, *Here They Dug the Gold* (New York: Brentano, 1931); William T. Stoll, *Silver Strike* (Boston: Little, Brown, 1932). See William S. Greever, *The Bonanza West.*

5. Paul, *Mining Frontiers of the Far West*; T. A. Watkins, *Gold and Silver in the West: The Illustrated History of an American Dream* (Palo Alto: American West Publishing Co., 1971).

6. Marvin D. Bernstein, *The Mexican Mining Industry, 1890–1950: A Case in the Interaction of Politics, Economics, and Technology* (Albany: State University of New York Press, 1964); Russell R. Elliott, *Nevada's Twentieth-Century Mining Boom: Tonopah, Goldfield, Ely* (Reno: University of Nevada Press, 1966); Duane A. Smith, *Colorado Mining: A Photographic History* (Albuquerque: University of New Mexico Press, 1977).

7. Eliot Lord, *Comstock Mining and Miners*, U.S. Geological Survey Monograph IV (Washington, D.C.: Government Printing Office, 1883); Dan De Quille (William Wright), *A History of the Comstock Silver Lode and*

Mines, Nevada and the Great Basin Region; Lake Tahoe and the High Sierras (Virginia City: F. Boegle, c. 1889).

8. Charles Howard Shinn, *Mining Camps: A Study in American Frontier Government* (New York: C. Scribner's Sons, 1885; paperbound ed., Harper Torchbooks, 1965); *The Story of the Mine, as Illustrated by the Great Comstock Lode of Nevada* (New York: D. Appleton and Co., 1896; paperbound ed., Reno: University of Nevada Press, 1980).

9. William J. Trimble, *The Mining Advance into the Inland Empire*, University of Wisconsin History Series Bulletin No. 638 (Madison, 1914).

10. John Walton Caughey, *Gold Is the Cornerstone* (Berkeley and Los Angeles: University of California Press, 1948); Rodman W. Paul, *California Gold: The Beginning of Mining in the Far West* (Cambridge: Harvard University Press, 1947; paperbound ed., Lincoln: University of Nebraska Press, 1975). For the sea routes, see Oscar Lewis, *Sea Routes to the Gold Fields: The Migration by Water to California in 1849-1852* (New York: Knopf, 1949); Octavius Thorndike Howe, *Argonauts of '49: History and Adventures of the Emigrant Companies from Massachusetts, 1849-1850* (Cambridge: Harvard University Press, 1923). Two of the best descriptions of overland travel to California are introductions to published diaries: David M. Potter (ed.), *Trail to California: The Overland Journal of Vincent Geiger and Wakeman Byarly* (New Haven: Yale University Press, 1945); Dale L. Morgan (ed.), *The Overland Diary of James A. Pritchard from Kentucky to California in 1849* (Denver: Old West Publishing Co., 1959). A recent comprehensive study of overland travel, 1840-60, includes gold rush Californians and renders obsolete other general treatments of the subject. See John D. Unruh, Jr., *The Plains Across: The Overland Emigrants and the Trans-Mississippi West, 1840-1860* (Urbana: University of Illinois Press, 1979).

11. Phyllis Flanders Dorset, *The New Eldorado: The Story of Colorado's Gold and Silver Rushes* (New York: Macmillan, 1970); Grant H. Smith, *The History of the Comstock Lode, 1850-1920*, University of Nevada Bulletin Vol. 37, No. 3, Geology and Mining Series 37 (Reno, 1943); George D. Lyman, *The Saga of the Comstock Lode* (New York: C. Scribner's Sons, 1937; paperbound ed., Sausalito, Calif.: Comstock Editions, 1976); Watson Parker, *Gold in the Black Hills* (Norman: University of Oklahoma Press, 1966; paperbound ed., Lincoln: University of Nebraska Press, 1982); Merle W. Wells, *Gold Camps and Silver Cities*, Idaho Bureau of Mines and Geology Bulletin 22 (Moscow, 1963); Merle W. Wells, *Rush to Idaho*, Idaho Bureau of Mines and Geology Bulletin 19 (Moscow, n.d.); Pierre Burton, *The Klondike Fever: The Life and Death of the Last Great Gold Rush* (New York: Knopf, 1958); R. N. De Armond, *The Founding of Juneau* (Juneau: Gastineau Chan-

nel Centennial Association, 1967); David Wharton, *The Alaska Gold Rush* (Bloomington: Indiana University Press, 1972); William R. Hunt, *North of 53°: The Wild Days of the Alaska-Yukon Mining Frontier, 1870-1914* (New York: Macmillan, 1974); William Bronson (with Richard Reinhardt), *The Last Great Adventure: The Story of the Klondike Gold Rush and the Opening of Alaska* (New York: McGraw-Hill, 1977). For a splendid collection of historic photographs of life on the Chilkoot Trail, see Robert L. Spude (comp.), *Chilkoot Trail* (Fairbanks: University of Alaska, 1980).

12. Duane A. Smith, *Rocky Mountain Mining Camps: The Urban Frontier* (Bloomington: Indiana University Press, 1967; paperbound ed. Lincoln: University of Nebraska Press, 1974); W. Turrentine Jackson, *Treasure Hill: Portrait of a Silver Mining Camp* (Tucson: University of Arizona Press, 1963); Duane A. Smith, *Silver Saga: The Story of Caribou, Colorado* (Boulder: Pruett Publishing Co., 1974); Don L. and Jean Harvey Griswold, *The Carbonate Camp Called Leadville* (Denver: University of Denver Press, 1951); Marshall Sprague, *Money Mountain: The Story of Cripple Creek Gold* (Boston: Little, Brown, 1953; paperbound ed. Lincoln: University of Nebraska Press, 1979); Larry Barsness, *Gold Camp: Alder Gulch and Virginia City* (New York: Hastings House, 1962); Watson Parker, *Deadwood: The Golden Years* (Lincoln: University of Nebraska Press, 1981); Paul Fatout, *Meadow Lake: Gold Town* (Bloomington: Indiana University Press, 1969; paperbound ed., Lincoln: University of Nebraska Press, 1974); James B. Allen, *The Company Town in the American West* (Norman: University of Oklahoma Press, 1966); Gunther Barth, *Instant Cities: Urbanization and the Rise of San Francisco and Denver* (New York: Oxford University Press, 1975); John Fahey, *Inland Empire: D. C. Corbin and Spokane* (Seattle: University of Washington Press, 1965); W. Hudson Kensel, "Inland Empire Mining and the Growth of Spokane, 1883-1905," *Pacific Northwest Quarterly* 50 (April 1969): 84-97.

13. Ralph Mann, "The Decade After the Gold Rush: Social Structure in Grass Valley and Nevada City, California, 1850-1860," *Pacific Historical Review* 41 (November 1972): 484-504; Mann, "National Party Fortunes and Local Political Structure: The Case of Two California Mining Towns, 1850-1870," *Southern California Quarterly* 57 (Fall 1975): 271-96; C. Eric Stoehr, *Bonanza Victorian: Architecture and Society in Colorado Mining Towns* (Albuquerque: University of New Mexico Press, 1975); Harold Kirker, "Eldorado Gothic: Gold Rush Architects and Architecture," *California Historical Society Quarterly* 38 (March 1959): 31-46; Clair E. Willson, *Mines and Miners: A Historical Study of the Theater in Tombstone*, University of Arizona Bulletin Vol. 6, No. 7 (Tucson, 1935); Melvin Schoberlin, *From Candles to Footlights: A Biography of the Pike's Peak Theatre, 1859-1876* (Denver:

Old West Publishing Co., 1941); Margaret G. Watson, *Silver Theatre: Amusements of the Mining Frontier in Early Nevada, 1850 to 1864* (Glendale: Arthur H. Clark Co., 1964); Elliott West, *The Saloon on the Rocky Mountain Mining Frontier* (Lincoln: University of Nebraska Press, 1979); Marion S. Goldman, *Gold Diggers and Silver Miners: Prostitution and Social Life on the Comstock Lode* (Ann Arbor: University of Michigan Press, 1982).

14. Michael P. Malone, *The Battle for Butte: Mining and Politics on the Northern Frontier, 1864-1906* (Seattle: University of Washington Press, 1981). The standard, published accounts of Anaconda Copper's role in Montana politics are dated: C. P. Connolly, *The Devil Learns to Vote* (New York: Covici Friede, 1938), and Carl B. Glasscock, *The War of the Copper Kings* (New York: Bobbs-Merrill, 1935). Studies of western free-silver politics include Thomas A. Clinch, *Urban Populism and Free Silver in Montana* (Missoula: University of Montana Press, 1970), and Mary Ellen Glass, *Silver and Politics in Nevada, 1892-1902* (Reno: University of Nevada Press, 1969).

15. John Welling Smurr, "The Montana Tax 'Conspiracy' of 1889," *Montana: The Magazine of Western History* 5 (Spring 1955): 46-53; (Summer 1955): 47-56; Gordon Bakken, "The Taxation of Mineral Wealth and the Nevada Constitutional Convention of 1864," *Nevada Historical Society Quarterly* 12 (Winter 1969): 5-15; William Graebner, *Coal-Mining Safety in the Progressive Period* (Lexington: University Press of Kentucky, 1976); Herbert H. Lang, "Uranium Mining and the AEC: The Birth Pangs of a New Industry," *Business History Review* 36 (Autumn 1962): 325-33; Robert L. Kelley, *Gold vs. Grain: The Hydraulic Mining Controversy in California's Sacramento Valley* (Glendale: Arthur H. Clark Co., 1959).

16. Leonard J. Arrington and Wayne K. Hinton, "The Horn Silver Bonanza," in Gene M. Gressley (ed.), *The American West: A Reorientation* (Laramie: University of Wyoming Publications, 1966), pp. 35-54; Leonard J. Arrington and Gary B. Hansen, *"The Richest Hole on Earth": A History of the Bingham Copper Mine* (Logan: Utah State University Press, 1963); Roy N. Lokken, "Stock Companies at the Placer Mines: The Alaska Gold Mining Company," *Pacific Northwest Quarterly* 49 (July 1958): 89-98; W. Turrentine Jackson, "The Irish Fox and the British Lion," *Montana: The Magazine of Western History* 9 (April 1959): 28-42; Clark C. Spence, "The Montana Company, Limited," *Business History Review* 33 (Summer 1959): 190-203; H. Lee Scamehorn, *Pioneer Steelmaker in the West: The Colorado Fuel and Iron Company, 1892-1903* (Boulder: Pruett Publishing Co., 1976); John Fahey, *The Days of Hercules* (Moscow: University of Idaho Press, 1978);

Kenneth Baxter Ragsdale, *Quicksilver: Terlingua and the Chisos Mining Company* (College Station: Texas A & M University Press, 1976).

17. Robert Glass Cleland, *A History of Phelps Dodge, 1834-1950* (New York: Alfred A. Knopf, 1952); Issac F. Marcosson, *Metal Magic: The Story of the American Smelting and Refining Company* (New York: Farrar, Straus and Co., 1949); Joseph H. Cash, *Working the Homestake* (Ames: Iowa State University Press, 1973); Issac Marcosson, *Anaconda* (New York: Dodd, Mead and Co., 1957); Robert H. Ramsey, *Men and Mines of Newmont: A Fifty Year History* (New York: Farrar, Straus and Giroux, 1973). Other candidates for business histories include Kennecott, Duval Corporation, AMEX (American Metal Climax), Alaska Juneau Mining Company, Golden Cycle Corporation, Mountain Copper Company, and Hecla Mining Company. See David Lavender, *The Story of Cyprus Mines Corporation* (San Marino: Huntington Library, 1962).

18. K. Ross Toole, "When Big Money Came to Butte: The Migration of Eastern Capital to Montana," *Pacific Northwest Quarterly* 44 (January 1953): 23-29; Toole, "The Anaconda Copper Mining Company: A Price War and a Copper Corner," *Pacific Northwest Quarterly* 41 (October 1950): 312-29; Clark C. Spence, *British Investments and the American Mining Frontier, 1860-1901* (Ithaca: Cornell University Press, 1958); W. Turrentine Jackson, *The Enterprising Scot: Investors in the American West after 1873* (Edinburgh: Edinburgh University Press, 1968); Joseph E. King, *A Mine to Make a Mine: Financing the Colorado Mining Industry, 1859-1902* (College Station: Texas A & M University Press, 1977); Marian V. Sears, *Mining Stock Exchanges, 1860-1930: An Historical Survey* (Missoula: University of Montana Press, 1973).

19. For examples of good beginnings, see Glen W. Barrett, "When Big Money Came to Owyhee," *Idaho Yesterdays* 13 (Spring 1969): 2-9, 22-29; Duane A. Smith, "The Promoter, the Investor, and the Mining Engineer: A Case Study," *Huntington Library Quarterly* 39 (August 1976): 385-401; James E. Fell, Jr., "Rockefeller's Right-hand Man: Frederick T. Gates and the Northwestern Mining Investments," *Business History Review* 52 (Winter 1978): 537-61; David M. Pletcher, *Rails, Mines, and Progress: Seven American Promoters in Mexico, 1867-1911* (Ithaca: Cornell University Press, 1958); Lewis Atherton, "The Mining Promoter in the Trans-Mississippi West," *Western Historical Quarterly* 1 (January 1970): 35-50; Atherton, "Structure and Balance in Western Mining History," *Huntington Library Quarterly* 30 (November 1966): 55-84; John Fahey, *The Ballyhoo Bonanza: Charles Sweeney and the Idaho Mines* (Seattle: University of Washington Press,

1971); C. L. Sonnichsen, *Colonel Greene and the Copper Skyrocket* (Tucson: University of Arizona Press, 1974).

20. Peterson, *The Bonanza Kings*; Allen Weinstein, "The Bonanza King Myth: Western Mine Owners and the Remonetization of Silver," *Business History Review* 42 (Summer 1968): 195-218.

21. The most recent of four biographies of Ralston is the best: David Lavender, *Nothing Seemed Impossible: William C. Ralston and Early San Francisco* (Palo Alto: American West Publishing Co., 1975). Likewise, the latest study of Tabor supplants at least two earlier ones. See Duane A. Smith, *Horace Tabor: His Life and the Legend* (Boulder: Colorado Associated University Press, 1973). For Stratton, Mackay, and Thompson, see Frank Waters, *Midas of the Rockies: The Story of Stratton and Cripple Creek* (New York: Covici Friede, 1937); Ethel Manter, *Rocket of the Comstock: The Story of John William Mackay* (Caldwell: Caxton Printers, 1950); Oscar Lewis, *Silver Kings: The Lives and Times of Mackay, Fair, Flood and O'Brien, Lords of the Nevada Comstock Lode* (New York: Knopf, 1947); Hermann Hagedorn, *The Magnate: William Boyce Thompson and His Time* (New York: Reynal and Hitchcock, 1935); Robert E. and Mary F. Stewart, *Adolph Sutro: A Biography* (Berkeley: Howell-North, 1962); Sarah McNelis, *Copper King at War: The Biography of F. Augustus Heinze* (Missoula: University of Montana Press, 1968). For a less than comprehensive treatment of William Stewart, see Effie Mona Mack, "William Morris Stewart, 1827-1909," *Nevada Historical Society Quarterly* 7 (1964): 9-110.

22. General works on the Guggenheims include Harvey O'Connor, *The Guggenheims: The Making of an American Dynasty* (New York: Covici Friede, 1937); Edwin P. Hoyt, Jr., *The Guggenheims and the American Dream* (New York: Funk and Wagnalls, 1967), neither of which precludes a systematic study of the family and their mining interests. Completely inadequate is Fremont and Cora Older, *The Life of George Hearst, California Pioneer* (San Francisco: for William Randolph Hearst, by William Wilke, 1933). H. Minar Shoebotham, *Anaconda, Life of Marcus Daly, the Copper King* (Harrisburg: Stackpole Co., 1956) is adulatory. William R. Mangam's two muckrake works on William A. Clark are bitingly critical: *The Clarks of Montana* (Washington, D.C.: Service Printing, 1939), and *The Clarks, an American Phenomenon* (New York: Silver Bow Press, 1941). On the other hand, James High's sketch of Clark is too sympathetic: "William Andrews

Clark, Westerner: An Interpretive Vignette," *Arizona and the West* 2 (Autumn 1960): 245-64.

23. Spence, *Mining Engineers and the American West.* There is an excellent biography of geologist Clarence King; mediocre ones of engineers Charles W. Merrill and Louis D. Ricketts: Thurman Wilkins, *Clarence King* (New York: Macmillan, 1958); David W. Ryder, *The Merrill Story* (n.p.: Merrill Co., 1958); Walter R. Bimson, *Louis D. Ricketts (1859-1940)* (New York: Newcomen Society, 1949). Other important engineers or geologists who are fitting subjects for serious biography include Raphael Pumpelly, Pope Yeatman, Joshua E. Clayton, Hennen Jennings, Arthur D. Foote, James D. Hague, Philip Argall, the Janin brothers (Alexis, Henry, and Louis), and the Hoffmanns (Charles F. and his four sons, George, John, Karl, and Ross).

24. Otis E. Young, Jr., "Philipp Deidesheimer, 1832-1916, Engineer of the Comstock," *Southern California Quarterly* 57 (Winter 1975): 361-69; Rodman W. Paul, "Colorado as a Pioneer of Science in the Mining West," *Mississippi Valley Historical Review* 47 (June 1960): 34-50; Robert L. Romig, "Stamp Mills in Trouble," *Pacific Northwest Quarterly* 44 (October 1954): 166-76; Ernest Oberbillig, "Development of Washoe and Reese River Silver Processes," *Nevada Historical Society Quarterly* 10 (Summer 1967): 3-43.

25. Otis E. Young, Jr., *Western Mining,* and *Black Powder and Hand Steel: Miners and Machines on the Old Western Frontier* (Norman: University of Oklahoma Press, 1975); Lewis Green, *The Gold Hustlers* (Anchorage: Northwest Publishing Co., 1977), is a history of both dredge technology and corporate machination. John C. Boswell, *History of Alaskan Operations of the United States Smelting, Refining and Mining Company* (Fairbanks: University of Alaska, 1979), is sketchier but includes much technical information. See also Clark C. Spence, "The Golden Age of Dredging: The Development of an Industry and Its Environmental Impact," *Western Historical Quarterly* 11 (October 1980): 401-14.

26. James E. Fell, Jr., *Ores to Metals: The Rocky Mountain Smelting Industry* (Lincoln: University of Nebraska Press, 1979). The volume is not as broad as its title.

27. Harold F. Williamson and Kenneth H. Myers, *Designed for Digging: The First 75 Years of Bucyrus-Erie Company* (Evanston: Northwestern University Press, 1955); H. William Axford, *Gilpin County Gold: Peter McFarlane, 1848-1929, Mining Entrepreneur in Central City, Colorado* (Chicago:

Swallow Press, 1976). See also Albert E. Seep, "History of the Mine and Smelter Supply Company," *Colorado Magazine* 23 (May 1946): 128-34; Ellsworth C. Mitick, "A History of Mining Machinery Manufacture in Colorado," *Colorado Magazine* 24 (November 1947): 225-41, and (March and May 1948): 75-94, 136-42.

28. Kenneth M. Johnson, *The New Almaden Quicksilver Mine* (Georgetown, Calif.: Talisman Press, 1963); Henry Winfred Splitter, "Quicksilver at New Almaden," *Pacific Historical Review* 26 (February 1957): 33-49.

29. Arthur P. Van Gelder and Hugh Schlatter, *History of the Explosives Industry in America* (New York: Columbia University Press, 1927), sketches the opening of Pacific Coast powder factories and discusses briefly the significance of explosives for western mining; K. Ross Toole and Edward Butcher, "Timber Depredations on the Montana Public Domain, 1885-1918," *Journal of the West* 7 (July 1968): 351-62.

30. See Thomas M. Marshall, "The Miners' Laws of Colorado," *American Historical Review* 25 (April 1920): 426-39; Joseph Ellison, "The Mineral Land Question in California, 1848-1866," *Southwestern Historical Quarterly* 20 (July 1926): 34-55; Beulah Hershiser, "The Influence of Nevada on the National Mining Legislation of 1866," Nevada Historical Society, *Third Biennial Report* (1911-12): 126-67. An interesting study of the use of miners' regulations to control local claims is Harwood P. Hinton, "Frontier Speculation: A Study of the Walker Mining Districts," *Pacific Historical Review* 29 (August 1960): 245-55. Also interesting, but dealing not with mining law as such but rather the carryover of eastern property protection precepts on the route to California, is John Phillip Reid, *Law for the Elephant: Property and Social Behavior on the Overland Trail* (San Marino: Huntington Library, 1980). Along with many available manuscript collections, historians would find helpful the very detailed, often multivolume legal interpretations and compilations written for other attorneys by such specialists as Gregory Yale, Robert S. Morrison, Curtis H. Lindley, Charles H. Shamel, and George P. Costigan, Jr.

31. Paul F. Brissenden, *The I.W.W.: A Study of American Syndicalism* (New York: Columbia University Press, 1919); Melvyn Dubofsky, *We Shall Be All: A History of the Industrial Workers of the World* (Chicago: Quadrangle Books, 1969), is sympathetic but the best study of the I.W.W. See also Joseph R. Conlin, *Big Bill Haywood and the Radical Union Movement* (Syracuse: Syracuse University Press, 1969); Vernon H. Jensen, *Heritage of Conflict: Labor Relations in the Nonferrous Metals Industry up to 1930* (Ithaca:

Cornell University Press, 1950). A sequel volume by Jensen addresses itself to Communist infiltration of the leadership of the western-oriented International Union of Mine, Mill and Smelter Workers: *Nonferrous Metals Industry Unionism, 1932-1954: A Story of Leadership Controversy* (Ithaca: Cornell University, 1954). Robert Wayne Smith, *The Coeur d'Alene Mining War of 1892: A Case Study of an Industrial Dispute* (Corvallis: Oregon State University Press, 1961); George G. Suggs, Jr., *Colorado's War on Militant Unionism: James H. Peabody and the Western Federation of Miners* (Detroit: Wayne State University Press, 1972).

    32. George S. McGovern and Leonard F. Guttridge, *The Great Coalfield War* (Boston: Houghton Mifflin, 1972); Barron B. Beshoar, *Out of the Depths: The Story of John R. Lawson, a Labor Leader* (Denver: Colorado Labor Historical Committee of the Denver Trades and Labor Assembly, 1942); Arnon Gutfeld, *Montana's Agony: Years of War and Hysteria, 1917-1921* (Gainesville: University Presses of Florida, 1979); John H. Lindquist and James Fraser, "A Sociological Interpretation of the Bisbee Deportation," *Pacific Historical Review* 37 (November 1968): 401-22.

    33. Cash, *Working the Homestake*; James R. Kluger, *The Clifton-Morenci Strike: Labor Difficulty in Arizona, 1915-1916* (Tucson: University of Arizona Press, 1970); Richard E. Lingenfelter, *The Hardrock Miners: A History of the Mining Labor Movement in the American West, 1863-1893* (Berkeley and Los Angeles: University of California Press, 1974 paperbound ed., 1980).

    34. Mark Wyman, *Hard Rock Epic: Western Miners and the Industrial Revolution, 1860-1910* (Berkeley and Los Angeles: University of California Press, 1979); Brown, *Hard-Rock Miners*.

    35. Otis E. Young, Jr., "The Spanish Tradition in Gold and Silver Mining," *Arizona and the West* 7 (Winter 1965): 299-314; Young, "The Southern Gold Rush: Contributions to California and the West," *Southern California Quarterly* 62 (Summer 1980): 127-41; Richard Henry Morefield, "Mexicans in the California Mines, 1848-1853," *California Historical Society Quarterly* 35 (March 1956): 37-46; Jay Monaghan, *Chile, Peru, and the California Gold Rush of 1849* (Berkeley: University of California Press, 1973). Much of the literature on Spanish-speaking people in early California concerns itself less with their role in mining than with the discrimination against them. See Leonard M. Pitt, *The Decline of the Californios, 1846-1890* (Berkeley: University of California Press, 1966); Richard H. Peterson, *Manifest Destiny in the Mines: A Cultural Interpretation of Anti-Mexican Nativism in California, 1848-1853* (San Francisco: R & E Research Associates, 1975); William

R. Kenny, "Mexican-American Conflict on the Mining Frontier, 1848-1852," *Journal of the West* 6 (October 1967): 582-92; Sister M. Colette Standart, "The Sonoran Migration to California, 1848-1856: A Study in Prejudice," *Southern California Quarterly* 57 (Fall 1976): 333-57; James J. Rawls, "Gold Diggers: Indian Miners in the California Gold Rush," *California Historical Quarterly* 55 (Spring 1976): 28-45; Rudolph M. Lapp, *Blacks in Gold Rush California* (New Haven: Yale University Press, 1977); W. Sherman Savage, "The Negro on the Mining Frontier," *Journal of Negro History* 30 (January 1945): 30-46. Savage, in his *Blacks in the West* (Westport, Conn.: Greenwood Press, 1976), devotes ten pages to the mining industry; Kenneth W. Porter, *The Negro on the American Frontier* (New York: Arno Press, 1971), gives less than two.

36. Most general studies of the Chinese in the West contain but limited material on them and mining. For pertinent accounts see Ted C. Hinckley, "Prospectors, Profits and Prejudice," *American West* 2 (Spring 1965): 58-65; Ping Chiu, *Chinese Labor in California, 1850-1880: An Economic Study* (Madison: State Historical Society of Wisconsin, 1963); David V. Dufault, "The Chinese in the Mining Camps of California, 1848-1870," *Historical Society of Southern California Quarterly* 41 (June 1959): 155-70; Pat K. Ourada, "The Chinese in Colorado," *Colorado Magazine* 29 (October 1952): 273-83; Betty Derig, "Celestials in the Diggings," *Idaho Yesterdays* 16 (Fall 1972): 2-23; Paul Crane and T. A. Larson, "The Chinese Massacre," *Annals of Wyoming* 12 (January and April 1940): 47-55, 153-61. See John Rowe, *The Hard-Rock Men: Cornish Immigrants and the North American Mining Frontier* (Liverpool: Liverpool University Press, 1974). More sprightly but less thorough is A. L. Rowse, *The Cousin Jacks: The Cornish in America* (New York: C. Scribner's Sons, 1969). A third study, containing much material that is not always digested, is Arthur Cecil Todd, *The Cornish Miner in America: The Contribution to the Mining History of the United States by Emigrant Cornish Miners—The Men Called Cousin Jacks* (Truro: D. Bradford Barton; Glendale, Calif.: Arthur H. Clark Co., 1967). The relationship of European immigrants to the mineral industry has not been drawn together. Most histories of specific or regional groups include pertinent information of a more general nature. See, for example, Andrew F. Rolle, *The Immigrant Upraised: Italian Adventurers and Colonists in an Expanding America* (Norman: University of Oklahoma Press, 1968), and Wilbur S. Shepperson, *Restless Strangers: Nevada's Immigrants and Their Interpreters* (Reno: University of Nevada Press, 1970). See also: Abraham P. Nasatir, *The French in the California Gold Rush* (New York: American Society of the French Legion of

Honor, 1934); Phillip I. Earl, "Nevada's Italian War, July–Sept., 1879 (Sometimes Known as the 'Charcoal War,' or the 'Coal Burner's War')," *Nevada Historical Society Quarterly* 12 (Summer 1969): 47–87; and three articles by Helen Zeese Papanikolas, "The Greeks of Carbon County," *Utah Historical Quarterly* 22 (April 1954): 143–64; "Life and Labor Among the Immigrants of Bingham Canyon," *Utah Historical Quarterly* 33 (Fall 1965): 289–315; and "Toil and Rage in a New Land: The Greek Immigrants in Utah," *Utah Historical Quarterly* 38 (Spring 1980): 99–203.

37. Ira B. Joralemon, *Romantic Copper: Its Lure and Lore* (New York: D. Appleton-Century Co., 1934), is an interesting and chatty approach by an able engineer but has no pretensions to scholarship. Thomas R. Navin, *Copper Mining and Management* (Tucson: University of Arizona Press, 1978), contains much business history of the major copper companies and is valuable to those concerned with corporate development. See also Gary B. Hansen, "Industry of Destiny: Copper in Utah," *Utah Historical Quarterly* 31 (Summer 1963): 262–79; Melody Webb Grauman, "Kennecott: Alaskan Origins of a Copper Empire," *Western Historical Quarterly* 9 (April 1978): 197–213; Joseph Schafer, *The Wisconsin Lead Region* (Madison: Historical Society of Wisconsin, 1932); James E. Wright, *The Galena Lead District: Federal Policy and Practice, 1824–1847* (Madison: Historical Society of Wisconsin, 1966); Arrell M. Gibson, *Wilderness Bonanza: The Tri-State District of Missouri, Kansas, and Oklahoma* (Norman: University of Oklahoma Press, 1972); James D. Norris, *AZn:PA History of the American Zinc Company* (Madison: State Historical Society of Wisconsin, 1968); an exception is Scamehorn's study of early Colorado Fuel and Iron, already noted. Also, a few articles serve as infrequent guideposts: Richard H. Kesel, "The Raton Coal Field: An Evolving Landscape," *New Mexico Historical Review* 41 (July 1966): 231–50; Thomas G. Alexander, "From Dearth to Deluge: Utah's Coal Industry," *Utah Historical Quarterly* 31 (Summer 1963): 235–47; Rita McDonald and Merrill G. Burlingame, "Montana's First Commercial Coal Mine," *Pacific Northwest Quarterly* 47 (July 1956): 23–28; Robert A. Chadwick, "Coal: Montana's Prosaic Treasure," *Montana: The Magazine of Western History* 23 (Autumn 1973): 18–31; William B. Evans and Robert L. Peterson, "Decision at Colstrip: The Northern Pacific Railway's Open Pit Mining Operation," *Pacific Northwest Quarterly* 71 (July 1970): 129–36; Marilyn Tharp, "Story of Coal at Newcastle," *Pacific Northwest Quarterly* 48 (October 1957): 120–26; Dwight F. Henderson, "The Texas Coal Mining Industry," *Southwestern Historical Quarterly* 68 (October 1964): 207–19; Robert N. Manley, "Wealth Beneath the Prairie: The Search for Coal in Nebraska," *Nebraska*

History 47 (June 1966): 157-76; Leonard J. Arrington, "Planning an Iron Industry for Utah, 1851-1858," *Huntington Library Quarterly* 21 (May 1958): 237-60; Gustive O. Larson, "Bulwark of the Kingdom: Utah's Iron and Steel Industry," *Utah Historical Quarterly* 31 (Summer 1963): 247-61. For commercial gem mining, see Richard M. Pearl, "Gem Mining in Colorado," *Colorado Magazine* 16 (November 1939): 213-20; and W. Turrentine Jackson, "Her Britannic Majesty and Montana's Elusive Bonanza: Sapphires and Rubies," *Montana: The Magazine of Western History* 14 (October 1964): 57-67. Of the substantial body of literature on the diamond fraud, much of it trash, the best is Bruce A. Woodard, *Diamonds in the Salt* (Boulder: Pruett Press, 1967).

38. Pathbreaking in these areas has been limited: Miles P. Romney, "Utah's Cinderella Minerals: The Nonmetallics," *Utah Historical Quarterly* 31 (Summer 1963): 220-34; Duane Vandenbusche, "Marble: Past to Present," *Colorado Magazine* 46 (Winter 1969): 16-39; Edith E. Bucco, "Founded on Rock: Colorado's Stout Stone Industry," *Colorado Magazine* 51 (Fall 1974): 317-35; James A. Sayre, "A Bonanza in Borax: The Story of John Wemple Searles and Searles Lake," *Journal of the West* 3 (July 1964): 277-90; Kathleen Bruyn, *Uranium Country* (Boulder: University of Colorado Press, 1955); T. M. McKee, "Early Discovery of Uranium Ore in Colorado," *Colorado Magazine* 32 (July 1955): 191-203; Don Sorensen, "Wonder Mineral: Utah's Uranium," *Utah Historical Quarterly* 31 (Summer 1963): 280-91; Herbert H. Lang, "Uranium Also Had Its 'Forty-Niners,'" *Journal of the West* 1 (October 1962): 161-69.

39. Jerome O. Steffen, *Comparative Frontiers: A Proposal for Studying the American West* (Norman: University of Oklahoma Press, 1980); Jay Monaghan, *Australians and the Gold Rush: California and Down Under, 1849-1854* (Berkeley and Los Angeles: University of California Press, 1966); William Parker Morrell, *The Gold Rushes* (London: A. and C. Black, 1940).

Chapter Seven

W. *Turrentine Jackson*

Transportation in
the American West

Historical research and literature pertaining to western transportation is fragmentary, perhaps more than in any other area of the history of the American West. A great mass of information has been collected and hundreds of books and articles have been published. It is a field that has attracted the attention not only of professional historians but also of scholars in allied disciplines, as well as numerous amateurs dedicated to enhancing the historical importance of locality and region. An overall thesis or synthesis has yet to be suggested. Emphasis has been on the accumulation of facts rather than on interpretation, and the romantic aspects have been overemphasized. Since transportation studies have had a tendency to be narrative rather than conceptual and analytical, one encounters difficulty in tracing changing patterns of interpretation. Seeking a unifying theme for the field and noting the nature of contemporary research may be more rewarding.

Any student wishing to study transportation in the American West would do well to start with the works of Oscar O. Winther. First interested in stagecoaching in California, he expanded his research into the Pacific Northwest and in 1964 summarized his lifetime of scholarly inquiry in *The Transportation Frontier, 1865–1890.* Winther's work is distinctive because he displayed exceptional ability to place a large amount of historical material in its proper perspective. He recognizes the interrelationship of water transportation with roads and rails throughout the total West. He deals with subjects one would anticipate: steamboats on western rivers, stagecoaches delivering mails and express, wagons carrying freight, and railroads. Terminating his study in 1890, he does not discuss the development of the highway system other than to note the importance of the bicycle craze at the end of the century, the organization of the League of American Wheelmen that led, in turn, to the

National League for Good Roads. In addition to his commendable attempt at summation, Winther was an avid bibliographer, and his references in *The Transportation Frontier* list the significant scholarship up to the time of publication. His *Classified Bibliography of the Periodical Literature of the Trans-Mississippi West, 1811–1957* is also a valuable research tool.[1]

Another helpful introduction to the literature of prerailroad transportation is the annotated bibliography of Henry Pickering Walker published in *Arizona and the West* in 1976. He notes that because of the lack of scholarly work, it is essential for the student to turn to several nonscholarly classics for information. Walker's emphasis is on the movement of peoples and their goods over long distances during the nineteenth century, and he therefore elects to omit such subjects as the surveying and construction of wagon roads.[2]

The most meaningful theme pertaining to all aspects of transportation in the American West in the nineteenth and twentieth centuries is the interrelationship and comparative significance of government and private enterprise. No aspect of prerailroad transportation has inspired as much interest among regional and local historians as river transportation and steamboats. Here the entrepreneurial spirit prevails. A sound and scholarly background can be obtained from Lewis C. Hunter, *Steamboats on Western Rivers: An Economic and Technological History.* He deals with the technical matters of construction and operation of steamboats, problems of navigation, the business aspects of their operation, life aboard steamers, and the competition with railroads for the transportation trade.[3] His primary concern is with the Mississippi River eastward. It is regrettable that a comparable overall study does not exist for the region to the west.

Two notable studies of transportation on far western rivers should be noted. William E. Lass has explored in scholarly fashion the subject of steamboating on the Upper Missouri, tracing the impact of railroad construction on shortening steamboat service farther upstream. Dorothy O. Johansen's classic study of the Oregon Steam Navigation Company has explained the difficulties and importance of navigation along the Columbia River into the gold camps of Idaho and provides an excellent example of business enterprise in transportation.[4]

Every major western river has attracted the attention of at least one historian. William J. "Steamboat Bill" Petersen introduced the trend in his early studies of the Mississippi and Missouri rivers. His personal identification with this area of research and writing made him well known in professional circles. His work and personality were a contributing factor to the decision to use the steamboat as a symbol on the cover of the publication of the Mississippi Valley Historical Association, a tradition that has been continued to the present day by the *Journal of American History,* published by the Organization of American Historians.[5]

Regional and state journals have published numerous accounts of steamboat travel. The Missouri River, quite naturally, first attracted the interest of many western historians. Early studies are descriptive and factual in nature, usually emphasizing the relationship between steamboat service on the western rivers and railroad construction. More recent studies have concentrated on the impact of these transportation services on such specific communities as Bismarck and Yankton.[6] Steamboating on the Red River of the North has been summarized in articles in the *North Dakota Historical Quarterly* and in *Minnesota History.* Kansas publications have revealed the difficulties of navigation on the Kansas River. The *Arkansas Historical Quarterly* contains information on the history and importance of water transportation on the various rivers of that state. Special emphasis has been given to the Colorado River of the West, not only because of steamboating activity that brought supplies to the military posts but also because of its importance to Mormon trade and settlement. Leonard Arrington, among the most distinguished of professional historians, has recently been interested in this subject, noting the plan of Brigham Young to ship goods by water up the lower Colorado, thence by wagon road to Salt Lake, rather than using only overland transportation. Richard E. Lingenfelter has made a major contribution in *Steamboats on the Colorado River, 1852-1916,* wherein he traces the significance of the steamboat in the economic and social development of an isolated, and somewhat inhospitable, region. He does not confine his investigation to the lower portions of the river where earlier scholars have concentrated their attention, but includes development schemes on the upper Colorado and its tributaries. The study is a definitive source for Colorado River history.[7]

In the Pacific Northwest the history of steamboating has included not only activity on the Columbia River but within Puget Sound. A comprehensive account of the construction and operation of steamboats in California has been provided by Jerry MacMullen, *Paddle Wheel Days in California.* Other writers have concentrated on such specific waters in the state as San Francisco Bay, Clear Lake, and Owens Lake.[8]

Interest in river transportation continues. Having emphasized the success stories on the major water arteries, historians have more recently told of great expectations that were unfulfilled, as in the case of navigation on the Des

Moines River. The *Alaska Journal* has reprinted accounts of steamboating on the Yukon River during the first decade of the twentieth century, in response to contemporary interest in all aspects of transportation in that state.[9]

A new departure in the scholarship of the 1970s concerning steamboating on western rivers has been an attempt by economists and economic historians to analyze the rise, decline, and profitability of steamboating enterprises. Initial studies have concentrated on the "old west" east of the Mississippi in the pre-Civil War period, but here we have a hopeful beginning that may produce a westward movement of scholarly inquiry.[10]

In the area of land transportation, including the location, improvement, and use of roads for the delivery of passengers, mail, express, and freight, by packtrains, wagons, and stagecoaches, the comparative importance of government sponsorship and subsidy of western transportation and that of private entrepreneurs has been clearly delineated. Three standard works are available on the role of the government: the exploration of the American West by the United States Army ostensibly for the location of military roads in the trans-Mississippi West between the Mexican and Civil wars; and the financial underwriting of mail deliveries by the federal government. William H. Goetzmann has dignified this attempt to explain the national government's relationship to the westward movement as the work of a new "Imperial School" of western historians.[11]

Among the military roads located by the federal government, none has received more attention than the trace located by John Mullan connecting the Missouri River at Fort Benton with the Columbia at Walla Walla. Perennial interest in the subject is illustrated by a recent article in the *Pacific Northwest Quarterly* explaining the economic impact of the road on the development of Walla Walla in eastern Washington.[12]

Stagecoaching as a business enterprise has received more attention, both by professional and amateur historians, than any other aspect of prerailroad transportation. Here the theme of the comparative importance of government sponsorship and entrepreneurial activity has been thoroughly explored. LeRoy R. Hafen's study of the overland mail is the standard work that should first be consulted on that subject. An in-depth account of the Southern Overland Mail published by Roscoe P. and Margaret B. Conkling, in three volumes, illustrates the extensive amount of information available both in governmental and private archives. The best illustration of the biographical approach to interrelationships between the delivery of mails and the transportation of passengers by stagecoach, as well as an example of business leadership, is found in James V. Frederick's biography of Ben Holladay, the stagecoach king.[13]

Popular histories, widely read, should be consulted because of the impact they have made upon the public concerning the nature of stagecoach operations in the West. Among the more notable are the Bannings' survey of stagecoaching in the American West; Root and Connelley's volume on overland mail, composed of the rambling and romantic reminiscences of Frank A. Root; Ralph Moody's *Stagecoach West,* based on reliable source materials; and the histories of Wells, Fargo and Company by Edward Hungerford and by Noel M. Loomis.[14]

The importance of stagecoaches for delivery of mails and express on the Pacific Slope was also noted some years ago by Winther. Often overlooked have been the studies concerned with stagecoach operations in Nevada and Idaho and the enduring struggle between San Francisco and Portland to dominate the channel of communication into the Idaho mining camps. In fact, the most neglected region where research on stagecoaching is concerned is the Pacific Northwest, a striking contrast to the interest there in water transportation. One significant book by Arthur L. Throckmorton should be examined. His study of Oregon business enterprise and its leaders devotes attention to many aspects of transportation including river steamers, packtrains, freight wagons, and stagecoaches.[15] A recent significant contribution to the history of stagecoaching and the delivery of the mails, not considered by Hafen, is Morris F. Taylor's *First Mail West: Stagecoach Lines on the Santa Fe Trail.*[16]

The most acrimonious debate over the interpretation of western transportation was instigated by Waddell F. Smith, a descendant of one of the partners in the freighting firm of Russell, Majors and Waddell, when he attacked Wells Fargo Bank advertising, insisting that Wells Fargo played no significant role in the Overland Mail Company or the Pony Express and that it never owned and operated a stagecoach in California. Smith's contention was supported by Raymond W. Settle and Mary L. Settle, who had written an admirable history of Russell, Majors and Waddell. W. Turrentine Jackson, using for the first time manuscript minute books of the boards of directors of both the Overland Mail Company and Wells, Fargo and Company, documented the fact that the financial support for the Southern Overland Mail, chiefly on the western third of the route, came from Wells, Fargo and Company; that its representatives on the board were instrumental in removing Butterfield from the presidency; and that by the time the mail service was moved to the central route, the express and banking firm had a major voice in selecting personnel and determining policy.[17]

The role of Russell, Majors and Waddell in establishing the Pony Express and operating it during the early months of the service as a promotional venture and without government subsidy, much to the firm's financial disadvantage, is well known and again described by the Settles. The literature on the Pony Express is voluminous. Roy Bloss emphasized the fact that, once the overland mail was moved to the central route and made a daily service, the Pony Express as a part of the government contract was subsidized. Moreover, Wells, Fargo and Company, at that time dominant in the mail operation, assumed responsibility for the Pony Express during the last third of its existence, especially west of Salt Lake City. Jackson's research has confirmed that this reinterpretation by Bloss is substantially correct. Jackson has meanwhile continued his studies on the history of Wells, Fargo and Company in Montana, Colorado, and the Pacific Northwest.[18]

Travel accounts of those who came west via stagecoaches are legion. Historians have repeatedly quoted descriptions from Horace Greeley, J. F. Rusling, Demas Barnes, Samuel Bowles, J. W. Clampitt, Waterman L. Ormsby, William Tallack, and others. This genre has been most effectively utilized by two distinguished scholars in producing syntheses of observations by other types of travelers in the West. A similar summation of the experiences of stagecoach passengers in the American West, based upon the above accounts of participants, has quite recently been written.[19]

Freighting by packtrains and wagons has long been a subject of interest to western historians. That the role of the U.S. Army in supplying western forts stimulated freighting enterprise is well known. The story of the largest of all the freighting firms, Russell, Majors and Waddell, has been twice told by the Settles. Two historians' interest in the subject of freighting began with the preparation of theses and dissertations written some years ago: Walker D. Wyman on the Santa Fe trade and Joseph A. McGowan on California. The Dakota story has been told by Harold E. Briggs. Throughout the literature we have the continuing theme of the comparative importance of service provided for the government on the one hand, and private business enterprise on the other.[20]

Standard reminiscences by Josiah Gregg, Alexander Majors, and William F. Hooker provide a romantic, descriptive base for freighting activities. Two of the most recent studies of freighting in the West have attempted an overall view. Henry Walker in *The Wagonmasters* has described long-haul freighting from the Missouri frontier across the High Plains to the various population centers. William E. Lass has concentrated on wagon freighting along the Platte River route, researching a diversity of sources, largely reminiscences of participants, thereby providing a readable survey.[21]

Most studies of freighting have emphasized the route from east to west. A departure, noting the importance of routes from south to north, will be found in Paul F. Sharp's study of trade and supply routes across the international boundary between Montana and western Canadian outposts. The most recent study of freighting by Betty M. and Brigham D. Madsen reminds us again of the importance of north-south freighting, in this case from Salt Lake to Montana. Interesting insights into toll routes and ferries are also provided. The perennial interest of the scholar in the army's role in freighting operations is illustrated by a recent article in the *Southwestern Historical Quarterly* by Emmett Essin.[22]

Overland migration on the Santa Fe, Oregon, and California trails, while not directly an aspect of transportation, does illustrate the overriding theme of mobility in the West. Neither professional historians nor skilled amateurs tire of delving into the subject. Jack D. Rittenhouse has provided us with a thorough bibliography of writings about the Santa Fe Trail. Beginning with R. L. Duffus's *The Santa Fe Trail* in 1930, popular histories followed, written by Stanley Vestal and Hiram Martin Chittenden. A long line of professional historians, including John E. Sunder, Max Moorehead, Otis E. Young, Leo E. Oliva, and Robert M. Utley, have dealt with the military use of the trail and the observations of travelers, surveyors, and diplomats. W. J. Ghent published *The Road to Oregon* as early as 1929. Notable authors including Jay Monaghan, Ralph Moody, Marshall Sprague, and David Lavender have also contributed to our understanding. Dale Morgan offered a meticulously edited two-volume work on the diaries in a single year, 1846, illustrating how much historians know about the migration. David M. Potter, another distinguished scholar, contributed a penetrating analysis of the nature of overland migration. Events on the California Trail have been told beginning with the earliest of travelers, John Bidwell, and engagingly summarized in the works of George R. Stewart.[23]

When it seemed that historians had exhausted the subject and that public consumption had been saturated, a new look suddenly appeared in the 1970s. This renascence took two forms: first, monumental studies of source materials by Merrill J. Mattes in *The Great Platte River Road* and by Louise Barry in *The Beginnings of the West*, which attempts to chronicle every overland party crossing the state of Kansas; and second with revisionary, interpretive works reflecting the interests and concerns of the contemporary generation of historians, most notably *The Plains Across* by John D. Unruh, Jr., and *Women and Men on the Overland Trail* by John Mack Faragher. In an exceptionally detailed treatment, Unruh considers migration on the overland trails as the experience changed through time. He suggests that a positive sense of community evolved among the participants. For example, Indian-white contact is pictured not as a story of conflict and violence but of cooperation and assistance. The book is a monument to scholarship. Faragher asserts that men and women on the trail experienced tension over power, that women were held in virtual bondage largely because of the differing roles of the sexes in the nineteenth century. He writes with empathy toward women and with an attempt to set the record straight. Julie Roy Jeffrey suggests that frontier women were comfortable in their domestic roles, even on the trails, that shielded them from greater responsibilities, but having reached a destination in the West they attempted to recreate the society and institutions they had known in the East. Other historians, Sandra L. Myres and Glenda Riley, reject attempts to stereotype western women and insist that their roles and attitudes were just as variable as those of men but with different priorities and concerns. Three views have emerged of white women on the overland trails: the self-sacrificing, long-suffering "saint in a sunbonnet," the contrasting picture of the exploited, overworked, and misunderstood drudge, and the more balanced suggestion that women's perceptions of themselves, their associates, and their experience were as diverse as those of men.[24]

Turning to the historical literature on railroads, the reader is likely to be overwhelmed by the abundance of primary and secondary sources. Background information will be found in the pioneering works by Robert E. Riegel and Robert R. Russel. A more recent, well-written overall account of *American Railroads* by John F. Stover contains several excellent chapters on western lines. Ira G. Clark's study of railroads in the Southwest provides a model for future investigators.[25]

The role of the federal government in conducting surveys for the transcontinental railroad has been a subject for historical inquiry for more than eighty years. For a penetrating analysis of the subject, William H. Goetzmann's *Army Exploration in the American West* should be read. So should Carter Goodrich, who has traced the continuing role of the government in subsidizing the construction and operation of the railroad network.[26]

Each major railroad line and system has had its historian. Two studies are worthy of special mention. Richard C. Overton's study of the Burlington line, based on the archives of that company, provides an objective, scholarly account that marked a significant departure from earlier company-sponsored, journalistic accounts of individual railroads. The second work based on company archives is Robert G. Athearn's *Union Pacific Country.* This study is not concerned with the transcontinental line but with the feeder lines constructed later and their importance in the settlement and economic development of the West. Athearn contributes to our suggested theme of the comparative importance of government and private enterprise in transportation development by suggesting that the entrepreneurial ability of the company's executives was curtailed by governmental regulations and interference. Several historians have approached the subject of railroad transportation from the biographical viewpoint, with varying success.[27]

The most enduring illustration of the comparative importance of government subsidy vis-à-vis business enterprise is the controversy that has raged over the importance of land grants by the government in aiding construction. In the late 1940s and 1950s numerous advocates and historians, including Robert S. Henry, David Maldwyn Ellis, Paul W. Gates, William S. Greever, Ray H. Mattison, John B. Rae, and a host of others became involved in the bitter debate. While historians of the American West appear to have concluded that the controversy is no longer rewarding, economists and economic historians renewed the debate in the 1970s, using methodologies characteristic of their disciplines. Robert W. Fogel has applied formal economic theory to his analysis of the Union Pacific Railroad as an example of premature enterprise, has assessed the role of government sponsorship of railroad construction, and has analyzed the social benefits that resulted. He suggests that governmental construction might have been the most desirable method of obtaining a Pacific railroad, selling it immediately after completion to private individuals. Social benefits would have been identical, the Union Pacific would have been a sounder corporation, and the government would have reaped a profit from the sale.[28]

Lloyd J. Mercer, writing in the *Journal of Economic History,* provides a detailed economic analysis of the Central Pacific system and concludes that private investors would not have built the railroad without land grants, that land subsidy hastened construction and, in the case of the Central Pacific, benefited society. An opposing view concerning the impact of land grants on regional development can be read in John F. Due's study of wagon road land grants in central Oregon. Mercer has also examined the history of land grant railroads to determine whether or not they were built ahead of demand as a result of federal subsidy; he concludes that the Central Pacific and Union Pacific were, in a superficial sense, and that others were in a more substantive way. William R. Petrowski has studied the promoter's profits from the building of the Kansas Pacific and Denver Pacific railroads and concludes that the builders took little risk, largely because of the U.S. bond subsidy loan, and that they manipulated these securities to obtain maximum profits. Heywood Fleisig has again raised the question as to whether land grants were necessary to build the Central Pacific Railroad and concludes that they were not. He argues that government loans through bonds were sufficient. An even larger issue is raised concerning "how frequently and to what extent have the existing possessors of wealth used the power of the government to win for themselves gains which they could not secure unaided in the market place?" A contrary view is presented in J. Hayden Boyd and Gary M. Walton, who have examined the social savings of rail passenger service in the nineteenth century in *Explorations of Economic History;* they conclude that "it is difficult to think of any other innovation that rendered economic gains of a similar magnitude." So the debate appears never to be over.[29]

The penetrating studies by another group of historians, though not regional in emphasis, should not be overlooked by historians of the American West: those of Robert H. Wiebe, Gabriel Kolko, and Albro Martin. Wiebe, in an initial study, suggested that business, rather than being villains opposed to the reformist thrust of the Progressive period, was actually involved and supportive in many ways. Broadening his investigation to include the years 1877–1920, Wiebe suggested that this period represented a shift in American values whereby the nation departed from rural standards and embraced those of the bureaucratic middle class. The Progressives are seen not as crusaders for a more democratic and honest government, nor those seeking to recoup the lost status of the middle class in the struggle between capital and labor, but as individuals attempting to institute a new set of values for older, established American beliefs. This type of revisionist thinking has been applied to the relationship between the government and the railroads by Kolko and Martin. Kolko contends that the railroads, rather than resenting government intervention and regulation, welcomed the development largely because control over transportation was maintained thereby in a way the railroads had been unable to achieve themselves. The Interstate Commerce Commission, he asserts, was aligned with the railroads. Thus, the regulations of the Progressive period were viewed not as an attempt to redress the balance of economic power, but as an effort to create stability in the railroad industry by political means. Martin disagrees with Kolko, suggesting that the unwillingness of the Interstate Commerce Commission to grant needed rate increases for the railroads during the Progressive period prevented the flow of investment funds to keep pace with the needs of the expanding system and eventually led to the financial collapse of railroad enterprise.[30]

An examination of the listing of "Recent Articles" in the first issue of the *Western Historical Quarterly* reveals that the centennial celebration of the first transcontinental railroad's completion led to an outburst of historical literature. Several contemporary approaches to railroad history can be ascertained. First, there is interest in such lesser-known personalities as Thomas Ewing, Jr., for his work in financing the Kansas Pacific Railway Company, Frank Seiberling for his role in planning the Midland Continental Railroad from Winnipeg south to the Texas Gulf ports to provide access for wheat shippers making connections with the ocean shipping headed for the Panama Canal, and George Brackett for his career in the Pacific Northwest, western Canada, and the Yukon.[31]

Second, there is a new look at the regional impact of railroad building. Richard V. Francaviglia traces in positive terms how the railroad network in Minnesota moved into virgin territory and led to settlement, agricultural growth, and town building. John S. Cochran maintains that the establishment of transcontinental connections for the Pacific Northwest was of the greatest significance, perhaps greater than for any other region of the West, and was an essential condition for the Northwest's dynamic growth at that time. W. H. Hutchison explores the myth and reality concerning the Southern Pacific and insists that every surge of California's unprecedented growth has been stimulated or accompanied by an improvement in transportation. He suggests that historians should judge the railroads by nineteenth-century rather than by twentieth-century standards.[32]

Third, transportation developments in Alaska have provided a new field of investigation for historians, and railroad studies have thereby been broadened. The *Alaska Journal* has published a variety of articles on such subjects as the Wild Goose Railroad, built in 1898–1900 across the tundra near Nome; the relationship between the construction of the Alaska Railroad and the development of the tourist industry; and the abortive proposal of the Trans-Canadian, Alaska, and Western Railways to supply Alaska and the U.S.S.R. during World War II. Another significant study of the Alaska Railroad and its effort to spur agricultural colonization in Alaska is available in a recent issue of *Agricultural History.*[33]

Several additional articles on railroad history in the West should be noted. Robert Higgs has taken exception to the recent position of economic historians that the complaints of the farmer about high railroad rates during the Populist period were not consistent with the facts. He suggests that railroad rates did decline, but so did prices for farm products at an even faster rate, and Higgs asserts that the rejection of Populist complaints by recent scholars is unjustified. Ross R. Cotroneo has shifted discussion of the history of the Northern Pacific Railroad away from its contribution as a land seller and colonizer to that as a timber resource manager in a remarkably able and well-documented article, written from company records and published in the *Journal of Forest History*. M. Guy Bishop has added a new chapter to the contribution of the Mormons to railroad construction in his study of John W. Young, Brigham's son, who was a dynamic force in construction of the Utah Central, Utah Northern, and Utah Western roads, as well as a participant in the affairs of the transcontinental Union Pacific and Atlantic Pacific roads.[34]

The movement for surfaced roads that could be traveled year around came about through an alliance of bicycle enthusiasts and farmers. In 1892 the League of American Wheelmen merged into the National League for Good Roads, later known as the National Good Roads Association. The federal government became involved the following year with establishment of the Office of Road Inquiry in the Department of Agriculture. Introduction of the automobile made expansion and improvement of roads imperative, and states began to give financial aid for construction of hard-surfaced roads. In 1916 the Federal Aid Road Act was passed to provide matching funds for those states that had established a program whereby federal funds could be used effectively. The Bureau of Public Roads in the Department of Commerce acted for the federal government. By 1921 a national network of highways had evolved.

Nowhere was the modern highway system more important than in the trans-Mississippi West, where great distances had to be crossed, where tourists visited the scenic wonders of the national parks, and where motortruck service flourished. The history of the good roads movement and development of the modern highway systems provides another significant chapter illustrating the theme of government sponsorship and subsidy to the transportaton system in the trans-Mississippi West.

The impact of the League of American Wheelmen on the good roads movement is ably explained by Philip P. Mason, who first became interested in the subject while preparing a doctoral dissertation at the University of Michigan. Another more recent book discussing initial developments in the first two decades of the twentieth century is John B. Rae, *The Road and Car in American Life*. Several articles are available that deal with interesting aspects of early efforts to improve highways for automobile traffic in the Far West. Joe McCarthy has ably surveyed the history of the Lincoln Highway, an initial effort of public and private groups to build a transcontinental highway to the Pacific. Private effort pointed up the need, public money finished the job. Thomas H. Peterson, Jr., has explained the business changes in a single state, in the case of Arizona, that were inspired by the introduction and increasing use of the automobile.[35]

Two early attempts were made to survey the entire subject of the introduction of the automobile and the establishment of the modern highway system, one in 1938 and a second in 1950. Often overlooked by historians is the history of road building published in the *Transactions* of the American Society of Engineers in 1928. More recently, Philip P. Mason, a recognized authority, has given us an overall picture in his *History of American Roads*. Political ramifications of the construction of express freeways in the last decade have been analyzed by Mark H. Rose, who suggests that those desiring to impose professional standards, with funds coming from the federal government, triumphed. The U.S. government has recently issued a popular history of the federal aid program from colonial times to the present.[36] The best study of the diffusion of the automobile throughout the United States between 1895 and 1969 will be found in a doctoral dissertation written at the University of Michigan by George Kirkham Jarvis. Earl Pomeroy's study of tourism in the golden West, mentioned earlier, notes the changing pattern of that industry as the automobile displaced the railroad as the means of access to attractions of the region. Two recent books have also made a significant contribution to our understanding of the social impact of the automobile: Michael L. Berger in *The Devil Wagon in God's Country* traces changes brought about in rural America between 1893 and 1929, and Warren James Belasco in *Americans on the Road* describes the development of auto-camps and later motels between 1910 and 1945. Both volumes provide evidence of changes in the American West in the twentieth century.[37]

In contrast to many aspects of transportation and communication, twentieth-century highway construction for automobile use has generally been studied from the national standpoint rather than by region. There are exceptions. Two contemporary highways, in Alaska and Baja California, have attracted the interest of scholars. David O. Remley has written on construction of the Alaska Highway in a study largely based on oral interviews with those involved. He concludes that wartime needs forced speed in building, and that as a result standards of construction were lowered and wastefulness resulted. His work on this subject has also been published in book form that can best be described as nontraditional history. Jack N. Barkenbus has studied the economic and political consequences of the transpeninsular highway in Baja California and suggests that economic considerations were paramount while the impact on unspoiled wilderness is cause for concern.[38]

Nowhere has the automobile and freeway construction had a greater impact than in California. Of primary interest has been the location of routes from the San Francisco Bay area across the Sierra Nevada into Nevada. Two recent articles published by the California Historical Society emphasize interesting sidelights. One deals with development of the intercity bus industry, born in the state, and traces the conflict with the railroads, the emergence of the Motor Carrier Association, and the foundation of contemporary bus systems. A second expresses concern over the insensitivity of CalTrans, the state highway construction agency, in destroying significant historical sites in the process of relocating interstate freeways.[39]

Turning to airlines, a most significant means of transportation in the trans-Mississippi West, the historian can find a superb illustration of the comparative significance of entrepreneurial and governmental activity. In the beginning, innovative individuals dominated. Later, the federal government controlled the industry through subsidization for carrying the mails, by defense contracts, and by regulation of domestic service. Beginning with the Kelley Mail Act of 1925 and the Air Commerce Act of 1926, the U.S. government established the Civil Aeronautics Authority in 1938, placed it in the Department of Commerce two years later, and finally in the Federal Aviation Act of 1958 merged all the various bureaus, boards, and committees into the Federal Aviation Agency.

Several single-volume histories of aviation were published prior to 1970. Most recently, R. E. G. Davies has written *Airlines of the United States*. Western historians will find in this volume a reliable summary of the establishment of routes, noting specifically the role of the Post Office in the delivery of airmail. Special emphasis is placed on the establishment of regional airlines in the trans-Mississippi West, notably along the Pacific Coast and in Alaska. Carroll V. Glines's *Saga of the Air Mail* is a popular account of note, emphasizing the contribution of the airmail system to the development of aviation. The same theme is developed in a more recent professional monograph by Walter F. Wacht. Carl Solberg's study of commercial aviation suggests that air commerce promoted national unity and the national economy by allowing business to operate on a nationwide basis. He makes specific reference to the West.[40]

Although the approach to aviation history has been national in scope, emphasizing involvement of the government, there are studies pertaining specifically to the West. An interesting account dealing exclusively with California as the center of aviation development is Kenneth M. Johnson, *Aerial California,* which traces to World War I the early history of flight. Other studies concentrate on the development of the aircraft industry within the state during World War II. A popular history of Western Air Lines, which claims to be the oldest in the country, is available.[41]

An able study of the air age in Wyoming, noting the importance of Cheyenne, has recently been published. No western region has received more recent attention than Alaska, primarily from historians writing for the *Alaska Journal.* Jeanne Harbottle has told the story of Clyde Wann, "Father of Yukon Aviation," who pioneered airways in the 1920s without direct airmail subsidies. She has also discussed the role of the White Pass Company, which dominated transportation by rail, steamboat, and air between Skagway and Whitehorse. Mary M. Worthylake traces the history of Pacific International Airways, which started with an airmail contract and was soon purchased by Pan American Airways in 1932.[42]

Thus, the historian interested in transportation and communication in the trans-Mississippi West must come to grips with a century and a half of technological change, and recognize that it is a subject that has interested not only professional historians but scholars in related disciplines and popular writers, all of whom have had something to contribute to the subject. In the massive amount of literature, local and regional interest in a single type of transportation has led to excessive fragmentation of information. Only a limited number of publications have attempted to examine various phases of transportation with the entire western region in view. Throughout, as repeatedly suggested, is the theme of the contribution of the entrepreneurial spirit expressed by individual pioneers and business enterprise, on the one hand, and the sustaining role of government on the other. Throughout time, departments of the federal government, such as War, Interior and Commerce, have been heavily involved—only moderately so in the period of prerailroad transportation but ever greater with the coming of railroads, highways, and airlines.[43]

Contemporary, younger historians interested in the American West have not placed a high priority on the subject of transportation and communication; and so it is a fruitful field for further study, particularly for those interested in the twentieth-century West.

Notes

1. Oscar O. Winther, *Express and Stagecoach Days in California* (Stanford: Stanford University Press, 1950); Winther, *The Old Oregon Country: A History of Frontier Trade, Transportation, and Travel* (Stanford: Stanford University Press, 1950; paperbound ed., Lincoln: University of Nebraska Press, 1969); Winther, *The Transportation Frontier, 1865-1890* (New York: Holt, Rinehart and Winston, 1964; paperbound ed., Albuquerque: University of New Mexico Press, 1974); Winther, *A Classified Bibliography of the Periodical Literature of the Trans-Mississippi West, 1811-1957* (Bloomington: Indiana University Press, 1961).

2. Henry P. Walker, "Pre-railroad Transportation in the Trans-Mississippi West: An Annotated Bibliography," *Arizona and the West* 18 (1976): 53-80.

3. Lewis C. Hunter, *Steamboats on Western Rivers: An Economic and Technological History* (Cambridge: Harvard University Press, 1949; later ed., New York: Octagon Books, 1969).

4. William E. Lass, *A History of Steamboating on the Upper Missouri* (Lincoln: University of Nebraska Press, 1962); Dorothy O. Johansen, "The Oregon Steam Navigation Company: An Example of Capitalism on the Frontier," *Pacific Historical Review* 10 (1941): 179-88.

5. William J. Petersen, *Steamboating on the Upper Mississippi: The Water Way to Iowa* (Iowa City: State Historical Society of Iowa, 1968); Petersen, "Steamboating in the Upper Mississippi Fur Trade," *Minnesota History* 13 (1932): 221-43; Petersen, "Steamboating on the Missouri River," *Iowa Journal of History* 53 (1955): 97-120.

6. Sam T. Bratton, "Inefficiency of Water Transportation in Missouri—A Geographical Factor in the Development of Railroads," *Missouri Historical Review* 14 (1919): 82-88; Harold E. Briggs, "Pioneer River Transportation in Dakota," *North Dakota Historical Quarterly* 3 (1929): 159-81; Phil E. Chappell, "A History of the Missouri River," Kansas State Historical Society *Transactions* 9 (1905-06): 237-316; Jay Mack Gamble, "Up River to Benton," *Montana* 6 (1956): 32-41; Thomas J. Myrha, "The Economic Influence of Steamboats on Early Bismarck," *North Dakota History* 28 (1961): 55-78; Ralph E. Nichol, "Steamboat Navigation on the Missouri River with Special

Reference to Yankton and Vicinity," *South Dakota Historical Collections* 24 (1952): 181-221; Alton B. Oviatt, "Steamboat Traffic on the Upper Missouri River, 1859-1869," *Pacific Northwest Quarterly* 40 (1949): 93-105; H. A. Trexler, "Missouri-Montana Highways, I—The Missouri River Route," *Missouri Historical Review* 12 (1918): 67-80; Walker D. Wyman, "Missouri River Steamboatin'," *Nebraska History* 26 (1946): 92-103.

7. Fred A. Bill, "Steamboating on the Red River of the North," *North Dakota Historical Quarterly* 9 (1942): 69-85; Marion H. Herriot, "Steamboat Transportation on the Red River," *Minnesota History* 21 (1940): 245-71; Edgar Langsdorf, "A Review of Early Navigation on the Kansas River," *Kansas Historical Quarterly* 18 (1950): 140-45; Mattie Brown, "River Transportation in Arkansas, 1819-1890," *Arkansas Historical Quarterly* 1 (1942): 342-54; Walter Moffatt, "Transportation in Arkansas, 1819-1840," *Arkansas Historical Quarterly* 15 (1956): 187-201. See also James H. Thomas and Carl N. Tyson, "Navigation on the Arkansas River, 1719-1886," *Kansas History* 2 (1979): 134-41; Milton R. Hunter, "The Mormons and the Colorado River," *American Historical Review* 44 (1939): 549-55; Francis H. Leavitt, "Steam Navigation on the Colorado River," *California Historical Society Quarterly* 22 (1943): 1-25 and 141-74; Arthur Woodward, *Feud on the Colorado* (Los Angeles: Westernlore Press, 1955); Leonard J. Arrington, "Inland to Zion: Mormon Trade on the Colorado River, 1864-1867," *Arizona and the West* 8 (1966): 239-50; Richard E. Lingenfelter, *Steamboats on the Colorado River, 1852-1916* (Tucson: University of Arizona Press, 1978).

8. N. A. McDougall, "Indomitable John: The Story of John Hart Scranton and His Puget Sound Steamers," *Pacific Northwest Quarterly* 45 (1954): 73-84; Randall V. Mills, *Stern-Wheelers Up Columbia: A Century of Steamboating in the Oregon Country* (Palo Alto, Calif.: Pacific Books, 1947; paperbound ed., Lincoln: University of Nebraska Press, 1977); Earle L. Stewart, "Steamboats on the Columbia: The Pioneer Period," *Oregon Historical Quarterly* 51 (1950): 20-42; Fred W. Wilson, "The Lure of the River," *Oregon Historical Quarterly* 34 (1933): 1-18, 111-33; Jerry MacMullen, *Paddle Wheel Days in California* (Stanford: Stanford University Press, 1944); Roger Olmstead, "The Square-Toed Packets of San Francisco Bay," *California Historical Society Quarterly* 51 (1972): 35-58; Frederick J. Simons, "Development of Transportation Routes in the Clear Lake Area," *California Historical Society Quarterly* 33 (1953): 353-71; Richard E. Lingenfelter, "The Desert Steamers," *Journal of the West* 1 (1962): 149-60.

9. Dave Hubler, "Des Moines River Navigation: Great Expectations Unfulfilled," *Annals of Iowa* 39 (1968): 287-306; E. S. Harrison, "Steamboating

on the Yukon," *Alaska Journal* 9 (1979): 49-53; reprinted from *Alaska-Yukon Magazine,* May 1907.

10. Erik F. Haites and James Mak, "The Decline of Steamboating on the Ante-bellum Western Rivers: Some Evidence of an Alternative Hypothesis," *Explorations in Economic History* 2 (1973): 25-36; Jeremy Atack, Erik F. Haites, James Mak, and Gary M. Walton, "The Profitability of Steamboating on Western Rivers, 1850," *Business History Review* 39 (1975): 346-54.

11. William H. Goetzmann, *Army Exploration of the American West, 1803-1863* (New Haven: Yale University Press, 1959; paperbound ed., Lincoln: University of Nebraska Press, 1979); W. Turrentine Jackson, *Wagon Roads West* (Berkeley and Los Angeles: University of California Press, 1952; paperbound ed., Lincoln: University of Nebraska Press, 1979); LeRoy R. Hafen, *The Overland Mail, 1849-1869* (Cleveland: Arthur H. Clark, 1926).

12. Alexander C. McGregor, "The Economic Impact of the Mullan Road on Walla Walla, 1860-1883," *Pacific Northwest Quarterly* 65 (1974): 118-29.

13. Roscoe P. Conkling and Margaret B. Conkling, *The Butterfield Overland Mail, 1857-1869* (Glendale: Arthur H. Clark, 1942); James V. Frederick, *Ben Holladay: The Stagecoach King: A Chapter in the Development of Transcontinental Transportation* (Glendale: Arthur H. Clark, 1940).

14. William and George H. Banning, *Six Horses* (New York: Century Company, 1930); Frank A. Root and William Elsey Connelley, *The Overland Stage to California* (Topeka: the authors, 1901; Glorieta, N.Mex.: Rio Grande Press, 1970); Ralph Moody, *Stagecoach West* (New York: Thomas Y. Crowell, 1967); Edward Hungerford, *Wells Fargo: Advancing the American Frontier* (New York: Random House, 1949); Noel M. Loomis, *Wells, Fargo: An Illustrated History* (New York: Clarkson N. Potter, 1968).

15. Oscar O. Winther, *Express and Stagecoach Days in California; Winther, The Old Oregon Country;* Victor Goodwin, "William C. (Hill) Beachey: Nevada-California-Idaho Stagecoach King," *Nevada Historical Society Quarterly* 10 (1967): 3-46; Clarence F. Intosh, "The Chico and Red Bluff Route: Stage Lines from Southern Idaho to the Sacramento Valley, 1865-1867," *Idaho Yesterdays* 6 (1962): 12-15, 18-19; Arthur L. Throckmorton, *Oregon Argonauts: Merchant Adventurers on the Western Frontier* (Portland: Oregon Historical Society, 1961).

16. Morris F. Taylor, *First Mail West: Stagecoach Lines on the Santa Fe Trail* (Albuquerque: University of New Mexico Press, 1971).

17. Waddell F. Smith, "Stage Lines and Express Companies in California," *The Far Westerner: Quarterly Publication of the Stockton Corral of West-*

erners (1965); Raymond W. Settle and Mary L. Settle, *Empire on Wheels* (Stanford: Stanford University Press, 1949); Settle and Settle, *War Drums and Wagon Wheels* (Lincoln: University of Nebraska Press, 1966); W. Turrentine Jackson, "A New Look at Wells Fargo, Stagecoaches and the Pony Express," *California Historical Society Quarterly* 45 (1966): 291–323; Jackson, "Wells Fargo: Symbol of the Wild West," *Western Historical Quarterly* 3 (1972): 179–96.

18. Raymond W. Settle, "The Pony Express: Heroic Effort: Tragic End," in Waddell F. Smith, *The Story of the Pony Express* (San Francisco: Hesperian House, 1960); Raymond W. Settle and Mary L. Settle, *Saddles and Spurs: The Pony Express Saga* (Harrisburg, Pa.: Stackpole Co., 1955; paperbound ed., Lincoln: University of Nebraska Press, 1972); Arthur Chapman, *The Pony Express: The Record of a Romantic Era in Business* (New York: G. P. Putnam's Sons, 1932); Roy S. Bloss, *Pony Express–Great Gamble* (Berkeley: Howell North, 1959); W. Turrentine Jackson, "Wells Fargo's Pony Expresses," *Journal of the West* 11 (1972): 405–36; Jackson, "Wells Fargo Staging Over the Sierra," *California Historical Society Quarterly* 49 (1970): 99–133; Jackson, "Stages, Mails and Express in Southern California: The Role of Wells, Fargo and Company in the Pre-railroad Period," *Southern California Quarterly* 56 (1974): 233–72; Jackson, *Wells Fargo Stagecoaching in Montana Territory* (Helena: Montana Historical Society Press, 1979).

19. Robert G. Athearn, *Westward the Briton* (New York: Charles Scribner's Sons, 1953); Earl S. Pomeroy, *In Search of the Golden West* (New York: Knopf, 1957); Elliott West, "Splendid Misery: Stagecoach Travel in the Far West," *American West* 18 (1981): 61–65, 83–86.

20. Ralph B. Bieber, "Some Aspects of the Santa Fe Trail, 1848-1890," *Missouri Historical Review* 18 (1924): 158–66; Averam B. Bender, "Military Transportation in the Southwest, 1848-1860," *New Mexico Historical Review* 32 (1957): 123–50; Joseph A. McGowan, "Freighting to the Mines in California, 1849-1859" (Ph.D. diss., University of California, 1949); Walker D. Wyman, "Freighting, a Big Business on the Santa Fe Trail," *Kansas Historical Quarterly* 1 (1931): 17–27; Harold E. Briggs, "Early Freight and Stage Lines in Dakota," *North Dakota Historical Quarterly* 3 (1929): 229–61.

21. Josiah Gregg, *Commerce of the Prairies,* ed. Max Moorhead, American Exploration and Travel Series, no. 17 (Norman: University of Oklahoma Press, 1954); Alexander Majors, *Seventy Years on the Frontier* (Chicago: Rand McNally, 1893); William F. Hooker, *The Prairie Schooner* (Chi-

cago: Saul Brothers, 1918); Howard R. Driggs (ed.), *The Bullwhacker: Adventures of a Frontier Freighter* (Yonkers-on-Hudson, N.Y., Chicago: World Book Company, 1925); Henry Pickering Walker, *The Wagonmasters: High Plains Freighting from the Earliest Days of the Santa Fe Trail to 1880* (Norman: University of Oklahoma Press, 1966); William E. Lass, *From the Missouri to the Great Salt Lake: An Account of Overland Freighting* (Lincoln: Nebraska State Historical Society, 1972).

22. Paul F. Sharp, *Whoop-Up Country: The Canadian-American West, 1865-1885* (Minneapolis: University of Minnesota Press, 1955; paperbound ed., Norman: University of Oklahoma Press, 1978); Betty M. and Brigham D. Madsen, *North to Montana* (Salt Lake City: University of Utah Press, 1980); Emmett Essin, "Mules, Pack and Packtrains," *Southwestern Historical Quarterly* 74 (1970): 52-60.

23. Jack D. Rittenhouse, *The Santa Fe Trail: A Historical Bibliography* (Albuquerque: University of New Mexico Press, 1971); R. L. Duffus, *The Santa Fe Trail* (New York: Longmans, Green and Co., 1930); Stanley Vestal, *The Old Santa Fe Trail* (Boston: Houghton Mifflin, 1939); Hiram Martin Chittenden, *The American Fur Trade of the Far West*, 3 vols. (New York: Barnes and Noble, 1935); John E. Sunder (ed.), *Matt Field on the Santa Fe Trail* (Norman: University of Oklahoma Press, 1960); Max L. Moorhead, *New Mexico's Royal Road: Trade and Travel on the Chihuahua Trail* (Norman: University of Oklahoma Press, 1958); Otis E. Young, *The First Military Escort on the Santa Fe Trail* (Glendale, Calif.: Arthur H. Clark, 1952); Leo E. Oliva, *Soldiers on the Santa Fe Trail* (Norman: University of Oklahoma Press, 1967); Robert M. Utley, "Fort Union and the Santa Fe Trail," *New Mexico Historical Review* 31 (1961): 36-48; W. J. Ghent, *The Road to Oregon* (New York: Thomas Y. Crowell, 1963); Marshall Sprague, *The Great Gates: The Story of Rocky Mountain Passes* (Boston: Little, Brown, 1964; paperbound ed., Lincoln: University of Nebraska Press, 1981); David Lavender, *Westward Vision: The Story of the Oregon Trail* (New York: McGraw-Hill, 1963; paperbound ed., 1971); Dale Morgan (ed.), *Overland in 1846: Diaries and Letters of the California-Oregon Trail*, 2 vols. (Georgetown, Calif.: Talisman Press, 1963); David M. Potter (ed.), *Trail to California: The Overland Journal of Vincent Geiger and Wakeman Bryarly* (New Haven: Yale University Press, 1945); John Bidwell, *A Journey to California* (San Francisco: J. H. Nash, 1937); George R. Stewart, *The California Trail: An Epic with Many Heroes* (New York: McGraw-Hill, 1962), and *Ordeal by Hunger: The Story of the Donner Party* (Boston: Houghton Mifflin, 1960).

24. Merrill J. Mattes, *The Great Platte River Road: The Covered Wagon*

Mainline via Fort Kearny to Fort Laramie (Lincoln: Nebraska State Historical Society, 1969); Louise Barry, *The Beginnings of the West: Annals of the Kansas Gateway to the American West, 1540–1854* (Topeka: Kansas State Historical Society, 1972); John D. Unruh, Jr., *The Plains Across: The Overland Emigrants and the Trans-Mississippi West, 1840–1860* (Urbana: University of Illinois Press, 1979); John Mack Faragher, *Women and Men on the Overland Trail* (New Haven: Yale University Press, 1979); Julie Roy Jeffrey, *Frontier Women: The Trans-Mississippi West, 1840–1880* (New York: Hill and Wang, 1979); Sandra L. Myres (ed.), *Ho for California! Women's Overland Diaries from the Huntington Library* (San Marino, Calif.: Huntington Library, 1980); Glenda Riley, *Frontierswomen: The Iowa Experience* (Ames: Iowa State University Press, 1981); and "Women in the West," *Journal of American Culture* 3 (1980): 311–29.

25. Robert E. Riegel, *The Story of the Western Railroads* (New York: Macmillan, 1926; paperbound ed., Lincoln: University of Nebraska Press, 1964); Robert E. Russel, *Improvement of Communication with the Pacific Coast as an Issue in American Politics, 1783–1864* (Cedar Rapids, Iowa: Torch Press, 1948); John F. Stover, *American Railroads* (Chicago: University of Chicago Press, 1969); Ira G. Clark, *Then Came the Railroad: The Century from Steam to Diesel in the Southwest* (Norman: University of Oklahoma Press, 1958).

26. William H. Goetzmann, *Army Exploration in the American West, 1803–1863* (New Haven: Yale University Press, 1959; paperbound ed., Lincoln: University of Nebraska Press, 1979); Carter Goodrich, *Government Promotion of American Canals and Railroads, 1800–1890* (New York: Columbia University Press, 1960; paperbound ed., Greenwood, 1974).

27. L. L. Waters, *Steel Rails to Santa Fe* (Lawrence: University of Kansas Press, 1950); Robert G. Athearn, *Rebel of the Rockies: A History of the Denver and Rio Grande Western Railroad* (New Haven: Yale University Press, 1962; paperbound ed. Lincoln: University of Nebraska Press, 1977); Richard C. Overton, *Gulf to Rockies: The Heritage of the Fort Worth and Denver-Colorado and Southern Railways, 1861–1898* (Austin: University of Texas Press, 1953); Richard C. Overton, *Burlington West* (Cambridge: Harvard University Press, 1965); Robert G. Athearn, *Union Pacific Country* (Chicago: Rand McNally, 1971; paperbound ed., Lincoln: University of Nebraska Press, 1976); Henrietta M. Larson, *Jay Cooke, Private Banker* (Cambridge: Harvard University Press, 1936); James B. Hedges, *Henry Villard and the Railways of the Northwest* (New York, 1930); G. T. Clark, *Leland Stanford* (Stanford: Stanford University Press, 1930); Albro Martin, *James J.*

Hill and the Opening of the Northwest (New York: Oxford University Press, 1976); David Lavender, *Collis P. Huntington, the Great Persuader* (Garden City, N.Y.: Doubleday, 1970).

28. Robert S. Henry, "The Railroad Land Grant Legend in American History Texts," *Mississippi Valley Historical Review* 32 (1945): 171–94; David Maldwyn Ellis, "The Forfeiture of Railroad Land Grants, 1867–1894," *Mississippi Valley Historical Review* 33 (1946): 27–60; Ellis, "The Oregon and California Railroad Land Grant, 1866–1945," *Pacific Northwest Quarterly* 39 (1948): 253–83; Paul W. Gates, "The Railroad Land-Grant Legend," *Journal of Economic History* 14 (1954): 143–46; William S. Greever, "A Comparison of Land-Grant Policies," *Agricultural History* 25 (1951): 83–90; Greever, *Arid Domain: The Santa Fe Railroad and Its Western Land Grant* (Stanford: Stanford University Press, 1954); Ray H. Mattison, "The Burlington Tax Controversy in Nebraska Over Federal Land Grants," *Nebraska History* 28 (1947): 110–31; John B. Rae, "The Great Northern's Land Grant," *Journal of Economic History* 12 (1952): 140–45; Ralph N. Traxler, "The Texas and Pacific Railroad Land Grants: A Comparison of Land Grant Policies of the United States and Texas," *Southwestern Historical Quarterly* 61 (1958): 359–70; Robert W. Fogel, *The Union Pacific Railroad: A Case of Premature Enterprise* (Baltimore: Johns Hopkins Press, 1960).

29. Lloyd J. Mercer, "Rates of Return for Land-Grant Railroads: The Central Pacific System," *Journal of Economic History* 30 (1970): 602–26; John F. Due, "Dangers of the Use of the Subsidation Technique: The Central Oregon Wagon Road Grants," *Land Economics* 46 (1970): 105–17; Lloyd J. Mercer, "Building Ahead of Demand: Some Evidence for the Land Grant Railroads," *Journal of Economic History* 34 (1974): 492–500; William R. Petrowski, "Kansas City to Denver to Cheyenne: Pacific Railroad Construction Costs and Profits," *Business History Review* 48 (1974): 206–24; Heywood Fleisig, "The Central Pacific Railroad and the Railroad's Land Grant Controversy," *Journal of Economic History* 35 (1975): 552–66; J. Hayden Boyd and Gary M. Walton, "The Social Savings from Nineteenth-Century Rail Passenger Services," *Explorations in Economic History* 9 (1972): 233–54.

30. Robert H. Wiebe, *Businessmen and Reform: A Study of the Progressive Movement* (Cambridge: Harvard University Press, 1962; paperbound ed., Chicago: Quadrangle, 1968); and Wiebe, *The Search for Order, 1877–1920* (New York: Hill and Wang, 1967; paperbound ed., Westport, Conn.: Greenwood, 1980); Gabriel Kolko, *Railroads and Regulation, 1877–1916* (Princeton: Princeton University Press, 1965; paperbound ed., New York: Norton,

1970); Albro Martin, *Enterprise Denied: Origins of the Decline of American Railroads, 1897-1917* (New York: Columbia University Press, 1971; paperbound ed., 1979).

31. David G. Taylor, "Thomas Ewing, Jr. and the Origins of the Kansas Pacific Railway Company," *Kansas Historical Quarterly* 42 (1976): 155-79; H. Roger Grant, "Frank A. Seiberling and the Formative Years of the Midland Continental Railroad, 1912-1920," *North Dakota History* 43 (1976): 28-36; Edwin C. Bearss and Bruce M. White, "George Brackett's Wagon Road," *Minnesota History* 45 (1976): 43-57.

32. Richard V. Francaviglia, "Some Comments on the Historic and Geographic Importance of Railroads in Minnesota," *Minnesota History* 33 (1972): 58-62; John S. Cochran, "Economic Importance of Early Transcontinental Railroads: Pacific Northwest," *Oregon Historical Quarterly* 71 (1970): 27-98; W. H. Hutchinson, "Southern Pacific: Myth and Reality," *California Historical Quarterly* 48 (1969): 325-34.

33. Alice Osborne, "Rails Across the Tundra," *The Alaska Journal* 2 (1972): 2-12; William H. Wilson, "Ahead of Times: The Alaskan Railroad and Tourism, 1924-1941," *The Alaska Journal* 7 (1977): 18-24; Lyman L. Woodman, "The Trans-Canadian, Alaska and Western Railways," *The Alaska Journal* 4 (1974): 194-202; William H. Wilson, "The Alaska Railroad and the Agricultural Frontier," *Agricultural History* 50 (1978): 263-79.

34. Robert Higgs, "Railroad Rates and the Populist Uprising," *Agricultural History* 44 (1970): 291-97; Ross R. Cotroneo, "Timber Marketing by the Northern Pacific Railway, 1920-1952," *Journal of Forest History* 20 (1976): 120-31; M. Guy Bishop, "Building Railroads for the Kingdom: The Career of John W. Young, 1867-1891," *Utah Historical Quarterly* 48 (1980): 66-80.

35. Philip P. Mason, *The League of American Wheelmen and the Good Roads Movement, 1880-1905* (Ann Arbor: University of Michigan Press, 1958); John B. Rae, *The Road and Car in American Life* (Cambridge: M.I.T. Press, 1971); Joe McCarthy, "The Lincoln Highway," *American Heritage* 25 (1974): 32-37, 89; Thomas H. Peterson, Jr., "Danger: Sound Klaxon— The Automobile Comes to Territorial Arizona," *The Journal of Arizona History* 15 (1974): 249-68.

36. J. W. Gregory, *The Story of the Road from the Beginning to the Present Day* (London: A and C Black, 1938); Jean Labatut and Wheaton J. Lane (eds.), *Highways in Our National Life* (Princeton: Princeton University Press, 1950); T. H. MacDonald, "History of the Development of Road Building in the United States," *Transactions of the American Society of Civil*

Engineers 93 (1928); Philip P. Mason, *A History of American Roads* (Chicago: Rand McNally, 1967); Mark H. Rose, *Interstate: Express Highway Politics, 1941-1956* (Lawrence: Regents Press of the University of Kansas, 1979); U.S. Department of Transportation, Federal Highway Administration, *America's Highways 1776-1976: A History of the Federal Aid Program* (Washington, D.C.: Government Printing Office, 1976).

37. George Kirkham Jarvis, *The Diffusion of the Automobile in the United States, 1895-1969* (Ann Arbor: University of Michigan, 1972); Michael L. Berger, *The Devil Wagon in God's Country: The Automobile and Social Change in Rural America, 1893-1929* (Hamden, Conn.: Archon, 1979); Warren James Belasco, *Americans on the Road: From Autocamp to Motel, 1910-1945* (Cambridge: M.I.T. Press, 1979).

38. David O. Remley, "The Crooked Road: Oral History of the Alaska Highway," *The Alaska Journal* 4 (1974): 113-21; Remley, *Crooked Road: The Story of the Alaska Highway* (New York: McGraw-Hill, 1976); Jack N. Barkenbus, "The Trans-Peninsular Highway: A New Era for Baja California," *Journal of Inter-American Studies and World Affairs* 16 (1974): 259-73.

39. Eli Bail, "California by Motor Stage," *California Historical Society Quarterly* 55 (1976): 306-25; Paul B. Smith, "Highway Planning in California's Mother Lode: The Changing Townscape of Auburn and Nevada City," *California History* 59 (1980): 204-21; Larry D. Givens, "The California Highway Commission and the Truckee River Route," *Nevada Historical Society Quarterly* 17 (1974): 153-64.

40. R. E. G. Davies, *Airlines of the United States Since 1914* (London: Putnam Co., 1972); Carroll V. Glines, *The Saga of the Air Mail* (Princeton, N.J.: D. Van Nostrand Co., 1968); Walter F. Wacht, *The Domestic Transportation Network in the United States,* University of Chicago Department of Geography Research Paper No. 154 (Chicago, 1974); Carl Solberg, *Conquest of the Skies: A History of Commercial Aviation in America* (Boston: Little, Brown, 1979).

41. Kenneth M. Johnson, *Aerial California* (Los Angeles: Dawson's Book Shop, 1961); *Wings Over the West: The Story of America's Oldest Airline* (n.p., 1951).

42. Gerald M. Adams, "The Air Age Comes to Wyoming," *Annals of Wyoming* 52 (1980): 18-29; Jeanne Harbottle, "Clyde Wann, Father of Yukon Aviation," *The Alaska Journal* 3 (1973): 237-45; Harbottle, "White Pass Aviation and Its Rivals," *The Alaska Journal* 4 (1974): 233-41; Mary M. Worthylake, "Pacific International Airways," *The Alaska Journal* 2 (1972): 41-48.

43. A recent issue of the *Red River Valley Historical Review* (Summer

1981), entirely devoted to "Highways of Adventure: Transportation Frontiers in Oklahoma," may indicate a renewal of interest in western transportation. The ten contributions to this volume follow the organization of this chapter, with Arrell M. Gibson discussing the waterways of Oklahoma, followed by six articles emphasizing various land routes across the future state, the coming of the railroads, and finally the highways. W. Edwin Derrick and James Smallwood organized and edited the volume. William P. Corbett's "Politics and Pavement: The Formative Years of the Oklahoma State Highway Department" is thoroughly researched in archival materials and is a significant contribution to scholarship.

Chapter Eight

Kenneth N. Owens

Government and Politics in the Nineteenth-Century West

Western government and politics: the phrase defines a research field that has interested many first-rate scholars, but a field whose boundaries are not yet clearly charted. At its center, all will agree, must be placed the history of the West's major political institutions, the agencies of territorial, state, and federal government. Beyond these central concerns, the lines of definition become blurred by themes that lead in every direction. Political concerns and political influences in the West, perhaps more than elsewhere in the American nation, seemed to pervade virtually every sector of social and economic activity during the nineteenth century. Indian affairs and land policy, labor movements and the temperance movement, the campaigns for government subsidy of silver mining, reclamation, and irrigation, the anti-Mormon movement and the anti-Chinese movement, social banditry, the conservation movement, the women's suffrage movement—all these subjects and many others can be found on this field's topical borderlands.

New scholarship may help to draw the boundaries more precisely. Meanwhile the puzzled historiographer is left to make some selection of topics, however arbitrary. This essay deals only with government and politics under Anglo-American authority, excluding any comparative view of the colonial governments that preceded Anglo-American rule in the West. It excludes from consideration such broad areas of public administration as Indian affairs and natural resources policy, covered for the most part by other essays in this volume. At the risk of some overlap with Richard Maxwell Brown's essay on western violence and Frederick Luebke's treatment of western ethnic and minority history, this chapter does give attention to political violence, to ethnic issues in western politics, and particularly to works that treat violence and ethnicity together as political subjects.

Overall, the essay is organized according to three main themes: first, proto-governments and proto-politics; second, the formal institutions of government; and third, the political protest and reform movements of the 1880s and 1890s. This organization, with appropriate topical subdivisions, establishes an approximate chronological sequence, from the expansionist era of the 1840s to the decade of Populist agitation at the century's end.

Western proto-governments, official and unofficial, were creatures of expediency: short-lived, ad hoc arrangements, contrived to meet an immediate need. Following the 1846 conquest of New Mexico and California, the U.S. Army formed one type of proto-government as a means to provide temporary legal and political authority for civilian populations in these areas. There is but one comparative examination of frontier military rule, a 1904 Columbia University Ph.D. dissertation by David Y. Thomas. In this outdated study, Thomas emphasized the problems of military administration, reaching conclusions that were critical both of the army's policies and the leadership it provided during the earliest stage of western political growth.[1]

The two modern historians who write with greatest authority about New Mexico's territorial politics, Howard R. Lamar and Robert W. Larson, are scarcely less critical. In Lamar's *The Far Southwest,* a magisterial treatment of New Mexico, Colorado, Arizona, and Utah territories, the chapter on the conquest era concludes that American politicians cooperated with the army to establish a military dictatorship in New Mexico. Larson, in *New Mexico's Quest for Statehood,* describes the efforts of local politicians to substitute civilian for military rule. He portrays the 1850 statehood movement, which Congress rejected, partly as a reaction to military autocracy and partly as an outgrowth of factional rivalries and personal ambitions.[2]

Theodore Grivas, the principal historian of army rule in California, finds less reason to be critical. In a volume entitled *Military Governments in California, 1846–1850,* Grivas contends that military control was successful in California, just as in New Mexico, since the army held the territory, maintained order, and supplied government where it was otherwise lacking. Despite some popular outcry, he declares, California's people were never seriously oppressed or mistreated by the military authorities. By implication a revisionist argument, Grivas's claims may be balanced against the view that early statehood for California became necessary in part because of popular opposition to military government. This view is presented for example in the widely used study by William Henry Ellison, *A Self-Governing Dominion: California, 1849-1860.*[3]

Before Congress authorized a legitimate territorial authority, another kind of proto-government, the so-called squatter governments, appeared in many western areas. These temporary commonwealths, sometimes labeled provisional governments, preceded territorial rule in at least nine different places. Similar in origin, they shared a generally similar history. In districts of settlement that already were secure within the boundaries of the United States, they served merely as political devices, a kind of tactical tool to prod Congress toward the early creation of a new federal territory. Once Congress acted, each faded away with scarcely a trace.

Because their objectives were limited and short-term, and because their sponsors seldom left documentary records, these provisional governments have attracted scant historical attention. A notable exception will be found in the writings of Howard Lamar. In *Dakota Territory,* the first of his territorial histories, Lamar supplies a highly informative chapter on Dakota's episode of squatter rule. His subsequent major study, *The Far Southwest,* offers similar accounts of the Colorado movement to create Jefferson Territory, Arizona's self-constituted territorial administration, and the Mormon campaign to establish a State of Deseret prior to the creation of Utah Territory. Another example of squatter government is described briefly by Russell R. Elliott in his *History of Nevada* under the apt title "Political Chaos, 1857-61."[4]

In the Oregon country different circumstances produced a distinctive movement for self-government during the 1830s and early 1840s. An area of international rivalry, held then under joint occupancy with Great Britain, the region was also the scene of controversies among different groups of American settlers. The customary historical view, emphasizing the international issue, is presented in Dorothy O. Johansen and Charles M. Gates, *Empire of the Columbia.* After an exhaustive reexamination of the sources, Robert J. Loewenberg argues for another interpretation in *Equality on the Oregon Frontier: Jason Lee and the Methodist Mission, 1834-43.* Loewenberg, narrating the role of Lee and his Methodist community, stresses the local issues that the makers of the provisional government meant to compromise and ends by calling the organization "a nongovernment or even an antigovernment."[5]

The Anglo-Texan independence movement, a proto-government that repudiated the authority of the Mexican Republic, brought still more distinctive, significant consequences. In the sequel, of course, the Texans' experiment in self-rule became the Lone Star Republic and finally the twenty-eighth state of the Union. An extensive literature awaits the student of this movement, beginning with Stanley Siegel's carefully researched volume, *A Political History of the Texas Republic*. Important also is the 1951 series of lectures by William C. Binkley published as *The Texas Revolution*. Other essential titles include Llerena B. Friend's biography of the republic's first citizen, *Sam Houston, the Great Designer;* a now classic study by William Ransom Hogan, *The Texas Republic: A Social and Economic History*; and for the breadth of its perspective, the stimulating essay by historical geographer D. W. Meinig, *Imperial Texas*.[6]

Throughout the West, the spirit of voluntary association at the local level gave rise to a variety of proto-government organizations, formed to meet special needs. Interesting comparisons might be drawn, for example, between land claim associations, mining district associations, the range associations of western ranchers, and early irrigation associations. Organizations of this type have received no more than passing notice in recent writings, with one exception. The transient form of proto-government in overland wagon trains on the Oregon and California trails has become the subject of three recent works: *The Plains Across* by John D. Unruh, Jr., *Women and Men on the Overland Trail* by John Mack Faragher, and John Phillip Reid's *Law for the Elephant: Property and Social Behavior on the Overland Trail*. The most pertinent of the three, Reid's study demonstrates the urge toward order and security of property that inspired many voluntary associations in western frontier communities. Serious students will also want to see in this regard John Willard Hurst's 1956 publication, *Law and the Conditions of Freedom in the Nineteenth-Century United States*, an outstanding interpretive work.[7]

Claims associations, wagon train law, and squatter governments, as well as the other forms of western proto-government, all had origins within the Anglo-American social and political tradition. So too did a series of popular frontier movements to exclude Hispanic, black, and Asian peoples from a role as social equals, and to deny these peoples access to political power or economic opportunity in the West. These popular movements became a pioneer form of proto-politics. On the part of Anglo-Americans they expressed short-term opportunism, immediate political tactics, and longstanding cultural prejudices. At times these movements led to riot and mob rule; at other times they operated within a quasi-legal framework. But the objective was similar in every case: to intimidate and victimize the members of a specific group, set apart by their racial or ethnic identity, and to make of them a political underclass, deprived of power and lacking the legal or political means to seek remedy against outrage.

From the era of Anglo-American conquest during the Mexican War, Hispanic peoples became the target of frontier proto-politics throughout the Southwest. Leonard Pitt's detailed original study, *The Decline of the Californios*, documents the anti-Hispanic campaign that reshaped economic and political power in California between 1846 and 1890. Two perceptive recent works provide a closer regional analysis, utilizing quantitative as well as narrative sources: Albert Camarillo's *Chicanos in a Changing Society*, an account of the Hispanic peoples of the Santa Barbara and southern California regions from 1848 to 1930; and Richard Griswold del Castillo's *The Los Angeles Barrio, 1850–1890: A Social History*. In both these volumes, as in Pitt's earlier account, there appears abundant evidence that the Anglo-American legal and political system served as a powerful weapon for dispossessing and subordinating Hispanic Californians. But Camarillo and Griswold del Castillo both emphasize as well the continuing vitality of Hispanic communities in southern California.

The corresponding experiences of Hispanos in Texas, New Mexico, and Arizona have yet to find their historians, although recent studies reveal some parts of the record. In *Los Primeros Pobladores*, Frances Swadesh describes the impact of the American conquest and later events upon the Hispanic communities in the New Mexico–Colorado borderlands, the area she designates as the Ute frontier. Roxanne Dunbar Ortiz examines in careful detail the Anglo-American assault upon the land-based economy of both Native Americans and Hispanic New Mexicans in *Roots of Resistance: Land Tenure in New Mexico, 1680–1980*. The proto-politics of ethnic relations is also summarized in Mario Barrera's *Race and Class in the Southwest*, a rather polemical book that purports to describe the formation of the Hispanic working class.[8]

Black migration into the West, both before and after the Civil War, likewise prompted strong assertions of white privilege. Eugene H. Berwanger's volume, *The Frontier Against Slavery: Western Anti-Negro Prejudice and the Slavery Extension Controversy*, relates the pre–Civil War campaign to exclude black people from the western territories and states. Berwanger summarizes the exclusion movement in the constitutional conventions of California, Oregon, and Kansas, and refers to similar efforts in Utah, Colorado, New Mexico, and Nebraska. Rudolph Lapp's 1977 publication, *Blacks in Gold*

Rush California, gives a detailed account of the struggle by black pioneers to avoid repression in this one frontier state. Briefer coverage will be found in W. Sherman Savage, *Blacks in the West,* which includes a chapter entitled "The Fight for Civil Rights."[9]

Chinese immigrants into California and adjacent areas became a third group to encounter popular hostility and political enmity. Among modern accounts, Gunther Barth's *Bitter Strength,* describing the Chinese experience in the United States from 1850 to 1870, offers a general summary with a chapter entitled simply "Strive." Two other monographs by non-Chinese scholars add to our knowledge: Elmer C. Sandmeyer, *The Anti-Chinese Movement in California,* and Alexander Saxton, *The Indispensable Enemy: Labor and the Anti-Chinese Movement in California.* Because federal law barred the naturalization of Chinese immigrants, their lack of civil rights made them vulnerable targets for legal and extralegal discrimination. Chinese laborers, lacking the law's protection and harshly exploited by Chinese merchant capitalists, were left to take the role of mudsill in California's pioneer society. But additional studies are needed to document the internal political history of the West's Chinese communities.[10]

For Anglo-Americans of the pioneer generation, the new conditions of western society often reinforced their old cultural and ethnic prejudices. Consequently the Anglo-American majority found ways to limit or exclude Hispanic, black, and Chinese minorities from participating equally in the West's political development. Economic discrimination and legal disabilities went hand in hand with the lack of access to political power. On the other hand, according to a few recent publications, Irish, Italian, and Jewish immigrants did not find the extreme kinds of prejudice in western regions or the bitter political enmity that they commonly faced in the eastern United States.[11] Western proto-politics created political structures that were far less than fully democratic for blacks, Chinese, and Hispanics, yet political life in the West proved more open for European ethnic groups than in eastern regions.

The American territorial system provided a framework of federal administration and national supervision of politics for the organized territories of the United States. A system of temporary colonial rule, it extended in time to every part of the American West except only Texas and California, which bypassed territorial status and entered the Union directly as states. In a few areas favored by rapid population growth or unique political circumstances, the territorial period was brief and the transition to statehood a goal soon achieved by local political leaders. Elsewhere, the period of territorial pupilage (to borrow a nineteenth-century term) lasted for decade after decade. Overall, territorial government remained the established political form for a large part of the West from the 1850s until the 1890s.

The history of territorial administration and frontier politics attracted little attention during the generation of Turner and the generation of Webb, when western historians devoted their attention mainly to social and economic themes. Three gifted researchers began to remedy this neglect during the 1930s and 1940s. First Clarence E. Carter, then Earl Pomeroy and W. Turrentine Jackson demonstrated that the National Archives and related depositories held rich collections of manuscript sources for territorial history.

In 1931, shortly after the creation of the National Archives, Carter accepted a position with the fledgling agency to compile, organize, and begin editing that series of distinguished volumes entitled *The Territorial Papers of the United States.* Carter and his small staff made the project a landmark for the development of editorial practice and the publication of primary historical sources. To sum up the historical insights he had gained in the course of this work, in 1948 Carter contributed to the *South Atlantic Quarterly* an article entitled "Colonialism in [the] Continental United States," his appraisal of the territorial system as a bureaucratic entity.[12]

While Carter was concentrating upon the materials for the early history of the territorial system, especially the territories of the Old Northwest and the Old Southwest, Earl Pomeroy began to investigate federal records related to the territories of the Far West. From these sources came a 1939 Ph.D. dissertation that, in revised form, won the Beveridge Prize and came to print in 1947 under the title *The Territories and the United States, 1861–1890: Studies in Colonial Administration.* Before this volume appeared, Pomeroy published in 1944 an article of great importance, "The Territory as a Frontier Institution." The territorial system, he explained in this interpretive summary, became more than a device for colonial rule. It served in frontier regions as an agency of Americanization, aiding settlement, promoting self-government, and extending American values and ideals.[13]

These publications by Pomeroy and Carter defined a federal perspective for territorial history, emphasizing the positive accomplishments of the federal territorial system. A second, rather different view also emerged during the 1940s, appearing in a series of articles by W. Turrentine Jackson. Not concerned primarily with administrative history, Jackson found in the National Archives a splendid body of sources for the study of western pioneer politics in the territories. The result was a series of articles that described political episodes in Idaho, Dakota, Montana, and Wyoming territories, illustrating many of the vagaries in federal policies and the failures in federal leadership. To these studies Jackson added another with great historiographical significance, "Territorial Papers of Wyoming in the National Archives," important because it first described a class of materials that would entice other scholars to specialize in territorial history.[14]

The two distinct approaches to territorial history that appeared in these early works, the federal perspective taken by Pomeroy and Carter and the territorial perspective adopted by Jackson, have remained basic to all later territorial studies. For the first, one other interpretive essay should be grouped with the writings of Pomeroy and Carter in defining the federal government's role in western territorial history: William M. Neil, "The American Territorial System Since the Civil War: A Summary Analysis."[15]

The influence of federal agencies and the impact of federal administrative programs upon the western territories still await a comprehensive assessment. The possibilities are shown by Thomas G. Alexander's outstanding regional study, *A Clash of Interests: Interior Department and Mountain West, 1863–1896.* For the territories of Idaho, Utah, and Arizona, Alexander examines federal activities in three major policy areas that fell within the Interior Department's administrative realm: territorial policy, land policy, and Indian policy. A related title, less comprehensive in scope, is the carefully researched volume by Victor Westphall, *The Public Domain in New Mexico, 1854–1891.* Both of these studies document the strains imposed upon federal efforts by the tug and pull of regional interests, and by the steady pressure of western politicians seeking to control the federal patronage.[16]

Local battles over patronage and political influence were the very life's blood of territorial government, a fact repeatedly emphasized by works that examine western political history from a territorial perspective. Following W. Turrentine Jackson's earlier articles, Howard Lamar demonstrated the potential for a narrative political history of a territory in his 1956 publication, *Dakota Territory, 1861–1889: A Study in Frontier Politics.* This volume, which displays a broadly cynical attitude toward Dakota's federal appointees and local officeholders alike, has become a design model for other studies. Lamar followed this model in his later work, *The Far Southwest,* which brings together in one volume the separate histories of New Mexico, Arizona, Utah, and Colorado territories. Jay J. Wagoner supplements Lamar's account with his more detailed investigation, *Arizona Territory, 1863–1912: A Political History.* Another volume in this same genre is Lewis Gould's *Wyoming: A Political History, 1868–1912,* a splendid summary and political analysis that emphasizes the role of Wyoming's most successful political entrepreneur of the era, Francis E. Warren.[17]

In the category of territorial histories, one more work should be singled out for special mention. Clark C. Spence, a well-known scholar who has published widely in many areas of western history, brought out in 1975 a major study, *Territorial Politics and Government in Montana, 1864–1889.* More successfully than any earlier territorial account, Spence's volume unites political narrative with a clear, detailed analysis of the local territorial administration, its operations and its costs and benefits in this one western locale. Spence's treatment of territorial Montana should set a new standard for students of pioneer government in the West.[18]

Territorial political movements also receive narrative treatment in a number of substantial topical studies. For example, Robert Larson's exacting investigation, *New Mexico's Quest for Statehood,* portrays the vicissitudes of territorial political life when lagging growth and partisan sentiment made it impossible to achieve statehood. The manipulation of religious and social intolerance for political purposes sets the theme for a detailed, balanced study by Merle W. Wells, *Anti-Mormonism in Idaho, 1872–1892,* an account of the political movement that dominated Idaho's party struggles through the earliest years of statehood. A related work by Gustive O. Larson, *The "Americanization" of Utah for Statehood,* centers on the conflict over polygamy and the accommodation by Mormon church leaders that finally made possible Utah's admission to the Union. Another impressive account is Danny Goble's *Progressive Oklahoma: The Making of a New Kind of State.* A broadly conceived social, economic, and political history, Goble's study describes the growth of Oklahoma from the 1889 land rush through the territorial period, concluding with an analysis of the 1906 constitutional convention and the first state election.[19]

Though we still lack full-scale political histories for Oregon and Washington territories, biographical and topical studies help fill the gap. In *Joe Lane of Oregon,* James E. Hendrickson traces the career of the man who dominated Oregon politics as the first territorial governor, organizer of the Democratic "Salem Clique," delegate, and later U.S. senator, until his prosouthern stance brought his political ruin in 1860. The 1979 biography by Kent D. Richards, *Isaac I. Stevens: Young Man in a Hurry,* offers a fresh, generally judicious view of Lane's protégé and ally in Washington Territory, a figure at the storm center of that territory's political turbulence from his arrival as governor in 1853 until his departure in 1861. The political crisis of the late 1850s in Oregon and Washington is described in the 1955 volume by Robert

W. Johannsen, *Frontier Politics and the Sectional Conflict,* an account drawn largely from newspaper sources that emphasizes the impact of national issues upon local party alignments. For a later political era in Washington Territory, Alan Hynding adds to our knowledge with his biographical account, *The Public Life of Eugene Semple,* describing the career of a regional businessman and promoter who became governor during the Cleveland administration, but who could not achieve the sort of leadership role earlier taken by Lane and Stevens.[20]

Biographical studies also supplement territorial histories for the Southwest. Victor Westphall's wide-ranging account, *Thomas Benton Catron and His Era,* presents a sympathetic portrayal of New Mexico's most capable and rapacious political leader during the territorial era. No less sympathetic is Oscar D. Lambert's life of Catron's close associate, *Stephen Benton Elkins: American Foursquare.* Lawrence R. Murphy describes a different sort of career in *Frontier Crusader—William F. M. Arny.* A Free Soil colonist in Kansas Territory, Arny moved on to New Mexico, where he spent most of his career in the Indian service as an advocate of humanitarian reform policies but also served two terms as territorial secretary.[21]

Colorado's first two territorial governors, each renowned outside political circles, have found modern biographers. Thomas L. Karnes is the author of *William Gilpin: Western Nationalist,* a life of the short-term governor, adventurer, editor, and theorist of western expansion who has been called America's first geopolitician. Gilpin's successor was a more practical man whose career is recounted sympathetically in Harry E. Kelsey, Jr., *Frontier Capitalist: The Life of John Evans.* A Chicago-area physician, land speculator, railroad promoter, and philanthropist, prominent in both the Methodist church and the Republican party, Evans carried to Colorado a prestigious reputation that failed to survive his term as territorial governor. Another notable Colorado biography is the study by Elmer Ellis, *Henry Moore Teller, Defender of the West,* a classic portrayal of the lawyer, mining entrepreneur, and political craftsman whose success during the territorial period made him Colorado's first U.S. senator, a position he kept from 1876 until his retirement in 1909.[22]

The judicial branch of government in the territories has attracted only slight attention. This subject is best introduced by William Baskerville Hamilton's erudite essay on the nature and place of territorial courts in the federal court system included in his volume *Anglo-American Law on the Frontier: Thomas Rodney and His Territorial Cases.* Although this study deals mainly with Mississippi Territory, Hamilton's constitutional and legal analysis applies as well to the courts in the western territories. Interested scholars will find an examplary history of the territorial courts in John D. W. Guice, *The Rocky Mountain Bench,* a nicely designed examination of the territorial judges and the accomplishments of their courts in Colorado, Montana, and Wyoming. Guice makes a persuasive case, discarding the carpetbagger stereotype, for valuing the contributions of the territorial courts toward the elaboration of a western legal system. A less convincing argument on behalf of local justice of the peace courts appears in John Wunder, *Inferior Courts, Superior Justice,* an investigation of the J.P. system in Washington Territory.[23]

As partners of the territorial judiciary, the federal marshals had the more perilous role in developing the frontier legal system. Against the mass of popular writings, incorporating romantic fantasies and unsubstantiated oral traditions, may be set but two substantial, straightforward historical treatments. The more general work is Frank Richard Prassel's informative volume, *The Western Peace Officer,* which describes local, territorial, and state law agencies during the nineteenth century. A more detailed account of federal lawmen appears in Larry D. Ball's regional study, *The United States Marshals of New Mexico and Arizona Territories, 1846–1912.* Ball's book, based on massive research, helps to restore a measure of sober historical truth to our understanding of the federal marshals' place as a pioneer law force.[24]

Western territorial history, this survey indicates, has become a lively topic for scholarship during the past two decades. The result has been, in Gene Gressley's phrase, some of the most able historiography on the West. But few authors thus far have ventured any attempt at synthesis or general analysis of territorial history. Despite the promise implicit in the title, Ray C. Colton's *The Civil War in the Western Territories* concerns only the former Mexican territories in the Southwest and deals only casually with their political history. In his recent work *The West and Reconstruction,* Eugene H. Berwanger deals with the issue of black suffrage in the territories and the western states, and he includes a one-chapter summary of western politics during the Reconstruction era. For the most part, however, the volume concentrates on western interest and western opinion related to national political events in this period. Although the topics are attractive, no one has yet undertaken a full comparative account of the 1850s political crisis in the territories, the struggle for political control between Radical Republicans and Home-Rule Democrats during the 1860s and 1870s, or the campaign for territorial reform led by the Cleveland administration during the 1880s.[25]

A solitary effort to deduce some broad, unifying traits in the territories' political history may be found in Kenneth N. Owens's "Pattern and Structure in Western Territorial Politics." This essay maintains that every frontier territory displayed first a pattern of chaotic factionalism in its politics, then developed a system of either one-party, two-party, or no-party rule. The author describes the emergence of these systems in individual territories, relating them to common structures of western social and political demography.[26]

In his introduction to the 1969 reprint edition of *The Territories and the United States,* Earl Pomeroy commented on the many additional topics he would like to include in his study, were he to write it afresh. His list, representing more than enough work to fill an additional volume or two, marked the progress of territorial studies between 1947 and 1969—a progress greatly expedited by Pomeroy's original work. And since 1969 other historians have continued to advance our knowledge of territorial history at a very respectable rate. But there are still many topics open to investigation, many problems left to be solved. Additional political narratives need to be written. Potential subjects for biographies abound in the territories. Detailed administrative studies are required to fill out our knowledge of the interplay between federal and territorial agencies. Some determined, ambitious scholar should give us an appraisal of territorial voting patterns, based in part upon statistical analysis of voting data that has not yet been collected. A related project might be the analysis of leadership elites in the territories. And, underlying many of these kinds of topics, there remains the problem of discovering how various economic and social interest groups managed to influence public policy and achieve power over the West's pioneer governments. Because the evidence is abundant to address these themes, we may expect that territorial studies will remain for many years a premier field in western history.

Texas and California, the two western states that bypassed federal territorial status during the nineteenth century, each have a unique historiography. Texas was the only western region where black racial slavery had become firmly established prior to the Civil War. In 1861 Texas seceded from the Union, of course, and joined the Confederacy. Four years later, when the Civil War ended, Texas began an era of political reconstruction that lasted until 1876. Thus the state's political history often took a more southern than western direction during the nineteenth century. And Texas historians during the twentieth century have continued to reflect in their writings many of the same strong sentiments, the political and social passions that unsettled the southern region's political life before 1900.

The years from statehood through the end of Reconstruction are the subject of Ernest Wallace's political synthesis, *Texas in Turmoil: The Saga of Texas, 1849-1875*. Based partly on extensive primary research, this work may be classed as a history of public affairs, emphasizing government and Indian relations. No full-scale modern studies supplement Wallace's account either for the antebellum period or the Civil War era, but Texas historiography is rich in Reconstruction studies. John L. Waller's biography, *Colossal Hamilton of Texas*, describes the career of Andrew Jackson Hamilton, a Texas Unionist who became the state's military governor and then served as provisional governor from 1865 to mid-1866. The carefully detailed volume by W. C. Nunn, *Texas Under the Carpetbaggers*, concentrates on the administration of Edmund J. Davis, a Texas Radical who served as governor between 1870 and 1874. In addition to narrating the political events, Nunn describes the state's economic and social history during the closing years of Reconstruction. Another work by Ernest Wallace should also be noted, *The Howling of the Coyotes: Reconstruction Efforts to Divide Texas*. This book narrates the abortive movement by disaffected Republican Radicals to create a separate state of West Texas in 1868-69, a movement that failed for lack of popular support and indifference in Congress.[27]

Three outstanding studies document the post-Reconstruction era in Texas political history. Heading the list is Alwyn Barr's fine work, *Reconstruction to Reform: Texas Politics, 1876-1906*, which makes a discerning analysis of the economic, ethnic, religious, and personal interests that shaped political events during this era. Second is Lawrence D. Rice's perceptive account of the state's largest minority group during this period, *The Negro in Texas, 1874-1900*. With an emphasis upon politics, Rice traces the declining status of Texas blacks from the end of Reconstruction through the abridgment of the franchise and the advent of Jim Crow laws by the 1890s. Third is Robert C. Cotner's volume, *James Stephen Hogg: A Biography*, which examines the career of the Democratic reform governor who held office from 1891 to 1895. The author portrays Hogg, quite believably, as a Progressive leader comparable to Robert LaFollette of Wisconsin.[28]

California's early political history has attracted surprisingly little attention in recent decades. For an introductory summary, researchers should consult the cooperative volume put together under the general editorship of Royce D. Delmatier, Clarence F. McIntosh, and Earl G. Waters, *The Rumble of California Politics, 1848-1970*. The first four chapters in this volume concern the state's political development during the nineteenth century. Earl Pomeroy provides a sound interpretive appraisal of the pre–Civil War period in his article "California, 1846–1860: The Politics of a Representative Frontier State." An impressionistic outline appears in a volume entitled *The Governors of California* by H. Brett Melendy and Benjamin F. Gilbert, which offers biographical sketches of each governor and a brief description of each gubernatorial administration. More analytical is the nicely crafted study by R. Hal Williams, *The Democratic Party and California Politics, 1880–1896*. A product of meticulous research, this book includes a notable treatment of the divisions among the Democratic faithful during the Cleveland administration, and it adds a trenchant reappraisal of the Southern Pacific Railroad's political activities during the 1890s. In their volume *Political Change in California*, Michael P. Rogin and John L. Shover apply the methods of political analysis derived from the works of V. O. Key, Jr. Their first chapter examines in detail the election of 1896 and the pattern of voter realignments in California.[29]

As in other areas, biographical studies enrich California's political historiography. A famous personal and political quarrel of the 1850s is recounted in the biographies of the two principals: A. Russell Buchanan, *David S. Terry of California: Dueling Judge*, and David A. Williams, *David C. Broderick: A Political Portrait*. Political life in the gold rush era receives attention also in Carl Brent Swisher, *Stephen J. Field, Craftsman of the Law*, a biography of the Connecticut lawyer who became California's chief justice, then chief justice of the U.S. Supreme Court. California's Republican Civil War governor, later railroad magnate and U.S. senator, is the subject of Norman E. Tutorow's *Leland Stanford, Man of Many Careers*. The life of the state's Populist "boss" is briefly sketched by Harold F. Taggart in "Thomas Vincent Cator: Populist Leader of California," in the *California Historical Society Quarterly*. An informative, fascinating examination of local politics appears in the recent publication by William A. Bullough, *The Blind Boss and His City: Christopher Augustine Buckley and Nineteenth-Century San Francisco*, a skilled portrayal of the Irish saloonkeeper who rose to be the chief power broker in the bay city's Democratic party during the 1880s.[30]

Aside from these publications related to Texas and California, modern scholarship has produced few studies of western state government and politics for the years prior to the 1890s. Substantial summaries of nineteenth-century political events appear in some recent one-volume surveys of state history, including William F. Zornow's *Kansas: A History of the Jayhawk State*, James C. Olson's *History of Nebraska*, and Russell R. Elliott's *History of*

Nevada. Territorial and state history receives a thorough treatment in other one-volume works such as Herbert S. Schell's *History of South Dakota,* Elwyn B. Robinson's *History of North Dakota,* T. A. Larson's *History of Wyoming,* and an especially distinguished volume by Michael P. Malone and Richard P. Roeder, *Montana: A History of Two Centuries.*[31]

Biographical studies of men who took part in western state politics prior to the 1890s are extremely rare. One example is Francis P. Weisenburger's 1965 publication, *Idol of the West: The Fabulous Career of Rollin Mallory Daggett,* which memorializes a California and Nevada journalist who served one term as a congressman from Nevada. Another is the 1871 volume by Mark A. Plummer, *Frontier Governor: Samuel J. Crawford of Kansas,* concerning a military hero who became governor at age twenty-nine, then failed in later years to win any other high office. A final item in this category is the 1975 biography of a person prominent in Kansas politics from the earliest, strife-torn territorial days through the 1880s: Don W. Wilson, *Governor Charles Robinson of Kansas.*[32]

During the 1890s an array of divergent, often contradictory and conflicting social issues found their political expression in the Populist movement, a protest effort that attempted to combine a wide spectrum of causes within a single, rather doctrinaire party program. John D. Hicks first described this unique episode in American political history in *The Populist Revolt,* a 1931 publication that won immediate acclaim. Populism, as Hicks interpreted it, was a movement of distressed western farmers who sought remedies for their economic grievances through political action. The farmers' program, according to Hicks, was basic and direct: they meant to capture political power, then to impose their primitive agrarian nostums upon the entire society.[33]

The Populist Revolt fixed Hicks's interpretation in American historical thought for nearly a generation. In time other scholars, notably Richard Hofstadter and Norman Pollack, challenged certain conclusions about Populist ideology and the nature of the Populist reform coalition that they found expressed in the Hicks volume. But they left unchallenged that work's central argument about the social and economic basis for the movement. Like Hicks, these critics assumed that Populism was the product of radical agrarianism in the West, caused by falling farm prices and rising farm costs.[34]

At an early point regional historians found it difficult to apply this analysis of Populism in the Rocky Mountain and Pacific Coast states. Protest movements in these areas, also identified with Populism during the 1890s, failed to match the pattern of agrarian revolt in Kansas and Nebraska. The result was not a challenge to Hicks, but instead a selective, pointed neglect of the Populist era in the historiography of these areas.

Only recently has neglect given way to a renewed interest, demonstrated by a few scholarly works that report new research and fresh conceptual analysis. In 1974 Robert Larson published a major contribution: *New Mexico Populism: A Study of Radical Protest in a Western Territory.* Another outstanding study matched his volume in the same year, James Edward Wright's *The Politics of Populism: Dissent in Colorado.* Both these authors have addressed the issues raised by Hicks, Hofstadter, and Pollack. Both found the Populism of their areas to be a complex, deeply rooted phenomenon not explained by any one single set of generalizations. In origin, in growth, and in impact, both authors contend, Populism can best be understood in terms of local politics and the shifting political alignments of local ethnic and social groups, affected in diverse ways by the economic dislocations of the 1880s and 1890s. For New Mexico, Larson demonstrates, the critical issues included land and cattle monopoly, Anglo encroachment upon Hispanic communal lands, the financial problems of petty capitalist farmers, and the effect of an industry-wide depression in silver mining upon working class miners. In Colorado, Wright points out, agrarian protest and the radicalism of silver mine laborers formed the basis for a farm-labor coalition; but this alliance split by 1894, when farm voters failed to support the advanced reform, pro-union program of Populist governor Davis H. Waite and his labor allies. As a political movement, both authors contend, Rocky Mountain Populism developed because of the failures of the traditional two-party system.[35]

The importance of the local political situation is made obvious by other recent books concerning the 1890s in the Rocky Mountain and Intermountain West. Mary Ellen Glass, for example, describes the record of factional politics that linked mining capitalists with reform candidates in her volume *Silver and Politics in Nevada, 1892–1902.* The dominant influence of Mormon-related issues in the politics of Idaho and Utah during this same period is made plain by two volumes previously cited, *Anti-Mormonism in Idaho* by Merle Wells, and *The "Americanization" of Utah for Statehood* by Gustive Larson. Another case study in coalition politics appears in Thomas A. Clinch's work, *Urban Populism and Free Silver in Montana,* a study that tends to reinforce Wright's observations about Populism in Colorado.[36]

Pacific Coast Populism, from the start a heterodox mix of urban and rural elements, is a topic still without its historian. The People's party enjoyed a large measure of success in Washington State but failed to shake the power of the regular party machines in Oregon and California. For these areas the interested student can find an outline of events in a scattered, mismatched collection of unpublished graduate papers, articles, and monographs, but there remains a need for a thorough reexamination that will bring forth, we may hope, a composite, analytical account.[37]

For Kansas and Nebraska, traditionally regarded as the very heartland of the Populist movement, recent historiography has provided a cluster of important works. A broad-ranging treatment, including a mass biographical examination of state Populist leaders, will be found in O. Gene Clanton, *Kansas Populism: Ideas and Men.* Walter T. K. Nugent's more sharply focused study of Populist attitudes announces the author's thesis in its title: *The Tolerant Populists: Kansas Populism and Nativism.* The changes, ideological and organizational, that overtook Kansas Populism during the 1890s are emphasized in a quasi-biographical study by Peter H. Argersinger, *Populism and Politics: William Alfred Peffer and the People's Party.* In *Persevering Populist: The Life of Frank Doster,* Michael J. Brodhead describes the career of a small-town lawyer who became Kansas's leading Populist intellectual, and whose radicalism persisted long after Populism had faded away.[38]

The social analysis of politics, carried out through detailed statistical investigations of the electorate and the elected, has particular prominence in the historiography of Nebraska during the Populist era. With an excellent use of statistics, Frederick C. Luebke charts the political behavior of the largest ethnic group among Nebraska's foreign-born in his 1969 monograph, *Immigrants and Politics: The Germans of Nebraska, 1880–1900.* In response to a variety of cultural and social influences, Luebke demonstrates, German voters moved first one way, then another, and finally came to fill the Republican ranks during the 1896 campaign. Stanley B. Parsons applies statistical analysis to identify Nebraska's political power structure in his outstanding 1973 volume, *The Populist Context: Rural versus Urban Power on a Great Plains Frontier.* While the farmers argued, Parsons reports, the locus of power remained with the merchants, professional men, and local business promoters in Nebraska's villages and towns. The conclusions of Luebke and Parsons are modified, refined, and extended in a third work based upon statistical analysis, Robert W. Cherny's 1981 publication *Populism, Progressivism, and the Transformation of Nebraska Politics, 1885–1915.* The "transformation" of Cherny's title involves a massive shift in party alignments marked by the rise and decline of the People's party, changes in leadership, and the professionalization of the state's political system by men who made politics their career. With their statistical methodologies, these three works bring to the study of western politics a new precision and sophistication. Only James Wright's Colorado study, *The Politics of Populism,* draws upon statistical analysis as well for any other western area.[39]

Populism and the reform movement in Nebraska of course highlight the early career of that state's most renowned political figure, the Great Commoner, William Jennings Bryan. For Bryan's career we are fortunate to have the superb three-volume biography by Paolo E. Coletta. The first volume, *William Jennings Bryan: Political Evangelist, 1860-1908,* keynotes Bryan's rise to prominence with his own remark that he entered politics by accident and remained by design. Before Coletta's study came into print, Paul W. Glad published in 1960 *The Trumpet Soundeth: William Jennings Bryan and His Democracy, 1896-1912.* This work is best characterized as a cultural and intellectual history of the Bryan cause. Bryan's stature as a reform spokesman, Glad urges, did not rest primarily upon economic or social belief. Instead, it derived from the moral faith of the Midwest that he shared with his supporters.[40]

Finally, a significant revisionary study has recently influenced historical thought about the reform agitation of the 1890s. The author is Lawrence Goodwyn; his book is *Democratic Promise: The Populist Movement in America.* As Goodwyn perceives it, the cooperative crusade of the Farmers Alliance during the 1880s, strongest among the rural poor of Texas and the South, became an essential radicalizing experience that created among its participants a powerful demand for economic and political reforms. As the cooperative crusade began to fail, due largely to the opposition of capitalist institutions, the Alliance activists turned into radical critics of the capitalist system, demanding change through political action. In states like Kansas and Nebraska where the Alliance cooperative movement had not become strong, Goodwyn further claims, the People's party movement lacked the radical integrity demonstrated in Texas and the South. Populism on the middle border was thus little more than a political fad, easily diverted by opportunists toward the issue of free silver and the tactic of fusion, the causes of the movement's demise.[41]

Goodwyn's volume makes a strong, rather convincing challenge to the conventional interpretation of Populism. But from a western perspective, it may be pointed out, he still shares the assumption of Hicks, Hofstadter, and others that Populism in the Far West was "simply silverism," and so can somehow be dismissed as no authentic movement for reform. The studies by Larson and Wright, as already indicated, lead to a different conclusion: there existed in both New Mexico and Colorado an authentic protest movement, not merely a publicity campaign led by a clique of wealthy silver mine owners.[42] If other scholars are attracted to the logic of Goodwyn's case, they will want to reexamine the radicalizing impact of union activity in the West during the 1880s and the 1890s, particularly among those who joined the Knights of Labor and the Western Federation of Miners. These union organizations, also meeting the increased hostility of capitalist institutions by the 1890s, may have provided in the Far West an analogue to the Farmers Alliance cooperative movement in other regions. Certainly the continued radicalism of the western working class after 1896 makes an argument, prima facie, for the possibilities in such a thesis.

As a growing body of historical literature demonstrates, the social and economic growth of the American West took place within a well-defined framework of government and politics. Although romantic myth has suggested otherwise, pioneer westerners sought for their communities a governed condition. Not anarchists and not utopian reformers, historians are demonstrating, they meant to secure their own interests through traditional political institutions and familiar political ways. Anglo-Americans early asserted their dominance on the West's political frontiers, achieving control when necessary by excluding other groups from participation in the political process. In control, the first generation of western political leaders worked to maximize their own power over regional affairs, hoping to influence policy and command local patronage. Military rule and territorial status they found obnoxious just to the extent that these forms of government frustrated local ambitions. For the most influential western groups, statehood marked a stage in their consolidation of political power.

From all of the relevant recent works, one must conclude that western politics remained staidly traditional until the 1890s. Then, as the rapid growth rates of the frontier era began to slacken, economic and social dislocations brought immediate political consequences throughout the West. Political protest, some historians have made clear, temporarily upset the established party system in a few localities. Elsewhere the old party leaders either made accommodations with reform demands, or reform forces brought forward their own leadership talent to take over the party machinery. As David Rothman remarks in his study of the United States Senate, *Politics and Power*, only a few western political magnates were able to withstand the tumult of the 1890s.[43] But, seen at the local level, the West's political institutions not only survived, they may have been broadened and strengthened by new democratic influences. At the same time, a few studies indicate, the institutions of party government were becoming professionalized and bureaucratized as never before.

By the beginning of the twentieth century, western government and politics achieved a kind of maturity that showed the region's frontier identity had nearly disappeared. Local distinctions aside, an historiographical survey strongly suggests, the West exhibited a political structure not too different from any other part of the nation. Reform movements had brought some alterations, but political authority still conferred power upon the powerful. Government still acted as a mechanism of economic privilege, white racial dominance, and male legal autocracy. And, like the citizens of other regions, western people continued to regard their political system both as an agency for change and a safeguard for the status quo.

Notes

1. David Y. Thomas, *A History of Military Government of the Newly Acquired Territory of the United States* (New York: Columbia University Press, 1904; reprint ed., AMS Press, 1967).

2. Howard Roberts Lamar, *The Far Southwest, 1846-1912: A Territorial History* (New Haven: Yale University Press, 1966; paperbound ed., Norton, 1970); Robert W. Larson, *New Mexico's Quest for Statehood, 1846-1912* (Albuquerque: University of New Mexico Press, 1968).

3. Theodore Grivas, *Military Governments in California, 1846-1850: With a Chapter on Their Prior Use in Louisiana, Florida and New Mexico* (Glendale, Calif.: Arthur H. Clark, 1963); William Henry Ellison, *A Self-Governing Dominion: California, 1849-1860* (Berkeley and Los Angeles: University of California Press, 1950). Both these authors, it should be pointed out, consider mainly the Anglo-American population in California and disregard the effects of martial law and military rule upon Hispanic Californians. For comparative purposes, some students will also want to consult two works related to military rule in Alaska: Ted C. Hinckley, *The Americanization of Alaska, 1867-1897* (Palo Alto, Calif.: Pacific Books, 1972), and Stanley Ray Remsberg, "The United States Administration of Alaska: The Army Phase, 1867-1877: A Study of Federal Governance of an Overseas Possession" (Ph.D. diss., University of Wisconsin, 1975).

4. Howard Roberts Lamar, *Dakota Territory, 1861-1889: A Study of*

Frontier Politics (New Haven: Yale University Press, 1956); Russell R. Elliott, *History of Nevada* (Lincoln: University of Nebraska Press, 1973), pp. 57–61. In his dissertation Kent D. Richards makes a comparative study of western proto-government in a limited few cases: "Growth and Development of Government in the Far West: The Oregon Provisional Government, Jefferson Territory, Provisional and Territorial Nevada" (Ph.D. diss., University of Minnesota, 1966).

5. Dorothy O. Johansen and Charles M. Gates, *Empire of the Columbia: A History of the Pacific Northwest* (New York: Harper and Bros., 1957; rev. ed., 1967); Robert J. Loewenberg, *Equality on the Oregon Frontier: Jason Lee and the Methodist Mission, 1834–43* (Seattle: University of Washington Press, 1976).

6. Stanley Siegel, *A Political History of the Texas Republic* (Austin: University of Texas Press, 1956); William C. Binkley, *The Texas Revolution* (Baton Rouge: Louisiana State University Press, 1951); Llerena B. Friend, *Sam Houston, the Great Designer* (Austin: Texas State Historical Society, 1954; reprint ed., University of Texas Press, 1969); William Ransom Hogan, *The Texas Republic: A Social and Economic History* (Norman: University of Oklahoma Press, 1946; reprint ed., University of Texas Press, 1969); and D. W. Meinig, *Imperial Texas: An Interpretive Essay in Cultural Geography*, paperbound ed. (Austin: University of Texas Press, 1969). Two additional biographical works merit citation: Stanley Siegel, *The Poet President of Texas: The Life of Mirabeau B. Lamar, President of the Republic of Texas* (Austin: Jenkins Publishing Company, The Pemberton Press, 1977), and Herbert Gambrell, *Anson Jones, the Last President of Texas* (Garden City, N.Y.: Doubleday, 1948).

7. John D. Unruh, Jr., *The Plains Across: The Overland Emigrants and the Trans-Mississippi West, 1840–60* (Urbana: University of Illinois Press, 1979); John Mack Faragher, *Women and Men on the Overland Trail* (New Haven: Yale University Press, 1979); John Phillip Reid, *Law for the Elephant: Property and Social Behavior on the Overland Trail* (San Marino, Calif.: Huntington Library, 1980); John Willard Hurst, *Law and the Conditions of Freedom in the Nineteenth-Century United States* (Madison: University of Wisconsin Press, 1956).

8. Leonard Pitt, *The Decline of the Californios: A Social History of the Spanish-Speaking Californians, 1846–1890* (Berkeley and Los Angeles: University of California Press, 1966); Albert Camarillo, *Chicanos in a Changing Society: From Mexican Pueblos to American Barrios in Santa Barbara and Southern California, 1848–1930* (Cambridge: Harvard University Press, 1979);

Richard Griswold del Castillo, *The Los Angeles Barrio, 1850–1890: A Social History* (Berkeley and Los Angeles: University of California Press, 1979); Frances Leon Swadesh, *Los Primeros Pobladores: Hispanic Americans of the Ute Frontier* (Notre Dame: University of Notre Dame Press, 1974); Roxanne Dunbar Ortiz, *Roots of Resistance: Land Tenure in New Mexico, 1680–1980* (Los Angeles: University of California, 1980); Mario Barrera, *Race and Class in the Southwest: A Theory of Racial Inequality* (Notre Dame: University of Notre Dame Press, 1979). Mention may be made also of Alvin R. Sunseri, *Seeds of Discord: New Mexico in the Aftermath of the American Conquest, 1846–1861* (Chicago: Nelson-Hall, 1979), a book that demonstrates more sentiment than research.

9. Eugene H. Berwanger, *The Frontier Against Slavery: Western Anti-Negro Prejudice and the Slavery Extension Controversy* (Urbana: University of Illinois Press, 1967); Rudolph Lapp, *Blacks in Gold Rush California* (New Haven: Yale University Press, 1977); W. Sherman Savage, *Blacks in the West* (Westport, Conn.: Greenwood Press, 1976). Two additional titles may have interest: James A. Rawley, *Race and Politics: "Bleeding Kansas" and the Coming of the Civil War* (Philadelphia: J. B. Lippincott Company, 1969; paperbound ed. Lincoln: University of Nebraska Press, 1979), a volume that emphasizes the element of racial prejudice in the Kansas issue; and Douglas Henry Daniels, *Pioneer Urbanites: A Social and Cultural History of Black San Francisco* (Philadelphia: Temple University Press, 1980), which documents the survival of an elite black community from the gold rush era to the mid-twentieth century.

10. Gunther Barth, *Bitter Strength: A History of the Chinese in the United States, 1850–1870* (Cambridge: Harvard University Press, 1964); Elmer C. Sandmeyer, *The Anti-Chinese Movement in California* (Urbana: University of Illinois Press, 1939; paperbound ed., 1973); Alexander Saxton, *The Indispensable Enemy: Labor and the Anti-Chinese Movement* (Berkeley and Los Angeles: University of California Press, 1971; paperbound ed., 1975).

11. See particularly R. A. Burchell, *The San Francisco Irish, 1848–1880* (Berkeley and Los Angeles: University of California Press, 1980); Andrew Rolle, *The Immigrant Upraised: Italian Adventurers and Colonists in an Expanding America* (Norman: University of Oklahoma Press, 1968); Robert E. Levinson, *The Jews in the California Gold Rush* (New York: KTAV Publishing House, 1978); and Moses Rischin, "Immigration, Migration, and Minorities in California: A Reassessment," *Pacific Historical Review* 41 (February 1972): 71–90.

12. Clarence E. Carter, "Colonialism in [the] Continental United States,"

South Atlantic Quarterly 47 (January 1948): 17-28. Carter's career is sketched by an admiring former colleague, Philip D. Jordan, in "A Dedication to the Memory of Clarence Edwin Carter, 1881-1961," *Arizona and the West* 10 (Winter 1968): 309-12. Jordan and another former associate, Harold W. Ryan, also published personal reminiscences of Carter in *Prologue: The Journal of the National Archives* 1 (Winter 1969): 46-47 and 48-50.

13. Earl S. Pomeroy, "The Territory as a Frontier Institution," *The Historian* 7 (Autumn 1944): 29-41. The original edition of *The Territories and the United States* was published by the University of Pennsylvania Press. In 1969 the University of Washington Press brought out a reprint edition, with a new introduction by the author.

14. W. Turrentine Jackson, "Territorial Papers of Wyoming in the National Archives," *Annals of Wyoming* 16 (January 1944): 45-55. Research materials for territorial history are broadly summarized in two more recent articles: Kenneth N. Owens, "Research Opportunities in Western Territorial History," *Arizona and the West* 8 (Spring 1966): 7-18; and Norman E. Tutorow and Arthur B. Abel, "Western and Territorial Research Opportunities in Trans-Mississippi Federal Records Centers," *Pacific Historical Review* 40 (November 1971): 501-18. A list of Jackson's early publications on territorial history can be found in the Owens article cited in n. 26 below.

15. William M. Neil, "The American Territorial System Since the Civil War: A Summary Analysis," *Indiana Magazine of History* 40 (September 1964): 219-40. Two additional works by Neil help to fill out our knowledge of the territories' administrative history: "The Territorial Governor in the Rocky Mountain West" (Ph.D. diss., University of Chicago, 1952) and "The Territorial Governor as Indian Superintendent in the Trans-Mississippi West," *Mississippi Valley Historical Review* 43 (September 1956): 213-37. Also noted should be Jack Ericson Eblen, *The First and Second United States Empires: Governors and Territorial Government, 1784-1912* (Pittsburgh: University of Pittsburgh Press, 1968), a diffuse work that deals mainly with territorial executives in the Old Northwest and the Midwest, giving only slight attention to the Far West. Another helpful reference is John W. Smurr's compendious study, "Territorial Constitutions: A Legal History of the Frontier Governments Erected by Congress in the American West, 1878-1900" (Ph.D. diss., University of Indiana, 1960). Kenneth N. Owens, "Frontier Governors: A Study of the Territorial Executives in the History of Washington, Idaho, Montana, Wyoming, and Dakota Territories" (Ph.D. diss., University of Minnesota, 1959), describes administrative activities within their political context.

16. Thomas G. Alexander, *A Clash of Interests: Interior Department and*

Mountain West, 1863–1896 (Provo, Utah: Brigham Young University Press, 1977); Victor Westphall, *The Public Domain in New Mexico, 1854–1891* (Albuquerque: University of New Mexico Press, 1965).

17. Jay J. Wagoner, *Arizona Territory, 1863–1912: A Political History* (Tucson: University of Arizona Press, 1970); Lewis Gould, *Wyoming: A Political History, 1868–1912* (New Haven: Yale University Press, 1968). Lamar's two volumes are fully cited in nn. 2 and 4 above.

18. Clark C. Spence, *Territorial Politics and Government in Montana, 1864–1889* (Urbana: University of Illinois Press, 1975). Serious scholars should also see the following unpublished studies among recent works on western territories: James Byron Potts, "Nebraska Territory, 1854–1867: A Study of Frontier Politics" (Ph.D. diss., University of Nebraska, 1973), a work that demonstrates the severe factional antagonisms of the era; Herbert T. Hoover, "History of the Republican Party in New Mexico, 1867–1952" (Ph.D. diss., University of Oklahoma, 1966), which documents the influence of federal appointees throughout the territorial period; Ronald H. Limbaugh, "The Idaho Spoilsmen: Federal Administrators and Idaho Politics, 1863–1890" (Ph.D. diss., University of Idaho, 1967), a descriptive narrative of factional and party battles; and James L. Thane, "Montana Territory: The Formative Years, 1862–1870" (Ph.D. diss., University of Iowa, 1972), a work that relies too heavily on the previous research of other students.

19. Robert Larson's *New Mexico* is fully cited in n. 2 above. Merle W. Wells, *Anti-Mormonism in Idaho, 1872–1892* (Provo, Utah: Brigham Young University Press, 1978), incorporates a very substantial body of research that Wells has published in an array of articles during the last two decades. Gustive O. Larson, *The "Americanization" of Utah for Statehood* (San Marino, Calif.: Huntington Library, 1971); Danny Goble, *Progressive Oklahoma: The Making of a New Kind of State* (Norman: University of Oklahoma Press, 1980). The problems of Mormon Utah during the 1850s are the focus of two other special studies: Norman F. Furniss, *The Mormon Conflict, 1850–1859* (New Haven: Yale University Press, 1960), and J. Keith Melville, *Conflict and Compromise: The Mormons in Mid-Nineteenth Century American Politics* (Provo, Utah: Brigham Young University Press, 1974). Another recent work with a strong political emphasis is E. B. Long, *The Saints and the Union: Utah Territory during the Civil War* (Urbana: University of Illinois Press, 1981), a narrative that stresses Utah's strategic importance. The topic of statehood movements, central to many of these studies, deserves more detailed attention. For background see Bayrd Still, "An Interpretation of the Statehood Process, 1800 to 1850," *Mississippi Valley Historical Review* 23 (September

1936): 189-204. The two pertinent modern studies are both found as dissertations: David Alan Johnson, "Pioneers and Politics: Statemaking in the Far West, 1845-1865" (Ph.D. diss., University of Pennsylvania, 1977), a comparison of the process of constitution writing in California, Nevada, and Oregon; and Gordon Morris Bakken, "Rocky Mountain Constitution-Making, 1850-1912" (Ph.D. diss., University of Wisconsin, 1970), a comparable study for the Rocky Mountain region.

20. James E. Hendrickson, *Joe Lane of Oregon: Machine Politics and the Sectional Crisis, 1849-1861* (New Haven: Yale University Press, 1967); Kent D. Richards, *Isaac I. Stevens: Young Man in a Hurry* (Provo, Utah: Brigham Young University Press, 1979); Robert W. Johannsen, *Frontier Politics and the Sectional Conflict: The Pacific Northwest on the Eve of the Civil War* (Seattle: University of Washington Press, 1955; paperbound ed., 1966); Alan Hynding, *The Public Life of Eugene Semple, Promoter and Politician of the Pacific Northwest* (Seattle: University of Washington Press, 1973).

21. Victor Westphall, *Thomas Benton Catron and His Era* (Tucson: University of Arizona Press, 1973); Oscar D. Lambert, *Stephen Benton Elkins: American Foursquare* (Pittsburgh: University of Pittsburgh Press, 1955); Lawrence R. Murphy, *Frontier Crusader–William F. M. Arny* (Tucson: University of Arizona Press, 1972).

22. Thomas L. Karnes, *William Gilpin: Western Nationalist* (Austin: University of Texas Press, 1970); Harry E. Kelsey, Jr., *Frontier Capitalist: The Life of John Evans* (Denver: State Historical Society of Colorado and Pruett Publishing Company, 1969); Elmer Ellis, *Henry Moore Teller, Defender of the West* (Caldwell, Idaho: Caxton Printers, 1941).

23. William Baskerville Hamilton, *Anglo-American Law on the Frontier: Thomas Rodney and His Territorial Cases* (Durham, N.C.: Duke University Press, 1953); John D. W. Guice, *The Rocky Mountain Bench: The Territorial Supreme Courts of Colorado, Montana, and Wyoming, 1861-1890* (New Haven: Yale University Press, 1972); John R. Wunder, *Inferior Courts, Superior Justice: A History of the Justices of the Peace on the Northwest Frontier, 1853-1889* (Westport, Conn.: Greenwood Press, 1979). Two related books on the territorial judiciary are Aurora Hunt, *Kirby Benedict, Frontier Federal Judge* . . . (Glendale, Calif.: Arthur H. Clark, 1961), the biography of a two-term appointee to New Mexico's territorial bench; and John Nicolson (ed.), *The Arizona of Joseph Pratt Allyn: Observations and Travels of a Pioneer Judge, 1863-1866* (Tucson: University of Arizona Press, 1974), a collection of letters, accompanied by a biographical sketch, from an Illinois judicial pilgrim who served two years on the Arizona bench.

24. Frank Richard Prassel, *The Western Peace Officer: A Legacy of Law and Order* (Norman: University of Oklahoma Press, 1972); Larry D. Ball, *The United States Marshals of New Mexico and Arizona Territories, 1846–1912* (Albuquerque: University of New Mexico Press, 1978).

25. Ray C. Colton, *The Civil War in the Western Territories* (Norman: University of Oklahoma Press, 1959); Eugene H. Berwanger, *The West and Reconstruction* (Urbana: University of Illinois Press, 1981). Gressley's remark appears in *West by East: The American West in the Gilded Age*, Charles Redd Monographs in Western History No. 1 (Provo, Utah: Brigham Young University Press, 1972), p. 40, n. 12.

26. Kenneth N. Owens, "Pattern and Structure in Western Territorial Politics," *Western Historical Quarterly* 1 (October 1970): 373–92. This piece also appears in John P. Bloom (ed.), *The American Territorial System* (Athens: Ohio University Press, 1973), a compilation of papers from a 1969 conference on the territories sponsored by the National Archives. Other pertinent papers in this volume are studies of the territorial courts by John D. W. Guice and William Lee Knecht, and an account of the federal land survey system in the Mountain West by Thomas G. Alexander.

27. Ernest Wallace, *Texas in Turmoil: The Saga of Texas, 1849–1875* (Austin, Tex.: Steck-Vaughn Company, 1965); John L. Waller, *Colossal Hamilton of Texas* (El Paso: Texas Western Press, The University of Texas at El Paso, 1968); W. C. Nunn, *Texas Under the Carpetbaggers* (Austin: University of Texas Press, 1962); Ernest Wallace, *The Howling of the Coyotes: Reconstruction Efforts to Divide Texas* (College Station: Texas A & M University Press, 1979). Another recent work that explains the Radical Republican program in great detail is Carl H. Moneyhon, *Republicanism in Reconstruction Texas* (Austin: University of Texas Press, 1980). Notable also is Ronald Norman Gray, "Edmund J. Davis: Radical Republican and Reconstruction Governor of Texas" (Ph.D. diss., Texas Tech University, 1976).

28. Alwyn Barr, *Reconstruction to Reform: Texas Politics, 1876–1906* (Austin: University of Texas Press, 1971); Lawrence D. Rice, *The Negro in Texas, 1874–1900* (Baton Rouge: Louisiana State University Press, 1971); Robert C. Cotner, *James Stephen Hogg: A Biography* (Austin: University of Texas Press, 1959).

29. Earl Pomeroy, "California, 1846–1860: The Politics of a Representative Frontier State," *California Historical Society Quarterly* 32 (December 1953): 291–302; Royce D. Delmatier, Clarence F. McIntosh, and Earl G. Waters, *The Rumble of California Politics, 1848–1970* (New York: John Wiley and Sons, 1970); H. Brett Melendy and Benjamin F. Gilbert, *The*

Governors of California (Georgetown, Calif.: Talisman Press, 1965); R. Hal Williams, *The Democratic Party and California Politics, 1880–1896* (Berkeley and Los Angeles: University of California Press, 1973); Michael P. Rogin and John L. Shover, *Political Change in California: Critical Elections and Social Movements, 1890–1966,* Contributions in American History No. 5 (Westport, Conn.: Greenwood Press, 1970).

30. A. Russell Buchanan, *David S. Terry of California: Dueling Judge* (San Marino, Calif.: Huntington Library, 1956); David A. Williams, *David C. Broderick: A Political Portrait* (San Marino, Calif.: Huntington Library, 1959); Carl Brent Swisher, *Stephen J. Field, Craftsman of the Law* (Washington, D.C.: Brookings Institution, 1930; reprint ed., University of Chicago Press, 1969); Norman E. Tutorow, *Leland Stanford, Man of Many Careers* (Menlo Park, Calif.: Pacific Coast Publishers, 1971); William A. Bullough, *The Blind Boss and His City: Christopher Augustine Buckley and Nineteenth-Century San Francisco* (Berkeley and Los Angeles: University of California Press, 1979); Harold F. Taggart, "Thomas Vincent Cator: Populist Leader of California," *California Historical Society Quarterly* 27 (December 1948): 311–18; and 28 (March 1949): 47–55.

31. William F. Zornow, *Kansas: A History of the Jayhawk State* (Norman: University of Oklahoma Press, 1957); James C. Olson, *History of Nebraska* (Lincoln: University of Nebraska Press, 1955; paperbound ed., 1974); Elliott, *History of Nevada;* Herbert S. Schell, *History of South Dakota,* 3d ed., rev., paperbound (Lincoln: University of Nebraska Press, 1975); Elwyn B. Robinson, *History of North Dakota* (Lincoln: University of Nebraska Press, 1966); T. A. Larson, *History of Wyoming,* 2d ed., rev. (Lincoln: University of Nebraska Press, 1978); Michael P. Malone and Richard P. Roeder, *Montana: A History of Two Centuries* (Seattle: University of Washington Press, 1976; paperbound ed., 1980). A highly interpretive treatment of Nevada's political development appears in Gilman M. Ostrander, *Nevada: The Great Rotten Borough, 1859–1964* (New York: Knopf, 1966).

32. Francis P. Weisenburger, *Idol of the West: The Fabulous Career of Rollin Mallory Daggett* (Syracuse, N.Y.: Syracuse University Press, 1965); Mark A. Plummer, *Frontier Governor: Samuel J. Crawford of Kansas* (Lawrence: University Press of Kansas, 1971); and Don W. Wilson, *Governor Charles Robinson of Kansas* (Lawrence: University Press of Kansas, 1975). Burton J. Williams, *Senator John James Ingalls: Kansas' Iridescent Republican* (Lawrence: University Press of Kansas, 1972), is a biography of the sharp-tongued U.S. senator from Kansas who served from 1873 to 1891, but this

work gives relatively little attention to state politics.

33. John D. Hicks, *The Populist Revolt: A History of the Farmers' Alliance and the People's Party* (Minneapolis: University of Minnesota Press, 1931; paperbound ed., Lincoln: University of Nebraska Press, 1961).

34. Richard Hofstadter, *The Age of Reform: From Bryan to F.D.R.* (New York: Knopf, 1955; paperbound ed., Vintage–Random House, n.d.); Norman Pollack, *The Populist Response to Industrial America: Midwestern Populist Thought* (Cambridge: Harvard University Press, 1962; paperbound ed., Norton, 1966).

35. Robert Larson, *New Mexico Populism: A Study of Radical Protest in a Western Territory* (Boulder: Colorado Associated University Press, 1974);. James Edward Wright, *The Politics of Populism: Dissent in Colorado* (New Haven: Yale University Press, 1974).

36. Mary Ellen Glass, *Silver and Politics in Nevada, 1892–1902* (Reno: University of Nevada Press, 1969); Thomas A. Clinch, *Urban Populism and Free Silver in Montana* (Missoula: University of Montana Press, 1970). The Wells and Larson volumes are cited in nn. 2 and 19 above.

37. Unpublished works that can contribute to such an account include the following: William J. Gaboury, "Dissension in the Rockies: A History of Idaho Populism" (Ph.D. diss., University of Idaho, 1966); Donald E. Walters, "Populism in California, 1889–1900" (Ph.D. diss., University of California, Berkeley, 1952); and James A. Halseth, "Social Disorganization and Discontent in Late Nineteenth Century Washington" (Ph.D. diss., Texas Tech University, 1974). A wide-ranging narrative summary of the Populist movement in eight western states and territories—California, Oregon, Washington, Idaho, Colorado, Montana, Utah, and Wyoming—appears in David B. Griffiths, "Populism in the Far West, 1890–1900" (Ph.D. diss., University of Washington, 1967). This study, perhaps too ambitious for a dissertation project, is based largely on other secondary sources and limited newspaper research. Another study with an ambitious scope is Karel D. Bicha, *Western Populism: Studies in an Ambivalent Conservatism* (Lawrence, Kan.: Coronado Press, 1976), a volume of inconsistent design. In the first half, Bicha summarizes the careers of four prominent Populists from Kansas, Nebraska, and Colorado. In the second, more valuable part of the book, the author presents a partial analysis of Populist influence upon reform legislation in seven western legislatures between 1891 and 1897, and a prosographic summary of western Populists in Congress between 1891 and 1899. In general Bicha concludes that the Populist leaders, especially as the movement matured, acted more like

party politicians than like the fanatic hayseed radicals of their opponents' imagery.

38. O. Gene Clanton, *Kansas Populism: Ideas and Men* (Lawrence: University Press of Kansas, 1969); Walter T. K. Nugent, *The Tolerant Populists: Kansas Populism and Nativism* (Chicago: University of Chicago Press, 1963); Peter H. Argersinger, *Populism and Politics: William Alfred Peffer and the People's Party* (Lexington: University Press of Kentucky, 1974); and Michael J. Brodhead, *Perservering Populist: The Life of Frank Doster* (Reno: University of Nevada Press, 1970).

39. Frederick C. Luebke, *Immigrants and Politics: The Germans of Nebraska, 1880-1900* (Lincoln: University of Nebraska Press, 1969); Stanley B. Parsons, *The Populist Context: Rural versus Urban Power on a Great Plains Frontier* (Westport, Conn.: Greenwood Press, 1973); Robert W. Cherny, *Populism, Progressivism, and the Transformation of Nebraska Politics, 1885-1915* (Lincoln: University of Nebraska Press, 1981). An important unpublished study for Nebraska is David S. Trask, "The Nebraska Populist Party: A Social and Political Analysis" (Ph.D. diss., University of Nebraska, 1971).

40. Paolo E. Coletta, *William Jennings Bryan: Political Evangelist, 1860-1908* (Lincoln: University of Nebraska Press, 1964); Paul W. Glad, *The Trumpet Soundeth: William Jennings Bryan and his Democracy, 1896-1912* (Lincoln: University of Nebraska Press, 1960; paperbound ed., 1966).

41. Lawrence Goodwyn, *Democratic Promise: The Populist Movement in America* (New York: Oxford University Press, 1976). This work also appears in an abridged version under a different title: *The Populist Moment: A Short History of the Agrarian Revolt in America*, paperbound ed. (New York: Oxford University Press, 1978). The subtitle of course displays one of Goodwyn's preconceptions about his topic. For Texas Populism an important 1933 study has been reprinted: Roscoe C. Martin, *The People's Party in Texas: A Study in Third Party Politics* (Austin: University of Texas Press, in cooperation with the Texas State Historical Association, 1970).

42. In an article that has appeared just in time for inclusion here, Robert W. Larson states a similar conclusion on the basis of a review of the Populist movement in Montana, Wyoming, Colorado, and New Mexico, giving more detailed attention to the secondary literature cited in this essay: "Populism in the Mountain West: A Mainstream Movement," *Western Historical Quarterly* 13 (April 1982): 143-64.

43. David J. Rothman, *Politics and Power: The United States Senate, 1869-1901* (Cambridge: Harvard University Press, 1966), pp. 172-73.

Chapter Nine

Robert C. Carriker

The American Indian from the Civil War to the Present

American treatment of Indians from the Civil War forward has followed two parallel avenues. One avenue was acculturation, the other was war. Not surprisingly, the literature dealing with the subject has traditionally concentrated on these two concepts. Consequently, the written history of American Indians from 1860 to 1980 suffers from a slight imbalance. During most of the early period, military historians dominated the field with reminiscences or summaries of nearly one thousand armed conflicts between the two races, and this from an almost exclusively white point of view. Official historians later concentrated on the record of federal Indian policies. But the growing popular interest in things Indian more recently has prompted academicians and so-called Indian historians to seek new approaches to the uneven and bewildering history of Native Americans over the past 120 years.

Events at Fort Sumter, South Carolina, in April 1861 dramatically changed the role of the U.S. Army in the West. Previously the military presence beyond the Mississippi had served as a stabilizing influence, defending white settlements from Indians, and simultaneously protecting Indians from unscrupulous white men. But the withdrawal of regular army troops from western garrisons forced local authorities to assume responsibility for Indian affairs. The subsequent series of wars were largely due to an obvious conflict of interest by the volunteers, who had much to gain by the defeat of area tribes. Typical of events that followed were the campaigns against the Santee Sioux in 1862, the Navajos in 1863, and the Cheyennes at Sand Creek, Colorado, in 1864.

At the conclusion of the Civil War, regular army troops once again occupied the western forts abandoned in 1861. But conditions would never be the same because of the many atrocities committed by both sides during the war years. Thus, for the next quarter of a century the U.S. Army would retaliate against the Indians in campaign after campaign. Federal troops at first tried to police the frontier by reacting to specific situations; but the volunteers' excesses, plus the population shift to the Far West stimulated by the end of the Civil War, by the Homestead Act, by mineral discoveries in the Rocky Mountains, and by the building of the transcontinental railroad created problems that could not be solved easily. By the 1870s the army was deploying highly trained commands to ferret out and destroy the irreconcilables. So successful was this approach that by the next decade only small renegade bands remained outside the reservations. An era came to an end at Wounded Knee, South Dakota, on December 29, 1890, in what is generally considered one of the most dishonorable events in U.S. military history.

The two major trends that dominated Indian historiography during the post–Civil War Indian campaigns were reminiscences and regionalism. Both were greatly influenced by the recent war, and even the best works were slightly parochial in nature. This penchant to write military history immediately after the fact is, of course, a universal one. So it was that veterans of frontier campaigns recorded their experiences soon after the sound of battle had faded. For example, at least a dozen books eventually appeared by participants in the Santee Sioux uprising. The same was true of the Modoc War, the Nez Perce War, and various other Indian expeditions. Publication outlets for such reminiscences included both state historical "proceedings" and a variety of military service journals, the most important of which were the *Army and Navy Journal* and the *Cavalry Journal*.[1] In addition, several dozen correspondents for the *Chicago Times, Harper's Weekly,* and other nineteenth-century publications wrote some excellent accounts of numerous engagements between the Indians and state and federal troops.[2]

The Spanish-American War rekindled the martial spirit in America and at the same time brought a renewed interest in the frontier experience. Participants who had been in their mid-twenties during the post–Civil War Indian campaigns were now approaching their fiftieth year and wanted their contributions to the so-called winning of the West and "solution to the Indian problem" recorded for posterity. Historian Don Rickey, Jr., has located and catalogued approximately four hundred published and unpublished manuscripts by Indian war veterans.[3] The usefulness of such materials varies considerably, and one has to take into account the accuracy of events based upon "constructed memory." Men naturally have a tendency to exaggerate their personal role in historic developments and often confuse facts with fancy. This undoubtedly explains why scholars are reluctant to rely too heavily upon this type of primary data. Indeed, reminiscences by veterans of Indian wars have gradually lost favor with the general public, and publishers are hesitant to invest in such manuscripts, even though some are well written or carefully edited.

The Indian wars involved a dozen recognized campaigns, in which approximately twenty-five thousand troops participated in nearly one thousand battles and skirmishes. Among the most publicized were Adobe Walls, Washita, the Arikaree, Summit Springs, Hayfield, and Wagon Box fights, Dull Knife's raid, and the Fetterman massacre. Analyzing such engagements, fought as they were over vast stretches of the American West, proved difficult for historians. It was almost a case of not being able to see the forest, the overall picture, for the trees, or local engagements. The tendency for both amateur and professional historians to depend heavily on personal reminiscences and to reflect local prejudices continued even as interest in Indian wars declined.[4]

Professional writers also had their turn at glamorizing the Indian wars, but they too tended to emphasize regions. Paul I. Wellman gave the public *Death on the Prairie* and *Death in the Desert* in the 1930s, and even thirty years later writers like Ralph K. Andrist concentrated on the Plains Indians in *The Long Death.*[5] Authors were simply overwhelmed by the epic proportions of the events. The retreat of Chief Joseph in 1877, for example, involves sorting out treaty complexities dating from 1863, a personality cult surrounding Joseph himself, the details of four major battles spread over nearly two thousand miles, and official reports totaling more than one hundred thousand words, to say nothing of at least two dozen memoirs by participants.

The Civil War Centennial created the next renaissance of interest in military history. Inasmuch as the observance was just as much an Indian wars celebration for the West as it was a Civil War celebration in the East, there was also a surge of interest in frontier military history. Historians now began to consult official records in the National Archives and even oral accounts by the Indians themselves. New sources and a more professional perspective helped elevate military history to a more sophisticated level than it had previously enjoyed. Moreover, authors increasingly came from outside the region of which they wrote and tended to be broader and more objective in their approach. William H. Leckie's *The Military Conquest of the Southern Plains,* Keith A. Murray's *The Modocs and Their War,* and nearly a dozen excellent re-creations of such battles as Sand Creek, Beecher's Island, the Hancock expedition, and the Red River War by Lonnie J. White in various quarterlies are all examples of what are now considered classics in the field.

The new professionalism of the 1960s was not limited to those with academic appointments. Dan Thrapp wrote *The Conquest of Apacheria;* Stan

Hoig, *The Sand Creek Massacre*; and Oliver Knight, *Following the Indian Wars*; all had journalism backgrounds. A cadre of National Park Service historians similarly produced an impressive block of serious scholarship without the taint of government document drabness. Notable among them were Robert M. Utley's *Last Days of the Sioux Nation,* Merrill D. Beal's *"I Will Fight No More Forever": Chief Joseph and the Nez Perce War,* and Don Rickey's scrutiny of the enlisted man in the Indian wars, entitled *Forty Miles a Day on Beans and Hay.*[6]

Perhaps the best single volume of this genre is *The Last Days of the Sioux Nation* by Robert M. Utley, published in 1963. Challenging, yet supplementing James Mooney's *Ghost Dance Religion* published sixty-seven years earlier, Utley applies the perspective of a trained historian to the complex events surrounding the tragic battle of Wounded Knee Creek and the subsequent repression of the Ghost Dance uprising of the Sioux Indians. The Ghost Dance, prompted as it was by unfulfilled government promises, crop failures, and reduced rations, turned "sullen resentment into violent protest." Utley concludes that Wounded Knee was intended by neither the Indians nor the military, and yet both sides share in the blame for this "tragic accident." Whereas historical regionalists emphasize personalities, vendettas, and arguments over who fired the first shot, Utley takes into consideration governmental policy and reservation conditions as basic causes.[7]

Utley has also produced the best single treatment of the Indian wars in the West after the Civil War. *Frontier Regulars,* published in 1973, is the comprehensive history military historians had been seeking since J. P. Dunn, Jr., first wrote his influential *Massacres of the Mountains: A History of the Indian Wars of the Far West, 1815–1875* in 1886.[8] In *Frontier Regulars* Utley balances the stereotype of the frontier military as an advance guard of manifest destiny with that of the military as butchers and unmitigated haters of Indians. He utilizes selected reminiscences of both officers and enlisted men, brings together dozens of regional studies, and chinks in the gaps between them with documentary evidence from government sources.

Although the book is the standard reference on the subject, it also points up the need for Native American viewpoints in the history of the Indian wars. *Frontier Regulars* is Indian history taken from the traditional vantage point of white contact, relying almost exclusively upon white sources. Significantly, at the same time that Utley was writing his book other historians were calling for an Indian-Indian orientation to Native American history, or at least a greater consideration of personal accounts by Indians as a counterweight to white recollections.[9] But where to find the Indian viewpoint, so as not to reflect Roy Harvey Pearce's observation that white Americans in writing about Indians have usually been writing for themselves about themselves?

The greatest impetus to gathering the Indian side of the wars in the West comes from the most unlikely of sources. No event in the Indian wars of the United States has attracted more public interest than the Little Big Horn defeat. The personal animosity between Custerphiles and Custerphobes has long colored the literature on this battle. Every facet of Custer's movements and intentions, the Indians' tactics, and the blame for the events that followed have been examined repeatedly.[10] Regardless of one's opinion regarding George Armstrong Custer, it should be recognized that this event is a landmark in the history of Indian-white relations.

As with almost all significant Indian battles, personal accounts of the Little Big Horn battle seemed to generate spontaneously. Many of these accounts were contradictory in important points and challenged the "official" history of the Sioux campaign.[11] No one was more active than Elizabeth Bacon Custer, who idolized her husband and who would devote the half-century of her widowhood to preserving his memory. It was not beyond her to use influence to prevent the publication of manuscripts damaging or detrimental to the reputation of her husband. Mrs. Custer died in 1933, and within a year a sudden increase of publications critical of the colonel appeared.[12] The history of the Indian wars now had its first revisionist writings. Of sorts. What the complete telling of the events at Little Big Horn needed, it was quite obvious, was the Indian viewpoint.

Time for the Indians now to come forward and tell their side of the story was long overdue. But the problem proved more difficult than it first appeared, especially since the Indians' concept of history differed considerably from white people's. For one thing, their culture was based on entirely different traditions. Instead of filing a formal written report with a war chief, Indians recorded events associated with a particular battle or campaign in a series of pictographs. Or they relied heavily upon oral traditions, something that most trained historians dismissed as inadequate, slanted, or purposely distorted.

Indians present at the Little Big Horn quickly became adept at telling the white man what he wanted to hear, no matter how irresponsible a comment it might have been. Rain-in-the-Face and Two Moon were particularly talkative to newspaper reporters, and they provided several gruesome descriptions of Indians mutilating the bodies of fallen Seventh Cavalry soldiers. Chief Gall later told his tale of the Little Big Horn to the *Army and Navy Journal* at the tenth anniversary of the battle. By the end of the century, tales of "last survivors" among the Indians were as numerous as "only survivors" among the whites.[13]

Interviews of Indian warriors by newspaper correspondents eventually ran their course. The practice of questioning Indians, however, did not disappear. Quite the contrary. During the second decade of the twentieth century, numerous professional men, not necessarily historians, went into the field and gathered Indian testimony. This was an early practice of oral history, a major source of information for today's Indian historian, and the beginning of a sustained emphasis on recording the Indian account of his own history.[14]

Skills in oral history in the 1920s and 1930s were primitive in comparison with today's advanced technology in recording devices and interviewing techniques. But some men were surprisingly successful in dealing with Indian participants in the wars. Among those with noteworthy skills was Walter S. Campbell, a journalism professor at the University of Oklahoma who wrote under the name Stanley Vestal. Campbell was skillful at oral history, and among his works on the Sioux was a biography of Chief White Bull entitled *Warpath: The True Story of the Fighting Sioux,* published in 1934. Two years earlier John G. Neihardt wrote *Black Elk Speaks,* about an Oglala medicine man who witnessed the massacre at Wounded Knee, and Frank B. Linderman used interviews of Pretty-shield, wife of one of Custer's Crow scouts, to prepare *Red Mother.* All these works have become classics in their field and have even been accepted by modern Indians.[15]

Indian reminiscences will continue to be suspect among historians of the Indian wars, and with justification. But as the writing of Indian war history progressed from history-by-reminiscence to a reliable military history in the 1960s, a critical evaluation of sources was stressed. The public could still be duped, as they were in 1971 with *The Memoirs of Chief Red Fox,* but not historians, who quickly identified the book as a fraud by using elementary tests of primary source material.[16]

A highlight in Indian wars history was achieved in 1967 with the publication of *The Life of George Bent: Written from His Letters* by George E. Hyde. Hyde's manuscript, a narrative of information taken from a lengthy correspondence with George Bent, a mixed-blood Cheyenne who nevertheless thought and acted like a full-blood, was rescued from obscurity in an attic in Omaha and prepared for publication by Savoie Lottinville. Previously overlooked by most historians, these letters offered military historians the opportunity to add a new, Indian dimension to a dozen battles, including the Washita, Sand Creek, Summit Springs, and Adobe Walls.[17]

Since the mid-1960s a virtual army of researchers has taken to the field to interview hundreds of Indians. Opinions have been given on a wide variety of topics, but relatively few of the thousands of tapes recorded recount episodes from the Indian wars. Though progress is being made in gathering the Indian viewpoint, technology arrived too late to record the comments of those who once lived the Indian wars. Unfortunately, that segment of Indian history is doomed to uncertainty.

The problem can be illustrated by considering the question of casualties during the Indian wars. For the white man there is a precise count compiled in Francis B. Heitman's *Historical Register and Dictionary of the United States Army,* Joseph P. Peters's *Indian Battles and Skirmishes on the American Frontier,* and the army's official *Chronological list of actions, etc. with Indians from January 15, 1837, to January, 1891.* The total army casualties in 930 engagements with Indians between 1866 and 1891 were 932 officers and enlisted men killed and 1,061 wounded. The army also lists 461 civilians killed and 116 wounded.[18]

Calculating the Indian losses cannot be as precise, since the Indian left no compilation. The army reported 5,519 Indians killed or wounded, but its record is suspect simply because various combat officers reported events as they would like them to be seen by a promotion board. Moreover, Indians almost always tried to carry their own dead and wounded from the field of battle.

Stanley Vestal in his *New Sources on Indian History* believes the army figures are greatly exaggerated. His Indian informants claim that among the Sioux, in a dozen battles between 1865 and 1876, only 69 warriors were killed and 102 wounded. Similarly, in the War on Powder River, contemporary whites estimate Indian losses at somewhere between 400 and 1,000, while George Hyde in *Red Cloud's Folk* says the Sioux suffered only six killed and six more wounded. Various so-called Indian authorities have estimated as many as one million Indians killed by white men in the conquest of the West. Author Don Russell, however, looked into such figures as prepared by the "liberal academic establishment," as he called it, and concluded there were only a maximum of 3,000 Indian deaths at the hands of the military and no more than 1,000 caused by civilians.[19]

Though Robert Utley did not make maximum use of Indian sources when he prepared *Frontier Regulars,* Dee Brown certainly gave the impression that he did when he wrote *Bury My Heart at Wounded Knee* in 1970. This book made a tremendously favorable impression on the American public and drew an equal but opposite reaction in the scholarly community. Brown, a librarian and successful professional writer, wrote what he intended to be a new story of injustice to Indians from "almost forgotten oral history" sources. The subtitle, "An Indian History of the West," appealed to uncritical newsmagazine and newspaper reviewers, and the general public responded by making the book a best seller. Historians were dismayed that a one-dimensional book glorifying the Indians and indicting every action of the white people vis-à-vis the Indians—based as it was on selective research and unsound methods of scholarship—should achieve so much popularity. The demeanor of professional historians toward the book was so stern that it retained little credibility in the academic community.[20]

Future historians of the Indian wars will, indeed, find it necessary not only to evaluate critically white and Indian accounts of battles and events, but also to correct some of the deficiencies in regionalistic treatments. John C. Ewers of the Smithsonian Institution has urged historians to consider seriously the role of intertribal warfare and its relationship to Indian-white warfare, a recommendation that can no longer be overlooked. Future accounts must also pay closer attention to the noncombative functions of the frontier military men. Their role as builders of towns and roads is well known, but not so their activities in protecting the Indian reservations from white encroachment, whiskey peddlers, or horse thieves. Military deficiencies have been overemphasized to the point that the accomplishments are obscured.[21]

Historians have already come to recognize the role of individual military officers in seeking just treatment of defeated tribesmen. In 1967 James T. King wrote "George Crook: Indian Fighter and Humanitarian," a pacesetting article that demonstrated Crook's concern for the Indian both while a general officer and in later years. Since then King's thesis has been echoed by other authors, who constitute the "Humanitarian General" school of interpretation, urging another look at the decent, fair treatment of Indians by numerous high-ranking military officers in the Indian wars, not the least of whom were Nelson A. Miles, Oliver O. Howard, and John Pope.[22] The final step in this process will come when future military historians of the Indian wars incorporate in their writings the themes of concurrent national policy toward the red man.

While the War Department was seeking its solution to the "Indian question," the Interior Department's Bureau of Indian Affairs was equally concerned. National policy in the second half of the nineteenth century remained fixed on the assimilation of the Indian, but achievement of that goal required several shifts in emphasis. Immediately following the Civil War the federal government responded to the Indian wars on the plains with peace commissions. The lack of success of this plan, however, prompted President Ulysses S. Grant to initiate a new Indian policy.

For eight years Grant's "Peace Policy" remained the guideline for federal response to the disturbing state of Indian affairs. The treaty system, whereby each tribe was considered a separate legal entity, was discontinued. All tribes were to be placed on reservations, and efforts would be renewed to acculturate, Christianize, and educate them. Furthermore, Grant followed the recommendation of a group of Quakers by selecting Indian agents from within the ranks of religious men nominated by various churches.

During these decades humanitarian reformers watched with dismay and revulsion as tribe after tribe was defeated by General of the Army William T. Sherman and his military units. Voices critical of military action against tribesmen came from a variety of churchmen, do-gooders, and congressmen. While they were never loud enough to drown out the sounds of battle produced by the War Department, they nevertheless were persistent and as unified as a chorus. After Grant's administration, reformers were left to their own devices to protect Indians from the twin evils of military extermination in the field and duplicity on the reservation. Their goal was to see tribesmen enjoy the benefits and virtues of both Christianity and an agricultural life based on private property.

For the literate American reader of the 1870s and 1880s, the multivolume works produced by Hubert Howe Bancroft and Francis Parkman portrayed the Indian as a romantic, tragic figure. But Theodore Roosevelt's four-volume epic, *The Winning of the West,* contradicted that impression and typified frontier impatience with humanitarian crusades. Like another popular author of the times, Richard I. Dodge in *Our Wild Indians,* Roosevelt emphasized the Indian's innate warlike character and the perversity of his culture. "Filthy," "lecherous," and "faithless" were adjectives he used to describe the Indian warrior. "All men of sane and wholesome thought," he wrote, "must dismiss with impatient contempt the plea that these continents should be reserved for the use of scattered savage tribes, whose life was but a few degrees less meaningless, squalid, and ferocious than that of the wild beasts with whom they held joint ownership."[23]

Even so, reformers held firm their ideals. Sincere friends of the Indian had long advocated individual ownership of land as the salvation of tribes. Not-so-sincere friends of the Indian also encouraged individual ownership of land because it would free millions of acres of land for the white man. Since both groups wished the same end, though for different reasons, bills to that effect were introduced in Congress as early as 1879. Eventually, Congress enacted the Severalty Act sponsored by Senator Henry L. Dawes, and President Grover Cleveland signed it in 1887. Critics said that the act balanced white and Indian interests unusually well, inasmuch as it helped the whites the most while injuring the Indians the least.

The law generally provided for the allotment of reservation land to individual adult and minor Indians in amounts of 160 acres. The land was to be held in trust by the government for twenty-five years, after which the Indian would be granted title in fee simple. All surplus lands on the former reservations would be bought by the government and eventually opened to white settlement.

The Severalty Act, or General Allotment Act, failed to assimilate the Indians, but it certainly freed their land for white acquisition. In 1887 Indian tribes owned some 138 million acres on 133 reservations in twenty states and territories. Before the repudiation of the Severalty Act in 1934, nearly 91 million acres belonging to the Indians had passed into white ownership. Loopholes in the legislation allowed the Indians to be legally swindled, and attempts by Congress to improve the act only made a bad law worse.[24]

Evaluation of the reform era in Indian affairs, 1865–1900, is a relatively recent development for historians. They seemed instinctively to avoid the period because they knew the result of the humanitarian labors was failure in the abuses of the Severalty Act. For decades the only literature on the development and administration of American Indian policy in this period was the numerous treatises, specialty journals, and annual reports of organizations such as the Indian Rights Association, the Lake Mohonk Conference, and the Women's National Indian Association. For the fifty years between 1914 and 1964, for example, only three books appraised the reform period in Indian policy. Two of those books, *Uncle Sam's Stepchildren* by Loring B. Priest and *The Movement for Indian Assimilation* by Henry E. Fritz, were excellent historical accounts of the period, but for the most part the scholarly community relegated the subject to graduate student dissertations or brief articles. It was not until the 1970s that Indian policy of a century before came under close scrutiny.[25]

Robert W. Mardock wrote *Reformers and the American Indian* in 1971, but the best work, *American Indian Policy in Crisis* (1976), was by Francis Paul Prucha, S.J. It was a book to replace, not duplicate, previous scholarship in the field of reform movements after the Civil War. Prucha used 172 contemporary reformist publications, plus other primary data, to correct the notion that reformers were merely warmed-over pre–Civil War abolitionists seeking a new cause. He argued that the reformers of the 1870s and 1880s were literate, educated Christians whose programs for the Indians were righteous, if not always correct. The failure of the movement occurred because humanitarians did not understand Indian culture, nor did they include it as a consideration in their education programs.[26]

Prucha followed up his *American Indian Policy in Crisis* with *The Churches and the Indian Schools, 1888–1912* in 1979. Education of the red man was a cardinal precept of the Indian reform movement, yet Prucha showed that the Indian was sometimes nothing more than a pawn in struggles between religious denominations. This theme has subsequently been examined by Clyde A. Milner in *With Good Intentions: Quaker Work Among the Pawnees, Otos, and Omahas in the 1870s* (1982), and in the research conference sponsored by the National Endowment for the Humanities and entitled "Churchmen and Western Indians." At this meeting, questions were raised regarding the goals of not only the Quaker and Catholic missionaries, but also of the Presbyterian, Methodist, Episcopalian, and Mormon missionaries.[27]

Investigations of other aspects of reservation life up to and through the Dawes Act have also seen their greatest motivation come in the past decade. Edmund J. Danziger's *Indians and Bureaucrats* is an excellent study of the administration of Indian affairs during the Civil War. Danziger was less concerned with the formulation of reservation policy by desk-bound clerks than with the actual events in the field. The conclusion he reached is that, yes, the Indians suffered greatly during the period, but probably not as much as they could have without the presence of the Indian Office, despite its many shortcomings.[28]

In several articles and a book on the Cheyenne-Arapaho reservation, Donald J. Berthrong made some equally important observations on the influences of economic forces on tribal systems already strained by military conquest and defeatist attitudes. He found that in the case of leases to cattlemen, Cheyenne Dog Soldiers led the tribal opposition. This respected warrior society enforced its will on the agents, the mixed-bloods, and the Indians who were already adapted to white institutions. The point is that the traditional tribal structure was not completely destroyed by the reservation experience. Berthrong's conclusions regarding the persistence of tribal culture run contrary to what had been presupposed by historians without heretofore actually examining the records. Similarly, William T. Hagan examined available documents for the Kiowa-Comanche reservation, also in Indian Territory, and published them in *United States–Comanche Relations: The Reservation*

Years, covering the years 1867–1906. His conclusions about the cultural aberrations suffered by this great tribe as it stumbled toward assimilation are as cogent as Berthrong's findings for the Comanches' Indian Territory neighbors. Both books are more than case studies of single tribes; they are prototypes for reservation policy studies in the future.[29]

Hagan and Berthrong had much to say about Indian agents, though in an indirect way. This is one subject that has not fared well among scholars studying Indian administration between the Civil War and the end of the nineteenth century. Indian agents have been habitually characterized as greedy, despicable parasites preying on helpless Indian wards. William E. Unrau in "The Civilian as Indian Agent: Villain or Victim?" even listed several reasons why Indian agents have been incorrectly viewed in American history. Doubtless, some agents were corrupt, but others were not and they patiently wrote their personal experiences to refute just such criticisms. Lawrie Tatum and Thomas C. Battey, among others, left memoirs; probably the best example is James McLaughlin, who wrote *My Friend the Indian.* McLaughlin worked for the Bureau of Indian Affairs as an agent and inspector for nearly half a century, including appointments to Devils Lake Agency from 1876 to 1881 and Standing Rock in the crucial years 1881 to 1895. In addition to his autobiographical apologia, McLaughlin left his personal papers; his career can be followed in the microfilm edition of these and in the somewhat laudatory biography by Father Louis Pfaller. It is clear from all these sources that McLaughlin performed his duties as agent in a manner quite the opposite of the stereotypical corrupt, incompetent politically appointed agent.[30]

Historians, however, remain intrigued with that stereotype. Unrau's search for an "alternate interpretation" has not yet produced one. Father Paul Prucha, likewise, made an appeal to a National Archives research conference in 1970 asking, "Where are the analytical studies of the office of agent and the effect of the agents on Indian matters?"[31] Perhaps the answer has to do with the research proclivities of historians as the field of American Indian history moves slowly through a transition period of maturing scholarship. It is no accident that most tribal histories trail off at 1880, that there are few reservation histories from the 1880s forward, or that the Dawes Act has been studied as a policy decision but seldom as an actuality of allotment to the Indians. The difficulty has to do not with scarcity of materials, but with an overabundance of them.

There are millions of pages of documents dealing with Indian affairs, Indian agents, and Indian tribes in federal, state, and university depositories. Hagan's book on *United States–Commanche Relations,* for example, is the product of more than 750,000 pages of manuscript material taken from the Western History Collections at the University of Oklahoma, the Oklahoma State Historical Society, and the National Archives. So little work had been previously accomplished in the realm of Comanche reservation history that 92 percent of Hagan's 558 source notes were from primary documents in either Oklahoma or the National Archives. Part of the answer to the query, where are our new analytical studies in Indian history, then, has to do with an embarrassment of research riches and the will power needed to come to grips with this immense body of material.[32]

The Dawes Act was unfortunate for Indians in many respects, but perhaps the least anticipated result of the law was the depreciation in public concern for the Indian which it fostered. Coming as it did, at the general time of the Battle of Wounded Knee, the final hostile act of the Plains tribes, the Dawes Act was thought by most American citizens and many congressmen to be the long-awaited merger of the two avenues of Indian policy, acculturation and war, in a final settlement. Presumably, the Indian would now become a farmer in the best traditions of rural America and the nation could turn its attention to other matters.

The first forty volumes of the *Mississippi Valley Historical Review* (1914–54) contain only a score of articles on Indians, an indication of the status of the Indian in history circles at that period. But one of them was especially important. Ralph C. Downes wrote "A Crusade for Indian Reform, 1922–1934," tracing the reawakening of Americans to the deplorable state of the Indians. Downes emphasized the roles of humanitarian reformers, the public press, single-issue lobbyists in Congress, and government investigations in reversing Indian policy under the Dawes Act. That the Wheeler-Howard (Indian Reorganization) Act was ultimately enacted in 1934, he wrote, was to the collective credit of all who finally persuaded the government that the "rugged individualism" of the Dawes Act was not applicable to the times.[33]

The New Deal for Indians under the Indian Reorganization Act, administered by Commissioner of Indian Affairs John Collier, 1933–45, emphasized community relief, self-help, social and educational renewal on the reservations, a revival of Native American religion, dances, dress, and crafts, plus an end to the allotment of tribal land. For decades historians took a lackadaisical attitude toward the Indian New Deal, generally accepting Collier's own assessment of the program as a series of successes that revitalized tribal society, rehabilitated Indian lands, and promoted Indian culture.[34]

By the mid-1970s scholars were ready to challenge the Collier concept and to examine the Indian New Deal as history rather than current events.

Lawrence C. Kelly, in "The Indian Reorganization Act: The Dream and the Reality," was among the first historians to cut through the mystique of the Indian New Deal. His revisionist article on the subject demonstrated that the Indian Reorganization Act fell far short of the revolutionary changes attributed to it. A year later Donald Parman completed a case study, *The Navajos and the New Deal*, a critical look at Collier's conservation policies and how they not only failed, but actually restrained the culture of the tribe. Kenneth Philp's biography of John Collier in 1977 similarly pointed out the uneven success of the Indian New Deal.[35]

Through the 1940s the federal government continued to push assimilation as a policy, but at a slower pace. After World War II strong voices questioned the success of that policy. Among other things, in 1946 Congress passed the Indian Claims Commission Act. The immediate purpose of the legislation was to correct past violations of tribal rights, but it also anticipated the day when all federal control over the Indians would be withdrawn. In 1953 Congress grew impatient with Indian affairs once again and tried to accelerate the assimilation process by demanding termination of all federal obligations to tribes. Simultaneously, Congress encouraged the movement of Indians from the reservation to the city. The tragic policy of termination remained the unofficial policy of Congress through 1961, though its after-effects could be seen for at least another decade. In response, Indians espoused the new philosophy of Red Power. Indian newspapers and intertribal organizations flourished, as did Indian confrontations with whites at places like Alcatraz Island and Puget Sound, Washington. Red Power meant freedom for the tribes to make their own decisions and to end the paternalistic attitude of the Bureau of Indian Affairs.[36]

While Indians' political and cultural affairs were proceeding from the New Deal to Red Power, historians were themselves achieving a growing maturity in their treatment of these events. Central to this advancement was the historians' recognition that documents, their chief resource, were sometimes written by unskilled and often prejudiced soldiers, traders, captives, agents, missionaries, and others whose emotional responses thwarted perception of Indian culture. Documentary history was questioned as being only the history of Indians as they affected whites.

The new orientation was toward culture as expressed in anthropology rather than documents. During the Indian Claims Commission cases of the 1950s, historians listened to testimony offered by anthropologists, and a respect for their observations on Indian culture and society grew. Ethnohistory, a blending of anthropology and history, became the most prominent new idea in the study of Native American culture. Historians increasingly sought out folklore, religion, and other influences to provide insights into the Indian character as well as his history. "The specimen under the glass did not change," wrote Calvin Martin, "only the perspective on him changed when the historian scrutinized him through another lens."[37]

Edward H. Spicer's *A Short History of the Indians of the United States* is indicative of this redirection in Indian history. The transition from traditional subjects to more analytical treatments of new concepts can be better observed, however, by comparing the special issues devoted to Indians published by several historical journals. In 1964 *Montana: The Magazine of Western History* and *Colorado Magazine* ran special issues on the Indian. The emphasis was on Indian wars and warriors, Sand Creek, the Nez Perce retreat, and so on. In 1971 the *Pacific Historical Review, Utah Historical Quarterly,* and *Kansas Quarterly* also featured the Indian theme. This time articles appeared on Indian historiography, the political context of a "new Indian history," comparative studies, reservation case studies, evaluations of Indian commissioners, and presentations by Native Americans themselves.[38]

In the three "Indian issues" of the journals produced in 1971, thirty-three different authors wrote articles. Their numbers were indicative of historical writing in the early 1970s, when Indian authorities began to appear from every direction. One practice was to dust off an old Ph.D. dissertation and send it to an eager publisher. It was not unusual to see published books based on research a quarter of a century old. Publishers, too, were caught up in Indian history as a growth industry; Arno Press, Ross and Haines, Greenwood Publishing Company, AMS Press, and Garland Publishing joined several well-known university presses in issuing reprints of "classic" Indian volumes. Some new editions had corrective footnotes; other reprints did not.[39]

Surveys were another quick method to break into print. In the 1960s three excellent histories opened the field of Indian history to general survey approaches. Historian William T. Hagan wrote *American Indians* as part of the University of Chicago Press's History of American Civilization Series; anthropologist Edward H. Spicer wrote *Cycles of Conquest,* emphasizing Indians of the Southwest; and William Brandon wrote the narrative for *The American Heritage Book of Indians.* By the early 1970s these editions were reputed to be out of date in their approach toward Indian culture and a new set of surveys appeared on the market. Unfortunately, most of the new efforts were not equal to the volumes they intended to replace. Angie Debo's *History of the Indians of the United States* relied on decades of previous research on the Five Civilized Tribes in Oklahoma, proving that the history of Oklahoma Indians cannot be generalized to apply to American Indians as a whole. Other surveys were by D'Arcy McNickle, an Oxford-educated Flathead Indian who republished in 1973 as *Native American Tribalism* a book that first appeared in 1962, and S. Lyman Tyler, who wrote *A History of Indian Policy* under contract with the Bureau of Indian Affairs. These volumes demonstrated that the substance of a survey depends upon the quality of monographs in the field, and in the early 1970s that vital area of Indian studies was only beginning to blossom.[40]

By the middle of the decade some of the worst abuses of "quickie" publication had dissipated, and there was an upward trend. In 1975 *The Indian in America* by Wilcomb Washburn appeared. This was particularly significant because it was a volume in the prestigious New American Nation Series, a recognition of the upgraded status of the field. Washburn, a prolific author of Indian books and staunch defender of ethnohistory, wrote a measured, comprehensive history of Indians from their coming to America to their search for identity in the 1970s.

Historians generally congratulated Washburn for his reasonable position. He believed that neither the Indian nor the white man could be totally blamed for the zigzag of American Indian policy in the past. Some ethnohistorians, however, felt that Washburn was being too "reasonable." They accused him of vague generalizations and of falling into an "acculturation syndrome" that would restore American Indian scholarship to a pre-1960 position.[41]

Indian history, then, was a rich field in the 1970s, alive to many publishing possibilities. But just as it began to divide along ethnohistorical concepts, so too there was interest in a new political context in writing the history of Indians. The "New Indian History" was best argued by Robert F. Berkhofer, Jr., in his 1971 article in the special issue of the *Pacific Historical Review*. He urged an Indian-Indian history, a record of ethnic survival as the red man trod the twin trails of Indian policy: acculturation or annihilation.[42]

More and more Indians wanted to write, and were capable of writing, for themselves. They wrote not as historians, anthropologists, or ethnologists, but as Indians. Vine Deloria, Jr., demanded as much in *Custer Died for Your Sins* in 1969. A witty but curious brand of contemporary history that threw barbs at social scientists, missionaries, bureaucrats, and Indian leaders, the book was less a history than a protest. N. Scott Momaday, a Kiowa, was one of several articulate Native Americans to approach history through literature. Indian programs were developed on college campuses; research libraries, most notably the Newberry Library, responded with special programs for Native American scholars.[43] The results have been encouraging.

But when Indians take the stance that only Indians are capable of writing Indian history, then there is discouragement, too. Among the most tribalistic of Indians are the Nez Perces. In *Noon-Me-Poo (We, the Nez Perces): Culture and History of the Nez Perces,* a book that acknowledges no sources and gives no citations for even direct quotes from tribal documents, the tribal historian states: "We have no sympathy with those who have written derogatory books about us and have chosen to ignore most of them. They are not our friends."[44] Such attitudes contribute little to the growth of Indian scholarship.

Documentary publications abounded during the 1970s. There were reprints of the annual reports of both the commissioner of Indian affairs and the Bureau of American Ethnology, plus the writings of the Friends of the Indians and other major reform organizations. There were also extensive microfilm editions of the expert testimony before the Indian Claims Commission.[45]

The next development in Indian historical literature came after the Bicentennial year, when an increasing number of reference works began to appear. Plans for the Smithsonian Institution-sponsored *Handbook of North American Indians* were begun in 1965, but the first volume did not appear until 1978. There will be twenty volumes in all, and each will be an encyclopedic summary by region of what is known about the prehistory, history, and culture of North American Indians. Meanwhile, in 1976 the Newberry Library Center for the History of the American Indian began to publish small bibliographies on tribes and topics. And in 1977 Francis Paul Prucha issued his *Bibliographical Guide to the History of Indian-White Relations in the United States,* covering books and articles issued through 1974. A supplement to that bibliography lists works published from 1975 to 1980.[46]

To have read a variety of historical journals dealing with frontier and Indian interests, perused their book review sections, and attended historical association meetings in the late 1970s, one would have thought Indian history had no direction. Military historians competed with acculturation historians and advocates of a new approach to Indian history for the limelight. But, in retrospect, Indian history had merely proceeded through several stages of development: contemporary reformist literature dominated for a time; then came a lag in interest in Indian policy problems; and, finally, there was a renaissance of interest that grew in stages, from a quick gratification of the market demands to making primary sources available and, at last, the emergence of substantive, mature scholarship.[47]

By the close of the 1970s, Indians and ethnohistorians were writing about "Indianness" in several Indian-oriented or activist journals. More traditional historians of Indian affairs, meanwhile, continued to publish the products of their research on the allotments of reservations, the Indian New Deal, the Indian Claims Commission, termination, and like subjects. New Indian historians were more concerned with Indian water rights, mineral resources on reservations, educational matters, urbanization, and legal aspects of the pan-Indian movement. The award-winning article by Norris Hundley, Jr., "The Dark and Bloody Ground of Indian Water Rights: Confusion Elevated to Principle," and the social science–oriented analysis, *The Indian Office: Growth and Development of an American Institution, 1865-1900*, by Paul Stuart, epitomize some of the original and controversial scholarship published on the threshold of the 1980s.[48]

As Indian history moved into the 1980s, it was increasingly interdisciplinary in its outlook. The field continues to emphasize white history with white documents, but less than it did a decade ago. Encouraged by the leading scholars in the field—Prucha, Hagan, Washburn, and Berkhofer among others—historians will continue to rethink their judgments on sources for Native American history. Anthropologist John C. Ewers argues that the archaeologist's spade, the oral historian's tape recorder, maps, paintings, and photographs all "yield data quite as important to an understanding of Indian history as the archivist's shelves of manuscripts."[49]

Native Americans themselves will also play a greater role in the research and writing of their own history. Accomplished scholars like R. David Edmunds, along with Veronica Tiller, Terry Paul Wilson, and Clifford Trafzer, are quietly making an impact on the writing of Indian history that will soon exceed the protests of Vine Deloria, Jr.[50]

Tribal histories have traditionally been a valuable genre of Indian history. The Civilization of the American Indian Series, begun in 1932 by the University of Oklahoma Press and now numbering over 150 volumes, is staying abreast of current interest by treating modern tribal problems as well as historical ones. *Menominee Drums: Tribal Termination and Restoration, 1954-1974* by Nicholas C. Peroff, for example, complements Patricia K. Ourada, *The Menominee Indians*, in the same series. Though most of the histories in this and other tribal series are in the traditional white-historical format, there is increased use of ethnohistorical approaches and more Indian authorship. The volumes by David Baird on *The Quapaw Indians* and R. David

Edmunds on *The Potawatomis* not only are solid history but are indicative of the redirection of Indian history.[51]

Comparative studies will probably be an important part of the Indian history of the 1980s. Wilbur Jacobs predicted as much in 1971 in his article, "The Fatal Confrontation: Early Native-White Relations on the Frontiers of Australia, New Guinea, and America—A Comparative Study." A comparison of American and Canadian policy toward Native Americans is the most logical outlet for this approach to Indian history. But for the moment a full-scale treatment must await greater progress by the Canadians as they assess their own policies.[52]

Finally, the interdisciplinary approach to Indian history will, in the future, rely heavily on the oral history collections at the universities of South Dakota, Utah, Oklahoma, and New Mexico. These collections are important contributions to an Indian-Indian orientation to Native American history. Some Indians, like N. Scott Momaday and Vine Deloria, Jr., are already disillusioned with the value of oral history, but its future significance seems assured to most others.[53]

The prospect that there will be major contributions to the literature of Indian history during the 1980s is great. Already, work is in progress exploring relationships, making comparisons, and testing theses on such wide-ranging topics as education, legal status, and environmentalism as it affects the Native American. Historians, ethnologists, and Native Americans are working together to shape a reliable, usable history of the Indian in America.

Notes

1. No comprehensive bibliography listing the reminiscences, recollections, diaries, or correspondence of participants in the Indian wars has yet been compiled. Francis Paul Prucha, *A Bibliographical Guide to the History of Indian-White Relations in the United States* (Chicago: University of Chicago Press, 1977), pp. 154–89, lists many personal accounts of the battles during the Civil War and after. See also the *United States Army and Navy Journal*, 1864–1964; *Journal of the Military Service Institution*, 1880–1917; *Army and Navy Register*, 1882–1962; *Cavalry Journal*, 1888–1944; *Army and Navy Journal*, 1866–85; John M. Carroll (ed. and comp.), *The Papers of the Order of Indian Wars* (Fort Collins, Colo.: Old Army Press, 1975). Complete files of the Order of Indian Wars are at the U.S. Military History Institute at Carlisle Barracks, Pennsylvania. The Order of Indian Wars was founded in 1896 to

"perpetuate the memories of the services rendered by the military forces of the United States in their conflicts and wars against hostile Indians."

2. Oliver H. Knight, "A Revised Check List of Indian War Correspondents, 1866-91," *Journalism Quarterly* 68 (Winter 1961): 81-82. The subject of Indian wars correspondents was effectively introduced by Knight, *Following the Indian Wars: The Story of Newspaper Correspondents Among the Indian Campaigns* (Norman: University of Oklahoma Press, 1960). The most recent volume is Daniel L. Thrapp (ed.), *Dateline Fort Bowie: Charles Fletcher Lummis Reports on an Apache War* (Norman: University of Oklahoma Press, 1979). Perhaps the best account by a correspondent is De Benneville Randolph Keim, *Sheridan's Troopers on the Borders: A Winter Campaign on the Plains* (Philadelphia: Claxton, Remsen and Haffelflinger, 1870). Keim reported on the 1868 campaign in the pages of the *New York Herald* and then added his personal experiences in greater detail for the book.

3. Don Rickey, Jr., *Forty Miles a Day on Beans and Hay: The Enlisted Soldier Fighting the Indian Wars* (Norman: University of Oklahoma Press, 1963; paperbound ed., 1977). The turn of the century also brought a rush of reminiscences by Old Army wives. Elizabeth Custer, Margaret Carrington, Lydia Lane, Frances M. Roe, Alice Baldwin, Ellen Biddle, and Mrs. Orsemus Boyd all published their personal accounts of life on the frontier. For additional information, see Sandra L. Myres, "Women in the West," in this book.

4. The treatment of the Sand Creek Massacre could serve as an illustration. A wide variety of Colorado participants, other citizens, and novelists wrote about that November dawn in 1864, a pattern that was especially characteristic of the period from the turn of the century to the mid-1920s. The first full-length treatment, however, did not appear until 1961, because previous writers had obscured the importance of the whole affair with endless debates on such questions as the guilt or innocence of Governor John Evans, agent Albert G. Boone, or Colonel John M. Chivington; whether the Indians were peaceful at Sand Creek or openly hostile; whether there was a conspiracy to expel all white settlers; and whether Black Kettle had an American flag flying before his tent when the troopers struck the village. See Michael A. Sievers, "Sands of Sand Creek Historiography," *Colorado Magazine* 49 (Spring 1972): 116-42.

5. Ralph K. Andrist, *The Long Death: The Last Days of the Plains Indians* (New York: Macmillan, 1964; paperbound ed., 1969); Paul I. Wellman, *Death on the Prairie: The Thirty Years' Struggle for the Western Plains* (New York: Macmillan, 1934), and *Death in the Desert: The Fifty Years' War for the Great Southwest* (New York: Macmillan, 1935). Wellman's two books were

later published together as *Death on Horseback: Seventy Years of War for the American West* (Philadelphia: J. B. Lippincott Co., 1947) and as *Indian Wars of the West* (Garden City, N.Y.: Doubleday, 1954). Both Wellman and Andrist wrote eminently readable books in the "Lo, the Poor Indian" style, with research limited to secondary sources.

6. William H. Leckie, *The Military Conquest of the Southern Plains* (Norman: University of Oklahoma Press, 1963); Keith A. Murray, *The Modocs and Their War* (Norman: University of Oklahoma Press, 1959; paperbound ed., 1976); Lonnie J. White, "The Battle of Beecher Island: The Scouts Hold Fast on the Arickaree," *Journal of the West* 5 (January 1966): 1-24, and other articles; Dan L. Thrapp, *The Conquest of Apacheria* (Norman: University of Oklahoma Press, 1967; paperbound ed., n.d.); Stan Hoig, *The Sand Creek Massacre* (Norman: University of Oklahoma Press, 1961; paperbound ed., n.d.); Knight, *Following the Indian Wars;* Robert M. Utley, *The Last Days of the Sioux Nation* (New Haven: Yale University Press, 1963; paperbound ed., n.d.); Merrill D. Beal, *"I Will Fight No More Forever":* Chief *Joseph and the Nez Perce War* (Seattle: University of Washington Press, 1963; paperbound ed., 1966); Rickey, *Forty Miles a Day.*

7. Utley, *The Last Days of the Sioux Nation,* p. 230; James Mooney, *The Ghost-Dance Religion and the Sioux Outbreak of 1890* (Washington, D.C.: Government Printing Office, 1896). Utley's interpretive differences with other historians can be seen in Michael A. Sievers, "The Historiography of 'The Bloody Field . . . That Kept the Secret of the Everlasting Word': Wounded Knee," *South Dakota History* 6 (Winter 1975): 33-54.

8. Robert M. Utley, *Frontier Regulars: The United States Army and the Indian, 1866-1891* (New York: Macmillan, 1973). In 1977 the book was reprinted in paperback by Indiana University Press. That same year Utley coauthored, with Wilcomb Washburn, *The American Heritage History of the Indian Wars* (New York: American Heritage Publishing Co., 1977), a coffee table book without footnotes, but essentially the same material as *Frontier Regulars.* J. P. Dunn, Jr., *Massacres of the Mountains: A History of the Indian Wars of the Far West, 1815-1875* (New York: Harper and Bros., 1886). Capricorn Books reissued the book in 1970, calling it the "definitive work . . . of the epic struggles of the American Indian."

9. At the time Utley was researching and writing *Frontier Regulars,* Wilcomb Washburn and Robert F. Berkhofer, Jr., among others, were vigorously urging a reorientation of traditional Indian history to an Indian-Indian emphasis. Wilcomb E. Washburn, "The Writing of American Indian History: A Status Report," *Pacific Historical Review* 40 (August 1971): 261-76; Robert

F. Berkhofer, Jr., "Native Americans and United States History," in *The Reinterpretation of American History and Culture,* ed. William H. Cartwright and Richard L. Watson, Jr. (Washington, D.C.: National Council for the Social Studies, 1973), pp. 37-52.

10. George A. Custer is the single most publicized figure in the Indian wars and more than a thousand books and articles have appeared on him. The best account of the battle of the Little Big Horn is considered to be Edgar I. Stewart, *Custer's Luck* (Norman: University of Oklahoma Press, 1955; paperbound ed., n.d.); the most balanced account of the man is Jay Monaghan, *Custer: The Life of General George Armstrong Custer* (Boston: Little, Brown, 1959; paperbound ed., Lincoln: University of Nebraska Press, 1971); also see W. A. Graham (ed.), *The Custer Myth: A Source Book of Custeriana* (Harrisburg, Pa.: Stackpole Company, 1953).

11. Before the Little Big Horn affair, officers who subsequently wrote of their experiences reserved their derogatory remarks for their Indian opponents. Now, army officers were outspoken in either their condemnation of Custer for disobeying orders by attacking the Sioux village when he did, or laudatory to the "boy general" for an act of heroism. The debate peaked in the 1890s, but not before it raised the question of the efficiency of America's military arm on the frontier.

12. Frederick F. Van de Water, *Glory Hunter: A Life of General Custer* (Indianapolis: Bobbs-Merrill, 1934) portrayed Custer as an "impetuous and irresponsible egotist." For an analysis of the Custer image, see Paul A. Hutton, "From Little Bighorn to Little Big Man: The Changing Image of a Western Hero in Popular Culture," *Western Historical Quarterly* 7 (January 1976): 19-45; Michael A. Sievers, "The Literature of the Little Bighorn: A Centennial Historiography," *Arizona and the West* 18 (Summer 1976): 149-76.

13. The press, as early as July 12, 1876, reported that Rain-in-the-Face had cut the heart from Custer's body. Writers followed the account as gospel truth and multiplied its savagery many times over. In 1894 Rain-in-the-Face, under the influence of liquor, confirmed the story. He later recanted, according to Charles Eastman, "Rain-in-the-Face," *Outlook,* October 27, 1906, pp. 507-12.

14. George Bird Grinnell presented a highly pro-Indian military account in *The Fighting Cheyennes* (New York: C. Scribner's Sons, 1915; reprint ed., Norman: University of Oklahoma Press, 1977). Some other early practitioners of oral history among the Indians, especially relating to the Little Big Horn matter, were Orin G. Libby, a professor at the University of North Dakota; Dr. Thomas Marquis, a lawyer and government physician in Montana whose

story of Wooden Leg is the clearest account of Indian movements on June 26, 1876, and whose criticism of Custer's men was not published until 1976; and Walter Camp, an engineer. Orin G. Libby (ed.), *The Arikara Narrative of the Campaign Against the Hostile Dakotas, June, 1876* (Bismarck: State Historical Society of North Dakota, 1920); Thomas B. Marquis, *Wooden Leg: A Warrior Who Fought Custer* (Minneapolis: Midwest Book Company, 1931; paperbound ed., Lincoln: University of Nebraska Press, 1962); Thomas B. Marquis, *Keep the Last Bullet for Yourself: The True Story of Custer's Last Stand* (New York: Two Continents Publishing Group, 1976); Kenneth Hammer (ed.), *Custer in '76: Walter Camp's Notes on the Custer Fight* (Provo, Utah: Brigham Young University Press, 1976).

15. Stanley Vestal, *Warpath: The True Story of the Fighting Sioux Told in a Biography of Chief White Bull* (Boston: Houghton Mifflin, 1934); John G. Neihardt, *Black Elk Speaks: Being the Life Story of a Holy Man of the Oglala Sioux* (New York: William Morrow and Company, 1932); Frank B. Linderman, *Red Mother* (New York: John Day Company, 1932); reprinted as *Pretty-Shield, Medicine Woman of the Crows* (Lincoln: University of Nebraska Press, 1974). Donald J. Berthrong does not see Campbell as a major interpreter of the Indian viewpoint; see Berthrong, "Walter Stanley Campbell: Plainsman," *Arizona and the West* 7 (Summer 1965): 91–104.

16. A nadir in Indian reminiscences was achieved when *Montana* published what appeared to be the *final* final interviews with survivors of Chief Joseph's retreat. Indians aged ninety-three and ninety-five recalled experiences when they were five and ten years of age. Rowena L. Alcorn, "Old Nez Perce Recalls Tragic Retreat of 1877," *Montana: The Magazine of Western History* 13 (January 1963): 66–74; and Rowena L. Alcorn and Gordon D. Alcorn, "Aged Nez Perce Recalls the 1877 Tragedy," *Montana: The Magazine of Western History* 15 (October 1965): 54–67. These veterans, however, turned out to be only the penultimate personal accounts when "Chief" Red Fox of the Sioux professed to be 101 years old and plagiarized James H. McGregor, *The Wounded Knee Massacre from Viewpoint of the Sioux* (Baltimore: Wirth Brothers, 1940), as *The Memoirs of Chief Red Fox* (New York: McGraw-Hill, 1971). See *New York Times*, March 10, 1972. Useful in the matter of Indian reminiscences and biographies is H. David Brumble III, *An Annotated Bibliography of American Indian and Eskimo Autobiographies* (Lincoln: University of Nebraska Press, 1981).

17. Savoie Lottinville (ed.), *Life of George Bent: Written from His Letters*, by George E. Hyde (Norman: University of Oklahoma Press, 1967).

18. Francis B. Heitman (comp.), *Historical Register and Dictionary of*

the United States Army, 2 vols. (Washington, D.C.: Government Printing Office, 1903); Joseph P. Peters (comp.), *Indian Battles and Skirmishes on the American Frontier* (New York: Arno Press, 1966); *Chronological List of Actions, etc. with Indians from January 15, 1837 to January, 1891,* intro. Dale E. Floyd (Fort Collins: Old Army Press, 1979) is a reprint of official army compilations.

19. Referring to his rather astounding figures of only 69 Sioux warriors killed and 102 wounded in a dozen encounters between 1865 and 1876, Vestal writes: "There is . . . uncertainty as to the exact number of Indians wounded. But there is *no* vagueness as to the number of dead. I consider the figures given for Indian dead . . . quite as accurate as the figures given by officers for white soldiers killed." Stanley Vestal (ed.), *New Sources of Indian History, 1850-1891* (Norman: University of Oklahoma Press, 1934), p. 102; George E. Hyde, *Red Cloud's Folk: A History of the Oglala Sioux Indians* (Norman: University of Oklahoma Press, 1937; paperbound ed., 1977); Don Russell, "How Many Indians Were Killed? White Man versus Red Man: The Facts and the Legend," *The American West* 10 (July 1973): 42-47, 61-63.

20. Dee Brown, *Bury My Heart at Wounded Knee: An Indian History of the American West* (New York: Holt, Rinehart and Winston, 1970; paperbound ed., New York: Bantam, 1972). See the laudatory reviews by Geoffrey Wolff in *Newsweek,* February 1, 1971, p. 69; R. Z. Sheppard in *Time,* February 1, 1971, pp. 80-81; and N. Scott Momaday in *New York Times Book Review,* March 7, 1971. See other reviews by Henry E. Fritz in *Pacific Historical Review* 41 (Fall 1972): 538-39; and especially by Francis Paul Prucha in *American Historical Review* 77 (Fall 1972): 589-90. See also letter of Lawrence C. Kelly in *Journal of American History* 58 (September 1971): 560-65.

21. John C. Ewers, "Intertribal Warfare as the Precursor of Indian-White Warfare on the Northern Great Plains," *Western Historical Quarterly* 6 (October 1975): 397-410; Ewers, "Introduction," in Dwight L. Smith (ed.), *Indians of the United States and Canada: A Bibliography* (Santa Barbara, Calif.: American Bibliographical Center-Clio Press, 1973); Michael L. Tate, "The Multi-purpose Army on the Frontier: A Call for Further Research," in *The American West: Essays in Honor of W. Eugene Hollon,* ed. Ronald Lora (Toledo: University of Toledo, 1980), pp. 171-208; Robert M. Utley, "The Contribution of the Frontier to the American Military Tradition," in *The American Military on the Frontier,* ed. James P. Tate (Washington, D.C.: Office of the Air Force History and United States Air Force Academy, 1978), pp. 3-13.

22. James T. King, "George Crook: Indian Fighter and Humanitarian," *Arizona and the West* 9 (Winter 1967): 333–48; Richard N. Ellis, "The Humanitarian Generals," *Western Historical Quarterly* 3 (April 1972): 169–78; King, "'A Better Way': General George Crook and the Ponca Indians," *Nebraska History* 50 (Fall 1969): 239–56; Michael J. Brodhead, "Elliott Coues and the Apaches," *Journal of Arizona History* 14 (Summer 1973): 87–94; Thomas C. Leonard, "Red, White and the Army Blue: Empathy and Anger in the American West," *American Quarterly* 26 (May 1974): 176–90; Thomas C. Leonard, "The Reluctant Conquerors: How the Generals Viewed the Indians," *American Heritage* 27 (August 1976): 34–40.

23. Theodore Roosevelt, *The Winning of the West,* 4 vols. (New York: G. P. Putnam's Sons, 1889–96), 2:147–48 and 3:44. Roosevelt also had some hateful things to say about crusader Helen Hunt Jackson and her *Century of Dishonor: A Sketch of the United States Government's Dealings with Some of the Indian Tribes* (New York: Harper and Bros., 1881), an influential but overrated piece of literature. Yet, Roosevelt assisted Edward S. Curtis in finding a sponsor to publish *The North American Indian: Being a Series of Volumes Picturing and Describing the Indians of the United States, and Alaska,* ed. Frederick Webb Hodge, 20 vols. (Seattle: E. S. Curtis, 1907–30).

24. *United States Statutes at Large,* 24:388–91; *Indians Taxed and Indians Not Taxed in the United States at the 11th Census: 1890* (Washington, D.C.: Government Printing Office, 1894), pp. 24–28; "Indian Land Tenure, Economic Status, and Population Trends," in *Supplementary Report of the Land Planning Committee* (Washington, D.C.: Government Printing Office, 1935), pt. X; Alvin M. Josephy, Jr., "Toward Freedom: The American Indian in the Twentieth Century," in *American Indian Policy: Indiana Historical Society Lectures, 1970–1971* (Indianapolis: Indiana Historical Society, 1971), pp. 38–40. The Burke Act of 1906, for example, accelerated the allotment process by permitting the issuance of land titles to individual Indians as soon as they were judged competent.

25. Early treatments of the reform era include Elsie M. Rushmore, *The Indian Policy during Grant's Administrations* (Jamaica, N.Y.: Marion Press, 1914); Loring B. Priest, *Uncle Sam's Stepchildren: The Reformation of United States Indian Policy, 1865–1887* (New Brunswick, N.J.: Rutgers University Press, 1942; paperbound ed., Lincoln: University of Nebraska Press, 1975); Henry E. Fritz, *The Movement for Indian Assimilation, 1860–1890* (Philadelphia: University of Pennsylvania Press, 1963). The Board of Indian Commissioners published annual reports, 1869–1932; the Indian Rights Association issued annual reports, 1883–1934; but see *Papers of the*

Indian Rights Association, 1864 (1882-1968) (Glen Rock, N.J.: Microfilming Corporation of America, 1973); *Proceedings of the . . . Annual Meeting of the Lake Mohonk Conference of Friends of the Indian, 1883-1916* (New York: Clearwater Publishing Company, 1975). See *North American Indians: A Dissertation Index* (Ann Arbor, Mich.: University Microfilms International, 1977) with *Supplement I* to 1978.

26. Robert W. Mardock, *The Reformers and the American Indian* (Columbia: University of Missouri Press, 1971); Francis Paul Prucha, *American Indian Policy in Crisis: Christian Reformers and the Indian, 1865-1900* (Norman: University of Oklahoma Press, 1976).

27. Francis Paul Prucha, *The Churches and the Indian Schools, 1888-1912* (Lincoln: University of Nebraska Press, 1979); Clyde A. Milner, *With Good Intentions: Quaker Work Among the Pawnees, Otos, and Omahas in the 1870s* (Lincoln: University of Nebraska Press, 1982); "Churchman and Western Indians" was held August 5-7, 1982, at Utah State University, Logan, Utah.

28. Edmund J. Danziger, Jr., *Indians and Bureaucrats: Administering the Reservation Policy During the Civil War* (Urbana: University of Illinois Press, 1974).

29. Donald J. Berthrong, "Cattlemen on the Cheyenne-Arapaho Reservation, 1883-1885," *Arizona and the West* 13 (Spring 1971): 5-32; Berthrong, "White Neighbors Come Among the Southern Cheyenne and Arapaho," *Kansas Quarterly* 3 (Fall 1971): 105-15; Berthrong, *The Cheyenne and Arapaho Ordeal: Reservation and Agency Life* (Norman: University of Oklahoma Press, 1976); and Berthrong, "Legacies of the Dawes Act. Bureaucrats and Land Thieves at the Cheyenne-Arapaho Agencies in Oklahoma," *Arizona and the West* 21 (Winter 1979): 335-54. The influences of corporation economies on reservations in Oklahoma is assessed in H. Craig Miner, *The Corporation and the Indian: Tribal Sovereignty and Industrial Civilization in Indian Territory, 1865-1907* (Columbia: University of Missouri Press, 1976). William T. Hagan, *United States-Comanche Relations: The Reservation Years* (New Haven: Yale University Press, 1976); and Hagan, "Kiowas, Comanches, and Cattlemen, 1867-1906: A Case Study of the Failure of U.S. Reservation Policy," *Pacific Historical Review* 40 (August 1971): 333-35. Hagan has more than once pioneered investigations into significant aspects of reservation life. His *Indian Police and Judges: Experiments in Acculturation and Control* (New Haven: Yale University Press, 1966; paperbound ed., Lincoln: University of Nebraska Press, 1980) is a highly regarded treatment of how Indians themselves both aided and detracted from reservation harmony.

30. William E. Unrau, "The Civilian as Indian Agent: Villain or Victim?"

Western Historical Quarterly 3 (October 1972): 405-20. See p. 420 for the conclusion: "Herein, then, lies the crux of the problem. A pro-military bias toward Indian policy and the settlement of the West, a new executive department with conflicting perogatives and little public support, an oversimplified belief that an expanding nation could somehow get along without a corresponding growth in its administrative ranks, and sweeping generalizations regarding alleged conspiracies to defraud both the public and the Indian at the grassroots level have resulted in a distorted picture of the civilian agent's place in American history." Lawrie Tatum, *Our Red Brothers and the Peace Policy of Ulysses S. Grant* (Philadelphia: John C. Winston and Co., 1899; paperbound ed., Lincoln: University of Nebraska Press, 1970); Thomas C. Battey, *The Life and Adventures of a Quaker Among the Indians* (Boston: Lee and Shepard, 1875); James McLaughlin, *My Friend the Indian* (Boston: Houghton Mifflin, 1910); Louis Pfaller, *James McLaughlin: The Man With an Indian Heart* (New York: Vantage Press, 1978). The experiences of many other agents have been published as articles. See Prucha, *A Bibliographical Guide,* pp. 109-13, for a listing of nearly one hundred items by and about Indian agents.

31. Francis Paul Prucha, "New Approaches to the Study of the Administration of Indian Policy," *Prologue* 3 (Spring 1971): 15-19. An equally good question implied by Prucha was, where are the studies of military men who served as Indian agents?

32. Carmelita S. Ryan, "The Written Record and the American Indian: The Archives of the United States," *Western Historical Quarterly* 6 (April 1975): 163-73; Ryan, "Special Study of the Appraisal of Indian Records"; Angie Debo, "Major Indian Record Collections in Oklahoma"; and Oliver W. Holmes, "Indian-Related Records in the National Archives and Their Use: Observations Over a Third of a Century," all in *Indian-White Relations: A Persistent Paradox,* ed. Jane F. Smith and Robert M. Kvasnicka (Washington, D.C.: Howard University Press, 1976), pp. 13-42, 112-18; William T. Hagan, "Archival Captive—The American Indian," *American Archivist* 41 (April 1978): 135-42.

33. Ralph C. Downes, "A Crusade for Indian Reform, 1922-1934," *Mississippi Valley Historical Review* 32 (December 1945): 331-54. See also Kenneth R. Philp, *John Collier's Crusade for Indian Reform, 1920-1954* (Tucson: University of Arizona Press, 1977); and Philp, "John Collier and the Crusade to Protect Indian Religious Freedom, 1920-1926," *Journal of Ethnic Studies* 1 (Spring 1973): 22-38.

34. D'Arcy McNickle, *They Came Here First: The Epic of the American Indian* (Philadelphia: J. B. Lippincott Co., 1949); D'Arcy McNickle and

Harold E. Fey, *Indians and Other Americans: Two Ways of Life Meet* (New York: Harper and Bros., 1959); William H. Kelley (ed.), *Indian Affairs and the Indian Reorganization Act: The Twenty Year Record* (Tucson: University of Arizona Press, 1954).

35. Lawrence C. Kelly, "The Indian Reorganization Act: The Dream and the Reality," *Pacific Historical Review* 44 (August 1975): 291–312; Kelly, "John Collier and the Indian New Deal: An Assessment," in *Indian-White Relations: A Persistent Paradox,* pp. 227–41; Philp, *John Collier's Crusade for Indian Reform, 1920–1954;* Donald J. Parman, *The Navajos and the New Deal* (New Haven: Yale University Press, 1976). Parman explains that Collier's plan to conserve the tribe's overgrazed land through livestock reduction contradicted the tribe's cultural heritage, which had always attached a great deal of prestige to the number of sheep owned by a family. See also Graham D. Taylor, *The New Deal and American Indian Tribalism: The Administration of the Indian Reorganization Act, 1934–45* (Lincoln: University of Nebraska Press, 1980); Clayton R. Koppes, "From New Deal to Termination: Liberalism and Indian Policy, 1933–1953," *Pacific Historical Review* 46 (November 1977): 543–66; D'Arcy McNickle, "The Indian New Deal as Mirror of the Future," in *Political Organization of Native North Americans,* ed. Ernest L. Schusky (Washington, D.C.: University Press of America, 1980), pp. 107–19.

36. Josephy, "Toward Freedom," pp. 38–42; Donald J. Berthrong, *The American Indian: From Pacifism to Activism* (St. Louis: Forum Press, 1973); William T. Hagan, "Tribalism Rejuvenated: The Native American Since the Era of Termination," *Western Historical Quarterly* 12 (January 1981): 5–16.

37. Calvin Martin, "Ethnohistory: A Better Way to Write Indian History," *Western Historical Quarterly* 9 (January 1978): 41–56. See also Nancy O. Lurie, "Ethnohistory: An Ethnological Point of View," *Ethnohistory* 8 (Winter 1961): 89; Robert C. Euler, "Ethnohistory in the United States," *Ethnohistory* 19 (Summer 1972): 201–7; Wilcomb E. Washburn, "Ethnohistory: History 'In the Round'" *Ethnohistory* 8 (Winter 1961): 31–48. Some of the anthropological work done at the turn of the twentieth century now of interest to historians includes the data collected by Robert H. Lowie, Alfred L. Kroeber, Clark Wissler, and George A. Dorsey.

38. Edward H. Spicer, *A Short History of the Indians of the United States* (New York: Van Nostrand Reinhold Company, 1969; paperbound ed.); *Montana: The Magazine of Western History* 14 (April 1964); *Colorado Magazine* 41 (Fall 1964); *Pacific Historical Review* 40 (August 1971); *Utah Historical Quarterly* 39 (Spring 1971); *Kansas Quarterly* 3 (Fall 1971). The

Pacific Historical Review issue has been expanded, revised, and reprinted in Wilcomb E. Washburn, et al., *The American Indian* (Santa Barbara, Calif.: American Bibliographical Center–Clio Press, 1974).

39. Typical was D. C. Otis, *The Dawes Act and the Allotment of Indian Lands,* ed. Francis Paul Prucha (Norman: University of Oklahoma Press, 1973), which was a reprint of an inconsequential government document first published in 1934. Worse was S. M. Barrett (ed.), *Geronimo's Story of His Life* (New York: Garrett Press, 1969), first issued in 1906, then republished in 1969 without so much as a new introduction or any corrective notes.

40. *The American Heritage Book of Indians,* editor in charge, Alvin M. Josephy, Jr., narrative by William Brandon (New York: American Heritage Publishing Company, 1961; text only edition by New York: Dell Publishing Company, 1964). The book was revised as William Brandon, *The Last Americans: The Indian in American Culture* (New York: McGraw-Hill, 1974). William T. Hagan, *American Indians* (Chicago: University of Chicago Press, 1961; rev. paperbound ed., 1979); Edward H. Spicer, *Cycles of Conquest: The Impact of Spain, Mexico and the United States on the Indians of the Southwest, 1533–1960* (Tucson: University of Arizona Press, 1962; paperbound ed.). Angie Debo, *History of the Indians of the United States* (Norman: University of Oklahoma Press, 1970); D'Arcy McNickle, *Native American Tribalism: Indian Survivals and Renewals,* revised ed., paperbound (New York: Oxford University Press, 1973); S. Lyman Tyler, *A History of Indian Policy* (Washington, D.C.: Department of the Interior, Bureau of Indian Affairs, 1973).

41. Wilcomb E. Washburn, *The Indian in America* (New York: Harper and Row, 1975; paperbound ed.). Review by Francis Paul Prucha, *Reviews in American History* (September 1975); Joseph Jorgensen and Richard Clemmer, "America in the Indian's Past: A Review," *Indian Historian* 11 (December 1978): 38–44.

42. Robert F. Berkhofer, Jr., "The Political Context of a New Indian History," *Pacific Historical Review* 40 (August 1971): 357–82; Berkhofer, "Native Americans and United States History," pp. 37–52. See P. Richard Metcalf, "Who Should Rule at Home? Native American Politics and Indian-White Relations," *Journal of American History* 61 (December 1974): 651–65, for an update on Berkhofer's proposal.

43. Vine Deloria, Jr., *Custer Died for Your Sins: An Indian Manifesto* (New York: Macmillan, 1969; paperbound ed., Avon, 1970). See also Vine Deloria, Jr., *Behind the Trail of Broken Treaties: An Indian Declaration of Independence* (New York: Delacorte Press, 1974; paperbound ed., Dell, 1974);

N. Scott Momaday, *House Made of Dawn* (New York: Harper and Row, 1968; paperbound ed., 1975); Momaday, *The Way to Rainy Mountain* (Albuquerque: University of New Mexico Press, 1969; paperbound ed., 1976). The Newberry Library Center for the History of the American Indian was established in 1972 and funded by grants from the National Endowment for the Humanities and other foundations. The center has academic fellowships for Indians and also publishes bibliographies, develops curricula, and offers seminars.

44. Alan P. Slickpoo, Sr., *Noon-Me-Poo (We, the Nez Perces): Culture and History of the Nez Perces* (Lapwai, Idaho: Nez Perce Tribe, 1973), p. viii.

45. See Richard N. Ellis, "Published Source Materials on Native Americans," *Western Historical Quarterly* 7 (April 1976): 189–92.

46. William C. Sturtevant, gen. ed., *Handbook of North American Indians*, 20 vols. projected (Washington, D.C.: Smithsonian Institution, 1978–). The Newberry Library Center for the History of the American Indian has already issued several seventy-five-page bibliographies on the Ojibwas, Navajos, Sioux, Apaches, and the Plains tribes, to name a few. Prucha, *A Bibliographical Guide*, and the sequel, *Indian-White Relations in the United States: A Bibliography of Works Published 1975-1980* (Lincoln: University of Nebraska Press, 1982). Prucha's two bibliographies are not only the best and most up-to-date listing of secondary works available, but they are also the most useful finding aid to primary sources. The volume issued in 1977, for example, cites more than three hundred catalogs, lists, and general guides to manuscript collections, government documents, and research libraries.

47. For appraisals of Indian historical literature, 1970–75, see Wilbur R. Jacobs, "The Indian and the Frontier in American History—A Need for Revision," *Western Historical Quarterly* 4 (January 1973): 43–56; Jacobs, "Native American History: How It Illuminates Our Past," *American Historical Review* 80 (June 1975): 595–609; Herman J. Viola, "Some Recent Writings on the American Indian," *American Archivist* 37 (January 1974): 51–54; Francis Paul Prucha, "An Awesome Proliferation of Writing About Indians," *Chronicle of Higher Education*, May 24, 1976, pp. 19–20; Prucha, "Books on American Indian Policy: A Half-Decade of Important Work, 1970-1975," *Journal of American History* 63 (December 1976): 658–69; Reginald Horsman, "Recent Trends and New Directions in Native American History," in *The American West: New Perspectives, New Dimensions*, ed. Jerome Steffen (Norman: University of Oklahoma Press, 1979), pp. 124–51.

48. Some of the best-known Indian periodicals of the 1970s were *American Indian Quarterly, American Indian Journal*, and *Wassaja/The Indian*

Historian. Prucha, *Indian-White Relations: A Bibliography,* pp. 16-19, lists eighteen publications on the Indian New Deal, eight on termination, fifteen on the Indian Claims Commission, thirteen on the Alaska Native Claims Settlement Act, and sixteen on the American Indian Policy Review Commission written between 1975 and 1980. By contrast, there are forty-six publications on water rights in the same period. Interest in Indian education is even more expansive. In Prucha's *A Bibliographic Guide,* covering all publications to 1974, there were 875 entries on education, but the second edition covers only five years yet lists another 397 citations. Norris Hundley, Jr., "The Dark and Bloody Ground of Indian Water Rights: Confusion Elevated to Principle," *Western Historical Quarterly* 11 (October 1978): 457-82; Paul Stuart, *The Indian Office: Growth and Development of an American Institution, 1865-1900* (Ann Arbor, Mich.: University Microfilms International Research Press, 1979). One of the by-products of Hundley's prodding was the publication of Michael L. Lawson, *Damned Indians: The Pick-Sloan Plan and the Missouri River Sioux, 1944-1980* (Norman: University of Oklahoma Press, 1982).

49. Ewers, Introduction to Smith, ed., *Indians of the United States and Canada,* p. xv.

50. R. David Edmunds (ed.), *American Indian Leaders* (Lincoln: University of Nebraska Press, 1980; paperbound ed.); Edmunds, *The Potawatomis: Keepers of the Fire* (Norman: University of Oklahoma Press, 1978). Veronica Tiller is a research consultant in Washington, D.C.; Terry P. Wilson directs the Native American Studies program at the University of California, Berkeley; and Clifford Trafzer is on the Native American Studies faculty at San Diego State University, and author of *The Kit Carson Campaign: The Last Great Navajo War* (Norman: University of Oklahoma Press, 1982).

51. Nicholas C. Peroff, *Menominee Drums: Tribal Termination and Restoration, 1954-1974* (Norman: University of Oklahoma Press, 1982); Patricia K. Ourada, *The Menominee Indians: A History* (Norman: University of Oklahoma Press, 1979); W. David Baird, *The Quapaw Indians: A History of the Downstream People* (Norman: University of Oklahoma Press, 1980); Edmunds, *The Potawatomis.* One of the finest examples of the traditional, white-oriented tribal histories is A. M. Gibson, *The Chickasaws* (Norman: University of Oklahoma Press, 1971). Interestingly, Gibson was the doctoral program advisor for both Baird and Edmunds at the University of Oklahoma.

52. Wilbur Jacobs, "The Fatal Confrontation: Early Native-White Relations on the Frontiers of Australia, New Guinea, and America—A Comparative Study," *Pacific Historical Review* 40 (August 1971): 283-309. See also W. Turrentine Jackson, "A Brief Message for the Young and/or Ambitious:

Comparative Frontiers as a Field for Investigation," *Western Historical Quarterly* 9 (January 1978): 12-14. The first scholarly account of white-native contact in any Canadian province is by a New Zealand anthropologist who writes history, Robin Fisher, *Contact and Conflict: Indian-European Relations in British Columbia, 1774-1890* (Vancouver: University of British Columbia Press, 1977).

53. The only published book-length collection of oral history transcripts is Joseph H. Cash and Herbert T. Hoover (eds.), *To Be an Indian: An Oral History,* paperbound ed. (New York: Holt, Rinehart and Winston, 1971). See also Richard N. Ellis, "The Duke Indian Oral History Collection at the University of New Mexico," *New Mexico Historical Review* 48 (July 1973): 259-63; Julia A. Jordan, "Oklahoma's Oral History Collection: New Source for Indian History," *Chronicles of Oklahoma* 49 (Summer 1971): 150-72; Alfonso Ortiz, "A Uniquely American Legacy," *Princeton University Library Chronicle* 30 (Spring 1969): 147-57. C. Gregory Crampton, "The Archives of the Duke Projects in American Indian Oral History," in *Indian-White Relations: A Persistent Paradox,* pp. 119-28. Indian disillusionment with oral history can be seen in Deloria, *Custer Died for Your Sins,* and N. Scott Momaday, "The Morality of Indian Hating," *Ramparts* 3 (Summer 1964): 29-40.

Chapter Ten

Gilbert C. Fite

The American West
of Farmers and Stockmen

Farming and ranching have provided a mainstay of western economic development since the days of earliest settlement. Within a decade after settlers arrived in Colorado, for instance, farming was producing more wealth than mining. Yet historians have given relatively little attention to the study of western agriculture and its place in the regional and national economy. Writers have concentrated on the seemingly more exciting topics of Indians, mining, the fur trade, railroads, exploration, gamblers, and cowboys. While it is true that ranching has not been neglected in the same way that dirt farmers have been ignored, the overall history of agriculture west of the 98th meridian still begs for broad historical treatment.

The main difficulty is the lack of works of synthesis and interpretation. There is, for instance, no general history of western agriculture and farming. Fortunately, source materials and specialized studies are abundant. The journal *Agricultural History* has been published since 1927, and it contains scores of articles on phases of western agricultural history. The index to these materials, "Agricultural History: An Index, 1927–1976," published by the Agricultural History Center at the University of California-Davis, provides ready access to this rich store of materials. The Agricultural History Center has also prepared a series of bibliographies that include extensive references to western agriculture. These guides are essential to anyone undertaking studies dealing with western agricultural development. Furthermore, students will find many valuable citations to agriculture in Oscar Winther's *Classified Bibliography of the Periodical Literature of the Trans-Mississippi West, 1811–1957*.[1]

The study of western agricultural history must begin with land policy. The type of farming and ranching that developed in the western United States depended not only on soil and climate, but on the amount of land that producers could acquire and operate. The question was whether westerners would be governed by land policies developed for farmers in the more humid region east of the 98th meridian. Would the older land system, based on the principle of small farms, be grafted onto a semiarid and arid West where, outside of irrigated areas, larger acreages were necessary? These were questions raised by both contemporary policymakers and by later historians.

Until the last half of the nineteenth century there was serious doubt if, without irrigation, the trans-Missouri West was suitable for farming at all. Perhaps as Stephen H. Long had reported in 1820, the region of the Great Plains, at least, would forever be the home of the buffalo and Indian. Much of the writing about western lands after passage of the Homestead Act in 1862 was either by those who believed much of the area beyond the 98th meridian was not suitable for farming, or by promoters who exaggerated the agricultural potential in order to lure farmers into the region. In 1878 John Wesley Powell published one of the earliest and most comprehensive surveys of the western lands in his *Report on the Lands of the Arid Region of the United States.* Powell argued that the Homestead Act, which provided for 160-acre farms, was totally unsuited to the semiarid and arid regions of the West unless irrigation were available on part of each farm or ranch. He recommended farms and ranches of at least 2,560 acres. Spokesmen for railroads, town site speculators, and other promoters of western settlement scoffed at Powell's assessment of how agriculture would fare throughout much of the West. Six years later Thomas Donaldson brought together large quantities of statistical data on land history in the *Public Domain,* which was published as a public document.[2]

While government agencies were producing raw data on the western lands, historical studies were slow in coming. It was not until 1924, after years in preparation, that the agricultural economist Benjamin H. Hibbard published the first survey of American land policy. Covering the period from the 1780s to the early twentieth century, Hibbard devoted about one-third of his book to western land policies. He was very critical of the Homestead Act and later land legislation, arguing that these measures encouraged speculation and an unhealthy concentration of landholdings. As Robert P. Swierenga pointed out many years later, Hibbard set the pattern followed by subsequent scholars for many years.[3]

In 1942, eighteen years later, Roy M. Robbins authored the second comprehensive history of American land policy. Entitling it *Our Landed Heritage: The Public Domain, 1776–1936,* Robbins devoted eleven chapters to the history of government land policy and disposition of the western public domain. Like Hibbard and a growing number of other scholars, Robbins was generally critical of government land policy and its administration. He did acknowledge, however, that federal lawmakers made some effort to adjust land policy to meet semiarid and arid conditions. Such legislation included the Newlands Act of 1902, which provided federal help to provide irrigation water for farmers, and the Enlarged Homestead Acts of 1909 and 1916, which permitted farmers in grazing areas to get larger acreages than allowed under the original Homestead Law. Robbins pointed out that land laws were so loosely drawn and poorly administered that individuals and corporations often acquired large bodies of land directly from the federal government at very cheap prices or through dummy entries. At about the same time, Harold H. Dunham carefully discussed the question of land law administration in *Government Handout: A Study in the Administration of the Public Lands, 1875-1891.*[4]

Meanwhile, Paul W. Gates was emerging as the nation's foremost student of public land policy. In 1936 he published his pace-setting article, "The Homestead Law in an Incongruous Land System." Sharply critical of the Homestead Act, Gates argued that by grafting this legislation onto previous land laws, Congress had failed to provide a form of land ownership that fit western geographic conditions or properly protected the interests of farmers and small stockmen. The Homestead Act, in other words, had failed as an instrument to promote economic democracy in the West.[5]

Gates's article, along with the earlier work of Hibbard, set the tone for western land studies for a generation. Subsequent writers tended to agree with Gates that the Homestead Act had not helped many farmers gain a new home on the public domain, and that it had, along with subsequent legislation, contributed to speculation and land monopoly. Robbins and Fred A. Shannon were among those strongly supporting this interpretation. By the time of the centennial of the Homestead Act in 1962, however, Gates had revised his earlier views. In "The Homestead Act: Free Land Policy in Operation, 1862-1935," he explained that the basic land law had played an important role in farm-making throughout much of the West. In his monumental study published in 1968, *History of Public Land Law Development,* Gates concluded: "That 1,322,107 homesteaders carried their entries to final patent after 3 or 5 years of residence is overwhelming evidence that, despite the poorly framed legislation with its invitation to fraud, the Homestead Law was the successful route to farm ownership of the great majority of settlers moving into the newer areas of the West after 1862." While many of these successful settlers were east of the 98th meridian, tens of thousands of them were west of that line.[6]

By the 1950s and 1960s an increasing number of scholars had rejected the earlier interpretations of Hibbard, Robbins, Gates, and others who had so sharply criticized the Homestead Act and other land laws. For example, Lawrence B. Lee showed how the Mormons successfully utilized the Homestead Act to establish farms in his article "Homesteading in Zion," as did Homer E. Socolofsky in his study of homesteading in Nebraska. The only general survey of western land policies in the first half of the twentieth century is E. Louise Peffer's *Closing of the Public Domain: Disposal and Reservation Policies, 1900–50.* Peffer's work is especially valuable, as she shows how the federal government moved to bring the public domain under more effective regulation and control.[7]

Policies that permitted thousands of acres to fall into the hands of railroad, ranching, and other corporations continued to arouse criticism from historians and social scientists. In a study completed in 1946, Walter Goldschmidt, an anthropologist, declared that concentration of landholdings in California not only hurt small farmers, but lowered the quality of community life as well. Recognition of Spanish land grants in California and New Mexico was partly responsible for monopolistic landholdings in those states. Studies by W. W. Robinson, *Land in California,* and by Victor Westphall, *The Public Domain in New Mexico, 1854–1891,* tell part of this story. Gates continued to emphasize the theme of the relationship between land policies and the development of large farms and ranches in California in his article "Public Land Disposal in California." He concluded that the land system in California helped to make that state "the land of the corporate-Agri-business farm." The history of one of the largest western landholdings, some 1.7 million acres in northern New Mexico, has been written by Jim B. Pearson. In *The Maxwell Land Grant,* Pearson discussed the conflicts, economic activity, and eventual disposition of this huge tract.[8]

As a result of federal and state land policies, the West contained an inordinate number of large agricultural operations from the 1880s onward. These included the bonanza farms of Dakota's Red River Valley, huge ranches in the plains and mountain states, and extensive farms and ranches in California.

While land policy was important in shaping agricultural development in the West, access to irrigation water in the arid and semiarid regions also played a key role. Without water for irrigation much of the West could not become agriculturally productive. Initially, farmers and ranchers settled along the creeks and rivers and diverted water to irrigate their adjacent fields of hay and grain. Much of the history of agricultural and ranching development west of the 100th meridian can be written in terms of the struggles to acquire water rights.

The federal government sought to encourage irrigation throughout the West. In 1877 Congress passed the Desert Land Act, which permitted settlers to acquire 640 acres of land for $1.25 an acre, providing part of the land was irrigated within three years. A settler had to pay only 25 cents an acre at the time of filing and the remaining $1 at the end of the three years. There were many abuses under the Desert Land Act. Much of the land filed on was not really desert at all, and little irrigation actually occurred as a result of the law. This legislation was more important in providing a means for ranchers and speculators to acquire large tracts at cheap prices.

The federal government's major effort to develop additional farms in the West through irrigation came with passage of the Reclamation Act of 1902. This law called for taking funds from the sale of public lands in sixteen western states and using the money to build irrigation facilities for western farmers. Farms receiving water from these newly created federal projects, however, were to be limited in size. The law stated that "no right to the use of water for land in private ownership shall be sold for a tract exceeding 160 acres to any one land holder." Here was an example of the federal government, through its water policy, planning agricultural development for family-type farmers in the West. This part of the statute, however, was never adequately enforced, and in some parts of the West, especially in California, large corporations and agribusiness firms gained control of huge acreages irrigated by water from federal projects, thus defeating the intention of preserving land and water rights for small farmers.

Western irrigation studies can be divided into at least three broad categories. First, there are the early government investigations that explored the prospects for irrigation in the West. One of the best of these surveys was done by a Senate committee in 1890 on the "irrigation and reclamation of arid lands." The investigators discussed the prospects of trying to farm in the West without irrigation and made suggestions for making water available to expand irrigated agriculture. Early promotional histories also fit into this category. Elwood Mead, one of the strongest supporters of irrigation, dealt with some of the early history and problems in *Irrigation Institutions.* In 1898 the Johns Hopkins University Studies in History and Political Science published Charles H. Brough's study, *Irrigation in Utah.* This was an optimistic account of how the Mormons had developed a sound agriculture based on the cooperative system of water distribution. William E. Smythe, another avid backer of irrigation expansion, published *The Conquest of Arid America* in 1905. This represented a further effort to promote irrigation.[9]

Another area of scholarship considered the questions of water rights and irrigation law. Three writers who have made distinctive contributions to the study of western irrigation and water policy are Robert G. Dunbar, Lawrence B. Lee, and Wells A. Hutchins. Hutchins discussed water law and how it affected western farmers in *Selected Problems in the Law of Water Rights in the West,* which appeared in 1942. Published as a government document, this study provided clear explanations of the doctrines of riparian rights versus prior appropriation and analyzed the problems arising from conflicting policies and interpretations of water law. Hutchins subsequently wrote a series of articles and pamphlets on water rights and problems in several states. Dunbar first concentrated his studies on Colorado and Montana. His articles on "The Origins of the Colorado System of Water-Right Control" and "Groundwater Property Rights and Controversies in Montana" are classic accounts. The latter study is important in that it outlines problems of conflict over groundwater rights between farmers and industrialists into the 1960s. Lee has emphasized the role of William E. Smythe and others in promoting irrigation in California and elsewhere in the 1890s, and has published articles dealing with conflicts over water rights. His *Reclaiming the American West: An Historiography and Guide* is absolutely essential for studying irrigation in the West. Michael C. Robinson's *The Bureau of Reclamation, 1902–1977* has a section that deals with the bureau's efforts to make water available for western irrigated farms.[10]

Most scholars who have written on western irrigation as it relates to agriculture have emphasized water rights and the irrigation movement rather than saying much about actual irrigation farming. Neither Paul W. Gates, who has a long chapter on water and reclamation policies in his book *History of Public Land Law Development,* nor Roy E. Huffman, in his *Irrigation Development and Public Water Policy,* has much to say on actual farming under irrigated conditions. The federal census in 1890 provided the first detailed account of the number, size, and production of western irrigated farms. Later censuses continued to provide extensive data on irrigated farming. Some of the best information on crop and livestock farming operations in the irrigated areas can be found in the various state agricultural experiment station bulletins. Much of the information found there has not been used by historians. One of the major conflicts over water use has been best discussed by Robert L. Kelley in *Gold vs. Grain: The Hydraulic Mining Controversy in California's Sacramento Valley.*[11]

Not all of the water for irrigation in the West came from streams and rivers requiring policies and laws for distribution to users. In parts of the Great Plains, California, and elsewhere, farmers turned to groundwater for irrigation. How deep-well irrigation developed on the southern Plains and how it effected agricultural development in that region has been told by Donald E. Green in his excellent *Land of the Underground Rain.* Subtitled *Irrigation on the Texas High Plains, 1910–1970,* Green's book deals with the early development of irrigation in the region, the technology associated with pump irrigation, expansion of irrigated agriculture, and the overall effect of irrigation on the region's agriculture. Moving farther north on the plains, R. Douglas Hurt has written about "Irrigation in the Kansas Plains Since 1930." Hurt shows how irrigation greatly increased farm productivity and how it caused land values to rise sharply; he then raises questions about future fuel costs and water supplies.[12]

The materials needed to understand general agricultural development in the West are even more scattered than the material that provides a view of western land and water policies and their effect on the development of western agriculture. As mentioned earlier, there is no general history of western farming. Indeed, many aspects of crop and livestock production, the importance of agriculture in western economic growth, rural life, labor, farm politics, marketing, irrigation, and other facets of the region's agriculture have not had full monographic treatment. For many topics relating to western agriculture, readers must rely on article-length studies. There is, of course, material on crop and livestock raising in the general studies of the West. Such works as those by Rupert N. Richardson and Carl Coke Rister, *The Greater Southwest* (1934), W. E. Hollon, *The Great American Desert Then and Now* (1966), and Robert G. Athearn, *High Country Empire: The High Plains and Rockies* (1960) all contain some discussion of settlement, land policies, water problems, crops, livestock, and other matters relating to western agriculture. Histories of the individual western states also include material on farming and ranching. But no overall picture emerges from any of these general histories which shows the extent and importance of western farming.[13]

The only attempt to survey the agricultural settlement of the West in the late nineteenth century is Gilbert C. Fite's *The Farmers' Frontier, 1865–1900.* In this volume Fite includes chapters on the settlement and early agricultural development of the western prairies and Great Plains, the Rocky Mountains, the Pacific Northwest, California, and West Texas and Oklahoma. The central theme of this study deals with the need for agricultural adjustment and experimentation in the semiarid and arid West. Fite concludes that in general farmers adjusted satisfactorily to the new environment. The basic importance of western agriculture, Fite says, was the great addition to the nation's farm output, especially in the production of wheat, livestock, and specialized fruit and vegetable crops.

While *The Farmers' Frontier* provides a synthesis of agricultural growth in the early years of western settlement, there is no work that carries the story into the twentieth century. However, Ladd Haystead and Fite have provided a good deal of information about western agriculture and its importance at mid-twentieth century in *The Agricultural Regions of the United States.* Four chapters in this volume are devoted to farming and ranching in the West. They are organized by region and emphasize the leading crops and livestock production. Statistical series showing trends in production, number and size of farms, value of products sold, and other data are included for individual western states. This study, however, is more descriptive than interpretive. The same is true of the excellent articles by Oliver E. Baker that appeared under the general title "Agricultural Regions of North America," published in *Economic Geography* between 1928 and 1932. There are thirteen chapters on western farming and ranching in Edward Higbee's *American Agriculture,* published in 1958. The volume of *Agricultural History* appearing in January 1975 and subtitled "Agriculture in the Development of the Far West," edited by James H. Shideler, contains thirty-eight articles, which grew out of an agricultural history symposium held at Davis, California, in 1974. Thomas R. Wessel edited the January 1977 issue of *Agricultural History,* which included twenty articles on Great Plains agriculture presented at a meeting at Montana State University in June 1976. Studies in these two volumes cover a wide variety of topics important in gaining a better understanding of agriculture in the Great Plains and Far West.[14]

If scholars have neglected to treat the agricultural history of the West in regional terms, they have done no better in writing state histories of agriculture. There is no modern scholarly history of agriculture for any western state. The best state study is Alvin T. Steinel's *History of Agriculture in Colorado* (1926), but it is sadly out of date. Nevertheless, this volume provides a fairly good account of Colorado's agricultural development from 1858 to 1926. Steinel covers such topics as early farm settlement, livestock raising, irrigation, sugar beet growing, and dry land farming. This volume is more a collection of facts than a historical synthesis, but it is a most valuable contribution to the West's agricultural history. Much can be learned about the development of agriculture in the West by viewing the photographic essay *Agricultural Technology and Society in Colorado* by David McComb. Claude B. Hutchison had edited a book entitled *California Agriculture,* which comes closest to providing an overall view of agriculture in that highly important farm state. Written by members of the College of Agriculture faculty at the University of California-Davis, the chapters deal with a broad variety of subjects, including a chapter on "The Historical Background of California Agriculture." Samuel L. Evans's doctoral dissertation, "Texas Agriculture, 1880–1930," provides the best survey of agricultural development in that state, and Verne S. Sweedlun has written on Nebraska agriculture. Donald E. Green edited a small volume on *Rural Oklahoma,* which contains some important articles on aspects of that state's agriculture.[15]

While failing to tackle a broad survey of western agricultural history, scholars have explored specific aspects of it in considerable detail. Much has been written on the problems faced by farmers as they moved onto the treeless prairies and plains west of the 98th meridian. The question was, how would farmers who came from the more humid Midwest and East adjust and adapt to the semiarid conditions found on the Great Plains?

In 1931 Walter Prescott Webb dealt with the broad question of adaptation in his book, *The Great Plains.* While Webb considered the impact of the Plains environment on aspects of life and institutions besides agriculture, he did emphasize that, if farmers were to succeed, they had to grow drought-resistant crops, implement dry farming techniques, and obtain larger acreages than they had in the forested areas.

It was James C. Malin, however, who wrote the most illuminating studies on the problems of necessary adjustments by Great Plains farmers. Beginning in 1936 with his article "The Adaptation of the Agricultural System to Sub-humid Environment," Malin examined the farm population and agricultural development in a township in Edwards County in western Kansas. This was one of the earliest studies based on the manuscript census material, as well as on accounts of a Farmer's Club in Edwards County. Malin showed how farmers shifted from corn to wheat growing, how they cultivated drought-resistant sorghum, and how they made other satisfactory adjustments to the semiarid region. In 1944 Malin expanded his themes in *Winter Wheat in the Golden Belt of Kansas.* His discussion of the introduction, acceptance by farmers, and expansion of hard red winter wheat in Kansas illustrates a major development in adaptation by farmers to a different agricultural environment. The Turkey Red variety was more hardy and drought-resistant, and it yielded better. In *The Great Plains in Transition* Carl Kraenzel dealt with the economic and social problems facing rural residents on the Great Plains in the mid-twentieth century.[16]

Pursuing the same theme of needed agricultural adjustment, Mary Wilma M. Hargreaves wrote an excellent book, *Dry Farming in the Northern Great Plains, 1900-1925.* In this study, Hargreaves dealt with the problems of recurrent drought, the promotional activities behind the dry farming movement, land policies, and climatic problems as they related to stable agricultural settlement. The best account of how farming developed on the Southern Plains, particularly the Texas Panhandle, is a series of four articles by Garry L. Nall published in the *Panhandle-Plains Historical Review* between 1972 and 1975. Beginning with a discussion of "The Farmers' Frontier in the Texas Panhandle," Nall takes the history of Panhandle agriculture through the 1930s. Much information can also be found in Charles M. Studness, "Development of the Great Plains Grain Farming Economy . . . to 1953," a doctoral dissertation completed at Columbia University in 1963. The promotion of agricultural settlement on the central Plains in the late nineteenth century has been discussed by David M. Emmons in *Garden in the Grasslands: Boomer Literature of the Central Great Plains.*[17]

The problems created by absentee farmers on the High Plains have been analyzed by Leslie Hewes, a geographer, in his book, *The Suitcase Farming Frontier.* Hewes examines the role of the nonresident farmer in western Kansas and eastern Colorado during the years from 1915 to 1968. The only general survey of farming in the Great Plains is Gilbert C. Fite's brief article, "Great Plains Farming: A Century of Change and Adjustment."[18]

Among the first serious studies of dust storms, a common occurrence on the plains, were three articles by James C. Malin that appeared in the *Kansas Historical Quarterly* covering the years from 1850 to 1900. The dust storms of the 1930s have been the subject of three books with widely differing views. Donald Worster argues in *Dust Bowl: The Southern Plains* that exploitation of the land by greedy farmers, especially wheat growers, paved the way for dust storms and soil losses, while in *The Dust Bowl: Men, Dirt, and Depression* Paul Bonnifield blames conditions on technology and New Deal agricultural planners. In his somewhat broader study, *The Dust Bowl: An Agricultural and Social History,* R. Douglas Hurt shows how the people and the region responded to this natural disaster.[19]

One part of the agricultural West that has been the subject of intense historical study is the Red River Valley of North Dakota. In 1964 Hiram M. Drache's *The Day of the Bonanza* appeared, and three years later Stanley

N. Murray's *The Valley Comes of Age* was published. Drache concentrated on the large bonanza farms of the 1870s and 1880s that were developed on railroad lands, explaining their operation and why they declined by the 1890s. Murray also deals with the large farms but gives attention to smaller operators as well. He discusses the history of agricultural development in that area up to about 1920. In 1970 Drache wrote a social history of farming and farm life in the Red River Valley entitled *The Challenge of the Prairie.*[20]

Several books deal with frontier farm life. Everett Dick's *The Sod-House Frontier* discusses economic and social conditions among settlers in late nineteenth-century Kansas and Nebraska. Another fine study is John Ise's *Sod and Stubble.* Based on the recollections of Ise's family, particularly his mother, this book reveals a great deal about day-to-day and year-to-year living on a farm in western Kansas during the 1870s and 1880s. Carl Coke Rister described farm homes, people at play, home health remedies, religion, education, and other aspects of rural life in *Southern Plainsmen.*[21]

Differences in land policies, climate, and geography produced tremendous variations in agriculture throughout the Rocky Mountain and Pacific Coast regions. One of the best regional studies that contains much about farming is Leonard J. Arrington's *Great Basin Kingdom: An Economic History of the Latter-day Saints, 1830–1900.* Arrington provides material on early irrigation, crops, and farm life in the intermountain region. Arrington's volume on *Beet Sugar in the West* is mainly an industrial history of the Utah-Idaho Sugar Company, but his book also contains a substantial amount of material on sugar beet growing in the West. Statistical information on agriculture and how it relates to the rest of the economy in the mountain West has been presented by Arrington in *The Changing Economic Structure of the Mountain West, 1850–1950.*[22]

Dorothy O. Johansen and Charles M. Gates have presented a considerable amount of agricultural history of the Pacific Northwest in their book *Empire of the Columbia,* as did Oscar Winther in his study of *The Great Northwest.* More specialized studies on farms and crops are those by Robert C. Nesbit and Charles M. Gates, "Agriculture in Eastern Washington, 1890–1910" and Neil W. Johnson and Rex E. Willard, *Trends in Agriculture in Washington, 1900 to 1930.* Idaho Agricultural Experiment Station researchers did a study of *The Farming Business in Idaho,* which covers the years from about 1870 to the mid-1920s.[23]

Early wheat growing in the Pacific Northwest has been considered by Edwin S. Holmes, Jr., who wrote *Wheat Growing and General Agricultural Conditions in the Pacific Coast Region of the United States.* The Palouse country of eastern Washington and western Idaho became one of the greatest wheat-producing regions in the nation. James F. Shepherd has described this in "The Development of Wheat Production in the Pacific Northwest." He discusses production, marketing, mechanization, and scientific advances in wheat growing. *The Great Columbia Plain: A Historical Geography, 1805–1910* by D. W. Meinig contains a good deal of information on agricultural development in the Pacific Northwest.[24]

The history of California's agriculture is by no means commensurate with its importance as a farm state. As mentioned earlier, Hutchison's *California Agriculture* has much historical material, but it does not provide a full survey of agriculture in that state. Unfortunately, Lawrence J. Jelinek's *Harvest Empire: A History of California Agriculture* is too brief and general to fulfill the need for a solid history of farming in California. On early developments in the American period, *California Ranchos and Farms, 1846–1862*, edited by Paul W. Gates, provides some excellent descriptions of farming and ranching. Much of this material originally appeared in the contemporary farm press. Another good survey is Rodman W. Paul's "The Beginnings of Agriculture in California: Innovation vs. Continuity," in which he explains that farmers tried to emulate the farm practices previously known, especially in regard to wheat growing. A very brief survey of the broad changes that occurred in California farming has been written by Howard S. Reed in "Major Trends in California Agriculture." Some of the changes that occurred in southern California can be traced in "Transformation of Southern California to a Cultivated Land," by Hallock F. Raup. Another study worthy of attention is Osgood Hardy's "Agricultural Changes in California, 1860–1900," which appeared in the Pacific Coast Branch, American Historical Association Proceedings for 1929. The rise and decline of wheat growing can be followed in Kenneth A. Smith's doctoral dissertation, "California: The Wheat Decades." Wheat marketing can be studied in Rodman W. Paul's "The Wheat Trade Between California and the United Kingdom."[25]

Despite the fact that western farmers have been leaders in mechanizing their production, this story must be reconstructed from many sources. A good brief survey is Roy Bainer's "Science and Technology in Western Agriculture," which discusses different types of machinery, from the combine to the tomato harvester. Leo Rogin included scattered references to western farm mechanization in his *Introduction to Farm Machinery*. In his prize-winning study of *Steam Power on the American Farm*, Reynold M. Wik has discussed the use of large steam tractors for plowing and threshing in the late nineteenth century, particularly in the Dakotas and the Pacific Coast states. The best study of a specific machine is Wayne D. Rasmussen's "Advances in American Agriculture: The Mechanical Tomato Harvester as a Case Study."[26]

Unlike farming, western ranching has been the subject of extensive research and writing. The earliest books on the western cattle industry were written by contemporary observers and participants, and they tended to be mainly promotional. One of the earliest men to play an important role in the western cattle business was Joseph G. McCoy, who established Abilene, Kansas, in the late 1860s as the western shipping point for cattle trailed northward from Texas. In 1874 McCoy published *Historic Sketches of the Cattle Trade of the West and Southwest.* While McCoy gave an optimistic account of the cattle ranching in the Southwest, his was restrained compared with that in two other popular books. In 1881 General James S. Brisbin, who had commanded several western military posts, wrote *The Beef Bonanza; or, How to Get Rich on the Plains.* The book's subtitle states its main theme. Brisbin gave glowing accounts of the profits to be made in western cattle ranching. Four years later, Walter Baron von Richthofen's *Cattle Raising on the Plains of North America* dealt with some of the successful cattle kings in Colorado and provided further evidence of the money to be made on western ranches. Joseph Nimmo, Jr., did a study in 1885 that provided statistical evidence on the raising and marketing of western cattle.[27]

Between the late nineteenth century and the 1920s many books and articles appeared on various aspects of ranching and cowboy life. It was not until 1929, however, that high standards of ranching scholarship began to appear. Ernest S. Osgood, author of *The Day of the Cattlemen,* wrote the first scholarly survey of western ranching. Although Osgood concentrated on ranching on the northern Plains of Wyoming and Montana, he also discussed the general trends in the western cattle business during the late nineteenth century. Much could be learned about ranching on the southern Plains from J. Evetts Haley's *The XIT Ranch of Texas,* which also appeared in 1929. Based on a wide variety of sources, including company records, Haley wrote an excellent history of the XIT, the largest ranch in the country under fence. He described how this 3-million-acre operation was established, how ranching functions were carried out, how it made the transition from longhorns to thoroughbreds, and how farmers subsequently bought much of the XIT. The Osgood and Haley books encouraged many additional specialized studies of cattle ranching.[28]

In 1930 E. E. Dale, who had been a small rancher in Oklahoma before becoming a historian, published *The Range Cattle Industry.* Dale discussed the Texas cattle industry at the close of the Civil War, the long drives, ranching as it developed up to 1900 on the Central Plains and in Texas and Oklahoma. He also discussed the transition to fenced operations and explained the relationship between the range cattle business and feeders in the Corn Belt. Dale later wrote a social history of ranching, which was published under the title *Cow Country.*

The Cattlemen's Frontier by Louis Pelzer appeared in 1936. Although Pelzer dealt with many of the same subjects covered by Osgood and Dale, he gave special attention to the importance of the Wyoming Stock Growers Association and considered the importance of eastern and foreign capital in the western ranching business. Pelzer carried the story down to 1890. In 1939 O. B. Peake added detail to the history of the cattle business with his study of ranching in Colorado. Meanwhile, Mari Sandoz provided insights into ranch and farm life in northwest Nebraska, beginning in the 1880s, in her book *Old Jules.* This story of her father, a tough old pioneer, became a classic piece of western literature. Sandoz also wrote a popular account of ranching on the plains extending well into the twentieth century. *When Grass Was King* by Maurice Frink, W. Turrentine Jackson, and Agnes Wright Spring also deals with general aspects of the cattle industry in the late nineteenth century. Bringing the story up to the middle of the twentieth century, Charles L. Sonnichsen wrote of *Cowboys and Cattle Kings: Life on the Range Today.* The best account of the cattle business on the plains in the twentieth century is John T. Schlebecker's *Cattle Raising on the Plains, 1900–1961.* Schlebecker shows how cattlemen adjusted to the Great Plains environment and deals with new cattle breeds, science, and other aspects of the modern cattle industry.[29]

In the decade after 1929 the works of Osgood, Dale, Pelzer, and Peake provided excellent histories of the range cattle business, mainly on the Great Plains and during the period of virtually free grass. These books, along with Haley's study of the XIT ranch, stimulated a growing number of histories of individual ranches and special phases of the western cattle industry. Studies of the Matador Land and Cattle Company in West Texas, the Spur Ranch and the famous King Ranch in South Texas, the 101 Ranch in Oklahoma, the Swan Land and Cattle Company of Wyoming, and the Irvine Ranch in California all added greatly to a better understanding of the ranching business in the late nineteenth and early twentieth centuries.[30]

Studies of individual ranchers also contributed greatly to the scholarly literature on the cattle business. Besides his book on the XIT, Haley wrote biographies of two prominent Texas cattlemen, Charles Goodnight and

George Littlefield. Less has been done on twentieth-century cattlemen, but Donald E. Green's biography of Henry C. Hitch, rancher in the Oklahoma Panhandle, is an excellent study. But the best discussion of large ranchers in the late nineteenth century, the kind of people they were, and the impact they made on their society is Lewis E. Atherton's *The Cattle Kings.* The relationship between the cattle business and the development of western towns has been told by Robert R. Dykstra in *The Cattle Towns.* He shows that the cattle trade did not have a very lasting effect on western town building. An important aspect of the background of western ranching has been treated by Terry G. Jordan in *Trails to Texas: Southern Roots of Western Cattle Ranching.*[31]

Early ranching in California has been covered by Robert G. Cleland in *The Cattle on a Thousand Hills: Southern California, 1850–1880,* and in "A History of California's Range Cattle Industry, 1770–1912," a doctoral dissertation by Hazel A. Pulling. J. Orin Oliphant, the leading authority on the cattle business in the Pacific Northwest during the late nineteenth century, has brought together years of research in *On the Cattle Ranges of the Oregon Country.*[32]

Much has been written on financing the cattle business by eastern and foreign capitalists. Herbert O. Brayer's article published in 1949 on "The Influence of British Capital on the Western Range-Cattle Industry" set the pattern for a series of additional studies. The best account is *Bankers and Cattlemen* by Gene M. Gressley. Dealing mainly with financing the cattle business in the 1880s, Gressley has provided careful detail of eastern investments in the western cattle business and what this meant to the industry. W. Turrentine Jackson has written about Scottish investments.[33]

Works on aspects of ranching in the mid-twentieth century include Mont Saunderson's *Western Stock Ranching,* Marion Clawson's *The Western Range Livestock Industry,* and Phillip O. Foss's *Politics and Grass,* which is a study of the background of Taylor Grazing Act of 1934 and an explanation of how ranchers utilize the public domain. Charles L. Wood, *The Kansas Beef Industry,* covers the period after 1890 in that state and discusses many phases of the modern cattle business, including the development of large feedlots.[34]

Cowboys and their role in the ranching enterprises have been the subject of numerous books and articles. One of the earliest studies of the cowboy, published in 1898, was Emerson Hough's *The Story of the Cowboy.* Although Hough discussed the life and work of cowboys on the range, his book presented a rather romantic view. *My Life on the Range,* written in 1924 by John Clay, was a first-hand account of cowboy and ranch life. The best overall study of the western cowboy, however, is *The American Cowboy: The Myth and the Reality* by Joe B. Frantz and Julian Ernest Choate. Contemporary newspaper and magazine accounts have been brought together in *Trailing the Cowboy: His Life and Lore as Told by Frontier Journalists,* while a group of other writings have been edited by Lon Tinkle and Allen Maxwell in *The Cowboy Reader.* There is also a substantial amount of material on cowboys in Wayne Gard's *The Chisholm Trail* and Donald E. Worcester's *Chisholm Trail: High Road of the Cattle Kingdom.* Philip Durham and Everett L. Jones have discussed black cowboys. Scarcely any aspect of the West has gripped the interest and imagination of Americans as has the real or imagined life and character of the cowboy. Two books by William W. Savage, Jr., both published in the 1970s, deal with the myths and imagery that grew up around the cowboy in American history. *Cowboy Life: Reconstructing an American Myth* is an edited volume that shows how romantic views about cowboys developed. In *The Cowboy Hero: His Image in American History and Culture,* Savage follows the image through advertising, the movies, and other mass media. He seeks to debunk the popular cowboy image.[35]

The literature on the sheep industry is relatively meager. In a special study done by the Bureau of Animal Husbandry, H. A. Heath and John Minto wrote an extensive account of the western sheep industry which was published in 1892. The only two books that provide fairly broad treatment of the sheep business are *Shepherd's Empire* by Charles W. Towne and Edward N. Wentworth, and Edward N. Wentworth's *America's Sheep Trails.* In the latter volume Wentworth deals with feeding, ranch management, disease, predatory animals, and other matters relating to sheep raising in the United States. *The Golden Hoof: The Story of Sheep of the Southwest* is a popular and interesting account.[36]

It is clear that many aspects of western farming and ranching have been treated well by historians. The need continues, however, for books on many of the main topics and a synthesis of the region's overall agricultural development. The bibliographies prepared by the Agricultural History Center at the University of California-Davis will both point the way and greatly assist in completing these important scholarly tasks. Moreover, there are many manuscript and other primary sources available whose wider use would greatly enhance the study of western agricultural and ranching history. Although there is no single depository for these materials, they may be found in such depositories as the state historical societies in the western states, the National Archives in Washington and at the regional centers, and in places like the

Huntington Library at San Marino, California. The abundance of both secondary and primary materials pose both challenges and opportunities for scholars.

Notes

1. These bibliographies are mimeographed and include Michael L. Olsen (comp. and ed.), "A Preliminary List of References for the History of Agriculture in the Pacific Northwest and Alaska" (Davis, Calif., 1968); Earl M. Rogers (comp.), "A List of References for the History of Agriculture in the Mountain States" (Davis, Calif., 1972); Richard J. Orsi, "A List of References for the History of Agriculture in California" (Davis, Calif., 1974); and Earl M. Rogers, "A List of References for the History of Agriculture in the Great Plains" (Davis, Calif., 1976). See also John T. Schlebecker (ed.), *Bibliography of Books and Pamphlets on the History of Agriculture in the United States, 1607–1967* (Santa Barbara, Calif.: ABC-Clio, 1969). Oscar O. Winther, *A Classified Bibliography of the Periodical Literature of the Trans-Mississippi West, 1811–1957* (Bloomington: Indiana University Press, 1961).

2. John Wesley Powell, *Report on the Lands of the Arid Region of the United States with a More Detailed Account of the Lands of Utah,* House Executive Document No. 73, 45th Cong., 2d sess., serial 1805 (Washington, D.C.: Government Printing Office, 1878); Thomas Donaldson, *The Public Domain,* House Miscellaneous Document No. 45, Part IV, 47th Cong., 2d sess., serial 2158 (Washington, D.C.: Government Printing Office, 1884).

3. Benjamin H. Hibbard, *A History of the Public Land Policies* (New York: Macmillan, 1924); Robert P. Swierenga, "Land Speculation and Its Impact on American Economic Growth and Welfare: A Historiographical Review," *Western Historical Quarterly* 8 (July 1977): 283–302.

4. Roy M. Robbins, *Our Landed Heritage: The Public Domain* (Princeton: Princeton University Press, 1942; 2d ed. rev., paperbound, Lincoln: University of Nebraska Press, 1976); Harold H. Dunham, *Government Handout: A Study in the Administration of the Public Lands, 1875–1891* (Ann Arbor, Mich.: Edwards Brothers, 1941). Other important books and articles that are important in studying western land policies and how they relate to agricultural development include Paul W. Gates, *Fifty Million Acres: Conflicts Over Kansas Land Policy, 1854–1890* (Ithaca, N.Y.: Cornell University Press, 1954); Charles L. Green, *The Administration of the Public Domain in South Dakota,* South Dakota Historical Collections, Vol. 20 (1940); Addison E. Sheldon, *Land Systems and Land Policies in Nebraska,*

Nebraska Historical Collections, Vol. 22 (1936); Reuben McKitrick, *The Public Land System of Texas, 1823-1910* (Madison, Wis., 1918); Thomas L. Miller, *The Public Lands of Texas, 1519-1970* (Norman: University of Oklahoma Press, 1972); Jerry A. O'Callaghan, *The Disposition of the Public Domain in Oregon* (Washington, D.C.: Government Printing Office, 1960); and Fredrick J. Yonce, "Public Land Disposal in Washington" (Ph.D. diss., University of Washington, 1969).

5. Paul W. Gates, "The Homestead Law in an Incongruous Land System," *American Historical Review* 41 (July 1936): 652-81.

6. Fred A. Shannon, *The Farmer's Last Frontier* (New York: Rinehart and Co., 1945); Paul W. Gates, "The Homestead Act: Free Land Policy in Operation, 1862-1935," in Howard W. Ottoson (ed.), *Land Use Policy and Problems in the United States* (Lincoln: University of Nebraska Press, 1963); and Gates, *History of Public Land Law Development* (Washington, D.C.: Government Printing Office, 1968), p. 798.

7. Lawrence B. Lee, "Homesteading in Zion," *Utah Historical Quarterly* 28 (January 1960): 29-38; Homer E. Socolofsky, "Success and Failure in Nebraska Homesteading," *Agricultural History* 42 (April 1968): 103-7. See also Socolofsky's "Land Disposal in Nebraska, 1854-1906: The Homestead Story," *Nebraska History* 48 (Autumn 1967): 225-48, and Lee's *Kansas and the Homestead Act, 1862-1905* (New York: Arno Press, 1979). E. Louise Peffer, *The Closing of The Public Domain: Disposal and Reservation Policies, 1900-50* (Stanford: Stanford University Press, 1951).

8. Walter Goldschmidt, *As You Sow* (Glencoe, Ill.: Free Press, 1947); W. W. Robinson, *Land in California: The Story of Mission Lands, Ranchos, Squatters, Mining Claims, Railroad Grants, Land Scrip, and Homestead* (Berkeley: University of California Press, 1948); Victor Westphall, *The Public Domain in New Mexico, 1854-1891* (Albuquerque: University of New Mexico Press, 1965); Jim B. Pearson, *The Maxwell Land Grant* (Norman: University of Oklahoma Press, 1961); Paul W. Gates, "Public Land Disposal in California," *Agricultural History* 49 (January 1975): 155-78.

9. *Report of the Special Committee of the United States Senate on the Irrigation and Reclamation of Arid Lands*, vol. 3, Senate Report 928, 51st Cong., 1st sess., serial 2708 (Washington, D.C.: Government Printing Office, 1890). In this same document see Richard J. Hinton, *Irrigation in the United States*. See also Elwood Mead, *Irrigation Institutions: A Discussion of the Economic and Legal Questions Created by the Growth of Irrigated Agriculture in the West* (New York: Macmillan, 1903); Charles H. Brough, *Irrigation in Utah*, Johns Hopkins University Studies in History and Political Science,

extra vol. 19 (Baltimore: Johns Hopkins University Press, 1898); William E. Smythe, *The Conquest of Arid America* (New York: Macmillan, 1905).

10. Wells A. Hutchins, *Selected Problems in the Law of Water Rights in the West,* USDA Miscellaneous Publication no. 418 (Washington, D.C.: Government Printing Office, 1942). Other works by Hutchins include studies of water rights in Idaho, Montana, Nevada, New Mexico, and Kansas. Robert G. Dunbar, "The Origins of the Colorado System of Water-Right Control," *Colorado Magazine* 27 (October 1950): 241-62; and Dunbar, "Groundwater Property Rights and Controversies in Montana" (Bozeman: Montana State University, 1976). Lawrence B. Lee, "William Ellsworth Smythe and the Irrigation Movement: A Reconsideration," *Pacific Historical Review* 41 (August 1972): 289-311; and Lee, *Reclaiming the American West: An Historiography and Guide* (Santa Barbara, Calif.: ABC-Clio, 1979). Michael C. Robinson, *The Bureau of Reclamation, 1902-1977* (Chicago: Public Works Historical Society, 1979).

11. Roy E. Huffman, *Irrigation Development and Public Water Policy* (New York: Ronald Press, 1953); Bureau of the Census, *Report on Agriculture by Irrigation in the Western Part of the United States,* Eleventh Census, 1890 (Washington, D.C.: Government Printing Office, 1894), and later censuses; Robert L. Kelley, *Gold vs. Grain: The Hydraulic Mining Controversy in California's Sacramento Valley* (Glendale, Calif.: Arthur H. Clark, 1959); see also H. E. Selby, "The Importance of Irrigation in the Economy of the West," *Journal of Farm Economics* 31 (November 1949): 955-64. Other developments relating to western irrigation and farming also appear in this issue of *The Journal of Farm Economics.* On a major irrigation project see Robert de Roos, *The Thirsty Land: The Story of the Central Valley Project* (Stanford: Stanford University Press, 1948).

12. Donald E. Green, *Land of the Underground Rain: Irrigation on the Texas High Plains, 1910-1970* (Austin: University of Texas Press, 1973); R. Douglas Hurt, "Irrigation in the Kansas Plains Since 1930," *Red River Valley Historical Review* 4 (Summer 1979): 64-72.

13. Rupert N. Richardson and Carl Coke Rister, *The Greater Southwest* (Glendale, Calif.: Arthur H. Clark, 1934); W. Eugene Hollon, *The Great American Desert Then and Now* (New York: Oxford University Press, 1966; paperbound ed., Lincoln: University of Nebraska Press, 1975); Robert G. Athearn, *High Country Empire: The High Plains and Rockies* (New York: McGraw-Hill, 1960; paperbound ed., Lincoln: University of Nebraska Press, 1965).

14. Gilbert C. Fite, *The Farmers' Frontier, 1865-1900* (New York: Holt,

Rinehart and Winston, 1966; paperbound ed., Albuquerque: University of New Mexico Press, 1977); Ladd Haystead and Gilbert C. Fite, *The Agricultural Regions of the United States* (Norman: University of Oklahoma Press, 1955); Oliver E. Baker, "Agricultural Regions of North America," *Economic Geography*, part VI, The Spring Wheat Region, 4, no. 4 (October 1928): 399–433; part VIII, The Pacific Subtropical Crops Region, 6, no. 2 (April 1930): 166–90; part IX, The North Pacific Hay and Pasture Region, 7, no. 2 (April 1931): 109–53; part X, The Grazing and Irrigated Crops Region, 7, no. 4 (October 1931): 325–64; and part X continued, The Grazing and Irrigated Crops Region, 8, no. 4 (October 1932): 326–77; Edward Higbee, *American Agriculture: Geography, Resources, Conservation* (New York: John Wiley and Sons, 1958).

15. Alvin T. Steinel, *History of Agriculture in Colorado . . . , 1858 to 1926* (Fort Collins: State Agricultural College, 1926); David McComb, *Agricultural Technology and Society in Colorado* (Fort Collins: Colorado State University, 1981); Claude B. Hutchison, *California Agriculture* (Berkeley: University of California Press, 1946); Samuel L. Evans, "Texas Agriculture, 1880–1930" (Ph.D. diss., University of Texas, 1960); Verne S. Sweedlun, "A History of the Evolution of Agriculture in Nebraska, 1870–1930" (Ph.D. diss., University of Nebraska, 1940); Donald E. Green (ed.), *Rural Oklahoma* (Oklahoma City: Oklahoma Historical Society, 1977).

16. Walter Prescott Webb, *The Great Plains: A Study of Institutions and Environment* (Boston: Ginn, 1931; paperbound ed., Lincoln: University of Nebraska Press, 1981); James C. Malin, "The Adaptation of the Agricultural System to Subhumid Environment," *Agricultural History* 10 (July 1936): 118–39; and *Winter Wheat in the Golden Belt of Kansas: A Study in Adaptation to Subhumid Geographical Environment* (Lawrence: University of Kansas Press, 1944). See also Robert G. Dunbar, "Agricultural Adjustments in Eastern Colorado in the Eighteen-Nineties," *Agricultural History* 18 (January 1944): 41–52; Carl Kraenzel, *The Great Plains in Transition* (Norman: University of Oklahoma Press, 1955; paperbound ed., 1970).

17. Mary Wilma M. Hargreaves, *Dry Farming in the Northern Great Plains, 1900–1925* (Cambridge: Harvard University Press, 1957); Garry L. Nall, "The Farmers' Frontier in the Texas Panhandle," *Panhandle-Plains Historical Review* 45 (1972): 1–20; and in the same journal "Panhandle Farming in the 'Golden Era' of American Agriculture," 46 (1973): 68–93; "Specialization and Expansion: Panhandle Farming in the 1920s," 47 (1974): 44–69; "Dust Bowl Days: Panhandle Farming in the 1930s," 48 (1975): 42–63. Charles M. Studness, "Development of the Great Plains Grain Farming Economy:

Frontier to 1953" (Ph.D. diss., Columbia University, 1963). David M. Emmons, *Garden in the Grasslands: Boomer Literature of the Central Great Plains* (Lincoln: University of Nebraska Press, 1971).

18. Leslie Hewes, *The Suitcase Farming Frontier: A Study in the Historical Geography of the Central Great Plains* (Lincoln: University of Nebraska Press, 1973); Gilbert C. Fite, "Great Plains Farming: A Century of Change and Adjustment," *Agricultural History* 51 (January 1977): 244-56.

19. James C. Malin, "Dust Storms: Part One, 1850-1860," *Kansas Historical Quarterly* 14 (May 1946): 129-44; "Dust Storms: Part Two, 1861-1880," *Kansas Historical Quarterly* 14 (August 1946): 265-96; "Dust Storms: Part Three, 1881-1900," *Kansas Historical Quarterly* 14 (November 1946): 391-413; Donald Worster, *Dust Bowl: The Southern Plains in the 1930s* (New York: Oxford University Press, 1979); Paul Bonnifield, *The Dust Bowl: Men, Dirt and Depression* (Albuquerque: University of New Mexico Press, 1979); R. Douglas Hurt, *The Dust Bowl: An Agricultural and Social History* (Chicago: Nelson Hall, 1981).

20. Hiram M. Drache, *The Day of the Bonanza: A History of Bonanza Farming in the Red River Valley of the North* (Fargo: North Dakota Institute for Regional Studies, 1964); and Drache, *The Challenge of the Prairie: Life and Times of Red River Pioneers* (Fargo: North Dakota Institute for Regional Studies, 1970); Stanley N. Murray, *The Valley Comes of Age: A History of Agriculture in the Valley of the Red River of the North, 1812-1920* (Fargo: North Dakota Institute for Regional Studies, 1967).

21. Everett Dick, *The Sod-House Frontier, 1854-1890* (New York: Appleton-Century Co., 1937; paperbound ed., Lincoln: University of Nebraska Press, 1979); John Ise, *Sod and Stubble: The Story of a Kansas Homestead* (New York: Wilson-Erickson, 1936; paperbound ed., Lincoln: University of Nebraska Press, 1967); Carl Coke Rister, *Southern Plainsmen* (Norman: University of Oklahoma Press, 1938).

22. Leonard J. Arrington, *Great Basin Kingdom* (Cambridge: Harvard University Press, 1958; paperbound ed., Lincoln: University of Nebraska Press, 1966); Arrington, *The Changing Economic Structure of the Mountain West, 1850-1950,* Monograph Series, Utah State University Press, Logan, Utah, vol. 10, no. 3 (June 1963); and Arrington, *Beet Sugar in the West: A History of the Utah-Idaho Sugar Company, 1891-1966* (Seattle: University of Washington Press, 1966).

23. Dorothy O. Johansen and Charles M. Gates, *Empire of the Columbia: A History of the Pacific Northwest* (New York: Harper and Row, 1957; rev. ed., 1967); Oscar Winther, *The Great Northwest: A History* (New York:

Knopf, 1947); Robert C. Nesbit and Charles M. Gates, "Agriculture in Eastern Washington, 1890-1910," *Pacific Northwest Quarterly* 37 (October 1946): 279-302; Neil W. Johnson and Rex E. Willard, *Trends in Agriculture in Washington, 1900-1930*, Washington State Agricultural Experiment Station Bulletin 300 (June 1934); *The Farming Business in Idaho*, Idaho Agricultural Experiment Station Bulletin 151 (July 1927).

24. Edwin S. Holmes, Jr., *Wheat Growing and General Agricultural Conditions in the Pacific Coast Region of the United States*, USDA, Division of Statistics, Miscellaneous Series, Bulletin 20 (Washington, D.C.: Government Printing Office, 1901); James F. Shepherd, "The Development of Wheat Production in the Pacific Northwest," *Agricultural History* 49 (January 1975): 258-71; D. W. Meinig, *The Great Columbia Plain: A Historical Geography, 1805-1910* (Seattle: University of Washington Press, 1968).

25. Lawrence J. Jelinek, *Harvest Empire: A History of California Agriculture* (San Francisco: Boyd and Fraser, 1979); Paul W. Gates, *California Ranchos and Farms, 1846-1862* (Madison: State Historical Society of Wisconsin, 1967); Rodman W. Paul, "The Beginnings of Agriculture in California: Innovation vs. Continuity," *California Historical Quarterly* 52 (Spring 1973): 16-27; Howard S. Reed, "Major Trends in California Agriculture," *Agricultural History* 20 (October 1946): 252-55; Hallock F. Raup, "Transformation of Southern California to a Cultivated Land," *Annals of the Association of American Geographers* 49 (September 1959): 58-79; Osgood Hardy, "Agricultural Changes in California, 1860-1900," *American Historical Association, Pacific Coast Branch, Proceedings* (1929): 216-30. Kenneth A. Smith, "California: The Wheat Decades" (Ph.D. diss., University of Southern California, 1969); Rodman W. Paul, "The Wheat Trade Between California and the United Kingdom," *Mississippi Valley Historical Review* 35 (December 1958): 391-412; Edward James Wickson's *Rural California* (New York: Macmillan, 1923) is old but still useful.

26. Roy Bainer, "Science and Technology in Western Agriculture," *Agricultural History* 49 (January 1975): 56-72; Leo Rogin, *The Introduction of Farm Machinery* (Berkeley: University of California Press, 1931); Reynold M. Wik, *Steam Power on the American Farm* (Philadelphia: University of Pennsylvania Press, 1953); Wayne D. Rasmussen, "Advances in American Agriculture: The Mechanical Tomato Harvester As a Case Study," *Technology and Culture* 9 (October 1968): 531-43.

27. Joseph G. McCoy, *Historic Sketches of the Cattle Trade of the West and Southwest* (Kansas City, Mo.: Ramsey, Millett and Hudson, 1874); James S. Brisbin, *The Beef Bonanza* (Philadelphia: J. B. Lippincott Co.,

1881); and Walter Baron von Richthofen, *Cattle Raising on the Plains of North America* (New York: D. Appleton and Co., 1885); Joseph Nimmo, Jr., *The Range and Ranch Cattle Traffic of the United States,* House Executive Document 267, 48th Cong., 2d sess., serial 2304 (Washington, D.C.: Government Printing Office, 1885).

28. Ernest S. Osgood, *The Day of the Cattleman* (Minneapolis: University of Minnesota Press, 1929; paperbound ed., Chicago: University of Chicago Press, 1957); J. Evetts Haley, *The XIT Ranch of Texas and the Early Days of the Llano Estacado* (Chicago: Lakeside Press, 1929).

29. E. E. Dale, *The Range Cattle Industry* (Norman: University of Oklahoma Press, 1930); and Dale, *Cow Country* (Norman: University of Oklahoma Press, 1942); Louis Pelzer, *The Cattlemen's Frontier: A Record of the Trans-Mississippi Cattle Industry from Oxen Trains to Pooling Companies, 1850-1890* (Glendale, Calif.: Arthur H. Clark, 1936); O. B. Peake, *The Colorado Range Cattle Industry* (Glendale, Calif.: Arthur H. Clark, 1937); Mari Sandoz, *Old Jules* (Boston: Little, Brown, 1935; paperbound ed., Lincoln: University of Nebraska Press, 1962); and *The Cattlemen From the Rio Grande Across the Far Marias* (New York: Hastings House, 1958); Maurice Frink, W. Turrentine Jackson, and Agnes Wright Spring, *When Grass Was King* (Boulder: University of Colorado Press, 1956); Charles L. Sonnichsen, *Cowboys and Cattle Kings: Life on the Range Today* (Norman: University of Oklahoma Press, 1950); John T. Schlebecker, *Cattle Raising on the Plains, 1900-1961* (Lincoln: University of Nebraska Press, 1963).

30. Tom Lea, *The King Ranch,* 2 vols. (Boston: Little, Brown, 1957); William C. Holden, *The Spur Ranch* (Boston: Christopher, 1934); Ellsworth Collings, *The 101 Ranch* (Norman: University of Oklahoma Press, 1937); W. M. Pearce, *The Matador Land and Cattle Company* (Norman: University of Oklahoma Press, 1964); Harmon R. Mothershead, *The Swan Land and Cattle Company Ltd.* (Norman: University of Oklahoma Press, 1971); Robert G. Cleland, *The Irvine Ranch of Orange County, 1810-1950* (San Marino, Calif.: Huntington Library, 1952); Lester F. Sheffy, *The Francklyn Land and Cattle Company: A Panhandle Enterprise, 1882-1957* (Austin: University of Texas Press, 1963).

31. J. Evetts Haley, *Charles Goodnight: Cowman and Plainsman* (Boston: Houghton Mifflin, 1936), and *George W. Littlefield, Texan* (Norman: University of Oklahoma Press, 1943); Donald E. Green, *Panhandle Pioneer: Henry C. Hitch, His Ranch, and His Family* (Norman: University of Oklahoma Press, 1979); Lewis E. Atherton, *The Cattle Kings* (Bloomington: Indiana University Press, 1961; paperbound ed., Lincoln: University of

Nebraska Press, 1972); Robert R. Dykstra, *The Cattle Towns* (New York: Knopf, 1968; paperbound ed., Lincoln: University of Nebraska Press, 1983); Terry G. Jordan, *Trails to Texas: Southern Roots of Western Cattle Ranching* (Lincoln: University of Nebraska Press, 1981).

32. Robert G. Cleland, *The Cattle on a Thousand Hills: Southern California, 1850–1880* (San Marino, Calif.: Huntington Library, 1964); Hazel A. Pulling, "A History of California's Range Cattle Industry, 1770–1912" (Ph.D. diss., University of Southern California, 1944); J. Orin Oliphant, *On the Cattle Ranges of the Oregon Country* (Seattle: University of Washington Press, 1968).

33. Herbert O. Brayer, "The Influence of British Capital on the Western Range-Cattle Industry," *Journal of Economic History* 9, supplement (1949): 85–98; Gene M. Gressley, *Bankers and Cattlemen* (New York: Knopf, 1966; paperbound ed., Lincoln: University of Nebraska Press, 1971). W. Turrentine Jackson, *The Enterprising Scot: Investors in the American West after 1873* (Edinburgh: Edinburgh University, Press, 1968). Among the early scholars on the range cattle industry, Louis Pelzer probably gave the most attention to financing the business. His article "Financial Management of the Cattle Ranges," *Journal of Economic and Business History* 2 (August 1930): 723–41, is a good early study.

34. Mont H. Saunderson, *Western Stock Ranching* (Minneapolis: University of Minnesota Press, 1950), and Saunderson, *Western Land and Water Use* (Norman: University of Oklahoma Press, 1950); Marion Clawson, *The Western Range Livestock Industry* (New York: McGraw-Hill, 1950); Phillip O. Foss, *Politics and Grass: The Administration of Grazing on the Public Domain* (Seattle: University of Washington Press, 1960); Charles L. Wood, *The Kansas Beef Industry* (Lawrence: Regents Press of Kansas, 1980).

35. Emerson Hough, *The Story of the Cowboy* (New York: D. Appleton and Co., 1898); John Clay, *My Life on the Range* (Chicago: privately printed, 1924); Joe B. Frantz and Julian E. Choate, *The American Cowboy: The Myth and the Reality* (Norman: University of Oklahoma Press, 1955); Philip Durham and Everett L. Jones, *The Negro Cowboys* (New York: Dodd, Mead and Co., 1965); Clifford P. Westermeier, *Trailing the Cowboy: His Life and Lore as Told by Frontier Journalists* (Caldwell, Idaho: Caxton Printers, 1955); Lon Tinkle and Allen Maxwell (eds.), *The Cowboy Reader* (New York: David McKay Company, 1959); William W. Savage, Jr., *Cowboy Life: Reconstructing a Myth* (Norman: University of Oklahoma Press, 1975); Savage, *The Cowboy Hero: His Image in American History and Culture* (Norman:

University of Oklahoma Press, 1979); Wayne Gard, *The Chisholm Trail* (Norman: University of Oklahoma Press, 1954); Don Worcester, *The Chisholm Trail: High Road of the Cattle Kingdom* (Lincoln: University of Nebraska Press, 1980).

36. H. A. Heath and John Minto, "Condition of the Sheep Industry West of the Mississippi River," Part II of U.S. Bureau of Animal Husbandry, *Special Report on the History and Present Condition of the Sheep Industry of the United States,* House Miscellaneous Document 105, 52d Cong., 2d sess., serial 3124 (Washington, D.C.: Government Printing Office, 1892), pp. 701–991; Charles W. Towne and Edward N. Wentworth, *Shepherd's Empire* (Norman: University of Oklahoma Press, 1945); Edward N. Wentworth, *America's Sheep Trails* (Ames: Iowa State University Press, 1948); Winifred Kupper, *The Golden Hoof: The Story of Sheep of the Southwest* (New York: Knopf, 1945).

Chapter Eleven

Richard Maxwell Brown

Historiography of Violence in the American West

Introduction

It is a deeply ingrained cultural fact that the popular image of the history of the American West is focused on violence. In film, fiction, and on television the dominant symbol has been the six-gun, and the prototypical westerner has been the gunfighter. Obviously the popular image of western history represents an exaggeration of the factor of violence. Cultural and intellectual historians have produced some outstanding studies that examine the dichotomy between the myth and the reality of the violent westerner. Another approach has been to observe the violent western experience—as mediated through folklore, fiction, and film—in relation to the broader context of American values. The prototypical myth-versus-reality study was Henry Nash Smith's very influential book of 1950, *Virgin Land: The American West as Symbol and Myth,* one of the finest books about the West ever published.[1] By no means focusing only on the violent aspect of western history (although he did highlight Kit Carson and the emergence of the blood-and-thunder dime novel), Smith's stunning book was virtually a primer for later intellectual historians to use in their employment of the technique of image analysis.

Because of the vast amount of folklore and mythology that has enveloped their subject, almost all serious students of western outlaws and gunfighters must emphasize the contrast between myth and reality; one prime example is the study by William A. Settle, Jr., of Jesse James and his criminal colleagues. Especially notable in the Smith tradition of scholarship is Kent Ladd Steckmesser's model study of *The Western Hero in History and Legend* (1966). Steckmesser's probing sketches of Billy the Kid and Wild Bill Hickok are among the best that have ever been done on the myth and reality of those two violent western heroes. He concludes his impressive book with the well-documented assertion that claims of epic significance for western heroes far outran historical reality, but the myths nevertheless filled the public's need to identify with a heroic ideal. Folklorist Américo Paredes provides a subtle contrast of myth and reality in his book *"With His Pistol in His Hand"* (1958), a study of the balladry of resistance that grew up around the Hispanic gunslinger Gregorio Cortez, who bravely opposed the oppressive tactics of Anglo law enforcers in south Texas of the early twentieth century. A broader application of the same approach is John O. West's study of the "good" outlaw tradition in the Southwest, wherein figures like Cortez and California's mythic Joaquin Murieta serve as folk champions for underdog groups like the Hispanos of the region.[2]

The prototypical work of scholarship that investigates literary and popular images of the violent West in regard to American values is Richard Slotkin's *Regeneration through Violence: The Mythology of the American Frontier, 1600–1860* (1973). Slotkin emphasized both serious authors like James Fenimore Cooper, as did Henry Nash Smith, and myth in popular culture as exemplified by the legend of Daniel Boone. Other historians and critics likewise deal with both serious authors of western fiction (for example, Walter Van Tilburg Clark and his 1940 novel on western vigilantism, *The Ox-Bow Incident*) and the formula Western in print and on film.[3] Indeed, critical and historical studies of western fiction and films has become a minor intellectual industry in recent years as dozens of books and articles have come rolling off the presses. This work is of generally high quality, and its practitioners tend to specialize either in western literature (both serious and popular) or in the western film. The perspective of many of these authorities, who often appear in the pages of the journal *Western American Literature,* is almost exclusively critical and therefore not relevant to this discussion of western American historiography.

Two notable experts whose viewpoint, however, is strongly historical are Richard W. Etulain and John G. Cawelti. In dealing with western fiction and films, such scholars as Etulain and Cawelti are not concerned alone with the imaginary treatment of violence; but, as some of the book titles indicate, the gunfighter and the six-gun are central to the subject of media-made western life. Starting out with a study of the formula-Western writer Ernest Haycox, Etulain has become a prolific author and editor on the print dimension of the popular Western. Cawelti has contributed two influential studies of violence-oriented western films and fiction. Among the most recent of studies analyzing western films in the intellectual tradition of Slotkin and Cawelti is John H. Lenihan's timely book on western movies since World War II: *Showdown: Confronting Modern America in the Western Film* (1980).[4]

An article by the British scholar Eric Mottram is a bitter indictment of the mythic significance of Billy the Kid in relation to our country's gun culture, while Werner J. Einstadter has turned to a newspaper of the Old West to show, suggestively, that in this case (Great Falls, Montana) journalistic coverage played down crime in the interest of the town elite's attempt to establish order and social control by deemphasizing crime and viewing it primarily as the work of outsiders. Fortunately, Ray Allen Billington lived to complete his badly needed study of the European image of the nineteenth-century American frontier, in which a salient chapter deals with the old country's insatiable appetite for writing on western lawlessness and vigilantism in the nineteenth century.[5]

The scholarly literature on images of western violence is large and impressive, but what of the historical reality of western violence? In his provocative study of *Cultural Regions of the United States* (1975), Raymond D. Gastil compared the homicide rates of western states with those in other American regions and found homicide to be more prevalent in the West than in the North and East but less frequent than in the South. An interesting anthropological case study of murder in contemporary Houston placed the homicide rate of that city, recently among the highest in the nation, squarely within the historic Texas tradition of violent personal redress, and I have noted that a transition in legal doctrine from the English duty-to-retreat to the American stand-one's-ground doctrine (originating in the frontier and western states) has given our country a more permissive attitude to homicide than is to be found among the other industrialized democracies of the Western world, which have lower rates of homicide. The factor of homicide in American western violence is reflected by two recent trends: the notable increase in multiple murders (or multicides) in the West as part of a national pattern and the West's formidable linkage with presidential assassination or assassination attempts. Ann Rule has treated the phenomenon of multicide as exemplified by the series of deaths in Colorado, Utah, and Washington that have been connected with Theodore Robert Bundy. Of all the western episodes of violence involving our presidents, the assassination in Dallas in 1963 of President John F. Kennedy has been the most traumatic death in American history since Franklin D. Roosevelt died in 1945. The definitive treatment of the assassination of John F. Kennedy may never be written, but the best, so far, of a vast outpouring of writings is the provocative *Conspiracy* (1980) by Anthony Summers.[6]

Historical writing on western violence in the more distant past falls into three broad categories: (1) the crime wars of the West, involving the violence of vigilantism, legal law enforcement, personal redress, and those favorites of the popularizers—outlaws and gunfighters; (2) the land and labor wars of the West, involving various permutations of violence among large, medium, and small property holders and wage earners; (3) the racial and religious wars of the West in which antagonistic factors of race and religion flared into violence. An examination of historical works thus subdivided is followed below by some concluding generalizations about the needs and opportunities in the study of western violence. (For conflict between whites and Indians, see the chapters in this book by Herbert T. Hoover and Robert C. Carriker.)

Crime in the West

The creation of new western communities has attracted some of the finest efforts of scholars, from Frederick Jackson Turner and Josiah Royce to Earl Pomeroy and Robert V. Hine in our own time. The creation of these communities in the flux of boom and bust and surges of settlement marked by the land and mining rushes of the West posed problems of order and stability for some and opportunities of tumult and disorder for others. For the propertied and the orderly among the settlers, crime was both a reality to be fought and a negative symbol upon which the ambitious pioneers could focus their hopes and fears. Outlaws and gunfighters were a constant irritant (or so it seemed), and in the interest of probity and property the upright placed against them an array of vigilantes and legal law enforcers. As an index of the determination of new settlers to impose old patterns of order and stability, the violence of vigilantism was even more significant than the violence of legal law enforcement.[7]

Historians have been prolific in their treatment of vigilantism in the West, beginning especially with two classic contemporary accounts by Thomas J. Dimsdale and Hubert Howe Bancroft. Dimsdale's *Vigilantes of Montana* (1866) was at once a history and a justification of the Bannack and Virginia City vigilantes of 1863–64 who had shattered the road-agent gang led by the false sheriff Henry Plummer. Later books by Nathaniel Pitt Langford (1890) and Hoffman Birney (1929) continued the adulatory tradition, although

Birney's book is still useful because it is the most complete treatment of the subject. More recent historians have dropped the provigilante bias in favor of an analytical stance as exemplified in the treatments by John W. Smurr, Barton C. Olson, and Merrill G. Burlingame. A similar transformation has occurred in the interpretation of the deadliest of all western vigilante movements, that led by Granville Stuart in an 1884 campaign that took a record number of lives (perhaps as many as thirty-five Montanans). The provigilante viewpoint of Oscar O. Mueller (1951) has been replaced by the much more complete analysis of Richard K. Mueller.[8]

Hubert Howe Bancroft's massive two-volume *Popular Tribunals* (1887) was a compendious history of vigilantism throughout the Far West, but it devoted an entire volume to the San Francisco vigilance committee of 1856, a movement headed by many of Bancroft's friends among the mercantile aristocracy. Its strongly provigilante bias aside, Bancroft's volume on the 1856 movement is, in effect, a primary source on the subject because so much of it is based on the interviews he conducted among his erstwhile vigilante friends who were members of the largest and the most prototypically significant of all western vigilante movements. The provigilante theme was perpetuated in two biographies that badly need redoing: Stanton A. Coblentz's on William Tell Coleman, the great leader of the 1856 vigilantes, and James A. B. Scherer's on James King of William, whose murder inspired the formation of the movement. The recent trend toward a conceptually oriented scholarship that has little sympathy for the vigilantes was foreshadowed by William H. Ellison's book on early California as a self-governing dominion, but not until 1969 did the first of a cluster of analytical treatments appear. All of these latter scholars—Richard Maxwell Brown, Roger W. Lotchin, Robert M. Senkewicz, Peter R. Decker, and Robert A. Burchell—emphasize the theme of conservative mercantile domination of the vigilante movement, but with differing shades of emphasis: ethnic rivalry (Brown, Burchell), urban development and municipal reform (Lotchin), business enterprise (Senkewicz), and the context of urban social structure (Decker). There is less work on the smaller, simpler San Francisco vigilante movement of 1851. George R. Stewart's 1964 narrative makes the subject come alive, but by far the best analytical study, with its stress on the theme of social control on the frontier, is Mary Floyd Williams's Ph.D. dissertation, published in 1921. Through a model use of the quantitative method, Sherman M. Ricards and George M. Blackburn have demonstrated that the target group of the 1851 vigilantes, the Australian immigrants, were unjustly stigmatized as the crime-prone "Sydney Ducks."[9]

Despite the key roles played by California and Montana in western vigilantism, it was Texas that had more vigilante movements (at least fifty-two) than any other western state. Although there is no overall book-length study of Texas vigilantism, there are general interpretations that link some Texas vigilante movements to that state's bumptious feuding tradition and see vigilantism as an integral factor in the historic culture of violence of central Texas. Indeed, vigilantism was pervasive in late nineteenth-century western history. With the exception of Utah, all of the contiguous western states had one or more major vigilante movements. I have quantified them, listed major sources, and interpreted them in terms of the use of the deeply embedded regulator-vigilante tradition to establish new western communities under the domination of the local elites of power. Vigilantism also tinctured a number of conflict situations in the West, including such land wars as that in Johnson County, Wyoming, and many other instances of rural, urban, and industrial strife. Adhering also to the vigilante tradition was the violence-prone moralistic Ku Klux Klan of the 1920s in Texas, which has been the subject of a monograph by Charles C. Alexander. John W. Caughey's apt documentary collection, *Their Majesties the Mob* (1960), connects the vigilante tradition of California and the West to the Cold-War era onslaught against American civil liberties in the 1940s and 1950s.[10]

Although it is often difficult to separate regular law enforcement from vigilantism in the Old West, there are a number of significant writings that focus only on the legally established agencies of law and order. This literature is headed by two very fine studies by Frank R. Prassel and Larry D. Ball. Dealing with the entire spectrum of sheriffs, marshals, police, and rangers is Prassel's landmark publication of 1972, *The Western Peace Officer,* a thorough, discriminating work. A more specialized study and one that is avowedly more tolerant of the flaws in legally constituted western law enforcement is Ball's book on the U.S. marshals in Arizona and New Mexico territories. Ball amasses much evidence to support his thesis that the U.S. marshals, in their impact, exemplified Robert H. Wiebe's theme of growing order and centralization in the decades around 1900.[11]

As good as any study that we have in the entire realm of western violence is Robert R. Dykstra's treatment of Abilene, Dodge City, and the other leading cattle towns of Kansas in the post–Civil War era. Dykstra innovatively linked the problem of interpreting cattle-town violence with his conceptual perspective of frontier community building and found that the entrepreneurial elites who controlled these bumptious towns structured a situation of law enforcement that allowed for the necessary modicum of cowboy high spirits while preserving the degree of order and stability essential to the reaping of the profits of the cattle trade. In a conclusion that holds true for much of the West in the pre-1900 era, Dykstra emphasized that social conflict, sometimes flaring into violence, was a normal aspect of urban growth. Philip D. Jordan's well-crafted collection of essays on *Frontier Law and Order* (1970) deals mainly with the Mississippi Valley.[12]

One of the most historically and socially significant of all western law enforcing bodies is the Texas Rangers. The starting point in the literature is, of course, Walter Prescott Webb's encyclopedic study *The Texas Rangers,* first published in 1935. Despite, or perhaps because of, its profusion of picturesque detail, it is Webb's only disappointing book: it is the book in which Webb fails, intellectually, to break free of the obsessive perspective of his rural, old-time Texas-Anglo background. We are told that at the time of his death in 1963, Webb was revising the book to purge it of the evident anti-Hispano bias of the original work. Indeed, this major flaw (among several) in Webb's *Texas Rangers* is relevant to a recently published, fair and impassioned (although thinly researched) indictment of anti-Hispano prejudice by the Rangers, especially for the period since 1960. The subject of Ranger violence against the Hispanic people of the Rio Grande Valley was first opened up for scholarly consideration in Ben H. Procter's significant essay of 1969. James R. Ward's study of the Rangers from 1919 to 1935 not only updates Webb's coverage for this period but emphasizes the retention of old Ranger traditions in the midst of a transition to modern methods of police science.[13]

Much more work needs to be done on the judicial phase of western law enforcement, but two pioneering studies reveal the analytical gains that can be made in this promising new field for the deeper study of western violence. The two works are John D. W. Guice's book on the territorial supreme courts of the Rocky Mountain states of Colorado, Montana, and Wyoming, and John R. Wunder's brisk volume on justices of the peace in Washington Territory. In finding that the supreme court justices and the J.P.s of their respective studies both performed relatively well, Guice and Wunder revise the commonly held stereotype of the mediocrity and irregularity of the western judiciary. Of course, more studies will be needed before the Guice-Wunder perception is established; one dramatic example of a case that badly needs the sort of sophisticated legal-history perspective of Guice and Wunder is that of the famous "Hanging Judge," Isaac C. Parker, whose federal district of western Arkansas included the violence-torn Indian Territory of present eastern Oklahoma. Until someone does a study of Parker's judicial administration that embraces the new legal-history perspective, the two solid but traditional books by Fred Harvey Harrington and Glenn H. Shirley must suffice.[14]

In somewhat the same fashion, another dimension of legal law enforcement in the West that cries out for scholarly investigation is the activities of the private detective agencies. The role of the great Pinkerton Detective Agency, from its vendetta against the entourage and family of Jesse James to the pervasive activities of the Denver regional office supervised by James McParlan, is one that appears often in the pages of *The Pinkertons* (1968) by James D. Horan and in many a publication on western violence. Still, the role of the Pinkertons and other western private detectives is yet to be studied in depth. Also neglected by scholars are the state-authorized, local anti-horse-thief associations of Kansas, Oklahoma, and elsewhere in the West. These local bodies existed by the hundreds and thousands and were a significant supplement to the undermanned police and sheriffs of the rural counties and towns.[15]

Finally, there is the role of the individual or the family in the preservation of order. Many westerners saw the enforcement of law (as they understood it) to be best carried out by the individual, or by members of an aggrieved family. Far back in American frontier history, Andrew Jackson's mother had admonished him never to "tell a lie, nor take what is not yours, nor sue . . . for slander" but to *"settle them cases for yourself."* In the West itself the violence-prone, Texas-born New Mexico rancher Oliver Lee invoked this ethic to justify his career as a killer: "I never in my life willingly hurt man, woman, or child—unless they hurt me first. Then I made them pay." No historian of the West has better handled the theme of violent personal redress in the full depths of human frailty and tragedy than C. L. Sonnichsen, especially in four books: *I'll Die Before I'll Run* (1951) and *Ten Texas Feuds* (1957), dealing with the great feuds of central and western Texas; *Outlaw* (1965), the story of Bill Mitchell, who killed for personal vengeance and spent fifty-two years of his life as a fugitive from justice; and *Tularosa* (1960), treating the violent region of south-central New Mexico. Like Bill Mitchell, whose outlaw career was the product of a central-Texas vendetta, the Suttons, Taylors, and other feudists about whom Sonnichsen wrote were motivated by the idea of personal redress.[16]

Often crossing the pages of C. L. Sonnichsen's writings on western violence are the outlaws and gunfighters who have such a high profile in popular ideas about western history. Indeed, historical publication on western outlaws and gunfighters has been vast, much of it lacking the grace and perceptiveness of Sonnichsen's work. Books like Dane Coolidge's *Fighting Men of the West*

(1932) and Eugene Cunningham's *Triggernometry: A Gallery of Gunfighters* (1934) were long on colorful description and short on analysis. Two attempts to offer meaningful generalizations about western gunmen are Joseph G. Rosa's thoughtful *The Gunfighter: Man or Myth?* (1969) and a series of encyclopedia sketches of leading outlaws and gunslingers published in 1977 by Gary L. Roberts. Although it has not been received with universal acclaim, Bill O'Neall's *Encyclopedia of Western Gunfighters* (1979) provides biographical sketches of 255 men who engaged in 587 gunfights in the period of 1865–1900. A monumental contribution is the four incomparable works of bibliography by the late Ramon F. Adams.[17]

Two conceptually focused essays offer thematic treatments of gunfighters: in the *American West,* Gary L. Roberts wrote of "the West's gunmen" as violent participants in the deadly serious social and economic conflicts that shook the late nineteenth century. Richard White perceptively treats the pervasive outlaws of Missouri and Oklahoma with his own original adaptation of E. J. Hobsbawm's social-bandit concept. In a popular treatment, Paul I. Wellman, with some apt documentation, supported his intriguing thesis that *A Dynasty of Western Outlaws* (1961) ruled an illicit crime kingdom in Missouri, Kansas, Oklahoma, and Arkansas from the 1860s to the 1930s. Wellman contended that the outlaw technique of the southwest originated in the guerrilla tactics of William C. Quantrill's band of Civil War irregulars and was handed down through young guerrillas like the Jameses and Youngers to such outlaw successors as Belle and Henry Starr, the Daltons, and, finally, Pretty Boy Floyd. The Wellman thesis was given credibility by one of the best books on the outlaw-gunfighter phenomenon and one of the few by a Ph.D.-trained historian: *Jesse James Was His Name . . .* (1966) by William A. Settle, Jr. Although the Jesse James legend is of prime concern to Settle, his book is in reality a study in depth of the James-Younger gang of bank and train robbers that plagued Missouri and neighboring states after the Civil War. On the basis of very strong research, Settle put the actual exploits of the gang in the context of their Confederate-guerrilla origins, the developing folklore about Jesse James and his criminal colleagues, and the political context of Democratic-Republican rivalry in post–Civil War Missouri.[18]

James B. (Wild Bill) Hickok is the subject of a solid biography by Joseph G. Rosa, while the publications on Wyatt Earp, for example, vary greatly in quality. A work of great skill and salience is a documentary compilation of contemporary Kansas newspaper stories on Hickok, Earp, Bat Masterson, and eighteen other *Great Gunfighters of the Kansas Cowtowns, 1867–1886* (1963) by Nyle H. Miller and Joseph W. Snell. Although undocumented, a valuable work is Frank H. Latta's massive compendium of source materials on the California bandit Joaquin Murieta. One of the most prolific and dependable writers on western outlaws and their opponents is Glenn H. Shirley, who has made his specialty the criminal "Oklahombres" of 1870–1920 and the law officers who tirelessly fought them.[19]

While the traditional gunfight of the Old West is seldom replicated nowadays, the West's tradition of organized crime and outlaw activity is as vigorous as ever. Typical of heavily reported careers of lone operators are three who have been the subjects of major books by Truman Capote and Norman Mailer. Both *In Cold Blood* (1965) by Truman Capote (a study of outlaws Richard E. Hickok and Perry E. Smith, who robbed and murdered the four members of the Clutter family of Holcomb, Kansas, in 1959) and *The Executioner's Song* (1979) by Norman Mailer (the story of the Oregon-Utah outlaw Gary Gilmore, who was executed by a Utah firing squad in a recent legal *cause célèbre*) rise to the level of contemporary social history. In its double focus on Great Plains small-town life of the 1950s and the typical small-time criminal careers of Hickok and Evans, Capote's stunning book is a double contribution to the social history of the West. Mailer's massive book, although a vivid treatment of Gilmore's hapless outlaw life, is also something more: a study of the often hard-working, often floundering struggle of lower-middle-class whites to survive in today's anomic world of western apartment lots, fast-food shops, and dead-end jobs.[20]

Organized crime has flourished all through the twentieth century. Aside from the Great Plains bank robbers of the 1920s and 1930s (depicted, for example, in a vivid case study, *The Santa Claus Bank Robber* by A. C. Greene), it has had a heavily urban character. Yet big-time organized crime did not come into its own until after World War II, when syndicate criminals began to flourish in southern California, the San Francisco Bay area, and America's gambling mecca, Las Vegas, Nevada. Ovid Demaris has chronicled the rise of syndicate operations in these locales in two books. A graphic personal portrait of the Bonannos' syndicate-crime family in the postwar Sun Belt boom cities of Tucson and San Jose has been given by Gay Talese. Organized violence of a different sort is a result of the burgeoning post–World War II outlaw motorcycle gangs centered in California; Hunter S. Thompson's description, *Hell's Angels* (1967), is a classic of social reportage. Just as nineteenth-century western outlaws came to be reflected in popular fiction (see Introduction, above), the like has happened with twentieth-century western crime. Dashiell Hammett drew on his background as a western Pinkerton agent to craft the first of the novels—*Red Harvest* (1929), whose setting,

"Poisonville," was Hammett's fictionalized version of the tough smelter city, Anaconda, Montana—in the widely praised genre of "hard-boiled" detective fiction which has been dominated by California authors Hammett, Raymond Chandler, Ross Macdonald, and most recently Joseph Wambaugh and Stephen Greenleaf.[21]

Land, Labor, and Minority Group Violence in the West

The violence of vigilantes, gunfighters, and legal enforcers of the law often overlapped the land and labor wars of the West; the latter represented pervasive conflict over landed and industrial property that lasted well into the twentieth century. High in the public consciousness were the land wars, exemplified by the most famous of them all—the Johnson County War of Wyoming in 1892. This conflict occurred just one year before Frederick Jackson Turner read his brilliant paper, "The Significance of the Frontier in American History," at the Chicago World's Fair of 1893. Given the heavy emphasis on the factor of land in his remarkable conceptual framework for western historiography, it is ironic that Turner virtually ignored the role of land in generating an enormous amount of conflict and violence within the West. This aspect of land in the West was, however, of major concern to one of Turner's great contemporaries, Henry George of San Francisco. George focused on the problem of land monopoly in a number of publications during the 1870s that were climaxed by his reform masterpiece, *Progress and Poverty*, first published in 1879.[22]

In general, the trauma that the West went through after 1865 was a long-term crisis in land, population, and wealth. Increasing population pressure on the land arising from the settling activities of farmers and ranchers of small means was counterpointed by what were, in effect, the land-enclosing tactics of the super-landholders—railroads, big ranchers, and politically powerful syndicates. In case after case, the settlers often fought back against the oppression of the land enclosers, and violence was frequently the result. Conforming to this pattern was the Johnson County War, which has been best described by Helena Huntington Smith in her book *The War on Powder River* (1966), offering a nuanced treatment of the arrogant social pretensions of the aristocratic British and American ranching nabobs who mounted a vigilante campaign against their rustler–small rancher–small farmer antagonists. In his political history of late-nineteenth-century Wyoming, Lewis L. Gould has traced the electoral backlash against the Republican-aligned big cattle-men in the aftermath of the Johnson County War.[23]

No state exceeded New Mexico's conflict over land in its territorial era. Jim B. Pearson's careful study of *The Maxwell Land Grant* (1961) focuses on the machinations of the Maxwell Land Grant Company of wealthy New Mexicans and Coloradoans that provoked the Colfax County War in northern New Mexico, a conflict pervaded with assassinations and vigilantism as the local settlers resisted the company. The role of Billy the Kid in the Lincoln County War of southern New Mexico has kept the printing presses churning out a huge amount of romantic balderdash; four studies by Maurice G. Fulton, William A, Keleher, Frederick W. Nolan, and Harwood P. Hinton, Jr., probe the economic and political realities that underlay the violence in Lincoln County. C. L. Sonnichsen and Arrell M. Gibson, while differing at times, have sensitively treated a later violent conflict of southern New Mexico: that in the Tularosa country that pitted the Republican party/big rancher faction headed by Colonel Albert J. Fountain against the Democratic party/small rancher faction headed by Oliver Lee and Albert B. Fall. Indis-pensable for an understanding of the broad political context that was so productive of violence in New Mexico (and its neighbor, Arizona) is Howard R. Lamar's excellent study, *The Far Southwest, 1846-1912* (1966).[24]

In Oregon a sensational event resulting from deep tension was the murder of the cattle king Peter French in 1897—the climactic event in Peter K. Simpson's penetrating, social-science oriented study of the conflict between homesteaders and big cattlemen in the southeastern part of the state. A similar alignment found the Olive family as the big-rancher protagonists of two deadly struggles in Texas and Nebraska, as related in Harry E. Chrisman's *The Ladder of Rivers* (1965), focusing on the violence-prone family patriarch I. P. (Print) Olive. The animosity of sheepmen and cattlemen was one factor of many in another bitter, lethal range vendetta, Arizona's Pleasant Valley War of 1886–92, which is the subject of Earle R. Forrest's classic piece of western Americana, *Arizona's Dark and Bloody Ground* (1936), as well as of a recent revisionist treatment by Clara T. Wood and Milton L. Schwartz. The full story of the sheep-cattle wars that pervaded the West is yet to be told by any scholar, but *America's Sheep Trails* (1948) by Edward N. Wentworth presents a substantial account of the heavy violence in Wyoming and Colo-rado in the 1890–1910 era.[25]

Three widely divergent conflicts produced violence in response to the land-enclosing trend. Seven deaths resulted from the Mussel Slough shootout near Hanford, California, on May 11, 1880. The violence arose from a dispute between hundreds of wheat-growing settlers and the Southern Pacific Railroad. The railroad claimed the farmers' land under the terms of a congressional land grant whose validity the settlers denied on the grounds of preemption rights. To countless Americans of the time, the May 11th shootout, climaxing several years of antirailroad protest and violence engendered by settlers, was a symbol of land-monopolizing capitalist oppression by a major American corporation owned by the Big Three of Collis P. Huntington, Leland Stanford, and Charles Crocker (Mark Hopkins of the original Big Four had died in 1878). With five of their number killed in the gun battle, the farmers also lost in the judicial chambers and were eventually ousted from the land. Both Josiah Royce and Frank Norris based novels on the Mussel Slough tragedy, which was a microcosm of the social, economic, and political tensions gripping America and the West in the late nineteenth century. Although there is a small book on the subject, historians as yet have not given adequate treatment to this conflict.[26]

Land enclosure by a combination of rich Anglo and Hispanic operators at the expense of poor Hispanic graziers led to the violent White Cap uprising of northern New Mexico in 1890, in which the "pauvres" resisted the "ricos" with nightriding guerrilla activity. This episode was treated by Robert W. Larson's article of 1975 and is highlighted in Robert J. Rosenbaum's sophisticated, conceptually oriented book of 1981, *Mexicano Resistance in the Southwest: "The Sacred Right of Self-Preservation,"* dealing with New Mexico, California, and Texas from 1848 to 1916. The fence-cutting violence of 1880-1900 in central Texas, which peaked in the Fence-Cutters' War of 1883-84, has been the subject of articles by R. D. Holt and Wayne Gard. As large ranchers crowded out small ranchers and some farmers by fencing in the open range, the small property holders responded by the sort of fence-cutting that was also resorted to by the New Mexico White Caps.[27]

Population pressure on the land was, as in previous cases, central to the Green Corn Rebellion of August 1917 that traumatized the well-to-do landlords and townspeople of eastern Oklahoma. Although the actual violence represented by the Green Corn Rebellion was minor, it has rightly attracted much attention by historians. Partly this is because the Green Corn Rebellion was but the last event in a trend of violence, including barn burnings, night riding, and bank robbing, that overspread the region in the 1910s. More fundamentally, it is because the Green Corn Rebellion and the violence that preceded it was symptomatic of the abnormally high rates of farm tenancy, illiteracy, and poverty, which gave rise to the largest movement of rural socialism in American history. Of several theses, that of John Womack, Jr., well captures the atmosphere of the turbulent Oklahoma countryside of this era. H. C. Peterson and Gilbert C. Fite, taking note of the antidraft element in the August 1917 uprising of poor farmers and tenants, place the event in the context of their inclusive study of the opponents of World War I. James R. Green and Garin Burbank, in their two books, go most deeply into the factors of agrarian discontent motivating the Oklahoma dissidents in their violence during the 1910s. In his sensitive, searching study of grassroots radicalism in the Southwest, Green interprets the Green Corn Rebellion and its 1910s background in terms of E. J. Hobsbawm's concept of the "social bandit"—that is, in the context of the indigenous outlaw and vigilante tradition of Oklahoma and the Southwest. In friendly disagreement with Green, Burbank discounts the former's emphasis on radical ideology and the social-bandit theme in favor of an interpretation that the Green Corn Rebels epitomized a much simpler tradition of backward-looking localist country people. Of related significance was the use of violence in an east Texas county to break up an interracial, white-black movement of Populists, an episode that Lawrence C. Goodwyn analyzed in the *American Historical Review* in 1971 and one that was cognate with some of the violent county conflicts described in C. L. Sonnichsen's writings about Texas.[28]

In contrast to the land wars of the West, with their violence focused on property disputes involving range and farm land, the labor wars of the West occurred in the arena of industrial conflict. Aligned against each other in outbreak after outbreak were the forces of capital and labor. The conflict usually took the form of labor disputes that culminated in strikes and lockouts. Violence was often the result.

No industry in the West exceeded the violence that occurred in the far-flung mining operations of the region, and within the mining industry the bulk of the violence afflicted the hard-rock mine and mill activities. A leading historian of western labor relations, Vernon H. Jensen, has delineated the pattern of conflict and violence up to 1930. A younger scholar, Richard E. Lingenfelter, has noted the way in which, due to management's co-optation of state power and labor's consequent frustration, increasing industrialization in the West led to increasing violence, just as it did in the East. Lingenfelter's thesis is well supported by the outburst of violence that shook the mining West especially in the period from 1890 to 1910. Much of this violence was found in the strife in the Coeur d'Alenes of Idaho, studied by Robert W. Smith, and in what George S. McGovern has called Colorado's "Thirty Years' War" of industrial violence. Deep in the Idaho and Colorado conflict was the militant Western Federation of Miners (WFM) headed by William D. (Big Bill) Haywood, whose 1906–07 trial (and acquittal) for the 1905 assassination of former Idaho Governor Frank Steunenberg was a national *cause célèbre*, an event that has been the subject of a study by David H. Grover. Earlier, Stewart H. Holbrook did a book on the self-confessed WFM bomber Harry Orchard, whose testimony failed to sway the jury against Haywood in the latter's trial.[29]

George C. Suggs's recent book is an impeccable study of Colorado Governor James H. Peabody's management-oriented vendetta against the WFM early in the twentieth century. Colorado's "Thirty Years' War" climaxed in 1913–14 with the greatest example of industrial violence in western history. At issue was the strike of southern Colorado coal miners, the subject of one of the best books in the literature of western violence, *The Great Coalfield War* (1972) by George S. McGovern (whose South Dakota senatorial career was preceded by a Northwestern Ph.D. in history supervised by Arthur S. Link) and Leonard F. Guttridge. With its stress on the intransigence of management, the desperation of the miners, the trauma of ethnic conflict, and the role of the Rockefeller family, *The Great Coalfield War* illustrates salient factors in western industrial violence in the decades just before and after 1900. Two other dramatic examples of western labor violence occurred in Los Angeles and San Francisco, respectively. The dynamiting of Harrison Gray Otis's *Los Angeles Times* building in 1910 (with the loss of many lives) by the McNamara brothers of the steel erectors' union has yet to receive the book-length study it deserves, but Graham Adams's treatment of it in his *Age of Industrial Violence, 1910–1915* (1966) is valuable. In 1916 a bomb exploded in San Francisco's Preparedness Day parade, killing ten, and this led to the conviction and imprisonment of the radical labor activist Tom Mooney. The controversy over Mooney's guilt or innocence continued until his pardon in 1939. *The Mooney Case* (1968) by Richard Frost is a fine study.[30]

Violence in the lumber industry of the West paralleled that in the mining industry, although apparently on a smaller scale. Vernon H. Jensen has provided an overview of the turbulent labor relations in the wood products field, taking due note of episodes of violence. Before 1920 some of the violence involved the activities of the Industrial Workers of the World (IWW). Melvyn Dubofsky has successfully argued that the IWW's reputation for labor violence was unduly exaggerated; but at times the union was clearly linked with violence in the West, especially in regard to its celebrated free-speech campaigns of 1909–16, conducted in western cities from Spokane to San Diego.[31]

One of the latter events resulted in a major case of violence when in Everett, Washington, the IWW supported a shingle-weavers' strike with a free-speech drive. Although a recently discovered eye-witness account calls in question the accuracy of the traditional term "Everett Massacre," at least seven persons and perhaps as many as nineteen died after Wobblies and citizen-deputies exchanged shots at an Everett dock on November 5, 1916. The Everett violence is the central episode in a richly textured, conceptually sophisticated social history of the city by Norman H. Clark. With his sensitive study of the tensions that divided Everett early in the twentieth century, Clark has not only provided the social and economic context of the Everett killings but has produced an incomparable study of a western community in the boom era of eighty years ago. Broader in scale are Robert L. Tyler's chapters on violence in his able study of the IWW in the Pacific Northwest. A solid article by Phillip I. Earl treats the strike in 1879 that led to the killing of five Italian-Swiss charcoal burners near Eureka, Nevada. The ethnic factor was important in this uprising of the hundreds of ill-paid workers who provided charcoal for the smelters of Eureka.[32]

Although Kenneth W. Porter and W. Sherman Savage had been publishing articles on the role of the blacks in the West for many years, it was two books of the 1960s that not only rescued blacks from the invisibility of their residence in the Old West but also emphasized the often violent activities of ubiquitous black cowboys and the frequent involvement of black cavalry with civilian violence in the West. While mythmakers had frozen blacks out of the legend of the West, the historical writers—Porter, Savage, Phillip Durham and Everett L. Jones, and William H. Leckie—were at last incorporating them into the reality (with its violent dimension) of the pioneer West.[33]

Texas was one state where, going back to the days of slavery and Civil War and Reconstruction, the role of blacks in such violent episodes as slave uprisings and Reconstruction turbulence has been chronicled—by Alwyn Barr and other writers. Arthur I. Waskow and Lawrence D. Rice are among those historians who have dealt with mob violence against Texas blacks after the period of Reconstruction, while Robert V. Haynes's engrossing study, *A Night of Violence* (1976), treats the riotous 1917 uprising of black soldiers in Houston. Daniel F. Littlefield, Jr., and Lonnie E. Underhill have shown that the supposed Crazy Snake uprising in Oklahoma, 1909, was in reality an episode of violent white aggression against blacks and Creek Indians.[34]

The vast movement of blacks to urban California in World War II and the postwar period led to black-white tensions that erupted in the massive violence of the six-day riot that ravaged the Watts section of Los Angeles in

August 1965. Indeed, the impact of the Watts riot was felt far beyond Los Angeles and the West, for it was the first of the super riots of black ghetto Americans that shook the country from coast to coast in the 1965–70 period. The literature, both popular and scholarly, on the Watts riot is large. Noteworthy works are Robert Conot's stunning reportage in his *Rivers of Blood, Years of Darkness* (1967), which brilliantly employs the oral-history method; historian Robert M. Fogelson's compilation, *The Los Angeles Riots* (1965); Nathan Cohen's collection of interdisciplinary social-science studies; and the study by David O. Sears and John B. McConahay. One of the main problems in the study of the 1965–70 super riots was assessing the scope of the damage, and an article by Joseph Boskin and Victor Pilson on the Watts riot underscored the police department's overestimate of the number who were wounded. Yet, this is relative, for both in Watts and elsewhere from 1965 to 1970 the black-ghetto uprisings were truly cataclysmic. The significance of the Watts riot must be calculated in terms of two general studies of the 1965–70 riot era that have been contributed by Joe R. Feagan and Harlan Hahn and by James W. Button.[35]

Related to the mood of black protest in the 1960s and 1970s were two episodes of terrorism that afflicted California in the 1970s. One was the racially motivated series of murders of whites in San Francisco known as the Zebra murders, the subject of a book by Clark Howard. The other was the campaign of the Symbionese Liberation Army, a black-white coterie of violent radicals whose murderous career was topped by a national media sensation, the kidnapping of heiress Patricia Hearst. Vin McLean and Paul Avery produced a book that compellingly illuminates the twisted fanaticism of the Symbionese Liberation Army.[36]

The analogies between the status of blacks in the late-nineteenth-century South and the status of Chinese in the West in the same period are arresting. Both racial minorities were the victims of widespread discrimination, which in each case took the form of legislative enactments and violence. In each section, too, anti-black and anti-Chinese sentiment had the effect of uniting the lower strata of the white majority population. This is a point made in Alexander Saxton's conceptually brilliant study of labor and the anti-Chinese movement in California. Although he gives due attention to violence, Saxton's book is valuable chiefly for its presentation of the historical context in which anti-Chinese violence occurred. Regarding violence itself, Chinese, in contrast to blacks in the South, were seldom the targets of lynch mobs, possibly because the Chinese were generally so mild and unobtrusive in their relations with whites on the individual level. But Chinese were the victims of major riots in California, Washington, and Wyoming, events in which popular prejudice with a strong working-class tincture was vented. Curiously, one of the greatest riots of all—in which about twenty Chinese died in Los Angeles in October 1871—has yet to have extended scholarly study; but the riots of Wyoming and Washington have not been ignored. The riot at Rock Springs, Wyoming, on September 2, 1885, was more a massacre than anything else, as from twenty-two to fifty Chinese died in the explosive context of ill feeling between competing white and Chinese miners. An article by Paul Crane and T. A. Larson and a thesis by Arlen R. Wilson have treated this sordid event.[37]

The Chinese loss of life was much lower in the subsequent riots in Seattle and Tacoma in 1885–86. Robert E. Wynne's study of the reaction to Chinese in the Pacific Northwest includes substantial accounts of the outbreaks in Seattle and Tacoma as well as in Vancouver, British Columbia. Jules A. Karlin has done articles on the Seattle-Tacoma riots. In an unpublished paper Carlos A. Schwantes has placed violent anti-Chinese feeling in the Northwest in the fresh context of his concept of the "North Pacific Industrial Frontier" and its web of social, economic, and political tensions. A book by Richard H. Dillon, *The Hatchet Men* (1962), a narrative of San Francisco's turn-of-the-century Tong wars, reminds us that division within the Chinese community itself could occasionally turn violent.[38]

Significant Hispanic violence in the West goes back at least as far as the Taos rebellion of Hispanos and Indians in January 1847. Violence in New Mexico has flared up as recently as 1967, when the protest movement of Reies Tijerina, aggrieved especially over the historic large-scale loss of land ownership in northern New Mexico by the indigenous Hispanic population, conducted a raid on the county courthouse in the town of Tierra Amarilla. Although one life was eventually lost, the violence stemming from Tijerina's movement was not heavy; but it was significant as a symbol of widespread discontent among the Hispanic population of northern New Mexico in the 1960s. The social drama involved in the courthouse raid inspired fine books by Peter Nabokov and Richard Gardner, studies that make evident the resemblance of the 1967 uprising to the 1890s White Cap insurgency in northern New Mexico. Tension between Hispanos and Anglos in Texas has often peaked in violence. One of the earliest protagonists of violent protest against American rule in Texas was Juan N. Cortina, the so-called Robin Hood of the Rio Grande. Cortina became a Hispanic folk hero for the forays he conducted along the border in the mid-nineteenth century, and he has been the subject of the book whose subtitle refers to the controversy over whether Cortina was simply a brutal bandit or a Hispanic patriot. Clarence C. Clendenen also treated the Hispano-Anglo conflict that produced group violence in the border country of Texas as late as the Norias raid of 1915.[39]

In the Golden State, the loss of Hispanic power following the American takeover bred episodes of violence that have been perceptively treated by Leonard Pitt in his moving book, *The Decline of the Californios* (1966). The most glaring instances treated by Pitt are the pervasive bandit activity of Joaquin Murieta; the "Downieville Horror," in which the American miners of that gold-digging camp lynched the Mexican woman Juanita in 1851; and ethnic conflict of Americans and Mexicans in Los Angeles, 1850–56. Nearly a hundred years later Los Angeles was again the scene of violent conflict: this time between Americans, primarily World War II servicemen stationed in the area, and the youthful Pachucos of the Hispanic community. The "Zoot Suit Riot" of 1943 has been the subject of a study by Mauricio Mazón in which the violent aggressiveness of the servicemen is probed in depth.[40]

Religious conflict is often mixed with racial and ethnic antagonisms, and indeed Protestant-versus-Catholic animosity frequently accompanied the Anglo-versus-Hispanic conflict noted above. Similarly, religious antipathies aligning Irish Catholics against Anglo-Saxon Protestants were a factor in the San Francisco vigilante outbreak of 1856. Yet, religiously motivated violence in the West seems not to have been as great as in the eastern half of the United States, but one deep blot on western history comes right out of the tradition of fanatic religiosity: the Mountain Meadows Massacre, in which some one hundred twenty gentiles perished in an attack by Mormons and Indians headed by Latter-day Saints hierarch John D. Lee in southwest Utah in 1857. Of course, it must not be forgotten that the atrocity of Mountain Meadows was the culmination in a violent chain of events that went back to gentile persecution of the Mormons in Missouri and Illinois. Indeed, it was the cowardly assassination of Joseph Smith and the violent destruction of Nauvoo that led to the L.D.S. exodus to Utah. The violent events in Missouri and Illinois are of necessity featured in all histories of the Mormons; but one fine work of scholarship in particular, *Nauvoo* (1965) by Robert B. Flanders, focuses at the end on the debacle in the Mormons' Illinois capital.[41]

On Mountain Meadows itself there is an inspiring example of scholarship in the work of Juanita Brooks. The massacre is, of course, a matter of profound regret and an unpleasant subject for those of the Mormon faith, an event that a Mormon historian might understandably wish to avoid. Such has not been the case, however, with Brooks, whose book *The Mountain*

Meadows Massacre (1950; rev. 1962) and whose biography of John D. Lee make up an impeccable body of scholarship that does not hesitate to link fairly the massacre with the leadership of Brigham Young. There may thus be no better example in western historiography of a historian's rising above the constrictions of personal background than Brooks's work on Mountain Meadows, which has by no means been superseded by the superficial, strongly anti-Mormon 1976 study of the subject by William Wise. Essential to understanding the mood of desperation which swept over the world of the Mormons in the 1850s and contributed strongly to the inception of the Mountain Meadows Massacre is Norman F. Furniss, *The Mormon Conflict, 1850–1859* (1960), a study of federal military intervention in Utah under President Buchanan.[42]

Conclusion: Toward a New Historiography of Western Violence

The substantive findings of the historiography of western violence are important. Among the most significant are the pervasiveness of vigilantism in regard to the creation of new communities, and its extension into the land, labor, racial, and religious wars of the West. Notable, also, has been the prevalence of the theme of personal redress. The role of Civil War–induced antagonisms crops up again and again, as does the role of partisan political conflict. The achievements of scholarship on western violence in both volume and quality are impressive. Yet when the subject is considered as a whole, it is evident that the sum of the scholarship is less than its parts.

One reason for this is that there is no overall explanatory paradigm of western history that includes violence within its framework. Frederick Jackson Turner emphasized political conflict between the West and the East in his paradigm of frontier history, but he virtually ignored conflict, and therefore violence, *within* the West. Despite the many exceptions cited in this essay, scholars have tended to ignore violence in their writings on the West. In the leading textbooks on western history, only Robert V. Hine's *The American West* (1973) adequately treats violence; the result is that the textbooks as a whole significantly neglect not only violence but the entire subject of conflict within western history.[43]

There is a ready explanation as to why leading historians of the West have largely avoided the subject of violence. The explanation is the artificial but understandable dichotomy between the Wild West and the Workaday West. By the late nineteenth century, most of the writing on the West was really writing on the so-called Wild West, the cowboys and Indians, the outlaws and gunfighters; it provided highly colored images of the romantic West in the public mind. So much of the writing on the Wild West, whether historical or fictional, was marked by the meretricious and sunk in superficiality that serious historians of the West, headed by Turner, avoided the Wild West. Understandably fearing intellectual guilt by association, professional historians of the West turned from the Wild West to the Workaday West of farm fields, ranch lots, mine shafts, millrooms, city streets, and legislative halls.

In giving low priority to western violence, Turner and the succession of conceptually oriented historians established the legitimacy of western history, for Turner's luminous essay of 1893 not only certified the seriousness of western historiography but gave the history of the West a central role in the perceptions of American intellectuals. In our own time Earl Pomeroy's emphasis on cities and the twentieth century has given western historiography a crucial intellectual updating that has kept our subject in phase with the dominant urban reality of twentieth-century American life.[44] But with the credibility of western historical scholarship long since established, it is now high time for analytical historians more fully to give western violence its due.

What is needed is a new conceptual framework for future research and writing on western violence. The new historiography of western violence should unite the Wild West with the Workaday West, should exemplify the unique character of western history, and should be cognate with the latest scholarship in the history and social science of violence.

Uniting the Wild West with the Workaday West

In reality the Wild West and the Workaday West were never separated. The participation of the Earp brothers in factional infighting for the political domination of Cochise County, Arizona, is an example of the reality of the union of the Workaday West and the Wild West. Occasionally scholars have treated the symbiosis of Wild West and Workaday West, as Lewis L. Gould has done with the political aspect of the Johnson County War and Robert R. Dykstra has done with his study of the merchant princes and gunfighters of the Kansas cattle towns.[45] These efforts are, however, but straws in the shifting wind of the historiography of western violence. The entire subject needs to be redone from this perspective.

Violence and the Unique Character of Western History

With his stress on political and cultural continuity between East and West and conservatism in western society and politics, Earl Pomeroy has ended the sharp separation between East and West that was a major aspect of Frederick Jackson Turner's paradigm of western history.[46] Recognition of the unity of America and the West has deeply enriched our knowledge of western history, but the distinctive historical reality of the West remains and must be blended into any new paradigm of western violence. Here the role of the authentic western tradition is crucial in terms, for example, of the institution of vigilantism and the tendency to personal redress which early on became embedded in frontier society.

The West and the Latest Scholarship in the History and Social Science of Violence

The publication in 1969 of *Violence in America: Historical and Comparative Perspectives,* edited by Hugh Davis Graham and Ted Robert Gurr, epitomized more than any other work the scholarly subdiscipline of violence studies to which European and American historians were making a major contribution. In the wake of *Violence in America,* a number of conceptual issues and problems have emerged in the interpretation of violence in the tradition of Western European and American civilization.[47] Future work in western American violence must be gauged against these issues and problems as follows.

First is the role of the crowd in violent episodes such as lynchings, riots, or local conflicts. The work of European scholars George Rudé, E. J. Hobsbawm, and E. P. Thompson, supported by American authorities, has postulated a goal-oriented, rationally motivated, ideologically conscious crowd that is the conceptual opposite of the long accepted prototype of the mindless mob developed by Charles Le Bon.[48] What, then, has been the behavior and background of the crowd in particular cases of western group violence? Much of the new scholarship on crowd behavior rests on new methods and techniques of research such as quantitative analysis and prosopography (or collective biography). It goes almost without saying that these and other new methodologies, such as oral history, should be included in the research repertoires of historians of western violence.

Second, the new approach to ideology goes beyond the traditional definitions of pure ideas or simply ideas in their social context to Clifford Geertz's concept of ideology as a cultural system in which ideas comprise a web of beliefs and perceptions through which people filter the meaning of their experiences and structure their actions. The Old Whig or Commonwealth ideology possessed by Americans in the 1760s and 1770s was basic to that Revolutionary generation. Ideology in this sense can be observed among the violent westerners of the past in, for example, the Homestead Ethic, which often motivated western vigilantes and opponents of land enclosers in the land wars, the Producer ethic through which violent whites viewed the Chinese, and the ideology of capitalist development, which caused the Big Three of Huntington, Stanford, and Crocker to stand firm against the violence-prone Mussel Slough settlers of California. It is evident, too, that ideology plays a key role in the phenomenon of crowd behavior discussed above.[49]

Third, the long-term trend of crime nationally and wordwide has been investigated by Ted Robert Gurr, Roger Lane, and others. They are showing that the rates of crime and violent death, having been high in western and northern Europe and in America until the early nineteenth century, fell steadily from the 1840s to the 1940s and have been rising steadily (with short-term interruptions) since the middle and late 1950s. The reason for the century-long decline in crime and violent death from the 1840s to the 1940s seems to have been the inherent social discipline and the rationalizing pressures of industrialization, urbanization, and modernization. Conversely, the emergence of postindustrial society during the 1950s and 1960s has led to a weakening of the bonds of society and a relaxation of the rationalizing pressures of industrialization. The result is a new long-term rise in crime and violent death from which, among major nations, only Japan has been relatively immune. A significant new study of crime and punishment in urbanizing Alameda County, California, 1870–1910, conforms to this pattern, but more such studies of western communities are needed to see if the West, generally, matches the paradigm.[50]

Fourth, the comparative prevalence of violence, both geographically and historically, is a key problem. The quantitative research of Gurr and others has well established that the United States is the most violent nation among its peer group of the industrialized modern democracies of the world. As noted above, scholars are also showing that, in historical terms, the late twentieth century has exceeded the late nineteenth century in the realm of crime and violent death. A few historians of the West have considered the comparative question. On the basis of his study of Kansas cattle towns, Robert R. Dykstra felt that the prevalence of western violence has been exaggerated, while in even broader terms a major theme in W. Eugene Hollon's *Frontier Violence* (1974) is that, contrary to myth, eastern violence surpassed western violence in the nineteenth century. On the other hand, in his case study of two towns of the pioneer West (Aurora, Nevada, and Bodie, California), Roger McGrath investigated the problem of frontier violence in relation to our own time and obtained a mixed result. In contrast to America of the 1970s and 1980s, nineteenth-century Bodie and Aurora rarely saw robbery and rape; but McGrath found quantitative validation for the myth of the Wild West in the very high murder rate in these two towns, which he found to be six times higher than in the most murder-prone cities of the United States in 1976. McGrath attributed the extremely high rate of murder in Bodie and Aurora, as well as the local prevalence of vigilantism, to the presence of authentic bad men and the vigor of the gunfight tradition of the West.[51]

Fifth, the success question: that is, does goal-oriented violence generally succeed or does it usually fail? In 1969 Hugh Davis Graham and Ted Robert Gurr concluded that violence was ordinarily counterproductive. Recently, however, a new view has been advanced in terms of what might be called the Tilly-Gamson thesis that violence, although regrettable, is a fairly normal part of the struggle for power in any society and that more often than not the use of violence will succeed.[52] The Tilly-Gamson thesis certainly seems to be borne out by western violence, at least in the period from 1865 to 1930. Aside from the plethora of episodes already cited, there were other cases where violence was introduced as an arbiter in western struggles for power: the violence-prone claim clubs organized in defense of squatters' rights; the county-seat wars that were at their most destructive in Kansas; and the dynamiting campaign of Owens Valley residents in defense of their water against the exactions of the city of Los Angeles.[53] All in all, it may well be that there is no better example of the workings of the Tilly-Gamson thesis in American history than the West.

If pursued by historians, the suggested agenda—uniting the Wild West with the Workaday West, viewing violence in terms of the unique character of western history, and relating the West to the latest scholarship in the field of violence studies—would indeed produce a new historiography of western violence. Besides its inherent interest, western violence is of particular importance to conceptually oriented historians because violence is the irremediable expression of conflict and tension that has been the fate of nearly all societies.

Violence, then, is the tracer that alerts the historian to the existence of conflict within a society. Consensus interpretations of western society, from
Turner (liberal consensus) to Pomeroy (conservative consensus), have dominated western historiography, as indeed they should; for despite the existence
of pervasive conflict and violence, the social bond in the American West, although often battered, has never been broken. Yet, as in the case of vigilantes
and many others, violence was used to bolster consensus in the West.

Conflict itself needs to be more emphasized by the analytical historians
of the West, and this will almost inevitably occur. As it does, historians will
of course do even more work on violence in western history. Some of the
greatest interpretive gains stand to be made in the study of western outlaws
and gunfighters, whom professional historians have neglected. Up until now
the western outlaws and gunfighters have survived in American consciousness
primarily for the entertainment of those who have turned to them in film
and fiction for escape from the strains and stresses of modern life. Yet, the
escapist function of popular images of western violence has had a most significant—and most noxious—byproduct in its implicit message that brutal
power is the determinant in human relations.[54] In the future, conceptual
historians will do more to depict the reality of the violent role, which outlaws
and gunfighters performed, in the struggles for economic and political power
that were the true story of the winning of the West.

Notes

1. Henry Nash Smith, *Virgin Land: The American West as Symbol and
Myth* (Cambridge: Harvard University Press, 1950; paperbound ed., 1970).

2. William A. Settle, Jr., *Jesse James Was His Name* . . . (Columbia: University of Missouri Press, 1966 paperbound ed., Lincoln: University of Nebraska Press, 1977); Kent Ladd Steckmesser, *The Western Hero in History
and Legend* (Norman: University of Oklahoma Press, 1965); Americo Paredes,
"With His Pistol in His Hand": A Border Ballad and Its Hero (Austin: University of Texas Press, 1958); John O. West, "To Die Like a Man: The 'Good'
Outlaw Tradition in the American Southwest" (Ph.D. diss., University of
Texas, 1964).

3. Richard Slotkin, *Regeneration Through Violence: The Mythology of
the American Frontier, 1600-1860* (Middletown: Wesleyan University Press,
1973); Walter Van Tilburg Clark, *The Ox-Bow Incident* (New York: Random
House, 1940; paperbound ed., Signet Classics, n.d.).

4. Richard W. Etulain, "Ernest Haycox: The Literary Career of a Western Writer, 1899-1950" (Ph.D. diss., University of Oregon, 1966); Etulain, "The Origins of the Western," *Journal of Popular Culture* 5 (Spring 1972): 799-805; Etulain, *Owen Wister* (Boise: Boise State College, 1973); and Etulain and Michael T. Marsden (eds.), *The Popular Western* . . . (Bowling Green, Ohio: Bowling Green University Popular Press, 1974); John G. Cawelti, *The Six-Gun Mystique* (Bowling Green, Ohio: Bowling Green University Popular Press, 1971); Cawelti, "The Western: A Look at the Evolution of a Formula," chap. 8 in Cawelti, *Adventure, Mystery, and Romance* . . . (Chicago: University of Chicago Press, 1976); John H. Lenihan, *Showdown: Confronting Modern America in the Western Film* (Urbana: University of Illinois Press, 1980).

5. Earl Mottram, "The Persuasive Lips: Men and Guns in America, the West," *Journal of American Studies* 10 (April 1976): 53-84; Werner J. Einstadter, "Crime News in the Old West: Social Control in a Northwestern Town, 1887-1888," *Urban Life* 8 (October 1979): 317-34; Ray Allen Billington, *Land of Savagery, Land of Promise: The European Image of the American Frontier in the Nineteenth Century* (New York: W. W. Norton, 1980).

6. Raymond D. Gastil, *Cultural Regions of the United States* (Seattle: University of Washington Press, 1975; paperbound ed., n.d.), pp. 107-8; Henry P. Lundsgaarde, *Murder in Space City: A Cultural Analysis of Houston Homicide Patterns* (New York: Oxford University Press, 1977); Richard Maxwell Brown in *Vanderbilt Law Review* 32 (January 1979): 232-33; Ann Rule, *The Stranger Beside Me* (New York: W. W. Norton, 1980); Anthony Summers, *Conspiracy* (New York: McGraw-Hill, 1980).

7. Frederick Jackson Turner, *The Frontier in American History* (New York: Holt, 1920; paperbound ed., Krieger, 1976); Josiah Royce, *California, from the Conquest in 1846 to the Second Vigilance Committee in San Francisco* . . . (Boston: Houghton Mifflin, 1886); Earl Pomeroy, "Josiah Royce, Historian in Quest of Community," *Pacific Historical Review* 40 (February 1971): 1-20; Robert V. Hine, *Community on the American Frontier* . . . (Norman: University of Oklahoma Press, 1980). For an overview of American and western vigilantism: Richard Maxwell Brown, *Strain of Violence: Historical Studies of American Violence and Vigilantism* (New York: Oxford University Press, 1975; paperbound ed., 1977), chaps. 4-6.

8. Thomas J. Dimsdale, *The Vigilantes of Montana* (Virginia City, Mont.: Montana Post Press, 1866; paperbound ed., Norman: University of Oklahoma Press, 1978); Nathaniel Pitt Langford, *Vigilante Days and Ways,* 2 vols. (Boston: J. G. Cupples, 1890; reprint ed., Missoula: University of Montana Press,

1957); Hoffman Birney, *Vigilantes* (Philadelphia: Penn, 1929); John W. Smurr, "Afterthoughts on the Vigilantes," *Montana: The Magazine of Western History* 18 (Spring 1958): 8-20; Merrill G. Burlingame, "Montana's Righteous Hangmen: A Reconsideration," *ibid.* 28 (Autumn 1978): 36-49; Barton C. Olsen, "Lawlessness and Vigilantes in America . . . Emphasizing California and Montana" (Ph.D. diss., University of Utah, 1968); Oscar O. Mueller, "The Central Montana Vigilante Raids of 1884," *Montana: The Magazine of Western History* 1 (January 1951): 23-35; Richard K. Mueller, "Granville Stuart and the Montana Vigilantes of 1884" (M.A. thesis, University of Oregon, 1980). Oscar O. and Richard K. Mueller are not related.

9. Hubert Howe Bancroft, *Popular Tribunals*, 2 vols. (San Francisco: History Co., 1887); Stanton A. Coblentz, *James King of William and Pioneer Justice in California* (New York: Barnes, 1961); James A. B. Scherer, *"The Lion of the Vigilantes": William T. Coleman and the Life of Old San Francisco* (Indianapolis: Bobbs-Merrill, 1939); William H. Ellison, *A Self-Governing Dominion: California, 1849-1860* (Berkeley: University of California Press, 1950); Richard Maxwell Brown, "Pivot of American Vigilantism: The San Francisco Vigilance Committee of 1856," in John A. Carroll (ed.), *Reflections of Western Historians* (Tucson: University of Arizona Press, 1969), pp. 105-19; Roger W. Lotchin, *San Francisco, 1846-1856* . . . (New York: Oxford University Press, 1974; paperbound ed., Lincoln: University of Nebraska Press, 1979), chaps. 8-9; Robert M. Senkewicz, "Business and Politics in Gold Rush San Francisco, 1851-1856" (Ph.D. diss., Stanford University, 1974); Peter R. Decker, *Fortunes and Failures: White-Collar Mobility in Nineteenth-Century San Francisco* (Cambridge: Harvard University Press, 1978), pp. 125-43; Robert A. Burchell, *The San Francisco Irish, 1848-1880* (Berkeley and Los Angeles: University of California Press, 1980), chap. 7; George R. Stewart, *Committee of Vigilance: Revolution in San Francisco, 1851* (Boston: Houghton Mifflin, 1964); Mary Floyd Williams, *History of the San Francisco Committee of Vigilance of 1851* . . . (Berkeley: University of California Press, 1921); Sherman M. Ricards and George M. Blackburn, "The Sydney Ducks: A Demographic Analysis," *Pacific Historical Review* 42 (February 1973): 20-31.

10. C. L. Sonnichsen, *I'll Die Before I'll Run* (New York: Devin-Adair, 1962); and Sonnichsen, *Ten Texas Feuds* (Albuquerque: University of New Mexico Press, 1957); Brown, *Strain of Violence*, chaps. 4, 8; Charles C. Alexander, *Crusade for Conformity: The Ku Klux Klan in Texas 1920-1930* (Houston: Gulf Coast Historical Association, 1962); John W. Caughey (ed.), *Their Majesties the Mob* (Chicago: University of Chicago Press, 1960).

11. Frank R. Prassel, *The Western Peace Officer* . . . (Norman: University

of Oklahoma Press, 1972); an older general work is Wayne Gard, *Frontier Justice* (Norman: University of Oklahoma Press, 1949); Larry D. Ball, *The United States Marshals of New Mexico and Arizona Territories, 1846-1912* (Albuquerque: University of New Mexico Press, 1978).

12. Robert R. Dykstra, *The Cattle Towns* (New York: Knopf, 1968; paperbound ed., New York: Atheneum, 1970), chap. 3 and *passim*; Philip D. Jordan, *Frontier Law and Order* (Lincoln: University of Nebraska Press, 1970).

13. Walter Prescott Webb, *The Texas Rangers: A Century of Defense* (Boston: Houghton Mifflin, 1935); in 1965 the University of Texas Press published a posthumous, unrevised second edition with a new foreword by Lyndon B. Johnson; Julian Samora *et al., Gunpowder Justice: A Reassessment of the Texas Rangers* (Notre Dame: University of Notre Dame Press, 1979); Ben H. Procter, "The Modern Texas Rangers: A Law Enforcement Dilemma in the Rio Grande Valley," in Carroll, *Reflections of Western Historians,* pp. 215-31; James R. Ward, "The Texas Rangers, 1919-1935 . . ." (Ph.D. diss., Texas Christian University, 1972).

14. John D. W. Guice, *The Rocky Mountain Bench . . . 1861-1890* (New Haven: Yale University Press, 1972); John R. Wunder, *Inferior Courts, Superior Justice . . .* (Westport, Conn.: Greenwood Press, 1979); Glenn H. Shirley, *Law West of Fort Smith . . .* (New York: Holt, 1957; paperbound ed., Lincoln: University of Nebraska Press, 1968); Fred Harvey Harrington, *Hanging Judge* (Caldwell, Idaho: Caxton, 1951).

15. James D. Horan, *The Pinkertons . . .* (New York: Crown, 1968); Brown, *Strain of Violence,* pp. 125-26; Patrick B. Nolan, "Vigilantes on the Middle Border: A Study of Self-Appointed Law Enforcement in the States of the Upper Mississippi from 1840 to 1880" (Ph.D. diss., University of Minnesota, 1971).

16. Marquis James, *Andrew Jackson: The Border Captain* (Indianapolis: Bobbs-Merrill, 1933), p. 30; Sonnichsen, *I'll Die Before I'll Run*; Sonnichsen, *Ten Texas Feuds*; Sonnichsen, *Outlaw: Bill Mitchell, Alias Baldy Russell . . .* (Denver: Sage, 1965); and Sonnichsen, *Tularosa: Last of the Frontier West* (New York: Devin-Adair, 1960). Besides the works already cited, other notable books by C. L. Sonnichsen on western violence are *Pass of the North* (El Paso: Texas Western Press, 1968), a salient treatment of very violent El Paso; *Billy King's Tombstone* (Tucson: University of Arizona Press, 1972); *From Hopalong to Hud: Thoughts on Western Fiction* (College Station: Texas A&M Press, 1978); with William V. Morrison, *Alias Billy the Kid* (Albuquerque: University of New Mexico Press, 1955), on Brushy Bill Roberts, who claimed to have been Billy the Kid; and *The Grave of John*

Wesley Hardin: Three Essays on Grassroots History (College Station: Texas A & M Press, 1979).

17. Dane Coolidge, *Fighting Men of the West* (New York: Dutton, 1932); Eugene Cunningham, *Triggernometry* (Caldwell: Caxton, 1940); a colorful earlier work was Emerson Hough, *The Story of the Outlaw* (New York: Grosset and Dunlap, 1907); Joseph G. Rosa, *The Gunfighter: Man or Myth?* (Norman: University of Oklahoma Press, 1969); Howard R. Lamar (ed.), *The Reader's Encyclopedia of the American West* (New York: Crowell, 1977); Bill O'Neall, *Encyclopedia of Western Gunfighters* (Norman: University of Oklahoma Press, 1969); all published by the University of Oklahoma Press in Norman are Ramon F. Adams, *Six Guns and Saddle Leather: A Bibliography of Books and Pamphlets on Western Outlaws and Gunmen* (1954), *Burs under the Saddle: A Second Look at Books and Histories of the West* (1964), *More Burs under the Saddle: Books and Histories of the West* (1979), and *A Fitting Death for Billy the Kid* (1981).

18. Gary L. Roberts, "The West's Gunmen," *American West* 8 (January 1971): 10–15, 64; (March 1971): 18–23, 61–62; Richard White, "Outlaw Gangs of the Middle Border: American Social Bandits," *Western Historical Quarterly* 12 (October 1981): 387–408; Paul I. Wellman, *A Dynasty of Western Outlaws* (Garden City, N.Y.: Doubleday, 1961). On the Civil War guerrillas see Don R. Bowen, "Guerrilla War in Western Missouri, 1862–65: Historical Explanations of the Relative Deprivation Hypothesis," *Comparative Studies in History and Society* 19 (January 1977): 30–51; Settle, *Jesse James Was His Name.* See also Richard Patterson, "Train Robbery . . . ," *American West* 14 (March/April 1977): 48–53.

19. Joseph G. Rosa, *They Called Him Wild Bill . . . ,* 2d ed. (Norman: University of Oklahoma Press, 1964). Nyle H. Miller and Joseph W. Snell, *Great Gunfighters of the Kansas Cowtowns, 1867–1886* (paperbound ed., Lincoln: University of Nebraska Press, 1967; originally published under the title *Why the West Was Wild* by the Kansas State Historical Society, Topeka, 1963). Frank F. Latta, *Joaquin Murrieta* [sic] *and His Horse Gangs* (Santa Cruz: Bear State Books, 1980); Glenn H. Shirley, *West of Hell's Fringe: Crime, Criminals, and the Federal Peace Officers in Oklahoma Territory* Norman: University of Oklahoma Press, 1977). Space does not permit discussion of all of the worthy books and articles on leading outlaws and gunfighters of the West, but the standard works by Leon Metz, Ed Bartholomew, F. Stanley, Lewis Nordyke, Wayne Gard, J. Evetts Haley, and many others are cited in the bibliography of O'Neall, *Encyclopedia of Western Gunfighters.* Typical of ongoing revisionist scholarship is Jack Burrows, "John Ringo: The Story of a Western Myth," *Montana: The Magazine of Western History* 25 (Autumn 1980): 2–15.

20. Truman Capote, *In Cold Blood* (New York: Random House, 1965); Norman Mailer, *The Executioner's Song* (Boston: Little, Brown, 1979).

21. A. C. Greene, *The Santa Claus Bank Robbery* (New York: Knopf, 1972); Ovid Demaris, *The Last Mafioso: The Treacherous World of Jimmy Fratianno* (New York: New York Times, 1981), an important work, but Fratianno's recollections must be used with caution; Ed Reid and Ovid Demaris, *The Green Felt Jungle* (New York: Trident, 1963); Gay Talese, *Honor Thy Father* (New York: World, 1971; paperbound ed., Dell, n.d.); Hunter S. Thompson, *Hell's Angels* (New York: Ballantine, 1967); Dashiel Hammett, *Red Harvest* (New York: Alfred A. Knopf, 1929; paperbound ed., Random House, n.d.).

22. Henry George, *Progress and Poverty* (San Francisco: Hinton, 1879; paperbound ed., Canaan, N.H.: Phoenix Pub., 1979); see also, George, *Our Land and Land Policy* (San Francisco: White and Bauer, 1871).

23. Helena Huntington Smith, *The War on Powder River* (New York: McGraw-Hill, 1966; paperbound ed., Lincoln: University of Nebraska Press, 1967); Lewis L. Gould, *Wyoming: A Political History, 1868–1896* (New Haven: Yale University Press, 1968), chap. 6.

24. Jim B. Pearson, *The Maxwell Land Grant* (Norman: University of Oklahoma Press, 1961); Maurice G. Fulton, *History of the Lincoln County War*, ed. Robert N. Mullin (Tucson: University of Arizona Press, 1968); William A. Keleher, *Violence in Lincoln County, 1869–1881* (Albuquerque: University of New Mexico Press, 1957); Frederick W. Nolan, *The Life and Death of John Henry Tunstall* (Albuquerque: University of New Mexico Press, 1965); Harwood P. Hinton, Jr., "John Simpson Chisum, 1877–84," *New Mexico Historical Review* 31 (July 1956): 177–205; 31 (October 1956): 310–37; 32 (January 1957): 53–65; Arrell M. Gibson, *The Life and Death of Colonel Albert Jennings Fountain* (Norman: University of Oklahoma Press, 1965); Sonnichsen, *Tularosa*; Howard R. Lamar, *The Far Southwest, 1846–1912: A Territorial History* (New Haven: Yale University Press, 1966; paperbound ed., Norton, 1970).

25. Peter K. Simpson, "A Social History of the Cattle Industry in Southeast Oregon, 1869–1912" (Ph.D. diss., University of Oregon, 1973); Harry E. Chrisman, *The Ladder of Rivers: The Story of I. P. (Print) Olive* (Denver: Sage, 1965); Earle R. Forrest, *Arizona's Dark and Bloody Ground* (Caldwell: Caxton, 1953); Clara T. Woody and Milton L. Schwartz, "War in Pleasant Valley . . . ," *Journal of Arizona History* 18 (Spring 1977): 43–68; Edward N. Wentworth, *America's Sheep Trails . . .* (Ames: Iowa State College Press, 1948), chap. 23.

26. Josiah Royce, *The Feud of Oakfield Creek* (Boston: Houghton

Mifflin, 1887); Frank Norris, *The Octopus* . . . (New York: Doubleday, Page, 1901; paperbound ed., Signet/NAL, n.d.); James L. Brown, *The Mussel Slough Tragedy* (n.p., 1958). Representing my own book in progress on the Mussel Slough conflict are two unpublished papers: "Vigilantism and the Ideology of the Western Crowd: Perspectives on the Mussel Slough Conflict in California, 1878-1880" (University of Oregon, May 16, 1977); "Seven Dead: The Mussel Slough Gunfight of May 11, 1880" (Western History Association, San Diego, October 18, 1979).

27. Robert W. Larson, "The White Caps of New Mexico . . . ," *Pacific Historical Review* 44 (May 1975): 171-85; Robert J. Rosenbaum, *Mexicano Resistance in the Southwest: "The Sacred Right of Self-Preservation"* (Austin: University of Texas Press, 1981); R. D. Holt, "The Introduction of Barbed Wire into Texas and the Fence Cutting War," *West Texas Historical Association Yearbook* 6 (1930): 70-75; Wayne Gard, "The Fence-Cutters," *Southwestern Historical Quarterly* 51 (July 1947): 1-15.

28. John Womack, Jr., "Oklahoma's Green Corn Rebellion" (B.A. thesis, Harvard College, 1959); H. C. Peterson and Gilbert C. Fite, *Opponents of War, 1917-1918* (Madison: University of Wisconsin Press, 1957); James R. Green, *Grass-Roots Socialism: Radical Movements in the Southwest, 1895-1943* (Baton Rouge: Louisiana State University Press, 1978), chaps. 8-9; Garin Burbank, *When Farmers Voted Red* . . . (Westport, Conn.: Greenwood, 1976), chap. 7; Lawrence C. Goodwyn, "Populist Dreams and Negro Rights: East Texas as a Case Study," *American Historical Review* 77 (December 1971): 1435-56; Sonnichsen, *I'll Die Before I'll Run* and *Ten Texas Feuds*.

29. Vernon H. Jensen, *Heritage of Conflict: Labor Relations in the Nonferrous Metals Industry up to 1930* (Ithaca, N.Y.: Cornell University Press, 1950); Richard E. Lingenfelter, *The Hard Rock Miners* . . . *in the American West, 1863-1893* (Berkeley: University of California Press, 1974), pp. 66-106, 196-218; Robert W. Smith, *The Coeur d'Alene Mining War of 1892* . . . (Corvallis: Oregon State University Press, 1961); George S. McGovern, "The Colorado Coal Strike, 1913-1914" (Ph.D. diss., Northwestern University, 1953); David H. Grover, *Debaters and Dynamiters: The Story of the Haywood Trial* (Corvallis: Oregon State University Press, 1964); Stewart H. Holbrook, *The Rocky Mountain Revolution* (New York: Holt, 1956).

30. George C. Suggs, Jr., *Colorado's War on Militant Unionism: James H. Peabody and the Western Federation of Miners* (Detroit: Wayne State University Press, 1972); George S. McGovern and Leonard F. Guttridge, *The Great Coalfield War* (Boston: Little, Brown, 1972); Graham Adams, Jr., *Age of Industrial Violence, 1910-1915* . . . (New York: Columbia University

Press, 1966); Herbert Shapiro, "The McNamara Case . . . ," *Southern California Quarterly* 59 (Fall 1977): 271–87; Richard H. Frost, *The Mooney Case* (Stanford, Calif.: Stanford University Press, 1968).

31. Melvyn Dubofsky, *We Shall Be All: A History of the Industrial Workers of the World* (Chicago: Quadrangle, 1968; paperbound ed., New York: Times Books, 1972); Vernon H. Jensen, *Lumber and Labor* (New York: Farrar and Rinehart, 1945).

32. William J. Williams, "Bloody Sunday Revisited," *Pacific Northwest Quarterly* 71 (April 1980): 50–62; Norman H. Clark, *Mill Town: A Social History of Everett, Washington* . . . (Seattle: University of Washington Press, 1970; paperbound ed., 1972); Robert L. Tyler, *Rebels of the Woods: The I.W.W. in the Pacific Northwest* (Eugene: University of Oregon, 1967), chaps. 3, 6, and *passim*; Phillip I. Earl, "Nevada's Italian War, July–September 1879," *Nevada Historical Society Quarterly* 12 (Summer 1969): 47–87. The sensational lynching of a labor organizer is treated in Arnon Gutfeld, "The Murder of Frank Little: Radical Labor Agitation in Butte, Montana, 1917," *Labor History* 10 (Spring 1969).

33. Philip Durham and Everett L. Jones, *The Negro Cowboys* (New York: Dodd, Mead, 1965), chap. 11 and *passim*; and William H. Leckie, *The Buffalo Soldiers: A Narrative of the Negro Cavalry in the West* (Norman: University of Oklahoma Press, 1967); Kenneth Wiggins Porter, *The Negro and the American Frontier* (New York: Arno, 1971); and W. Sherman Savage, *Blacks in the West* (Westport, Conn.: Greenwood, 1976).

34. Alwyn Barr, *Black Texans . . . 1528–1971* (Austin: Jennings, 1973), pp. 27–34, 48–50; and, for example, Frank H. Smurr, "Unionism, Abolitionism, and Vigilantism in Texas, 1856–1865" (M.A. thesis, University of Texas, 1961); Arthur I. Waskow, *From Race Riot to Sit-In, 1919 and the 1960s* . . . (Garden City, N.Y.: Doubleday, 1967), pp. 16–20 and *passim;* Lawrence D. Rice, *The Negro in Texas, 1874–1900* (Baton Rouge: Louisiana State University Press, 1971), pp. 250–54; Robert V. Haynes, *A Night of Violence: The Houston Riot of 1917* (Baton Rouge: Louisiana State University Press, 1976); Daniel F. Littlefield, Jr., and Lonnie E. Underhill, "The 'Crazy Snake Uprising' of 1909: A Red, Black, or White Affair?" *Arizona and the West* 20 (Winter 1978): 307–24.

35. Robert Conot, *Rivers of Blood, Years of Darkness* (New York: Bantam, 1967); Robert M. Fogelson (comp.), *The Los Angeles Riots* (New York: Arno, 1969); Nathan Cohen (ed.), *The Los Angeles Riots: A Socio-Psychological Study* (New York: Praeger, 1970): David O. Sears and John B. McConahay, *The Politics of Violence: The New Urban Blacks and the Watts Riot*

(Boston: Houghton Mifflin, 1973); Joseph Boskin and Victor Pilson, "The Los Angeles Riot of 1965: A Medical Profile of an Urban Crisis," *Pacific Historical Review* 39 (August 1970): 353-65; Joe R. Feagin and Harlan Hahn, *Ghetto Revolts: The Politics of Violence in American Cities* (New York: Macmillan, 1973); James W. Button, *Black Violence: Political Impact of the 1960s Riots* (Princeton: Princeton University Press, 1978).

36. Clark Howard, *Zebra* . . . (New York: Marek, 1979); Vin McLean and Paul Avery, *The Voices of Guns* (New York: Putnam, 1977).

37. Alexander Saxton, *The Indispensable Enemy: Labor and the Anti-Chinese Movement in California* (Berkeley: University of California Press, 1971); see also Elmer C. Sandmeyer, *The Anti-Chinese Movement in California* (Urbana: University of Illinois Press, 1939); Paul Crane and T. A. Larson, "The Chinese Massacre," *Annals of Wyoming* 12 (1940): 47-55, 153-60; Arlen R. Wilson, "The Rock Springs, Wyoming, Massacre, 1885" (M.A. thesis, University of Wyoming, 1967).

38. Robert E. Wynne, "Reaction to the Chinese in the Pacific Northwest and British Columbia, 1850-1910" (Ph.D. diss., University of Washington, 1964); Jules A. Karlin, "The Anti-Chinese Outbreaks in Seattle, 1885-1886," *Pacific Northwest Quarterly* 39 (April 1948): 103-30; and Karlin, "The Anti-Chinese Outbreak in Tacoma, 1885," *Pacific Historical Review* 23 (August 1954): 271-83; Carlos A. Schwantes, "Outcasts in a Promised Land: The Origins of Labor Militancy in Washington and Oregon, 1885-1886" (unpublished paper, Pacific Northwest History Conference, Victoria, B.C., April 24, 1981); Richard H. Dillon, *The Hatchet Men* . . . (New York: Coward-McCann, 1962).

39. Peter Nabokov, *Tijerina and the Courthouse Raid,* 2d ed. rev. (Albuquerque: University of New Mexico Press, 1969); Richard Gardner, *Grito! Reies Tijerina and the New Mexico Land Grant War of 1967* (Indianapolis: Bobbs-Merrill, 1972); José T. Canales, *Juan N. Cortina: Bandit or Patriot?* (San Antonio: Artes Gráficas, 1951); Clarence C. Clendenen, *Blood on the Border* . . . (New York: Macmillan, 1969), chap. 2 and *passim*; Charles C. Cumberland, "Border Raids in the Lower Rio Grande Valley," *Southwestern Historical Quarterly* 57 (January 1954): 285-311; see also Rosenbaum, *Mexicano Resistance.*

40. Leonard Pitt, *Decline of the Californios: A Social History of Spanish-Speaking Californians, 1846-1890* (Berkeley: University of California Press, 1966), chaps. 4, 9, 10; Mauricio Mazón, "Social Upheaval in World War II: 'Zoot Suiters' and Servicemen in Los Angeles, 1943" (Ph.D. diss., University of California, Los Angeles, 1976). For anti-Filipino violence in California,

see Howard A. DeWitt, "The Watsonville Anti-Filipino Riot of 1930 . . . ," *Southern California Quarterly* 61 (Fall 1979): 291-302.

41. Brown, "Pivot of American Vigilantism"; Burchell, *San Francisco Irish,* chap. 7; Robert M. Senkewicz, "Religion and Non-Partisan Politics in Gold Rush San Francisco," *Southern California Quarterly* 61 (Winter 1979): 351-78; Robert B. Flanders, *Nauvoo* . . . (Urbana: University of Illinois Press, 1965); see also the significant study by Dallin H. Oaks and Marvin S. Hill, *Cathage Conspiracy: The Trial of the Accused Assassins of Joseph Smith* (Urbana: University of Illinois Press, 1975).

42. Juanita Brooks, *The Mountain Meadows Massacre,* rev. ed. (Norman: University of Oklahoma Press, 1962); and Brooks, *John Doyle Lee* . . . (Glendale, Calif.: Arthur H. Clark, 1972); William Wise, *Massacre at Mountain Meadows* (New York: Crowell, 1976); Norman F. Furniss, *The Mormon Conflict, 1850-1859* (New Haven: Yale University Press, 1960; paperbound ed., Westport, Conn.: Greenwood, 1977).

43. Frederick Jackson Turner, *The Frontier in American History* (New York: Holt, 1920); Robert V. Hine, *The American West: An Interpretive History* (Boston: Little, Brown, 1973; paperbound ed.). Two leading reference works in western history give prominent treatment to violence: Lamar, *Reader's Encyclopedia*; Rodman W. Paul and Richard W. Etulain, *The Frontier and the American West* (Arlington Heights, Ill.: AHM, 1977), a comprehensive bibliography.

44. Warren I. Susman, "The Useless Past: American Intellectuals and the Frontier Thesis, 1910-1930," *Bucknell Review* 11 (March 1963): 1-20; Earl Pomeroy, "The Urban Frontier of the Far West," in John G. Clark (ed.), *The Frontier Challenge* . . . (Lawrence: University Press of Kansas, 1971), pp. 7-29; and Pomeroy, *The Pacific Slope* . . . (New York: Knopf, 1965; paperbound ed., Seattle: University of Washington Press, 1975), chaps. 8-13.

45. See nn. 12 and 23, above.

46. Earl Pomeroy, "Toward a Reorientation of Western History: Continuity and Environment," *Mississippi Valley Historical Review* 41 (March 1955): 579-600.

47. Hugh Davis Graham and Ted Robert Gurr (eds.), *The History of Violence in America* . . . (New York: Praeger, 1969), is a more readily accessible edition than the Government Printing Office edition of 1968. In 1979 a new, revised edition with the original title, *Violence in America* . . . , was published by Sage of Beverly Hills, and it deals with some of the issues I am discussing.

48. George Rudé, *The Crowd in the French Revolution* (Oxford: Clarendon Press, c. 1959); Rudé, *The Crowd in History: . . . France and England, 1730–1848* (New York: Wiley, 1964); Rudé, *Paris and London in the Eighteenth Century: Studies in Popular Protest* (New York: Viking, 1971); E. J. Hobsbawm and George Rudé, *Captain Swing* (New York: Pantheon, 1968); Hobsbawm, *Primitive Rebels . . .* (New York: Norton, 1965); E. P. Thompson, "The Moral Economy of the English Crowd in the Eighteenth Century," *Past and Present* 50 (February 1971): 76–136; and Thompson, *Whigs and Hunter . . .* (New York: Pantheon, 1975); Richard Maxwell Brown, "The Archives of Violence," *American Archivist* 61 (October 1978): 431–43.

49. Clifford Geertz, "Ideology as a Cultural System," in Geertz, *The Interpretation of Cultures . . .* (New York: Basic Books, 1973); Richard Maxwell Brown, "Back Country Rebellions and the Homestead Ethic . . . ," in Brown and Don E. Fehrenbacher, eds., *Tradition, Conflict, and Modernization . . .* (New York: Academic Press, 1977), chap. 4; and Brown, "The Homestead Ethic and No Duty to Retreat: Rural Violence in America and the Old West" (unpublished paper, Conference on Violence in American Society, Dallas, April 27, 1980); Saxton, *Indispensable Enemy*, pp. 21–22, 40–42, 51–52, 94, 96–101, 265–69, 274; see Richard J. Orsi, "*The Octopus* Reconsidered: The Southern Pacific and Agricultural Modernization in California, 1865–1915," *California Historical Quarterly* 55 (Fall 1975): 197–220.

50. Ted Robert Gurr, Peter N. Grabosky, and Richard C. Hula, *The Politics of Crime and Conflict . . .* (Beverly Hills: Sage, 1977); Gurr, "On the History of Violent Crime in America," in Graham and Gurr, *Violence in America* (1979 ed.), chap. 13; Roger Lane, *Violent Death in the City . . .* (Cambridge: Harvard University Press, 1970), esp. chap. 6; Lawrence M. Friedman and Robert V. Percival, *The Roots of Justice: Crime and Punishment in Alameda County, California, 1870–1910* (Chapel Hill: University of North Carolina Press, 1981).

51. Dykstra, *Cattle Towns*, chap. 3; W. Eugene Hollon, *Frontier Violence: Another Look* (New York: Oxford University Press, 1974); Roger McGrath, "Frontier Violence in the Trans-Sierra West" (Ph.D. diss., University of California, Los Angeles, 1978).

52. Graham and Gurr, "Conclusion," in *Violence in America* (1969 ed.); Charles Tilly, "Collective Violence in European Perspective," in Graham and Gurr, *Violence in America* (1979 ed.). Among Tilly's many other relevant publications see also Charles, Louise, and Richard Tilly, *The Rebellious Century, 1830–1930* (Cambridge: Harvard University Press, 1975); and Charles Tilly, *From Mobilization to Revolution* (Reading, Mass.: Addison-

Wesley, 1978); William A. Gamson, *The Strategy of Social Protest* (Homewood, Ill.: Dorsey, 1975); Graham, "The Paradox of American Violence," in Graham and Gurr, *Violence in America* (1979 ed.), p. 486.

53. Allan G. Bogue, "The Iowa Claim Clubs: Symbol and Substance," in Vernon Carstenson (ed.), *The Public Lands* . . . (Madison: University of Wisconsin Press, 1963); Homer E. Socolofsky, "County-Seat Wars in Kansas," *Trail Guide* 9 (December 1964): 1-8; William L. Kahrl, "The Politics of California Water: Owens Valley and the Los Angeles Aqueduct, 1900-1927," *California Historical Quarterly* 55 (Spring 1976): 2-25; (Summer 1976): 98-120.

54. Cf. George Gerbner *et al.,* "Television Violence, Victimization, and Power," in *American Behavioral Scientist* 23 (May-June 1980): 705-17.

Chapter Twelve

William L. Lang

**Using and Abusing
Abundance: The Western
Resource Economy
and the Environment**

Western history thrives on superlatives. Nothing, it seems, can be merely
large; it must be massive. Writers describe the prairies as endless or boundless,
not just broad; mountains become towering ranges rather than high peaks.
The penchant for using adjectives of size affects popular writer and scholar
alike, and in this they repeat the descriptive excesses of the actual participants in the nation's westward movement. The men and women who settled
the trans-Mississippi West and made an economy for themselves often portrayed their environment in those larger-than-life terms. The source for all
of this, back in the last century and today, is the western environment
itself: it is a region of impressive dimension. Western historians can be for-
given if they mirror something of the atmosphere of the region they chronicle
and interpret, but in that proclivity there is a truth about the history of the
West and the frontier that concerns the subject of this essay.

Nearly three decades ago, in a series of brilliant essays, David M. Potter
directed our attention to an often overlooked aspect of American history. He
discussed a factor that he believed permeated the development of the American national character throughout our history and that had a dominant role
in the westward course of our continental empire. The aspect he identified
was economic abundance, the constant promise of greater personal and
national wealth. Potter called us a "people of plenty," meaning that our culture, our ways of thinking, our expectations, and more have all been profoundly affected by our riches. His singular point, and the one that carried
the weight of his arguments, was that economic abundance is not and never
has been an incidental or accidental feature of American life: it is integral to
the whole.[1]

It was economic abundance in natural resources that drew so many of the migrants westward, and it was a rare diarist in the West who did not remark on the region's immense size and abundance. As one recent scholar of overland migration has pointed out, travelers on the Oregon Trail regularly noted exposed coal seams, inviting water power sites, or virgin stands of timber as genuine economic opportunities. Hundreds of miles from civilization and with little idea how they might capitalize on what they saw, they spoke of two things in the same breath: the great abundance of what they observed and their inclinations to see the main chance, the economic possibilities.[2]

Although we can debate whether it was the "pull" of abundance in the West or the "push" of conditions in the East that stimulated the migrations, Potter is correct when he argues that Americans were and are a people with plenty, because they chose to develop their resources with an ingenuity that reflected their constant search for opportunity.[3] The key interrelationship is between the resource-rich environment and the aggressive capitalists who developed it. As Potter explains, this relationship has been a symbiotic one; our experience in developing resources has directly affected our views of the environment and, conversely, the environment's abundance has affected our thinking.

There are classic examples of this symbiotic relationship in the economic history of the West. Decisions by mine promoters, lumbermen, oilmen, and other entrepreneurs reflect the interplay between their aggressive pursuit of development and the natural resource environment they tilled for wealth. This is particularly true of the natural resource industries that are the focus of this essay: the forest products, oil, coal, fishing, and tourist industries that all have grown enormously during the last one hundred years. Fur trading, metal mining, transportation, and other economic pursuits that affected the environment are covered in other essays in this volume. The natural resource industries discussed here took advantage of the major changes in the American economy in the last two decades of the nineteenth century, not the least of which was the expansion of rail transportation in the West. With access to national and international markets and the infusion of new capital, these natural resource industries were primed for rapid growth by the turn of the century.[4]

The rise of these industries coincided with the first awareness, on the part of a few Americans, that the abundance of the West could be in jeopardy if development continued unabated. The uneasy questioning of unrestrained exploitation of western resources increased apace with resource development until the idea of conservation became more than an infrequent demand voiced by critics. It was the beginning of an era in western economic history, one that continues to the present and provides example upon example of David Potter's point about economic abundance and the American character. Western economic history in the last one hundred years is a broad-gauged and immensely complex story of dialogues between the exploiters of the national domain and those pledged to protect it, between government agencies and policies that were in disagreement, and recently between those who fear environmental disaster and those who predict economic disaster.

Our point of departure in reviewing what has been written and should be written about western economic and environmental history is an elementary one. Perhaps Arthur A. Ekirch's axiomatic statement in his seminal *Man and Nature in America* says it best: "Man *and* nature is the basic fundamental fact of history. The relationship is mutual and necessary." There are few works that approach the subject from this broad viewpoint; most studies deal with pieces of this larger picture. In this literature far more has been written about the environment in its broadest context, particularly on the subject of conservation, than about the economic development of the West. The research opportunities in western economic history are truly great. In state historical societies and regional depositories throughout the West, the records of thousands of businesses, banks, and factories are housed waiting for historians to write the economic history of the American West. The proposition here is that the focus should be on the changing economic conditions in the West over the last one hundred years and how the intertwining of economic and environmental factors have made westerners act as they have. And this should be carried out in general as well as case studies, in regional as well as local history.

In the relatively scanty literature in western natural resource economic history, one field stands out as drawing the most attention—forest history. From lumberjack tales to forest conservation politics, much more has been written about the forest products industry than any other natural resource industry.[5] "Lumber, gentlemen, is your greatest resource today," James J. Hill told dinner guests in Everett, Washington, in 1892. Hill knew the promise of the great northwestern forests and what capital and efficient transportation could mean. When he introduced Frederick Weyerhaeuser to the opportunity that beckoned from the abundant stands of Douglas fir and hemlock on the western slopes of the Cascades and Weyerhaeuser then responded, a new era in American logging began. Building the largest lumber mill in the world in 1900 on the shore of Port Gardner Bay at Everett, Weyerhaeuser expanded a business into the beginnings of an empire. That story—the Weyerhaeuser story—is one of the best examples of what coincident combinations of abundant resources, available capital, transportation, and enterprising will can do in an open field. The Weyerhaeuser expansion in the Northwest, best documented in Ralph Hidy, Frank Hill, and Allan Nevins, *Timber and Men: The Weyerhaeuser Story* (1963), was part of the timber industry's aggressive movement west from the Lake Plains at the turn of the century.[6]

There had been a lumber industry in the West, of course, long before Weyerhaeuser entered the field. Nineteenth-century Pacific Coast lumbermen, as Thomas R. Cox has explained in his important book *Mills and Markets* (1974), were very competitive. Operating relatively small firms along the coast, they competed for a changing lumber market that extended across the nation and to international buyers. These firms—their logging operations and mills—totally dominated the local economies in their lumber-port towns. Much of this changed, as Cox points out, when the transcontinental railroads penetrated the region. Small gave way to large, and only the companies that controlled logging and milling operations in their locales and had access to the best ports survived.[7]

The literature on the western lumber industry concentrates on the Pacific Northwest, where the largest concerns cut into the virgin timber that seemed to stretch forever. Works on the other western timber regions need much more attention. There is, however, a fairly large and growing literature on the redwoods of California, most notably studies by Howard B. Melendy and Susan R. Schrepfer, and other significant timber operations in northern California.[8] Similarly, historians have researched the lumber industry of east Texas, Arkansas, and Iowa, but little has been done on the industry in Colorado, Nevada, New Mexico, and Montana.[9] Lumber operations in many western states may have been marginal or local in character, especially when compared with the great Pacific Northwest industries, but they too deserve study.

Company-dominated lumber towns continued to be the mainstay of the western lumber industry well into this century, as the larger timber companies cut into the abundant forests. Histories of twentieth-century corporate logging are important to chart the changes in industry economics, but the greater need is to document the broader history of lumbering in those medium and small mill towns throughout the West. Norman Clark's superlative *Mill Town* (1970), for example, does more than document the Weyerhaeuser, Clough, and Hartley companies. Clark tells a fuller story of Everett's growth as the world's premier lumbertown, what that growth meant to local economics and politics, and the community's tragic labor struggles. The sources for this kind of history, especially since 1910, are in local records, U.S. Forest Service documents, company business records, and particularly in the memoirs of participants. The substantial oral history collection at the Forest History Society, gathered in large part by Elwood Maunder over the last two decades, is an especially rich source.[10]

The history of the logging frontier and the development of the western timber industry is also the history of men and women who worked in the woods. Increasingly, in articles published in the Forest History Society's *Journal of Forest History* and other journals, historians are writing about life in lumber camps, the conditions of work, and the travails of labor organizations. Biographies and autobiographies, such as David T. Mason's "Memoirs of a Forester," do more than fill in the missing details. They explain that late-nineteenth-century and early-twentieth-century western lumbermen had to adjust to a new type of logging, one that demanded new technologies and new methodologies. They were responding to the environment they had invaded, from which some would build empires. It is also clear that the logging frontier did not move in lockstep fashion into the West; development went where the opportunity was, and at the speed that capital and will allowed. The maturation of the industry continued well into this century, from the advent of donkey steam engines to high-lead logging; with these changes came changes in the lives of loggers. These changes need more documentation, if we are to understand the interplay between working men and women and the environment that shaped an industry.[11]

The aggressive exploitation of western forests, however, created its own countervailing force. The first questions raised about the seemingly unrestricted harvest of timber on the public domain came in the late 1880s and resulted in federal legislation that gave the president power in 1891 to establish forest reserves. This was the faint beginning of a western forest conservation movement, hardly enough to dull a faller's ax. And there is some question, as raised by Sherry Olson in *The Depletion Myth* (1971), whether the large private corporations charged with exploiting the forests actually were as wasteful as popular opinion then held and historians have since accepted. Olson argues persuasively that the railroads did not leave only stumps in their wake, that in fact they practiced conservation and reforestation. But there is no question that timber companies competed for short-term gains and cut the forests accordingly. Even taxation of standing timber, as Richard White notes in his recently published study of Island County, Washington, might encourage lumbermen to cut all that stood.[12]

For historians of forest conservation it is difficult to overrate the importance of the first two decades of the twentieth century. Central to the action is Gifford Pinchot, first head of the nascent U.S. Forest Service, self-proclaimed originator of the term "conservation," and confidant of conservation-minded President Theodore Roosevelt. Pinchot's famous dispute in 1910 with William Howard Taft's Secretary of the Interior Richard Ballinger brought him and the question of conservation instant national attention. Those who feared the despoilation of the nation's resources, particularly the western forest reserves, applauded Pinchot's resolve and feisty confrontation with Ballinger. Pinchot led a growing number of Americans, including many westerners, who demanded federal conservation efforts. The affair left Ballinger with the reputation of a despoiler and a tool of the corporate exploiters. Pinchot's autobiographical *The Fight for Conservation* (1910) and *Breaking New Ground* (1947) argue this line most effectively. But recent investigations cast doubt on how easily we should put the black hat on one antagonist and the white on the other. Beginning with *The Politics of Conservation* (1962) by Elmo R. Richardson and buttressed by *Progressive Politics and Conservation* (1968) by James L. Penick, Jr., the view of Pinchot has changed. He has emerged as politically more adept than Ballinger, but Ballinger is given credit for being very much a conservationist, too.[13]

If the Ballinger-Pinchot struggle over the limits of federal power and control was the real controlling issue of the conservation movement, the movement's importance in the early twentieth century would have remained essentially a political question. But there was much more to the movement than that. What did the conservationists think they were doing and what motivated them? Two answers that have been given to these questions are related to our discussion. Samuel P. Hays has argued that conservationists were essentially interested in scientific resource management. They wanted to manage American abundance and limit access to it on agreed-upon and professional grounds. J. Leonard Bates, on the other hand, has emphasized that conservationists expected the elimination of waste and the establishment of an honest administration of natural resources to help fulfill American democracy. Bates's conservationists, then, wanted access to our resource abundance to be equitable, to be fair, and not to be confined to the hands of the "interests."[14]

In both views, utilization of American abundance seems to be a foregone conclusion, and for most Americans this was accepted as a matter of course. Voices were raised, of course, protesting the threatened opening of *all* of the forests to development, whether on a scientific or equitable basis. Of that group, which was much smaller in 1910 than it would become in later decades, we shall hear more. At this point we need interject two other queries. Where did the conservation impulse originate, and were westerners significant in the movement?

The accepted answer on the origins of the movement has long been that concerned foresters, the first trained forest managers in the United States, became alarmed at timber depredations and depletion and so they agitated for some conservation measures. John F. Reiger in *American Sportsmen and the Origins of Conservation* disputes that claim, arguing that hunters, not foresters, were the first conservationists. Using sources that exhibit the thoughts of game hunters at the turn of the century, Reiger maintains that George Bird Grinnell, Theodore Roosevelt, and others—the men who founded the Boone and Crockett Club—set about protecting game habitat through private hunting clubs and also pressed for governmental conservation efforts. Reiger is undoubtedly right that outdoorsmen contributed to the early conservation movement, but clearly it was that group that Gordon Dodds labels the "economic conservationists" who really spurred the movement. They were the professionals managing and working in the natural resources and they were reacting to a perceived threat to abundance. Their resolve was self-interested but also protective of what they knew to be a renewable yet potentially threatened resource. They saw themselves, government forester and timber manager alike, as acting in behalf of a people of plenty.[15]

Westerners, of course, looked at conservation with a legitimate and vested interest; they lived in the natural resource region, and many wanted first access to opportunity, not unlike contemporary Northern Plains residents who are eager to strip off the region's coal. But as Lawrence Rakestraw has pointed out, those who invoked the antifederal anthem in 1907-15 and wrapped themselves in their own state flags were not always anticonservationists. Many, like Governor Marion Hay of Washington, believed that conservation was crucial to the economic stability of their areas, but they also wanted to control the conservation programs.[16]

The disputes in the first two decades of this century over this question point up the need for additional study of state and local conservation ideas and action. How did local industrialists, commercial groups, and county and municipal bodies react to federal conservation or to the lack of any conservation? Some recent studies of conflicts over the establishment of national parks indicate that the disagreements were often extreme and protracted and that a full range of resource management disputes were present. In some cases, as accounts of the tree-farm movement and corporate sustained-yield programs show, timber companies took the initiative. We need to know more about these local developments if we are to get the full story of the interplay between man and environment, between the users of abundance and the concern for the source of that abundance.[17]

In the western timber country, the anger aimed at the federal government often had a single target, the U.S. Forest Service. Federal forest policy often did not coincide with industry plans for cutting stands on the public lands. Early histories of the forest service, like John Ise, *The United States Forest Policy* (1920), stressed its conservationist ethic, paying little attention to contrary opinion. Stressing the development of preservationist policies from Bernard Fernow's success in establishing forest reserves in 1891 on through the tenures of Gifford Pinchot and Henry Graves as forest service chiefs, this standard view portrayed the forest service as more conservationist than it really was. But recent revisionist works, especially Jack Shepherd's *Forest Killers* (1975) and Daniel R. Barney's *The Last Stand* (1974), err in the opposite direction. To charge, as Barney does, that the U.S. Forest Service is merely the tool of the timber corporations is a distortion.[18]

Harold K. Steen's quasi-official *The U.S. Forest Service: A History* (1976), the latest history of the agency, is a corrective to previous studies. Pinchot and other early leaders of the forest service were not preservationists, although some lumbermen saw them at best as obstructionists. The history of increasing economic demands placed on the West's natural resources tells much of the story. Throughout the twentieth century the forest service has been pressed by interest groups that have wanted the fewest obstacles between themselves and lucrative natural resources. At the highest administrative levels, the essential focus of Steen's account, the sustained-yield policies, the formulation of the Multiple-Use Act of 1960, and other decisions have been as much political in nature as economic or environmental. The important story of the precise effect forest service policies have had on western economic history, however, will not be told until sound histories of individual forest service regions and districts are written.[19]

If the Pinchot-Ballinger flap turned national attention to the broad question of conservation and the proper disposition of western abundance, the infamous Teapot Dome scandal of the early 1920s became a natural resource bombshell. The heart of the scandal contained twin exacerbating problems: official malfeasance and the avaricious machinations of oilmen with designs on the national reserves in Wyoming and California. Years before the famous controversy erupted, as J. Leonard Bates has documented in *The Origins of*

Teapot Dome (1963), the oil companies had tried to manipulate federal bureaucrats to allow pumping from the naval oil reserves.[20] It was one of the classic struggles between the conservationists and the exploiters over a vital western natural resource.

The Teapot Dome affair, however, is a very small part of the larger history of the western oil industry, a history that has been poorly documented. Gerald D. Nash has called it "an unexplored field." The nineteenth-century oil industry was based, of course, in the eastern fields. Although engineers, investors, and anyone who had stumbled upon one of the many oil springs in the West knew there was oil west of Pennsylvania, it was not until the first decade of this century that western oil production challenged and soon overwhelmed the eastern sources. Since then, oil in America has been primarily a western resource industry. The importance of oil to the western economy, as Gerald T. White and others have noted, goes far beyond cash value per barrel or investment in technology. The crude oils of the West were especially valuable for the production of gasoline. The economic benefit and the economic changes resulting from the automobile age had a profound impact on the West. Oil has dominated the modern economies of Texas, California, Oklahoma, and Louisiana, and all but a handful of western states have contributed significantly to national oil production.[21]

The discoveries of oil fields in California's San Joaquin Valley, at Spindletop in Texas, and in Oklahoma just after 1900 set off frantic oil booms, not unlike the nineteenth-century gold rushes. Although the science and technology was more sophisticated in these booms than in the gold placer rushes, the effect was much the same: a sudden exploitation of a natural resource where little if any development previously existed. Large corporations dominated the investment in the first years, but the western fields generated more new companies and significantly increased competition. As Gerald White notes in his study of the California oil industry, the famous court-ordered dissolution of the Standard Oil Trust in 1911 had already been achieved in reality through competition from the new California fields.[22]

Those new companies formed in the western oil fields would soon become giants in their own right. Union Oil Company, Conoco, Texaco, Gulf, Humble Oil and Refining, and several other firms began in the West. Their rise to national and international prominence needs to be documented in solid corporate histories like the superb *History of Humble Oil and Refining Company* (1959) by Henrietta M. Larson and Kenneth Wiggins Porter. Biographies on the order of W. H. Hutchinson's study of the Union Oil Company's creator, Thomas Robert Bard, and Anne Morgan's book on Robert S. Kerr are needed to fill the enormous gaps in our knowledge about how the western oil industry grew from mere pumpers of oil seeps to America's energy combines. To the list of needs we can add biographies of oil promoters, geologists, and studies of speculative oil prospecting.[23]

What is clear about the western oil industry is that it faced a dilemma much different from that confronted by the Pacific Northwest lumber industry. The oil industry's resource was abundant, like timber, but it was nonrenewable. Further, the expansion of the oil industry, particularly in refining capacity, raised the question of conservation. Unlike the timber industry's natural resource, which could be easily tabulated by standing board feet, the oil industry's statistics on what had been discovered, what had been pumped, and what might remain were considered corporate possessions. How much oil was there? Should there be forced, government-policed conservation? Was a precious national resource being squandered? Although the federal government had surveyed much of the known oil discoveries in the West before 1910, the great production boom of the World War I years and the 1920s led to genuine concern on the part of producing companies and the oil-rich states. Their oil abundance was threatening economic stability. As the price of crude oil dropped with increasing production, the self-interested became conservationists. Oklahoma and Texas tried to limit oil production but failed; that failure led to the creation of the Interstate Oil Compact Commission in 1935.[24]

The federal government's policies, as Gerald Nash points out in his *United States Oil Policy, 1860-1964* (1968), have had an enormous regional impact because the great majority of production is in the West. And western oil has been affected by developments and dislocations in world oil competition and supply, as E. Anthony Copp has documented in *Regulating Competition in Oil* (1976). For the West, recent changes in the national oil pricing structure and the intensive exploration of the so-called overthrust belt of potential oil and gas deposits in the northern Rockies are having a significant contemporary impact. The western oil industry, according to some estimates, has a very limited future as known reserves dwindle. Others, however, predict that oil shale and oil sand deposits are good for several generations. Either outcome will make a considerable difference in the shape of the western economy.[25]

Coal, today the West's primary energy competitor with oil, has a much different history as a resource industry. Noted by the Lewis and Clark Expedition and nearly every other subsequent survey of the West, coal was used in fur trading posts as fuel and was "harvested" from exposed seams by early plains settlers. It has always been recognized as one of the West's great natural resources. As ubiquitous as coal is in many areas of the trans-Mississippi West, documentation of the history of its mining is meager. It is one of the least, if not the least, documented industries in the United States, and it is one of the great opportunities for research in western economic history.[26]

Coal provided a cheap source of fuel for western railroads and prompted them to develop coal mines near their main and branch lines. The Denver and Rio Grande, Northern Pacific, and Union Pacific railroads operated sizable mines in Colorado, Utah, Wyoming, and Montana. Some of these mines have been studied; the rest need to be. Coal mining in isolated locations in the West like Coalfield (Utah), Rock Springs (Wyoming), Ludlow (Colorado), and Red Lodge (Montana) produced small tonnages by comparison with the large strip mines now operating on the northern plains, but they did create unique communities. Experienced miners from eastern districts and from foreign countries made these towns into ethnically mixed industrial settlements smack in the middle of rural and almost wilderness settings. The bloody Ludlow coal strike of 1913 and subsequent strikes in the Colorado fields have drawn attention, as have strikes in eastern Washington and other locales, but solid histories of western coal-mining communities are yet to be written.[27]

Coal mining in the West has changed its face and technology. The deep mines, where still operating, contribute smaller and smaller proportions of the total production. Although open-pit coal mines could be found on the western plains fifty years ago, today's large-scale strip mining operations are of recent origin. The West's renewed coal industry is controversial and has generated considerable national debate. Cheaper than foreign oil, the strippable coal in the western states is expected to play a major role in providing the nation with a reliable energy source for the future. But the environmental costs may be too high and the social costs too great for western states that sit on the largest and most accessible deposits. Portions of Montana, Wyoming, and North Dakota's semi-arid plains cover the largest of them, the Fort Union Coal Formation, which is estimated to contain 1.3 trillion tons of highly prized low-sulphur coal. The investments in mining technology and mine-mouth steam-generation electrical plants will constitute the largest private investments in the history of the northern plains states.

To get the coal, huge draglines must scrape off up to 250 feet of overburden, thereby altering the landscape forever and threatening other traditional economies, particularly livestock raising. But more than that, the critics of strip mining claim, the production of electricity will rob the region of its most precious resource, water. So the contemporary argument rotates on the issue of the nation's need for more energy and is pulled at the extremes by the desire to expand the regional economy and the demand that the fragile plains environment be left undisturbed. In government reports, both state and federal, in industry studies, and in informed commentary, there is a body of information that will give historians one of the best opportunities to document a major western industry. Most difficult in this history, as David Potter suggested, will be the evaluation and explanation of how the abundance of western coal altered the thinking and actions of westerners who have contended with the most vexatious decisions about the future of their land.[28]

Even more neglected by historians than the western coal industry is documentation of heavy industry and manufacturing in the West. Although the West has never contested the Northeast or the Great Lakes area for industrial superiority, there has been an industrial presence in the trans-Mississippi West almost from the beginning. Sawmills, flour mills, foundries, and small factories that served limited western markets have dotted the western states since the 1870s, and in some areas even earlier. Concentration on metal mining and the railroad industry has kept historians from pursuing these topics except as adjuncts to urban or commercial history.[29]

Large-scale manufacturing and heavy industries in the West have developed in relatively few locations. The forest products, aluminum, and aircraft industries located, respectively, in the Northwest and in southern California, Texas, and Kansas because of economic and environmental factors. The Pacific Coast furniture industry is another example of manufacturing concerns' locating near raw materials and markets. In the aircraft industries and associated electronics industries of California and Texas, one manufacturing enterprise generates others nearby, and they all contribute to an economically interrelated industrial region. Some of these have been studied, particularly the paper and plywood industries, but much more needs to be done.[30] These future studies should try to determine which factors led to the location of the industries, established their tenure, and encouraged development. In short, why were they successful? We need to know what combination of natural resources, capital, and development of markets proved successful. The need, in general, is for a model upon which our understanding of western industrial history might build.

Lee Scamehorn's studies of the Colorado Fuel and Iron Company, Leonard Arrington's work on Salt Lake City industrialists and the Utah sugar beet industry, and histories of Oregon's woolen mills suggest that individual investors, managers, and even speculators have had a great deal to do with industrial success in the West.[31] Yet, though the importance of individual entrepreneurs is not to be denied, these studies and others still come back to western natural resources as the basis for industrial development.

On the Pacific Coast the fishing industry is an excellent example of the manufacturing function's coming to the natural resource. The coastal canning industry, from California to Alaska, has been significant in local economies for well over one hundred years. It is also one of the many neglected fields of study in western economic history. Here, in the story of fisheries, is the history of fishing towns, cannery workers, international diplomacy, and conservation. Of the fisheries, the salmon was the acknowledged king, the great cash crop from the sea. The story of salmon fishing is one of unrelenting harvest, of failure to foresee decline, and of the failure of conservation. In Richard A. Cooley's *Politics and Conservation: The Decline of the Alaska Salmon* (1963), the federal government ends up taking the blame; but fishermen, Pacific rim nations, state governments, and canneries all share in the guilt. Men like R. D. Hulme, the subject of Gordon Dodds's *The Salmon King of Oregon* (1959), wore two hats, one as developer and the other as conservator. Hulme pioneered in the artificial propagation of salmon. There was concern expressed over the need for conservation, but still the salmon pack declined from its peak in the 1930s to just one-quarter that amount by the 1960s. Of Hulme and some of the other large canners we know a little, but the coastal fishing industry awaits general study.[32]

Western natural resource abundance, in case after case, was threatened by overdevelopment. If not dominated by the cut-and-run philosophy, the resource industries like oil and fisheries let competition drive them to near panic for conservation or some measure of production control. These resources, renewable and nonrenewable, were in turn part of a much larger resource—the western scenic landscape. From the southwestern deserts and California's sun-baked beaches to Rocky Mountain lakes and the Gulf Coast, the West presented something for others to see. As Samuel Bowles wrote in 1869, "The eastern half of America offers no suggestion of its western half."[33]

It was primarily because of that western attraction that easterners and Europeans toured the West, beginning one of the region's great and growing industries. The tourist industry is a good example of what David Potter calls the "creation by society of a secondary environment," in which Americans have taken advantage of environmental conditions and developed a resource, utilizing their abundance. Western state tourist promotion bureaus testify to how important tourism is to their economies; in several western states tourism is one of the top three or four industries. And some states have artificially aided tourism, as in Nevada, where divorce laws were liberalized to attract visitors and then, in 1931, the state legalized full-scale gambling, making it a tourist mecca. Most western tourism, however, is based on the region's expansive splendor, its monumental scenery, and its natural wonders.[34]

Beginning in the 1840s with what were probably the first paying western tourists, hunters in the Rockies, the tourist industry grew as westerners began serving travelers. Robert Athearn's *Westward the Briton* (1953) and Richard A. Van Orman's *A Room for the Night: Hotels of the Old West* (1966) describe this history through travelers' accounts. The hostelries were often crude, although it was not long before railroads invested in substantial hotels and turned scenic spots into resort areas. Earl Pomeroy in his *In Search of the Golden West* (1957) covers that period of the history of western tourism, from the 1870s to the 1920s. The automobile era in western tourism, however, has gone undocumented. And, with the exception of Pomeroy's book, the general history of tourism in the West has gone begging for historical treatment.[35]

Much of the draw of the West, as evidenced by the popularity of Wild West shows that toured the East at the turn of the century, was its frontier character. Begun by Howard Eaton at his famous Custer Trail Ranch in the Dakotas in 1881, dude ranching has been a mainstay of the western tourist industry for one hundred years. Ranchers, who capitalized on more than the stock-raising potential of their western setting, opened their spreads to paying guests who wanted a genuine western experience. Contrary to the popular image, dude ranches are not posh resorts for well-heeled easterners and urban desk workers. They try, in fact, to create a true ranch life experience for their "dudes." What we know about the dude ranches established in Wyoming, Colorado, Montana, California, and across the Southwest comes from memoirs and a few articles. There is no general history of dude ranching in the West. The history of that great western sport attraction, the rodeo, has received some coverage, but we need to know much more about its origins and growth. Finally, a general western theme which has had almost nothing written on it is recreational history, from early mountain climbing to the flashy post–World War II resorts.[36]

On the last leg of their historic exploration of the area that would soon become Yellowstone National Park, Charles W. Cook hoped aloud to his companions that "something . . . be done" to preserve the area and allow everyone the chance to see its natural wonders. Three years later, in 1872, Congress set aside an enormous acreage as the world's first national park, establishing it "as a public park or pleasuring-ground for the benefit and enjoyment of the people." Of all the great attractions of the West, undoubtedly the national parks historically rank first, but in their history there is more than the story of "pleasuring-ground" and economic boons to western tourism. National parks are very much in the mainstream of conservation and environmental history, and their origins in the United States go back to Henry David Thoreau's and Ralph Waldo Emerson's praiseful songs of nature.[37]

In the life and work of John Muir, the great inspirational figure of the early conservation movement and progenitor of the later wilderness movement, the two central aspects of American national park history coalesce. For Muir, national parks were not only necessary to give modern civilization an opportunity to experience "the healing powers of nature," but also to offer the prime chance to preserve nature rather than use it. The dispute over preservation or utilization of the environment has long been identified as the crucial split in the conservation movement of the early twentieth century. John Muir's disagreements with Gifford Pinchot, particularly over the controversial damming of the beautiful Hetch Hetchy Valley in Yosemite in 1913, have been considered the epitome of the arguments between the "preservationists" and the "multiple-use" advocates. It was also a struggle that brought up an old question for westerners: How should the environment be best used? In this case it came down to preservation of scenery versus water for San Francisco. The developers won, and seemingly the preservationists lost ground. Lawrence Rakestraw and other historians have questioned how complete the split was between Muir and Pinchot, noting that neither was singularly oriented toward preservation or development. Regardless of how clearly that line between the two philosophies can be drawn, it is certain that by 1916, when the National Park Service was created, those who had long argued for preservation of scenic areas had achieved something of a victory.[38]

The national parks in the early years, as Duane Hampton explains in *How the U.S. Cavalry Saved Our National Parks* (1971), were threatened by economic interests, poachers, and even vandals. Historians writing on the parks agree that the establishment of the National Park Service and the influence of its first director, Stephen Mather, were critical to the parks movement. Yet, as Robert Shankland in *Steve Mather of the National Parks* (1951) and Donald Swain in *Wilderness Defender* (1970) have stressed, the first directors of the parks promoted travel to the parks, upgraded tourist facilities, and generally made them popular attractions. The national parks were developed as tourist attractions—"pleasuring-ground"—not wilderness preserves.[39]

The literature on national parks, particularly Yellowstone, Yosemite, and Grand Canyon, is voluminous, from natural histories and guidebooks to monographs on specific aspects of park administration. Generally these histories have stressed the importance of parks as special preserves and as economic benefits to the West and nation. Alfred Runte, in *National Parks: The American Experience* (1979), calls this entire historical tradition into question. The origins of the national parks, Runte maintains, are not to be found in the transcendental views of nature found in Thoreau and Emerson or in the rhapsodic praises to mountains written by Muir; they are not even to be found purely in the promotion of tourism. Lacking historical monuments of civilization like European nations, Runte argues, Americans borrowed nature's scenic wonders in the West as "earth monuments" to suffice where human history had provided no monuments. But Americans also wanted to develop the West, to use their abundance; and before parks were designated, so Runte's argument proceeds, they had to be certain that the lands were "worthless." Further, he argues that the preservation of ecologically complete areas has been neglected because of this fixation with monumentalism and with the preservation of the "wonders" of nature instead of ecological areas that deserve protection. Runte's work has received criticism, and surely his argument is overdrawn at points, but his thesis is sound on two items. The first parks clearly were designated because of their unique scenery, and the park service has been slow in recognizing the importance of protecting entire ecological areas.[40]

As Donald Swain, Elmo Richardson, and other scholars have noted, the entire conservation movement went through significant changes in the twentieth century. Swain, in particular, has corrected the view that the 1920s was a conservation wasteland. As much conservation activity as there was in the 1920s, there is no question that the New Deal years gave conservation its second wind, particularly as the federal presence throughout the West grew through the U.S. Forest Service and the Department of Interior. Historical investigations of the development of American resource policy in the mid-twentieth century indicate that the decisions affecting the western environment, economies, and resources have become *national* decisions of increasing political and scientific complexity.[41]

No better illustration of this can be found than in the tangled and complicated history of water resources in the West. Studies of federal conservation policies associated with building dams, reclaiming lands, irrigating, and allocating precious water supplies have increased our knowledge, but much more needs to be done. Elmo Richardson's *Dams, Parks and Politics* (1973) admirably discusses the tensions arising between federal resource policy and western politics and conservation. And Norris Hundley's path-breaking study, *Water and the West* (1975), has set a high standard. In his treatment of the famous Colorado River Compact, Hundley demonstrates how complicated water resource history is, how critical technology has been to the development of reclamation, and how volatile water politics can be. The subject is central to western economic and environmental history. Donald Worster's challenging volume on the Dust Bowl of the 1930s, *Dust Bowl* (1979), asks one of the more difficult questions about water resources and the treatment of land in the West: What has man's exploitation of the environment wrought? Worster answers that the drive of the people of plenty for more on the southern plains led directly to the Dust Bowl catastrophe. His thesis is controversial, laying the blame at the doorstep of American capitalism; but it suggests that unrestricted development of western resources may well lead to ecological disaster.[42]

The general concern for the environment, from water resources to pesticide use, is part of a newer conservation movement, one that has its roots in a branch of the older conservation enthusiasm. John Muir's pleas for the environment during the great conservation battles over Yosemite and the involvement of the Sierra Club fueled an enthusiasm in the conservation movement that historians have labeled "esthetic conservation." Esthetic conservationists, as contrasted with "utilitarian conservationists," were concerned about the preservation of man's natural surroundings. They placed the protection of western natural abundance above its development, and in that proposition they were not in accord with most westerners.[43]

The development of esthetic conservation, from John Muir to the likes of Arthur Carhart, Aldo Leopold, Robert Marshall, and Rachel Carson, spawned several other movements, including the contemporary environmental and wilderness organizations. The history of these organizations, their philosophies, origins, personnel, and methodologies is in its infancy. Most important of the works on this subject is Roderick Nash's *Wilderness and the American Mind* (1967). In this seminal work, Nash explains why the nineteenth-century calls for preservation of wilderness fell on deaf ears but the twentieth-century environmentalists and wilderness advocates gained a hearing. The success of esthetic conservationists and wilderness proponents like Bob Marshall, Howard Zahniser, and Benton McKaye was the result of their abilities to develop successful political strategies. Rather than appealing to conscience and love of nature alone, Nash argues, the new conservationists organized to protect what remained of America's wild lands. Donald Fleming, in an important article published in 1972, concurs with Nash, emphasizing the importance of environmental studies by Rene Dubos, Rachel Carson, and Garrett Hardin.[44]

Robert Marshall, one of the founders of the Wilderness Society and principal political organizers of the wilderness movement, put the case for wilderness plainly in an important article that appeared in 1930. The westward expansion of the nation, Marshall reminded, had no place for wilderness because wild nature "was an enemy of diabolical cruelty and danger, standing as a great obstacle to industry and development." Marshall, Leopold, Carhart, and others had come to the conclusion by the 1920s and 1930s that "the fate of wilderness must be decided . . . by deliberate rationality and not by personal prejudice." More important for our consideration here, the wilderness advocates had arrived at that conclusion after years of work as foresters, wildlife biologists, and naturalists. They had seen what westerners had done with their natural abundance. The limits of the environment and its fate in the hands of development in no small way inclined them to think about the importance of preservation. It was part of the fundamental interplay between man and environment that is at the heart of western economic and environmental history.[45]

The post–World War II wilderness movement became part of a much broader concern for American environmental quality. Books like Stewart L. Udall's *The Quiet Crisis* (1963) ushered in what Michael McCloskey has called conservation's "third wave." The passage of the Wilderness Act in 1964, the questioning of the potential harm from pesticide use, and the disastrous Santa Barbara oil spill in 1969 were developments that led to a new environmental awareness among westerners and Americans in general. The history of these concerns, now just being studied and written, will expand our knowledge considerably about the interaction of the increasingly technological western economy and environment. More importantly, as Wilbur Jacobs wrote in an important recent article, historians need to look at the entire sweep of western history from an environmental viewpoint. Historians need to explode fallacies, as John Opie has noted, such as the notion that "the land was a perpetual cornucopia," and to recognize "the role man plays in his ecosystem."[46]

If David Potter was right about the importance of American abundance, and the literature reviewed here suggests that he was, historians need to look more carefully at the interactions between man and the western environment. The conclusions reached may be much different from Potter's, and it is likely that they will not agree with Frederick Jackson Turner's or Walter Prescott

Webb's. What will result is a broader understanding of the development of the western economy and the realization that the story of subduing nature and exploiting it is only a portion of the saga. To some extent, Americans see the last part of this century much the way Turner viewed the frontier's end. A corner seems to have been turned: perhaps abundance itself is threatened. Our historical perspective is one of the few viewpoints that can ascertain the truth of our national condition.

Notes

1. David M. Potter, *People of Plenty: Economic Abundance and the American Character* (Chicago: University of Chicago Press, 1954; also paperbound).

2. John D. Unruh, *The Plains Across: The Overland Emigrants and the Trans-Mississippi West, 1840-60* (Urbana: University of Illinois Press, 1979), pp. 397–401.

3. Potter, *People,* pp. 78–90. For an important discussion of why migrants came west, see Dorothy O. Johansen, "A Working Hypothesis for the Study of Migrations," *Pacific Historical Review* 36 (February 1967): 1-12.

4. For discussions of the importance of the 1870-1900 period for the economic development of the West, see W. Turrentine Jackson, *The Enterprising Scot: Investors in the American West after 1873* (Edinburgh: University of Edinburgh Press, 1968); Gene M. Gressley, *Bankers and Cattlemen* (New York: Knopf, 1966; paperbound ed., Lincoln: University of Nebraska Press, 1971); Clark C. Spence, *British Investments and the American Mining Frontier, 1860-1901* (Ithaca, N.Y.: Cornell University Press, 1958). Charles M. Gates, "A Historical Sketch of the Economic Development of Washington Since Statehood," *Pacific Northwest Quarterly* 39 (July 1948): 214-32; and Gerald D. Nash, "Stages in California's Economic Growth, 1870-1970: An Interpretation," *California Historical Society Quarterly* 51 (Winter 1972): 315-30, both discuss the stages of development in regional economies in the West, concluding that specific environmental realities combined with new sources of capital and improved transportation account for the progressive stages of development.

5. Arthur A. Ekirch, *Man and Nature in America* (New York: Columbia University Press, 1963; paperbound ed., Lincoln: University of Nebraska Press, 1973), p. 1. For challenging discussions on the interaction between environment and human activity and how that interaction has affected

socioeconomic development, see Harold and Margaret Sprout, *The Ecological Perspective on Human Affairs* (Princeton: Princeton University Press, 1965); and D. W. Meinig, *The Great Columbia Plain* (Seattle: University of Washington Press, 1968).

6. Ralph Hidy, Frank Ernest Hill, and Allan Nevins, *Timber and Men: The Weyerhaeuser Story* (New York: Macmillan, 1963). The indispensable source for published forest history is Ronald J. Fahl's bibliography, *North American Forest and Conservation History* (Santa Cruz, Calif.: Forest History Society, 1977). For manuscript sources see Richard C. Davis (ed.), *North American Forest History: A Guide to Archives and Manuscripts in the United States and Canada* (Santa Cruz, Calif.: Forest History Society, 1977).

7. Thomas R. Cox, *Mills and Markets: A History of the Pacific Coast Lumber Industry to 1900* (Seattle: University of Washington Press, 1974). Two good case studies of nineteenth-century mills are Richard C. Berner, "The Port Blakely Mill Company, 1876-89," *Pacific Northwest Quarterly* 57 (October 1966): 158-71; and Thomas R. Cox, "William Kyle and the Pacific Lumber Trade: A Study in Marginality," *Journal of Forest History* 19 (January 1975): 4-14.

8. On redwoods see Howard Brett Melendy, "Two Men and a Mill: John Dobleer, William Carson and the Redwood Lumber Industry in California," *California Historical Society Quarterly* 38 (March 1959): 59-71; Melendy, "One Hundred Years of the Redwood Lumber Industry, 1850-1950" (Ph.D. diss., Stanford University, 1953); Susan R. Schrepfer, "A Conservative Reform: Saving the Redwoods, 1917 to 1940" (Ph.D. diss., University of California at Riverside, 1971); Frank M. Stanger, *Sawmills in the Redwoods: Logging on the San Francisco Peninsula, 1949-1967* (San Mateo, Calif.: San Mateo County Historical Society, 1967); Sherwood D. Burgess, "The Forgotten Redwoods of the East Bay," *California Historical Society Quarterly* 30 (March 1951): 1-14; Emanuel Fritz, *California Coast Redwood: An Annotated Bibliography* (San Francisco: Foundation for American Resource Management, 1957). Literature on northern California lumber operations includes William H. Hutchinson, *California Heritage: A History of Northern California Lumbering* (Santa Cruz, Calif.: Forest History Society, 1974); and Hyman Palais and Earl Roberts, "The History of the Lumber Industry in Humboldt County," *Pacific Historical Review* 19 (February 1950): 18-27.

9. On Texas see Ruth Alice Allen, *East Texas Lumber Workers: An Economic and Social Picture, 1870-1950* (Austin: University of Texas Press, 1961); and Robert S. Maxwell, "Lumbermen on the East Texas Frontier," *Forest History* 9 (April 1965): 12-16. On other states see George B. Hartman,

"The Iowa Sawmill Industry," *Iowa Journal of History and Politics* 40 (January 1942): 52-93; Carolyn Blanks, "Industry in the New South: A Case History," *Arkansas Historical Quarterly* 11 (Autumn 1952): 164-75; Patricia Roppel, "Alaskan Lumber for Australia," *Alaska Journal* 4 (Winter 1974): 20-24.

10. Another good corporate history, besides the excellent *Timber and Men*, is Edwin Truman Coman and Helen M. Gibbs, *Time, Tide and Timber: A Century of Pope and Talbot* (Stanford: Stanford University Press, 1949). An example of the many brief and popular corporate histories is Stewart Holbrook, *Green Commonwealth: A Narrative of the Past and a Look at the Future of One Forest Products Community, 1895-1945* [Simpson Timber Company] (Seattle: Simpson Logging Company, 1945). Studies of mill towns include Norman Clark, *Mill Town: A Social History of Everett, Washington, From Its Earliest Beginnings on the Shores of Puget Sound to the Tragic and Infamous Event Known as the Everett Massacre* (Seattle: University of Washington Press, 1970; paperbound ed., 1972); Stephen Dow Beckham, "Asa Mead Simpson: Lumberman and Shipbuilder," *Oregon Historical Quarterly* 68 (September 1967): 259-73, which deals with Coos Bay, Oregon; Patricia Roppel, "Gravina," *Alaska Journal* 2 (Summer 1972): 13-15; James B. Allen, *The Company Town in the American West* (Norman: University of Oklahoma Press, 1966). For the importance of company records see Elwood R. Maunder, "Writing the History of Forest Industries," *Pacific Northwest Quarterly* 48 (October 1957): 127-33.

11. David C. Smith, "The Logging Frontier," *Forest History* 18 (October 1974): 96-106, notes the lack of any general work on the logging frontier and points out how important the involvement of eastern lumbermen was in western logging. An excellent biography of an important lumberman-politician in the Northwest who had a significant impact on the forest products industry is Robert E. Ficken, *Lumber and Politics: The Career of Mark E. Reed* (Seattle: University of Washington Press, 1980). Autobiographical sources include David T. Mason, "Memoirs of a Forester," oral history interview by Elwood Maunder, *Forest History* 10 (January 1967): 6-12, 29-35; "Memoirs Part II" *Forest History* 13 (April/July 1969): 28-39; James W. Girard, *The Man Who Knew Trees: The Autobiography of James Girard*, introduction by Rodney C. Loehr (St. Paul: Forest Products History Foundation, Minnesota Historical Society, 1949); William B. Greeley, *Forests and Men* (Garden City, N.Y.: Doubleday, 1951); and Thomas Emerson Ripley, *Green Timber: On the Flood Tide to Fortune in the Great Northwest* (Palo Alto, Calif.: American West Publishing Co., 1968). For an interesting view of women's roles in

logging camps, see Anna M. Lind, "Women in Early Logging Camps: A Personal Reminiscence," *Journal of Forest History* 19 (July 1975): 128-36. The classic study of labor in lumbering is Vernon H. Jensen, *Lumber and Labor* (New York: Farrar and Rinehart, 1945); and an excellent labor history is Harold M. Hyman, *Soldiers and Spruce: Origins of the Loyal Legion of Loggers and Lumbermen* (Los Angeles: University of California Press, 1963).

12. Sherry H. Olson, *The Depletion Myth: A History of Railroad Use of Timber* (Cambridge: Harvard University Press, 1971). For another revisionist view of railroad control of forest lands see Ross R. Cotroneo, "Western Land Marketing by the Northern Pacific Railway," *Pacific Historical Review* 37 (August 1968): 299-320. Gary D. Libecap and Ronald N. Johnson, "Property Rights, Nineteenth-Century Timber Policy and the Conservation Movement," *Journal of Economic History* 39 (March 1979): 129-42, argues that federal land policy was responsible for fraud and timber theft. See also Richard White, *Land Use, Environment, and Social Change: The Shaping of Island County, Washington* (Seattle: University of Washington Press, 1980).

13. Gifford Pinchot, *The Fight for Conservation*, introduction by Gerald D. Nash (1910; Seattle: University of Washington Press, 1968); Pinchot, *Breaking New Ground*, introduction by James L. Penick, Jr. (1945; Seattle: University of Washington Press, 1972); Elmo R. Richardson, *The Politics of Conservation: Crusades and Controversies, 1897-1913* (Berkeley: University of California Press, 1962); James L. Penick, Jr., *Progressive Politics and Conservation: The Ballinger-Pinchot Affair* (Chicago: University of Chicago Press, 1968); Alpheus T. Mason, *Bureaucracy Convicts Itself: The Ballinger-Pinchot Controversy of 1910* (New York: Viking Press, 1941), presents the classic argument against Ballinger. The best study of Pinchot as forester is Harold T. Pinkett, *Gifford Pinchot: Private and Public Forester* (Urbana: University of Illinois Press, 1970).

14. Samuel P. Hays, *Conservation and the Gospel of Efficiency: The Progressive Movement, 1890-1920* (Cambridge: Harvard University Press, 1959; paperbound ed., Atheneum, 1969); J. Leonard Bates, "Fulfilling American Democracy: The Conservation Movement, 1970-1921," *Mississippi Valley Historical Review* 44 (June 1957): 29-57.

15. Henry Clepper (ed.), *Leaders of American Conservation* (New York: Ronald Press, 1971); and Clepper, "The Ten Most Influential Men in American Forestry," *American Forests* 56 (May 1950): 10-13, 30, 37-39, provide biographical sketches of many foresters who were conservation leaders. John F. Reiger, *American Sportsmen and the Origins of Conservation* (New York: Winchester Press, 1975); Gordon Dodds, "The Historiography of American

Conservation, Past and Prospects," *Pacific Northwest Quarterly* 56 (April 1965): 75-80. Robert E. Ficken, "Gifford Pinchot Men: Pacific Northwest Lumbermen and the Conservation Movement, 1902-1910," *Western Historical Quarterly* 13 (April 1982): 165-78.

16. Lawrence Rakestraw, "The West, States' Rights, and Conservation," *Pacific Northwest Quarterly* 48 (July 1957): 89-99; H. J. Bergman, "The Reluctant Dissenter: Governor Hay of Washington and the Conservation Problem," *Pacific Northwest Quarterly* 62 (January 1971): 27-33.

17. Elmo R. Richardson, "Olympic National Park: Twenty Years of Controversy," *Forest History* 12 (April 1968): 6-15; Arthur D. Martinson, "Mountain in the Sky: A History of Mount Rainier National Park" (Ph.D. diss., Washington State University, 1966); Ralph R. Widner (ed.), *Forests and Forestry in the American States: A Reference Anthology* (Washington, D.C.: National Association of Foresters, 1968), has articles on each state, many of which deal with conservation. See also Henry E. Clepper and Arthur B. Meyer (eds.), *American Forestry: Six Decades of Growth* (Washington, D.C.: Society of American Foresters, 1960). On tree farms see Paul F. Sharp, "The Tree Farm Movement: Its Origin and Development," *Agricultural History* 23 (January 1949): 41-45; and on tree planting see the interesting book by Wilmon H. Droze, *Trees, Prairies, and People: A History of Tree Planting in the Plains States* (Denton, Texas: Texas Women's University Press, 1977). On sustained-yield forest planning, see Roy O. Hoover, "Public Law 273 Comes to Shelton: Implementation of the Sustained-Yield Forest Management Act of 1944," *Journal of Forest History* 22 (April 1978): 86-101.

18. John Ise, *The United States Forest Policy* (New Haven: Yale University Press, 1920); also see Jenks Cameron, *The Development of Governmental Forest Control in the United States* (Baltimore: Johns Hopkins University Press, 1928), for a general overview of forest service policies; Samuel T. Dana, *Forest and Range Policy: Its Development in the United States* (New York: McGraw-Hill, 1956); and Charles Van Hise, *The Conservation of Natural Resources in the United States* (New York: Macmillan, 1910), for contemporary thinking on forest conservation. Some of the more critical studies of the forest service are Jack Shepherd, *The Forest Killers: The Destruction of the American Wilderness* (New York: Weybright and Talley, 1975); Daniel R. Barney, *The Last Stand: Ralph Nader's Study Group Report on the National Forests* (New York: Grossman Publishers, 1974); Glen O. Robinson, *The Forest Service: A Study in Public Land Management* (Baltimore: Johns Hopkins University Press, 1960); and Michael Frome, *Whose Woods These Are: The Story of the National Forests* (Garden City, N.Y.: Doubleday, 1962).

19. Harold K. Steen, *The U.S. Forest Service: A History* (Seattle: University of Washington Press, 1976); see Arthur H. Carhart, *The National Forests* (New York: Knopf, 1959), for a description of forest service regions and some history of their operations. Clyde P. Fickes, *Recollections by Clyde P. Fickes, Forest Ranger Emeritus* (Missoula: U.S.F.S. Northern Region, 1972), is a good personal account of the history of one forest service region. Judith K. Steen (comp.), *A Guide to Unpublished Sources for a History of the United States Forest Service* (Santa Cruz, Calif.: Forest History Society, 1973), is a superb reference work.

20. J. Leonard Bates, *The Origins of Teapot Dome: Progressives, Parties and Petroleum, 1909-1921* (Urbana: University of Illinois Press, 1963); Burl Noggle, *Teapot Dome: Oil and Politics in the 1920's* (Baton Rouge: Louisiana State University Press, 1962; paperbound ed., Norton, 1965), deals with the political aspects of the scandal itself.

21. See articles in *Pacific Historical Review*'s special issue, "The Petroleum Industry," Vol. 39 (May 1970), especially Gerald T. White, "California's Other Mineral," pp. 135-54; Arthur M. Johnson, "California and the National Oil Industry," pp. 155-70; Ralph Andreano, "The Structure of the California Petroleum Industry, 1895-1911," pp. 171-92; and Gerald D. Nash, "Oil in the West: Reflections on the Historiography of an Unexplored Field," pp. 193-204. See also Walter Rundell, Jr., "Centennial Bibliography: Annotated Selections on the History of the Petroleum Industry in the United States," *Business History Review* 32 (Fall 1959): 429-47.

22. Carl Coke Rister, *Oil: Titan of the Southwest* (Norman: University of Oklahoma Press, 1949); Gerald T. White, *Formative Years in the Far West: A History of the Standard Oil Company of California and Predecessors Through 1919* (New York: Appleton-Century-Crofts, 1962). See also Paul H. Giddens, "One Hundred Years of Petroleum History," *Arizona and the West* 4 (Summer 1962): 127-44; for the best bibliography, consult E. B. Swanson, *A Century of Oil and Gas in Books* (New York: Appleton-Century-Crofts, 1960).

23. Henrietta M. Larson and Kenneth Wiggins Porter, *History of Humble Oil and Refining Company: A Study in Industrial Growth* (New York: Harper Bros., 1959). For other corporate histories see the uncritical *Conoco: The First One Hundred Years* (New York: Dell Publishing Co., 1975), Harold D. Roberts, *Salt Creek, Wyoming: The Story of a Great Oil Field* (Denver: Midwest Oil Corporation, 1956), and the solidly researched John L. Loos, *Oil on Stream: A History of Interstate Oil Pipe Line Company, 1909-1959* (Baton Rouge: Louisiana State University Press, 1959). Three

good biographical studies are: William H. Hutchinson, *Oil, Land, and Politics: The California Career of Thomas Robert Bard,* 2 vols. (Norman: University of Oklahoma Press, 1965); Anne H. Morgan, *Robert S. Kerr: The Senate Years* (Norman: University of Oklahoma Press, 1980); and Gerald T. White, "California Oil Boom of the 1860's: The Ordeal of Benjamin Silliman, Jr.," *The American West: A Reorientation,* ed. Gene M. Gressley (Laramie: University of Wyoming Publications, 1966), pp. 1–32.

24. Gene M. Gressley, "G.O.S., Petroleum, Politics and the West," in *The Twentieth Century West: A Potpourri* (Columbia: University of Missouri Press, 1977), pp. 102–38, discusses the career of George Otis Smith, director of the U.S. Geological Survey. For the oil compact see Interstate Oil Compact Commission, *The Compact's Formative Years, 1931–1935* (Oklahoma City: Interstate Oil Compact Commission, 1954).

25. Gerald D. Nash, *United States Oil Policy, 1860–1964: Business and Government in Twentieth Century America* (Pittsburgh: University of Pittsburgh Press, 1968); E. Anthony Copp, *Regulating Competition in Oil: Government in the U.S. Refining Industry, 1948–1975* (College Station: Texas A&M University Press, 1976). See also John M. Blair, *The Control of Oil* (New York: Patheon, 1977), for coverage of oil prices and world politics. On oil shale see Paul L. Russell, *History of Western Oil Shale* (East Brunswick, N.J.: The Center for Professional Management, 1980).

26. Robert F. Munn, *The Coal Industry in America: A Bibliography and Guide to Sources* (Morgantown: West Virginia University Press, 1965); Gerald D. Nash, "Research in Western Economic History—Problems and Opportunities," *The American West: An Appraisal,* ed. Robert G. Ferris (Santa Fe: Museum of New Mexico Press, 1963), pp. 61–69. See also Eugene McAuliffe, *Early Coal Mining in the West* (New York: Newcommen Society, 1948).

27. Good state and local studies include Sam T. Bratton, "Coal in Missouri," *Missouri Historical Review* 22 (January 1928): 150–56; Cassius A. Fisher, "Geology of the Great Falls Coal Fields, Montana" (Washington, D.C.: Government Printing Office, 1909); Union Pacific Coal Company, *History of the Union Pacific Coal Mines, 1868 to 1940* (Omaha: Colonial Press, 1940); Rita McDonald and Merrill G. Burlingame, "Montana's First Commercial Coal Mine," *Pacific Northwest Quarterly* 47 (January 1956): 23–28; Robert Chadwick, "Coal: Montana's Prosaic Treasure," *Montana the Magazine of Western History* 23 (October 1973): 18–31; Thomas G. Alexander, "From Dearth to Deluge: Utah's Coal Industry," *Utah Historical Quarterly* 31 (Summer 1963): 233–47. On the Colorado strikes see Eugene O. Porter, "The Colorado Coal Strike of 1913: An Interpretation," *Historian* 12

(January 1949): 3-27; and Donal J. McClurg, "The Colorado Coal Strike of 1927–Tactical Leadership of the IWW," *Labor History* 4 (1963): 68-92.

28. William B. Evans and Robert L. Peterson, "Decision at Colstrip: The Northern Pacific Railway's Open Pit Mining Operation," *Pacific Northwest Quarterly* 61 (July 1970): 129-36; Wallace E. Tyner and Robert J. Kalter, *Western Coal: Promise or Problem* (Lexington, Mass.: Lexington Books, 1978). For a western historian's not unbiased appraisal of western strip mining of coal see K. Ross Toole's *The Rape of the Great Plains* (Boston: Atlantic, Little, Brown, 1976).

29. Nash, "Research in Western Economic History," pp. 61-63; Earl Pomeroy, "What Remains of the West?" *Utah Historical Quarterly* 35 (Winter 1965): 37-56.

30. Edwin J. Cohn, Jr., *Industry in the Pacific Northwest and the Location Theory* (New York: Columbia University Press, 1954); Douglass C. North, "Location Theory and Regional Economic Growth," *Journal of Political Economy* 63 (June 1955): 243-58. On pulp and papermaking, see N. K. Benson, *The Pulp and Paper Industry of the Pacific Northwest* (Seattle: University of Washington Experiment Station, 1929); J. Alfred Hall, *The Pulp and Paper Industry and the Northwest* (Portland: U.S. Forest Service, 1969); David C. Smith, *History of Papermaking in the United States* (New York: Lockwood Publishing Co., 1970).

31. Lee Scamehorn, *Pioneer Steelmaker in the West: The Colorado Fuel and Iron Company, 1872-1903* (Boulder: Pruett Publishing Co., 1976); Scamehorn, "John C. Osgood and the Western Steel Industry," *Arizona and the West* 15 (Summer 1973): 133-48; Leonard J. Arrington, *Beet Sugar in the West: A History of the Utah-Idaho Sugar Company, 1891-1966* (Seattle: University of Washington Press, 1966); Arrington, *David Eccles: Pioneer Western Industrialist* (Logan: Utah State University Press, 1975); Peter A. Shroyer, "Oregon Sheep, Wool and Woolen Industries," *Oregon Historical Quarterly* 67 (June 1966): 125-38; Alfred L. Lomax, *Later Woolen Mills in Oregon: A History of the Woolen Mills Which Followed the Pioneer Mills* (Portland: Binfords and Mort, 1974).

32. Vernon Carstenson, "The Fisherman's Frontier on the Pacific Coast: The Rise of the Salmon-Canning Industry," *The Frontier Challenge: Responses to the Trans-Mississippi West*, ed. John G. Clark (Lawrence: University of Kansas Press, 1971); Richard A. Cooley, *Politics and Conservation: The Decline of the Alaska Salmon* (New York: Harper and Row, 1963); Gordon B. Dodds, *The Salmon King of Oregon: R. D. Hulme and the Pacific Fisheries* (Chapel Hill: University of North Carolina Press, 1959). For fishing

on the Columbia, see T. E. Craig and R. L. Hacker, *History and Development of the Fisheries of the Columbia* (Washington, D.C.: Bureau of Fisheries, 1940).

33. Samuel Bowles, *Our New West* (Hartford: Hartford Publishing Co., 1869), quoted in Alfred Runte, *National Parks: The American Experience* (Lincoln: University of Nebraska Press, 1979), p. 11.

34. Potter, *People,* p. 90; Oscar Lewis, *Sagebrush Casinos* (Garden City, N.Y.: Doubleday, 1953).

35. Robert G. Athearn, *Westward the Briton* (New York: C. Scribner's Sons, 1953); Richard A. Van Orman, *A Room for the Night: Hotels of the Old West* (Bloomington: Indiana University Press, 1966); Earl Pomeroy, *In Search of the Golden West: The Tourist in Western America* (New York: Knopf, 1957).

36. M. Struthers Burt, *The Diary of a Dude Wrangler* (New York: C. Scribner's Sons, 1924); L. W. Randall, *Footprints Along the Yellowstone* (San Antonio: Naylor Company, 1961); Lawrence R. Borne, "Dude Ranches and the Development of the West," *Journal of the West* 17 (July 1978): 83–94. On the rodeo see Max Kegley, *Rodeo: The Sport of Cow Country* (New York: Hastings House, 1942); and Clifford P. Westermeier, *Man, Beast, Dust: The Story of Rodeo* (New York: World Press, 1947). A solid history of a resort area is W. Turrentine Jackson and Donald J. Pisani, *From Resort Area to Urban Recreation Area: Themes in the Development of Lake Tahoe* (Davis: University of California at Davis, 1973). Periodicals like the *Journal of Sport History* are beginning to stimulate more interest in the field. For skiing see Jack Benson, "Before Skiing Was Fun," *Western Historical Quarterly* 8 (October 1977): 431–41.

37. Roderick Nash, "The American Invention of National Parks," *American Quarterly* 22 (Fall 1970): 726–35.

38. Elmo R. Richardson, "The Struggle for the Valley: California's Hetch Hetchy Controversy, 1905–1913," *California Historical Society Quarterly* 38 (September 1959): 249–58; Lawrence Rakestraw, "Sheep Grazing in the Cascade Range: John Minto vs. John Muir," *Pacific Historical Review* 27 (November 1958): 371–82. On John Muir see Linnie Marsh Wolfe, *Son of the Wilderness: The Life of John Muir* (New York: Knopf, 1945); Holway R. Jones, *John Muir and the Sierra Club: The Battle for Yosemite* (San Francisco: Sierra Club, 1965); and the revisionist work by Stephen Fox, *John Muir and His Legacy: The American Conservation Movement* (Boston: Little, Brown, 1981). For other views of the Muir-Pinchot split see Lawrence Rakestraw, "Conservation Historiography: An Assessment," *Pacific Historical*

Review 61 (August 1972): 271-88; and Grant McConnell, "The Conservation Movement—Past and Present," *Western Political Quarterly* 7 (September 1954): 463-78.

39. H. Duane Hampton, *How the U.S. Cavalry Saved Our National Parks* (Bloomington: Indiana University Press, 1971); Robert Shankland, *Steve Mather of the National Parks*, 3d ed. (New York: Knopf, 1970); Donald C. Swain, *Wilderness Defender: Horace M. Albright and Conservation* (Chicago: University of Chicago Press, 1970). For the earliest survey of the park service, see Jenks Cameron, *The National Park Service: Its History, Politics and Organization* (New York: Appleton, 1922); and for a modern conservationist view, consult John Ise, *Our National Park Policy: A Critical History* (Baltimore: Johns Hopkins University Press, 1961).

40. Alfred Runte, *National Parks: The American Experience* (Lincoln: University of Nebraska Press, 1979); for critical reviews of Runte's book see Gordon Chappell in *Arizona and the West* 23 (Spring 1981): 66-68, and Robert W. Righter in *Montana, The Magazine of Western History* 31 (April 1981): 70-71. For partial support of Runte's viewpoint see Carl P. Russell, "Wilderness Preservation," *National Parks Magazine* 71 (April/June 1944): 3-28; H. Duane Hampton, "Opposition to National Parks," *Journal of Forest History* 25 (January 1981); 36-45, explains how opposition to national parks has delayed their establishment and limited their growth.

41. A prime source for conservation history is Frank E. Smith *et al.* (eds.), *Conservation in the United States: A Documentary History*, 5 vols. (New York: Chelsea House, 1971); Donald C. Swain, *Forest Conservation Policy, 1921-1933* (Berkeley: University of California Press, 1963); Swain, "The National Park Service and the New Deal, 1933-1940," *Pacific Historical Review* 61 (August 1972): 312-32. Richard Polenberg, "Conservation and Reorganization: The Forest Service Lobby, 1937-38," *Agricultural History* 39 (October 1965): 230-39; and Polenberg, "The Great Conservation Contest," *Forest History* 10 (January 1967): 13-23, discuss conflicts within and between federal agencies over conservation politics in the 1930s. For discussions of federal conservation policy in the New Deal and after, see Elmo R. Richardson, "The Interior Secretary as Conservation Villain: The Notorious Case of Douglas 'Giveaway' McKay," *Pacific Historical Review* 61 (August 1972): 333-45; Richardson, "Was There Politics in the Civilian Conservation Corps?" *Forest History* 16 (July 1972): 12-21; John A. Salmond, *The Civilian Conservation Corps, 1933-1942: A New Deal Case Study* (Durham: Duke University Press, 1967).

42. Elmo R. Richardson, *Dams, Parks and Politics: Resource Development*

and Preservation in the Truman-Eisenhower Era (Lexington: University of Kentucky Press, 1973), discusses Department of Interior policies affecting water resources and water power. For reclamation see special issue of *Pacific Historical Review* 37 (November 1978), particularly Lawrence B. Lee, "100 Years of Reclamation Historiography," pp. 507-64. For the Colorado River Compact, see Norris Hundley, Jr., *Water and the West: The Colorado River Compact and the Politics of Water in the West* (Berkeley: University of California Press, 1975); also consult Abraham Hoffman, *Vision or Villainy: Origins of the Owens Valley-Los Angeles Water Controversy* (College Station, Texas: Texas A & M University Press, 1980); William L. Kahrl, "The Politics of California Water: Owens Valley and the Los Angeles Aqueduct, 1900-1927," *California Historical Society Quarterly* 60 (Spring 1976): 2-25 and (Summer 1976): 98-120; and Donald C. Swain, "The Bureau of Reclamation and the New Deal, 1933-1940," *Pacific Northwest Quarterly* 61 (July 1970): 137-46; Donald Worster, *Dust Bowl: The Southern Plains in the 1930s* (New York: Oxford University Press, 1979). For a sweeping review of U.S. land policy and conservation see William K. Wyant, *Westward in Eden: The Public Lands and the Conservation Movement* (Berkeley: University of California Press, 1982).

43. Douglas Hillman Strong, "The Rise of American Esthetic Conservation: Muir, Mather and Udall," *National Parks Magazine* 44 (February 1970): 4-9.

44. Roderick Nash, *Wilderness and the American Mind* (New Haven: Yale University Press, 1967; paperbound ed., 1973); Donald Fleming, "Roots of the New Conservation Movement," *Perspectives in American History* 6 (1972): 7-94. For the classic studies of Americans' views on nature see Ekirch, *Man and Nature in America*; Hans Huth, *Nature and the American: Three Centuries of Changing Attitudes* (Berkeley: University of California Press, 1957; paperbound ed., Lincoln: University of Nebraska Press, 1972). A modern proponent of the transcendental view is David Brower, for years president of the Sierra Club. On Brower see John McPhee, *Encounters with the Archdruid* (New York: Farrar, Straus and Giroux, 1971); and on the Sierra Club see Susan Schrepfer, "Conflict in Preservation: The Sierra Club, Save-the-Redwoods League, and Redwood National Park," *Journal of Forest History* 24 (April 1980): 60-77; and Schrepfer, "Perspectives on Conservation: Sierra Club Strategies in Mineral King," *Journal of Forest History* 20 (October 1976): 176-90.

45. Robert Marshall, "Problem of the Wilderness," *Scientific Monthly* 30 (February 1930): 141-48; on Aldo Leopold consult Susan L. Flader, *Think-*

ing Like a Mountain: Aldo Leopold and the Evolution of an Ecological Attitude Toward Deer, Wolves and Forests (Columbia: University of Missouri Press, 1974; paperbound ed., Lincoln: University of Nebraska Press, 1978); and on Arthur Carhart see Donald N. Baldwin, *The Quiet Revolution: The Grass Roots of Today's Wilderness Preservation Movement* (Boulder: Pruett Publishing Company, 1972); and Roderick Nash, "Arthur Carhart: Wildland Advocate," *Living Wilderness* 44 (December 1980): 32-34.

46. Stewart L. Udall, *The Quiet Crisis* (New York: Holt, Rinehart and Winston, 1963); Michael McCloskey, "Wilderness Movement at the Crossroads, 1945-1970," *Pacific Historical Review* 41 (August 1972): 346-61; Wilbur Jacobs, "The Great Despoliation: Environmental Themes in American Frontier History," *Pacific Historical Review* 67 (February 1978): 1-26; John Opie, "Frontier History in Environmental Perspective," *The American West: New Perspectives, New Dimensions,* ed. Jerome O. Steffen (Norman: University of Oklahoma Press, 1979; paperbound ed., 1981), pp. 20-21. On recent environmental political history see Richard H. K. Vietor, "The Evolution of Public Environmental Policy: The Case of 'Non-Significant Deterioration,'" *Environmental Review* 3 (Winter 1979): 3-19; and Joseph M. Petulla, *American Environmentalism: Values, Tactics, Priorities* (College Station, Texas: Texas A & M University Press, 1980).

Chapter Thirteen

F. Alan Coombs

**Twentieth-Century
Western Politics**

In a recent book review, the author of the foremost textbook on the American West in the twentieth century noted with unfortunate accuracy that "politics in the twentieth-century West is still a relatively obscure subject." Notwithstanding the fact that the last two decades of the century are already upon us—and that, by most quantitative measures, the American West as here defined has experienced most of its history since 1900—historians have still devoted by far the greatest part of their labors to the saga of the frontier. Gerald Nash feels that "before historians can begin to generalize about the structure, the problems, and the personalities in western politics, . . . more detailed studies will be needed," but fools rush in where wiser scholars fear to tread.[1]

The reasons for the paucity of serious works on the politics of the American West are not hard to discern; virtually all relate to the vast geographical expanse of the region and its considerable heterogeneity, both formidable obstacles to generalization. The nineteen states included in this survey collectively account for nearly two-thirds of the nation's land area and an amazing variety of climates, natural resources, historical developments, and peoples. Even within individual states, stark contrasts are common. Regardless of the rule propounded, then, exceptions will be manifest. Some have been blunt enough to question whether, in the post–World War II era, the West even constituted a well-defined political entity.[2]

If scholars have had their doubts, so apparently have westerners themselves. Over forty years ago, Carey McWilliams observed in Ray West's survey of *Rocky Mountain Cities* that the West "doesn't know quite what it is," and at the beginning of John F. Kennedy's presidency Neal Maxwell found the region's representatives in Congress still harboring "a certain ambivalence" about their common interests. Even as he wrote, there were signs of growing regional self-awareness in the form of institutions such as the Western States Governors' Conference, the Conference of Western Senators, the Western States Democratic Conference, and the Republican Western Conference. There is reason to suppose that the more the inhabitants of the area feel their growing political power, the more they may be tempted to act in some concerted fashion to achieve mutual objectives.[3]

As these lines are written, the smoke has hardly cleared from the elections of 1980 with their momentous message for the future of American politics. It is not yet clear, to be sure, precisely what that message *was*, but a brief recapitulation of some of the more notable results will indicate that the West will have a major role in articulating it. Begin with the most evident fact: the new president of the United States is Ronald Reagan of California, elected with his vice-presidential running mate, George Bush of Texas. Add to that the positions of power occupied by western members of the new Republican-controlled U.S. Senate, with important committees chaired by Mark Hatfield of Oregon, Robert Dole of Kansas, John Tower of Texas, Jake Garn and Orrin Hatch of Utah, and James McClure of Idaho. Then one finds Senator Paul Laxalt of Nevada, Mr. Reagan's national campaign chairman and transition adviser, ready to serve as the chief executive's personal link with the Congress, making him "overnight one of Washington's most powerful men." In the House of Representatives, where the Democrats retain a majority, James Wright of Texas will continue to discharge the duties of majority leader.[4]

A part of this enhanced influence of the West on Capitol Hill stems from demographic shifts. "South and West Goes the Nation," reads the headline carrying the news of the preliminary totals for the 1980 census. Growth rates in the past ten years of 63.5 percent for Nevada, 53.1 percent for Arizona, and 41.6 percent for Wyoming merely lead the way. Of the nineteen states defined herein as the West, only four (the Great Plains states of North Dakota, South Dakota, Nebraska, and Kansas) exhibit modest rates of growth ranging from 3.6 to 5.6 percent; every other state in the region found its population expanding faster than the national average. Of the twelve fastest growing states, only one, Florida, was *not* a part of the American West. Clearly, these numbers point to augmented political strength starting with eleven new House seats after reallocation. Some pundits have already perceived that, even if Texas goes Democratic in a presidential contest, Republican candidates in recent decades (save Barry Goldwater) have been able to count on a block of roughly 120 electoral votes from the West, just under half the 270 required for election. As recently as two decades ago, Frank Jonas wrote that "the West simply does not have the vote to determine its own destiny." That day has passed.[5]

It is appropriate, then, that scholars once again consider what elements, if any, in the political behavior of the western states tend to make them distinctive. This is not the place to undertake an extensive chronological survey of the region's political history, but its historical development is obviously one key to understanding that behavior. The Populist Revolt of the 1890s unquestionably left its imprint on the Great Plains and the Mountain West, and Progressivism affected the political institutions of the Pacific Coast states far more profoundly than it did some other parts of the country. In terms of partisan preference, however, the dominant record of the West in twentieth-century American politics is that of a "swing" section that usually goes with the winner in national elections. The majority of westerners voted for conservative Republican presidents in the 1920s, for Franklin Roosevelt and the New Deal in the 1930s, for Harry Truman in 1948, and for Dwight Eisenhower in the 1950s. This role of political bellwether was abandoned in 1960 when the West preferred Richard Nixon to John Kennedy and again in 1976 when it expressed a preference for Gerald Ford over Jimmy Carter, but analysts of the region's voting habits need to cope with the question of how much distinctiveness can be claimed for a group of states that usually vote the same way as the rest of the nation.

With that brief overview, let us consider what has been written about the politics of the West in this century. The general syntheses, as Gerald Nash observed, are few and far between. To his credit, he endeavored to allot some space in each major time period in his *American West in the Twentieth Century* to identification of the essential character of the region's politics for that period, but political history was only one of Nash's concerns and not necessarily the primary one. As a consequence, some readers may find descriptions of the 1920s as years of conservatism which included "muted reform" too vague to be very helpful. A generation before Nash's text, the field was largely dominated by journalists writing popular accounts for a more-or-less mass market. The Sage of Emporia, Kansas, William Allen White, contributed *The Changing West* in 1939, an interesting book written in the author's engaging style, long on charm and short on hard evidence. Also avowedly popular was John Gunther's *Inside U.S.A.* (1947). Although amateurish by the standards of some recent scholars, Gunther's methodology—moving into a community, determining who the most knowledgeable people in town were, and asking them who actually wielded the power—had something to recommend it; and the work still has its value as an historical source.[6] In a similar vein a decade and a half later was a book by San Diego newspaperman Neil Morgan entitled *Westward Tilt: The American West Today.* The title derived from Frank Lloyd Wright's theory "that America is tilted, and everything loose was sliding into Southern California," and Morgan's own observation that in the early 1960s "an awesome hunk of America has come loose," making "the move to Western America . . . the largest migration in the history of the world." Drawing on his long experience and acute eye for detail, Morgan delivered some perceptive analyses of the politics and cultural distinctiveness of the region.[7]

A worthy successor to this tradition in recent years has been *Washington Post* columnist Neal Peirce. It was Peirce's avowed purpose in the early 1970s to retrace the ground Gunther had broken as he prepared his book on *The Mountain States of America,* which appeared in 1972. The subtitle was descriptive: *People, Politics, and Power in the Eight Rocky Mountain States.* Within the next two years, Peirce had also completed two companion volumes, *The Pacific States of America* (surveying California, Oregon, Washington, Alaska, and Hawaii) and *The Great Plains States of America* (encompassing the central tier of states straddling the 98th meridian plus Minnesota, Iowa, and Missouri). As a former political editor of the *Congressional Quarterly* and author of an excellent book on the electoral college system, Peirce was especially able in dealing with the political aspects of his subject. If he ended up repeating most of the conventional wisdom of the states he traveled through, he also talked to a large number of well-informed people who had been active in public life for a long time. The possibility always lurks that much of their conventional wisdom may be true.[8]

Surveys of more serious scholarly intent began to appear in the late 1940s, often from the labors of political scientists rather than historians. Specifically, in 1948 the *Western Political Quarterly* began a biennial series of analyses of elections in the West, soliciting reports from experts in each western state and endeavoring to find the common threads in a summary article. As one might expect from such a collective enterprise, the results were uneven, but the historian of today seeking to understand western political developments in the 1950s and 1960s will find the state-by-state summaries replete with insight and information. Many of the articles no doubt seemed impressionistic to political scientists of the behavioral persuasion. Some members of the journal's board of editors worried that the contributions lacked theoretical importance, and there was a concern that the focus should be on the politics of the region rather than on individual states. As a result, the series was abandoned in March 1971, and historians are poorer for that decision.[9]

Another early effort of some interest was produced by Alfred De Grazia in 1954, entitled *The Western Public, 1952 and Beyond.* For the purposes of this study, it is handicapped by its failure to include the states along the 98th meridian, but the research scheme involved no fewer than 452 "in-depth" interviews with westerners prior to the 1952 elections and 210 shorter interviews thereafter and thus introduced a more systematic approach to the study of western politics than had previously been employed. Moreover, De Grazia asked most of the right questions, beginning with the matter of whether or not the West was "peculiar." His conclusion was not designed to win the hearts of those who cherish the idea of the American West as a distinctive region, but it had the ring of truth: "That there is a great area of sameness between the West and the rest of the country can be affirmed straightaway. It will also be shown that many popular beliefs about the West are greatly exaggerated and sometimes completely unfounded. There are, too, some interesting differences about the West that can be demonstrated."[10] In at least one instance, his judgment that people in the West had the same emotional commitment to their chosen political parties as Americans in other sections, De Grazia's findings may have been flawed, but a quarter of a century after its publication his book is still provocative.

One enterprising contributor to the periodic election analyses in the *Western Political Quarterly* was Frank H. Jonas, political scientist at the University of Utah. In 1961, having engaged the services of other stalwarts in the *Western Political Quarterly* series such as Totton James Anderson of the University of Southern California, Hugh A. Bone of the University of Washington, Boyd A. Martin of the University of Idaho, and Curtis Martin of the University of Colorado, Jonas put together a volume under the title *Western Politics* which strove to assess the past and present politics of thirteen western states, individually and collectively as a region. As in the case of De Grazia's study, the central tier of states was omitted, but nothing quite so detailed or comprehensive had been attempted before. A follow-up volume, *Politics in the American West,* with the same essential schema, appeared in 1969. Both books suffer from some of the same problems mentioned in connection with the *Western Political Quarterly* articles, but most of the contributors knew the politics of their states, including the local mythology, and had much to say to students eager to comprehend the mysteries of western practices.[11]

Even more recently, and somewhat less directly, there is the work of Daniel J. Elazar. In his bold and imaginative book *American Federalism: A*

View from the States, originally published in 1966, three basic varieties of American political culture were identified ("moralistic," "individualistic," and "traditionalistic"), and eventually the states were grouped by the dominant political culture within their borders. Accordingly, North Dakota, Colorado, Utah, and Oregon emerged with the designation "moralistic" (in which "the concept of serving the community is the core of the political relationship" and politicians "are expected to adhere to it even at the expense of individual loyalties and political friendships"); and South Dakota, Kansas, Montana, Idaho, Washington, and California were assigned to the "moralistic-individualistic" category. "Individualistic," as Elazar uses the term, refers to regional cultures that emphasize "the conception of the democratic order as a marketplace. In its view, government is instituted for strictly utilitarian reasons, to handle those functions demanded by the people it is created to serve." A "traditionalistic" political culture, on the other hand, traces of which he finds in Oklahoma, Texas, New Mexico, Arizona, and Hawaii, "is rooted in an ambivalent attitude toward the marketplace coupled with a paternalistic and elitist conception of the commonwealth. It reflects an older, precommercial attitude that accepts a substantially hierarchical society as part of the ordered nature of things, authorizing and expecting those at the top of the social structure to take a special and dominant role in government." The author dealt with migrational patterns to help explain these tendencies and also classified the various states according to their traditions of centralism and localism. The sociocultural component that Elazar provided, some historians found illuminating. Others were surely tempted to add one more "istic"—namely, "*simpl*istic."[12]

Elazar was only one of several scholars of the 1970s trying to establish a more meaningful regional typology. As the decade began, Ira Sharkansky, who was generally impressed with Elazar's work, was publishing his own *Regionalism in American Politics,* a study that noted quite properly that a basic problem with the literature on regionalism was that "almost every piece deals with an individual region without making a serious effort to determine empirically how that region actually differs politically from other parts of the United States." In his view, when an author failed to make such a comparison, it was impossible to "accept any claim that his region is peculiar." He also faulted previous students of the subject for defining the political process too narrowly in terms of electoral behavior rather than including other significant factors such as governmental structure and policy. Sharkansky's research produced a multiplicity of regions and subregions, but while some of the latter—most notably the "Mountains" of Montana, Wyoming,

Colorado, Idaho, and Utah–demonstrated a high degree of uniformity, the larger "Transmississippi" region (encompassing the area of our own study except for Alaska and Hawaii and adding Minnesota, Iowa, and Missouri) ranked the lowest of any region when it came to internal similarity. A few years later, Raymond Gastil, an historical geographer using the culture area concept, proceeded to divide the country into thirteen regions, subdivided into subregions, districts, and areas, according to an interesting combination of cultural indices. Although the historical background of each region may be inadequate for the tastes of many historians, Gastil's approach was challenging inasmuch as it questioned the older practice of drawing cultural boundaries along state borders. Although his technique appears valid for many purposes, the fact remains that states are *political* entities in which specific elections are held; so for the political historian the Gastil contribution may present more problems than it solves.[13]

Beyond the general syntheses, one finds a number of studies that might be termed "subregional." The most famous of these is probably Walter Prescott Webb's classic work, *The Great Plains*. Even though it was written half a century ago (and therefore can hardly take note of changes wrought by the Great Depression, World War II, and postwar affluence and anxiety), the author's marvelous identification with his territory and gift of literary expression retain their value for the early period. When Webb describes the political radicalism of the Great Plains as a function of the farmer's "economic maladjustment" rather than some psychological reaction to his decline in status, he speaks with an authority that still commands attention. A similar note is sounded in Russel B. Nye's 1959 volume, *Midwestern Progressive Politics*. Defining the Midwest as including everything from Ohio west to North and South Dakota, Nebraska, and Kansas, Nye began by quoting Woodrow Wilson's remark that "the voice of the West is a voice of protest" and went on to consider "the political contentiousness that seemed to affect the settlers as soon as they crossed the outermost fringe of settlement." As in Webb, a significant role is assigned to economic motivation; the midwesterner's dominant political trait has been an intense desire to protect his own interests.[14]

Daniel Elazar, in a recent article entitled "Political Culture on the Plains," appears to disagree. Applying the typology he established in *American Federalism*, he calls the conception of democratic order as a marketplace– Webb's and Nye's prime motivator–"individualistic," but finds in North Dakota, South Dakota, and Kansas a greater "moralistic" cultural base. Beyond that generalization, he was handicapped by certain complexities of the region he chose to examine, a fifteen-state area he called the "prairie-plains heartland" stretching from Montana to Louisiana and including Wyoming, Colorado, and New Mexico. The complexities ranged from "local political subcultural pockets" in Nebraska to the observation that "Kansas differs substantially from all the states which surround it. . . ." It is not difficult to find fault with Elazar's approach in some respects. It *is* difficult to fault him for trying to introduce a systematic approach that lends itself to some badly needed generalizations.[15]

The Great Plains are obviously only a portion of the sprawling area in which this survey is interested. Another important subregion was the focus of a volume on *Rocky Mountain Politics* produced by Thomas C. Donnelly, in which Donnelly, Frank Jonas, and six other contributors discussed the politics of Utah, Colorado, Nevada, Wyoming, Idaho, Montana, New Mexico, and Arizona. By the standards of the 1980s some of these articles may seem quaint and subjective, but historians are often in the position of having to rely on the best available evidence, and contemporary accounts continue to have their relevance. The late 1940s brought Ray West's compendium on *Rocky Mountain Cities,* affording an interesting if less-than-scholarly look at some of the political movers and shakers operating in the West's urban areas in the first half of the century, and, just as important, glimpses of the cultural milieu in which they operated.[16]

Concerning the desert Southwest, the work of two authors merits special attention. In 1961, W. Eugene Hollon published *The Southwest: Old and New* and followed it up five years later with *The Great American Desert Then and Now.* In these volumes Hollon called attention to the social problems created in that arid land by its climate and geography. He also worried about the ability of states like New Mexico and Arizona to deal with those problems so long as they were "poorly governed," and he observed that "the caliber of their legislatures is not high, their state constitutions are outmoded, and better administrative personnel are badly needed." Linked to that concern was the author's awareness of the growth of right-wing pressure groups and their capacity for blocking needed legislation. In a thoughtful article that appeared shortly before *The Great American Desert,* John W. Caughey had suggested that one difficulty might be the failure of the inhabitants of that geographical area to see themselves as part of a distinct region. "Whereas millions proclaim 'I am a Texan,' or 'I am a Californian,' almost no one boasts 'I am a Southwesterner.'" Considering the changes in this part of the West effected by the pell-mell growth of the last twenty years, it is fair to view the politics of the Southwest as a neglected field of study.[17]

The Pacific Coast has fared somewhat better at the hands of historians, although there, too, work remains to be done. *Empire of the Columbia: A History of the Pacific Northwest,* coauthored by Dorothy Johansen and Charles Gates a generation ago, contains such specific sections as "Politics of the Progressive Era" and "Forty Years of Politics, 1916–1956" in its thirty-seven-chapter regional study. It is textbook-ish in its organization and style and is often more narrative than analytical, but it still provides a starting place for readers with a special interest in Washington, Oregon, and Idaho. The same territory plus California, Utah, and Nevada is covered more felicitously in Earl Pomeroy's masterful treatment, *The Pacific Slope.* This is a beautifully written and exhaustively researched volume in which, despite the author's vast knowledge of the six states surveyed, the details never obscure the larger picture or Pomeroy's "feel" for the region. Even though the scope of the narrative is broad, considerable attention is given to politics, which is portrayed as fluid with "frequent migrations across the lines of parties and doctrines"—the ideal setting for the "extroverted individualism" of a Wayne Morse. There is also a suggestion that the Far West is becoming increasingly like the rest of the United States, but what the ultimate significance of that trend may be is not altogether clear. All in all, Pomeroy's work could easily serve as a model for studies of other more-or-less homogeneous aggregations of states.[18]

To proceed from the general to the more particular: it is true that virtually all the states have their own general histories, which cover political developments and the behavior of the electorate with varying degrees of sophistication. The aforementioned biennial state-by-state summaries in the *Western Political Quarterly,* 1948 through 1971, fall into this category, as do the Jonas books. Following the 1952 presidential election, three political scientists, Paul David, Malcolm Moos, and Ralph Goldman, produced a five-volume cooperative survey, *Presidential Nominating Politics in 1952,* which contains excellent description and commentary on the political processes of the several states at mid-century as well as brief characterizations of the voters in each state. Some state historical journals seem more inclined to publish articles on political subjects than others; in this regard, *California History, Idaho Yesterdays, North Dakota History, Southern California Quarterly,* and the *Annals of Wyoming* may deserve special mention, although the list of publications that accept occasional contributions on political topics is much longer. The *Pacific Historical Review,* the *Pacific Northwest Quarterly,* and the *Western Historical Quarterly* are regional periodicals that regularly print additional pieces of the West's political puzzle.[19]

It is hardly surprising that California has attracted a lot of attention from political scientists and historians. One might begin with Carey McWilliams's treatment in *California, the Great Exception*, first published in 1949. As the title indicates, he regarded the Golden State as normally an exception to most of the rules that might otherwise be set down about national or even sectional politics, but he also understood that it was becoming less so. Walton Bean's *California: An Interpretive History*, appearing in 1968, provided good topical coverage for the twentieth century, including such chapters as "The Roots of Reform," "The Republican Progressives in Power," "The Triumph of Conservatism," "Water, Power, and Politics," "The Great Depression and Politics," "Republican Ascendancy," and "Democratic Revival." Written in an agreeable style, the book also devotes considerable attention to the economic and social-cultural context in which the state's political developments occurred. The selections in two edited works, *California Politics and Policies: Original Essays*, by Eugene P. Dvorin and Arthur J. Misner, and *California Politics and Parties*, by John Robert Owens, Edmond Costantini, and Louis F. Weschler, examine and skillfully define the state's political peculiarities. In 1970 Royce Delmatier, Clarence McIntosh, and Earl Waters (a political scientist, a historian, and a state official, respectively) published *The Rumble of California Politics*, a useful narrative covering a broad expanse of time. At the conclusion of their labors, the authors remained impressed with the analytical difficulties of their subject, observing that "California's population and its moods are in such constant flux that its course can only be charted from the stern for it can only see where it has been and not where it is going." Finally, that same year, Michael P. Rogin and John L. Shover collaborated on *Political Change in California: Critical Elections and Social Movements, 1890–1966*, a book which is undeniably stimulating while drawing some critical fire.[20]

California has naturally enjoyed the spotlight because of its size and political importance, but it is not the only western state so investigated by scholars. In 1967 Jack E. Holmes authored *Politics in New Mexico*, a volume based on careful research and containing more substantial evidence about the political behavior of the Land of Enchantment than had been gathered into a single work before. Warren Beck's earlier *New Mexico: A History of Four Centuries* also remains useful, noting in a chapter entitled "Things Political" that New Mexico "may be in the United States but is not of the United States" owing to the unusual nature of its political past and particularly its penchant for spoilsman politics reminiscent of the Age of Jackson. Montana has been similarly well served by Michael Malone and Richard Roeder in their *Montana: A History of Two Centuries*, which paints a vivid and balanced picture of a state with the habit of voting for liberal members of Congress while electing conservative political leaders at the state level. The emphasis given to twentieth-century affairs is especially praiseworthy and the authors make it clear that the state's political culture is now much too complex to allow it to operate as a subsidiary of Anaconda Copper.[21]

A state as large as Texas merits better treatment from serious historians than it has received. The work of Seth Shepard McKay in the 1940s and 1950s sought to fill some gaps but was primarily narrative, based for the most part on newspapers and other periodicals; it left room for improvement both methodologically and stylistically. An undergraduate course requirement in the state apparently encouraged production of a number of textbooks on Texas government and politics, and some of them contain copious quantities of information, some analysis, and even some historical perspective—but textbooks they remain. In 1971 Dan Nimmo and William Oden published a volume, *The Texas Political System,* in which the last word of the title is especially significant; the authors attempted a simplified systems analysis of the politics of the Lone Star State within the larger context of other state systems and those of the nation. They also complained that in searching for empirical studies to validate their theories they found "that much of what passes for knowledge about Texas is based more on legend than research." Their book is decidedly more systematic and analytical than most, sometimes employing Elazar's typology, but it will strike some readers as a bloodless document that misses the human factor and the excitement of the political arena.[22]

Good coverage of other individual states is afforded by several volumes published by the University of Nebraska Press. Noteworthy in this regard for the time it spends on political questions is T. A. Larson's *History of Wyoming*; knowing personally so many of the Cowboy State's political power brokers over the past four decades gave Professor Larson, now a member of the state legislature during his "retirement" years, a perspective often unavailable to academics. Other volumes in this excellent series include Russell R. Elliott, *History of Nevada*; James C. Olson, *History of Nebraska*; Elwin P. Robinson, *History of North Dakota*; and Herbert S. Schell, *History of South Dakota.* The bicentennial histories of each state produced during the period 1976–78 by W. W. Norton and Company and the American Association for State and Local History, which often contain important interpretive overviews, may also be consulted with profit. Moreover, a growing number of Ph.D. dissertations are appearing in the field, and these works are conveniently listed from time to time in the *Western Historical Quarterly.*[23]

Obviously, geographical grouping does not preclude other studies from emphasizing special time periods or topics. Since it could be argued that modern western politics really began with the Populists, one should not neglect such venerable standards as John D. Hicks's *The Populist Revolt*, especially valuable for those interested in the agrarian radicalism of the Great Plains, and the book Theodore Saloutos published with the assistance of Hicks, *Agricultural Discontent in the Middle West, 1900–1939*. The last decade has seen scholars probing more deeply into the Populist phenomenon in specific locations with works like Peter Argersinger's *Populism and Politics: William Alfred Peffer and the People's Party*; James Edward Wright, *The Politics of Populism: Dissent in Colorado*; and Robert Larson's *New Mexico Populism: A Study of Radical Protest in a Western Territory*, which appears to contradict Richard Hofstadter's assumption that Populism in the mountain states was motivated almost entirely by silver.[24]

In the Progressive Era after the turn of the century, the West often took the lead in the drive to restore the reins of government to the people, and George Mowry's study of *The California Progressives* in 1951 represented an undertaking so compelling that it clearly bore significance for other states as well. Whether Mowry's profile of the typical Progressive leader was in fact typical of all Progressives or merely of all leadership elites during that period, it has left its imprint on the historical profession's perception of Progressivism as an essentially middle-class movement. Others might disdain his high estimate of the reformers, but the book contains some special insights into California politics in the early years of the century. Close on the heels of Mowry's book came Walton Bean's tale of *Boss Ruef's San Francisco*, a well-documented and fascinating account of the kind of turn-of-the-century municipal corruption against which many Progressives were rebelling. Nor has California-style Progressivism been the only variety investigated by scholars. In the middle 1950s Robert Morlan wrote what is still probably the finest account of the Non-Partisan League between 1915 and 1922, entitled *Political Prairie Fire*. The book is especially commendable considering that some relevant manuscript sources were still closed to the author at the time it was written. Lewis Gould's focus was toward the south in *Progressives and Prohibitionists: Texas Democrats in the Wilson Era*, a nicely written study, based on work in an impressive quantity of manuscript collections, in which the author identified Prohibition as a major conditioning factor in the larger reform movement in Texas and called it the "most important achievement" of Progressives there. Important monographs have also been contributed by Danny Goble, *Progressive Oklahoma: The Making of a New Kind of State* (1980), and Robert Sherman La Forte, whose 1974 survey of the *Leaders of Reform: Progressive Republicans in Kansas, 1900–1916* sheds new light on the politics of the Sunflower State.[25]

The 1920s represent an opportunity for more extensive investigation by historians of the American West, but some interesting analyses of specific questions have already appeared. David Sarasohn, for example, has evaluated the realigning effect of the 1916 presidential election in the Mountain West and has noted that the farther west one looked in 1924, the higher the percentage of the vote captured by Robert M. La Follette under the Progressive banner. David Burner, in his *Politics of Provincialism,* points out quite accurately that it was as much Al Smith's insensitivity—an eastern brand of "provincialism"—that hampered his candidacy in the West as it was any narrow-mindedness on the part of the voters of the region. The political strength of the Ku Klux Klan in the twenties in such states as Oregon and Colorado is easier to assess because of the work of Eckard Toy and Robert Goldberg.[26]

The years of the Great Depression and the New Deal, on the other hand, have received substantial scrutiny. An instructive survey of the New Deal in the western states was the theme of an entire issue of the *Pacific Historical Review* in August 1969, capped by challenging articles by James T. Patterson and Leonard Arrington. In a 1975 work entitled *The New Deal,* edited by John Braeman, Robert H. Bremner, and David Brody, the second volume of which examines *The State and Local Levels,* the particular experiences of Oklahoma, Wyoming, Montana, Colorado, New Mexico, and Oregon during the 1930s were considered in chapters by Keith L. Bryant, Jr., F. Alan Coombs, Michael P. Malone, James F. Wickens, William Pickens, and Robert E. Burton, respectively. That helped supplement earlier studies such as Robert E. Burke's deft account of *Olson's New Deal for California.* Now Ronald Feinman has added a nicely crafted version of an old story in *Twilight of Progressivism: The Western Republican Senators and the New Deal,* in which the growing disenchantment of old Progressive warhorses such as William Borah and Hiram Johnson with F.D.R. and his programs is detailed.[27]

The 1970s ushered in several new monographs dealing with a range of different topics. Robert Burton's *Democrats of Oregon: The Pattern of Minority Politics, 1900–1956* (1970) was one such effort; *Shall the People Rule? A History of the Democratic Party in Nebraska Politics, 1854–1972* by James F. Pedersen and Kenneth D. Wald was another. Two significant examinations of the radical element in western politics in the first half of the twentieth century were Garin Burbank's *When Farmers Voted Red: The Gospel of Socialism in the Oklahoma Countryside, 1910–1924,* and James R. Green's *Grass-Roots Socialism: Radical Movements in the Southwest, 1895–1943,* in which the focus is on Arkansas and Louisiana as well as Texas and Oklahoma. By the end of the decade George Norris Green's *The Establishment in Texas Politics: The Primitive Years, 1938–1957* had appeared. The author's antipathy toward "The Establishment" may occasionally distort the picture, but he is knowledgeable, the story is interesting, and similar studies for other states in the region would go far toward raising the curtain of ignorance.[28]

One other genre of historical literature deserves mention: biography. What other region, after all, can boast a more colorful array of political characters? Still entertaining are the sketches done in the early 1930s by Ray Tucker and Frederick R. Barkley of the U.S. Senate's *Sons of the Wild Jackass,* most of whom came from the region dealt with in this survey. Since that time, three major biographies of William E. Borah have appeared, beginning with the hagiographic and disappointing volume by Claudius Johnson while the senator was still alive and supplemented by more balanced treatments by Marian McKenna (1961) and Leroy Ashby (1972). Richard Lowitt's monumental work on George W. Norris occupies a rather special place in this category because of its sweep and erudition; most public figures will not require or justify three volumes, and most historians will not have the endurance to paint their subjects on such a scale. Meanwhile, competent studies already exist for Hugh Butler, Arthur Capper, Edward P. Costigan, Thomas P. Gore, Robert S. Kerr, Franklin K. Lane, William Lemke, Maury Maverick, Peter Norbeck, Key Pittman, C. Ben Ross, Glen H. Taylor, Kenneth Wherry, and Samuel Yorty, and the stories of those men inevitably enhance our understanding of the region's politics.[29]

In addition to Borah and Norris, several other western politicians have attained the prominence necessary to receive the concentrated attention of more than one author. William Jennings Bryan's story has been recounted in three volumes by Paolo Coletta, impressive for its research if less so for its style and interpretation. In the middle 1960s Lawrence Levine illuminated the last (and in many ways least happy) decade of the Great Commoner's life, and as the 1970s began Charles Morrow Wilson and Louis W. Koenig produced one-volume treatments of his long career.[30] Already Lyndon Johnson has been the subject of lengthy studies by Eric Goldman (who probably made too much of L.B.J.'s rustic and humble beginnings as a handicap during his presidency) and, more intimately, by Doris Kearns, who, with the assistance of a series of long interviews with Johnson after his retirement, may have come closer than anyone else to explaining what psychological factors made the thirty-sixth president act the way he did. Not always flattering but containing numerous insights into Johnson's complex personality is Merle Miller's 1980 "oral biography."[31]

Richard Nixon will no doubt provide copy for historians, and perhaps especially psychohistorians, for years to come. Bruce Mazlish and Fawn Brodie have already made their contributions in this regard with books very nearly as controversial as Nixon himself. There is a natural tendency when dealing with figures so important in the nation's history to dwell on their activities in Washington and around the world while neglecting their regional political roots.[32]

So, to the extent that getting acquainted with the cast of characters is an important part of comprehending any historical problem, progress in this area has been made—but more remains to be done. Full-length scholarly portraits of people as significant as Hiram Johnson, Thomas J. Walsh, Burton K. Wheeler, Bronson Cutting, Carl Hayden, Nellie Tayloe Ross, Mike Mansfield, and William Knowland still need to be completed. Nevertheless, the necessary spadework is being done and twentieth-century western politics is no longer quite the "virgin field" Nash described just a few years ago.[33]

What are the principal themes that emerge from this body of literature? What is it that makes the political history of the West since 1900 different and what questions remain to be answered? A thorough analysis of the subject is clearly beyond the scope of this study, but a few summary comments may suggest promising directions for future scholarship. The single most pervasive idea encountered is that of the West as a region of political independence and individualism, given to ticket-splitting by the voters and intense factionalism in already weak political parties. At the same time, westerners have often been more politically active than their neighbors in the East and the South.

The region's distinctive geography, including an abundance of natural resources (most significantly, for the late twentieth century, energy resources) and a scarcity of water, will continue to influence its political attitudes and behavior. So too will the West's self-image, particularly the myth of rugged individualism and the legacy of the frontier. How does one explain the apparent paradox of that myth's survival in a region containing a number of chronically vulnerable industries and agricultural commodities and which has, in truth, been dependent in large measure on eastern capital and assistance from the federal government? Finally, why do California and some of the other western states often appear to be leading the rest of the nation in setting new social and political trends when they were obviously settled at a much later point in our national experience than their eastern counterparts?

There will be answers to those problems once the right hypotheses are formulated and the requisite evidence is marshaled. What is necessary is a new appreciation of the unique characteristics of the American West in the twentieth century and a sensitive appraisal of the factors that cause it to behave the way it does. Given that attention, the result should be a flowering of important new monographs which may, in turn, yield a much-needed synthesis of western politics from the Populists to the era of Ronald Reagan and beyond.[34]

Notes

1. Gerald D. Nash, review of *Robert S. Kerr: The Senate Years,* by Anne Hodges Morgan, in *Pacific Historical Review* 49 (May 1980): 395-96.

2. It has been noted that California, although only the third-largest state in the region, has a greater land area than each of seventy-five members of the United Nations, and yet it is sharply divided into "several Californias," each with its own economic, social, and political character. See John Roberts Owens, Edmond Costantini, and Louis F. Weschler, *California Politics and Parties* (London: Macmillan and Company; Collier-Macmillan Limited, 1970), p. 11. Carey McWilliams once described Idaho as a "geographical monstrosity" in the Introduction to Ray B. West (ed.), *Rocky Mountain Cities* (New York: W. W. Norton, 1949), p. 14. Gerald D. Nash, *The American West in the Twentieth Century: A Short History of an Urban Oasis* (Englewood Cliffs, N.J.: Prentice-Hall, 1973; paperbound ed., Albuquerque: University of New Mexico Press, 1977), p. 249; Charles G. Bell, "Politics in the West," *Western Political Quarterly* 28 (June 1975): 237.

3. West, *Rocky Mountain Cities,* p. 24; Neal A. Maxwell, "The West on Capitol Hill," in *Western Politics,* ed. Frank H. Jonas (Salt Lake City: University of Utah Press, 1961), p. 358; Totton J. Anderson, "The Political West in 1960," *Western Political Quarterly* 14 (March 1961): 290.

4. "The Conservatives Are Coming!" *Time,* November 24, 1980, pp. 14-16; Virginia Robicheaux, "As Election Dust Settles, West Moves to Washington," *Salt Lake Tribune,* November 10, 1980, p. D3. An entire issue of *Social Science Journal* has been devoted to rendering a preliminary reading on the meaning of the 1980 election returns, with individual reports from specialists in eleven different western states. Noting the "rising Republicanism

in the West," the editors of that issue pose the question of whether the returns signaled "a regional tide or harmonic state waves"—and then concluded
that a host of idiosyncratic factors meant "the answer to this question is not
clear." Cal Clark and B. Oliver Walter (eds.), "A Symposium on Politics in the
West: The 1980 Election," *Social Science Journal* 18 (October 1981): 6.

5. "South and West Goes the Nation," *Salt Lake Tribune,* December 17,
1980, p. A5; *The World Almanac and Book of Facts, 1982* (New York: News-
paper Enterprise Association, 1981), pp. 196–97; "Where We Are," *Time,*
December 29, 1980, p. 16; "Census Indicates U.S. Grew 10.8%, Political
Clout Shifting to Sunbelt," *Salt Lake Tribune,* December 25, 1980, p. A9;
Patricia O'Brien, "Census Shows Exodus From Cities to Country," *Salt Lake
Tribune,* December 25, 1980, p. F1; Tom Wicker, "Carter's Wasting His Time
in West," *Salt Lake Tribune,* September 28, 1980, p. 14A; Joseph Kraft, "'80
Campaign Shows Regional Politics Still in Flux," *Salt Lake Tribune,* June 2,
1980, p. A7; and Jonas, *Western Politics,* p. 19.

6. Nash, *American West,* p. 109; William Allen White, *The Changing West:
An Economic Theory About Our Golden Age* (New York: Macmillan, 1939),
p. 25; and John Gunther, *Inside U.S.A.,* rev. ed., 2 vols. (New York: Bantam
Books, 1952; orig. Harper and Bros., 1947).

7. Neil B. Morgan, *Westward Tilt: The American West Today* (New York:
Random House, 1963), p. 3.

8. Neal R. Peirce, *The Mountain States of America: People, Politics, and
Power in the Eight Rocky Mountain States* (New York: W. W. Norton, 1972);
*The Pacific States of America: People, Politics, and Power in the Five Pacific
Basin States* (New York: W. W. Norton, 1972); and *The Great Plains States
of America: People, Politics, and Power in the Nine Great Plains States* (New
York: W. W. Norton, 1973).

9. See "Editorial Comment," *Western Political Quarterly* 28 (June 1975):
236.

10. Alfred De Grazia, *The Western Public, 1952 and Beyond* (Stanford,
Calif.: Stanford University Press, 1954), p. 156.

11. Jonas, *Western Politics*; and *Politics in the American West* (Salt Lake
City: University of Utah Press, 1969).

12. Daniel J. Elazar, *American Federalism: A View from the States,* 2d ed.
(New York: Thomas Y. Crowell, 1972; paperbound), pp. 93–99, 117.

13. Ira Sharkansky, *Regionalism in American Politics* (Indianapolis and
New York: Bobbs-Merrill, 1970), pp. 178–79, 24, and 67; and Raymond
D. Gastil, *Cultural Regions of the United States* (Seattle: University of
Washington Press, 1976; paperbound ed., n.d.). The research spurred by these

studies continues, suggesting that their most valuable contribution may have been as a stimulant to further scholarship. See Sharkansky, "The Utility of Elazar's Political Culture: A Research Note," *Polity* 2 (Fall 1969): 66–83, in which Elazar is described as "a perceptive—if sometimes abstruse—observer of state cultures"; Edward J. Clynch, "A Critique of Ira Sharkansky's 'The Utility of Elazar's Political Culture,'" *Polity* 5 (Fall 1972): 139–41; Timothy D. Schiltz and R. Lee Rainey, "The Geographic Distribution of Elazar's Political Subcultures among the Mass Population: A Research Note," *Western Political Quarterly* 31 (September 1978): 410–15; and Robert L. Savage, "Looking for Political Subcultures: A Critique of the Rummage-Sale Approach," *Western Political Quarterly* 34 (June 1981): 331–36.

14. Walter Prescott Webb, *The Great Plains* (Boston: Ginn, 1931; paperbound ed., Lincoln: University of Nebraska Press, 1981); and Russel B. Nye, *Midwestern Progressive Politics: A Historical Study of Its Origins and Development, 1870–1958* (New York: Harper and Row, 1959; paperbound ed., n.d.), pp. 3, 5, 14.

15. Daniel J. Elazar, "Political Culture on the Plains," *Western Historical Quarterly* 11 (July 1980): 261, 282, 281. See also Carl Frederick Kraenzel, *The Great Plains in Transition* (Norman: University of Oklahoma Press, 1955; paperbound ed., 1970), for a pointed analysis of the problems of the region by a rural sociologist.

16. Thomas C. Donnelly (ed.), *Rocky Mountain Politics* (Albuquerque: University of New Mexico Press, 1940); West, *Rocky Mountain Cities*. Also helpful for capturing the tone of the Mountain West, which helps to explain its politics, are Wallace and Page Stegner, "Rocky Mountain Country," *Atlantic*, April 1978, pp. 44–64, 70–91; and Robert G. Athearn, *High Country Empire: The High Plains and the Rockies* (New York: McGraw-Hill, 1960; paperbound ed., Lincoln: University of Nebraska Press, 1965).

17. W. Eugene Hollon, *The Southwest: Old and New* (New York: Knopf, 1961; paperbound ed., Lincoln: University of Nebraska Press, 1968); and Hollon, *The Great American Desert Then and Now* (New York: Oxford University Press, 1966; paperbound ed., Lincoln: University of Nebraska Press, 1975), p. 195. John W. Caughey, "The Spanish Southwest: An Example of Subconscious Regionalism," in *Regionalism in America*, ed. Merrill Jensen (Madison: University of Wisconsin Press, 1965), p. 184.

18. Dorothy O. Johansen and Charles M. Gates, *Empire of the Columbia: A History of the Pacific Northwest* (New York: Harper and Bros., 1957; 2d ed., 1967); and Earl Pomeroy, *The Pacific Slope: A History of California, Oregon, Washington, Idaho, Utah, and Nevada* (New York: Knopf, 1965;

paperbound ed., Seattle: University of Washington Press, 1975), pp. 330, 327. See also Lancaster Pollard, "The Pacific Northwest," in Jensen (ed.), *Regionalism in America.*

19. Paul T. David, Malcolm Moos, and Ralph M. Goldman (eds.), *Presidential Nominating Politics in 1952*, 5 vols. (Baltimore: Johns Hopkins Press, for the American Political Science Association with the cooperation of the Brookings Institution, 1954). See especially Vol. 3: *The South*; Vol. 4: *The Middle West*; and Vol. 5: *The West.*

20. Carey McWilliams, *California, the Great Exception* (New York: Current Books, 1949); Walton Bean, *California: An Interpretive History* (New York: McGraw-Hill, 1968; 3d ed., 1978); Eugene P. Dvorin and Arthur J. Misner (eds.), *California Politics and Policies: Original Essays* (Palo Alto: Addison-Wesley Publishing Co., 1966); Owens, Costantini, and Weschler (eds.), *California Politics and Parties;* Royce D. Delmatier, Clarence F. McIntosh, and Earl G. Waters (eds.), *The Rumble of California Politics, 1848–1970* (New York: John Wiley and Sons, 1970); and Michael P. Rogin and John L. Shover, *Political Change in California: Critical Elections and Social Movements, 1890–1966* (Westport, Conn.: Greenwood Press, 1970). Cf. Jackson K. Putnam, "Political Change in California: A Review Essay," *Southern California Quarterly* 53 (December 1971): 345–55.

21. Jack E. Holmes, *Politics in New Mexico* (Albuquerque: University of New Mexico Press, 1967); Warren A. Beck, *New Mexico: A History of Four Centuries* (Norman: University of Oklahoma Press, 1962), p. 296; Michael P. Malone and Richard B. Roeder, *Montana: A History of Two Centuries* (Seattle: University of Washington Press, 1976; paperbound ed., 1980).

22. See Seth Shepard McKay, *W. Lee O'Daniel and Texas Politics, 1938–1942* (Lubbock: Texas Tech Press, 1947); McKay, *Texas Politics, 1906–1944* (Lubbock: Texas Tech Press, 1952); and McKay, *Texas and the Fair Deal, 1945–1952* (San Antonio: Naylor Co., 1954). Textbooks include James E. Anderson, Richard W. Murray, and Edward L. Farley, *Texas Politics: An Introduction*, 3d ed. (New York: Harper and Row, 1979); Wilbourn E. Benton, *Texas: Its Government and Politics*, 3d ed. (Englewood Cliffs, N.J.: Prentice-Hall, 1972); and Clifton McCleskey, with the assistance of T. C. Sinclair and Pauline Yelderman, *The Government and Politics of Texas*, 3d ed. (Boston: Little, Brown, 1969); Dan D. Nimmo and William Oden, *The Texas Political System* (Englewood Cliffs, N.J.: Prentice-Hall, 1971). Paul D. Casdorph, *A History of the Republican Party in Texas, 1865–1965* (Austin: Pemberton Press, 1965), is a disappointing work, based almost entirely on printed secondary sources and largely on newspaper accounts. The author tried

to tell a lot of the "what" but other scholars will need to supply the "why."

23. T. A. Larson, *History of Wyoming,* 2d ed., rev. (Lincoln: University of Nebraska Press, 1978); Russell R. Elliott, *History of Nevada* (Lincoln: University of Nebraska Press, 1973); James C. Olson, *History of Nebraska,* 2d ed. (Lincoln: University of Nebraska Press, 1966); Elwyn P. Robinson, *History of North Dakota* (Lincoln: University of Nebraska Press, 1966); and Herbert S. Schell, *History of South Dakota,* 3d ed., rev. (Lincoln: University of Nebraska Press, 1975).

24. John D. Hicks, *The Populist Revolt: A History of the Farmers' Alliance and the People's Party* (Minneapolis: University of Minnesota Press, 1931; paperbound ed., Lincoln: University of Nebraska Press, 1961); Theodore Saloutos and John D. Hicks, *Agricultural Discontent in the Middle West, 1900–1939* (Madison: University of Wisconsin Press, 1951; republished Lincoln: University of Nebraska Press, n.d., under the title *Twentieth-Century Populism*); Peter H. Argersinger, *Populism and Politics: William Alfred Peffer and the People's Party* (Lexington: University Press of Kentucky, 1974); James Edward Wright, *The Politics of Populism: Dissent in Colorado* (New Haven: Yale University Press, 1974); and Robert W. Larson, *New Mexico Populism: A Study of Radical Protest in a Western Territory* (Boulder: Colorado Associated University Press, 1974).

25. George E. Mowry, *The California Progressives* (Berkeley and Los Angeles: University of California Press, 1951; paperbound ed., Times Books, 1972); Walton Bean, *Boss Ruef's San Francisco* (Berkeley and Los Angeles: University of California Press, 1952); Robert L. Morlan, *Political Prairie Fire: The Non-Partisan League, 1915–1922* (Minneapolis: University of Minnesota Press, 1955); Lewis L. Gould, *Progressives and Prohibitionists: Texas Democrats in the Wilson Era* (Austin: University of Texas Press, 1973); Danny Goble, *Progressive Oklahoma: The Making of a New Kind of State* (Norman: University of Oklahoma Press, 1980); and Robert Sherman La Forte, *Leaders of Reform: Progressive Republicans in Kansas, 1900–1916* (Lawrence: University Press of Kansas, 1974).

26. David Sarasohn, "The Election of 1916: Realigning the Rockies," *Western Historical Quarterly* 11 (July 1980): 285–305; David Burner, *The Politics of Provincialism: The Democratic Party in Transition, 1918–1932* (New York: Knopf, 1968); Eckard V. Toy, Jr., "The Ku Klux Klan in Tillamook, Oregon," *Pacific Northwest Quarterly* 53 (1962): 60–64; and Robert A. Goldberg, *Hooded Empire: The Ku Klux Klan in Colorado* (Urbana: University of Illinois Press, 1981).

27. *Pacific Historical Review* 38 (August 1969); John Braeman, Robert

H. Bremner, and David Brody (eds.), *The New Deal,* vol. 2, *The State and Local Levels* (Columbus: Ohio State University Press, 1975); Robert E. Burke, *Olson's New Deal for California* (Berkeley and Los Angeles: University of California Press, 1953); Ronald L. Feinman, *Twilight of Progressivism: The Western Republican Senators and the New Deal* (Baltimore: Johns Hopkins University Press, 1981). See also Gary M. Fink, "Northern Great Plains Senators in the New Deal Era," *Capitol Studies* 3 (Fall 1975): 129-51; and James F. Wickens, *Colorado in the Great Depression* (New York and London: Garland Publishing, 1979).

28. Robert E. Burton, *Democrats of Oregon: The Pattern of Minority Politics, 1900-1956* (Eugene: University of Oregon Books, 1970); James F. Pedersen and Kenneth D. Wald, *Shall the People Rule? A History of the Democratic Party in Nebraska Politics, 1854-1972* (Lincoln: Jacob North, 1972); Garin Burbank, *When Farmers Voted Red: The Gospel of Socialism in the Oklahoma Countryside, 1910-1924* (Westport, Conn.: Greenwood Press, 1976); James R. Green, *Grass-Roots Socialism: Radical Movements in the Southwest, 1895-1943* (Baton Rouge: Louisiana State University Press, 1978); and George Norris Green, *The Establishment in Texas Politics: The Primitive Years, 1938-1957* (Westport, Conn.: Greenwood Press, 1979).

29. Ray Tucker and Frederick R. Barkley, *Sons of the Wild Jackass* (Seattle and London: University of Washington Press, 1970; orig. L. C. Page and Company, 1932); Claudius O. Johnson, *Borah of Idaho* (New York, 1936; reprinted Seattle: University of Washington Press, 1967); Marian C. McKenna, *Borah* (Ann Arbor: University of Michigan Press, 1961); Leroy Ashby, *The Spearless Leader: Senator Borah and the Progressive Movement in the 1920s* (Urbana: University of Illinois Press, 1972); Richard Lowitt, *George W. Norris: The Making of a Progressive, 1861-1912* (Syracuse, N.Y.: Syracuse University Press, 1963); *George W. Norris: The Persistence of a Progressive, 1913-1933* (Urbana: University of Illinois Press, 1971); and *George W. Norris: The Triumph of a Progressive, 1933-1944* (Urbana: University of Illinois Press, 1978); Justus F. Paul, *Senator Hugh Butler and Nebraska Republicanism* (Lincoln: Nebraska State Historical Society, 1976); Homer F. Socolofsky, *Arthur Capper: Publisher, Politician, and Philanthropist* (Lawrence: University of Kansas Press, 1962); Fred Greenbaum, *Fighting Progressive: A Biography of Edward P. Costigan* (Washington: Public Affairs Press, 1971); Monroe L. Billington, *Thomas P. Gore: The Blind Senator from Oklahoma* (Lawrence: University of Kansas Press, 1967); Anne Hodges Morgan, *Robert S. Kerr: The Senate Years* (Norman: University of Oklahoma Press, 1977); Keith W. Olsen, *Biography of a Progressive: Franklin K. Lane,*

1864-1921 (Westport, Conn.: Greenwood Press, 1979); Edward C. Blackorby, *Prairie Rebel: The Public Life of William Lemke* (Lincoln: University of Nebraska Press, 1963); Richard B. Henderson, *Maury Maverick: A Political Biography* (Austin: University of Texas Press, 1970); Gilbert C. Fite, *Peter Norbeck: Prairie Statesman* (Columbia: University of Missouri Press, 1948); Fred Israel, *Nevada's Key Pittman* (Lincoln: University of Nebraska Press, 1963); Michael P. Malone, *C. Ben Ross and the New Deal in Idaho* (Seattle: University of Washington Press, 1970); F. Ross Peterson, *Prophet Without Honor: Glen H. Taylor and the Fight for American Liberalism* (Lexington: University Press of Kentucky, 1974); Marvin E. Stromer, *The Making of a Political Leader: Kenneth S. Wherry and the United States Senate* (Lincoln: University of Nebraska Press, 1969); and John C. Bollens and Grant B. Geyer, *Yorty: Politics of a Constant Candidate* (Pacific Palisades, Calif.: Palisades Publishers, 1973).

30. Paolo Coletta, *William Jennings Bryan,* vol. 1: *Political Evangelist, 1860-1908*; vol. 2: *Progressive Politician and Moral Statesman, 1909-1915*; and vol. 3: *Political Puritan, 1915-1925* (Lincoln: University of Nebraska Press, 1964-69); Lawrence W. Levine, *Defender of the Faith: William Jennings Bryan: The Last Decade, 1915-1925* (London: Oxford University Press, 1965; paperbound ed., 1968); Charles Morrow Wilson, *The Commoner: William Jennings Bryan* (Garden City, N.Y.: Doubleday, 1970); and Louis W. Koenig, *Bryan: A Political Biography of William Jennings Bryan* (New York: G. P. Putnam's Sons, 1971). See also Paul W. Glad, *The Trumpet Soundeth: William Jennings Bryan and His Democracy, 1896-1912* (Lincoln: University of Nebraska Press, 1960; paperbound ed., 1966).

31. Eric F. Goldman, *The Tragedy of Lyndon Johnson* (New York: Knopf, 1969); Doris Kearns, *Lyndon Johnson and the American Dream* (New York: Harper and Row, 1976; paperbound ed., New York: Signet, 1976); and Merle Miller, *Lyndon: An Oral Biography* (New York: G. P. Putnam's Sons, 1980).

32. Bruce Mazlish, *In Search of Nixon: A Psychohistorical Inquiry* (Baltimore: Penguin Books, 1973; orig. Basic Books, 1972); and Fawn M. Brodie, *Richard Nixon: The Shaping of His Character* (New York: W. W. Norton, 1981). Students should keep in mind that autobiographies and memoirs, while generally self-serving, often contain important information. See Richard Nixon, *Six Crises* (New York: Pyramid Books, 1968; orig. Doubleday, 1962); Lyndon B. Johnson, *The Vantage Point: Perspectives of the Presidency, 1963-1969* (New York: Holt, Rinehart and Winston, 1971); and Barry M. Goldwater, *With No Apologies: The Personal and Political Memoirs of United*

States Senator Barry M. Goldwater (New York: William Morrow and Company, 1979).

33. Nash, *American West*, p. 44n.

34. Monroe Lee Billington, *The Political South in the Twentieth Century* (New York: Charles Scribner's Sons, 1975), might serve as something of a model with a bit more emphasis on conceptual framework and the insights of the new social science. Finally, it should be noted that locating the primary sources for such a project will not be easy, for there is no single volume that covers the subject satisfactorily in the way that Rodman W. Paul and Richard W. Etulain, compilers, *The Frontier and the American West*, Goldentree Bibliography in American History (Arlington Heights, Ill.: AHM Publishing Corp., 1977) have tried to do for secondary sources. Until such a book is produced, scholars will have to "mine" the Library of Congress Manuscripts Division, the National Archives and Federal Records Centers, the presidential libraries, the various state archives, and university libraries—wherever manuscript collections, records, newspapers, and oral history transcripts are housed. Helpful historiographical information, some of it bearing on political subjects, is also provided by Gerald D. Nash, Kent D. Richards, Eugene H. Berwanger, Thomas G. Alexander, Jessie L. Embry, and James T. Stensvaag in the *Pacific Historical Review* 50 (November 1981) under the subtitle "Western States Historiography: A Status Report."

Chapter Fourteen

Bradford Luckingham

**The Urban Dimension
of Western History**

Frederick Jackson Turner appreciated the significance of both the frontier and the city. His famous paper, "The Significance of the Frontier in American History," delivered at the annual meeting of the American Historical Association in 1893, omitted any mention of urban development as an integral part of the westward movement, but eventually he viewed the city as a major force in American life. Over the years he urged his students at Wisconsin and Harvard to deal with the emergence of western cities and their role in the expansion process. Few of them did, but at one point Turner began an essay entitled "The Significance of the City in American History." He never finished it, but he knew other historians would develop the theme. "There seems likely to be an urban reinterpretation of our history," he wrote to his friend Arthur M. Schlesinger in 1925.[1]

A reconsideration of American history from an urban point of view was slow in coming, but in 1938 at the annual meeting of the American Historical Association, Schlesinger delivered a paper entitled "The City in American History." Two years later it was published in the *Mississippi Valley Historical Review,* and Schlesinger became the "father of American urban history." In his seminal article Schlesinger declared that a "true understanding of America's past" demanded a "balanced view—an appreciation of the significance of both the frontier and the city." In discussing the "westward movement of the urban frontier" and noting the importance of "urban rivalry" and "urban imperialism," the Harvard professor brought attention to an essential dimension of the western experience.[2]

Seven years earlier in 1933, Bayrd Still, a graduate student doing research in western history under the direction of Frederick Paxson, Turner's successor at Wisconsin, discovered that "there was a society with urban characteristics on the cutting edge of the frontier, even beyond the outer edge of the farmer frontier, in some instances." Looking at the early life of Chicago, Still found evidence of economic pursuits and cultural amenities that related to an urban rather than a rural society, and it appeared to him that "urbanization was a development correlative with the expansion of the frontier, often an integral part of it." In 1935 Still published his interpretation of the Chicago experience in an Illinois journal, and in a 1941 *Mississippi Valley Historical Review* article he elaborated on the theme that the "growth of cities" was a "significant aspect of the history of the West." A comparative study of Buffalo, Cleveland, Detroit, Chicago, and Milwaukee during the period 1830 to 1870, the article was instructive. According to Still, "on many a frontier the town builder was as conspicuous as the farmer pioneer," and the "western city, through the efforts of its founders to extend its economic hinterland, actually facilitated the agrarian development of the West." The "opportunities attending city growth as well as those afforded by cheap farm lands contributed to the dynamic sense of abundance felt by Americans of the mid-nineteenth century."

Still's conclusion that the city was an integral part of the westward movement would become a major theme in the study of urban history. He also noted that western cities showed "a willing dependence upon eastern sources in the transmission of culture," and "a studied imitation of tested forms of municipal practice and urban service." Still emphasized that the establishment of frontier communities was often a conservative process, and the notion that urban pioneers worked to reproduce familiar city patterns in the new country also became an important theme in the urban history of the West.[3]

Another vital topic, urban rivalry, gained attention in 1947 with the appearance of Wyatt W. Belcher's account of the 1850 to 1880 battle between St. Louis and Chicago for control of the vast Mississippi Valley. The key factor in this contest, according to Belcher, was the difference in attitude taken by business leaders in each city. In Chicago they promoted railroad development, while in St. Louis they were more conservative, preferring to retain their faith in river transportation. The "iron horse" prevailed, and by 1880 Chicago emerged the victor. Throughout the struggle, in virtually every aspect of promotion, St. Louis business leaders proved less willing to take risks and pursue bold policies than did their Chicago counterparts. They did not learn in time that the "hazards of venturesome business activity were far 'less deadly than the mould and mildew of stagnating caution.'" Belcher's book made historians more aware of the close relationship between innovations in transportation and the growth of urban centers, and it made clear that the outcome of urban rivalry often depended on the quality of the people who lived in and promoted western cities.[4]

The year Belcher's book was published Schlesinger was urging his students in a seminar at Harvard to explore urban topics. One of them, Richard C. Wade, impressed with the ideas of both Turner and Schlesinger, decided to do a dissertation on "the urban dimension of the frontier." He examined the history of five cities in the Ohio Valley from 1790 to 1830, and he published his findings in article form in 1958, and in 1959 in *The Urban Frontier: The Rise of Western Cities*. Reflecting the influence of Schlesinger and Still, Wade developed the thesis that the cities served as "spearheads of the frontier." Urban developers, acting as generative agents in the new region, often preceded rural pioneers, and from the start Pittsburgh, Cincinnati, Lexington, Louisville, and St. Louis represented a prominent force in the Ohio Valley. Urban centers not only attracted settlers to the West, but they also helped transport culture to that region. In cultural matters, as in other areas, the urban West tried to emulate the East, and imitation rather than innovation prevailed. Urban rivalry and urban imperialism injected, according to Wade, an "extraordinary dynamic into city growth." Ambitious and aggressive, these centers of progress, "by spreading their economic power over the entire section, by bringing the fruits of civilization across the mountains, and by insinuating their ways into the countryside, speeded up the transformation of the West from a gloomy wilderness to a richly diversified region." Others, notably Still, had demonstrated the importance of the city in the westward movement, but it was Wade who inspired the most recognition of this necessary corrective to Turner's frontier thesis.[5]

Following the publication of *The Urban Frontier,* historians began to pay more attention to the history of the city in the West, and the works that emerged during the next two decades followed a variety of interests, including those developed by Wade. To begin with, Charles N. Glaab's contributions on the significance of nineteenth-century urban promoters and promotion in the early West made it clear that historians may have neglected the role of the city in the new country, but contemporaries were quick to appreciate it. Jesup W. Scott, William Gilpin, and other city spokesmen in the area celebrated the vitality of the urban frontier, and they foresaw an urban future for the region and the nation. They viewed the city as the "exemplar of American growth and progress." As Scott declared in 1848: "All people take pride in their cities. In them naturally concentrate the great minds and the great wealth of the nation. There the arts that adorn life are cultivated, and from them flows out the knowledge that gives its current of thought to the national mind."[6]

The most effective city boosters, usually visionary businessmen willing to combine private interests with community interests, directed their attention to economic promotion and cultural development. In *The Americans: The National Experience,* Daniel J. Boorstin illustrated the indispensable role of the human element in urban manifest destiny by examining the careers of a number of urban pioneers whose booster spirit often reflected the success or failure of an upstart city in the West. William B. Ogden, for example, arrived in Chicago from New York in 1835. The town census of that year listed a population of 3,265, most of whom were recent arrivals, and Ogden quickly sensed the opportunities that were emerging. He entered the real estate business, and in 1837 he was elected the first mayor. As a business and political leader, he promoted Chicago, and as the city grew so did Ogden's economic and social status. As he later recalled, "In 1844 I purchased for $8,000 what 8 years thereafter sold for 3 millions of dollars." He continued to acquire land in choice locations, and as Chicago developed into a city of over 100,000 population by 1860, Ogden reaped fantastic material benefits. In his opinion, to boost one's city showed not only good business sense, but community spirit, and there was hardly a public improvement in which Ogden did not play a leading role. "Perhaps the most striking trait of his character," noted a contemporary, "was his absolute faith in Chicago. He saw in 1835, not only the Chicago of today, but Chicago the great city of the future. From that early day, his faith never wavered. Come good times or come bad times, Chicago's great future was to him a fixed fact." And the Ogden story, as Boorstin pointed out in his important book, was repeated in many variations as the city moved west.[7]

Scholars interested in the city wanted to show that urban pioneers deserved as much credit for developing the American West as the trappers, miners, cowboys, and farmers most often dwelled upon by historians. Living in modern America, an urban nation, and searching for a "usable past," many of them found more meaning in an urban West with an urban past; to them the urban frontier deserved at least as much attention as the rural frontier. The prevailing interpretation of the West as an image of the American past left too much out; it failed to give adequate emphasis to the urban frontiersmen as generators of economic and cultural life.

Economic growth was the primary goal of urban pioneers, but evidence of urban maturity gave support to that goal. The attempts of urban boosters to promote their cities as cultural as well as economic centers was often motivated by the desire to create a proper image. As Wade, Glaab, and others pointed out, to be the Boston, New York, or Philadelphia of the West was a prime consideration in that it indicated a sense of arrival. From the earliest days, western urban dwellers wanted to recreate the best of the past, and a stimulating cultural environment was considered a valuable attribute. Businessmen, in fact, often became cultural agents as well as affluent entrepreneurs in the urban West. In Chicago, St. Louis, Denver, San Francisco, and other rising centers, they promoted and supported libraries, concert halls, museums, and theaters, believing they would bring the facilities of civilization to their cities, make intellectual resources available to the inhabitants, and give "rational amusement" to those who wished it. These amenities contributed to a city's aura of stability and permanency and increased its ability to attract desirable newcomers and capital investment. Some of these institutions became models of regional culture, and generally they helped refine the West.[8]

Even in Texas patterns of urbanization were established during the middle years of the nineteenth century. According to Kenneth W. Wheeler, Houston, Galveston, Austin, and San Antonio came of age during this period. City growth in Texas accompanied or preceded the opening of rural frontiers; urban rivalry existed as businessmen and editors engaged in promotional battles; and cultural conservatism was evident. The urban influence in Texas was prominent, asserts Wheeler, for "upon all the cities focused the major cultural, social, economic, and political activities of the state." Texans looked to the cities "for guidance in art, architecture, music, the theatre and literature. They read urban newspapers, sought out urban society, borrowed money, traded raw materials and purchased goods from urban merchants. They used urban industrial production." On the "last frontier of the Old South," all roads converged upon the urban centers of Houston, Galveston, Austin, and San Antonio because they were the paramount points around which Texas developed.[9]

In *Cities of the American West*, a survey of frontier urban plans and planning, John W. Reps contributed additional material supporting the theme that the founding of towns on the various frontiers preceded rural settlement or took place at the same time, and that the establishment of urban communities stimulated the development of the rural West. The towns, as vanguards of settlement, shaped the structure of society in the new country. They were the "spearheads of the frontier" not only in the trans-Appalachian West, but also in the trans-Mississippi West, and to overlook this crucial aspect of life in the region is to tell but part of the story. By 1890 in virtually every aspect of life, urban residents and institutions "dominated western culture and civilization." Moreover, by that year western cities resembled in many ways the older eastern centers; imitation had continued to be a stronger force than innovation in the urbanization of the West, and by the end of the century, Reps declared, the "gap between the urban and rural West was far greater in every aspect than whatever differences may still have distinguished a western city from its eastern counterpart."

Reps also noted that the history of the urban West is replete with "lost opportunities" for truly attractive or beneficial planning. The boosters of the young cities of the West were determined to reach metropolis status at any cost, an approach that often resulted in unfortunate consequences. As the twentieth century dawned, "virtually all Americans and especially those living in the West remained convinced that to grow bigger was to become better." This belief "shaped the policies of the region's growth," and "order and beauty continued to be subordinated to wealth and size as the frontier era passed into history and a new stage of urban development began."

Reps wrote about the "dreams of power, wealth, freedom, conquest, and opportunity that led men into the American West to people it with towns and cities." The lure of the urban West is a compelling theme, and it is clearly evident in his treatment of the beginnings of urbanization in the Ohio and Mississippi valleys, the appearance of Hispanic and Anglo settlements in Texas, the Southwest, and California, the emergence of Mormon towns, the creation of urban centers in the Pacific Northwest, Great Plains, and mountain states, and the rise of "overnight cities" in Oklahoma. Reps paid special attention to well-planned towns and cities of the caliber of Colorado Springs and Salt Lake City, and he indicated what "might have been" produced throughout the West with "orderly design and managed development." Yet he considered San Francisco, despite the "deficiencies of its planning," the "most attractive, diversified, and cosmopolitan of American western communities."[10]

Reps's book supported Lawrence H. Larsen's thesis in *The Urban West at the End of the Frontier* that in many ways "the frontier cities were similar to those throughout the rest of the nation." The challenge of the western environment did not produce in the urban West a "new society." At the end of the frontier, western cities in almost all respects looked and functioned like cities in the East. In his brief but instructive book, Larsen surveyed the condition of twenty-four cities that made up the region in 1880, including many that have remained dominant. Problems as well as prospects were covered. Utilizing a variety of sources, but especially social statistics obtained from the 1880 U.S. Census, Larsen analyzed data relating to economic and political development, ethnic and religious composition, occupational and residential structure, social and recreational life, architecture and urban planning, communication and transportation facilities, and city services such as municipal water, fire, and police departments, schools, public health and sanitation systems. According to Larsen, the data made it clear that an urban civilization in western America was quite visible in 1880, for city life familiar to easterners had moved west with the people. Adopting a host of urban characteristics, western cities drew on the history of the older centers. Occasionally a western city would lead the way in innovation, but more common was the fact that as the United States became an urban nation the characteristics of western cities resembled those of their eastern counterparts. The urban frontier was not an area demanding experiment, but it did provide an opportunity for the extension and proliferation of existing trends. As a result, Larsen concluded, "little was unique or new about the young cities of the West." At the same time, he portrayed with vigor and competence the paramount influence of urban pioneers and urban centers in the development of the trans-Mississippi country.[11]

Even the mining camps and the cattle towns exhibited the refinements as well as the problems of an urban civilization. Both the mining camps and the cattle towns emerged in the latter half of the nineteenth century, and Duane A. Smith and Robert A. Dykstra have modified traditional concepts concerning their evolution. According to Smith, the Rocky Mountain mining towns resembled in many ways earlier urban frontiers, only on a smaller scale. The urban pioneer on the mining frontier wanted his camp, the "germ of a city," to reflect the image he held of the older urban centers, and he worked to that end. The heyday of unlimited chaos so often depicted in the popular media was a relatively short interval in the life span of a typical mining camp, as the maturing communities, led by businessmen and editors, quickly established more positive urban institutions. Dykstra provided important material on the social process of cooperation and conflict within the cattle towns, also pointing out in his analysis of violence the moderate occurrence of homicide, thus giving a conservative touch to the tenacious Wild West image. For example, in fifteen years, 1870–85, in the five Kansas cattle towns studied, only forty-five homicides were recorded. This averages out to three a year, less than one per year per town. Dodge City, with the highest murder rate, had an average of only one homicide per year. As Dykstra put it, "Legend does the cattle town people a double injustice—falsely magnifying the periodic failures of their effort to suppress violence while altogether refusing to take account of its internal complexities." The "urban impulse" pervaded the Kansas cattle towns, and leading citizens in each of them promoted growth and development as they sought the "prize of city status."[12]

Most aspiring towns in the American West did not achieve big-city status. On the Rocky Mountain mining frontier, for example, few made it beyond the town or small-city stage. At the same time, the Rocky Mountain towns contained a number of familiar urban institutions, including the "drinking house." According to Elliott West, early in the life of a mining town the multifunctional saloon became the "conspicuous feature of the streets." It was the most versatile place in town, the "social heart-centre of the camp." The saloon, at least in the beginning, often served as an all-purpose community center. In time, if the town survived, other institutions arrived to provide services the saloon had handled by default in the early days, but the saloon never lost the traditional role it had played from the start as "a place of amusement and relaxation." As the town grew, its drinking houses began, like the town, to look more refined and permanent. With maturity, a town offered a variety of drinking establishments with different atmospheres and styles; its collection of saloons gradually came to resemble those of most American cities.

Leaders in places like Leadville, Colorado, or Jacksonville, Illinois, had dreams of their towns' achieving urban prominence, but they failed to materialize. When failure became apparent, an inverted form of boosterism often emerged. For instance, leaders of the town of Jacksonville, according to Don Doyle in *The Social Order of a Frontier Community*, created a promising place, but it never fulfilled its early expectations. They worked to make it an economic and cultural center, but their efforts fell short, and Jacksonville remained a small town. When attempts to stimulate manufacturing in Jacksonville failed in the 1860s and the town lost the University of Illinois to Champaign during the same decade, it was all over. Following 1870, a local history tradition developed to justify the failure of Jacksonville by pointing to its small-town existence as "chosen success." Local leaders now nurtured the "ideal" of small-town life. An "unspoken agreement was made to deny that Jacksonville had ever wanted to be anything else." As a local historian put it in 1885, "Our city has not been in a hurry to climb the hill of fame." Jacksonville did not attain urban prominence, but it did make the attempt, and Doyle did an excellent job of constructing the frontier community's "struggle for success." Moreover, noted Doyle, Jacksonville was typical of most frontier towns in that it aspired to "urban greatness" with only moderate success. For every Kansas City, Denver, or Seattle, there were hundreds of Jacksonvilles whose ambitions were thwarted, and Doyle's book may well serve as a model for the study of such towns.[13]

Differences in the urban experience often involved time and scale. Some urban centers developed faster than others; for example, San Francisco and Denver have been described by Gunther Barth as "instant cities" because of the suddenness of their evolution. Urban centers also varied in importance as economic generators and civilizing agents. Early San Francisco was the home of dynamic city builders who contributed greatly to the welfare and refinement of their society. Individually and collectively they worked to make San Francisco the metropolis of the Pacific Coast, and like older urban centers, San Francisco soon exerted a powerful influence over a vast hinterland. As Henry George declared in 1868, there existed "not a settler in all the Pacific States and Territories but must pay San Francisco tribute; not an ounce of gold dug, a pound of ore smelted, a field gleaned, or a tree felled in all their thousands of square miles, but must add to her wealth." By 1880 San Francisco was the largest city west of Chicago, a business and cultural center of major significance. It became known as "the City," and as one observer noted at the time, "the greater part of the West was so poor in resources for enjoyment that most of the luxury of the slope has collected in and about San Francisco. The people from the wide region between the British and Mexican lines west of the Rocky Mountains have come here for twenty years to seek compensation for the toils and privations of frontier life."[14]

The San Francisco experience was dramatic, but the quest for prominence remained important also among the other major cities of the Far West, and each of them eventually achieved a high rank in the urban hierarchy. As Earl Pomeroy, a pathfinder in pointing out the vital contribution of the city in the region, has observed: "From the time of the first American settlements, the Pacific slope was significantly urban. Even those far westerners who did not live in cities looked to them to an unusual degree; even in states and areas where population was sparse, society was remarkably urbanized." In a chapter entitled "The Power of the Metropolis" in his 1966 study, *The Pacific Slope,* which remains the best survey available, Pomeroy described the history and influence of San Francisco, Salt Lake City, Portland, Seattle, Los Angeles, and other important cities of the region, leaving no doubt as to their crucial role. In an exploratory article in 1971, "The Urban Frontier of the Far West," he added more depth and understanding to his argument that historians have been slow to recognize the urban dimension of the American Far West. This area did not evolve from rural beginnings to city endings, but had cities at the same time it had ranches, farms, and mines; and the urban centers proved dominant.[15]

In the Far West, urban rivalry existed as city promoters competed for valuable hinterlands, and urban imperialism continued to reflect cultural as well as economic goals. In many respects reminiscent of earlier city boosters, far western urban pioneers were imitators rather than innovators. For example, in the nineteenth century leading citizens in San Francisco and Denver, according to Gunther Barth, inaugurated and maintained "a style and tone of life characteristic of great cities," and they fostered "a quality of urban behavior symptomatic of large centers." Thus, modes of class distinction and norms of cultural excellence which were standardized in the older cities to the east were imposed by the young western elites as they sought to transplant stereotypes of American society. As Barth put it, "The elites' role in San Francisco and Denver as well as the cities' positions as metropolitan centers on the coast and in the mountains clarify the part played by the urban environment in extending recognized status symbols to the West." For better or worse, far western urban pioneers imposed accepted eastern norms throughout the region. "After the East itself," Pomeroy asserted, the Far West was "the most Eastern part of America." A "large part of western opportunity was the opportunity to imitate an older society." Whether it involved economic establishments, public services, or cultural pursuits, the direction traveled was mainly west by east, and a familiar American business and social structure developed.[16]

Although most far western cities experienced familiar urban patterns in their development, certain amenities were available in parts of the region that were nonexistent in most other areas. The use of climate to promote immigration provides a prime example. In 1872, for instance, Los Angeles was described as "the Garden of Paradise." There was no reason, argued the *Los Angeles Star*, why, when the truth were known, climate should not attract thousands of people, and it did. Promotion campaigns emphasizing the therapeutic effect of the climate prompted, as John E. Baur pointed out, a "health rush" to the City of the Angels and its environs. The promotion in general, as Oscar O. Winther detailed, was endless. One advocate declared: "Land of the glorious sunset, thou art truly the Valley of the Angels. Here it is, that morning, noon and night, throughout the changing year, the temperature is even and unvariable, the skies are beautiful and the atmosphere pure." One of countless publicity pamphlets noted that "all the best conditions for which mankind may reasonably hope, meet and center here in Los Angeles." The chamber of commerce proudly asserted in 1892 that "we sell the climate at so much an acre and throw in the land free." The result was the arrival of thousands of people in search of an "earthly Heaven."[17]

Los Angeles, in fact, stands as an excellent example of the impact of amenities on regional urban growth. After 1880, according to Robert M. Fogelson in *The Fragmented Metropolis,* thousands of people from points east made their way to the California sunshine center in search of the "good life." No New York or Chicago for them. The great majority of them were native Americans who viewed suburban life as the ideal way to live, and the advent of the electric railways in 1880 meant that expansion was possible. In the 1920s the automobile replaced the railways as the principal mode of transportation in Los Angeles; and residential dispersal, along with the de-centralization of business and industry, increased considerably. The result was urban sprawl, an environment, declared one developer, "uncontaminated by urban vices and conducive to rural virtues." And here, as Fogelson pointed out in the best available historical account of urban sprawl, was a departure from familiar patterns. An urban form emerged that would make its mark on the future despite critics who viewed the rise of Los Angeles as a collection of suburbs in search of a city. By 1930 the West Coast metropolis had more single-family and fewer multifamily dwellings than any comparable American city. Nowhere else in the country did suburbs extend so far into the country-side and business districts become so widely placed. And this process, which reflected the preference of newcomers, the practices of subdividers, and the inclination of businessmen, proved to be perpetual.[18]

The horizontal development of Los Angeles did not prevent the emergence of familiar urban enclaves. Black Americans, for example, also moved west-ward, carrying with them the same aspirations as the dominant white major-ity, but their movement within the city of Los Angeles was effectively checked. As in their past experience, they became an excluded group. By 1900 Los Angeles was the focal point in the West for black settlement, and by 1930 the dynamics of the ghetto were well established. Legal and extra-legal restrictions, ranging from race covenants to outright violence, were used to contain blacks in a few isolated areas. By 1930, out of fourteen assembly districts, one housed more than 70 percent of the city's blacks. This segre-gation, along with economic and social discrimination, persisted, culminating in the tragic episodes of the 1960s. The spatial ghetto in Los Angeles differed somewhat from the ghettos of New York, Chicago, and other large cities to the east; but as Lawrence B. De Graaf pointed out, the overall situation was much the same.[19]

Mexican Americans also were located in certain areas as new western cities emerged. Until recently Mexican American, or Chicano, urban history was largely ignored by historians, but by 1980 several of them had correctly focused on Chicanos, both in the past and present, as an urban rather than a rural people. Albert Camarillo and Richard Griswold del Castillo led the way, providing valuable accounts of the changes that transformed two important Mexican pueblos into Chicano urban barrios. According to Camarillo and Griswold del Castillo, a sense of ethnic identity and cultural awareness, along with patterns of discrimination and segregation, encouraged barrio development in Santa Barbara and Los Angeles. Mario T. Garcia, in his study of the Mexican population of El Paso from 1880 to 1920, also contributed to our understanding of Chicano life in the American West. All three works help historians who appreciate the role of western cities to recognize the significance of Chicanos in them.[20]

As the twentieth century evolved, the Far West, led by its urban centers, became more prominent in the life of the nation. During the Great Depression and World War II, the federal government became increasingly involved in the growth of the region, and this development, along with new as well as traditional technological and social factors, gave impetus to the unprecedented economic boom and population explosion that the area experienced in the 1950s. During that decade and beyond, according to Gerald D. Nash, the metropolitan Far West, notably in California, led the way in making the region "a pacesetter for the nation."[21]

That the cities led the way in making the Far West "a pacesetter for the nation" in the post-World War II years emphasized the persistent role of urban centers in the westward movement. Some 25 million people moved across the Mississippi River from 1945 to 1965, and the vast majority of them settled in the urban West. By 1965 more than two-thirds of the inhabitants of the American West were urban dwellers; as the cities grew and developed, they steadily increased their dominance over their respective hinterlands.[22]

This pattern of urban dominance may be seen in the history of individual cities. Recent biographies of Kansas City, Denver, and Seattle may serve as illustrations. In each of the emerging cities of the nineteenth century, pioneers worked to attract railroads and capital, and they hoped to create centers of civilization. Opportunities and amenities were promoted. Economic and cultural prominence enabled the cities to continue to drive for urban supremacy. To neglect to boost growth and development for a city and its hinterland was to deny progress and risk decline and defeat. Attitude was most important on the urban frontier, for cities succeeded not only because of natural advantages, but also because of aggressive, ambitious leaders who were intent on seeing their particular urban centers emerge as winners in the race for urban status.

By the turn of the century, Kansas City, Denver, and Seattle were well established as leading urban centers in the West. Regional economic and cultural leaders, they continued to develop despite problems of growth. With the coming of the automobile age they became metropolitan centers, and during and after World War II the combination of federal investment and private enterprise encouraged economic booms and population explosions. At the same time, more urban problems came along with progress and prosperity, leading to conflicting opinions over present and future goals.[23]

Recent studies also indicate a pattern of urban dominance in the Southwest, a region defined by the eminent geographer D. W. Meinig as Arizona, New Mexico, and the western promontory of Texas. Since the beginnings of Spanish settlement in the seventeenth century, urban centers have played a significant role in the Southwest. While the English established towns on the East Coast and in the interior, Spanish pioneers were creating Santa Fe, Paso del Norte, Albuquerque, and Tucson on the northern frontier of New Spain. Outposts of civilization and spearheads of the desert frontier, the oasis towns served as key factors in the life of the region. Urban growth accompanied or preceded the opening of the surrounding country, and the towns acted as links between vast hinterlands and the outside world.

In 1821 Mexico won its independence from Spain, and in 1846 war broke out between the United States and Mexico. Following the conflict, Anglos in the westward movement increasingly found their way to the urban nodes of the American Southwest. They joined with local Hispanos in the further development of El Paso, Albuquerque, and Tucson, and in 1867 Anglo pioneers created Phoenix. By 1880 promoters of all four of these communities were involved in the coming of the railroads, the key to their emergence as the four principal cities of the Southwest.

With the coming of the railroads, the four desert towns turned into thriving small cities, with El Paso in front. Difficulties arose, including the deterioration of Anglo-Mexican relations as Anglos became dominant, but urban growth continued with little disruption to the Great Depression. Along the way the builders of the urban Southwest worked to make the cities transportation hubs, business centers, military outposts, health meccas, and tourist attractions while they encouraged and supported the cotton, cattle, copper, and other interests of the hinterlands.

Each of the four cities suffered less from the Great Depression than many of their counterparts elsewhere, and, with the exception of El Paso, they all increased their populations in the 1930s. During the decade a strong relationship developed between the federal government and the urban Southwest, especially because of New Deal programs. During and after World War II the relationship continued as the cities of the region became major military and high technology defense centers.

New military bases, government agencies, and manufacturing plants, along with the progress of traditional economic factors, caused people from all directions to flock to the "sunshine cities" of the Southwest. A robust multiplier effect took hold, giving impetus to the economic boom and population explosion of the 1950s. Rapid urban growth prompted an exhibit of the exploitative but historical philosophy of progress, and problems emerged during the decade; but by the 1960s the air-conditioned desert hubs, offering opportunities and amenities as well as problems, and led by Phoenix, the largest city in the Southwest, were making strides toward metropolis status. In the process, they increased their dominance over the region.[24]

Cities have been important in the history of the American West, and they are likely to become even more so in the future. The urban growth and development of the region emphatically points out the current and future direction of the American people. The lure of the "urban frontier" remains a compelling theme, and it is hoped that historians will continue to involve themselves in the research and presentation of the dominant role played by cities in the evolution of the modern American West. An urban perspective is necessary before a fuller understanding of that region and the nation can be obtained.

Notes

1. Ray Allen Billington, *Frederick Jackson Turner: Historian, Scholar, Teacher* (New York: Oxford University Press, 1973), pp. 492-93; Arthur M. Schlesinger, "The City in American Civilization," in Schlesinger, *Paths to the Present* (New York: Macmillan, 1949), p. 210.

2. Arthur M. Schlesinger, "The City in American History," *Mississippi Valley Historical Review* 27 (June 1940): 43-66.

3. Bruce M. Stave (ed.), *The Making of Urban History: Historiography Through Oral History* (Beverly Hills, Calif.: Sage, 1977), pp. 66-68; Bayrd Still, "Evidences of the 'Higher Life' on the Frontier, as Illustrated in the History of Cultural Matters in Chicago, 1830 to 1850," *Journal of the Illinois Historical Society* 28 (July 1935): 81-99; and Still, "Patterns of Mid-

Nineteenth Century Urbanization in the Middle West," *Mississippi Valley Historical Review* 28 (September 1941): 187-206. In 1953 Constance McLaughlin Green, another pioneer in American urban history, wrote that "migrations westward brought new cities into being as rapidly as farmers brought virgin land under cultivation or as miners, ranchers and lumbermen developed new sources of wealth." Indeed, Green declared, "frequently it was the rise of new cities and their promotors' efforts to make them grow greater that hastened the peopling of the country roundabout. The ideas and the aspirations that created an urban America originated not on the farms and in the forests of the backcountry but in the cities themselves." Moreover, in the emerging region, the "pattern of urban influence repeated that of the seaboard, and the cities of the New West became magnets attracting the ambitious and the gifted who felt stifled on the farms." Constance McLaughlin Green, *American Cities in the Growth of the Nation* (New York: Harper and Row, 1957), pp. 242-43.

4. Wyatt W. Belcher, *The Economic Rivalry Between St. Louis and Chicago, 1850-1880* (New York: Columbia University Press, 1947), pp. 193-206, *passim.*

5. Stave, *Oral History*, pp. 163-67; Richard C. Wade, *The Urban Frontier: The Rise of Western Cities, 1790-1830* (Cambridge: Harvard University Press, 1959), pp. 341-42; and Wade, "Urban Life in Western America, 1790-1830," *American Historical Review* 64 (October 1958): 14-30.

6. Charles N. Glaab, "Jesup W. Scott and a West of Cities," *Ohio History* 73 (Winter 1964): 3-12; and Glaab, "Visions of Metropolis: William Gilpin and Theories of City Growth in the American West," *Wisconsin Magazine of History* 65 (Autumn 1961): 21-31. According to Glaab, "one of the more dynamic and vital aspects of the history of American urban growth has been the systematic and organized promotion of enterprise by the representatives of American cities." Glaab, "Historical Perspective on Urban Development Schemes," in *Social Science and the City,* ed. Leo F. Schnore (New York: Praeger, 1968), p. 219.

7. Daniel J. Boorstin, *The Americans: The National Experience* (New York: Random House, 1965), pp. 113-23. For good accounts of urban pioneers in a single city, see Charles N. Glaab, *Kansas City and the Railroads: Community Policy in the Growth of a Regional Metropolis* (Madison: Wisconsin State Historical Society, 1962); A. Theodore Brown, *Frontier Community: Kansas City to 1870* (Columbia: University of Missouri Press, 1963). For an informative essay on the notion that the "urban dream competed with the agrarian ideal as a symbol of opportunity for many pioneers," see

J. Christopher Schnell and Katherine B. Clinton, "The New West: Themes in Nineteenth Century Urban Promotion, 1815-1880," *Bulletin of the Missouri Historical Society* 30 (January 1971): 75-88.

8. Henry Nash Smith, *Virgin Land: The American West as Symbol and Myth* (Cambridge: Harvard University Press, 1950; paperbound ed., 1970); and Smith, "The West as an Image of the American Past," *University of Kansas City Review* 18 (Autumn 1951): 30-40; Charles N. Glaab, "The Historian and the American Urban Tradition," *Wisconsin Magazine of History* 66 (Autumn 1963): 13-25; Wade, *The Urban Frontier,* pp. 314-21; Bradford Luckingham, "Agents of Culture in the Urban West: Merchants and Mercantile Libraries in Mid-Nineteenth Century St. Louis and San Francisco," *Journal of the West* 17 (April 1978): 28-35.

9. Kenneth W. Wheeler, *To Wear a City's Crown: The Beginnings of Urban Growth in Texas, 1836-1865* (Cambridge: Harvard University Press, 1968), pp. 165-66, *passim.* For the history of the urban South, including Texas cities, see Blaine A. Brownell and David R. Goldfield (eds.), *The City in Southern History* (Port Washington, N.Y.: Kennikat, 1977). For a good biography of an individual city, see David G. McComb, *Houston: The Bayou City* (Austin: University of Texas Press, 1969).

10. John W. Reps, *Cities of the American West: A History of Frontier Urban Planning* (Princeton: Princeton University Press, 1979), pp. 667-94, *passim.* See also Bradford Luckingham, "The City in the Westward Movement: A Bibliographical Note," *Western Historical Quarterly* 5 (July 1974): 295-306. Rapid city growth in the West was viewed as fundamental to the development of the expanding nation; the urbanization of the region served as a significant nationalizing force. See, for example, the comments by Ronald L. Davis and Harry D. Holmes in the introduction to a "western urbanization" number of the *Journal of the West* 13 (July 1974): 1-5. See also Ronald L. Davis, "Western Urban Development: A Critical Analysis," in *The American West: New Perspectives, New Dimensions,* ed. Jerome O. Steffen (Norman: University of Oklahoma Press, 1979), pp. 175-96.

11. Lawrence H. Larsen, *The Urban West at the End of the Frontier* (Lawrence: Regents Press of Kansas, 1978), pp. xi, 120-21, *passim.* See also Lawrence H. Larsen and Robert L. Branyan, "The Development of an Urban Civilization on the Frontier of the American West," *Societas* 1 (Winter 1971): 33-50; J. Christopher Schnell and Patrick E. McLear, "Why the Cities Grew: A Historiographical Essay on Western Urban Growth, 1850-1880," *Bulletin of the Missouri Historical Society* 27 (April 1972): 162-77. Historians of the urban South have been addressing many of the same themes and reaching the

same conclusions. See, for example, Leonard P. Curry, "Urbanization and Urbanism in the Old South: A Comparative View," *Journal of Southern History* 40 (February 1974): 43-60; and Blaine A. Brownell, "Urbanization in the South: A Unique Experience?" *Mississippi Quarterly* 26 (Spring 1973): 105-20.

12. Duane A. Smith, *Rocky Mountain Mining Camps: The Urban Frontier* (Bloomington: Indiana University Press, 1967; paperbound ed., Lincoln: University of Nebraska Press, 1974), pp. 3-15, 242-52, *passim*; Robert A. Dykstra, *The Cattle Towns: A Social History of the Kansas Cattle Trading Centers Abilene, Ellsworth, Wichita, Dodge City and Caldwell, 1867-1885* (New York: Knopf, 1970; paperbound ed., Lincoln: University of Nebraska Press, 1983), pp. 112-48, *passim*. See also W. Turrentine Jackson, *Treasure Hill: Portrait of a Silver Mining Camp* (Tucson: University of Arizona Press, 1963); James B. Allen, *The Company Town in the American West* (Norman: University of Oklahoma Press, 1966); Stanley B. Parsons, *The Populist Context: Rural Versus Urban Power on a Great Plains Frontier* (Westport, Conn.: Greenwood Press, 1973); Gilbert A. Stelter, "The City and Westward Expansion: A Western Case Study," *Western Historical Quarterly* 4 (April 1973): 187-202. Even the mountain men had urban aspirations. See, for example, William H. Goetzmann, "The Mountain Man as Jacksonian Man," *American Quarterly* 15 (Fall 1963): 402-15.

13. Elliot West, *The Saloon on the Rocky Mountain Mining Frontier* (Lincoln: University of Nebraska Press, 1979), pp. 130-49, *passim*; Don Harrison Doyle, *The Social Order of a Frontier Community: Jacksonville, Illinois, 1825-1870* (Urbana: University of Illinois Press, 1978), pp. 255-59, *passim*. See also Oliver Knight, "Toward an Understanding of the Western Town," *Western Historical Quarterly* 4 (January 1973): 28-42.

14. Gunther Barth, *Instant Cities: Urbanization and the Rise of San Francisco and Denver* (New York: Oxford University Press, 1975), *passim*; Roger W. Lotchin, *San Francisco, 1846-1856: From Hamlet to City* (New York: Oxford University Press, 1974; paperbound ed., Lincoln: University of Nebraska Press, 1979), *passim*; Earl Pomeroy, *The Pacific Slope: A History of California, Oregon, Washington, Idaho, Utah, and Nevada* (New York: Knopf, 1966; paperbound ed., University of Washington Press, n.d.), chap. 6. San Francisco has been the object of more historical study than any other far western city. For two recent books, see William A. Bullough, *The Blind Boss and His City: Christopher Augustine Buckley and Nineteenth Century San Francisco* (Berkeley: University of California Press, 1979); and Judd Kahn, *Imperial San Francisco: Politics and Planning in an American City, 1897-*

1906 (Lincoln: University of Nebraska Press, 1979). See also the following three articles by Roger W. Lotchin: "The City and the Sword: San Francisco and the Rise of the Metropolitan-Military Complex, 1920-1942," *Journal of American History* 75 (March 1979): 996-1020; "The Metropolitan-Military Complex in Comparative Perspective: San Francisco, Los Angeles, and San Diego, 1919-1941," *Journal of the West* 18 (July 1979): 19-30; "The Darwinian City: The Politics of Urbanization in San Francisco Between the World Wars," *Pacific Historical Review* 68 (August 1979): 357-81.

15. Pomeroy, *Pacific Slope,* chap. 6; and Pomeroy, "The Urban Frontier of the Far West," in *The Frontier Challenge: Responses to the Trans-Mississippi West,* ed. John G. Clark (Lawrence: Regents Press of Kansas, 1971), pp. 7-29. See also Charles S. Peterson, "Urban Utah: Toward a Fuller Understanding," *Utah Historical Quarterly* 74 (Summer 1979): 227-35; Earl Pomeroy, "What Remains of the West?" *ibid.* 63 (Winter 1967): 39-55. For an early effort to treat urban pioneers and urban growth in the Far West, see Glenn C. Quiett, *They Built the West: An Epic of Rails and Cities* (New York: Appleton-Century, 1934). As on other urban frontiers, contemporary observers of the Far West noted the influence of the city. For example, in 1884, several years before Turner presented his famous essay, Josiah Strong declared that in the Far West "the city stamps the country, instead of the country stamping the city." Josiah Strong, *Our Country* (New York: Baker and Taylor, 1885), p. 157. In 1899 Adna Weber noted the high rate of urban growth in the West, and he declared it "astonishing that the development of cities in a new country should outstrip that of the rural districts which they serve. Yet in great regions of the West, the cities have grown entirely out of proportion to the rural parts." Adna Weber, *The Growth of Cities in the Nineteenth Century: A Study in Statistics* (Ithaca, N.Y.: Cornell University Press, 1963), p. 20.

16. Gunther Barth, "Metropolism and Urban Elites in the Far West: San Francisco and Denver," in *The Age of Industrialism in America: Essays in Social Structure and Cultural Values,* ed. Frederic Cople Jaher (New York: Free Press, 1968), pp. 158-87; Paul G. Merriam, "Urban Elite in the Far West: Portland, Oregon, 1870-1890," *Arizona and the West* 18 (Spring 1976): 41-52; Pomeroy, *Pacific Slope,* p. 3; Peter R. Decker, *Fortunes and Failures: White Collar Mobility in Nineteenth-Century San Francisco* (Cambridge: Harvard University Press, 1978), pp. 255-58.

17. John E. Baur, "Los Angeles County in the Health Rush, 1870-1900," *California Historical Society Quarterly* 31 (Spring 1952): 13-31; Oscar O. Winther, "The Use of Climate as a Means of Promoting Migration to Southern

California," *Mississippi Valley Historical Review* 33 (December 1947): 411–23.

18. Robert M. Fogelson, *The Fragmented Metropolis: Los Angeles, 1850–1930* (Cambridge: Harvard University Press, 1967), pp. 137–63, *passim*. See also Mark S. Foster, "The Model-T, the Hard Sell, and Los Angeles's Urban Growth: The Decentralization of Los Angeles during the 1920s," *Pacific Historical Review* 64 (November 1975): 459–84; and Foster, "The Western Response to Urban Transportation: A Tale of Three Cities, 1900–1945," *Journal of the West* 18 (July 1979): 31–39; John and La Ree Caughey, *Los Angeles: Biography of a City* (Berkeley: University of California Press, 1976).

19. Lawrence B. De Graaf, "The City of Black Angels: Emergence of the Los Angeles Ghetto, 1890–1930," *Pacific Historical Review* 39 (August 1970): 323–52. See also De Graaf, "Recognition, Racism, and Reflections on the Writing of Western Black History," *ibid.* 44 (February 1975): 22–51.

20. Albert Camarillo, *Chicanos in a Changing Society: From Mexican Pueblos to American Barrios in Santa Barbara and Southern California, 1848–1930* (Cambridge: Harvard University Press, 1979); Richard Griswold del Castillo, *The Los Angeles Barrio, 1850–1890: A Social History* (Berkeley: University of California Press, 1980); Mario T. García, *Desert Immigrants: The Mexicans of El Paso, 1880–1920* (New Haven: Yale University Press, 1981). See also Juan Gómez-Quiñones and Luis L. Arroyo, "On the State of Chicano History: Observations on Its Development, Interpretations, and Theory," *Western Historical Quarterly* 7 (April 1976): 155–85. For other ethnic groups, see Bradford Luckingham, "Immigrant Life in Emergent San Francisco," *Journal of the West* 12 (October 1973): 600–617; Moses Rischin, "Beyond the Great Divide: Immigration and the Last Frontier," *Journal of American History* 55 (June 1968): 42–53; Howard P. Chudacoff, *Mobile Americans: Residential and Social Mobility in Omaha, 1880–1920* (New York: Oxford University Press, 1972); John A Price, "The Migration and Adaptation of American Indians to Los Angeles," *Human Organization* 27 (Summer 1968): 168–75; S. Lyman Tyler, "The Recent Urbanization of the American Indian," in *Essays on the American West, 1973–1974*, ed. Thomas G. Alexander (Provo, Utah: Brigham Young University Press, 1975), pp. 43–62.

21. Gerald D. Nash, *The American West in the Twentieth Century: A Short History of an Urban Oasis* (Englewood Cliffs, N.J.: Prentice-Hall, 1973; 2d ed., University of New Mexico Press, 1977), pp. 6–7, *passim*. This book is the only survey of the American West in the twentieth century that gives adequate attention to the urban dimension, and in it the emphasis is on

California. Nash was influenced by Walter Prescott Webb, who had noted in 1957 that the West "is already an urban society." It "is today virtually an oasis civilization." Walter Prescott Webb, "The American West: Perpetual Mirage," *Harper's Magazine,* May 1957, p. 28. See also the articles on the urban West by Nash, Carl Abbott, Roger W. Lotchin, Mark S. Foster, Bradford Luckingham, Harold L. Platt, Howard N. Rabinowitz, and Lyle W. Dorsett in the *Journal of the West* 18 (July 1979). Few surveys of the westward movement in American history give suitable attention to the role of the city, but some have recognized its significance. "Clearly the city was not a product of a long evolutionary process on the frontier," Ray Allen Billington declared in 1966, "but an agency for the advancement of settlement no less important than the mine or farm." He urged historians to include this aspect of the story if they hoped to "visualize accurately the whole frontier process." Yet, almost ten years later, Richard A. Bartlett could note that "historians of the American frontier have consistently ignored urban places in their narratives of the developing new country, and this failure to take the cities into account has contributed to a distorted view of the American move West." Bartlett devoted only one chapter to urban pioneers and "urban places" in his social history of the frontier, but he concluded that "more even than the farm, ranch, mine, or lumber camp, the towns and cities were the symbols of civilization's advance into the new country." Ray Allen Billington, *America's Frontier Heritage* (New York: Holt, Rinehart and Winston, 1966), p. 45; and *idem, Westward Expansion: A History of the American Frontier* (New York: Macmillan, 1974), pp. 6–7; Richard A. Bartlett, *The New Country: A Social History of the American Frontier, 1776-1890* (New York: Oxford University Press, 1974; paperbound ed., 1976), chap. 7.

22. Jonathan Kendell, "Historians of West Are Shedding 'Cowboy' Image and Gaining Acceptance," *New York Times,* October 15, 1971; Luckingham, "The City in the Westward Movement," pp. 295–306; and Luckingham, "The American West: An Urban Perspective," *Journal of Urban History* 7 (November 1981): 99–105. In 1967, Wallace Stegner, new editor of *The American West,* urged contributors to be more aware of the urban dimension. As he put it, "The American West, whatever its frontier past, is in the twentieth century increasingly urban. The western American is, by the millions, a city dweller, even if he wears boots and a Stetson and grows whiskers for Frontier Days. Seven out of eight readers of this magazine are city dwellers." Wallace Stegner, editorial, *The American West* 4 (February 1967): 5.

23. A. Theodore Brown and Lyle W. Dorsett, *K. C.—A History of Kansas City, Missouri* (Boulder, Colo.: Pruett, 1979); Lyle W. Dorsett, *The Queen*

City: A History of Denver (Boulder, Colo.: Pruett, 1977); Roger Sale, *Seattle: Past to Present* (Seattle: University of Washington Press, 1976; paperbound ed., n.d.). The first two books are the initial volumes in the new Western Urban History Series published by Pruett. More city biographies of the same quality are promised. This series is encouraging to scholars who feel that serious problems have developed over the years because of the neglect of the city by western historians, and the neglect of the West by urban historians.

24. D. W. Meinig, *Southwest: Three Peoples in Geographical Change, 1600-1970* (New York: Oxford University Press, 1971), pp. 3-8; Bradford Luckingham, "Urban Development in Arizona: The Rise of Phoenix," *Journal of Arizona History* 22 (Summer 1981): 197-234; and Luckingham, *The Urban Southwest: A Profile History of El Paso, Albuquerque, Tucson, and Phoenix* (El Paso: Texas Western Press, University of Texas at El Paso, 1982); Howard Rabinowitz, "Growth Trends in the Albuquerque SMSA, 1940-1979," *Journal of the West* 18 (July 1979): 62-74; C. L. Sonnichsen, *Pass of the North: Four Centuries on the Rio Grande*, 2 vols. (El Paso: Texas Western Press, University of Texas at El Paso, 1980). For a good study of a Mexican border city, See Oscar J. Martinez, *Border Boom Town: Ciudad Juárez since 1948* (Austin: University of Texas Press, 1978).

Chapter Fifteen

Thomas G. Alexander

Toward the New Mormon History: An Examination of the Literature on the Latter-day Saints in the Far West

The written history of the Church of Jesus Christ of Latter-day Saints (LDS) has passed through four discrete but overlapping phases. The first phase—the Old Mormon History—began shortly after the Church's organization and derived from early attempts to attack, support, or explain the new movement. It consisted essentially of three types of literature: muckraking exposé, pietistic or apologetic defense, and travel curiosa. The common element in the three was the tendency to ignore careful research and analysis in order to support a case. The second and third phases originated shortly after the turn of the twentieth century in an attempt to apply more rigorous standards of evidence to the study of the Mormon past. The second phase, we might label the Venerative Scholars. Favorable to the Church like the pietistic group of Old Mormon Historians, the Venerative Scholars nevertheless brought new canons of scholarship to their research. The third phase also began in the early twentieth century with the exodus of a group of Mormon students in the social and behavioral sciences, the humanities, and history to universities outside the Mountain West. This might be called the phase of Progressive Scholarship since these writers were heavily influenced by the assumptions of the Beardian-Robinsonian school in their secularism, their affinity for economic interpretation, their application of social-scientific methodology, and their discounting of spiritual motivation. The fourth phase—the New Mormon History—started in the 1950s among both Mormon and non-Mormon scholars. It derived from a belief that secular and spiritual motivation coexist in human affairs and that a sympathetic but critical evaluation of the Mormon past, using techniques derived from historical, humanistic, social-scientific, and religious perspectives, could help in understanding what was at base a religious movement.[1]

These four phases should not be thought of as following after one another. Rather, although they began in succeeding times, each has continued to the present in one form or another and with varying intensity. Perhaps the most useful metaphor for the time relationship of these phases is that of the lagging juxtaposition of sine and cosine waves across the face of an oscilloscope. Each wave begins at a different place but fluctuates across the cathode ray tube on which it is projected. The following essay will examine the essential characteristics and identify some of the representative works of the various phases. The emphasis of the essay, however, will be on the last and most significant phase: the New Mormon History.

The first phase, the Old Mormon History, rested on essentially three sets of questions. The first group of questions asked how to discredit what appeared to be a deviant and immoral sect. The second set of questions derived from the opposite premise, how to defend the divinity of Christ's restored Church. The third category of questions asked, what is interesting to the general non-Mormon reader about the Utah Mormons?

Most easily identifiable of the Old Mormon History is the literature that attacked the Mormons. It includes such exposés as John H. Beadle's edition of the confessions of William Hickman. Hickman's charges led to the indictment of Brigham Young for murder, though the indictments were eventually thrown out of court. Beadle's introduction leaves the impression of an organized band of assassins, but Hickman's confessions do not allege that such a group existed. The value, for us today, of a work like Hickman's is to represent a point of view, certainly neither to determine the guilt or innocence of Brigham Young nor to assess the lasting effect of the Mormon contribution.[2]

Some exposés were written by apostates. Perhaps the best example is T. B. H. Stenhouse's *Rocky Mountain Saints,* which emphasized the sensational and bizarre. Here we have the story of blood atonement, the terrors of polygamy, and Brigham Young's authoritarianism. It was also a tract supporting the Godbeite or New Movement, a group of businessmen and spiritualists who broke with the orthodox Mormons in the late 1860s and early 1870s. In Stenhouse's work, as with most others of this type, the principal value is to provide insights for the present-day student into the point of view of a significant group that disagreed with the mainstream of Latter-day Saints. Stenhouse's criteria for selection of evidence seems to have been generally polemical and his interpretation quite prejudiced against the people he had abandoned. Some of the most recent examples of this exposé literature, while well written, allow rhetoric to supplant new research. William Wise's *Massacre at Mountain Meadows,* for instance, reviewed evidence already used by Juanita Brooks. By speculating beyond the evidence, however, he arrived at the unsubstantiatable conclusion that the events could never have taken place in Mormon Utah without Brigham Young's complicity (p. 175).[3]

Representative of the second set of works from the Old Mormon History— the pietistic or apologetic—is a broad range of literature that remains popular in the Mormon community. Brigham H. Roberts, for instance, produced a sympathetic and uncritical biography of John Taylor. Written without references, Roberts's book, which is still in print, nevertheless provides insight into the faith of Church members who revered President Taylor as a prophet, seer, and revelator, and also into their attitude toward the Gentiles and federal officeholders who opposed LDS beliefs and practices. This type of literature has continued into the twentieth century and is well represented by Preston Nibley's biography of Brigham Young, which manages the astounding feat of eulogizing the much-married Mormon prophet without mentioning polygamy in more than five hundred pages. Nibley had access to the Church archives in Salt Lake City but failed to apply the sort of critical scholarship that might have come from a careful, imaginative, and insightful use of those records.[4] His reasons probably have a great deal to do with his perception of the sensitivity of much of what he might say to substantial portions of the LDS community.

Some of the travel literature and curiosa from the third category of the Old Mormon History is still of value. John W. Gunnison's *The Mormons* was one of the first and most-cited firsthand descriptions of Utah Mormon society. Gunnison's work provides considerable insight into the obviously absurd but then-current attitude of non-Mormon observers that internal disunity would soon destroy the LDS Church. His description of Mormon "Theo-democracy" is often quoted and captures quite well the combination of personal and local autonomy on the one hand and central direction on the other which was essential to the success of the LDS enterprise. Perhaps the most frequently read travel work is Richard F. Burton's *City of the Saints.* Fascinated by the Mormons in Utah as he had been by the Moslems in the Middle East, Burton left a generally favorable impression of Utah society. He spent several weeks in Salt Lake City studying, conversing, and observing, and he produced an eminently readable and generally accurate account of the people he saw. As a contemporary observation, it still provides much of value to modern scholars.[5]

As one moves from the three categories of the Old Mormon History to other phases of Mormon historiography, it is important to distinguish the Venerative Scholars from the pietistic group of the Old Mormon History.

Unlike the earlier group, the Venerative Scholars have produced well-researched and reasonably argued studies. Their work exhibits little of the scissors-and-paste mélange of Preston Nibley's *Brigham Young,* for instance. Like the pious group, however, they have written for the general LDS community rather than for the larger group of Mormons and non-Mormons who want answers to the questions posed by the New Mormon History. More serious, however, is the general unwillingness of this group to make explicit comparisons with other religions or to draw on the social and behavioral sciences for insights.

Perhaps B. H. Roberts's work after 1900 best represents the work of these Venerative Scholars. His *Comprehensive History of the Church* has stood for fifty years as a factually reliable, well-researched history of the Mormons down to about 1900. The material on the thirty years between 1900 and 1930 tends to be sketchy, but it is nevertheless accurate. An indefatigable researcher, Roberts read virtually everything he could get his hands on— Mormon, non-Mormon, and anti-Mormon. He drew on these sources to produce an eminently readable and well-documented defense of the Saints. The major problem with the *Comprehensive History* is the way Roberts evaluated evidence on controversial matters. In dealing with the Mountain Meadows Massacre, for instance, Roberts placed virtually the entire blame on John D. Lee. While he faulted stake president Isaac C. Haight for not restraining Lee, the charge was one of omission rather than complicity. By adopting this interpretation, Roberts could deplore the carnage while absolving not only the General Authorities, as most studies have, but also the local Church leaders of any direct responsibility (4:160–80).[6]

Especially characteristic of the Venerative Scholars is the tendency to downplay problems or failures. Milton R. Hunter's *Brigham Young, The Colonizer,* for instance, was the first scholarly work to analyze in detail Young's colonizing methods and accomplishments. Begun as a doctoral dissertation at the University of California, Hunter's work presents significant information and interpretation on the colonizing ventures. Nevertheless, little is said about the failures or the difficulties that caused them. Since the Latter-day Saints were ultimately successful in colonizing a large area of western America, the events Hunter chronicles are quite significant, but the omissions leave a study lacking in balance.[7]

Like the works belonging to the Old Mormon History, studies by Venerative Scholars have continued to the present. Hugh Nibley's *Sounding Brass,* for instance, is a meticulous critique of two anti-Mormon writings. Nibley's book is most useful for the poorly informed who do not have the background to critique sensationalistic or popular works of questionable validity, like those of Ann Eliza Young and Irving Wallace. But it is a pointed and often sarcastic essay that emphasizes in great detail flaws already evident to the knowledgeable reader. The generally uninformed but orthodox Latter-day Saint will find this type of work supportive of his beliefs, but the Mormon who is familiar with critical methodology and with the history will prefer a synthesis of the events critiqued. Many scholars find this style of writing to be a sort of intellectual overkill, and it has not been particularly influential among historians.[8]

There is a tendency among the Venerative Scholars to play down internal conflict and differences within the LDS community, especially between members of the hierarchy. For example, Truman G. Madsen's biography of B. H. Roberts deemphasizes the battles between Roberts and others in the Church over politics to such an extent that Madsen finally concludes that Roberts—a highly partisan Democrat—was a political "independent." In presenting the controversy between Roberts and Joseph Fielding Smith over evolution, Madsen outlines some aspects of Roberts's views but never specifies Elder Smith's position. The reader is left with the impression that "the most essential elements" of Roberts's views were published in discourses. Nothing is mentioned about the significance of Roberts's thought to the continuing controversy over evolution within the LDS community. Nevertheless, Madsen's biography fills an important gap in the literature.[9]

In contrast to the Venerative Scholars, whose work continues in large quantities, there are very few Progressive Scholars still writing. The first books published by this group appeared in the early 1920s, though they were often based on works completed somewhat earlier. Born generally in the late nineteenth century, the founders of this school were trained in the Progressive tradition with its emphasis on secular, economic, and social-scientific interpretation. As rural progressives, they exhibited a tendency to praise the accomplishments of nineteenth-century Mormon communitarians and to posit a cleavage between the General Authorities and the Mormon people, often showing considerable sympathy for the people but antagonism toward the leadership. There is a tendency in such writing to emphasize sociological analysis and to neglect though not ignore the religious dimension of the LDS experience.

For the Progressive Scholars, the center of Mormon life was the town or *Mormon Village,* as Lowry Nelson called it. Their attitude toward developments in the twentieth century tended to be ambivalent, particularly as the Mormons began to face an increasingly urban and secular society. Concerned about the decline in agrarian values, they feared in an almost contradictory way that LDS responses to twentieth-century urban-industrial life had become dogmatic and uncreative. They seemed to fear that such attitudes would not allow the Mormon people to confront the realities of modern life. This is not to say that the Progressive Scholars have completely neglected the religious dimension of the Mormon experience. There is, however, a tendency to downplay that aspect in favor of sociological analysis. Nels Anderson, for instance, treated the Mormon Reformation of the late 1850s as essentially a social phenomenon rather than as a set of experiences that derived from the deep religious feelings of the Mormon people. His analysis of polygamy, likewise, emphasized the sociological and cultural aspects of the institution.[10]

One of the first of the Progressive Scholars, Ephraim E. Erickson, exhibited in his 1922 book what seems to have been the central tendency of the Progressives. His essay shows concern about what he saw as a failure to confront modern life. He lamented the direction toward which Mormon society seemed to be moving. On the one hand, he anticipated the development of "a sort of Mormon scholasticism," designed to "justify" Mormon "dogmas." On the other, he expected the development of a cadre of progressive scholars who could apply the scientific method to the study of Mormon institutions. He thought such study would lead to critical analysis and improvement in Mormon society. Although he anticipated that the critique might "inhibit natural expression of impulses" and "create friction" resulting "in the loss of energy," he was nevertheless willing to risk this tendency in order to confront what he viewed as serious social problems.[11]

Perhaps the best current example of Progressive Scholarship is the work of Samuel W. Taylor, whose *Rocky Mountain Empire* exhibits many of the characteristics of earlier studies of this school. Taylor's work is actually two books. The first deals quite harshly with the public activities of the Church leadership following statehood. Emphasis is on conflict, particularly over such problems as the political ambitions of Moses Thatcher, the question of new polygamy, and the seating of Senator Reed Smoot. Taylor's father, John W. Taylor, was one of the apostles who refused to end new plural marriage after President Joseph F. Smith prohibited it through the Second Manifesto of 1904. The author's point of view is essentially secular. In fact, the same sort of study could have been written about any large organization with internal and public relations problems.

The second half of Taylor's book contrasts quite sharply with the first. It is essentially a nostalgic and appreciative look at small-town life in Utah Valley and at Brigham Young University during the early twentieth century. Here Taylor exhibits a genuine love and concern for the people among whom he had lived and studied. It is clear that Taylor believes that the Cluff expedition to find Book of Mormon sites in Central America and the Koyle Dream Mine opened by a Spanish Fork bishop to save the Church both derived from deep religious convictions. For Taylor, then, among the people there is a deep religious faith; among the leaders there is politics and expediency.[12]

One of the most recent examples of Progressive Scholarship is Mark Leone's *Roots of Modern Mormonism*. Leone respects the Latter-day Saints' religious traditions, and like Taylor, he has written two books. Chapters 1, 2, 7, 8, 9, and part of 6 interpret the background and meaning of current Mormonism. Chapters 3 through 5 and part of 6 are the pro-agrarian chapters which provide an insightful and sympathetic analysis of Mormon life and institutions in the Little Colorado settlements of northern Arizona. Drawing upon the work of sociologists and anthropologists like Roy Rappaport, Robert Bellah, and Thomas Luckmann, Leone interprets the shift in Mormonism from a theocratic state in the nineteenth century to what he calls "a colonial religion" in the twentieth.[13]

For Leone, authentic Mormonism is to be found in its popular traditions. By focusing on these traditions, however, Leone has overemphasized the do-it-yourself nature of modern Mormonism. Contrary to his assertion, doctrine is, in fact, prescribed and regulated by the Church's authorities. They leave considerable individual and local latitude, as Leone intimates, on questions on which the First Presidency has taken no official position, but numerous Latter-day Saints are disciplined or even excommunicated for their insistence on preaching doctrines or continuing practices declared heretical. Certainly, as Leone has written, Latter-day Saints have used genealogy and other skills auxiliary to history to sustain their faith and rituals. But the record of the Progressive and Venerative Scholars and the New Mormon History ought to be sufficient to refute the claim that "very little of the record [of the Mormon past] has been interpreted and made into history" (p. 205).

That Mormon society is susceptible to anti-intellectualism as Leone indicates does not make it unique. As Richard Hofstadter has amply demonstrated, anti-intellectualism is characteristic of the larger American society as well.[14] No one, however, would assert that virtually all of American history has been of a do-it-yourself variety, despite the popular symbolism that often passes in the United States for the story of our past. Yet Leone makes that assertion for Mormon history. This view, it seems to me, is erroneous in the same way that the idea that Mormonism is "memoryless" is erroneous (p. 211). Both could equally be said of the American people, and both rely upon a definition of history that excludes the work of both scholars and popular historians.

On the other hand, Leone's analysis of the life of nineteenth-century Latter-day Saints in the agricultural villages of the Little Colorado is insightful and significant. His chapter on ecclesiastical courts is the best available on the subject. It shows a thorough understanding of the attitude held by nineteenth-century LDS leaders and members that the sacred and profane are inextricably bound together. Nineteenth-century courts, unlike those of today, had temporal as well as the religious jurisdiction. Indeed, the separation of the religious and secular so common to twentieth-century life would have been as unthinkable to nineteenth-century Mormons as to seventeenth-century Puritans. Decisions in Church courts were, as Leone indicates, then as today, based on inspiration, although he overemphasizes the ad hoc nature of each decision since Church doctrine and practice prescribe charges for which courts are to be held and appropriate punishment for particular offenses.

Some other works, though on the fringes, ought also to be included in the Progressive category. Unlike Leone's and Taylor's writings, these works give virtually no attention to religious motivation in Mormonism. In some cases, negative comments on contemporary Mormonism are present; in others, they are missing. Some of these works might be included in the anti-Mormon group of the Old Mormon History, but they tend to be more sophisticated in research and development. Beyond this, the lack of a clear concern for religious motivation and of a sympathetic understanding of the Mormon people and their traditions exclude this work quite clearly from either the Venerative School or the New Mormon History. Perhaps the best example is Laurel B. Andrew's *Early Temples of the Mormons.* Andrew emphasizes the secular aspect and has written with such a degree of clinical detachment that little of the intense otherworldliness and religious fervor of the temple experience comes through. Andrew's study is written as intellectual history, but the causal connections between the influences said to have produced the temple architecture and ritual are assumed rather than proved. The evidence for architectural influences is readily obtainable and has been used by such writers as Paul Anderson and Mark Hamilton.[15]

The lack of proved causal connections, however, provides considerable difficulty in Andrew's interpretation of the development of the temple ritual and of the symbolism of the temple and its interior and exterior space. She argues, for instance, for a close relationship between the LDS and Masonic rituals, but a careful comparison of the two reveals only the most superficial similarity. The ritual theme of the Masonic ceremony concerns the events surrounding the construction of Solomon's Temple, while that of the Latter-day Saints' temple ceremony revolves around the fall of Adam and the redemption through Jesus Christ. By using a post hoc argument, Andrew finds it unnecessary to account for the differences, since Mormon leaders were active in the Masonic order in Nauvoo.

Andrew's discussion of agrarianism is more enlightened and, in fact, much more sophisticated than that of the early Progressive scholars like Nelson or Erickson. She reveals little of the nostalgia for rural life apparent in Nelson's work, for instance. Rather, she considers the presence of such universal themes as the garden of the world and the desert or wilderness myth, which was elaborated by Henry Nash Smith, whom she does not cite, and traced historically by Leo Marx, whom she does.[16] Her case for the presence of these themes in Latter-day Saints' thought and for their relationship to the location of temples in the Great Basin is quite persuasive.

It is important explicitly to understand the differences in point of view of the Progressives, Venerative Scholars, and the New Mormon Historians. Most representatives of each of the three groups received some academic training. All three groups tend to see Mormonism at least partly as a religious movement. There is, nevertheless, a greater tendency on the part of the Progressive Scholars to emphasize the sociological and cultural roots of Mormon institutions and to analyze Latter-day Saints' historical development from a secular point of view. Even when developments would seem to be clearly religious, the Progressive will often give more attention to their secular content.

This is not to say that the Venerative Scholars and the New Mormon Historians see everything as religious. They, too, recognize that Mormon institutions and history have a secular side. The question of the secular is rather a matter of degree, since the Venerative Scholars and the New Mormon Historians recognize to a much greater degree than the Progressives the continuing religious motivation for action within the LDS community. The principal difference between the Venerative Scholars and the New Mormon Historians, as indicated before, is the tendency of the former to report difficulties only in passing or without analysis or critical comment, or to ignore conflict altogether in order to emphasize what they evidently consider safe topics. The latter tend to confront and interpret problem areas much more readily, to analyze more conceptually, and to pay more attention to the relationship between Mormon and general U.S. historiography.

It is important to understand the degree to which an interpretation emphasizing religious commitment is inherent in the work of the New Mormon Historians. In a study of that most worldly topic—economic history—Leonard J. Arrington, a devout Mormon and former LDS Church Historian, in *Great Basin Kingdom* emphasized the religious basis of Mormon economic institutions and the religious motivation that led the Saints to develop their Kingdom. Similarly, Thomas F. O'Dea, a Catholic scholar, dealt insightfully in *The Mormons* with what might seem the secular problem of strain and conflict in Mormon society. Unlike Progressive scholars who have treated similar problems, however, O'Dea summed up his analysis with the comment: "It would seem a grave mistake for a religious movement to concentrate its attention on this-worldly activities, since it is precisely this-worldliness and activism that modern man appears to be finding inadequate" (p. 262). Likewise, Klaus J. Hansen, a somewhat independent Latter-day Saint, in *Quest for Empire* considered religious motives to have been the basis of the Latter-day Saints' attempts to develop what appeared to outsiders as a temporal empire. Most importantly, he related the development of the Mormon Kingdom of God to the decidedly religious concept of millennialism.[17]

It would not be too much to say that the earliest impulses for the New Mormon History came from active and devout Mormons anxious to understand their own roots. Perhaps the first example of New Mormon History was Juanita Brooks's exhaustive study of the *Mountain Meadows Massacre,* published in 1950. Brooks, a devout Latter-day Saint who grew up in the vicinity of the massacre, heard rumors of these events and learned that her own grandfather had been involved in some way. Unsatisfied with the currently available accounts both of the anti-Mormon variety which blamed the general Church leadership and the pro-LDS versions which laid the blame entirely on John D. Lee and the Indians, she spent a number of years trying to uncover every possible primary source. Her volume, while cluttered with too many verbatim transcripts by current literary standards, is a model of meticulous research and analysis.

In what seems to be a reasonable conclusion, she argues that the massacre derived both from the fears and excitement associated with the Utah War and from the deep commitment of Cedar City Mormons to the Church and its leadership. Clearly, John D. Lee was not solely, or perhaps even primarily, responsible. He was the military commander on the ground, but his orders had come from Isaac C. Haight, his military superior and stake president, and ultimately from William H. Dame, Haight's military commander. At the time, all of Utah Territory had been placed under martial law and was preparing for war with the U.S. government. Members of the Fancher wagon train were unfriendly and by their statements and actions helped ignite the fire that led to their own destruction. She demonstrates quite clearly, however, that Brigham Young and the general Church leadership bore no direct responsibility for the events. They were partly responsible for the fever pitch of emotions that accompanied the massacre and, in addition, did little to help in bringing all the perpetrators to justice, except eventually (1870) to excommunicate Haight and Lee. But Brooks's study is really a rather narrow one, and while she mentions such concepts as "mob psychology" and "war hysteria," there is really no systematic application or analysis of these syndromes.[18]

An explicit application of social-scientific concepts to a Mormon problem had to await what is probably the single most significant bellwether of the New Mormon History, Leonard J. Arrington's *Great Basin Kingdom*. Since the publication of Arrington's work, scholars have been unwilling to accept without critical comment the failure to apply systematic analysis through the comparative approach to the study of Mormon history. His work includes explicit comparisons with general American economic development and with the points of view of social scientists such as Max Weber who have studied the general relationship between economic development and religion. Arrington's book is also valuable because it analyzes Mormon economic life and because it is a case study of the interaction of a religious group carrying the ideals of a communitarian society with the predominantly market-oriented American economy.

In recent years, some chinks have developed in the communitarian armor that Arrington fashioned for the Mormon people. Recent studies by James Kearl, Clayne Pope, and Larry Wimmer, based on systematic analysis of income and wealth data, reveal that Utah society in its early years responded generally to market forces. In fact, they conclude that the single most important determinant of wealth was length of residence, not communitarian commitment. Beyond this, studies by Dwight Israelsen seem to show that communitarian institutions were probably not as important determinants of equality in the society as has previously been believed. In a comparison of United Order and non–United Order towns, he concluded that those with United Orders did not have any significantly higher degree of equality. His results are based on incomplete data, but I suspect that future research will show that the economic shift from the nineteenth century to the twentieth did not require as great a reversal of economic attitudes as Arrington believed, since Utah already had a basically market economy. The biggest economic challenges were probably to the relative self-sufficiency of the Mormon Kingdom rather than to Mormon communitarian ideals. These were, however, problems which Utah shared with other Mountain states as the western economy was integrated into the nation.[19]

In the political and social arena, the situation was much different, and the integration was probably much more difficult. This is quite evident in Norman Furniss's *The Mormon Conflict,* a study of the Utah War. Furniss recognized that blame for the war was shared by the officers of the U.S. government, who were intemperate, injudicious, and hasty in their actions, and by the Mormons, who were extreme in their language and whose actions made it clear that they wanted as little to do with the constituted authority as possible. On the whole, Furniss considered the Utah expedition a blunder of monumental proportions, but he recognized that its rather unheroic conclusion was simply a prelude to further clashes between Mormons and federal authorities.[20]

Like other New Mormon Historians, however, Furniss's interpretation incorporates the deep religious commitment of the Latter-day Saints. It is instructive to compare his treatment of the Reformation of the 1850s (pp. 92–94) with that of Nels Anderson (pp. 152–53), who emphasized the sensational and bizarre rather than the basic religious motivation that undergirded the effort to reform the Mormon community.

Important because of its integration of doctrinal concepts with political events is Klaus J. Hansen's *Quest for Empire.* Hanson believed that the idea of a temporal kingdom on earth established in preparation for Christ's second coming, rather than the more visible practice of plural marriage, was the main source of Latter-day Saints' uniqueness and the principal cause of Gentile opposition to the Church. Established in 1844 at Nauvoo, the governing body of the earthly Kingdom of God, the so-called Council of Fifty, was active during the exodus to the West. Technically separate from the Church organization itself, the Council of Fifty included some Gentiles, and Hanson's narrative leads one to believe that it was more important than the Church's General Authorities during the exodus and early years in Utah. Afterward, it went underground, but the Church leadership continued to govern in temporal affairs. Hansen is convinced that Gentiles objected to political dictation more than to any other Mormon practice.[21]

A recent study by Michael Quinn makes it necessary to modify some of Hansen's conclusions. Admittedly, it does seem clear that the idea of a political kingdom of God established on earth preparatory to Christ's second coming was important in Mormon thought and practice. Quinn has shown, however, that the Council of Fifty was dominated by Church leaders and that no Gentiles were members after 1845. More importantly, he raises some fundamental questions about the relative practical significance of the council. Quinn's analysis shows that the Council of Fifty was never particularly active after 1850 and that the Church leadership itself really governed in the political as well as the spiritual sphere.[22]

It seems probable, however, that we can draw some balance between these studies. Hansen probably overestimated the importance of the extra-Church Council of Fifty in dictating political affairs, especially in Utah. On the other hand, the Church leadership did control politics, and Latter-day Saints' millennial theology is quite explicit on the need for an organization here on earth to prepare for the second coming. Generally, as Hansen has pointed out, Church members have considered this temporal organization to be the Church itself. If that is so, it required no fundamental shift in principles to abandon a relatively inactive Council of Fifty in order to achieve statehood.

In his *"Americanization" of Utah for Statehood,* Gustive O. Larson has considered the question of the relative importance of polygamy and political dictation in the Gentile opposition to LDS institutions. He was convinced, as Hansen was, that the major objections to late-nineteenth-century Mormonism were leveled not at social institutions, but at political dictation by Church leaders. That Gentiles were concerned about Latter-day Saints' political power is clear. Elsewhere, however, authors such as Victoria Grover-Swank and I have questioned the view shared by both Larson and Hansen that non-Mormons were not particularly concerned with the continued practice of polygamy. The prevailing evidence seems to indicate rather that Victorian Americans saw plural marriage as immoral and as a threat to monogamy and Christian institutions.[23]

Aside from this objection, Larson's book has considerable value as a political and social study. His treatment of the life of the Latter-day Saints hiding out from pursuing U.S. marshals and informers is sensitive and insightful; it required for its writing a thorough understanding of the religious commitment of the Mormon people. In addition, his analysis of the efforts of Republican politicians to woo and win the heretofore antagonistic Latter-day Saints is revealing. Larson's study is significant as part of a reconsideration of the movement of Mormons into the political mainstream of American life and particularly into the close alliance with the Republican party that has characterized the Church leadership in recent years. A great deal more has been added to this subject by the completion of Leo Lyman's doctoral dissertation, which documents the shift of the Mormon leadership to the Republican party during the movement of statehood.[24]

Much of the New Mormon History we have considered to this point has been political or economic history—both rather traditional types. Quite significant, in addition, has been the work on less conventional subjects. In recent years we have seen articles on images of the Mormons, both as they perceived themselves and as they have been perceived. We have studies in intellectual history dealing with doctrines. The New Mormon History has insisted upon an understanding of development, rather than just doctrinal exegesis; and we now have discussions of the development of doctrine, including disputes over doctrinal positions within the Church and considerations of why and how doctrine has differed over time.[25]

Some significant work has been done on the lives and roles of Mormon women. Perhaps the best example is Claudia Bushman's edition of *Mormon Sisters*. Bushman's introductory essay, for instance, demonstrates that in the nineteenth and early twentieth centuries, LDS women participated in Pentecostal experiences that would generally be considered unacceptable today. Such spiritual manifestations as speaking in tongues, mystical experiences, and healings seem to have been common among early Mormon women. During the twentieth century, as conditions and expectations changed, the frequency of these types of experiences has declined.[26]

Since the publication of Kimball Young's *Isn't One Wife Enough?* in 1954, we have sufficient studies of various aspects of plural marriage that an elaborate synthesis is now possible and is long overdue. The use of Young's work is frustrating because of the lack of notes and bibliography as well as his technique of dealing with particular people and families anonymously. We have fairly reliable data on such problems as the fertility of polygamous wives, the reasons for entering plural marriage, the reaction of the community to the practice, and the lives of those who participated in polygamy. It seems clear, however, that a synthetic study using the available materials which conceives the topic broadly is needed. A start in this direction was made by Klaus Hansen in *Mormonism and the American Experience,* which ties the development of plural marriage clearly to Latter-day Saints' theological concerns such as the eternity of the family and the potential Godhood of mortal men and women. An insightful and important comparative study applying the techniques of the social sciences as well as historical analysis is Lawrence Foster's *Religion and Sexuality.* It is perhaps the best analysis of the currently available literature on the topic of Mormon polygamy. An important dimension of Foster's work is the explicit comparison of Mormon polygamy with Shaker celibacy and Oneida complex marriage.[27]

An important study using survey research techniques is Vicki Burgess-Olson's doctoral dissertation. It is somewhat more narrowly conceived than one would desire for a full-scale analysis, but it does consider such matters as family structure, reasons for entering, and status of polygamists. The sample on which the generalizations are based is relatively small (136 families), and not every question asked of the sources could be answered for all families. Nevertheless, we learn that religious commitment and third-party pressure led most to enter polygamy. In addition, we learn that polygamous wives tended to work in a variety of occupations outside the home, much more like modern women than like the nineteenth-century stereotype of the "true" woman.[28]

Another important contribution of the New Mormon History has been to an understanding of the LDS colonization process and of Mormons in outlying areas during the nineteenth century. Perhaps the best study of this type is Charles Peterson's *Take Up Your Mission,* which investigates the settlement and development of the Little Colorado area of northern Arizona. The principal strength of Peterson's monograph is the breadth of its conception. Not an antiquarian study of the settlements, the book considers such problems as the general process of settlement, reasons for mission (settlement) calls, the strengths and weaknesses of the settlers and leaders, and difficulties in meeting communitarian expectations in such programs as the United Order and irrigation development. Peterson's study reveals a complex and hazardous process undertaken by ordinary people with a strong commitment to the LDS Church. It is not the usual faith-promoting story since the warts are there with the dimples. It is a story of failure as well as of success and of backbiting as well as harmony. Carrying the history to about 1890, Peterson details the breakup of the politically and economically solid Arizona communities and the integration of the Mormons into local society.[29]

The flowering of the New Mormon History has been due in part to the availability of reliable primary sources. The best bibliography of those sources is Davis Bitton's *Guide to Mormon Diaries and Autobiographies.*[30] Significant collections of primary sources are found at Brigham Young University, the University of Utah, the Utah State Historical Society, and some depositories outside Utah such as the Huntington Library, the Bancroft Library, and the Library of Congress.

The largest repository of primary materials is the archives of the Church of Jesus Christ of Latter-day Saints in Salt Lake City. Use of the Church archives was quite restricted until the work of Earl E. Olson as Assistant Church Historian in the late 1960s. Access was broadened with the appointment of Leonard J. Arrington as Church Historian and Donald T. Schmidt as Librarian-Archivist in the early 1970s. A number of significant works could probably never have been written without the manuscripts in the Church archives. Examples which come readily to mind are E. B. Long's *The Saints and the Union,* a well-documented study of the relationship between the Mormons and the federal government during the Civil War, and Stanley B. Kimball's *Heber C. Kimball: Mormon Patriarch and Pioneer,*[31] an insightful biography of an important LDS leader.

Evidence indicates, however, that access to Church records is becoming increasingly restricted and that the work of scholars may be suspect. Some researchers report difficulty in securing access to papers of Church officials which were heretofore available for serious study. The abolition of the History Division and its relocation at Brigham Young University as the Joseph Fielding Smith Institute of Church History seems in part to have resulted from hostility to the New Mormon History in some quarters. On the positive side, the change will undoubtedly free the scholars connected with the institute to produce better-balanced studies. Reports indicate that President Spencer W. Kimball and some of the members of the Council of the Twelve are much in favor of the continuation of scholarly studies of the LDS past. Clear signals from some general authorities, including a recent rather undeserved broadside at Mormon historians by a member of the Council of the Twelve, indicate displeasure in some circles.[32]

To summarize work on the Mormons over the past one hundred and thirty years: it seems clear that each group of writers wants the answer to questions uppermost in its own mind. These groups do not correspond to generations nor are they easily categorized into Mormons and non-Mormons. They are, rather, best identified as cultural groups with particular biases and interests that dictate the questions asked and methodology used to secure satisfactory answers.

My own bias favors the work of the New Mormon Historians. From my point of view, the Progressives have been too prone to venerate a lost agrarian past and to posit wedges between the Mormon people and their leaders, when both were engaged in essentially the same enterprise for essentially the same reasons. The Venerative Scholars have been unwilling to probe the difficult areas; and while I realize that it is possible to overemphasize problems and areas of disagreement, this school seems to approach controversies with insufficient forthrightness. In some cases, they seem to overstate the obvious for what appears to be the need to reaffirm the faith of Latter-day Saints for whom they are writing.

Finally, it seems useful to ask what directions Mormon historiography ought to take in the future. The largest single need is currently being filled by Leonard Arrington, who is under commission from Alfred Knopf to write a biography of Brigham Young.[33] A second important need is for insightful and synthetic studies of Mormonism in the twentieth century. We have a rather sketchy beginning in the work of James Allen and Richard Cowan, together with the chapters in Arrington and Davis Bitton in *The Mormon Experience* and Allen and Glen Leonard in *The Story of the Latter-day Saints*. Jan Shipps is currently at work on such a study, and if her recent work on the creation of the Mormon world is any indication, it should be interpretive and insightful. We need a study of urban Mormonism since Mormons in the urban setting have become the rule rather than the exception. Some of the work of Armand Mauss on LDS attitudes is suggestive of questions that need to be probed. Still, much work needs to be done, and done in both a workmanlike and insightful way.[34]

Third, we need studies in which social, cultural, political, and economic history are woven together to probe the lives of the LDS people. A study of the LDS family is one example. In this same vein, studies of the work and lives of Mormon bishops and stake presidents are needed, together with general considerations of the development of wards and stakes. These must be broadly conceived, and the scholars who undertake them must use the tools of the social and behavioral sciences and of religious studies to make them of sufficiently insightful content to satisfy the need for comparative analysis.[35]

Fourth, similar studies are needed of a broad range of doctrinal and experiential topics. My studies of Wilford Woodruff and of the Progressive reinterpretation of LDS doctrine, Gary Bergera's discussions of the confrontation between Brigham Young and Orson Pratt, and James Allen's treatment of the changing doctrinal emphasis found in Joseph Smith's first vision are suggestions for the directions such studies might take, but they are admittedly incomplete and certainly not definitive. We need to know when and why the Pentecostal experiences so evident in the early LDS movement ceased to be acceptable and when and why the premillennial fervor of the early years abated. James Allen's work on the life of William Clayton offers some suggestions, as does some of the work done by Claudia Bushman and others on Mormon women, but certainly they too are not definitive. We need, also, to understand better the internalization by the LDS community of general American attitudes on so many issues, and why those attitudes seem to coexist with an embattled and communitarian mentality seeing Mormonism as the last bastion of basic Christian morality.[36]

Fifth, we also need to understand more of the method of interaction of the General Authorities: among themselves, with the local Church leaders, and with the general Church membership. Clearly, both the Progressive image of a sharp cleavage between leaders and people and the Venerative Scholar's image of little or no conflict are hardly credible. Michael Quinn's prosopographical work on the General Authorities has revealed some important aspects of the interaction within the hierarchy, but more work is needed.[37]

Given the number and variety of scholars currently at work on the history of the Latter-day Saints, it seems probable that the 1980s will provide answers to at least some of these questions. As conditions change, new questions will undoubtedly arise crying for satisfactory answers, and many old questions will have to be asked again since the answers satisfactory to one group of people may be found incomplete by another.[38]

Notes

1. The categories of the Old Mormon History and the early work on the Progressive School are based in part on Leonard J. Arrington, "Scholarly Studies of Mormonism in the Twentieth Century," *Dialogue: A Journal of Mormon Thought* 1 (Spring 1966): 15–32. The term "New Mormon History" seems to have been used first by Moses Rischin in *The American West* 5 (March 1969): 49. It was elaborated and explicated in more detail by Robert B. Flanders in "Some Reflections on the New Mormon History," *Dialogue* 9 (Spring 1974): 34–41. The two tensions that Richard Bushman elaborated in "Faithful History," *Dialogue* 4 (Winter 1969): 18, first between "the Church and the world," and second "between God and the Church," seem to correspond to some of the questions asked by the Venerative Scholars and the New Mormon Historians. I have benefited from reading the foregoing and a number of other historiographical essays, including: Leonard J. Arrington, "The Search for Truth and Meaning in Mormon History," *Dialogue* 3 (Summer 1968): 56–66; Rodman W. Paul, "The Mormons as a Theme in Western Historical Writing," *Journal of American History* 54 (December 1967): 511–23; Richard D. Poll, "God and Man in History," *Dialogue* 7 (Spring 1972): 101–9; Paul M. Edwards, "The Irony of Mormon History," *Utah Historical Quarterly* 41 (Autumn 1973): 393–409; and from Marvin S. Hill's "Survey: The Historiography of Mormonism," *Church History* 28

(December 1959): 418–26, though Hill's generalizations about the short-comings of Mormon historiography seem dated by the work of the intervening twenty-three years. In addition, I have benefited from the bibliographic essays in James B. Allen and Glen M. Leonard, *The Story of the Latter-day Saints* (Salt Lake City: Deseret Book, 1976); and Leonard J. Arrington and Davis Bitton, *The Mormon Experience* (New York: Knopf, 1979). Also, my work with James B. Allen on "The Mormons in the Mountain West: A Selected Bibliography," *Arizona and the West* 9 (Winter 1967): 365–84 proved helpful.

2. John H. Beadle (ed.), *Brigham's Destroying Angel: Being the Life, Confessions, and Startling Disclosures of the Notorious Bill Hickman, the Danite Chief of Utah* (New York: G. A. Crofutt, 1872). Other exposés include: Ann Eliza Young, *Wife No. 19; or, The Story of a Life of Bondage* (Hartford, Conn.: Dustin, Gilman and Co., 1876); and W. W. Bishop (ed.), *Mormonism Unveiled: The Life and Confessions of John D. Lee* (St. Louis: Bryan, Brand and Co., 1877). The most generally used history of the LDS Church of this genre is William A. Linn, *The Story of the Mormons* (New York: Macmillan, 1902).

3. T. B. H. Stenhouse, *The Rocky Mountain Saints: A Full and Complete History of the Mormons, from the First Vision of Joseph Smith to the Last Courtship of Brigham Young* (New York: D. Appleton and Co., 1873). Another example is Frank J. Cannon and Harvey J. O'Higgins, *Under the Prophet in Utah: The National Menace of a Political Priestcraft* (Boston: C. M. Clark, 1911); William Wise, *Massacre at Mountain Meadows: An American Legend and a Monumental Crime* (New York: Thomas Y. Crowell, 1976). Another example of this school is Stanley Hirshson, *Lion of the Lord: A Biography of Brigham Young* (New York: Knopf, 1969).

4. B. H. Roberts, *The Life of John Taylor* (Salt Lake City: George Q. Cannon and Sons, 1892); Preston Nibley, *Brigham Young: The Man and His Work* (Salt Lake City: Deseret News, 1936). More recently, although this type of work has dealt with such formerly taboo subjects as plural marriage, it often neglects recent scholarship on controversial topics and removes the complexity from the lives of its subjects. See for instance: Francis M. Gibbons, *Brigham Young: Modern Moses, Prophet of God* (Salt Lake City: Deseret Book, 1981) and Gibbons, *Heber J. Grant: Man of Steel, Prophet of God* (Salt Lake City: Deseret Book, 1979). Textbooks representing this genre include Joseph Fielding Smith, *Essentials in Church History*, 25th ed. (Salt Lake City: Deseret Book, 1972), frequently revised and republished; and William E. Berrett, *The Restored Church*, 7th ed. (Salt Lake City: LDS Dept. of Education, 1949), also frequently revised and republished.

5. John W. Gunnison, *The Mormons or Latter-day Saints, in the Valley of the Great Salt Lake* (Philadelphia: Lippincott, Grambo and Co., 1852); Richard F. Burton, *The City of the Saints and Across the Rocky Mountains to California* (London: Longman, Green, Longman and Roberts, 1861). There are numerous other books of this type, including Jules Remy and Julius Brenchley, *A Journey to Great Salt Lake City,* 2 vols. (London: W. Jeffs, 1861); Samuel Bowles, *Across the Continent: A Summer Journey . . .* (Springfield, Mass.: S. Bowles, 1865). Recent examples of this genre include William J. Whalen, *The Latter-day Saints in the Modern Day World* (New York: John Day, 1964); Robert Mullen, *The Latter-day Saints: The Mormons Yesterday and Today* (New York: Doubleday, 1966); and Wallace Turner, *The Mormon Establishment* (Boston: Houghton Mifflin, 1966), all journalistic accounts.

6. B. H. Roberts, *A Comprehensive History of the Church of Jesus Christ of Latter-day Saints, Century 1,* 6 vols. (Salt Lake City: Deseret, 1930). The best representative of a text in this style is Russel R. Rich, *Ensign to the Nations: A History of the Church From 1846 to the Present* (Provo, Utah: Brigham Young University Publications, 1972).

7. Milton R. Hunter, *Brigham Young, the Colonizer* (Salt Lake City: Deseret News, 1940). Another example of venerative scholarship begun as a dissertation is Richard Vetterli, *Mormonism, Americanism, and Politics* (Salt Lake City: Ensign Publishing Company, 1961).

8. Hugh Nibley, *Sounding Brass* (Salt Lake City: Bookcraft, 1963). Cf. Young, *Wife No. 19*; Irving Wallace, *The Twenty-seventh Wife* (New York: Simon and Schuster, 1961).

9. Truman G. Madsen, *B. H. Roberts: Defender of the Faith* (Salt Lake City: Bookcraft, 1980).

10. Lowry Nelson, *The Mormon Village: A Pattern and Technique of Land Settlement* (Salt Lake City: University of Utah Press, 1952), esp. pp. 275–85; Nels Anderson, *Desert Saints: The Mormon Frontier in Utah,* 2d ed. (Chicago: University of Chicago Press, 1966), esp. pp. 152–54.

11. Ephraim E. Ericksen, *The Psychological and Ethical Aspects of Mormon Group Life* (Salt Lake City: University of Utah Press, 1975; first published 1922), esp. pp. 98–99. Though I have included Thomas O'Dea with the New Mormon Historians, one essay completed shortly before his death suggests the possibility of the inclusion of some of his work with the Progressive Scholars. "Sources of Strain in Mormon History Reconsidered," in Marvin S. Hill and James B. Allen (eds.), *Mormonism and American Culture* (New York: Harper and Row, 1972), pp. 147–67.

12. Samuel W. Taylor, *Rocky Mountain Empire: The Latter-day Saints Today* (New York: Macmillan, 1978).

13. Mark P. Leone, *Roots of Modern Mormonism* (Cambridge: Harvard University Press, 1979).

14. Richard Hofstadter, *Anti-intellectualism in American Life* (New York: Knopf, 1963; paperbound ed., Random House/Vintage, 1966); on the question of Mormon anti-intellectualism, see Davis Bitton, "Anti-Intellectualism in Mormon History," and James B. Allen, "Thoughts on Anti-Intellectualism: A Response," *Dialogue* 1 (Autumn 1966): 111–40.

15. See, for example, Marilyn Warenski, *Patriarchs and Politics: The Plight of the Mormon Women* (New York: McGraw-Hill, 1978); Laurel B. Andrew, *The Early Temples of the Mormons: The Architecture of the Millennial Kingdom in the American West* (Albany: State University of New York Press, 1978); Paul L. Anderson, "William Harrison Folsom: Pioneer Architect . . . ," *Utah Historical Quarterly* 43 (Summer 1975): 240–59. For a more informed essay on the symbolism of the Salt Lake Temple, see C. Mark Hamilton, "The Salt Lake Temple: A Symbolic Statement of Mormon Doctrine," in Thomas G. Alexander (ed.), *The Mormon People: Their Character and Traditions* (Provo, Utah: Brigham Young University Press, 1980), pp. 103–27.

16. Leo Marx, *The Machine in the Garden: Technology and the Pastoral Ideal in America* (New York: Oxford University Press, 1964; paperbound ed., 1967); Henry Nash Smith, *Virgin Land: The American West as Symbol and Myth* (Cambridge: Harvard University Press, 1950; paperbound ed., 1970).

17. Leonard J. Arrington, *Great Basin Kingdom: An Economic History of the Latter-day Saints, 1830–1900* (Cambridge: Harvard University Press, 1958; paperbound ed., Lincoln: University of Nebraska Press, 1966); Thomas F. O'Dea, *The Mormons* (Chicago: University of Chicago Press, 1957; paperbound ed., 1964); Klaus J. Hansen, *Quest for Empire: The Political Kingdom of God and the Council of Fifty in Mormon History* (East Lansing: Michigan State University Press, 1967).

18. Juanita Brooks, *The Mountain Meadows Massacre*, 2d ed. (Norman: University of Oklahoma Press, 1970; 1st ed., 1950).

19. J. R. Kearl, Clayne L. Pope, and Larry T. Wimmer, "Household Wealth in a Settlement Economy: Utah, 1850–1870," *Journal of Economic History* 40 (September 1980): 477–96; L. Dwight Israelsen, "An Economic Analysis of the United Order," *BYU Studies* 18 (Summer 1978): 536–62. For a detailed analysis of the United Order movement and Mormon communitarianism, see Leonard J. Arrington, Feramorz Y. Fox, and Dean L. May, *Building the City of God: Community and Cooperation Among the*

Mormons (Salt Lake City: Deseret Book, 1976). On the change of one LDS corporation in the twentieth century, see Leonard J. Arrington, *Beet Sugar in the West: A History of the Utah-Idaho Sugar Company, 1891-1966* (Seattle: University of Washington Press, 1966). A recent study of a single Mormon community lends support to the private enterprise interpretation of Mormon community life. Michael S. Raber, "Religious Polity and Local Production: The Origins of a Mormon Town" (Ph.D. diss., Yale University, 1978).

20. Norman F. Furniss, *The Mormon Conflict, 1850-1859* (New Haven: Yale University Press, 1959).

21. Hansen, *Quest for Empire, passim.*

22. D. Michael Quinn, "The Council of Fifty and Its Members, 1844 to 1945," *BYU Studies* 20 (Winter 1980): 163-97. Ernest Sandeen, in *The Roots of Fundamentalism: British and American Millenarianism, 1800-1930* (Chicago: University of Chicago Press, 1970), p. 302, raises some questions about Hansen's understanding of millennialism. See also Louis G. Reinwand, "An Interpretive Study of Mormon Millennialism During the Nineteenth Century with Emphasis on Millennial Developments in Utah" (M.A. thesis, Brigham Young University, 1971), for a general study of millennialism. This should be reviewed against the research of Grant Underwood, "Seminal vs. Sesquicentennial Saints: A Look at Mormon Millennialism," *Dialogue* 14 (Spring 1981): 32-44.

23. Gustive O. Larson, *The "Americanization" of Utah for Statehood* (San Marino, Calif.: Huntington Library, 1971); Thomas G. Alexander, "On Utah's Struggle to Be Accepted by Victorian America," *Brigham Young University Today* 27 (December 1973): 10-11; Alexander, "A Conflict of Perceptions: Ulysses S. Grant and the Mormons," *Newsletter of the Ulysses S. Grant Association* 7 (July 1971): 29-42; Victoria Grover-Swank, "Sex, Sickness and Statehood: The Influence of Victorian Medical Opinion on Self-Government in Utah" (M.A. thesis, Brigham Young University, 1980). On the conflict between Mormons and non-Mormons in Idaho, see Merle W. Wells, *Anti-Mormonism in Idaho, 1872-92* (Provo, Utah: Brigham Young University Press, 1978). Views of the conflict from the Gentile point of view will be found in Robert Joseph Dwyer, *The Gentile Comes to Utah: A Study in Religious and Social Conflict (1862-1890),* 2d ed., rev. (Salt Lake City: Western Epics, 1971); and A. J. Simmonds, *The Gentile Comes to Cache Valley: A Study of the Logan Apostasies of 1874 and the Establishment of Non-Mormon Churches in Cache Valley, 1873-1913* (Logan, Utah: Utah State University Press, 1976).

24. For additional information on the Latter-day Saints in politics in the period of transition and the twentieth century, see Milton R. Merrill, *Reed Smoot: Utah Politician* (Logan, Utah: Utah State University Press, 1953); Edward Leo Lyman, "Isaac Trumbo and the Politics of Utah Statehood," *Utah Historical Quarterly* 41 (Spring 1973): 128–49; and Lyman, "The Mormon Quest for Utah Statehood" (Ph.D. diss., University of California at Riverside, 1981); Gene A. Sessions (ed.), *Mormon Democrat: The Religious and Political Memoirs of James Henry Moyle* (Salt Lake City: Historical Department of the Church of Jesus Christ of Latter-day Saints, 1975); Jan Shipps, "Utah Comes of Age Politically: A Study of the State's Politics in the Early Years of the Twentieth Century," *Utah Historical Quarterly* 35 (Spring 1967): 91-111; Shipps, "The Mormons in Politics: The First Hundred Years" (Ph.D. diss., University of Colorado, 1965); and Edward and Frederick H. Schapsmeier, *Ezra Taft Benson and the Politics of Agriculture: The Eisenhower Years, 1953-1961* (Danville, Ill.: Interstate Printers and Publishers, 1975).

25. Leonard J. Arrington, "An Economic Interpretation of the Word of Wisdom," *BYU Studies* 1 (Winter 1959): 37–49; Arrington and Jon Haupt, "Intolerable Zion: The Image of Mormonism in Nineteenth Century American Literature," *Western Humanities Review* 22 (Summer 1968): 243-60; Thomas G. Alexander, "The Reconstruction of Mormon Doctrine: From Joseph Smith to Progressive Theology," *Sunstone* 5 (July–August 1980): 24-33; Gary J. Bergera, "The Orson Pratt-Brigham Young Controversies: Conflict with the Quorums, 1853 to 1868," *Dialogue* 13 (Summer 1980): 7-49; Davis Bitton, "Double Jeopardy: Visual Images of Mormon Women to 1914," *Utah Historical Quarterly* 46 (Spring 1978): 184-202; Bitton, "Mormonism's Encounter with Spiritualism," *Journal of Mormon History* 1 (1974): 39-50; Bitton, "The Ritualization of Mormon History," *Utah Historical Quarterly* 43 (Winter 1975): 67-85; Bitton and Gary L. Bunker, "Mischievous Puck and the Mormons, 1904-1907," *BYU Studies* 18 (Summer 1978): 504-19. Bitton and Bunker are currently at work on a volume dealing with visual images of the Mormons.

26. Claudia L. Bushman (ed.), *Mormon Sisters: Women in Early Utah* (Cambridge, Mass.: Emmeline Press, 1976); see also Vicki Burgess-Olson (ed.), *Sister Saints* (Provo, Utah: Brigham Young University Press, 1978).

27. Kimball Young, *Isn't One Wife Enough?* (New York: Henry Holt, 1954); for an extended critical review of the literature of Mormon polygamy, see Davis Bitton, "Mormon Polygamy: A Review Article," *Journal of Mormon History* 4 (1977): 101-18; perhaps the best short article on the subject

is Stanley Ivins, "Notes on Mormon Polygamy," *Western Humanities Review* 10 (Summer 1956): 229–39; Klaus J. Hansen, *Mormonism and the American Experience* (Chicago: University of Chicago Press, 1981); Lawrence Foster, *Religion and Sexuality: Three American Communal Experiments of the Nineteenth Century* (New York: Oxford University Press, 1981).

28. Vicki Burgess-Olson, "Family Structure and Dynamics in Early Utah Mormon Families, 1847–1885" (Ph.D. diss., Northwestern University, 1975). This view has been questioned by Maureen Beecher in "Women's Work on the Frontier," *Utah Historical Quarterly* 49 (Summer 1981): 276–90.

29. Charles S. Peterson, *Take Up Your Mission: Mormon Colonizing Along the Little Colorado River, 1870–1900* (Tucson: University of Arizona Press, 1973); other worthwhile studies of colonization and regional development include: Donald W. Meinig, "The Mormon Culture Region: Strategies and Patterns in the Geography of the American West, 1847–1964," *Annals of the Association of American Geographers* 55 (June 1965): 191–220; Andrew Karl Larson, *I Was Called to Dixie: The Virgin River Basin; Unique Experiences in Mormon Pioneering* (Salt Lake City: University of Utah Press, 1961); Joel E. Ricks and Everett L. Cooley (eds.), *The History of a Valley: Cache Valley, Utah-Idaho* (Logan, Utah: Utah State University Press, 1956).

30. Davis Bitton, *Guide to Mormon Diaries and Autobiographies* (Provo, Utah: Brigham Young University Press, 1977).

31. E. B. Long, *The Saints and the Union: Utah Territory During the Civil War* (Urbana: University of Illinois Press, 1981); Stanley B. Kimball, *Heber C. Kimball: Mormon Patriarch and Pioneer* (Urbana: University of Illinois Press, 1981).

32. Boyd K. Packer, "The Mantle Is Far, Far Greater Than the Intellect," *BYU Studies* 21 (Summer 1981): 259–78.

33. I have not considered biography extensively in this essay since the biographies of Mormon subjects tend to follow the person quite closely and often fail to pay sufficient attention to the broader context in which the leader operated or the general historical literature of the period under consideration. Some of the better biographies include Andrew Karl Larson, *Erastus Snow: The Life of a Missionary and Pioneer for the Early Mormon Church* (Salt Lake City: University of Utah Press, 1971); Juanita Brooks, *John D. Lee: Zealot, Pioneer Builder, Scapegoat*, rev. ed. (Glendale, Calif.: Arthur H. Clark, 1972); Harold Schindler, *Orrin Porter Rockwell: Man of God, Son of Thunder* (Salt Lake City: University of Utah Press, 1966); and Leonard J. Arrington, *Charles C. Rich: Mormon General and Western Frontiersman* (Provo, Utah: Brigham Young University Press, 1974). James

Allen is currently at work on a biography of William Clayton which interprets his religious experiences and millennial expectations.

34. James B. Allen and Richard O. Cowan, *Mormonism in the Twentieth Century,* 2d ed. (Provo, Utah: Brigham Young University Press, 1967); Armand L. Mauss, "Moderation in All Things: Political and Social Outlooks of Modern Urban Mormons," *Dialogue* 7 (Spring 1972): 57–69.

35. Kenneth W. Godfrey has begun a study of the monogamous Mormon family and presented some of his conclusions in "The Mormon Monogamous Family, 1852–1890," paper presented at the symposium "A Mosaic of Mormon Culture," Brigham Young University, October 2, 1980.

36. James B. Allen, "One Man's Nauvoo: William Clayton's Experience in Mormon Illinois," *Journal of Mormon History* 6 (1979): 37–59; Allen, "Emergence of a Fundamental: The Expanding Role of Joseph Smith's First Vision in Mormon Religious Thought," *ibid.* 7 (1980): 43–61; Bergera, "The Orson Pratt-Brigham Young Controversies"; Linda King Newell, D. Michael Quinn, and Irene M. Bates, "A Gift Given, a Gift Taken: Washing, Anointing, and Blessing the Sick Among Mormon Women," and "Response," *Sunstone* 6 (September–October 1981): 16–28. Thomas G. Alexander, "Wilford Woodruff and the Changing Nature of Mormon Religious Experience," *Church History* 45 (March 1976): 56–69.

37. D. Michael Quinn, "The Mormon Hierarchy, 1832–1932: An American Elite" (Ph.D. diss., Yale University, 1976).

38. It is important to realize that much of the work of the New Mormon Historians adopts models from the social and behavioral sciences and from religious studies. Such models are abstractions used to provide analytical and comparative insights and to promote interdisciplinary, intercultural, and interreligious understanding. The use of such models has been criticized in contrasting and contradictory ways by some supporters of the Venerative Historians and the pious group of the Old Mormon History, on the one hand, and by some supporters of the Progressive School and the anti-Mormon group of the Old Mormon History, on the other. The former have argued that the use of models is illegitimate because they take religious concepts and reinterpret them in secular terms or introduce religious terms foreign to Mormonism. The latter have argued that such models discredit the Mormon faith because they demonstrate similarities with other movements and thus disprove the uniqueness and divinity of Mormonism. Both criticisms are unfounded, since they erroneously assume the reification of an abstraction and the equivalence of the model and the actual condition.

Chapter Sixteen

Sandra L. Myres

Women in the West

Nearly one hundred years after Turner's famous 1893 essay on the significance of the frontier, Americans still find the frontier experience exciting and significant, and they are still discovering new aspects of that experience which were not explored by Turner or his successors. Turner's approach to history was primarily geographic, political, and economic; and while Turnerian scholars subjected large sections of the American West to minute analysis and interpretation, they also bypassed many essential areas.

Nowhere was this trend more apparent than in the field of women's history.[1] Until recently, most western historians have not considered women a part of the frontier experience. Turner's frontiers were as devoid of women as the Great Plains were devoid of trees. Turner's pioneers were explorers, fur trappers, miners, ranchers, farmers—all of them male; and succeeding generations of western historians continued to interpret the westering movement as primarily a male enterprise in which women played a largely invisible and subordinate role. After all, as T. A. Larson pointed out in a 1974 article, because women "did not lead expeditions, command troops, build railroads, drive cattle, ride Pony Express, find gold, amass great wealth, get elected to high public office, rob stages or lead lynch mobs," most writers assumed they did not play a significant role in the building of the West.[2]

Ever since Turner's essay appeared, American high school and college students have read about the "winning of the West" in a series of well-written and often exciting texts that captured the adventure and romance, as well as part of the reality, of the westward movement, but which dismissed women as "invisible, few in number, and not important to the process of taming a wilderness." "I define the American Pioneer," historian George Parker wrote in 1922, "as the *man* who . . . crossed the mountains . . . swept on through the passes . . . solidified his settlement. . . . To me, this *man* reflects the character of the most effective single human movement in history" (italics mine).[3]

This male-dominated trend has continued. A 1974 survey of standard textbooks used in college and university courses in western history concluded that these texts "all come close to ignoring women entirely." As recently as 1976, a textbook on the West listed only three women (Helen Hunt Jackson, Queen Liliuokalani, and Sacajawea) in the index. Even Richard Bartlett, whose 1974 social history of the frontier paid lip-service to women's participation in the westward movement, concluded that "No one has even questioned, let alone analyzed the masculinity of the frontier society. Since it is as obvious as the sun in the daytime, the subject has not been discussed." Nor has the monographic literature been much more helpful. "Indeed," as Richard Jensen pointed out in a recent article, "it takes exhaustive searching in the pre-1970 literature to find even minor monographs on . . . frontier women." Again, as recently as 1979, a major new interpretive work on the overland trails contained only a few brief references to women.[4]

Even when historians acknowledged the presence of women on the western frontiers, they often portrayed them in ethereal, mysterious terms or presented a stereotypic portrait as false as that of the Hollywood Indian. Unfortunately, most of these perceptions of westering women were shaped by male writers who did not read what women themselves wrote about the West. Or, if they did read the many journals and reminiscences written by women, they chose to ignore them in favor of more dramatic legends and myths. Perhaps no image in American history and literature is more deeply imbedded in the American mind than that of the frightened and tearful woman wrenched from home and hearth and dragged off into the terrible West where she was condemned to a life of lonely terror among savage beasts and rapine Indians. Overworked and overbirthed, she lived through a long succession of dreary days of toil and loneliness until, at last, driven past the point of sanity, she resigned herself to a hard life and an early death. This tragic figure appeared so often that she assumed almost legendary status. From Hawthorne to Hemingway, American literature is replete with examples. Typical of this stereotype was Hamlin Garland's description of his mother: "Her life had been always on the border—she knew nothing of civilization's splendor of song and story. All her toilsome, monotonous days rushed through my mind with a roar like a file of gray birds in the night—how little—how tragically small her joys, and how black her sorrows, her toil, her tedium."[5]

Another part of this portrait was the isolation of the woman cut off from her own kind, from the network of womankind and sisterhood. The space, the wind, the emptiness of the prairies and plains drove her to melancholia and eventually to suicide or to an insane asylum. Such women appeared in the novels of O. E. Rölvaag and Dorothy Scarborough, and their story was retold in the pictures and newspaper accounts of insanity, suicide, and violent death in the recently published *Wisconsin Death Trip*. The image was that of a "refined lady" of a sensitive and emotional nature who, unable to adjust to the frontier way of life, was "dashed and buffeted by the winds of western life till her frail body broke."[6]

Unfortunately, these literary stereotypes found their way into historical portraits of frontier women. "It is a well known fact," one author wrote in 1940, "that women, as a rule find it harder to leave friends, relatives, and associations than do men." Women, especially western women, according to another male "authority," were conservative, home-loving creatures, "hating with a passion those three concomitants of the western frontier—poverty, physical hardship and danger." It was women, charged another historian, who were responsible for the "retreat from the frontier. . . . These solitary women, longing to catch a glimpse of one of their own sex, swept their eyes over the boundless prairie and thought of the old home in the East. They stared and stared across space with nothing to halt their gaze over the monotonous expanse. . . . Hollow-eyed, tired, and discouraged. . . . Some begged their husbands to hitch up the team, turn the wagon tongue eastward, and leave the accursed plains."[7]

Recently feminist historians have embellished this image with psycho-analytical overtones. Women's lives in the American West, one wrote, were dominated by the "patriarchy of masculine power and prerogatives." Women, he declared, "always controlled . . . always confined," resigned themselves to "a mild kind of rural American purdah." Another feminist historian, in a gloomy analysis of women's diaries, concluded that women were generally reluctant to go West, that their life there, whether on an isolated farm or in a frontier community, was one of unending toil and unnatural labor, that suicides and insanity were common, and that their trail journals "with their relentless record-keeping of the graves passed, were ultimately indictments of men."[8]

Concomitant with the image of the weary and forlorn frontier wife, a sort of helpless helpmate, was the stereotype of the westering woman as sturdy helpmate and civilizer of the frontier. She, too, was reluctant to go West, but once the decision was made, she trod westward with grim-faced determination, clad in gingham or linsey-woolsey, her face wreathed in a sunbonnet, baby at breast, rifle at the ready, bravely awaited unknown dangers and dedicated herself to removing wilderness from both man and land and restoring civilization as quickly as possible. She was a woman of some culture and refinement, "domestic, submissive but sturdy, moral," the guardian of all that was fine and decent. She was a hardy heroine, an example for others of her sex, and her story was familiar to nineteenth-century readers. An 1850s description of Catherine Sevier was typical of this genre: "tall in stature, erect in person, stately in walk with small piercing blue eyes, raven locks, a Roman nose, and firmness in her mouth and every feature. . . . It could be said of her without any question that she 'reverenced her husband' and she instilled the same Scriptural sentiment in the minds of his children. She relieved him of his cares at home, and applauded his devotion to the service of the people."[9]

The sturdy helpmate could fight Indians, kill the bear in the barn, make two pots of lye soap, and do a week's wash before dinnertime and still have the cabin neat, the children clean, and a good meal on the table when her husband came in from the fields—all without a word of complaint or even a hint of an ache or a pain. She was the Madonna of the Prairies, the Brave Pioneer Mother, the Gentle Tamer so familiar in western literature. We encountered her in James Fenimore Cooper's Esther and Emerson Hough's Molly Wingate, and we find her still in historian Richard Bartlett's 1974 portrait of the pioneer woman: "The new country woman held her head high, and her bright eyes searched the horizon for what lay ahead. She shared with her husband a faith in their future. . . . She was a builder, along with her husband; she knew her value."[10]

If this image seems more positive than that of the overburdened drudge, it still has its negative aspects. The Gentle Tamer was still fearful if somewhat self-sufficient, and she had to be protected from danger. Such women feared and hated wilderness and thus, by extension, they feared and hated Indians and other wild creatures. It was these women who, in their fear, insisted on killing or at least removing the "savage" with whom the lone white male once had a positive relationship. This popular image, according to historian Dawn Gherman, "led recent writers to identify the 'invasion of feminine sentiment' into the wilderness as the major cause of historic racism in America." Gherman went on to explore, in depth, the literary and historical images which led to this conclusion, and she pointed out that modern literary critics would go so far as to have us believe that it was the entrance of women into the wilderness that destroyed "the second Paradise" and brought about the destruction of both the woods and the Indians.[11]

The arrival of the Gentle Tamers in the wilderness also curtailed male freedom and forced unwanted control upon men's self-imposed rejection of civilized values. The frontier was a fine, free, male place until the petticoat pioneers arrived bringing law and order, cleanliness, and religion. Once women arrived, there was no more "zestful combat" with frontier dangers. "And to destroy these traditional testers of human endurance was to destroy something male in the race." Psychohistorian Erik Erikson went one step further and named the pioneer mother as the historical prototype of that twentieth-century horror, "Mom."[12]

There was yet a third image of the western woman prevalent in American literature, that of the "bad woman." Sometimes she was the backwoods belle, "hefty, grotesque, and mean with a pistol." Like the Prairie Rose described by nineteenth-century army officer and explorer Randolph Marcy, she was occasionally shocking in her speech and manners and "just as wild, untamed, and free from tyrannical conventionalities of society as the mustangs that roamed over the adjacent prairies." Or she was the soiled dove or female bandit, the Calamity Jane who drank, smoked, and cursed and was handy with a poker deck, a six-gun, and a horse. She was the antithesis of the civilizer-helpmate; she was more masculine than feminine in her behavior, but she always had "a heart of pure gold." In a less malevolent image, she was the backwoodswoman of eastern writers, unlettered, crude of manner, super-stitious. She displayed many strange habits of speech and dress; and although she was often kind and considerate, the image she projected was still primar-ily negative.[13] There were, and are, other images of the frontier woman, of course, but they were derived from these basic stereotypes.

Views of frontierswomen, then, were numerous and often contradictory. Whatever the frontier, women were there, but they were described by semi-romanticized and generally negative stereotypes that obscured their real lives and character. Such images were not based entirely on retrospective twentieth-century views. Rather, most of the stereotypes derived from nineteenth-century ideas of what women should be—"kind, gentle, passive, religious, domestic, pure, and refined." Nineteenth-century writers also portrayed westering as a male enterprise, and most doubted the ability of women to withstand the hardships of the westward journey and the early settlement period. Horace Greeley's advice to "Go West, young man" meant exactly that. Pioneering was fine for young, single males; but it was, as one eastern paper advised, "palpable homicide to attempt to send women and children."[14] The West was full of dangers, and delicate women should not be exposed to the suffering imposed by wilderness conditions.

Women did go West, of course, and they contended successfully with the problems imposed by frontier conditions. But it was assumed that women resented the new tasks that they were called upon to perform on the frontier and that they went West reluctantly, forced by male ambition to leave their comfortable homes and dear friends. The lesson of a later day was clear: the West was "hell on women and horses." This viewpoint dominated many nineteenth-century novels and short stories and led one modern historian to conclude: "The standard feminine figure in literature hates to leave civilization, is repelled by the wilderness landscape and hates and fears Indians." Another favorite theme of nineteenth-century novelists was the "bad girls." Penny dreadfuls and dime novels (many of them written by women) portrayed such interesting female characters as Hurricane Nell, the Trapper's Bride, and Zilla Fitz-James, the Bandit Queen. These works helped to enhance the reputation of "real" western women like Calamity Jane and Belle Starr.[15]

A few nineteenth-century histories also dealt with western women. Their authors displayed a strong "pioneer mother" bias similar to that in the description of Catherine Sevier quoted above. They pictured pioneer women as perfect ladies who were nonetheless capable of defending home and family and "holding the fort" until their husbands returned and who also brought enlightenment and civilization to the benighted redfolks and other denizens of the "dark and bloody" frontier.[16]

Early twentieth-century historians generally continued the established nineteenth-century patterns in describing frontier women or, following in the Turnerian tradition, ignored women as a part of the westward movement. Finally, during the 1940s and 1950s, a few new, scholarly studies of western women began to appear. Unfortunately, most were written from government documents and men's accounts or used only a few carefully selected women's journals and reminiscences. For example, Georgia Willis Read's "Women and Children on the Oregon-California Trail" (1944) was based on official reports and the observations of J. Goldsborough Bruff. Nancy Ross's *Westward the Women* (1944) and Helena Huntington Smith's "Pioneers in Petticoats" (1959) did use women's accounts; but their sample was very limited, and their interpretations, although more realistic than the nineteenth-century versions, were within the "brave pioneer mother" tradition.[17]

In a similar vein, Dee Brown portrayed western women as civilizers and culture bearers, an attitude reflected in his title, *The Gentle Tamers* (1958). Ray Allen Billington, who ignored women entirely in his popular and widely adopted textbook, *Westward Expansion* (first edition 1949), included two brief pages on the role of women in *America's Frontier Heritage* (1966).

Billington suggested that the frontier experience altered the relationship between men and women, but only insofar as women were more valued on the frontier. Like many other historians of the period, Billington believed that women were the "harbingers of civilization" and "desireable helpmates." Because they were few in number, "they were to be sought after, venerated, and pampered to a degree unrecognizable in areas with a more equitable ratio of the sexes."[18]

Other historians presented a different view. Walter Prescott Webb, after ignoring women in the first five hundred pages of *The Great Plains* (1931), finally included them among the "Mysteries of the Great Plains." According to Webb, the Plains were "strictly a man's country." Women dreaded and feared them, and they often refused to go West because frontier life, at least on the Plains, "precluded the little luxuries that women love and that are so necessary to them." William Sprague's book-length study, *Women and the West* (1940), utilized a number of women's source materials, but Sprague, like Webb, was influenced by the prevailing stereotypes of frontier women. For example, he contended that women suffered more than men from the fevers and ague prevalent in many frontier areas, that they endured greater hardships than men, and that their "real difficulties" came when they were deprived of "shipping facilities, material luxury and attention by men." A similar interpretation of frontier women as deprived and discouraged "drudges" was presented in Everett Dick's anecdotal *The Sod-House Frontier* (1937).[19]

In recent years, the interest in women's history has led to the publication of new studies of frontier women. A number of articles dealing with women's role on the overland trails and on the frontier have appeared in historical journals within the past decade, and several journals devoted entire issues to western women's history. Unfortunately, some of these authors, in an attempt to demolish the old myths about westering women, succeeded only in creating new ones.[20] Several authors, writing from a militant, feminist perspective, pictured western women as the victims of male exploitation and a male-dominated social ethic.

These authors contended that women on the frontiers were forced into unfamiliar, "demeaning" roles, and that although women in the western settlements continued to try to reinstate a culture of domesticity, their work as virtual hired hands prevented them from either returning to older, more familiar roles in the social structure or from creating positive new ones. Unable "to appropriate their new work to their own ends and advantage," the authors of one such article concluded, frontier women "remained estranged from their function as able bodies." A similar interpretation was offered by Lillian Schlissel in a 1977 article. Schlissel also saw a conflict between women's sense of "proper sphere" and the new roles and conditions imposed by the frontier. Women, she believed, "understood the westward migration as a masculine enterprise." Although Schlissel conceded that the frontier "seems in later stages to have yielded to newer social and legal forms for women," she also suggested that the frontier "worked against" women and failed to offer as many new opportunities for them as it did for men.[21]

Writing from a somewhat different perspective, David Potter and Robert V. Hine also questioned the application of Turner's thesis to women's frontier experiences and concluded that women did not share in the freedom and opportunities that the West offered to men. The frontier influenced "women as well as men," Potter agreed; but "If we accept Turner's own assumption that economic opportunity is what matters, and that the frontier was significant as the context within which economic opportunity occurred, then we must observe that for American women . . . opportunity began pretty much where the frontier left off." In a similar vein, Hine believed that although there were independent western women who may have been different from women in the urban East, "Industrialism and the city, not the western farm, opened new avenues for women." The frontier, according to Hine, was a "retrogressive force" which "strongly reinforced the traditional role of the sexes." Mill girls, he concluded, were likely to be far more "revolutionary" than their rural, western counterparts.[22]

In 1979 two important books on western women appeared that aroused a good deal of comment and controversy. John M. Faragher's *Women and Men on the Overland Trail* and Julie Roy Jeffrey's *Frontier Women: The Trans-Mississippi West, 1840-1860* took very different approaches and provided very different pictures of western women. The title of Faragher's book was misleading. Although his study focused on the overland immigrants, he was primarily interested in midwestern farm families at a particular point in time. Since there were few diaries and reminiscences of midwestern farm life, Faragher used the diaries which those folk who moved west wrote about the trail, and from those later writings he attempted to reconstruct family life before emigration. He also utilized a number of demographic techniques and an elaborate content analysis of diaries and memoirs as well as folksongs and folklore of the period as a basis for examining the roles of men and women and their own perceptions of those roles. Writing from a Marxist orientation, Faragher defined all relationships in terms of class, racial, and sexual struggle; within the sexual struggle, Faragher saw women as exploited, subordinate, and powerless. He viewed immigrant women as passive participants who "only reluctantly" went West "because of the terms of obedience which marriage had imposed. . . ." Like other radical feminist writers, he concluded that the West did not provide new opportunities or more equal status for women. Rather, "the frontier extended the impact that agricultural settings have historically had on relations between the sexes"; and westering women, like their midwestern sisters, remained "confined to the domestic space, left without social power . . . dependent for status upon their relations with their husbands."[23]

Jeffrey's study was based on a broader geographic area, and, using more traditional methodology, she reached very different conclusions. Although Jeffrey also failed to find a new egalitarianism for women in the West, she portrayed frontier women as spirited, if selfless, participants who were able to take advantage of some of the opportunities offered in the new country. She also pointed out that although western women remained conservative and that "few responded to the frontier by casting off convention," they played an active role in frontier life. "None thought to reject the civilizing mission they assumed they had consciously performed," she concluded, and they wrote of their contributions with pride and appreciation of their value: "Had they not known it before these women realized now how strong and successful they had been in meeting the challenges of frontier life. . . . They had been not weak but strong; they had been not passive but active. They had triumphed over frontier conditions heroically."[24]

Jeffrey's work and several other recent studies have done much to counterbalance the old nineteenth-century myths and the more recent feminist stereotypes of frontier women. Especially helpful are Glenda Riley's several articles and her recently published *Frontierswomen: The Iowa Experience,* which offer a new, more balanced approach to the study of western women. Riley has suggested, quite correctly, that frontierswomen cannot be characterized as "any one thing." Rather, frontierswomen, like their male counterparts, "were many things at many times and different things at different times." Riley also pointed out that women were not always exploited victims. Women's work she suggested, was often valued by their husbands and children. Like Jeffrey, Riley believed that women took a good deal of pride in their accomplishments. "Most frontierswomen were justifiably proud of their skills and their results," she noted in a recent article: "All of the frontierswomen's duties, from feeding a family through clothing them 'made plenty of work.' But on another level, the outcome of her labors also plainly indicated her degree of skill as an artisan in a society which judged a person by immediate results rather than by wealth, family name or social class." A similar interpretation of women's adjustment to and pride in their new duties was suggested in Sandra L. Myres, *Ho for California!* and *Westering Women and the Frontier Experience.*[25]

Riley and Myres also pointed out, as did Joan Jensen and Darlis Miller, that our notions about the scarcity of women on some frontiers need to be revised. Jensen and Miller noted that recent demographic studies simply do not support the contention that women were scarce in all areas of the West. "Rather," they found, "studies show that gender balance differed according to area and time, indicating that the ... generalization must always be qualified." Riley showed that in Iowa, for example, women were "a major part of Iowa's population right from the beginning of settlement." The "typical" Iowa pioneer "lived in households which averaged 5 to 6 members"; although men outnumbered women by a ratio of 4 to 3, the ratio changed during the frontier period and also varied from county to county.[26]

Other historians have begun to fill in many of the gaps in the literature pertaining to western women. T. A. Larson has provided a number of articles that redress the pro-eastern bias of most women's suffrage studies.[27] Patricia Stallard and Sandra Myres have contributed new insights on the role of army wives in the trans-Mississippi West; a number of authors have studied the contributions of western women in literature and the arts. D'Ann Campbell's careful, quantitative study of the values and attitudes of western women in the 1940s offered a useful model for further work in this almost unexplored area. Jeffrey is currently working on an analysis of women's diaries and reminiscences that will provide a more suitable framework for utilizing primary source materials.[28]

Other investigators have rescued minority women in the West from the almost complete historical oblivion to which they were consigned in the past. Jane Dysart, Darlis Miller, and Janet Lecompte have done pioneering work on Mexican-American women, and others have explored the experiences of westering black women. Riley is working on a new interpretation of the relationship between Indians and white women; Valerie Mathes is preparing an anthology on Indian women; and Myres has contributed a brief study on Indian women's relations with white women. There is also some preliminary work on female Asian immigrants.[29]

Obviously, work on women in the West has just begun. A number of important questions remain to be explored. But it should be pointed out that in contrast to the paucity of pre-1970 secondary studies, there are rich primary sources. Indeed, the number of letters, diaries, and reminiscences

written by frontierswomen is almost overwhelming. Many of these have recently been reprinted, and undoubtedly many more will soon be published
for the first time.[30] Many state historical journals are publishing women's
sources from state historical society collections.

Unfortunately, there is no comprehensive bibliography on western women.
The best available guides to the secondary literature are Sheryll and Gene
Patterson-Black, *Western Women,* and the extensive bibliographical notes in
Jensen and Miller, "The Gentle Tamers Revisited." Also helpful, although not
confined to western women, is Cynthia A. Harrison (ed.), *Women in Ameri-
can History: A Bibliography,* which provides a guide to the periodical litera-
ture. Of some assistance for minority women are Beatrice Medicine, "The
Role of Women in Native American Societies: A Bibliography"; Robert
Cabello-Arandona et al., *The Chicana: A Comprehensive Study*; Lenwood G.
Davis, *The Black Women in American Society*; and Rayna Green's article,
"Native American Women." An excellent guide to the manuscript sources
was recently prepared at the University of Minnesota under National Endow-
ment for the Humanities auspices: Andrea Hinding and Clarke Chambers,
Women's History Sources.[31]

The continuing interest in women's studies and the growing body of published literature should provide the basis for a number of new studies on
women in the West during the coming decades. There are still many questions to be addressed. For example: Were the experiences of seventeenth-
and eighteenth-century Spanish-Mexican and French frontierswomen significantly different from those of eighteenth- and nineteenth-century women
on the predominantly Anglo-American frontiers? How, if at all, did the
experience of European emigrant women differ from that of American
women from eastern communities? If women were not scarce in all sections
of the West, where were they living and how did sex ratios differ from place
to place and from one period to another? Did the frontier provide the same
opportunities for women that it did for men? If so, did women take advantage of such opportunities to the fullest possible extent? Did women play an
important role in the economic and political as well as in the social and
cultural development of the frontier? We can hope that studies addressing
these and other questions will help us better understand the differences
between the *reality* of women's lives on the frontier and the images and
stereotypes of westering women that developed from both earlier nineteenth-
and twentieth-century works and the newer feminist interpretations. More
importantly, by adding to our knowledge of yet another aspect of the westering experience, new work on western women will help us better evaluate

the significance and impact of the frontier and the West on American character and development.

Notes

1. Portions of this essay are published in Sandra L. Myres, "Women and the North American Wilderness: Myth and Reality," World Conference on Records, *Proceedings,* Series 319, vol. 3, *North American Family and Local History* (Salt Lake City: Genealogical Society of Utah, 1980), pp. 1–15. Other portions appear in *Westering Women and the Frontier Experience* (Albuquerque: University of New Mexico Press, 1982; paperbound ed.).

2. According to Richard Jensen, "A scan of 2,000 pages of Turner's published writing will reveal but a single paragraph on women. . . ." Richard Jensen, "On Modernizing Frederick Jackson Turner," *Western Historical Quarterly* 11 (July 1980): 316; T. A. Larson, "Women's Role in the American West," *Montana: The Magazine of Western History* 24 (Summer 1974): 4.

3. Joan M. Jensen and Darlis A. Miller, "The Gentle Tamers Revisited: New Approaches to the History of Women in the American West," *Pacific Historical Review* 49 (May 1980): 177; George F. Parker, *The American Pioneer and His Story* (Iowa City: State Historical Society of Iowa, 1922), p. 3, quoted in Glenda Riley, "Images of the Frontierswoman: Iowa as a Case Study," *Western Historical Quarterly* 8 (April 1977): 189.

4. Larson, "Women's Role," p. 4; Jensen and Miller, "The Gentle Tamers Revisited," p. 176; Richard Bartlett, *The New Country: A Social History of the American Frontier, 1776–1890* (New York: Oxford, 1974; paperbound ed., 1976), p. 343, quoted in Jensen and Miller, "The Gentle Tamers Revisited," p. 177; Jensen, "On Modernizing Frederick Jackson Turner," p. 317; John Unruh, Jr., *The Plains Across: The Overland Emigrants and the Trans-Mississippi West, 1840–60* (Urbana: University of Illinois Press, 1979).

5. Hamlin Garland, *A Pioneer Mother* (Chicago: The Bookfellows, 1922), p. 18.

6. O. E. Rölvaag, *Giants in the Earth: A Saga of the Prairie* (New York: Harper and Bros., 1927); Dorothy Scarborough, *The Wind,* reprint ed. (Austin: University of Texas Press, 1979); Michael Lesy, *Wisconsin Death Trip* (New York: Pantheon, 1973); Willie Newbury Lewis, *Between Sun and Sod,* reprint ed. (College Station: Texas A & M University Press, 1976), p. 41.

7. William F. Sprague, *Women and the West: A Short Social History*

(Boston: Christopher Publishing House, 1940), p. 30; Dee Brown, *The Gentle Tamers: Women of the Old Wild West* (New York: Putnam, 1958; paperbound ed., Lincoln: University of Nebraska Press, 1968), p. 297; Everett Dick, *The Sod-House Frontier, 1854–1890* (New York: D. Appleton-Century Company, 1937; paperbound ed., Lincoln: University of Nebraska Press, 1979), p. 234.

8. John M. Faragher, *Women and Men on the Overland Trail* (New Haven: Yale University Press, 1979), p. 181; Lillian Schlissel, "Women's Diaries on the Western Frontier," *American Studies* 18 (Spring 1977): 92; Schlissel, *Women's Diaries of the Westward Journey* (New York: Schocken Books, 1982), esp. pp. 3–102.

9. Riley, "Images of the Frontierswoman," p. 191; extended quotation is from Elizabeth Ellet, *Pioneer Women of the West* (New York: Charles Scribner, 1852), p. 35.

10. Bartlett, *The New Country*, p. 350.

11. Dawn Gherman, "From Parlour to Tepee: The White Squaw on the American Frontier" (Ph.D. diss., University of Massachusetts, 1975), pp. 20, 30–31. Gherman points out that both Richard Slotkin, *Regeneration Through Violence: The Mythology of the American Frontier, 1600–1860* (Middletown: Wesleyan University Press, 1973), and Leslie A. Fiedler, *The Return of the Vanishing American* (New York: Stein and Day, 1968), advance this general thesis.

12. Brown, *The Gentle Tamers*, p. 297; Erik H. Erikson, *Childhood and Society*, 2d ed. (New York: W. W. Norton, 1963; paperbound ed., 1964), pp. 290–95.

13. Beverly J. Stoeltje, "'A Helpmate for Man Indeed': The Image of the Frontier Woman," *Journal of American Folklore* 88 (January–March 1975): 32; Randolph B. Marcy, *Thirty Years of Army Life on the Border* (New York: Harper and Bros., 1866), p. 372. Stoeltje also explores other images of the frontierswoman, including the refined lady and the helpmate. These images appear frequently in the writings of Caroline Kirkland and Eliza Farnham. See, for example, Kirkland's description of Mrs. Danforth in *A New Home; or, Life in the Clearings*, reprint ed. (New York: Putnam's, 1953), pp. 32–43; and Farnham's description of an Iowa farm woman in *Life in Prairie Land* (New York: Harper and Bros., 1846), pp. 47–48.

14. Glenda Riley, "Through Women's Eyes: Indians in the Trans-Mississippi West," paper delivered at the 20th Annual Conference of the Western History Association, Kansas City, Mo., October 1980. The best discussion of the ideal nineteenth-century woman is Barbara Welter, "The Cult of True

Womanhood, 1820-1860," *American Quarterly* 18 (Summer 1966): 151-74; *New York Daily Tribune,* December 28, 1843, quoted in Unruh, *The Plains Across,* p. 39.

15. Gherman, "From Parlour to Tepee," p. v; Frank Starr, *Hurricane Nell, Queen of Saddle and Lasso* (New York: Frank Starr and Co., 1877); Percy B. St. John, *The Trapper's Bride: A Tale of the Rocky Mountains with the Rose of Wisconsin, Indian Tales* (London: John Mortimer, 1845); Zilla Fitz-James, *Zilla Fitz-James, the Female Bandit of the Southwest; or, the Horrible, Mysterious, and Awful Disclosures in the Life of the Creole Murdfress (!) . . . An Autobiographical Narrative,* ed. A. Richards (Little Rock: A. R. Orton, 1852).

16. See, for example, Ellett, *Pioneer Women;* William W. Fowler, *Women on the American Frontier* (Hartford: S. S. Scranton and Company, 1879); John Frost, *Heroic Women of the West* (Philadelphia: A. Hart, 1854); and H. Addington Bruce, *Women in the Making of America* (Boston: Little, Brown, 1912), pp. 115-55. There are also some recent additions to this genre, including Elinor Bluemel, *One Hundred Years of Colorado Women* (n.p.: n.p., 1973); Anne D. Pickrell, *Pioneer Women in Texas* (Austin: Jenkins Publishing Company, 1970); and Elinor Richey, *Eminent Women of the West* (Berkeley: Howell-North Books, 1975).

17. Georgia Willis Read, "Women and Children on the Oregon-California Trail in the Gold Rush Years," *Missouri Historical Review* 39 (October 1944): 1-23; Nancy Wilson Ross, *Westward the Women* (New York: Knopf, 1944); Helena Huntington Smith, "Pioneers in Petticoats," *American Heritage* 10 (February 1959): 36-39, 101-3.

18. Brown, *The Gentle Tamers;* Ray Allen Billington, *America's Frontier Heritage* (New York: Macmillan, 1966), pp. 215-17. Billington's *Westward Expansion* has now gone through five editions, 1949, 1960, 1967, 1974, and 1982.

19. Walter Prescott Webb, *The Great Plains* (New York: Grosset and Dunlap, 1931; paperbound ed., Lincoln: University of Nebraska Press, 1981), pp. 505-6; Sprague, *Women and the West,* p. 63; Dick, *Sod-House Frontier,* p. 234. For a similar assessment of Sprague's work, see Paula Treckel, "An Historiographical Essay: Women on the American Frontier," *The Old Northwest* 1 (December 1975): 393-95. Treckel also discusses the Frost and Fowler volumes (cited in n. 16 above), and Page Smith, *Daughters of the Promised Land: Women in American History* (Boston: Little, Brown, 1970), pp. 215-25.

20. The various articles and special issues on western women include:

Robert L. Munkres, "Wives, Mothers, Daughters: Women's Life on the Road West," *Annals of Wyoming* 42 (October 1970): 191-224; Jerena E. Giffin, "'Add a Pinch and a Lump: Missouri Women in the 1820s," *Missouri Historical Review* 65 (July 1971): 478-504; B. J. Zenor, "By Covered Wagon to the Promised Land," *American West* 11 (July 1974): 30-41; Ruth B. Moynihan, "Children and Young People on the Overland Trail," *Western Historical Quarterly* 6 (July 1975): 279-92; June Sochen, "Frontier Women: A Model for All Women?" *South Dakota History* 7 (Winter 1976): 36-56; Glenda Riley, "Women in the West," *Journal of American Culture* 3 (Summer 1980): 311-29; Mildred C. Fry, "Women on the Ohio Frontier: The Marietta Area," *Ohio History* 90 (Winter 1981): 54-73; the articles cited in Jensen and Miller, "The Gentle Tamers Revisited"; *Journal of the West* 12 (April 1973); *Montana, The Magazine of Western History* 24 (Summer 1974); *Heritage of Kansas* 10 (Spring 1977); *Utah Historical Quarterly* 46 (Spring 1978); and *Pacific Historical Review* 49 (May 1980); and forthcoming 1982 issues of *Journal of the West* and *New Mexico Historical Review*. For a fuller discussion of the new mythology, see Sandra L. Myres, "The Westering Woman," *Huntington Spectator* 1 (Winter 1980): 1.

21. Johnny M. Faragher and Christine Stansell, "Women and Their Families on the Overland Trail to California and Oregon, 1842-1867," *Feminist Studies* 2 (1975): 161; Schlissel, "Women's Diaries," 94-97; Schlissel, *Women's Diaries,* esp. pp. 103-14.

22. David M. Potter, "American Women and the American Character," in Edward N. Saveth (ed.), *American History and the Social Sciences* (Glencoe, Ill.: Free Press, 1964), pp. 431-32; Robert V. Hine, *The American West: An Interpretive History,* paperbound ed. (Boston: Little, Brown, 1973), p. 174.

23. Faragher, *Women and Men,* p. 187.

24. Julie Roy Jeffrey, *Frontier Women: The Trans-Mississippi West, 1840-1880* (New York: Hill and Wang, 1979; paperbound ed., n.d.), p. 202.

25. Riley's articles and books include: *Women on the American Frontier* (St. Louis: Forum Press, 1977); "'Not Gainfully Employed': Women on the Iowa Frontier, 1833-1870," *Pacific Historical Review* 49 (May 1980): 237-64; *Frontierswomen: The Iowa Experience* (Ames: State University of Iowa, 1981); "Iowa's Trail Women: A Paradigm for All Women," *Annals of Iowa* (Winter 1982): 167-97; and the articles, "Images of the Frontierswoman" and "Women in the West," cited above. The quotes are from *Women on the American Frontier,* p. 15, and "'Not Gainfully Employed,'" p. 257. Also see Sandra L. Myres, *Ho for California! Women's Overland Diaries from*

the *Huntington Library* (San Marino, Calif.: Huntington Library, 1980); and *Westering Women and the Frontier Experience.*

26. Jensen and Miller, "Gentle Tamers Revisited," p. 189; Riley, *Frontierswomen,* pp. 10-11; and Riley, "'Not Gainfully Employed,'" pp. 237-38.

27. T. A. Larson, "Petticoats at the Polls: Woman Suffrage in Territorial Wyoming," *Pacific Northwest Quarterly* 44 (April 1953): 74-79; "Woman Suffrage in Wyoming," *Pacific Northwest Quarterly* 56 (April 1965): 57-66; "Woman Suffrage in Western America," *Utah Historical Quarterly* 38 (Winter 1970): 7-19; "Dolls, Vassals, and Drudges—Pioneer Women in the West," *Western Historical Quarterly* 3 (January 1972): 5-16; "The Woman's Rights Movement in Idaho," *Idaho Yesterdays* 16 (Spring 1972): 2-15, 18-19; "Montana Women and the Battle for the Ballot," *Montana, The Magazine of Western History* 23 (January 1973): 24-41; "Idaho's Role in America's Woman Suffrage Crusade," *Idaho Yesterdays* 18 (Spring 1974): 2-17; "Woman Suffrage" in Howard Lamar (ed.), *The Reader's Encyclopedia of the American West* (New York: Thomas Y. Crowell, 1977), pp. 1283-84; "The Woman Suffrage Movement in Washington," *Pacific Northwest Quarterly* 67 (April 1976): 49-62; "Wyoming's Contribution to the Regional and National Women's Rights Movements," *Annals of Wyoming* 52 (Spring 1980): 2-14. Ruth B. Moynihan, "Dethroning the Idol Gold: The Radical Theories of Oregon's Abigail Scott Duniway," paper presented at the Pacific Northwest History Conference, April 17, 1980; and Moynihan, "Abigail Scott Duniway of Oregon: Woman and Suffragist of the American Frontiers," 2 vols. (Ph.D. diss., Yale University, 1979). There are a number of other studies on western women's suffrage; see Jensen and Miller, "The Gentle Tamers Revisited," pp. 202-3.

28. Patricia Stallard, *Glittering Misery: Dependents of the Indian Fighting Army* (San Rafael, Calif.: Presidio Press, 1978); Sandra L. Myres, "The Ladies of the Army—Views of Western Life," in *The American Military on the Frontier: Proceedings of the Seventh Military History Symposium* (Washington, D.C.: Office of Air Force History, 1978), pp. 135-54; and "Romance and Reality on the American Frontier: Views of Army Wives," *Western Historical Review,* forthcoming. An extensive list of articles on women in literature and the arts is in Jensen and Miller, "The Gentle Tamers Revisited," pp. 179-80; D'Ann Campbell, "Was the West Different? Values and Attitudes of Young Women in 1943," *Pacific Historical Review* 47 (August 1978): 453-63; Julie R. Jeffrey, "Frontier Letters: A Perspective on Women's

World," paper presented at the 20th Annual Conference of the Western History Association, Kansas City, Mo., October 1980.

29. Jane Dysart, "Mexican Women in San Antonio, 1830–1860: The Assimilation Process," *Western Historical Quarterly* 7 (October 1976): 365–76; Darlis Miller, "Cross-Cultural Marriages in the Southwest: The New Mexico Experience," *New Mexico Historical Review* 57 (October 1982): 335–60; Janet Lecompte, "The Independent Women of Hispanic New Mexico, 1821–1846," *Western Historical Quarterly* 12 (January 1981): 17–36; also see the short chapter on Mexican frontier women in Alfredo Mirandé and Evangelina Enríquez, *La Chicana: The Mexican-American Woman* (Chicago: University of Chicago Press, 1979), pp. 53–95; Sue Armitage, Theresa Banfield, and Sarah Jacobus, "Black Women and Their Communities in Colorado," *Frontiers* 2 (Summer 1977): 45–51; Lawrence B. de Graaf, "Race, Sex, and Region: Black Women in the American West, 1850–1920," *Pacific Historical Review* 49 (May 1980): 285–314; Yuji Ichioka, "*Amerika Nadeskiko*: Japanese Immigrant Women in the United States, 1900–1924," *Pacific Historical Review* 49 (May 1980): 339–57.

30. There are so many of these that it is impossible to even begin to list them all. A few of the most recent include: Ellen B. Holland, *Gay as a Grig: Memories of a North Texas Girlhood* (1970); Sallie R. Matthews, *Interwoven: A Pioneer Chronicle* (1977); Sarah Ellen Roberts, *Alberta Homestead: Chronicle of a Pioneer Family* (1968), from the University of Texas Press at Austin; Anita Kunkler, *Hardscrabble: A Narrative of the California Hill Country* (1975); Sarah E. Olds, *Twenty Miles From a Match: Homesteading in Western Nevada* (1978); Marvin Lewis, *Martha and the Doctor: A Frontier Family in Central Nevada* (1977), from University of Nevada Press at Reno; Lily Klasner, *My Girlhood Among Outlaws* (1972); Glen G. Boyer (ed.), *I Married Wyatt Earp: The Recollections of Josephine Sarah Marcus Earp* (1976), from the University of Arizona Press at Tucson; and over ten titles from the University of Nebraska Press, many of them in the paperback Bison Book series.

31. Sheryll and Gene Patterson-Black, *Western Women in History and Literature* (Crawford, Nebr.: Cottonwood Press, 1978); Cynthia A. Harrison (ed.), *Women in American History: A Bibliography* (Santa Barbara, Calif.: ABC-Clio, 1979); Beatrice Medicine, "The Role of Women in Native American Societies: A Bibliography," *Indian Historian* 8 (Summer 1975): 50–54; Robert Cabello-Arandona et al., *The Chicana: A Comprehensive Study*

(Los Angeles: University of California Chicano Studies, 1975); Lenwood G. Davis, *The Black Woman in American Society: A Selected Annotated Bibliography* (Boston: G. K. Hall, 1975); Rayna Green, "Native American Women," *Signs* 6 (Winter 1980): 248-67; and Andrea Hinding and Clarke Chambers, *Women's History Sources,* 2 vols. (New York: Bowker, 1979).

Chapter Seventeen

Frederick C. Luebke

**Ethnic Minority Groups
in the American West**

Many books and articles have been written on ethnic groups in the West.[1]
A substantial portion of this extensive literature consists of articles in state
history journals and collections, books published by obscure and sometimes
private presses, dozens of church or denominational histories, published
diaries and reminiscences, and unpublished master's theses and doctoral dissertations. Primarily factual in character and descriptive of separate ethnic
group experience, most of these materials fail to illuminate either internal
social structures or the intricate relationships of minorities to each other and
to the dominant or host society. Moreover, they often tend to be filiopietistic;
their purpose is to praise the great deeds of the ethnic fathers who led their
people through the wilderness to establish new homes in a strange land. They
recount in loving detail how this or that group settled here or there, established their distinctive institutions, and perpetuated their special cultural
forms. They record the bravery, fortitude, imagination, and skill with which
ethnic groups braved environmental hardship to become solid and respectable citizens. Analyses of failure, incompetence, mismanagement, intragroup
conflict, and stubborn refusal to adapt are less common in this literature.

Filiopietistic accounts that concentrate on the accomplishments of ethnic
group leaders or prominent members of the subsociety have a special tendency to mythologize the past. The history of ethnic groups in America is
first of all the story of large numbers of ordinary persons, not dramatic tales
of colorful or unusually talented leaders. To focus on an ethnic elite without
treating the character of the masses or examining the relationships between
leaders and followers is automatically to distort the history of immigrant
people. Some leaders, because of their own personal background and psychological needs, identify much more strongly with the ethnic group than do

rank-and-file members. Other persons, prominent because of individual accomplishment in the business, political, or intellectual worlds, tend to have rather exceptional social experiences and hence may have few meaningful ties with the ethnic group associated with them in the public mind. They may, in fact, shed ethnic attitudes and behaviors with remarkable speed. In either case, it is a mistake to apply generalizations from leadership or elite experience to the minority group as a whole, as has often happened in immigration history.

If the writings of amateurs and filiopietists have tended to lack adequate conceptual foundations, the work of academic and professional historians has been dominated by a point of view that tends to minimize the importance of ethnic history. Most historians of the West, understandably enough, have conceived of their work in terms of the frontier thesis, fathered by Frederick Jackson Turner and often graced with his name. The central assumption of this overarching thesis is that the exigencies of life in a frontier environment forced people, regardless of their origins and culture, to adapt their ways to the physical realities of the place they had chosen for their new home. The frontier environment is thus assumed to have been a crucible in which the cultural characteristics of newcomers were melted away. Out of the heat of this refining process, wrote Turner, emerged a new man, an American, who was different and probably superior in his strengths, qualities, values, and virtues compared to his forebears and contemporaries in Europe. In the American West, where barren deserts, rugged mountains, and treeless, semiarid plains dominate the landscape, environmental forces are commonly assumed to be especially powerful and capable of eradicating ethnocultural distinctions. In short, Turnerian theory predisposes the historian to emphasize the rapidity and ease with which ethnic groups were assimilated into American society and to ignore ethnocultural conflict and the persistence of immigrant attitudes, values, and behaviors.

It is not surprising, therefore, that historians of the West have tended to treat their subject as the story of an undifferentiated, English-speaking majority on a steady, civilizing march from the time of exploration and settlement toward the present, with its allegedly high levels of accomplishment. This is not to say that racial groups were absent from these accounts, which often describe how progress was generally obstructed by Indians, sometimes noble but usually savage, and in lesser ways by Mexicans and Chinese. But questions of the past were seldom framed in terms of differing cultures in collision and even more rarely in ways that fostered the analysis of ethnocultural variations within white society. This seems especially apparent in works that synthesize the history of the West or its major regions.

Walter Prescott Webb, the environmentalist historian of *The Great Plains* (1931), seemed oblivious to the substantial numbers of European immigrants who settled the region. He merely noted that they avoided the Great Plains and left the region to old-stock Americans of English and Scottish ancestry. Apparently he was unaware of the fact that in some parts of the plains European immigrants and their children constituted a majority of the population; he ignored entirely the numerous German pioneers who settled the hill country of central Texas, just a few miles from his home in Austin. Similarly, Everett Dick, the social historian of *The Sod-House Frontier* (1937), ignored the fact that from the time of the earliest settlements on the central plains a major portion of the population—one-eighth in Kansas, nearly a fourth in Nebraska, and more than a third in Dakota—was foreign-born. In his study of *The Great Northwest* (1965), Oscar Winther, himself the youngest son in a Danish immigrant family and author of several articles on English immigrants in the West, fails to treat ethnic group settlement and analyzes the immigrant presence in the twentieth century within the scope of ten pages. Earl Pomeroy provides a sensitive and judicious introduction to racial minorities in his history of *The Pacific Slope* (1965), but he surveys European immigrant groups in four paragraphs. Even John Hawgood, the author of an important book on German settlements on the midwestern frontier, fails to integrate ethnic peoples into his study of *America's Western Frontiers* (1967) and treats them only in a final chapter. Many other similar historiographical sins of omission could be identified, but to do so would obscure the point that most contributions have been conceived in ways that assume the dominance of environmental forces over the culture brought to the region by immigrants.[2]

In most instances these interpretations of western history may be attributed, directly or indirectly, to Turner's vision of the frontier. Turner was a master whose sweeping imagination and romantic style inspired scores of followers to write histories patterned on his famous thesis with its dominant strain of environmental determinism. But Turner also stressed the importance of method. Because he produced so few books and essays of a monographic character in his lifetime, his methodology does not emerge clearly from his published works. In his seminars, however, Turner led his students to data stored in census reports, commercial records, church registers, and the multifarious records compiled by county, city, and township governments; he taught them to sort, classify, and interpret quantitative evidence. Moreover, he emphasized the spatial differentiation that may be discovered in economic, social, and cultural evidence. Turner's workshop contained numerous maps that plotted election data, geological information, differences in soils, ethnic settlement patterns, literacy rates, church memberships—anything that might reveal geographical variation.[3] This was the Turner that stressed the significance of sections in American history. In contrast to the frontier thesis, which worked against the study of the ethnic variable, Turner's sectionalist doctrines were based on a methodology that was ideally suited for the study of ethnic minority groups in the American West.[4]

Nevertheless, it is a fact that Turner himself never pursued ethnocultural variables in a more than superficial way. He understood that ethnicity was capable of modifying a region's character to such an extent that it could be distinguished from the rest of the nation. Moreover, he often charted ethnic and religious groups on his maps, and he even wrote a series of popular articles on several immigrant groups for the *Chicago Record-Herald* in 1901.[5] Yet he never penetrated the subject deeply enough to analyze the significance of the variables he had discovered.[6] This could emerge most readily through the study of group conflict, but for Turner conflict occurred chiefly between regions rather than within them. Because of his preoccupation with variation on a sectional scale, he tended to slight class and group conflicts that were not fundamentally related to spatial distribution.[7]

But it took no great leap of the imagination to substitute ethnic minority groups for regions in Turner's sectionalist theories. Ethnic groups, like the people of each region within the United States, considered their culture to be superior and they expected the rest of the country to tolerate their ways, if not to emulate them. If, as Turner taught, the American political system provided a forum for the definition of regional interest and an arena for the resolution of sectional conflict through accommodation and compromise, it could also be understood as serving the same function for ethnic minority groups, though on a more local level. The question therefore arises whether any of Turner's students analyzed immigration or ethnic history in ways that transcended the confinements of the frontier thesis by employing the research methods Turner had fostered in his pursuit of sectionalism.[8]

Turnerian methodology is ably illustrated in the several works by Joseph Schafer, a Turner Ph.D. who became superintendent of the State Historical Society of Wisconsin in 1920. Though not an immigration historian, Schafer was much interested in the acculturation of Wisconsin's numerous ethnic groups, especially the Germans. During his two decades as superintendent

Schafer produced a series of microcosmic studies under the general title of *The Wisconsin Domesday Book.* It was an ambitious and novel enterprise. Ultimately he produced five volumes, of which three are attempts to understand the history of specific areas in Wisconsin—four lakeshore counties, the lead region, a river basin—in terms of the interaction of the people, including the many immigrants, with their specific environments. Schafer treated topography, soils, land use, migration and settlement, agriculture, politics, and population changes. Ethnic groups were always integral parts of his analysis, but as a devoted Turnerian conceptually committed to the frontier thesis, Schafer tended to emphasize the Americanization of the immigrants— how rapidly they were assimilated in the frontier environment, not how tenaciously they retained ethnic cultural characteristics.[9]

Schafer also tended to overstate the striving of immigrants toward the ideal of the socially acceptable American citizen, but he admitted that it was not necessary for them to discard all ethnic traits in order to become "good Americans."[10] No filiopietist, Schafer had a keen understanding of the assimilation process, its ethnic group variations, and the role in it of language, religion, and exogamy, even though he tended to overestimate the rate at which these factors operated. He employed unpublished census data, land office records, and surveyor reports to calculate for each immigrant group such variables as spatial diffusion, attitudes toward land, occupational distributions, family size, marriage rates, and income patterns compared with native-born persons. In short, Schafer's analysis was remarkably comprehensive for its time. He provided a model for research that has been all but ignored by later generations of historians interested in ethnicity.

One of the last of Turner's students at Harvard, Merle Curti, followed Schafer a generation later with a far more comprehensive and systematic case study. *The Making of an American Community* (1959) was designed to test objectively Turner's frontier thesis, most specifically the idea that the frontier experience promoted American democracy. This included the increasing participation of immigrants in the political process and the expansion of opportunities for them in economic and cultural affairs. Curti chose Trempealeau County, Wisconsin, as the subject for his study at least partly because its frontier population included significant numbers of German, Norwegian, and Polish immigrants. Thus, Trempealeau County provided a laboratory in which to verify Turner's metaphor of the frontier as a crucible in which the immigrants were to have been fused into a mixed race. Curti and his associates analyzed mobility data, indices of success in various occupations, changes in occupational structures, and measures of leadership, political participation, school attendance, and marriage patterns. He concluded that frontier conditions had in fact stimulated democracy in Trempealeau and that "decade by decade the foreign-born, including those from non-English speaking countries, were increasingly represented in political and also in cultural activities."[11]

Whether these findings supported Turner's general position, as Curti claimed, is less clear. He had in fact merely demonstrated that "Americanization" had occurred in Trempealeau County; he had not proved that this process occurred because of frontier conditions. It is possible that in an urban setting, for example, these same persons might have assimilated more rapidly than they did on the Wisconsin frontier. Moreover, the possibility remains that frontier conditions masked, or were mistaken for, variables with greater power to explain the process by which ethnic groups gradually lost their distinctive character and became indistinguishable from the majority. What was missing in Curti's research design was a series of comparisons with other appropriate communities; what was needed was a conceptual framework to replace the powerful imagery of Turner's frontier thesis.[12]

If Schafer and Curti were microscopic in their approaches, another Turner student, Marcus Lee Hansen, was telescopic. Hansen's perspective was intercontinental as he shifted attention in immigration history from the cultural contributions of immigrant leaders to the phenomenon of mass migration from Europe to America. This he achieved chiefly through two posthumously published books, *The Immigrant in American History* (1940) and *The Atlantic Migration, 1607–1860* (1940). Like Schafer, Hansen was the son of an immigrant, a great advantage in assessing ethnic experience. He remained steadfast in the Turnerian faith until his premature death, at age forty-five in 1938.

Hansen's work represents a laudable accomplishment in several respects, but for present purposes he must be identified as a major source of a misconception about immigrants on the frontier. Hansen taught that newcomers from Europe were not commonly found on the fringe of settlement because they lacked experience in coping with the problems of such an environment. The immigrant was not a frontiersman, wrote Hansen, and "had, in fact, an innate aversion to the wilderness with its solitude and loneliness and primitive mode of life. . . . Neither by experience nor temperament was the immigrant fitted for pioneering."[13] This notion is at least partly based on the fact that from 1775 to 1830 European immigration had virtually ceased. Hence, few immigrants from any country could possibly have participated in the settlement of the American frontier as it existed in those decades. After the 1830s, however, immigration increased spectacularly. Thus, when the trans-Mississippi West was settled, immigrants were present on the northern and western frontiers in proportions that were usually in excess of that for the United States as a whole.

The purpose of this discussion about Turner, his students, and their treatment of ethnic history is to suggest that the frontier thesis, which has tended to dominate thinking about the American West, is conceptually inadequate for the study of ethnic minorities on the frontier because it assumes the dominance of environments over culture and therefore predisposes the historian to emphasize the rapid assimilation of immigrants. It does not offer a framework for the study of the frontier as a place where environment and culture interact; instead, it postulates that the frontier environment is more powerful than the culture brought to it. It stimulates the consideration of evidence that supports the thesis and tends to ignore the rest; in effect, it makes a judgment before the evidence is brought forth.

In contrast to the frontier thesis, Turnerian methodology fosters the search for interpretive frameworks—alternatives to the frontier thesis—that encompass evidence for the persistence of ethnic culture as well as its disappearance, for slow assimilation as well as rapid, the study of the masses of immigrants as well as the leaders, for inquiry into conflict as well as accommodation to established norms. Above all, Turnerian methodology encourages the study of ethnicity in its relationships to environment, whatever they may be, rather than assuming the dominance of environment over ethnicity.

An immigrant community should be studied holistically because its history emerges from the interaction of its culture with the environment of its new home.[14] In order to understand ethnic behavior in America one must discover first who the immigrants were, where they came from, when and why they emigrated; one must comprehend the culture that immigrants brought with them—group values, attitudes, folkways, religions, and languages. The enormous variations possible within each group, as well as among different groups, must also be recognized.

Secondly, as Schafer's work suggests, the historian of ethnic minority groups must understand the physical and social environments in which the assimilative process occurred.[15] It was one thing, for example, for Norwegian immigrants to settle in the vast, sparsely populated prairie of North Dakota; it was quite another for them to join the Scandinavian stream to the Mormon Zion in the deserts of Utah; it was still another to participate in the development of Washington with its great forests and bustling seaports. In each environment Norwegian immigrants had different assimilative histories.[16]

The mode of settlement is also an essential part of immigration history. Did the immigrants come individually or in colonies? Did they come directly to the West or did they live elsewhere in the United States first? The collective experiences of Germans from Russia, for example, a large proportion of whom came directly to the Great Plains states in colonies, were significantly different from those of Germans from Germany, for whom the classic pattern of chain migration and resettlement in the West was standard.[17] What patterns of distribution in space were established by a given group? Were they farmers? Were they townsfolk? To what extent were distributive patterns influenced by the physical environment and to what extent by immigrant culture? Among Black Sea Germans, for example, inheritance customs were such that a high proportion of immigrants were enabled to reestablish themselves on farms on the Great Plains, but among Volga Germans a different inheritance custom had the effect of reducing the number of potential farmers in the West and forcing a large proportion to seek employment in cities, thereby creating a strikingly different settlement pattern.[18]

The question of the density of ethnic population holds special importance for the West, where small numbers of people are often thinly spread over vast areas. In order for ethnocultural forms to be sustained over time, they must have the support of institutions such as churches, schools, an immigrant-language press, social and cultural associations of all kinds, mutual benefit or insurance societies, and businesses that cater to the ethnic trade. A certain level of concentration in the ethnic population—"a critical mass"—must be attained before the supportive institutions can be generated. If they appear, ethnic culture and language will be maintained for a longer period of time; without their support, immigrants will tend to lose their ethnocultural characteristics and assimilate rapidly. Richard Etulain has shown that even among the Basques, a group having an unusually keen sense of identity, assimilation takes place more rapidly in small ethnic enclaves than in large ones. Gordon Hendrickson has found a similar pattern in Wyoming.[19] Obviously, such auxiliary institutions cannot be easily created or maintained in areas where the ethnic population is thinly distributed over a large area, as in much of the West. For the same reason the religious characteristics of a given ethnic minority are especially important. Churches were commonly the easiest of immigrant institutions to create; often they were the only ones in the sparsely populated West, where they often provided the nucleus of ethnic life and functioned as substitutes for the array of social and cultural societies that were available in urban centers.

The degree of concentration necessary for the maintenance of ethnic language and culture is also related to the social distance perceived by an ethnic group between its own distinctive way of life and what it discerns as the culture of the host or receiving society. In the United States the core culture may be described as having emerged from English and pietistic Protestant origins. The greater the difference perceived between immigrant group characteristics and those of the mainstream society, the greater will be the tendency for clustering. To illustrate, we may expect that Polish immigrants, as adherents of Roman Catholicism and speaking a Slavic tongue, will tend to congregate more readily than Swedes, whose language is a Teutonic relative of English and whose Lutheran Protestantism in America savored strongly of pietism. If the cultural distance were accompanied by discernible differences in physical appearance, as among Japanese or blacks, then the numbers of migrants required for the maintenance of ethnic language and culture will be reduced. For example, the Germans of Nebraska, an unusually heterogeneous group that historically was the largest in the state, may be unable to sustain their culture as readily as the Chicanos, a very small group by comparison.

"Critical mass" is thus also related to the internal cohesion of an ethnic group, its homogeneity, and its sense of peoplehood.[20] English immigrants in the West have almost no sense of themselves as an ethnic group, but the Chicanos speak of themselves as *La Raza*. Whereas one hundred ordinary German immigrants in a rural setting was rarely enough to produce a strong sense of communal identity, a hundred is near the maximum size of the communities of German-speaking Hutterites, a radical Protestant group from Russia that still organizes itself into communally owned agricultural colonies in South Dakota, Montana, and the Canadian prairie provinces.[21] Moreover, the greater the distance between the immigrant and core cultures, the greater will be the potential for conflict. For this reason the Hutterites try to avoid contact (and hence conflict and assimilation) by living in isolated colonies in areas of low population density. Even so, historical accident is capable of shattering their communal peace, as it did in World War I, when Hutterite pacifism clashed so intensely with American superpatriotism that a majority temporarily abandoned South Dakota for Canada.[22]

The history of an immigrant group in America is the story of its assimilation into the mainstream. So long as it sustains a separate cultural identity it will have an ongoing history; once its distinctiveness as a group disappears it ceases to exist as an ethnic minority group. For some groups this history is remarkably short, and it is shorter in some environments than in others. For other groups the process may be attenuated, and distinctive traits and behaviors may be retained over many generations. Research into ethnic minority history should therefore concentrate on how, why, and in what areas of life assimilative changes have taken place. One must ask how quickly or slowly the immigrant society adopts the dress, language, work habits, political behavior, marriage and family patterns, religion, and ultimately the values and attitudes of the host society. The pressures exerted by the physical and social environments in stimulating or forcing ethnic group adaptation or conformance cannot be ignored. Most important, questions of the past must be framed in ways that permit comparisons in space and time to be made. One must ask how a specific behavior of an immigrant group in a given place compared (1) to that of other groups, native or foreign-born, in the same environment; (2) to that of the same group in other environments; and (3) to what it became later in time. It is possible, of course, for excellent histories of ethnic groups to be written without comparisons being made on the basis of quantitative evidence. But since ethnic history is the study of change in a social grouping that is different in some ways from the larger society of which it is a part, the evolution of these changes often may be discovered and analyzed most efficiently in this way.

The systematic study of ethnic group history clearly ought to begin with the settlement process, but this subject has received remarkably little scholarly attention. Donald W. Meinig has traced major patterns of racial and ethnic group settlement and dispersion in Texas, New Mexico, and Arizona. I have attempted an overview for the Great Plains region, but nothing similar exists for other large parts of the West.[23] Maps showing the spatial distribution of racial and ethnic groups are essential, but only one state and one ethnic group has been treated in detail.[24] The first ethnic groups to attract scholarly attention are often those that are distinctive in some special way. Probably no Great Plains group has been studied more extensively than the Germans from Russia.[25] However, more typical European settlers, such as the Swedes, Czechs, or Irish, have received scant attention. But model studies are beginning to appear. For example, Robert C. Ostergren, a cultural geographer, has examined a small Swedish settlement in Dalesburg, South Dakota, in which he traces origins in Sweden, patterns of migration to the West, and spatial distribution in the settlement, with special reference to the immigrant churches as nuclei of the community.[26]

Another important question concerns the use ethnic groups make of the land on which they have settled and whether their practice of agriculture is distinctive. The remarkable affinity of the Basques for the sheep-grazing industry is a well-known phenomenon.[27] But agriculture in the West is another matter. For some ethnic groups, differences in agricultural practice are well known. Theodore Saloutos has shown, for example, that the Japanese, Italians, and Portuguese in California have tended to farm intensively, often using distinctive methods. But for the more numerous European groups, differences are less apparent in most parts of the West. Bradley Baltensperger, another cultural geographer, has compared the agricultural behavior of German, German-Russian, and Swedish farmers in Nebraska to discover only minor differences. In general, immigrants tended to adopt American cropping and livestock practices quickly.[28]

The most thorough study of ethnic agriculture in the West has been made by Terry G. Jordan, also a geographer, in his *German Seed in Texas Soil* (1966). After surveying agricultural practices in both the American South and Germany in the nineteenth century, Jordan introduces temporal and spatial comparisons as he examines German agriculture in two separate Texas districts with that of native-born farmers (chiefly from Alabama and Tennessee) from 1850 to 1880. He demonstrates that the German immigrants adapted readily to the Texas environment and that there were only minor differences between the two groups in settlement patterns, the crops they raised, and the livestock they grazed. German farmers quickly learned to cultivate such new crops as corn and cotton and to abandon imported varieties that were ill suited for Texas conditions. They displayed some distinctiveness in their tendency to farm more intensively and they invested more labor and capital in their operations than the native-born. In the western district—the German Hill Country near Austin where Germans were nearly the only settlers in the frontier period—cultural contacts with the native-born were less frequent, and consequently ethnic distinctiveness was more pronounced. In general, Jordan found that the Texas Germans assimilated rapidly, especially in economic and political affairs, but that they still retain remnants of their distinctive heritage in social and cultural matters.[29]

Ethnic agriculture has also attracted the interest of other geographers. D. Aidan McQuillan has studied the agricultural adaptation of three immigrant groups—Swedes, German-Russian Mennonites, and French Canadians—and compared them in a variety of ways with native-born American farmers in central Kansas over the half-century following the first settlements there in 1875. McQuillan has also systematically studied the pattern of mobility among ethnic farmers. He found that all groups, immigrants as well as native-born, had high rates of movement in and out of the area. Differences were slight in both the pioneer period and later. Neither poverty nor residence in the heart of the ethnic enclave were barriers to outmigration. In general, the most persistent farmers in all groups were older persons with greater wealth and larger families.[30]

Religion could also be influential in the practice of agriculture in the West. John A. Hostetler, an anthropologist, has shown that the Old Order Amish, a German-culture religious group from Pennsylvania, failed in their colonization efforts on the Great Plains because of a reluctance to modify their religiously rooted small-scale mechanized operations. At the same time, the equally separatistic Hutterites, theological cousins of the Amish who live exclusively in communally owned colonies in the northern plains, have experienced remarkable agricultural success.[31]

The political behavior of ethnic groups in the West has received little scholarly attention, compared with the work that has been done in the Midwest and East. The Populist era, however, has been the subject of much attention. In 1963 Walter T. K. Nugent introduced the ethnocultural dimension into the debate about western Populism. He demonstrated that, contrary to interpretations of the Populists as narrow, xenophobic protofascists, these agrarian radicals were tolerant of immigrants and welcomed their support. A decade later Stanley Parsons employed statistical methods in his study of Nebraska Populism. Although Parsons conceptualized his work in terms of a power struggle between rural and urban forces, he also attempted to integrate ethnocultural variables into his analysis.[32]

My own monograph on this subject, *Immigrants and Politics* (1969), is designed to examine the political acculturation of the German ethnic group in Nebraska over two decades. Through the use of the collective biography technique and correlations between voting data on a precinct level with census manuscript data, I sought to demonstrate that the heterogeneous Germans tended to display partisan preferences that reflected perceived differences between themselves and the presumed representatives of Anglo-American culture. Thus, for example, a German immigrant residing in town and employed in a skilled craft, business, or one of the professions, and affiliated with a pietistic Protestant denomination, would be more likely to vote Republican (the party of the "establishment" in Nebraska) than would a German Catholic or Lutheran farmer, whose relative isolation in a rural ghetto limited the number and quality of personal contacts with members of the host society. As the assimilation process ran its course, the German Americans tended to vote increasingly like the mainstream, except when ethnocultural issues such as prohibition, woman suffrage, Sabbatarianism, and the regulation of parochial schools impinged directly upon their group interest, as happened most clearly in 1890, when they helped to defeat a proposed prohibition amendment to the state constitution. By the end of the century the Germans of Nebraska were participating extensively and intelligently in the political process, even though ethnic politics would not disappear entirely for years to come.[33]

Other scholars have studied the voting behavior of all major ethnic groups within a given state. Nebraska has continued to attract attention. Robert W. Cherny, in his *Populism, Progressivism, and the Transformation of Nebraska Politics, 1885-1915* (1981), investigates ethnic voters and their leaders, using a variety of quantitative methods that assure appropriate comparisons in time and space. He demonstrates that in Nebraska in the 1880s political history is best understood in terms of ethnocultural conflict, with prohibition as the preeminent issue. The political system of that time was unidimensional, ritualistic, and symbolic in character. But it was transformed by the advent of Populism, a movement that strongly attracted voters in lower social and economic strata. Cherny shows that old ethnic lines of division were crossed as party loyalties were weakened. By the time of the Progressive era a new, multiple-issue political system had emerged in which ethnicity did not cease to be important, but continued as one of several factors determining the course of state political history.[34]

Traditional methodology is combined with a unique conceptual schema in *A People of Two Kingdoms* (1975) by James C. Juhnke. This model study treats the political acculturation of a small ethnoreligious group, the Mennonites of Kansas, most of whom were ethnic Germans who had emigrated from Russia after 1870. Central to Juhnke's thesis is the Anabaptist version of the doctrine of two kingdoms. In this view, the Mennonites, as subjects in the kingdom of Christ, were obligated to renounce war, the taking of oaths, and the holding of political office. But they were also required to obey the government, even though it was a part of the worldly kingdom of evil, because it was the agency ordained by God to maintain order. In Juhnke's interpretation, the political history of this people emerges from the conflicting demands made upon them by the two kingdoms.[35]

Tracing the immigrants through literature is another avenue to an understanding of ethnic groups in the West and their relationships with the rest of society. Wilbur S. Shepperson has provided an effective example of this approach in his *Restless Strangers: Nevada's Immigrants and Their Interpreters* (1970). Shepperson first establishes the character of the Nevada environment and shows how its barren mountains and deserts dictated a sparse and unevenly settled population, highly unstable and without a well-knit social structure. Immigrants from all parts of the world—Irish, Germans,

Italians, Basques, Mexicans, Chinese, East Indians—formed an exceptionally large proportion of the state's population. Shepperson reveals in great detail how the immigrants were interpreted by novelists, essayists, newspapermen, and biographers. While many sources recount tales of crime, violence, and debauchery, others present economic, social, and political success stories, as well as descriptions of discrimination and ethnic conflict. Shepperson concludes that even though the environment redirected the immigrants, it did not reshape them. Instead, Nevada was reshaped by its restless strangers.[36]

The settlement process, agriculture, political behavior, and literature are representative avenues for research that have been traveled by scholars to discover ethnic history in the West. There are other paths as well. Urban and labor history are especially important, as Robert A. Burchell's study, *The San Francisco Irish, 1848-1880* (1979) testifies.[37] Ethnic education is a theme that has attracted Canadian scholars, but curiously it has been ignored by American students of the West.[38] The related fields of nativism and public policy, however, have attracted much attention in the Pacific Coast states, where ethnocentric reaction to Asian and Mexican immigrants has been especially strong.[39] The advantage such studies have over histories of specific ethnic groups lies in their holistic approach; in this way immigrants are treated as minorities in larger societies, not as isolated people with separate histories.

The work of Donald W. Meinig, a cultural geographer, best illustrates a comprehensive regional approach. His *Imperial Texas* (1969) places the study of the many different peoples of that state—Hispanos, blacks, southerners, Germans—within the context of spatial and eivnronmental relationships. In *Southwest: Three Peoples in Geographical Change, 1600-1970* (1971), Meinig is even more attentive to ethnic factors as he traces the interaction of Indians, Hispanos, and Anglos in New Mexico and Arizona over four centuries. He shows that of these groups, the Hispanos are the most cohesive, bound together by language, religion, and social heritage. The Indians are really four groups—Pueblos, Pima-Papagos, Navahos, and Apaches. The Anglos are midwesterners, Texans, Californians, Mormons, and European immigrants, such as Cornish miners and Jewish merchants. Meinig pursues the economic, political, and demographic consequences of this ethnic mixture in the southwestern environment, but he does not attempt to explain in depth the culture of any one of the several groups.[40]

In contrast to studies like Meinig's that are conceptualized in topical or cross-ethnic terms, histories of specific minority groups in the West have the potential of offering greater depth of analysis and understanding of ethnic culture. At their worst, these histories are informed by no analytical purpose and consist of pleasant tales alternating with tedious lists of names. At their best, they are highly conceptualized and offer appropriate comparisons in time and space. Andrew Rolle, for example, in his study of *The Immigrant Upraised* (1968), argues that in the presumably free, tolerant, and open society of the West, Italian immigrants found acceptance rather than hostility, opportunity rather than alienation. His study is conceived in Turnerian terms and is intended as counterweight to Oscar Handlin's influential book *The Uprooted* (1951), which stresses the trauma of immigration and assimilation. Not all of Rolle's evidence, however, supports his interpretation. When the western environment permitted the concentration of many Italian immigrants in one place, assimilation was slowed and conflict with the host society was often sharp. When immigrant numbers were small, as circumstances frequently dictated, Italian immigrants quickly conformed to American behavior patterns.[41]

Other books on specific ethnic groups in the West tend to be narrower in their focus, treating specific times, places, and circumstances. To cite a few examples, Robert A. Levinson has studied the Jews in the California Gold Rush; T. Lindsay Baker has investigated the settlements of Poles in Texas; and Frederick Bohme has written a history of the Italians in New Mexico. There is even a history of Yugoslavs in Nevada.[42] In other instances, collections of articles have been published on individual states or regions. *The Peoples of Utah*, for example, is especially comprehensive and includes material not only on European immigrants, but also Indians, blacks, Chinese, Japanese, Arabs, and Mexicans.[43]

Non-European peoples have been especially numerous in parts of the West and have attracted the attention of many social scientists, in addition to historians. Their experiences have been fundamentally different from those of European immigrants and therefore deserve a much fuller treatment than can be provided here.

The history of Mexicans or Chicanos in the United States is distinctive because of the long, permeable boundary that stretches from San Diego to Brownsville, making their movement across the border, legal and otherwise, a relatively simple matter. The fact that the Southwest was a part of Mexico before 1848 also alters the relationship of Chicanos to American history. These circumstances are basic to the extensive bibliography that has developed on them in recent years. It has been analyzed intelligently and authoritatively by several scholars, notably Arthur F. Corwin and Juan Gomez-Quinones.[44]

Since the publication of the classic study by Carey McWilliams, *North From Mexico* (1949), a variety of monographs focusing on Chicano labor in the United States have appeared. A recent example is *Chicanos in a Changing Society* (1979) by Albert Camarillo. This history of the Chicanos in Santa Barbara is in several respects a model of the kind of monograph called for in this essay. Camarillo focuses on the history of common people, the unlettered poor who left no written records; he makes extensive use of occupational data contained in census manuscripts and city directories, in addition to oral histories; and he introduces a series of comparisons with other California cities and other non-Chicano workers over time. The result is an informative book that traces the profound changes that occurred as Mexican pueblos of the Southwest evolved into American barrios.[45]

Like the Chicanos, the several Asian groups in America settled chiefly in the West. Unlike them, however, they crossed a great ocean instead of a boundary line to get here. Vastly different in language and culture from old-stock Americans, most Asians, especially the Chinese, stoutly resisted assimilation, hoping to return home to their families as quickly as possible. Nevertheless, many stayed and acculturation did occur, though not without much strife and anguish.

The historical literature of the Asians has also received searching historiographical analysis.[46] No attempt is made here to survey the many contributions to Asian-American history, but one book illustrates many of the qualities effective minority group history ought to have. In *Bitter Strength* (1964), Gunther Barth interprets the first phase of the history of the Chinese in America as emerging from the abrasive contact between two very different cultures. The highly divergent goals of both the American settlers and the Chinese sojourners in California were shaped by the societies from which they came, and both sought easy riches in the West. While there was no permanent place for the Chinese in the California envisioned by most Americans, Barth shows that the Chinese, sustained by devotion to family and tightly controlled by their own society, also excluded themselves from the American mainstream. He describes the efforts of the humanitarians to expose the Chinese "to the liberating influence of American culture" and how, inevitably, increasing numbers of sojourners came into meaningful contact with Californians and were thus transformed into immigrants. Finally, Barth concludes with comparisons with Chinese experience in places other than California.[47]

Blacks in the West have also captured the attention of many historians in the past two decades. Since blacks were originally brought to this country as slave labor, their history will always be uniquely different from all other groups in this country. W. Sherman Savage has provided a sweeping synthesis with his *Blacks in the West* (1976); Lawrence B. DeGraaf has served admirably as historiographer.[48] DeGraaf points out that before 1960 the books and articles written on blacks in the West were virtually without effect on the standard syntheses of western history. Since then many books have been published which demonstrate that, even though blacks were never numerous in the West, they nevertheless played important roles in its development as frontiersmen, cowboys, miners, soldiers, farmers, town builders, and urban workers.[49] Because its aim has been to bring attention to the accomplishments of blacks in the West, most of this literature is traditional in concept and method. Usually lacking in comparisons with other minority groups, the dominant society, or blacks in other regions, it has often dwelt on white racism and oppression, with the result that we still have little understanding of black society in the West, urban or rural, compared with what recent studies have revealed about Negro life in the South or the cities of the Northeast.

I have attempted in this essay to show that since the mid-1960s there has been an enormous growth in the number and quality of studies treating historical aspects of ethnic minority life in the American West. Although much of this recent work bears similarities in its methods to what Frederick Jackson Turner taught in his famous seminars early in the century, its inspiration lies elsewhere, even though Turner's frontier thesis has been a dominating concept in western historiography. Turner provided the key to ethnic history in his methodology, but his students fumbled at the door. More attracted by the frontier thesis and its melting-pot corollary, they failed to integrate racial and ethnic minorities into their histories. For decades professionally trained historians left the field to amateurs and filiopietists. Only in the 1960s, when interest in the pluralistic character of American society flourished as it never had before, did the professionals turn to ethnic minority history. Almost none recognized an intellectual debt to Turner, unless it was through his latter-day students Hansen and Curti. Instead, their formulations emerged from the "new social history," "the new political history," or cross-disciplinary study in cultural geography, sociology, anthropology, and folklore.[50] Still others seem to have been stimulated by a new concern for local history and the changing character of life at the local level. The result of this new interest is an array of carefully conceptualized books, the best of which examine the process of change over time in ethnic minority group culture as it interacts with other groups, native and immigrant, within a specific physical and social environment. A review of the literature shows that much has been accomplished in a decade. But it is only a beginning.

Notes

1. An excellent introduction to historical thinking about ethnic groups in the West has been provided by Moses Rischin, "Beyond the Great Divide: Immigration and the Last Frontier," *Journal of American History* 55 (June 1968): 42-53. See also his "Immigration, Migration, and Minorities in California: A Reassessment," *Pacific Historical Review* 41 (February 1972): 72-90. The most useful general bibliography is John D. Buenker and Nicholas C. Burckel (eds.), *Immigration and Ethnicity: A Guide to Information Sources* (Detroit: Gale Research Company, 1977).

2. Walter Prescott Webb, *The Great Plains* (Boston: Ginn, 1931; paperbound ed., Lincoln: University of Nebraska Press, 1981), p. 509; Everett Dick, *The Sod-House Frontier, 1854-1890: A Social History of the Central and Northern Plains* (1937; paperbound ed., Lincoln: University of Nebraska Press, 1979); Oscar O. Winther, *The Great Northwest: A History,* 2d ed. rev. (New York: Knopf, 1950), pp. 417-26; Earl Pomeroy, *The Pacific Slope* (New York: Knopf, 1965; paperbound ed., Seattle: University of Washington Press, 1975), pp. 262-64; John A. Hawgood, *America's Western Frontiers: The Exploration and Settlement of the Trans-Mississippi West* (New York: Knopf, 1967). Most western state histories are also vulnerable to this criticism, but for a notable exception see Elwyn B. Robinson, *History of North Dakota* (Lincoln: University of Nebraska Press, 1966). More recently Richard Bartlett has made an admirable but not entirely successful effort to integrate immigrants into the social history of the nineteenth-century American frontier. See *The New Country* (New York: Oxford University Press, 1974; paperbound ed., 1976), esp. pp. 143-72.

3. Fulmer Mood, "The Development of Frederick Jackson Turner as a Historical Thinker," *Transactions of the Colonial Society of Massachusetts* 34 (1943): 328-51; Richard Jensen, "American Election Analysis," in *Politics and the Social Sciences*, ed. Seymour Martin Lipset (New York: Oxford University Press, 1969), pp. 232-35.

4. Merle Curti, "Frederick Jackson Turner," in *Wisconsin Witness to Frederick Jackson Turner,* comp. O. Lawrence Burnette, Jr. (Madison: State Historical Society of Wisconsin, 1961), pp. 202-4; Merle Curti, "The Section and the Frontier in American History: The Methodological Concepts

of Frederick Jackson Turner," in *Methods in Social Science,* ed. Stuart Rice (Chicago: University of Chicago Press, 1931), pp. 353–67; Avery O. Craven, "Frederick Jackson Turner," in *The Marcus W. Jernegan Essays in American Historiography,* ed. William T. Hutchinson (Chicago: University of Chicago Press, 1937), p. 265; Ray Allen Billington, *Frederick Jackson Turner: Historian, Scholar, Teacher* (New York: Oxford University Press, 1973), pp. 209–32.

5. Written in response to a request from the newspaper, six articles treated the immigration of Italians, Germans, Jews, and French-Canadians to the United States. They appeared in August, September, and October 1901. The best analysis of Turner in relation to immigration history is by Edward N. Saveth, *American Historians and European Immigrants, 1875–1925* (New York: Columbia University Press, 1948), pp. 122–37. See also Billington, *Turner,* pp. 171–73 and 486–89.

6. E.g., "The Old West," in *Frontier in American History* (New York: Henry Holt, 1921), esp. pp. 93–105.

7. See Richard Hofstadter's perceptive criticism of Turner's sectionalism in *The Progressive Historians: Turner, Beard, Parrington* (New York: Knopf, 1968; paperbound ed., 1970), pp. 95–105. *Western Historical Quarterly* has recently published three articles that relate to Turnerian sectionalism and the West: Jackson K. Putnam, "The Turner Thesis and the Westward Movement: A Reappraisal," *Western Historical Quarterly* 7 (October 1976): 377–404; Michael C. Steiner, "The Significance of Turner's Sectional Thesis," *Western Historical Quarterly* 10 (October 1979): 437–66; and Richard Jensen, "On Modernizing Frederick Jackson Turner: The Historiography of Regionalism," *Western Historical Quarterly* 11 (July 1980): 307–22. For present purposes Putnam's essay is the most valuable.

8. One of Turner's earliest graduate students at Wisconsin, Kate Everest, effectively studied German immigration to the state. Publication of her work actually preceded the presentation by Turner of his frontier thesis at the American Historical Association meeting of 1893. Unfortunately, Everest's work attracted little scholarly attention then or later. Kate Asaphine Everest, "How Wisconsin Came by Its Large German Element," *Collections of the State Historical Society of Wisconsin* 12 (1892): 299–334. See also Kate Everest Levi, "Geographical Origins of German Immigration to Wisconsin," *ibid.* 14 (1898): 343–50.

9. Clifford Lord and Carl Ubbelohde, *Clio's Servant: The State Historical Society of Wisconsin, 1846–1954* (Madison: State Historical Society of Wisconsin, 1967), pp. 257–63. The volumes of the Domesday series are *A History*

of Agriculture in Wisconsin (1922), *Wisconsin Domesday Book: Town Studies* (1924), *Four Wisconsin Counties: Prairie and Forest* (1927), *The Wisconsin Lead Region* (1932), and *The Winnebago-Horican Basin* (1937). All were published by the State Historical Society of Wisconsin. See also Schafer's *The Social History of American Agriculture* (New York: Macmillan, 1936), esp. pp. 209–21.

10. Schafer, *Social History*, p. 219.

11. Merle Curti *et al.*, *The Making of an American Community: A Case Study of Democracy in a Frontier County* (Stanford: Stanford University Press, 1959), p. 444.

12. The idea that social forces not inherently part of frontier conditions could explain American development received powerful exposition by the sociologist Everett S. Lee, who stressed the role of social mobility in "The Turner Thesis Re-examined," *American Quarterly* 13 (Spring 1961): 77–87. See also George W. Pierson, "The M-Factor in American History," *American Quarterly* 14 (Summer Supplement 1962): 275–89. Rowland Berthoff has examined the unsettling effect of social mobility in American history in his *An Unsettled People: Social Order and Disorder in American History* (New York: Harper and Row, 1971), though not explicitly as an alternative scheme to Turnerism.

13. Marcus Lee Hansen, *The Immigrant in American History* (Cambridge: Harvard University Press, 1940), pp. 65–68; *The Atlantic Migration, 1607–1860* (Cambridge: Harvard University Press, 1940), pp. 13–17; to illustrate Hansen's influence in this regard, see Hawgood, *America's Western Frontiers*, p. 393 n. 8, and his *The Tragedy of German-America* (New York: Putnam, 1940), pp. 22–23. Carlton Qualey, a student of Norwegian settlement in the United States, is sharply critical of Hansen. See his "Marcus Lee Hansen," *Midcontinent American Studies Journal* 8 (Fall 1967): 18–25. For a more favorable assessment of Hansen's importance for immigration history and Turnerian historiography, see Billington, *Turner*, pp. 487–89; Allan H. Spear, "Marcus Lee Hansen and the Historiography of Immigration," *Wisconsin Magazine of History* 54 (Summer 1961): 258–68; and Moses Rischin, "Marcus Lee Hansen: America's First Transethnic Historian," in *Uprooted Americans: Essays to Honor Oscar Handlin*, ed. Richard L. Bushman *et al.* (Boston: Little, Brown, 1979), pp. 319–47. Two other major historians of American immigration, George Stephenson and Carl Wittke, studied with Turner at Harvard. Neither, however, received encouragement from him to enter this field, nor is their work associated with the frontier thesis or with Turnerian methodology. See Rischin, "Hansen," p. 334.

14. Cf. Robert F. Berkhofer, Jr., "Space, Time, Culture, and the New Frontier," *Agricultural History* 38 (January 1964): 21–30.

15. James C. Malin has argued that one must master the ecology of a region before its history can be written. The study of environmental characteristics and their relationship to human occupance is the prolegomenon to history, in his view. See *Grassland of North America* (1947; Gloucester, Mass.: Peter Smith, 1967).

16. Carlton Qualey, *Norwegian Settlement in the United States* (1938; New York: Arno Press, 1970); William Mulder, *Homeward to Zion: The Mormon Migration from Scandinavia* (Minneapolis: University of Minnesota Press, 1957); Kenneth Bjork, *West of the Great Divide: Norwegian Migration to the Pacific Coast, 1847–1893* (Northfield, Minn.: Norwegian-American Historical Association, 1958); Jorgen Dahlie, "A Social History of Scandinavian Immigration, Washington State, 1895–1910" (Ph.D. diss., Washington State University, 1967).

17. Frederick C. Luebke, *Immigrants and Politics: The Germans of Nebraska, 1880–1900* (Lincoln: University of Nebraska Press, 1969), pp. 16–70; Richard Sallet, *Russian-German Settlements in the United States,* trans. Lavern J. Rippley and Armand Bauer (Fargo: North Dakota Institute for Regional Studies, 1974; orig. 1931).

18. Timothy Kloberdanz, "Plainsmen of Three Continents: Volga German Adaptation to Steppe, Prairie, and Pampa," in *Ethnicity on the Great Plains,* ed. Frederick C. Luebke (Lincoln: University of Nebraska Press for the Center for Great Plains Studies, 1980), p. 63.

19. Richard Etulain, "Basque Beginnings in the Pacific Northwest," *Idaho Yesterdays* 18 (Spring 1974): 26–32; Gordon Hendrickson, "Immigration and Assimilation in Wyoming," in *Peopling the High Plains: Wyoming's European Heritage,* ed. Gordon Hendrickson (Cheyenne: Wyoming State Archives and Historical Department, 1977), pp. 169–94. Several of the historiographical considerations raised here are explored further by Kathleen N. Conzen, "Historical Approaches to the Study of Rural Ethnic Communities," in *Ethnicity on the Great Plains,* ed. Luebke, pp. 1–18.

20. Kathleen N. Conzen, "Immigrants, Immigrant Neighborhoods, and Ethnic Identity: Historical Issues," *Journal of American History* 66 (December 1979): 603–15.

21. John A. Hostetler, *Hutterite Society* (Baltimore: Johns Hopkins University Press, 1974), p. 186.

22. Allan Teichroew, "World War I and the Mennonite Migration to Avoid the Draft," *Mennonite Quarterly Review* 45 (July 1971): 219–49.

23. Donald W. Meinig, *Imperial Texas: An Interpretive Essay in Cultural Geography* (Austin: University of Texas Press, 1969; paperbound ed., n.d.); Meinig, *Southwest: Three Peoples in Geographical Change, 1600–1970* (New York: Oxford University Press, 1971); Frederick C. Luebke, "Ethnic Group Settlement on the Great Plains," *Western Historical Quarterly* 8 (October 1977): 405–30, and Luebke, Introduction to *Ethnicity on the Great Plains,* pp. xi–xxxiii. For useful studies on the state level, see William C. Sherman, "Ethnic Distribution in Western North Dakota," *North Dakota History* 46 (Winter 1979): 4–12; and Douglas Hale, "European Immigrants in Oklahoma: A Survey," *Chronicles of Oklahoma* 53 (Summer 1975): 179–203.

24. J. Neale Carman, *Foreign-Language Units of Kansas,* vol. 1, *Historical Atlas and Statistics* (Lawrence: University of Kansas Press, 1962); Heinz Kloss, *Atlas of Nineteenth and Early Twentieth Century American Settlements* (Marburg, West Germany: N. G. Elwert, 1974). See also Terry G. Jordan, "*Annals* Map Supplement Number Thirteen: Population Origin Groups in Rural Texas," *Annals of the Association of American Geographers* 60 (June 1970): 404–5. Spatial distributions of ethnic groups in Oklahoma are mapped separately in the several volumes of the Newcomers to a New Land series. E.g., see Douglas Hale, *The Germans from Russia in Oklahoma* (Norman: University of Oklahoma Press, 1980), p. 23; and Kenny L. Brown, *The Italians in Oklahoma* (Norman: University of Oklahoma Press, 1980), pp. 15–16. Decennial census reports formerly included maps showing the distribution and density of the various racial and ethnic groups. For example, see U.S. Bureau of the Census, *Statistical Atlas, Twelfth Census of the United States, 1900* (Washington, D.C.: Government Printing Office, 1903), plates 55–75.

25. See esp. Sallett, *Russian-German Settlements,* and Albert J. Peterson, Jr., "German-Russian Catholic Colonization in Western Kansas: A Settlement Geography" (Ph.D. diss., Louisiana State University, 1970).

26. Robert C. Ostergren, "Prairie Bound: Migration Patterns to a Swedish Settlement on the Dakota Frontier," in *Ethnicity on the Great Plains,* ed. Luebke, pp. 73–91.

27. William A. Douglas and Jon Bilbao, *Amerikanuak: Basques in the New World* (Reno: University of Nevada Press, 1975); see also David A. Cookson, "The Basques in Wyoming," in *Peopling the High Plains,* ed. Hendrickson, pp. 95–120.

28. Theodore Saloutos, "The Immigrant in Pacific Coast Agriculture, 1880–1940," *Agricultural History* 49 (January 1975): 182–201; Andrew F. Rolle, *The Immigrant Upraised: Italian Adventurers and Colonists in an*

Expanding America (Norman: University of Oklahoma Press, 1968), pp. 251–92; Masakazu Iwata, "The Japanese Immigrants in California Agriculture," *Agricultural History* 36 (January 1962): 25–37; Bradley Baltensperger, "Agricultural Change among Nebraska Immigrants, 1880–1900," in *Ethnicity on the Great Plains*, ed. Luebke, pp. 170–89. For an early, excellent study of ethnic agriculture, see Russell W. Lynch, *Czech Farmers in Oklahoma*, Bulletin, Oklahoma Agricultural and Mechanical College, Stillwater, Oklahoma, 39 (June 1942). This volume effectively makes a series of comparisons of Czech with non-Czech practice, but it lacks a historical dimension.

29. Terry G. Jordan, *German Seed in Texas Soil: Immigrant Farmers in Nineteenth-Century Texas* (Austin: University of Texas Press, 1966). A recent Texas study that broadens the scope to include other ethnic groups but adds little to an understanding of ethnic agriculture is Winston Lee Kinsey, "The Immigrant in Texas Agriculture during Reconstruction," *Agricultural History* 53 (January 1979): 125–41.

30. D. Aidan McQuillan, "Adaptation of Three Immigrant Groups to Farming in Central Kansas, 1875–1925" (Ph.D. diss., University of Wisconsin-Madison, 1975); McQuillan, "The Mobility of Immigrants and Americans: A Comparison of Farmers on the Kansas Frontier," *Agricultural History* 53 (July 1979): 576–96.

31. John A. Hostetler, "The Old Order Amish: A Study in Cultural Vulnerability," in *Ethnicity on the Great Plains*, ed. Luebke, pp. 92–108; Hostetler, *Hutterite Society*, pp. 194–200.

32. Walter T. K. Nugent, *The Tolerant Populists: Kansas Populism and Nativism* (Chicago: University of Chicago Press, 1963); Stanley B. Parsons, Jr., *The Populist Context: Urban versus Rural Power on a Great Plains Frontier* (Westport, Conn.: Greenwood Press, 1973). See also David S. Trask, "The Nebraska Populist Party: A Social and Political Analysis" (Ph.D. diss., University of Nebraska, 1971). North and South Dakota ethnic groups from the Populist era to the 1950s are analyzed in Michael Paul Rogin, *The Intellectuals and McCarthy: The Radical Specter* (Cambridge, Mass.: MIT Press, 1967), pp. 104–67.

33. Luebke, *Immigrants and Politics*. John R. Kleinschmidt, "The Political Behavior of the Bohemian and Swedish Ethnic Groups in Nebraska, 1884–1900" (M.A. thesis, University of Nebraska, 1968) is patterned directly on my study. For other systematic approaches to the study of ethnic politics, see Clifford L. Nelson, *German-American Political Behavior in Nebraska and Wisconsin, 1916–1920* (Lincoln: University of Nebraska–Lincoln Publication No. 217, 1972); Burton W. Folsom II, "Ethnoreligious Response to

Progressivism and War: German Americans and Nebraska Politics, 1908–1924" (M.A. thesis, University of Nebraska, 1973); Robert W. Cherny, "Isolationist Voting in 1940: A Statistical Analysis," *Nebraska History* 52 (Fall 1971): 293–310. Relatively little of a systematic character has been produced for other parts of the West, but see Leslie W. Koepplin, "A Relationship of Reform: Immigrants and Progressives in the Far West" (Ph.D. diss., University of California at Los Angeles, 1971); and Michael Paul Rogin and John L. Shover, *Political Change in California: Critical Elections and Social Movements, 1890–1966* (Westport, Conn.: Greenwood, 1970). For a brief historiography of ethnocultural voting studies, see Paul Kleppner, "Immigrant Groups and Partisan Politics," *Immigration History Newsletter* 10 (May 1978): 1–5.

34. Robert W. Cherny, *Populism, Progressivism, and the Transformation of Nebraska Politics, 1885–1915* (Lincoln: University of Nebraska Press for the Center for Great Plains Studies, 1981).

35. James C. Juhnke, *A People of Two Kingdoms: The Political Acculturation of the Kansas Mennonites* (Newton, Kans.: Faith and Life Press, 1975).

36. Wilbur S. Shepperson, *Restless Strangers: Nevada's Immigrants and Their Interpreters* (Reno: University of Nevada Press, 1970), p. 6. In contrast to Shepperson, who depends upon nonimmigrant writers, Dorothy Burton Skårdal draws almost exclusively on literature produced by first and second generation immigrants from Norway, Sweden, and Denmark. See *The Divided Heart: Scandinavian Immigrant Experience through Literary Sources* (Lincoln: University of Nebraska Press, 1974). Skårdal does not distinguish Scandinavian experience in the West from that in other parts of the country.

37. Robert A. Burchell, *The San Francisco Irish, 1848–1880* (Manchester, England: Manchester University Press, 1979). For a perceptive analysis of cross-ethnic residential patterns in Omaha, Nebraska, see Howard P. Chudacoff, "A New Look at Ethnic Neighborhoods: Residential Dispersion and the Concept of Visibility in a Medium-Sized City," *Journal of American History* 60 (June 1973): 76–93. Other urban ethnic histories in the West tend to be traditional in approach, e.g., Max Vorspan and Lloyd P. Gartner, *History of the Jews of Los Angeles* (San Marino, Calif.: Huntington Library, 1970). Neil C. Sandberg, *Ethnic Identity and Assimilation: The Polish-American Community, Case Study of Metropolitan Los Angeles* (New York: Praeger, 1974), is an example of a sociological study. William Toll provides two fine examples of carefully conceptualized studies in his essays "Fraternalism and Community Structure on the Urban Frontier: The Jews of Portland, Oregon,"

Pacific Historical Review 47 (August 1978): 369–403; and "Voluntarism and Modernization in Portland Jewry: The B'nai B'rith in the 1920s," *Western Historical Quarterly* 10 (January 1979): 21–38.

38. See, for example, Jorgen Dahlie, "No Fixed Boundaries: Scandinavian Response to Schooling in Western Canada," in *Emerging Ethnic Boundaries,* ed. Danielle Lee (Ottawa: University of Ottawa, 1979), pp. 117–32; and Keith Macleod, "Education and the Assimilation of the New Canadian in the Northwest Territories and Saskatchewan, 1885–1934" (Ph.D. diss., University of Toronto, 1975). I have touched on the interaction of superpatriotism with ethnic education in "Legal Restriction on Foreign Languages in the Great Plains States, 1917–1923," in *Languages in Conflict: Linguistic Acculturation on the Great Plains,* ed. Paul Schach (Lincoln: University of Nebraska Press for the Center for Great Plains Studies, 1981), pp. 1–19. For a general survey of studies in ethnic education see Maxine S. Seller, "The Education of Immigrants in the United States: An Introduction to the Literature," *Immigration History Newsletter* 13 (May 1981): 1–8.

39. Robert F. Heizer and Alan J. Almquist, *The Other Californians: Prejudice and Discrimination under Spain, Mexico, and the United States to 1920* (Berkeley: University of California Press, 1971); Roger Daniels, *The Politics of Prejudice: The Anti-Japanese Movement in California and the Struggle for Japanese Exclusion* (Berkeley: University of California Press, 1962); Stuart C. Miller, *The Unwelcome Immigrant: The American Image of the Chinese, 1785–1882* (Berkeley: University of California Press, 1969); Roger Daniels, *Concentration Camps, USA: Japanese Americans and World War II* (New York: Holt, Rinehart, and Winston, 1971). For a fascinating study that combines nativism and labor history, see Alexander Saxton, *The Indispensable Enemy: Labor and the Anti-Chinese Movement in California* (Berkeley: University of California Press, 1971). A collection of published articles, *Racism in California* (New York: Macmillan, 1972), has been edited by Roger Daniels and Spencer Olin, Jr. See also Charles Wollenberg (ed.), *Ethnic Conflict in California History* (Santa Monica, Calif.: Tinnon-Brown, 1970).

40. See n. 23 above.

41. Andrew F. Rolle, *The Immigrant Upraised: Italian Adventurers and Colonists in an Expanding America* (Norman: University of Oklahoma Press, 1968); cf. Oscar Handlin, *The Uprooted: The Epic Story of the Great Migrations That Made the American People,* 2d ed., enlarged (1951; Boston: Little, Brown, 1973).

42. Robert A. Levinson, *The Jews in the California Gold Rush* (New

York: Ktav Publishing House, 1978); T. Lindsay Baker, *The First Polish Americans: Silesian Settlements in Texas* (College Station: Texas A&M University Press, 1979); Frederick G. Bohme, *A History of the Italians in New Mexico* (New York: Arno Press, 1975); Adam S. Eterovich, *Yugoslavs in Nevada, 1859–1900* (San Francisco: R and E Research Associates, 1973).

43. Helen Z. Papanikolas (ed.), *The Peoples of Utah* (Salt Lake City: Utah State Historical Society, 1976). See also Hendrickson (ed.), *Peopling the High Plains*; Luebke (ed.), *Ethnicity on the Great Plains*; James A. Halseth and Bruce A. Glasrud (eds.), *The Northwest Mosaic: Minority Conflicts in Pacific Northwest History* (Boulder, Colo.: Pruett, 1977); Sidney Heitman (ed.), *Germans from Russia in Colorado* (Ann Arbor: Western Social Science Association, 1978); Anne Loftis, *California–Where the Twain Did Meet* (New York: Macmillan, 1973), is a well-written synthesis treating all racial and ethnic groups in one state. In the case of Oklahoma, the University of Oklahoma Press has published a series of ten short ethnic histories, including the major European groups, Indians, blacks, and Mexicans.

44. Arthur F. Corwin, "Mexican-American History: An Assessment," *Pacific Historical Review* 42 (August 1973): 269–308; and Corwin, "The Study and Interpretation of Mexican Labor Migration: An Introduction," in *Immigrants–and Immigrants: Perspectives on Mexican Labor Migration to the United States,* ed. Arthur F. Corwin (Westport, Conn.: Greenwood Press, 1978), pp. 3–24; Juan Gomez-Quinones and Luis Leobardo Arroyo, "On the State of Chicano History," *Western Historical Quarterly* 7 (April 1976): 155–85.

45. Carey McWilliams, *North from Mexico: The Spanish-Speaking People of the United States* (1949; reprint ed., New York: Greenwood Press, 1968); Albert Camarillo, *Chicanos in a Changing Society: From Mexican Pueblos to American Barrios in Santa Barbara and Southern California, 1848–1930* (Cambridge, Mass.: Harvard University Press, 1979). Spatial comparisons are central to a brief study by Richard Griswold del Castillo, "Tucsonenses and Angelenos: A Socio-economic Study of Two Mexican-American Barrios, 1860–1880," *Journal of the West* 18 (January 1979): 58–66. A recent study that examines assimilational and settlement patterns is Lawrence A. Cardoso, *Mexican Emigration to the United States, 1897–1931* (Tucson: University of Arizona Press, 1980).

46. E.g., see Roger Daniels, "The Asian American Experience," in *Reconstruction of American History and Culture,* ed. William H. Cartwright and Richard L. Watson, Jr. (Washington, D.C.: National Council for the Social

Studies, 1973), pp. 139–48; and "American Historians and East Asian Immigrants," *Pacific Historian Review* 42 (November 1974): 449–72.

47. Gunther Barth, *Bitter Strength: A History of the Chinese in the United States, 1850–1870* (Cambridge: Harvard University Press, 1964). Easy introduction to literature on the Asians may be found in such surveys as Betty Lee Sung, *Mountain of Gold: The Story of The Chinese in America* (New York: Macmillan, 1967); and in collections of significant essays, such as Norris Hundley (ed.), *The Asian American: The Historical Experience* (Santa Barbara, Calif.: ABC-Clio, 1976); and Stanford M. Lyman, *The Asian in North America* (Santa Barbara, Calif.: ABC-Clio, 1977); but see also John Modell, *The Economics and Politics of Racial Accommodation: The Japanese of Los Angeles, 1900–1942* (Urbana: University of Illinois Press, 1977).

48. W. Sherman Savage, *Blacks in the West* (Westport, Conn.: Greenwood Press, 1976); Lawrence B. DeGraaf, "Recognition, Racism, and Reflections on the Writing of Western Black History," *Pacific Historical Review* 44 (February 1975): 22–51.

49. Kenneth W. Porter, *The Negro on the American Frontier* (New York: Arno Press, 1971); Philip Durham and Everett L. Jones, *The Negro Cowboys* (New York: Dodd, Mead and Co., 1965); Rudolph M. Lapp, *Blacks in Gold Rush California* (New Haven: Yale University Press, 1977); William H. Leckie, *The Buffalo Soldiers: A Narrative of the Negro Cavalry in the West* (Norman: University of Oklahoma Press, 1967); Arlen Fowler, *The Black Infantry in the West, 1869–1891* (Westport, Conn.: Greenwood Press, 1971); Kenneth G. Goode, *California's Black Pioneers* (Santa Barbara, Calif.: McNally and Loftin, 1973); Norman Crockett, *The Black Towns* (Lawrence: Regents Press of Kansas, 1979); Nell Irwin Painter, *Exodusters: Black Migration to Kansas after Reconstruction* (New York: Knopf, 1976); Robert G. Athearn, *In Search of Canaan: Black Migration to Kansas, 1879–80* (Lawrence: Regents Press of Kansas, 1978); and Jimmie L. Franklin, *The Blacks in Oklahoma* (Norman: University of Oklahoma Press, 1980).

50. Kathleen N. Conzen has pointed out to me that Curti provides a direct link between Turner and the "new urban history." Stephan Thernstrom, a pioneer in the latter field, was clearly aware of Curti's work on Trempealeau County, to which he compared his own discoveries in nineteenth-century urban social mobility. See Stephan Thernstrom, *Poverty and Progress: Social Mobility in a Nineteenth Century City* (Cambridge, Mass.: Harvard University Press, 1964), pp. 197–98.

Chapter Eighteen

Richard W. Etulain

Shifting Interpretations of Western American Cultural History

In the 1880s, James Bryce, the noted English traveler and writer, made two trips to the United States that included excursions into the West. Impressed with what he saw and experienced, he returned to England to complete *The American Commonwealth,* which contained his often-cited observation that the West was "the most American part of America; . . . the part where those features which distinguish America from Europe come out in the strongest relief. What Europe is to Asia, what England is to the rest of Europe, what America is to Europe, that the Western States and Territories are to the Atlantic States." Bryce revisited the West and noted later in 1910 that his first observations, completed in 1887, described "a phase of life which is now swiftly disappearing and may never be again seen elsewhere. Pioneer work in the Rocky Mountain and Pacific States is almost at an end; and these regions are becoming more like the older parts of the Republic."[1]

Bryce did not comment on several topics that have interested later historians writing about the West, but he did understand two relational questions central to western cultural life. Intrigued with the relationship between the West and East, he concluded, as Frederick Jackson Turner would in the 1890s, that the frontier West was sharply different from the eastern part of the United States. Second, he noted that the West was changing and moving from a frontier toward a postfrontier society. These two themes—the horizontal bearing between East and West and the vertical connection between frontier and postfrontier Wests—are pivotal concerns for a consideration of the changing interpretations of western American cultural history.[2]

Although Lord Bryce expressed interest in the cultural development of the frontier West, few American historians of his time were intrigued with the subject. For example, Hubert Howe Bancroft, the most important western historian writing before Frederick Jackson Turner, dealt with numerous facets of western life in his multivolume histories of the West, but he did not pay nearly as much attention to frontier literature, religion, education, or art as he did to military, political, and economic affairs. Nor did his brief discussions of western cultural history suggest that he wished to examine how much the East influenced the West.[3]

Even before Bancroft completed the synthetic essays contained in his final volumes, Turner began publishing his pathbreaking articles of the 1890s and early twentieth century. Turner's contention that the frontier was the major shaping force in American life prevailed in graduate schools for at least two generations. Similarly, the subjects that he stressed have been the topics most western historians emphasized until as recently as a decade or two after World War II. Although some commentators point to Turner's poetic style and his encouragement of his students to study cultural institutions as evidences that he was a humanistic historian, he was, on the contrary, primarily a social science historian more interested in statistics, demography, and geography than in the history of literature, religion, education, or art.[4]

Another factor that limited Turner's interest in cultural history was his continuing stress on the beginning years of frontier societies. Convinced that the farther a society moved from the East Coast the more it freed itself from Europe and the more American it became, Turner reiterated the importance of studying the early years of successive, westward-moving frontier societies. Because Turner's interpretations were so persuasive and popular, his students —and most other western historians in the past decades of the twentieth century—did not diverge from the topics he emphasized. There was, as William Goetzmann has written, a Turnerian "tyranny" in early western historiography.[5]

Turner's attitudes toward frontier societies retarded interest in western cultural history in still another way. He did not expect that the cultural activities of frontiersmen would amount to much. In writing that "a primitive society can hardly be expected to show the intelligent appreciation of the complexity of business interests in a developed society," he implied a good deal about the cultural achievements he expected from a frontier society.[6] In the 1890s Turner considered "civilization" in the trans-Mississippi West as young and immature, as no more than sixty or seventy years old. And in the few passages he devoted to western cultural history, he did not treat the cultural accomplishments of Hispanic settlements in the Southwest, Mormon communities in Utah, or those in northern California.

In the closing sections of his classic essay published in 1893, Turner was even more explicit in his interpretation of frontier culture. He mentioned here for the first time the importance of education, religion, and other intellectual activities in the West. Asserting that the East feared the isolation of the West, he noted that the East tried to civilize the West by flooding the region with preachers and teachers. These carriers of culture influenced the West, Turner admitted, but not so much as the absence of institutional hierarchies and restraints on the frontier. Just as he would in his other writings on the frontier, Turner concluded in his most famous essay that the open and free frontier atmosphere did more than eastern institutions to shape western cultural life.[7]

Finally, Turner was not much interested in the twentieth-century West. Although he continued to write until his death in 1932—forty years after the publication of his earliest essays—his books and major essays dealt with the pre-1890 period, even if his western history course at Harvard nudged past 1900 and a few of his less familiar writings treated twentieth-century subjects. Turner encouraged other scholars to study the contemporary West, but he was not sufficiently enamored to devote his time and energy to the post-1900 era.[8]

Most of Turner's contemporaries were as reluctant as he to deal with western cultural history. His successor at the University of Wisconsin when he left for Harvard in 1910, Frederic Logan Paxson, published a general account of the West the same year he came to Madison. Fourteen years later Paxson produced his Pulitzer Prize–winning *History of the American Frontier, 1763–1893*. Paxson's volumes carried full accounts of Indian-white relations, exploration and expansion, economic, political, and governmental developments, but he failed to devote even one of the eighty-three chapters in the two books to cultural history.[9]

Some of the same gaps are apparent in the writings of Herbert Eugene Bolton. Attracted to Spanish explorers and settlers who marched across what became the Gulf Coast states and the American Southwest, Bolton stressed the Borderlands concept and helped broaden subsequent discussions of western American history. But he did not provide extended discussions of literature, education, and the arts. Even in his well-known essay "The Mission as a Frontier Institution in the Spanish-American Colonies," he treated the mission primarily as a political, social, and military institution.[10]

Bolton's emphases in his classic essay are typical of many of his best-known writings: he was much more intrigued with economic, political, and military history than with cultural topics. What Spanish leaders experienced in New World expansion, what routes they took, what economic and social problems they faced—these questions occupied Bolton more than the literature the Spaniards wrote, what they taught in their schools, and what art and architecture resulted from their experiences. Indeed, when Bolton spoke of the priests and friars who spent their lives serving the Church and the Spanish Empire, he treated them more as agents of church and government than as bearers of culture.

Walter Prescott Webb was equally uninterested in cultural history in the early stages of his career. Trained in institutional history under Lindley Miller Keasby at the University of Texas, Webb followed his mentor's social scientific emphases, especially Keasby's interest in studying the relationships between environmental and institutional development. When Webb wrote *The Great Plains* (1931), he set out to trace the evolution of a unique civilization on the Great Plains, but in developing his provocative thesis, he devoted only one section to cultural history, a chapter on western literature.

Although he did not betray much interest in cultural history, Webb treated his subject in a manner that distinguished him from Turner. In the preface of *The Great Plains,* Webb made clear that he was interested in the Plains as frontier *and* region. He noted that his early interest in weapons, fencing, and water supply led him to ask whether new experiences on the Plains drew on older techniques of livelihood inherited from the East or whether new circumstances demanded new adaptations. Agreeing with Turner, he noted that "American institutions and cultural complexes that came from a humid and timbered region" were altered, and new kinds of societies and cultures emerged.[11]

But Webb moved beyond the innovating power of the Plains environment. Having determined that frontiersmen met new circumstances once they crossed the Mississippi, he began his story with the physical environment and the first human contacts with this environment. He then traced these layers of cultural contact from Indian societies to Anglo literature of the early twentieth century. Unlike Turner, however, Webb moved beyond frontier contacts and adaptations into a later period of regional development. Not satisfied to limit what he said to nineteenth-century experiences, he moved closer to the present than many Turnerians had. In short, Webb began to write about the Great Plains as a separate, identifiable region; and his definition of the Plains setting—"a geographic unity whose influences have been so powerful as to put a characteristic mark upon everything that survives within its borders"—should satisfy most scholars in search of an appropriate definition of regionalism. "The Plains country," Webb added, "was something apart, with aspects incommensurable with those of surrounding regions, where conditions were different" (p. vi).

At the outset of *The Great Plains* Webb showed his indebtedness to the Turnerian school of historiography. At the same time he hinted that he was also interested in something more than frontier history; he wanted to trace the evolution of a culture from its beginnings to its maturation as a regional culture. In this emphasis, Webb led the way in studying the West as a region.

Although western historians paid little attention to most cultural topics before 1930, a few writers were beginning to examine the literature of the frontier West. In the 1920s three book-length studies, all strongly influenced by Turner's ideas, became the first notable volumes on the American literary West. Ralph Leslie Rusk's two-volume *Literature of the Middle Western Frontier* and Dorothy Dondore's *The Prairie and the Making of Middle America* . . . emphasized accounts of exploration, travel narratives, and histories but slighted fiction and other forms of belletristic literature. Conversely, *The Frontier in American Literature,* a brief descriptive book by Lucy Lockwood Hazard, stressed fiction and dealt with early twentieth-century writers. None of these interpreters treated the West as a region, choosing instead to discuss western authors as frontier writers.[12]

Another indication of this nascent interest in western cultural history was evident in the first national conference convened to study the trans-Mississippi West. When the University of Colorado hosted the meeting in June of 1929, two plenary sessions were devoted to western missionaries and the West in American literature, and in the volume resulting from the meeting, six of the sixteen papers dealt with these two topics. Nearly all the essays on religion and literature reflect a pronounced Turnerian bias, but at least they treated topics that many other western historians overlooked.[13]

That few historians of the West emphasized cultural history before 1930 is not surprising; the same lacuna was evident in American historiography. The first courses in American cultural-intellectual history were not offered until the 1920s, and no interpretation of U.S. history stressed the history of ideas until the volumes of Vernon Louis Parrington's immensely influential *Main Currents in American Thought* appeared in 1927 and 1930. Before Parrington, progressive historians and advocates of the New History seemed to agree with scientific historians that literature and philosophy were not satisfactory bedfellows for history. These disciplines, commentators of the teens and 1920s implied, were too theoretical, too likely to stress the mythical and the unreal.

But new historical ideas swept through America in the 1930s, and by the

1950s cultural and intellectual histories proved extremely popular among professional historians. Voting in 1950 on the most important American historical works published since 1920, historians gave Parrington a commanding lead over Turner and listed Merle Curti's *The Growth of American Thought* (1943) as the best book appearing between 1936 and 1950. During the 1930s and 1940s, Parrington, Curti, Ralph Gabriel, Perry Miller, and Richard Hofstadter made lasting contributions to American historiography in the fields of cultural and intellectual history.[14]

In these same decades, western historians began to pay more attention to cultural history. Notable among these efforts is Franklin Walker's smoothly written *San Francisco's Literary Frontier* (1939), which is more comprehensive than the title suggests. A Rhodes Scholar and biographer of Frank Norris, Walker set out to write a study of San Francisco literary culture from the Gold Rush to the arrival of the transcontinental railroad in 1869. But in utilizing the methods of group biography and in emphasizing intellectual and social history, Walker enlarged his focus and produced the best volume of western cultural history published prior to World War II.

Although Walker confessed intellectual debts to Turner, Parrington, and Bernard DeVoto, his books on Norris and the literary activities of San Francisco, late-nineteenth-century southern California, and Carmel seem to owe less to these interpreters than to his own blend of biography, cultural history, and literary criticism. He suggested that rapid social change in northern and southern California in the latter half of the nineteenth century, particularly in those years following the arrival of the railroads, dramatically changed the culture of the state. Previously isolated and provincial, California became more culturally sophisticated once the railroads brought hosts of newcomers with varied backgrounds and opened the way for Californians to flee to the East Coast and Europe. Walker posits that California in the 1850s and 1860s produced a literature illustrative of its frontier experiences, characterized by boisterous satire, booster fiction and poetry, and numerous factual writings. While Walker centered on literary activity, he did not omit commentary on historical writing, the theater, churches and preachers, and other social and economic activities.[15]

In the same year that Walker's *San Francisco's Literary Frontier* appeared, Colin B. Goodykoontz, a student of Turner, published *Home Missions on the American Frontier,* one of the few full-length studies of religion in the West. Emphasizing the central roles of Congregationalists, Presbyterians, and the American Home Missionary Society, Goodykoontz traced the impact of New England religious ideas on the nineteenth-century western frontier. While the author briefly discussed the impact of the missionaries on schools, colleges, and society in general, most of his narrative was narrowly focused on institutional developments. But he was surprisingly non-Turnerian in concluding that the Home Missionary movement "was conservative in its tendencies and results," that it transplanted eastern ideas and religious life that took root in the West.[16]

What Franklin Walker accomplished in his books on California, Englishman Sidney Warren attempted for the Pacific Northwest in *Farthest Frontier*. Devoting fact-filled chapters to regional developments in education, literature, and journalism, he also provided sections on theater, music, art, and architecture. Terminating his coverage at 1910 because, he argued, that date divided the pioneer and modern periods of the Pacific Northwest, Warren stressed the rise of cultural institutions in the region. Though his book was more narrative than interpretive and more focused upon early than later cultural developments, Warren did conclude, in non-Turnerian fashion, that "westerners were, on the whole, imitators, not originators, and conformists rather than nonconformists."[17]

Focusing on a smaller region, Carey McWilliams's *Southern California Country* is a provocative analysis of the sociocultural life of California south of the Tehachapi. Divorcing himself from a good deal of traditional western historiography (he was a journalist), McWilliams moved quickly through the Spanish, Mexican, and frontier periods to emphasize the twentieth century. He noted the eastern and midwestern influences on the region, the urbanism of the area, and the confusion of cultures arising from southern California's complex heritage. While devoting extended sections to literature, religion, and art, he also included discussions of architecture, Hollywood, and ethnic cultures. More than previous interpreters of western American culture, McWilliams was fascinated with cultural geography. Indeed, the headnote of an important chapter entitled "The Cultural Landscape" was geographer Carl Sauer's assertion: "Culture is the agent, the natural area the medium, the cultural landscape the result." Though this stimulating book is well written, persuasively argued, and full of new information, it seems little known among many western historians.[18]

In the 1950s several important publications propounded novel approaches to the cultural history of the West. In 1955, in perhaps the most widely cited recent essay on western history, Earl Pomeroy called for a reorientation of western history with less emphasis on Turner's views of the frontier as a radically innovative environment and more stress on the West as a replicator of eastern views and experiences. Ten years later, Pomeroy practiced what he preached in *The Pacific Slope,* a unique interpretation of the Far West that noted many continuities between East and West, especially in political and economic developments. In addition, Pomeroy broke sharply with the tendency of western historians to focus on the pre-1900 era when he devoted more than half of his provocative volume to the first sixty-five years of the twentieth century. No one could claim that Pomeroy's revisionist views immediately won over most western historians, but his interpretations have been increasingly important in the 1960s and 1970s.[19]

In the same year that Pomeroy called for a reorientation of western history, Louis B. Wright, a distinguished scholar of English and American cultural history, published a series of six lectures entitled *Culture on the Moving Frontier.* Arguing that "children of light," especially those of Anglo-Saxon Protestant backgrounds, were culture bearers in successive westward moves across the continent, Wright dealt with frontier cultures on the Atlantic seaboard, in the Ohio Valley, in Kentucky, and in gold-rush California. Contrary to Turner's interpretation of the frontier as a powerful innovative and custom-breaking force, Wright asserted that American frontiers and frontiersmen were more conservative than innovative, that the West followed more than it deviated from cultural attitudes and experiences of Europe and the eastern United States.[20]

Even more influential than the interpretations of Pomeroy or Wright in western cultural historiography are the views of Henry Nash Smith, whose *Virgin Land: The American West as Symbol and Myth* appeared in 1950. No book published in the past thirty years has swayed thinking and writing about the American West more than this brilliant volume. The first monograph in what has become known as the American Studies movement, *Virgin Land* helped revolutionize interpretations of the West. Most of all, Smith urged scholars to take seriously myths about the frontier West that shaped and powered attitudes, ideas, and policies concerning the region in the eighteenth and nineteenth centuries. He showed in penetrating fashion that myths depicting the West as the Passage to India, as the home of the heroic Sons of Leatherstocking, as the Great American Desert, and as the Garden of the West were powerful symbols to Americans interested in the frontier. In his final chapter, Smith demonstrated how these symbols and myths influenced the thinking and writing of Frederick Jackson Turner.[21]

If Smith outlined a new way of looking at the West as symbol and myth, he also noted how the study of previously overlooked material could yield new insights about the mythic West. In addition to scrutinizing the writings of such well-known writers as Cooper, Whitman, and Garland, he gave close readings to government documents, dime novels, and historical essays and books that historians had dismissed or passed over lightly. In the three decades since the publication of *Virgin Land,* numerous western historians have drawn on Smith's volume for its novel insights as well as for its methods of research and analysis.

In the past two decades more studies of western literature have appeared than on any other facet of western cultural history. The establishment of the Western Literature Association in 1965 and the appearance of its journal, *Western American Literature,* have sparked much of this new interest in western writing. At the same time, publication of the brief pamphlets in the Steck-Vaughn Southwest Writers Series (1967-71) and the Boise State Western Writers Series (1972-), the appearance of numerous volumes on western authors in the Twayne United States Authors Series, and the organization of the Popular Culture Association and the publication of its periodicals, *Journal of Popular Culture* and *Journal of American Culture,* have also provided other outlets for scholars interested in the American literary West.

Although a new wave of scholarship on western literature has appeared in the 1960s and 1970s, most of these recent essays and books are the work of scholars in departments of English and American Studies and reflect the perspectives of literary and myth critics more often than the approaches of literary historians. Still, historians can learn a great deal from these critics. One of these scholars, John R. Milton, has recently revised some of his widely cited essays, added new readings of numerous western novels, and incorporated them into his important book *The Novel of the American West.* In defining the "Western" novel Milton stresses several themes: a land-based philosophy, intuitive perceptives, spiritual values, and "open" structures. Another major interpreter of western fiction, Max Westbrook, has presented his provocative views in a series of significant articles. A third writer, Don D. Walker, illustrates his training under Henry Nash Smith in *Clio's Cowboys,* which collects several of his essays on western literature and historiography. Also trained in American Studies, John G. Cawelti has encouraged students to study carefully the structures and social implications of popular western fiction. Although none of these critics has produced traditional literary history, all have sketched several paradigms useful to western literary historians.[22]

Recent studies of western art have been less numerous—and much less innovative—than commentaries on western literature. The two most widely cited overviews of western art are, in fact, curiously uninterpretive, when viewed in the light of changing currents of western historiography. In *Artists and Illustrators of the Old West, 1850–1900,* Robert Taft provides a series of biographical and topical chapters devoted to artists and illustrators of the Plains and Rockies. A professor of chemistry, Taft ransacked public and private archives, corresponded with numerous friends and relatives of the artists he discussed, and scrutinized numerous government documents to gather the extraordinary amount of factual information contained in his volume. But his book lacks any historiographical framework; it does not mention Turner nor include substantive references to other leading western historians. Likewise, *Artists of the Old West* (enl. ed., 1973) by ethnologist John C. Ewers contains useful biographical sketches of the major nineteenth-century artists (western and nonwestern) who painted the West and includes several attractive examples of each artist's work. The author makes comparisons and contrasts among these artists, but his discussions do not set these works in any cultural or historiographical circumference. Like these two books, most studies on western art have been narrative or pictorial in nature and have eschewed interpretation and analysis. Few areas in western cultural history offer more possibilities for further research and writing than the history of western art.[23]

Not many of the recent studies of western churches and religious leaders have been interpretive and broad based; most have been narrowly focused essays or books on single denominations or figures in one state. While sufficient materials are available for comprehensive and analytical studies, cultural historians and church annalists have seemed satisfied to write provincial institutional history with little attention given to the extensive impact of churches and ministers on western culture. In the only recent summary of religion in the West, Gary Topping concludes that eastern traditions and frontier environment were at a standoff in the West. As he puts it, "reciprocal processes of adaptation occurred," and from this marriage of conservative and innovative strains came new offspring: "the Spanish mission, the camp meeting, the circuit rider and the Mormon village." Topping also implies that if the full story of religion in the West were told, historians would have to pay more attention to the twentieth century, especially to developments in California.[24]

While historians have not paid a great deal of attention to education in the West, the field is more alive with fresh ideas and interpretations than is the religious history of the region. Historians of education in the last two decades have abandoned the narrowly focused and progressive outlook of Ellwood P. Cubberly, and a few revisionists are even castigating the work of such highly regarded scholars as Bernard Bailyn and Lawrence A. Cremmin. But the most important work on American education published in the last decade or so is that of David B. Tyack, whose essays and book, *The One Best System,* are extremely useful interdisciplinary studies. Although Tyack's monograph deals briefly with education in the West—he discusses schooling in Oregon and San Francisco—he provides paradigms and interpretations that should be tested in future studies of western education. His analysis of such topics as bureaucratization, pluralism, and centralism demonstrate how scholars could view educational practices and policies in light of shifting currents of American thought and culture.[25]

Some educationists and historians are beginning to realize that the West could be a new frontier for their scholarly studies. One historian of education, Sol Cohen, notes that American educational history has "slighted American regionalism. As far as most historians of education are concerned, the American West might be uninhabited. . . . No region of the United States has been so neglected by historians of education as that west of the Rockies." A recent, brief overview by Ronald Butchart, a historian of education, fills some of this large gap. His summary of educational developments in the nineteenth and twentieth centuries illustrates the kind of broad-based history of education that Tyack and other recent scholars have called for. And Butchart's point of view is clearly more on the side of continuity than innovation when he argues that "Western education faithfully mirrored contemporary Eastern practices," and "continuity has been a key aspect."[26]

Although most new commentaries on western cultural history discuss literature, religion, education, or art, a few noteworthy interpretations treat other aspects of the region's culture. Harold Kirker's studies of California architecture point out how much buildings in that state owe to eastern influences and frontier demands. Neither of the major histories of western films—that by George N. Fenin and William K. Everson or that by Jon Tuska—deals with these films or with Hollywood as "western" culture, but both fact-filled books are useful reference tools. Conversely, John H. Lenihan's solid study treats the Western film as a cultural document, as a barometer of shifting national moods. Western drama and music, which have received less attention than these topics, badly need full-length studies.[27]

Writers of western history textbooks have followed their colleagues in not emphasizing cultural history, but two notable exceptions should be mentioned. Robert V. Hine's *The American West: An Interpretive History* contains chapters on churches, schools, and writers, as well as sections on art and popular culture. While most competing textbooks emphasize economic, political, and social history, Hine stresses cultural history and in doing so provides the only western text with that emphasis.[28]

The other recent survey that gives considerable attention to cultural history is Gerald Nash's *The American West in the Twentieth Century*, the only overview of the recent West. Emphasizing the colonial and urban nature of the twentieth-century West before World War II, Nash argues that the West in the 1950s and 1960s became a cultural pacesetter for the United States. He discusses shifting currents in western literature, education, architecture, art, and popular culture in outlining the West's transition from colonial to pacesetting region. In stressing the modern West, Nash gives the fullest summary in print of cultural developments in the contemporary West.[29]

For future studies of western cultural history, two new interpretations should prove especially useful. In 1973 Kevin Starr, a native Californian and a product of the American Civilization program at Harvard, published his provocative *Americans and the California Dream, 1850–1915*. Building on the research of Franklin Walker and utilizing some of the theoretical framework of Henry Nash Smith's *Virgin Land*, Starr examines not only continuities between East and West but also analyzes the cultural and intellectual changes that occurred as California moved from frontier to province. Opening his volume with a discussion of Spanish and Mexican influences on California, he then outlines the transformations that took place after Americans arrived on the scene. By carrying his story to World War I and by dealing with interworkings among writers, churchmen, educators, artists, and architects, Starr shows in this comprehensive study how California gradually moved away from its non-American backgrounds and toward formation of its own provincial culture. No previous scholar has provided such a full and innovative reading of the shifting cultural currents of a western state or region.[30]

If Starr provides a synthetic model for western cultural studies, Julie Roy Jeffrey's *Frontier Women*, the first full-length analytical study of the topic, opens the way for the much-needed study of women's roles in western culture. Jeffrey notes that when women came west from 1840 to 1880, they brought with them a fixed set of attitudes and ideas. Once these women settled in the West, their cultural predispositions outlasted the pressures of the new environment. The frontier tested, bruised, and sometimes redirected these traditional ideals and values; but more often they endured, illustrating Earl Pomeroy's contention that the West accepted more eastern precedents than it rejected. Jeffrey emphasizes women's activities on agricultural, urban, mining, and Mormon frontiers but also includes commentary on women as teachers, church workers, prostitutes, and social and cultural activists. Because previous interpreters have overlooked many of the topics the author treats, this useful volume, like many recent studies of ethnic groups, should remind scholars to cast their nets wider and deeper before declaring they have defined the major facets of western culture.[31]

If the works of Starr and Jeffrey suggest novel approaches and new topics that historians could utilize and investigate, scholars should also not overlook the possibilities of cross-institutional research in western cultural history. Except for Franklin Walker, Sidney Warren, Carey McWilliams, and Kevin Starr, most historians have limited their works to the study of one cultural institution. They have not examined, for example, the influences of journalists on western fiction, the impact of churches on schools, or the bearing of artists on novelists or architects. Such cross-topical investigations could give western cultural studies a broader focus than they have had thus far.[32]

In addition to their hesitancy to study the influences of cultural institutions on one another, students of western culture, like most western historians, have not been very open to the research methods of other disciplines. Few treatments of western literary history completed before 1960 betray an acquaintance with New Criticism, and after that an understanding of myth criticism. As noted previously, most discussions of western art lack the close-reading techniques of art critics. And specialists on education and religion in the West seem reluctant to experiment with the structuralist theories of social scientist Claude Lévi-Strauss and the interpretations of cultural anthropologists Clifford Geertz and Marvin Harris. The approaches and findings of these scholars could broaden and sharpen the insights of western cultural historians. So might the recent research of political scientists and geographers like Ira Sharkansky, Donald Meinig, and Raymond Gastil, whose studies of regionalism should be assigned reading for historians of western regional culture.[33]

One must conclude that few fields in western history offer as many rich possibilities for research as western cultural history. At present the field seems largely undiscovered and uncultivated, but the increasing interest in the role of the West in the economic, political, and social life of the nation is likely to encourage scholars to pay more attention to the cultural history of the West. If this surmise proves true, one hopes that interpreters will produce less narrative history of the frontier period and fashion more analytical studies of the twentieth-century West. If these changes occur, western cultural studies will become an important part of the much-needed reorientation of western history.

Notes

1. James Bryce, *The American Commonwealth,* 2 vols. (London: Macmillan and Company, 1889), 2: 681; Bryce, *The American Commonwealth,* 2 vols. (New York: Macmillan, 1917; paperbound ed., Folcraft, 1978), 2: 891.

2. This essay emphasizes cultural topics that have engendered the most commentary: literature, religion, and education. Other recent interpreters, less inclined to view history as one of the humanities, have defined "cultural" in much broader and theoretical terms. For a stimulating overview of some of these views, see Robert Berkhofer, Jr., "Clio and the Culture Concept: Some Impressions of a Changing Relationship in American Historiography," *Social Science Quarterly* 53 (September 1972): 297-320. In the paragraphs that follow I have drawn upon but have tried to avoid merely repeating the observations in two of my previous essays: "The American Literary West and Its Interpreters: The Rise of a New Historiography," *Pacific Historical Review* 45 (April 1976): 311-48; and "Frontier, Region, and Myth: Changing Interpretations of Western Cultural History," *Journal of American Culture* 3 (Summer 1980): 268-84.

3. Bancroft includes brief comments on cultural topics throughout his many works, but see especially vols. 38 and 39 of *The Works of Hubert Howe Bancroft,* 39 vols. (San Francisco: The History Company, 1882-90), for several essays on cultural topics.

4. The best book on Turner is Ray Allen Billington, *Frederick Jackson Turner: Historian, Scholar, Teacher* (New York: Oxford University Press, 1973). I note briefly Turner's lack of interest in cultural history in "Frontier, Region, and Myth," pp. 268-71, 282.

5. William H. Goetzmann, "The West and the American Age of Exploration," *Arizona and the West* 2 (Autumn 1960): 278.

6. Frederick Jackson Turner, "The Significance of the Frontier in American History," *The Frontier in American History* (New York: Henry Holt and Company, 1920), p. 32.

7. *Ibid.,* pp. 35-38.

8. For Turner's interest in a vanishing frontier, see Ray A. Billington, "Frederick Jackson Turner and the Closing of the Frontier," *Essays in Western History in Honor of T. A. Larson,* ed. Roger Daniels (Laramie: University of Wyoming, 1971), pp. 45-56.

9. Frederic L. Paxson, *The Last American Frontier* (New York: Macmillan, 1910); and Paxson, *History of the American Frontier, 1763-1893* (Boston: Houghton Mifflin, 1924).

10. Herbert E. Bolton, "The Mission as a Frontier Institution in the Spanish-American Colonies," *American Historical Review* 23 (October 1917): 42-61.

11. Walter P. Webb, *The Great Plains* (Boston: Ginn, 1931; Grosset and Dunlap, [1931]; paperbound ed., Lincoln: University of Nebraska Press, 1981), p. vi. Subsequent quotes are from the Grosset and Dunlap edition. I am drawing here on the writings of Gregory M. Tobin: *The Making of a History: Walter Prescott Webb and "The Great Plains"* (Austin: University of Texas Press, 1976); and "Landscape, Region, and the Writing of History: Walter Prescott Webb in the 1920s," *American Studies International* 16 (Summer 1978): 7-18.

12. Ralph Leslie Rusk, *The Literature of the Middle Western Frontier*, 2 vols. (New York: Columbia University Press, 1925); Dorothy Anne Dondore, *The Prairie and the Making of Middle America: Four Centuries of Description* (Cedar Rapids, Iowa: Torch Press, 1926); and Lucy Lockwood Hazard, *The Frontier in American Literature* (New York: Thomas Y. Crowell, 1927). Less well known but deserving of attention as the first attempt to deal briefly with western regional literature is Carey McWilliams, *The New Regionalism in American Literature* (Seattle: University of Washington Book Store, 1930).

13. James F. Willard and Colin B. Goodykoontz (eds.), *The Trans-Mississippi West* (Boulder: University of Colorado, 1930).

14. Vernon L. Parrington, *Main Currents in American Thought*, 3 vols. (New York: Harcourt, Brace and Company, 1927, 1930; paperbound ed., 1954); Merle Curti, *The Growth of American Thought* (New York: Harper and Bros., 1943). For very useful commentary on trends in American cultural and intellectual historiography, consult Robert Allen Skotheim, *American Intellectual Histories and Historians* (Princeton: Princeton University Press, 1966); and John Higham, *History: Professional Scholarship in America* (New York: Harper Torchbooks, 1973). See also Higham (ed.), *New Directions in American Intellectual History* (Baltimore: Johns Hopkins University Press, 1979).

15. Franklin Walker, *San Francisco's Literary Frontier* (New York: Knopf, 1939; paperbound ed., Seattle: University of Washington Press, 1969); Walker, *A Literary History of Southern California* (Berkeley: University of California Press, 1950); *The Seacoast of Bohemia*, enl. ed. (Santa Barbara and Salt Lake City: Peregrine Smith, 1973). For Walker's comments on his craft, see his "On Writing Literary History," *Pacific Historical Review* 45 (August 1976): 349-56.

16. Colin B. Goodykoontz, *Home Missions on the American Frontier with*

Particular Reference to the American Home Missionary Society (Caldwell, Idaho: Caxton Printers, 1939), p. 425.

17. Sidney Warren, *Farthest Frontier: The Pacific Northwest* (New York: Macmillan, 1949), p. 329.

18. Carey McWilliams, *Southern California Country: An Island on the Land* (New York: Duell, Sloan and Pearce, 1946). Carl Sauer's statement appears on p. 138.

19. Earl Pomeroy, "Toward a Reorientation of Western History: Continuity and Environment," *Mississippi Valley Historical Review* 41 (March 1955): 579–600; *The Pacific Slope: A History of California, Oregon, Washington, Idaho, Utah, and Nevada* (New York: Knopf, 1965; paperbound ed., Seattle: University of Washington Press, 1975); "The Changing West," in *The Reconstruction of American History,* ed. John Higham (New York: Harper and Bros., 1962), pp. 64–81. I am indebted throughout this essay to the ideas of Earl Pomeroy.

20. Louis B. Wright, *Culture on the Moving Frontier* (Bloomington: Indiana University Press, 1955; paperbound ed., New York: Harper and Bros., 1961).

21. Henry Nash Smith, *Virgin Land: The American West as Symbol and Myth* (Cambridge: Harvard University Press, 1950; paperbound ed., 1970). See Smith's comments on his methods of analysis in the twentieth anniversary printing of the book (1970), pp. vii–x; and in his essay *"Virgin Land Revisited,"* *Indian Journal of American Studies* 3 (June 1973): 1–18. A useful volume that draws heavily on *Virgin Land* is James K. Folsom, *The American Western Novel* (New Haven, Conn.: College and University Press, 1966). Richard Slotkin enlarges upon some of Smith's notions but deals with eastern frontiers in his provocative volume *Regeneration Through Violence: The Mythology of the American Frontier, 1600–1860* (Middletown, Conn.: Wesleyan University Press, 1973). The most recent volume utilizing Smith's approach is Ray A. Billington's *Land of Savagery/Land of Promise: The European Image of the American Frontier in the Nineteenth Century* (New York: W. W. Norton, 1981).

22. John R. Milton, *The Novel of the American West* (Lincoln: University of Nebraska Press, 1980); Max Westbrook, "Conservative, Liberal, and Western: Three Modes of American Realism," *South Dakota Review* 4 (Summer 1966): 3–19; "The Practical Spirit: Sacrality and the American West," *Western American Literature* 3 (Fall 1968): 193–205; and "The Authentic Western," *Western American Literature* 3 (November 1978): 213–25; Don D. Walker, *Clio's Cowboys: Studies in the Historiography of the Cattle Trade*

(Lincoln: University of Nebraska Press, 1981); John G. Cawelti, *The Six-Gun Mystique* (Bowling Green, Ohio: Bowling Green University Popular Press, [1971]); and Cawelti, *Adventure, Mystery, and Romance: Formula Stories as Art and Popular Culture* (Chicago: University of Chicago Press, 1976). For a brief historical overview of western American literature, see Richard W. Etulain (ed.), *The American Literary West* (Manhattan, Kans.: Sunflower University Press, 1980). The most comprehensive listing of essays and books about western literature and western authors is Richard W. Etulain (ed.), *A Bibliographical Guide to the Study of Western American Literature* (Lincoln: University of Nebraska Press, 1982). For useful introductions to the life and works of the leading western writers, consult Fred Erisman and Richard W. Etulain (eds.), *Fifty Western Writers: A Bio-bibliographical Sourcebook* (Westport, Conn.: Greenwood Press, 1982).

23. Robert Taft, *Artists and Illustrators of the Old West, 1850-1900* (New York: Charles Scribner's Sons, 1953); and John C. Ewers, *Artists of the Old West*, enl. ed. (Garden City, N.Y.: Doubleday, 1973). Ben Merchant Vorpahl provides an imaginative study of western art and literature in *Frederic Remington and the West: With the Eye of the Mind* (Austin: University of Texas Press, 1978). A brief overview of western art is presented in Phillip Drennon Thomas, "The Art and Artists of the American West," *Journal of American Culture* 3 (Summer 1980): 389-406.

24. Gary Topping, "Religion in the West," *Journal of American Culture* 3 (Summer 1980): 330, 340. The best recent study of religion in America, which contains sections on frontier and western religious experiences, is Sydney E. Ahlstrom, *A Religious History of the American People* (New Haven: Yale University Press, 1975). Unfortunately, very little of William Warren Sweet's massive *Religion on the American Frontier . . . ,* 4 vols. (New York, 1931, 1936; Chicago, 1939, 1946), deals with the trans-Mississippi West; neither does Charles A. Johnson, *The Frontier Camp Meeting: Religion's Harvest Time* (Dallas: Southern Methodist University Press, 1955). Professor Ferenc Szasz of the University of New Mexico has underway a study of religion on the trans-Mississippi frontier, with special emphasis on the Great Plains and the Rockies.

25. David B. Tyack, *The One Best System: A History of American Urban Education* (Cambridge: Harvard University Press, 1974); "Bureaucracy and the Common School: The Example of Portland, Oregon, 1851-1913," *American Quarterly* 19 (Fall 1967): 475-98; "The Kingdom of God and the Common School: Protestant Ministers and the Educational Awakening in the West," *Harvard Educational Review* 36 (Fall 1966): 447-69; and Tyack,

"The Tribe and the Common School: Community Control in Rural Education," *American Quarterly* 24 (March 1972): 3-19.

26. Sol Cohen, "History of Education as a Field of Study: An Essay on Recent Historiography of American Education," in *History, Education, and Public Policy,* ed. Donald R. Warren (Berkeley, Calif.: McCutchan Publishing Corporation, 1978), pp. 35-49, 50-53 (quotation on p. 44). This volume contains several other useful historiographical essays on American education. Ronald Butchart, "Education and Culture in the Trans-Mississippi West: An Interpretation," *Journal of American Culture* 3 (Summer 1980): 351, 353.

27. Harold Kirker, *California's Architectural Frontier: Style and Tradition in the Nineteenth Century* (San Marino, Calif.: Huntington Library, 1960); and Kirker, "California Architecture and Its Relation to Contemporary Trends in Europe and America," *California Historical Quarterly* 51 (Winter 1972): 289-305. On the architecture of another region, see Thomas Vaughan and Virginia Guest Ferriday (eds.), *Space, Style, and Structure: Building in Northwest America,* 2 vols. (Portland: Oregon Historical Society, 1974). George N. Fenin and William K. Everson, *The Western: From Silents to the Seventies,* rev. ed. (New York: Grossman Publishers, 1973); Jon Tuska, *The Filming of the West* (Garden City, N.Y.: Doubleday, 1976); John H. Lenihan, *Showdown: Confronting Modern America in the Western Film* (Urbana: University of Illinois Press, 1980). The best survey of one aspect of western music is Ronald L. Davis, *A History of Opera in the American West* (Englewood Cliffs, N.J.: Prentice-Hall, 1965). Bill C. Malone deals with the cowboy image in western music and several other topics in *Country Music U.S.A.: A Fifty-Year History* (Austin: University of Texas Press, 1968).

28. Robert V. Hine, *The American West: An Interpretive History* (Boston: Little, Brown, 1973; paperbound ed.).

29. Gerald Nash, *The American West in the Twentieth Century: A Short History of an Urban Oasis* (Englewood Cliffs, N.J.: Prentice-Hall, 1973; paperbound ed., Albuquerque: University of New Mexico Press, 1977).

30. Kevin Starr, *Americans and the California Dream, 1850-1915* (New York: Oxford University Press, 1973; paperbound ed., Santa Barbara and Salt Lake City: Peregrine Smith, 1981). Starr is working on a companion volume dealing with the later twentieth century.

31. Julie Roy Jeffrey, *Frontier Women: The Trans-Mississippi West, 1840-1880* (New York: Hill and Wang, 1979). See also the special issue of *Pacific Historical Review* 49 (May 1980) devoted to "Women in the American West," especially Joan M. Jensen and Darlis A. Miller, "The Gentle Tamers Revisited: New Approaches to the History of Women in the American West," pp. 173-

213; and Glenda Riley, "Women in the West," *Journal of American Culture* 3 (Summer 1980): 311-29.

32. Two models for the kind of cross-disciplinary research called for here are Clive Bush, *The Dream of Reason: American Consciousness and Cultural Achievement from Independence to the Civil War* (New York: St. Martins Press, 1977); and Donald Ringe, *The Pictorial Mode: Space and Time in the Art of Bryant, Irving and Cooper* (Lexington: University Press of Kentucky, 1971).

33. See, for example, Claude Lévi-Strauss, *The Savage Mind* (Chicago: University of Chicago Press, 1966); and Lévi-Strauss, *Structural Anthropology*, 2 vols. (New York: Basic Books, 1976); Clifford Geertz, *The Interpretation of Cultures: Selected Essays* (New York: Basic Books, 1973); Marvin Harris, *Cultural Materialism: The Struggle for a Science of Culture* (New York: Random House, 1979). Ira Sharkansky discusses his views of regionalism in *Regionalism in American Politics* (Indianapolis: Bobbs Merrill, 1970). In addition to several important volumes on the West, D. W. Meinig has written "American Wests: Preface to a Geographical Interpretation," *Annals of the Association of American Geographers* 62 (June 1972): 159-84; and "The Continuous Shaping of America: A Prospectus for Geographers and Historians," *American Historical Review* 83 (December 1978): 1186-1205. Raymond Gastil presents a case study in "The Pacific Northwest as a Cultural Region," *Pacific Northwest Quarterly* 64 (October 1973): 147-56, 161-62; and broader perspectives in *Cultural Regions of the United States* (Seattle: University of Washington Press, 1975; paperbound ed., n.d.). Finally, consult Gene M. Gressley, "Regionalism and the Twentieth-Century West," in *The American West: New Perspectives, New Dimensions*, ed. Jerome O. Steffen (Norman: University of Oklahoma Press, 1979), pp. 197-234.

Contributors

Thomas G. Alexander is Professor of History and Director of the Charles Redd Center for Western Studies at Brigham Young University, Provo, Utah. His publications include *The Papers of Ulysses S. Grant,* vol. 5 (assistant editor, 1973); *A Dependent Commonwealth: Utah's Economy from Statehood to the Great Depression* (coauthor, 1974); *A Clash of Interests: Interior Department and Mountain West, 1863-96* (1977); and *Utah's History* (Associate editor, 1978).

Dennis E. Berge is Professor of History at San Diego State University. The author of articles on Mexican and California history, he has also translated and edited *Considerations on the Political and Social Situation of the Mexican Republic in 1847* (1975).

Richard Maxwell Brown is Beekman Professor of Northwest and Pacific History at the University of Oregon, Eugene. His numerous publications include *The South Carolina Regulators* (1963), *American Violence* (editor, 1970), *Strain of Violence: Historical Studies of American Violence and Vigilantism* (1975), and *Tradition, Conflict and Modernization: Perspectives on the American Revolution* (coeditor, 1977). Professor Brown served as a consultant to the National Commission on the Causes and Prevention of Violence.

Robert C. Carriker is Professor of History at Gonzaga University, Spokane, Washington. His writings include *Fort Supply, Indian Territory: Frontier Outpost on the Plains* (1970), *Kalispel People* (1973), and *An Army Wife on the Frontier* (editor, 1975).

F. Alan Coombs is Associate Professor of History at the University of Utah, Salt Lake City. He has published articles and essays on various subjects involving the recent West. Professor Coombs is completing a biography of Senator Joseph O'Mahoney of Wyoming.

Donald C. Cutter is O'Connor Professor of History at St. Mary's University of San Antonio, Texas. He is the author of many works, including *Malaspina in California* (1960), *Tadeo Haenke y el final de una vieja polémica* (coauthor, 1966), *The California Coast* (editor, 1969), and *Journal of Tomás de Suría of his Voyage with Malaspina to the Northwest Coast of America in 1791* (editor, 1980). Professor Cutter is a former president of the Western History Association, is currently president of the Pacific Coast Branch of the American Historical Association, and has been a Fulbright research fellow in Spain and a Fulbright lecturer in Mexico.

Gordon B. Dodds is Professor of History at Portland State University. Among his publications are *The Salmon King of Oregon* (1959), *Hiram Martin Chittenden: His Public Career* (1973), and *Oregon: A Bicentennial History* (1977).

Richard W. Etulain is Professor of History at the University of New Mexico, Albuquerque, and editor of the *New Mexico Historical Review*. His many writings include *Owen Wister* (1973), *The Popular Western: Essays Toward a Definition* (coeditor, 1974), *Fifty Western Writers: A Bio-Bibliographical Sourcebook* (coeditor, 1982), and *Bibliographical Guide to the Study of Western American Literature* (1982).

Gilbert C. Fite is Richard B. Russell Professor of American History at the University of Georgia, Athens. Professor Fite's voluminous writings include *Peter Norbeck: Prairie Statesman* (1948), *George N. Peek and the Fight for Farm Parity* (1954), *The Farmers' Frontier, 1865–1900* (1966), and *American Farmers: The New Minority* (1981). A former president of Eastern Illinois University, he has served as president of both the Agricultural History Society and the Southern Historical Association. He has been a Ford and Guggenheim Fellow and has twice received Fulbright awards to India.

Herbert T. Hoover is Professor of History at the University of South Dakota, Vermillion, and Acting Director of the Center for the History of the

American Indian at the Newberry Library, Chicago. His publications include *To Be an Indian* (coauthor, 1971), *The Practice of Oral History* (coauthor, 1975), *The Sioux: A Critical Bibliography* (1979), and *Bibliography of the Sioux* (coauthor, 1980).

W. Turrentine Jackson is Professor of History at the University of California at Davis. Among his many writings are *Wagon Roads West* (1952), *Treasure Hill: Portrait of a Silver Mining Camp* (1963), *The Enterprising Scot: Investors in the American West after 1873* (1968), and an ongoing series of monographs and articles on environmental history and on the Wells Fargo enterprises. He is a Fulbright, Rockefeller Foundation, and Guggenheim Fellow and a past president of the Western History Association.

William L. Lang is editor of *Montana: The Magazine of Western History*. He is the coauthor of *Montana: Our Land and People* (1979) and author of articles in the field of western American history.

Bradford F. Luckingham is Associate Professor of History at Arizona State University, Tempe. He has published numerous articles, mainly in the field of western urban history, and is the author of *The Urban Southwest: A Profile History of El Paso, Albuquerque, Tucson, and Phoenix* (1982).

Frederick C. Luebke is Professor of History at the University of Nebraska-Lincoln. Among his publications are *Immigrants and Politics: The Germans of Nebraska, 1880-1900* (1969), *Bonds of Loyalty: German Americans and World War I* (1974), and *The Great Plains: Environment and Culture* (editor, 1979). He is editor of the *Great Plains Quarterly* and has held fellowships from the Fulbright, Danforth, and Rockefeller programs.

Michael P. Malone is Professor of History and Dean of Graduate Studies at Montana State University, Bozeman. His publications include *C. Ben Ross and the New Deal in Idaho* (1970), *Montana: A History of Two Centuries* (coauthor, 1976), and *The Battle for Butte: Mining and Politics on the Northern Frontier, 1864-1906* (1981).

Sandra L. Myres is Professor of History at the University of Texas at Arlington. Among her publications are *The Ranch in Spanish Texas, 1690-1800* (1969), *Cavalry Wife: The Diary of Eveline M. Alexander* (editor, 1977), *Ho for California! Women's Overland Diaries from the Huntington*

Library (editor, 1980), and *Western Women and the Frontier Experience* (1982). Professor Myres is a Fulbright Fellow.

Kenneth N. Owens is Professor of History at California State University, Sacramento. He has published *Galena, Grant and the Fortunes of War* (1963), *The Wreck of the Sv. Nikolai: Two Narratives of the First Russian Expedition to the Oregon Country, 1808–1810* (coeditor, forthcoming), and numerous articles on western territorial politics and other subjects. He is a Danforth Associate and a Woodrow Wilson Fellow.

Rodman W. Paul is Edward S. Harkness Professor of History, Emeritus, at the California Institute of Technology, Pasadena. His books include *California Gold: The Beginning of Mining in the Far West* (1947), *Mining Frontiers of the Far West, 1848–1880* (1963), *A Victorian Gentlewoman in the Far West: The Reminiscences of Mary Hallock Foote* (editor, 1972), and *The Frontier and the American West* (coeditor, 1977). Professor Paul is a past president of the Western History Association and of the Pacific Coast Branch of the American Historical Association, and is a Guggenheim and Ford Foundation Fellow.

Clark C. Spence is Professor of History at the University of Illinois, Urbana. Among his voluminous writings are *British Investments and the American Mining Frontier, 1860–1901* (1958), *God Speed the Plow: The Coming of Steam Cultivation to Great Britain* (1960), *Mining Engineers and the American West* (1970), and *Territorial Politics and Government in Montana, 1864–89* (1975). He is a past president of the Western History Association and is a Ford and Guggenheim Fellow.

Index